JAMES K. POLK, *JACKSONIAN*

1795-1843

JAMES K. POLK

JACKSONIAN

1795-1843

BY CHARLES GRIER SELLERS, JR.

PRINCETON, NEW JERSEY
PRINCETON UNIVERSITY PRESS
1957

4-21-8

History

87755
MAY 1 '58

E
417
S46

For My

Mother and Father

PREFACE

THIS VOLUME frankly purports to be both biography and history. It rests, indeed, on the proposition that the two cannot be separated: that personality cannot be divorced from history, and that history cannot be divorced from personality. The current revival of the old-fashioned "life and times" type of historical biography means, I hope, that this proposition is coming to be more generally accepted.

The project appealed to me originally for its biographical value alone. Over thirty years ago Eugene I. McCormac's *James K. Polk: A Political Biography* so impressively demonstrated Polk's presidential services that he has come to be recognized as one of our strongest chief executives. Yet Professor McCormac left much to be revealed about Polk, the man, and his growth through the first forty-eight of his fifty-four years. Such a figure, I felt and still feel, deserves to be as fully known as the record permits.

I was not long in discovering the obstacles that perhaps led my predecessor to eschew the task of bringing to life the personality concealed behind Polk's disciplined public façade. While I have had no choice but to present Polk in the main as his contemporaries saw him, I have sought to convey also some sense of the dramatic inner developments that alone explain the kind of man he was. At the same time I have tried to relate Polk's personal growth at every stage to the historical circumstances that environed him.

As the story took shape, however, I came to value it as much for its illumination of the experience of his generation of Americans as for its revelation of Polk. In the life of his immediate family, such historical abstractions as the westward movement, the American Revolution, Jeffersonian Republicanism, land speculation, and frontier leadership are translated into concrete human terms. Polk himself, to a unique degree and quite aside from his intrinsic importance, was in the thick of the major political developments of his period: the rise of popular democracy, the Jacksonian struggles of the 1830's, and after 1835 the emergence of sectional animosities that eventually overrode the Jeffersonian-Jacksonian issues. Finally, in the climactic years beyond the present volume, the American people's passage from the Jacksonian epoch of their history into a new and fateful one was most vividly exemplified in Polk's presidential experiences as the last national leader who had a chance to apply the old Jeffersonian-Jacksonian convictions to solution of the sectional problem.

The labors of an army of able investigators have by now turned up most of the important information we shall ever have about these developments as general phenomena on a national scale. Yet historical events are inevitably distorted and oversimplified when approached exclusively at this generalized level, and in the absence of adequate state studies the particulars are too often inferred from the generalizations. The time has come for trained scholars to turn more of their attention from the national and general to the local and particular, from "the rise of popular democracy," for instance, to the particular circumstances that led particular people at particular times and places to demand a greater voice in the decisions of their magistrates, legislators, or congressmen. Only through careful investigation at the levels where ordinary human motivations are observable can we grasp the complex of convictions, aspirations, and interests that sustained, say, Jacksonian Democracy or the American System.

Polk's biography offers an unusual opportunity to bridge this gap between the nationally significant and the narrowly local, since Tennessee political history is documented with singular fullness in the voluminous Polk and Jackson papers. I have attached great importance to exploiting this opportunity, and I hope that readers will find the textbook clichés about the Jacksonian period sharpened by being tied to the actions of real people in concrete situations. The relationship between Polk, the doctrinaire Republican, and his brother-in-law James Walker, the entrepreneurial democrat, to take one example, personifies strikingly the ambivalent orientation of this whole generation of Americans: plunging headlong into the exploitation and transformation of a bountiful environment, yet drawn almost as powerfully back toward the simplicity and virtue of a half-imagined agrarian past, symbolized for Polk by Old Mecklenburg.

Since I have found the Old Mecklenburg theme to be a major motif in the Polk story, I should confess that I am, like Polk, a native of Mecklenburg County, North Carolina. And though by my day Polk's Old Mecklenburg had become a bustling, urbanized, newly rich showpiece of the New South, my family's roots in the surrounding countryside connect me more closely, perhaps, with the surviving vestiges of an older way of life. I have doubtless treated the Old Mecklenburg theme more sympathetically than others would, but I do not believe I have made it any more important in the life of Polk and his generation than it actually was.

I want to thank a host of librarians and archivists for the innumerable services and kindnesses that made pleasant and fruitful my visits to the institutions indicated in the notes to this volume. An equally indispensable obligation of another kind is owed to the Princeton University Research Fund for making possible the completion and publication of this study. My greatest debt of gratitude is to my friend Arthur Link, who sacrificed the progress of his own work to a painstaking reading of my manuscript, every page of which now bears the mark of his expert hand. Professors Clement Eaton and Arthur M. Schlesinger, Jr., and my colleague Professor Robert R. Palmer were also generous with their time and wisdom in reading the manuscript and suggesting improvements. Finally, I am deeply grateful to Professor Fletcher M. Green of the University of North Carolina, who guided the early evolution of this project as a doctoral dissertation and who, by precept, example, and friendship, continues to make historical scholarship exciting for his many present and former students.

CHARLES GRIER SELLERS, JR.

Princeton, New Jersey

CONTENTS

ILLUSTRATIONS

(Between pages 32 and 33)

PLATE I

JANE KNOX POLK. Painting in the Sam Polk House, Polk Memorial Association, Columbia, Tenn.

COLONEL WILLIAM POLK. Engraving from a painting, in *Year Book of the Society of Sons of the Revolution in the State of New York* (New York, 1893), 244.

THE UNIVERSITY OF NORTH CAROLINA. Detail from a lithograph made about 1861, owned by the University of North Carolina. The third floor of Old East on the left had been added since Polk's student days, as had Smith Hall, a corner of which is visible between Old East and New College.

PLATE II

FELIX GRUNDY. Engraving from a painting by Washington B. Cooper, in [James B. Longacre and James Herring,] *The National Portrait Gallery of Distinguished Americans: with Biographical Sketches* (4 vols., Philadelphia, 1856), III, plate 35.

SAM POLK HOUSE. Columbia, Tenn., Wiles-Hood Photographers, Nashville.

POLK'S LAW OFFICE. From an old newspaper photograph, Sam Polk House, Polk Memorial Association, Columbia, Tenn.

PLATE III

ANDREW JACKSON. Painting by Asher B. Durand, courtesy of The New-York Historical Society, New York City.

HUGH LAWSON WHITE. Painting in the Tennessee Historical Society, Nashville.

WILLIAM CARROLL. Painting by Washington B. Cooper, in the Tennessee Historical Society, Nashville.

CAVE JOHNSON. Engraving from a daguerreotype, in *The United States Magazine, and Democratic Review*, XVII (Oct. 1845), 242.

PLATE IV

JAMES KNOX POLK and SARAH CHILDRESS POLK. A pair of paintings in the Sam Polk House, Polk Memorial Association, Columbia, Tenn. These are probably the paintings made at Washington in the 1830's by Andrew Jackson's friend and "court painter," Ralph E. W. Earl. The circumstances are described as follows in Mrs. Polk's reminiscences: "The artist Earle had spent some time with General Jackson at the White House. During his stay there

xiii

the Tennesseans who were assembled one evening in the parlor of Mr. and Mrs. Polk proposed that they should have their portraits painted by him, and this proposition was soon carried into effect. Mrs. Polk's portrait, the earliest one of her, has preserved her youthful appearance, with the bright eyes, and raven hair hanging in clustering curls around her face." Anson and Fanny Nelson, *Memorials of Sarah Childress Polk: Wife of the Eleventh President of the United States* (New York, 1892), 38.

PLATE V

THE OLD HOUSE OF REPRESENTATIVES. Painting by Samuel F. B. Morse, in the Collection of the Corcoran Gallery of Art, Washington, D.C.

PLATE VI

JOHN BELL. Painting in the Tennessee Historical Society, Nashville.

RICHARD M. JOHNSON. Lithograph by Charles Fenderich, 1840, Library of Congress.

THE CITY OF WASHINGTON, 1833. Detail from an engraving of a painting by George Cooke, Library of Congress.

PLATE VII

EPHRAIM H. FOSTER. Painting in the Tennessee Historical Society, Nashville.

JAMES C. JONES. Painting by Washington B. Cooper, Tennessee Historical Society, Nashville.

THE COURTHOUSE AT NASHVILLE, MEETING PLACE OF THE TENNESSEE LEGISLATURE. An 1832 print, Tennessee State Library, Nashville.

PLATE VIII

POLK AS GOVERNOR. Lithograph by Charles Fenderich, about 1840, Library of Congress.

MAPS OF TENNESSEE

(Pages 34-35)

JAMES K. POLK, *JACKSONIAN*

1795-1843

SYMBOLS

DU   Duke University Library, Durham, N.C.

HEH   Henry E. Huntington Library and Art Gallery, San Marino, Calif.

HSP   Historical Society of Pennsylvania, Philadelphia.

JUL   Joint University Library, Nashville, Tenn.

LC   Library of Congress, Washington.

LM   McClung Collection, Lawson-McGhee Library, Knoxville, Tenn.

MHS   Massachusetts Historical Society, Boston.

NA   National Archives, Washington.

NCC   North Carolina Collection, University of North Carolina Library, Chapel Hill.

NCDAH   North Carolina Department of Archives and History, Raleigh.

NCSS   Office of the North Carolina Secretary of State, Raleigh.

NYHS   New-York Historical Society, New York City.

NYPL   New York Public Library, New York City.

PU   Princeton University Library, Princeton, N.J.

SHC   Southern Historical Collection, University of North Carolina Library, Chapel Hill.

THS   Tennessee Historical Society, Nashville.

1

OLD MECKLENBURG

ONE AUTUMN DAY in 1821 a seventy-three-year-old patriarch, with several stalwart sons and a band of slaves at his back, came marching along a trail through the wild Chickasaw country of West Tennessee. Years of toil and exposure had left their mark on this old man, but had not quenched the determination that drove him on to one last pioneering venture. Colonel Ezekiel Polk embodied all those qualities—restlessness, avarice, adventurousness, perhaps even idealism—that were impelling Americans in their rapacious conquest of a virgin continent. Ezekiel's latest destination lay on the banks of the Hatchie River, and here he cleared fields, built rude cabins, and settled his family.

Yet Ezekiel and his kind looked east as much as west, backward as often as forward. Only their faith in the verities of the snug worlds they had left behind made possible their headlong pursuit of the limitless possibilities lying always a little to the west and a little in the future; and ever again on successive frontiers they sought to recreate their points of origin. No sooner had a semblance of civilization come to Ezekiel's settlement on the Hatchie than he began planning a great eight-room house to stand symbolically as the destination of his lifelong westward striving. Ezekiel was dead before the façade rose in the forest, but he had lived long enough to name his mansion. "Mecklen" he called it, turning back in thought at the end of life to upcountry North Carolina and the county of Mecklenburg where he had begun his pilgrimage so many years before. For Ezekiel Polk, Mecklenburg had been both an end and a beginning; in a sense he had never left it.

So it was with many another pioneer. In Tennessee one was forever encountering the sons—sons in a more than physical sense—of what they always called "Old Mecklenburg," or if not Mecklenburg, then some other half-remembered, half-imagined Arcadia. Tennessee's most famous citizen, Andrew Jackson, never forgot that he had grown up on Mecklenburg's borders; and nearby another Tennessean destined for a large public role, Ezekiel's grandson James K. Polk, had spent his early years. The younger Polk was not a man to expound on his spiritual origins, yet his whole career would attest to the power of nostalgia in the life of his westering, enterprising generation.

If James K. Polk never put this mood in words himself, he found satisfaction in the company of those who did, especially his friend Doctor J. G. M. Ramsey, the historian of Tennessee's pioneer period. Ramsey had not been near North Carolina until he was half grown, but his mother had imprinted the image of Old Mecklenburg indelibly on his consciousness; and he devoted the best energies of a lifetime to historical writing that conveyed his vision of this older America. When Ramsey came to erect his own mansion among the hills of East Tennessee, where the Holston and French Broad join to form the Tennessee River, he christened it, by an internal necessity, "Mecklenburg." Here Polk came whenever he found himself in this part of the state.

What Old Mecklenburg meant to Polk and Ramsey, as they sat looking out over the westbound river and reminiscing of the bygone days back east, they could not have said with any precision. Only years later, after Polk had long departed the world and a catastrophic civil war had swept away the last reminders of the old way of life, did Ramsey attempt what had not before seemed necessary. Retreating in broken spirits to a farm in Mecklenburg County itself in 1866, and finding even here that change had done its work, Ramsey labored with a passion born of despair to make explicit the *mystique* of the Old Mecklenburg. "The primitive simplicity of the pastoral stage of society," as he finally put it in the pages of General D. H. Hill's unreconstructed magazine, *The Land We Love*, "with its calm, quiet and security, its freedom from care, from avarice and the rivalries of older communities, stamped the infant settlements with the impress of another Arcadia, pure, contented, free, enlightened, enterprising, virtuous and independent."[1] More than description, more than history, this was an invocation of the moral order that had given meaning to the lives of Ramsey, the Polks, and most of their contemporaries.

II

The idyllic land of simple virtues and steady habits evoked by

[1] Mnemonika [Dr. J. G. M. Ramsey], "Sketch of Mecklenburg County," *The Land We Love*, II (Dec. 1866), 130.

Doctor Ramsey's nostalgic description corresponded closely to the real Mecklenburg that James K. Polk knew for eleven childhood years. By the time of Polk's birth in 1795, Mecklenburg's frontier rawness had mellowed, and the turbulence of its Revolutionary days had receded almost a generation into the past. From his father's door little Jimmy Polk looked out on a vista of fertile and well-cultivated fields, spreading down a gentle slope into a wide bend of Little Sugar Creek; and any suggestion of isolation was dispelled by the friendly wisps of smoke rising from neighboring cabins at several points over the horizon. Even the exciting outside world of the far-away upcountry trading centers, Salisbury fifty miles to the north and Camden sixty miles to the south, did not seem quite so remote when the Great Post Road connecting them skirted the slope in front of Jimmy's house and crossed the creek on his father's bridge. True, the Great Post Road was but a narrow, rutted track, maintained by farmers along the way; yet watching every seven days the boy could see the carrier of the United States mail pass, northbound one week and southbound the next. Only rarely had Jimmy himself been farther up the road than the two miles to Grandfather Ezekiel Polk's plantation or perhaps the nine miles more to Charlotte, the little county seat that had recently impressed George Washington as "a trifling place."[2] Occasionally Jimmy and his playmates might still be frightened to see an Indian on the road, but the once powerful Catawbas had been reduced to a pitiful remnant huddled some ten miles away on the banks of the river to which they had given their name.

Jimmy's father, Sam Polk, provided well for his family. They lived in a log cabin, a fitting home for a boy who would one day aspire to the presidency, but it was of the "saddlebag" type that denoted well-being in early Mecklenburg. Actually there were two houses of hewn logs, with a common roof affording a covered passageway between them, and with mud-chinked chimneys of split sticks on either end. Sam Polk's "bottom lands" along Little Sugar Creek were among the most productive in the county, and no less an authority than President Washington had noted their "very rich

<hr/>

[2] John C. Fitzpatrick, ed., *The Diaries of George Washington, 1749-1799* (4 vols., Boston, 1925), IV, 185; Mecklenburg County, N.C., Minute Book, Court of Pleas and Quarter Sessions, 1796-1808, MS vol. (NCDAH; all other Mecklenburg County records hereafter cited are in the courthouse at Charlotte), entries for 26 Oct. 1796, 26 Apr. 1797; [Major Joseph Graham,] "A plan of Mclenburg and portions of joining Counties . . . January 16th 1789," MS map (NCDAH); Halifax *North Carolina Journal,* 15 Jan., 14 May 1798.

look" as he passed up the road on his way to spend the night with Uncle Thomas Polk at Charlotte four years before Jimmy was born.[3] Tobacco, wheat, corn, hemp, peas, barley, oats, and flax were the principal crops of the Carolina upcountry. The tobacco was hauled down to Camden for sale to Charleston merchants as the chief source of cash at first; but falling tobacco prices and the introduction of Eli Whitney's gin resulted in its virtual replacement by cotton around the turn of the century. As Sam prospered, he bought more land, until eventually he had a plantation of more than 400 acres. Like other well-to-do farmers, Sam doubtless worked in the fields alongside his handful of Negro slaves.[4]

For Jimmy Polk the years passed placidly enough, filled with the customary chores and amusements of country boys past and present. At home he had only his little sisters, Jane and Eliza, for playmates, with perhaps a Negro boy or two. Brothers Franklin and Marshall were still babies, but there were boys in the large families on neighboring farms to provide companionship for swims in the creek or rambles through the woods. Frequent gatherings of the Polk clan at Grandfather Ezekiel's afforded other outlets for youthful gregariousness, with the numerous grandchildren romping in high excitement from yard to barn to creek and back again, while their mothers gossiped in the shade of the porch and their fathers discussed crops and politics on the front steps.

It was about the time of Jimmy's fifth birthday that the political discussions grew most heated, for Mecklenburg was passionately involved in what historians have called the "revolution of 1800." He and other Mecklenburg boys may well have been impressed by the mixture of reverence and faith with which their fathers spoke of Tom Jefferson. For Mecklenburgers identified the Republican candidate with the defense of their way of life, of the individualistic America of plowing and planting, against the seldom-experienced but vividly feared machinations of Alexander Hamilton and his aristocratic merchant and banker friends.

The election doubtless made more of an impression on Jimmy Polk

[3] *Washington Diaries*, IV, 184-185; Cyrus Lee Hunter, *Sketches of Western North Carolina, Historical and Biographical* . . . (Raleigh, 1877), 92; Benson J. Lossing to [David L. Swain], 31 Dec. 1851, David L. Swain Papers (NCDAH).

[4] *Washington Diaries*, IV, 195; François André Michaux, *Travels to the West of the Alleghany Mountains*, in Reuben Gold Thwaites, ed., *Early Western Travels, 1748-1846* (32 vols., Cleveland, 1904-1907), III, 292-298; agreement between Gen. Thomas Polk and Elkanah Watson, 23 Oct. 1786, Polk-Yeatman Papers (SHC); Mecklenburg County, N.C., Record of Deeds, Second Series, Bk. 19, p. 487.

than on other Mecklenburg boys, for while Mecklenburg as a whole was overwhelmingly Republican, the Polk clan was deeply divided. Though Jimmy's father and grandfather were ardent Republicans, Cousin William Polk, the richest man in the county, was Mecklenburg's most conspicuous Federalist. Grandfather had never got along with Cousin William, but it was still upsetting to know that the leading member of one's own family was a traitor to Mecklenburg and all it valued. This bitter family quarrel was well calculated to implant the Republican dogmas deep in the mind of a small boy, despite his total inability to comprehend the nature of the issues.

Yet Jimmy's elders were no better able than he to detect their real enemy. In its Republican rejoicing over Jefferson's victory, Mecklenburg was oblivious to the advent of the nineteenth century and the forces unleashed by James Watt and Eli Whitney. None could have believed that Mr. Jefferson himself, and his chosen successors, would be forced to beat a strategic retreat before an economic dynamism that was soon to engulf the old values. Nor could any have guessed that Sam Polk's son would one day play an important part in a last futile attempt to reconcile these old American values of his boyhood Mecklenburg with the railroad-building, cotton-shipping, stock-jobbing, industrial actualities of the America that lay a few short decades ahead.

It is not after all so important what little Jimmy Polk experienced or understood directly; for the ethos that governed his mature years was made up out of the common experiences of his clan and the wider community of Old Mecklenburg, effortlessly absorbed around Sam Polk's fireplace on long winter evenings, or in the shade of the big cedars at Grandfather Ezekiel's, or on the benches beside the little log courthouse at Charlotte. On such occasions heroic fact and prosaic history blended into legend and myth, as old men and women recalled the clearing of the forests, the terror of the Indians, the bold stand for liberty, the years of skirmishing with British soldiers. From these epic narratives Jimmy Polk absorbed his image of Old Mecklenburg, a Mecklenburg old only in experience and recent enough in time to be a living reality.

III

The Polks had been in the thick of Mecklenburg affairs since the beginning. Scotch-Irish in derivation, the first American Polks had appeared late in the seventeenth century as substantial farmers along the broad creeks and estuaries of Maryland's Eastern Shore, where they helped organize the earliest Presbyterian congregations in the New World. It was some time before 1740 that one of these Maryland Polks, William by name, struck out for the Pennsylvania frontier and located himself in the Cumberland valley near the present site of Carlisle. Here his wife Margaret bore him eight children.[5]

By the early 1750's the good lands in the Cumberland valley were all occupied, and with William's older sons approaching the age when they would want farms of their own, the Polks began to think of joining the hundreds of Cumberland families who were already trekking down the Great Wagon Road through the Valley of Virginia into the empty southern upcountry. The third son, Thomas, "a young man of great athletickness, of much energy of both mind and body," led the way. Joining the southward procession in 1753, he pressed on until he left settlements behind as he crossed the Yadkin River in upcountry North Carolina. Finally, near the southern border of the province, he came upon a fertile country, watered by a network of creeks flowing south and west into the Catawba River. Here he cleared land, built one of the first cabins on Sugar Creek, and married a daughter of the first white settler west of the Yadkin.[6]

[5] This account is based on the autobiographical sketch written in the 1820's by Colonel William Polk of North Carolina and reproduced in William Henry Hoyt, ed., *The Papers of Archibald D. Murphey* (2 vols., Raleigh, 1914), II, 400-410. Colonel Polk, who undoubtedly got his information from his father, Thomas Polk, says that the family migrated from Ireland to the Eastern Shore of Maryland about 1722 and to the neighborhood of Carlisle, Pennsylvania, in 1740. According to [William Harrison Polk,] *Polk Family and Kinsmen* (Louisville, 1912), 3-93, the first Polks, or Pollocks as they were originally known, arrived on the Eastern Shore in the latter decades of the seventeenth century. A Polk Family Tree published in 1849 (copy in William Polk Papers, NCDAH) indicates that the William Polk who moved to Pennsylvania and became progenitor of the North Carolina Polks was a son of John Polk, the son of Robert Bruce Polk, the original seventeenth century immigrant to Maryland. More recent investigation by William Harrison Polk reveals that William, the son of John, the son of Robert Bruce, lived and died in Maryland. The same investigator suggests that William Polk of Pennsylvania was a hitherto unknown son of William Polk, another son of Robert Bruce Polk. *Polk Family and Kinsmen*, 16, 18, 204. This conclusion, however, is far from demonstrated. It seems that there were more branches of the Polk family in early eighteenth century Maryland than the genealogists have yet distinguished. Until better evidence is discovered, the statements of Colonel William Polk of North Carolina provide the most reliable information on his branch of the family. For the Scotch-Irish settlements in the Cumberland valley, see Wayland F. Dunaway, *The Scotch-Irish of Colonial Pennsylvania* (Chapel Hill, 1944), 60-64, 102-103, 107-108.

[6] *Murphey Papers*, II, 400.

Thomas was soon joined by the rest of his family, along with many of their Pennsylvania neighbors. Three of his mother's sisters had married members of the Alexander clan, and the Alexanders poured into the Catawba country in such numbers that they were to dominate it, numerically, politically, and socially, for many generations. Nearly 300 Alexanders, their Old Testament names—Ezra, Moses, Elias, Abraham, Hezekiah, Adam, Abijah, and many another—proclaiming their ardent Presbyterianism, were to be recorded in this area by the Census of 1790. Indeed, as Doctor Ramsey, whose mother had been a Mecklenburg Alexander, was to recall, there were not enough Biblical names to go around. "So numerous were the tribe of Alexanders," he wrote, that "they had to be designated by their office—their trade or their middle name." Thus Mecklenburgers referred to "Governor Nat" to distinguish Governor Nathaniel Alexander from "Fuller Nat" or "Red Head Nat," and to "Clerk Isaac" to avoid confusing the veteran county clerk with his kinsman "Long Creek Isaac" Alexander.[7]

"The whole tribe of these Alexanders," as the pious Doctor Ramsey noted proudly, "were remarkable for the tenacity with which they adhered to the doctrines and order of presbytery." Such sectarian zeal was not nearly so marked among the Mecklenburg Polks. Indeed this and much else in their character may be explained by their need to set themselves apart somehow from their numerous Alexander neighbors. Was it perhaps deliberately that William Polk eschewed the Alexandrian Biblicism in giving his older sons such conventional names as William, John, Thomas, and Charles? Only the youngest boy, Ezekiel, was christened under the Alexandrian spell, and he turned out to be a singularly inappropriate choice for this distinction.

Ezekiel was only six when the family made its long journey to the North Carolina frontier. William Polk the elder seems to have died shortly after reaching the new country, and the older children quickly left the parental roof to marry, clear farms, and raise families of their own. William's widow could hardly have supported herself and little Ezekiel from the occasional fees she received as a midwife, and it seems that both of them were taken into the household of Thomas, the most prosperous of the brothers.[8]

---

[7] William B. Hesseltine, ed., *Dr. J. G. M. Ramsey: Autobiography and Letters* (Nashville, 1954), 286-289; Bureau of the Census, *Heads of Families at the First Census Taken in the Year 1790* (12 vols., Washington, 1908), xi, 158-164.

[8] Ramsey, *Autobiography*, 3. For mention of the various Polks in North Carolina

IV

Though Virginians had been coming down the old Trading Path to barter with the Catawba and Cherokee Indians since the early part of the century, the pioneer farmers who arrived with the Polks found the gently rolling land still covered with hardwood forests and virgin savannahs. The wilderness quickly gave way as these vigorous Scotch-Irishmen cleared the bottom lands along the creeks. They found the red clay soil fertile, and their log cabins rose on the nearby slopes wherever springs afforded a convenient supply of clear, cold water.

Through the 1750's and 1760's the stream of Scotch-Irish immigrants into the southern uplands grew steadily larger, and as the choice locations in the Sugar Creek country were preempted, it poured over the provincial boundary. Among these later comers were the parents of Andrew Jackson, who stopped in the Waxhaw community only a few miles south of the Polks, and the parents of John C. Calhoun, who pushed on across the Catawba into the rolling hills of western South Carolina.

Presbyterians almost to a man, the Sugar Creek Scotch-Irish could not bear to be without regular worship according to the forms of their denomination. Makeshift preaching stands in the woods had to serve in the earliest days, but within a few years they were replaced by little meeting houses. Around these crude buildings were

---

see: affidavit of William Davidson in pension papers of Charles Polk, Veterans Administration Section (NA); Walter Clark, ed., *The State Records of North Carolina* (vols. xi-xxvi, Winston and Goldsboro, 1895-1905), xxii, 437; Bureau of the Census, *Heads of Families*, xi, 162; Polk entries in Card Index to Land Grants (NCSS); John Polk entries in Anson County, N.C., Index to Deeds, Grantees, 1749-1900, microfilm (NCDAH); Mecklenburg County, Record of Deeds, First Series, Bk. 2, pp. 637-639; *Polk Family and Kinsmen*, 192-195; receipt by Margaret Polk, 10 Aug. 1767, Estate of Samuel Bigers, in Mecklenburg County, N.C., Settlements of Estates (NCDAH).

The most reliable Polk genealogies are Wilmot Polk Rogers, "Ezekiel Polk and His Descendents," typescript copies (LC and THS); and Mrs. Frank M. Angellotti, "The Polks of North Carolina and Tennessee," *New England Historical and Genealogical Register*, lxxvii (1923), 133-145, 213-227, 250-270, lxxviii (1924), 33-53, 159-177, 318-330.

John Polk married in 1758 and Charles four years later. John settled near Rocky River, some miles to the east of Sugar Creek; he was later a government agent among the Catawba Indians, living in South Carolina, where in 1803 his widow recorded her will (York County, S.C., Will Book 1, p. 159, Courthouse, York, S.C.). Charles established himself above John's original farm on Rocky River. Both of these sites were in Anson County. Their brother William had married before coming to North Carolina, and where he lived has not been discovered. The three sisters married respectively Samuel McLeary, Benjamin Alexander, and Robert McRea.

organized the seven congregations that became the focal points of life in the Catawba country. Everyone, pious or not, attended church to learn the latest news, make trades, or simply visit, though the faithful tried strenuously to prevent such secular intrusions on the holy Sabbath, forbidding even the cracking of walnuts. Much of Saturday was devoted to preparation for the Sabbath. All the food that would be needed was prepared ahead of time, boots and shoes were blacked, and firewood was cut and piled near the door. All of this culminated Saturday evening in a family service of spiritual preparation, and for communion Sundays the preparation was extended back to Friday, when every communicant was expected to keep a fast and attend the meeting house to hear a preparation sermon.[9]

This stern piety made for strong men and women, the only kind who could prosper on the turbulent Catawba frontier. Indian raids in the 1750's were followed in the next decade by rioting over lands and taxes; and these troubles were hardly past when the Carolina upcountry was plunged into civil war. Callous exploitation by corrupt courthouse rings, in league with the province's dominant tidewater politicians, had goaded thousands of the humbler interior people into an open revolt that ended only in pitched battle at Alamance Creek in 1771. However the Scotch-Irish along the Catawba made an advantageous alliance with Governor William Tryon and the lowcountry leaders against the insurgent Regulators. The rebels complained bitterly that "the Gov. gives Commissions making one Col. Alexander, and another Capt. Alexander and another Alexander Esq. Justice of the Peace &c. &c.—and all this to take in a large body of Presbyterians"; but the protests did not deter the Polks and their neighbors from accepting these and other favors or from marching with the governor's army against their desperate countrymen.[10]

Ezekiel Polk grew up in the midst of this turbulence, for his

[9] Daniel A. Tompkins, *History of Mecklenburg County and the City of Charlotte from 1740-1903* (2 vols., Charlotte, 1903), I, 15-27; William Henry Foote, *Sketches of North Carolina, Historical and Biographical* . . . (New York, 1846), 79-81, 168-170, 183-190; Ramsey, *Autobiography*, 288.

[10] William K. Boyd, ed., *Some Eighteenth Century Tracts Concerning North Carolina* (Raleigh, 1927), 348; Tompkins, *Mecklenburg*, I, 8-14; Charles Town *South Carolina Gazette*, 21 July 1756, 12 May 1759; William L. Saunders, ed., *The Colonial Records of North Carolina* (10 vols., Raleigh, 1886-1890), VII, 6, 10, 14-35, 1004; Henry Eustace McCulloh to Edmund Fanning [April 1765], Fanning-McCulloh Letters (SHC).

brother Thomas was rapidly becoming the most prominent man in the Sugar Creek country. Thomas Polk was the chief promoter of the new county of Mecklenburg, formed in 1762, one of its original magistrates, and a captain in the provincial militia. The little county seat town of Charlotte was established under his sponsorship, and he served in Mecklenburg's delegation to the provincial assembly every year save one from 1766 to 1774.[11]

Captain Polk did more for his youngest brother than furnish him an example of backwoods leadership. By 1769, when Ezekiel was twenty-two, the frontier had moved so far toward the mountains that a new county was organized across the Catawba and named for the governor with whom the Polks had recently allied themselves. Thomas Polk's counterpart on the other side of the river was his brother-in-law, Captain Thomas Neal, and the two of them together seem to have controlled the new county's patronage. At any rate Ezekiel appeared at the first meeting of the Tryon County court bearing a commission from Governor Tryon naming him clerk of court, a lucrative and politically important office in eighteenth century local government.[12]

The young politician's new eminence enabled him to take a wife, Maria ("Nanny") Wilson, daughter of a wealthy farmer in the northern end of Mecklenburg. Establishing his bride on a 200-acre farm near the southern border of the new county, Ezekiel settled down to increase his worldly goods and political influence. His family was growing along with his local consequence. In 1770 Maria presented him with twins, Thomas and Matilda; and two years later a second son, Samuel, was born.[13]

Just at this auspicious moment Ezekiel's fair prospects were unexpectedly blasted. In 1772 the disputed provincial boundary was at last surveyed, and both Thomas Neal and Ezekiel found to their dismay that they were living in South Carolina. But these aggressive Scotch-Irishmen were not to be stopped by any such mischance. Within a year or two Thomas Neal was colonel and Ezekiel was

[11] Albert Ray Newsome, "Thomas Polk," in Allen Johnson and Dumas Malone, eds., *Dictionary of American Biography* (21 vols., New York, 1937), xv, 42; Tompkins, *Mecklenburg*, I, 31-34.

[12] Tryon County, N.C., Minute Book, Court of Pleas and Quarter Sessions, 1769-1779, microfilm (NCDAH), July Term, 1769.

[13] Chalmers G. Davidson, *Major John Davidson of "Rural Hill,"* . . . (Charlotte, 1943), 6-7. For the location of Ezekiel's Tryon plantation, see Land Book 22, p. 22 (NCSS); also, assignments of road overseers, Tryon Court Minutes, October Term, 1769, and April Term, 1771. Rogers, "Ezekiel Polk," 15, 24, 59, 66.

lieutenant colonel in the militia organization of the New Acquisition, as South Carolina called the district she had acquired under the boundary settlement.[14] But once again, just when Ezekiel's prospects were brightening, forces he could not control intervened, with unhappy consequences for his personal fortunes.

V

However unprepossessing the Mecklenburg of Jimmy Polk's boyhood may have seemed, Mecklenburgers were not apologetic. They had been, as they conceived, actors in history's most momentous drama, the war between tyranny and liberty; and they lived in the lingering glory of that great struggle. In 1800, heroes still walked among them, were indeed their neighbors, cousins, uncles, and brothers. Mecklenburgers never tired of recounting gleefully the rout of a sizeable British foraging party by a dozen farmers at the McIntyre place; or how, when the enemy was forced to evacuate Charlotte in 1780, a reluctant guide had got Lord Cornwallis's entire army lost in the tangled thickets along lower Sugar Creek. Naturally Mecklenburgers took pride in the epithet, "hornet's nest," that his lordship had bestowed upon their troublesome county.

Yet the Revolution was more than a hallowed memory. The liberty Mecklenburgers had fought for in the seventies was a way of life, an agrarian individualism, that still had to be defended. Their votes for Jefferson were a reaffirmation of the lofty principles so ringingly declared in 'seventy-five and so indelibly burned into their consciousness by seven years of privation, hatred, and bloodshed.

The sons and grandsons of Mecklenburg had special reason for this unusually passionate identification of their social values with the revolutionary heritage. Wherever they went they carried with them the conviction that their revolutionary forebears had been the first Americans anywhere to declare their independence from the British king. The news of fighting at Lexington and Concord had no sooner reached the Sugar Creek country than a meeting was called to adopt the celebrated resolves of May 31, 1775. "All Commissions, civil and military, heretofore granted by the Crown, to be exercised in these Colonies," the Mecklenburgers declared, "are wholly null and void, and the Constitution of each Colony wholly suspended."

---

[14] Marvin L. Skaggs, *North Carolina Boundary Disputes Involving Her Southern Line* (Chapel Hill, 1941), 74-97; Edward McCrady, *The History of South Carolina in the Revolution, 1775-1780* (New York, 1901), 11n.

Suiting their actions to the boldness of their words, they promptly created a revolutionary committee to supplant the legal county government constituted under Crown authority.[15]

The Polks had played a prominent part in these proceedings and in the fighting that followed. Thomas Polk was a ringleader in the initial revolutionary agitation, and it was he who had called the meeting to adopt the Mecklenburg Resolves. He and his son William became colonel and major respectively in the Continental line, and Thomas was subsequently commissary general for Horatio Gates' ill-fated southern army. Two of the other Polk brothers, Charles and John, served honorably as militia captains.[16]

Ezekiel's revolutionary career was more checkered. His youthful days in Thomas Polk's comfortable home had been, as he later admitted, "spent in pleasure," a result to which Thomas's pack of frolicsome sons no doubt contributed. Thomas had provided his youngest brother with a good education, and some people regarded Ezekiel as the most talented of all the Polks. Impulsive, nimble-witted, fiercely independent, and eloquent, he had an ability to sweep others along with him in his various enthusiasms. But he lacked the persevering qualities of the more commonplace members of his clan, and this failing was frequently his undoing.[17]

In the early months of the revolutionary crisis, Ezekiel joined heartily with the lowcountry leaders of the patriot party in South Carolina, attending the provincial congress at Charlestown in June 1775 and accepting a captain's commission in the mounted regiment organized to keep the upcountry from going over to the king. He had hardly reached the patriot camp, however, when he was enraged by an order to march the upcountry troops to the coast to meet a threatened invasion. His men had not enlisted to protect the plantations of lowcountry nabobs, snorted Captain Polk, and he "would

---

[15] William Henry Hoyt, *The Mecklenburg Declaration of Independence* . . . (New York, 1907), 271. This authoritative study of a long-vexed question demolishes the myth of a "Declaration of Independence" on 20 May 1775, but leaves unquestioned the radical resolves adopted on 31 May 1775.

[16] Newsome, "Thomas Polk," *loc.cit.*, 42; J. G. de R. Hamilton, "William Polk," *Dictionary of American Biography*, xv, 43-44; Pension Papers of Charles Polk and Charles Polk (of Texas), Veterans Administration Section (NA).

[17] Quotation from the epitaph Ezekiel composed for his own tombstone as printed in Jackson (Tennessee) *Gazette*, 13 Sept. 1824; [Tennessee Democratic Central Committee, comp.], *Vindication of the Revolutionary Character and Services of the Late Col. Ezekiel Polk, of Mecklenburg, N.C.*, pamphlet (Nashville [1844]), 14.

not sacrifice their Healths for no Council of Safety's Parading notions." Whereupon he marched his company home.[18]

This was treason, as Ezekiel quickly perceived, and it was only by taking charge of the ruthless coercion of neutrals and loyalists that he persuaded the patriot leaders to restore his commission. Though he participated creditably in several campaigns against the loyalists and Indians, Ezekiel was never able to regain the confidence of his patriot neighbors, and in 1776 he moved his family back to Mecklenburg. Buying a 260-acre farm from his brother Thomas, he settled down on the east side of Sugar Creek, some nine miles down the Great Post Road from Charlotte.[19]

Luckily for his family, Ezekiel's instability did not carry over into economic activities; to the accumulation of property he devoted himself with a single-mindedness worthy of the noblest cause. By this time the theater of war had moved off to the north, leaving Mecklenburg relatively undisturbed. Ezekiel was able to concentrate on farming, and in 1778 he opened a tavern on the courthouse square in Charlotte. His appointment the following year as justice of the

[18] Alexander S. Salley, Jr., ed., "Papers of the First Council of Safety of the Revolutionary Party in South Carolina, June-November, 1775," *South Carolina Historical and Genealogical Magazine,* I (1900), 69. Information on Ezekiel's career in South Carolina is drawn from the following: A. S. Salley, Jr., ed., "Historical Notes," *ibid.,* v (1904), 189-190, vii (1906), 103-107; "Extracts from the Journal of the South Carolina Provincial Congress of June, 1775," copied into a notebook in James K. Polk Papers, Second Series (LC; hereafter cited as Polk Papers, which refers to First Series unless otherwise indicated); McCrady, *S.C. in Revolution, 1775-1780,* 13-14, 37; "Journal of the Council of Safety for the Province of South Carolina, 1775," *Collections of the South Carolina Historical Society,* II (1858), 24-26, 37; "Papers of Council of Safety," *loc.cit.,* I (1900), 47, 69-71, 192, II (1901), 103, 261-262, III (1902), 3-4, 171; *Murphey Papers,* II, 201, 401-403; John Drayton, ed., *Memoirs of the American Revolution* . . . (2 vols., Charleston, 1821), I, 323; A. S. Salley, Jr., *The History of Orangeburg County, South Carolina, from Its First Settlement to the Close of the Revolutionary War* (Orangeburg, 1898), 389, 395, 406-407, 414, 416-419, 424-425, 434; R. W. Gibbes, ed., *Documentary History of the American Revolution* . . . (3 vols., Columbia, S.C., and New York, 1853-1857), I, 133, 137, 147, 151, 227, 240, II, 27; A. S. Salley, Jr., ed., *Col. William Hill's Memoirs of the Revolution* (Columbia, S.C., 1929), 29-30; *American Archives,* Fourth Series, IV, 28, 31, 33, 40-48, v, 578, Fifth Series, I, 458; *Vindication of Ezekiel Polk,* 14.

[19] A. S. Salley, Jr., ed., *Journal of the General Assembly of South Carolina, September 17, 1776–October 20, 1776* (Columbia, 1909), 161 and passim, shows that Ezekiel was elected to this body but did not attend. The deed from Thomas Polk to Ezekiel Polk, dated 3 Oct. 1776, of 260 acres for £300, lists both men as being "of Mecklenburg." Mecklenburg Deeds, Second Series, Bk. 5, p. 232. The family graveyard where Ezekiel buried his first wife and at least two of his children may be seen today in the dense woods about two miles northwest of the town of Pineville, just east of Sugar Creek, and fixes the location of his plantation.

peace indicated that for the third time in a decade he was winning consequence in a new community.[20]

It was not long, however, before the war again intervened in Ezekiel's fortunes. With Lord Cornwallis's invasion of South Carolina in the summer of 1780 and the disastrous American defeat at Camden in August, the Mecklenburg militia was called out for operations against the loyalists rallying west of the Catawba and for gallant guerrilla action against the inexorable advance of the enemy's main army. Though he took the field himself on several occasions, Ezekiel more characteristically joined the Presbyterian clergy in haranguing the militia and "exhorting them to be true to their country." But when, on September 26, the British army marched past his farm into Charlotte, Ezekiel's own patriotism failed. Cornwallis had chosen the only painted building in the village, Thomas Polk's "White House," as his headquarters, and there Ezekiel went to save his property by "taking protection," promising to remain peaceably at home and cooperate with the invaders.[21]

Eleven days later fortune again turned against Ezekiel. The annihilation of Cornwallis's left wing at Kings Mountain forced a British withdrawal, and only Ezekiel's family connections saved him from punishment by the resentful Whigs. Nevertheless he managed to restore himself to the good graces of his neighbors by some service in the final stages of the war, for in 1782 the Mecklenburg magistrates, with only two dissenting votes, elected him sheriff, the most important office at their disposal. But the day after his election he was back before the justices complaining loudly about the condition of the jail, and within three months the unpredictable Ezekiel had resigned.[22]

VI

With the war won and independence established, the victors pro-

[20] Mecklenburg Deeds, First Series, Bk. 36, p. 80; Mecklenburg County, N.C., Minute Book, Court of Pleas and Quarter Sessions, 1774-1785, entries for 16 Oct. 1778 and Oct. Term, 1779.

[21] Raleigh *North Carolina Standard*, 18 Sept. 1844; *Vindication of Ezekiel Polk*, 9-14; Thomas G. Polk to Bishop Leonidas Polk, 21 June [1852], and Benson J. Lossing to Bishop Leonidas Polk, 12 June 1852, Polk Family of North Carolina Papers (LC).

[22] *Vindication of Ezekiel Polk*, 9-13; Revolutionary Vouchers (NCDAH), Salisbury District, No. 5138, to Ezekiel Polk for militia services; Revolutionary Accounts (NCDAH), Vol. vi, fo. 88, p. 1, Vol. xii, fo. 26, p. 4, and fo. 31, p. 4, to Ezekiel Polk; Mecklenburg Court Minutes, 1774-1785, 10-11 Apr. 1782 and July Term, 1782.

ceeded to reap the spoils; in the sequel Ezekiel and his descendants were to become Tennesseans. The great prize was North Carolina's wilderness domain stretching west from the mountains to the Mississippi. Before the war was over the legislature set aside part of this territory to satisfy soldiers' land bounty warrants, most of which quickly fell into the hands of speculator-politicians. The rest of the vast area was disposed of by an act of 1783, under which millions of acres went for a song to a handful of insiders. The architect of this colossal grab was William Blount, an eastern politician with an eye to the main chance, and prominent among his associates was Thomas Polk of Mecklenburg.

Thomas Polk was typical of a large group of aggressive men who had come to the fore in the North Carolina backcountry. By virtue of the oligarchic structure of county government and through alliance with the tidewater leaders who ran provincial affairs, these men had been able to organize courthouse rings that dominated the interior. It was these oligarchs of tidewater and backcountry, irritated at British interference with their efforts to manage provincial affairs for their own benefit, who initiated and led the revolutionary movement in North Carolina. But to many other North Carolinians the Revolution meant a quickening and partial fulfillment of democratic aspirations, and this ambivalence of purpose paved the way for many future conflicts.

The popular element first emerged as a force in North Carolina politics at the 1776 election for a provincial congress to form a state constitution. In Mecklenburg this contest pitted Thomas Polk against a popular faction led by the Alexanders. The Alexanders won, mainly it seems by branding Polk as "a home-bred lord" who "has been much employed in public services, in all of which he was ever mindful of his own private emolument." What was at stake in this election was revealed more clearly when the Alexanders called a public meeting and drafted a set of radical instructions for the Mecklenburg delegates. The new constitution must provide, the delegates were told, for universal manhood suffrage, annual assemblies, direct election of local officials, and—a typically Alexandrian demand—strict religious qualifications for holding office. The conservatives, however, won a partial victory in the convention, and Thomas Polk retained his influence with the state leaders, despite his loss of support at home. So it happened that Thomas Polk was

17

on hand to join William Blount and other insiders in lobbying their grand speculative scheme through the legislature of 1783.[23]

The land act of 1783 ostensibly threw open most of what was to become the state of Tennessee for sale to all comers, but few outside the Blount circle were prepared to take advantage of its ingeniously drawn provisions. Payment was to be made in the discredited state and continental notes, which no one except the speculators had had the foresight to amass. A grant could be obtained only by: (1) employing a locator in the western country to prepare an entry, or rough description of a desirable tract; (2) then filing the entry with a special office at Hillsborough, hundreds of miles from the western country, and receiving a warrant of survey; (3) having the warrant surveyed by an official surveyor in the western country; and, finally, (4) returning the plat of survey to the North Carolina secretary of state. Since the various officials were themselves involved in the Great Speculation, they used this complicated procedure to bar interlopers, while winking at irregularities by their associates.

Planned with the utmost care, the Great Speculation was executed with remarkable dispatch. In May 1784 the Blount faction persuaded the legislature to suspend the land act and cede the whole western territory to the Confederation authorities, provided that they make good all warrants already issued, as well as any military warrants to be issued in the future. In seven short months more than three million acres had been entered, practically all of it by insiders who were organized and had locators in the field. These warrants of 1783, moreover, were to demonstrate an astonishing capacity for expansion and self-proliferation; by the time they were all perfected into grants, they would cover practically all the desirable acreage in the Tennessee country.[24]

The Polks were deeply involved in the Great Speculation as partners with the Blounts and as members of several land companies organized by other members of the Blount group. With advance

---

23 James H. Moore, *Defence of the Mecklenburg Declaration of Independence* . . . (Raleigh, 1908), 147-157; *ibid.*, 123-128; Hoyt, *Mecklenburg Declaration*, 113-116; Samuel A'Court Ashe, *History of North Carolina* (2 vols., Greensboro and Raleigh, 1925), i, 556-559; John H. Wheeler, *Historical Sketches of North Carolina* (reprint edn., 2 vols. in 1, New York, 1925), ii, 260-262.

24 Thomas P. Abernethy, *From Frontier to Plantation in Tennessee: A Study in Frontier Democracy* (Chapel Hill, 1932), 35-59; Alice Barnwell Keith, "Three North Carolina Blount Brothers in Business and Politics, 1783-1812," Ph.D. dissertation, University of North Carolina (1940), 267; Albert Lincoln Bramlett, "North Carolina's Western Lands," Ph.D. dissertation, University of North Carolina (1928), 91-93, 118-120, 131-136.

knowledge of what was coming, one of these companies had its locators in the field a full year before the scheme became law. As soon as the act was passed, Thomas Polk took his four sons into the western wilderness to join the race for the best lands, at the same time buying up soldiers' claims for location in the military district. Through the Blount influence, Thomas Polk was elected to the Council of State by this same legislature and reelected the next year. His brother Ezekiel was chosen as one of the surveyors to run the boundary of the military district, and his son William as one of the three official surveyors for the western country. So closely were the speculators tied in with the leaders of the infant settlements across the mountains that William Polk had no sooner reached his new post than he was elected to represent the frontier county of Davidson in the North Carolina assembly.[25]

Ezekiel Polk did not rank high enough in political circles to share directly in these fruits of liberty. He had been initiated into the charmed circle of provincial oligarchs back in his Tryon County days, but having lost his chance for prominence he now had to content himself with such favors as his powerful brother threw his way. The first of these, the appointment as surveyor of the military boundary in 1783, must have been especially gratifying to a man of Ezekiel's temperament. Not only did this expedition into the wilderness across the mountains appeal to his strong spirit of adventure, but also he was to receive a princely tract of land for his services. Though Indian raids soon forced the surveyors to return home, Ezekiel never got over this first venture into the verdant country. At the earliest opportunity he bought the military

[25] *N.C. State Records,* xix, 185, 571, xxii, 152; Keith, "Blount Brothers," 266-267, 285, 295; Bramlett, "Western Lands," 68-76; Albert V. Goodpasture, "The Boyhood of President Polk," *Tennessee Historical Magazine,* vii (Apr. 1921), 43; grant to Ezekiel Polk, Land Grants, Middle District, File No. 3 (NCSS); Maury County, Tenn., Minutes of Circuit Court, 1810-1815 (wherever Tennessee county records are cited herein, the typescript copies in the State Library at Nashville have been used), 141; Maury County, Minutes of County Court, 1808-1809, pp. 76-79, entry for 19 Sept. 1809; Williamson County, Tenn., Minutes of County Court, 1800-1812, entry for 14 Oct. 1806; *Murphey Papers,* i, 176n., ii, 408; "Directions to Col Polk in the case of Polk vs Polk," 10 Oct. 1826, Polk Family Papers; articles of agreement between Thomas Polk and Elijah Robertson, 1, 3 June 1784, Polk-Yeatman Papers; resolutions of Memucan Hunt and Co., 1 Apr. 1789, *ibid.;* Stockley Donelson to Col. William Polk, 15 May 1790, *ibid.;* Joseph Johnson, *Traditions and Reminiscences Chiefly of the American Revolution in the South* . . . (Charleston, 1851), 85.

For the grantees, see Card Index to Tennessee Land Grants (NCSS); and Book of Warrants Issued by John Armstrong's Office, in the Tennessee Land Office, Nashville. The latter is more nearly complete.

bounty right to a tract north of the Cumberland, on a branch of the Sulphur fork of the Red River, in what would later be Robertson County.[26]

Meanwhile Ezekiel's family was growing; his fourth daughter and eighth child was born in 1790. The placid life on the Sugar Creek plantation, however, only made Ezekiel more restless. In 1790 he secured an appointment as deputy surveyor of land grants in the western country, and in August he packed up his family for the arduous journey over the mountains to settle on the military grant he had bought a few years before.

The Great Speculation was just entering a new phase. Since most of the tracts claimed during those seven feverish months of 1783-1784 were in Indian country and could not be surveyed and granted for many years to come, the speculators were determined to control the area, so as to defend and, wherever possible, inflate their claims. Thus when the federal government organized the Tennessee country as the Southwest Territory in 1790, William Blount got himself appointed territorial governor. Blount and his associates, in fact, were to dominate the area, as territory and state, for three decades to come. As late as the 1820's, when James K. Polk entered public life, politics and legislation would still revolve around the same Great Speculation that led his grandfather west in 1790, just as the Southwest Territory was being organized. Ezekiel had no sooner reached his new home than Governor Blount, doubtless at Thomas Polk's instance, appointed him one of the nine magistrates for the county where his lands lay.[27]

Only ten years before, the original pioneers in the Red River country had been driven off by bloody Indian raids, but the Indian menace had abated temporarily, and immigrants were now coming in large numbers. Once he got his cabin built and his family established, Ezekiel was kept busy surveying tracts for other newcomers, leaving his older boys and the Negro slaves to clear fields for spring planting. Yet the winter's hard work went for naught when Ezekiel's beloved Maria became seriously ill. Hoping that old friends

---

[26] Grants to Ezekiel Polk, Land Grants, Middle District, File No. 3, and Davidson County, Tenn., File No. 220 (NCSS).

[27] Rogers, "Ezekiel Polk," 105; Stockley Donelson to Col. William Polk, 15 May 1790, Polk-Yeatman Papers; Ezekiel Polk's bond as deputy surveyor, 25 Aug. 1790, Polk Family Papers; Col. William Polk to Col. Robert Hays, 16 Aug. 1790, Miscellaneous Papers (NCDAH); Clarence E. Carter, ed., *The Territorial Papers of the United States*, Vol. IV, *The Territory South of the River Ohio, 1790-1795* (Washington, 1936), 441-442.

and familiar surroundings might arrest her decline, the Polks moved back to Mecklenburg before they were able to gather their first crop on the Red River.[28] But Maria was beyond recovery and died in the fall of 1791, leaving the disconsolate Ezekiel to record his grief in the eight lines of funereal verse he composed for her elaborately carved tombstone:

> Here unalarm'd at Death's last Stroke
> Lies in this tomb MARIA POLK
> A tender Mother virtuous Wife
> Resign'd in every Scene of life
> Truly pious without parade
> Where want appear'd she lent her Aid
> To heavenly Courts she did repair
> May those she lov'd all meet her there[29]

In less than a year, however, Ezekiel had married again. Not one of the several children his new wife bore him survived infancy, and again Ezekiel vented his grief in doggerel epitaphs:

> Beneath this Slab lies here Interr'd
> An Innocent that never Err'd
> A Mothers Hope in racking pain
> A Sixth time blasted are again
> April the 2d. 1793
> Still born son of EZEKIEL POLK[30]

Meanwhile the older sons and daughters were leaving the Sugar Creek plantation to marry and set up for themselves.

VII

The Polks were often the scandal of their more conventional neighbors. The influence of wives taken from among Wilsons, Spratts, and Alexanders was usually enough to keep the restive Polk men up to the minimum standards of behavior prescribed by a Presbyterian community and occasionally to produce sons and daughters of a circumspect Alexandrian cast. But now and again

---

[28] A deed dated 28 June 1791 lists Ezekiel Polk as being again a resident of Mecklenburg. For conditions on the Red River at this time, see Albert V. Goodpasture, "Beginnings of Montgomery County," *American Historical Magazine* (Nashville), VIII (July 1903), 193-205; and "The Correspondence of Gen. James Robertson," *ibid.*, I (Oct. 1896), 284-285.

[29] Gravestone of Maria Polk, Polk Graveyard, near Pineville, N.C.

[30] Gravestones of Eliza Polk and "Still born son of EZEKIEL POLK," Polk Graveyard. The name of Ezekiel's second wife is given variously as Bessie Davis and Polly Campbell.

an ungovernable strain in the family line would erupt in the impetuous enthusiasms of an Ezekiel Polk or the madcap pranks that distinguished Thomas Polk's son "Devil Charley" from another kinsman, "Civil Charley" Polk.[31]

Ezekiel's second son, Sam, turned out to be one of the sober, conventional Polks, though his conventionality took the form of a passion for this world's goods, rather than his neighbors' zeal for the Presbyterian God. Sam had had a good education for the time and place, probably at Charlotte's Liberty Hall Academy, and he developed into the sturdy, level-headed kind of youth upon whom careful fathers are not afraid to bestow their daughters. So like Ezekiel before him, he was able to seek a wife among the prosperous, orthodox farmers of Hopewell congregation in the northern end of Mecklenburg. It was probably on a visit to his Wilson kin, perhaps while attending church with them, that Sam met Jane Knox.

The Knoxes represented perfectly the Scottish Presbyterian tradition suggested by their family name. Jane's father, James Knox, impressed his neighbors as being "remarkable for his piety" and for "his extreme care and fidelity in the religious education and culture of his children in the doctrine and order of the Presbyterian Church." He had been a militia captain during the Revolution, and Mecklenburgers long celebrated his courageous charge up to the muzzle of a British cannon at the Battle of Hanging Rock. Since the war, hard work at farming and blacksmithing had made him well-to-do, and the Hopewell community recognized him as one of its leading citizens. His grandson and namesake, James Knox Polk, was to resemble him more than he would any other immediate ancestor, a resemblance which the younger man would acknowledge by taking special pride in his maternal grandfather, and more particularly in Grandfather Knox's military record, as contrasted with Grandfather Ezekiel Polk's.[32]

To the canny Captain Knox and his nineteen-year-old daughter, twenty-two-year-old Sam Polk must have seemed an excellent marital prospect; and Sam's courtship had almost won its object when suddenly, in October 1794, James Knox died in the full vigor of his middle years, leaving behind a wife and four children and a considerable estate, including ten slaves. The impatient young people de-

---

[31] Johnson, *Traditions and Reminiscences*, 83-85.

[32] Ramsey, *Autobiography*, 270-271; Hattie S. Goodman, *The Knox Family* . . . (Richmond, 1905), 30-35, 114, 118; *Vindication of Ezekiel Polk*, 9; *N.C. State Records*, XIX, 973-974.

layed their plans only ten weeks. Sam's older brother, Thomas, was also bringing his courtship of a Hopewell girl to a successful conclusion, and a double wedding was arranged for Christmas night. The ceremony was probably performed at the Widow Knox's and followed, as was the custom, by a big country party.[33]

Ezekiel presented his newly married sons with adjacent 250-acre farms on Little Sugar Creek, several miles south of his own plantation; while Jane received from her father's estate two Negro girls, a feather bed, three cows and calves, a mare, a saddle and bridle, a third of his household furniture, and a fifth of his undivided estate. So the young people were off to a flying start as they moved into their cabin and set about the business of raising crops and children. Brother Thomas and his wife stole a march on Sam with the birth of a daughter the following October, but Jenny Polk was not far behind, her oldest son being born about noon on the second of November, 1795. It was altogether fitting that Jenny was allowed to name this first child, who was to be so unlike the Ezekiels and the Devil Charleys of the Polk clan, James Knox Polk.[34]

The birth of her baby brought Jenny Polk face to face with an aspect of life among the Polks that would sadden the rest of her days. The thing people remembered about Jenny was her piety, "her theological acumen, her vigorous and masculine intellect, her great tenacity of Presbyterianism." Her chief pleasure, as Sam soon learned, was in "the Bible, the Confession of Faith, the Psalms and Watt's Hymns."[35] The first thing such a mother would think about was the baptism of her child, but as soon as this issue was raised, Jenny learned that she could never feel altogether at home with the Polks.

[33] Gravestone of James Knox, Cemetery of Hopewell Church, Mecklenburg County, N.C.; Mecklenburg County, N.C., Record of Wills, Bk. D, 135-137; Rogers, "Ezekiel Polk," 15, 59; *Polk Family and Kinsmen*, 192; Hunter, *Sketches of Western N.C.*, 93; Goodman, *Knox Family*, 114; J. B. Alexander, *Biographical Sketches of the Early Settlers of the Hopewell Section and Reminiscences of the Pioneers and Their Descendants by Families* (Charlotte, 1897), 92.

[34] Mecklenburg Deeds, Second Series, Bk. 14, pp. 163, 310; Mecklenburg Court Minutes, 1796-1808, entry for 26 Oct. 1796; Mecklenburg Wills, Bk. D, 135-137; Rogers, "Ezekiel Polk," 15, 59; Milo M. Quaife, ed., *The Diary of James K. Polk during His Presidency, 1845 to 1849* (4 vols., Chicago, 1910), I, 86, II, 216. Sam Polk's farm was not actually deeded to him until 1796, the consideration being five shillings.

It is possible that Jane Polk went back to her mother's to have her first child, though the highly circumstantial argument to this effect in J. B. Alexander, *Hopewell Section*, 92-94, is unconvincing. "It is sufficient to be born in Mecklenburg to entitle one to all that is good and patriotic," writes this local historian, "but to be born in the Hopewell boundary adds eclat to the fact."

[35] Ramsey, *Autobiography*, 270-271.

Sam had not been antireligious; indeed, in that first year of married life Jenny probably had little trouble persuading her devoted husband to take her the seven miles to Providence meeting house for Sunday services. Unfortunately Providence congregation was ruled by an iron-willed young parson, the Reverend James Wallis, who was described as "clear, strong, ardent, and more dreaded though less loved."[36] Wallis was little disposed to let any of his hearers rest comfortably in a state of religious indifference, and Sam doubtless took offense at the minister's pointed allusions to himself. Before long, Polk resentment of the Presbyterian clergy's theocratic pretensions was to produce an explosion that would rock the Sugar Creek country to its foundations.

When Jenny somehow persuaded Sam to take her baby to Providence for baptism, the infant James K. Polk became the focus for one of the most acerbating incidents in this mounting friction. Presbyterians had always insisted on a profession of faith by the parents of a child presented for baptism, and Parson Wallis was hardly the man to abate this requirement. The inevitable result was a violent quarrel between Sam and the parson. Little Jimmy was taken home unbaptized; and knowledge of this episode was to leave such deep scars that he would not receive the sacrament of baptism until he lay on his death bed.[37]

The matter might have ended in armed neutrality had Sam alone been concerned, for he was not by nature a radical. But Ezekiel Polk had his own reasons for taking a hand in the controversy, and he was not one for halfway measures. Outwardly Ezekiel had been orthodox enough up to the time of Maria's death, his nascent religious radicalism having been restrained by her piety, which was remarkable even for a daughter of Alexandrian Hopewell. "The last Exercises of her feeble voice," Maria's epitaph reported, "were employed in singing the 33rd Hymn of the 2d Book of Doctr. Watts Composition: in which, anticipating the Joys of the blessed Society above, she exchanged the earthly for the Heavenly Melody."

But Maria's departure and the death of all Ezekiel's children by his second wife produced a profound disillusionment with orthodoxy. The childbirth loss of his babies made the Presbyterian doctrine of infant damnation particularly abhorrent; and his characterization of one of these unfortunates as "An Innocent that never Err'd"

36 Foote, *Sketches of N.C.*, 248.
37 O. P. Fitzgerald, *John B. McFerrin: A Biography* (Nashville, 1893), 222, 230.

doubtless expressed a conscious dissent, especially since he appended to his own crude verses on the child's tombstone a ten-line verse from another source celebrating the infant's flight to heaven.[38]

Yet even those who knew him best were shocked when Ezekiel made himself the champion of that archheresy, deism, and proceeded to plunge Presbyterian Mecklenburg into a bitter broil. He and his neighbor Ezra Alexander, the family rebel, organized a debating society that met up and down Sugar Creek, turning the light of reason on Biblical revelation; and Ezekiel personally contributed a circulating library containing such deistic writers as Gibbon, Hume, and Paine. Parson Wallis and Samuel C. Caldwell, the pastor at nearby Sugar Creek church, led the counterattack from both pulpit and printing press, Wallis publishing an elaborate pamphlet to expose the errors of Paine's *Age of Reason.*

The controversy was rendered even sharper by various social and family rivalries that became involved, for both Wallis and Caldwell had consolidated their sacerdotal authority by marrying daughters of the leader of the Alexander clan. And the whole affair bore with added intensity on poor Jenny Polk when her mother, the Widow Knox, found a new husband in none other than Parson Wallis's father. The battle raged for five years, with first one side and then the other gaining an advantage.[39] First fall went to the orthodox, when a recurrence of Ezekiel's Tennessee fever enabled Parson Wallis to deal him a body blow.

VIII

During the summer of 1797, while the religious controversy was at fever pitch, a certain John Johnson arrived in Mecklenburg from Tennessee and began stirring up interest in a proposed settlement in the great bend of the Tennessee River near Muscle Shoals. The lands were a part of the notorious Yazoo grants made by the Georgia legislature two years before, but the grants lay in Indian territory where settlement was forbidden by federal law. This fact had not deterred Zachariah Cox, the father of the project, from attempting to raise a small army, or from building near Knoxville

---

[38] Gravestone of "Still born son of EZEKIEL POLK," Polk Graveyard.

[39] Foote, *Sketches of N.C.,* 248-249; J. B. Alexander, *The History of Mecklenburg County from 1740 to 1900* (Charlotte, 1902), 78, 281-282; James Wallis, *The Bible Defended . . .* (Halifax, N.C., 1797); William M. Clemens, comp., *North and South Carolina Marriage Records from the Earliest Colonial Days to the Civil War* (New York, 1927), 159; Mecklenburg Wills, Bk. A, 163.

a floating fortress armed with cannon to carry his men down the Tennessee River prepared to fight off Indians or anyone else who might try to bar their way. Cox's emissary was now promising a thousand acres to any man who would arm himself and stay with the enterprise for a year.[40]

When Johnson described this grandiose but illegal project in Mecklenburg, Ezekiel's combustible imagination was fired, with consequences that would set the new United States government in Philadelphia trembling. Ezekiel was able to enlist about twenty-five Mecklenburgers, and in July they set out to join Cox near Knoxville. Just at this moment Parson Wallis got wind of the matter and saw a chance to strike a blow for religion. Consulting prominent Federalists in the neighborhood, he rushed off to the federal district judge a deposition hinting darkly that "from the mysterious manner in which the business has been conducted, much more is contemplated by the authors of it than is promulged, or perhaps generally suspected."[41] The judge hurried a copy of the Wallis statement to Philadelphia, at the same time dispatching the federal marshal after Ezekiel and his followers.

The Adams administration was already nervous over an epidemic of unrest, plotting, and foreign intrigue in the turbulent Southwest. When Wallis's alarming information reached the capital, President Adams was at home in Massachusetts, but the jittery secretary of state, Timothy Pickering, dispatched him an urgent message pro-

40 For the Cox expedition and Ezekiel's part in it, see the following: Isaac J. Cox, ed., "Documents Relating to Zachariah Cox," Historical and Philosophical Society of Ohio, *Quarterly Publication*, viii (1913), 29-114; Samuel C. Williams, ed., "Executive Journal of Gov. John Sevier," East Tennessee Historical Society, *Publications*, No. 1 (1929), 144-146, No. 2 (1930), 144-149, No. 3 (1931), 159-160, No. 5 (1933), 165-166; *American State Papers, Public Lands*, i, 232, 244; Col. William Polk to Gen. William R. Davie, 9 Aug. 1797, photostat, and Oliver Wolcott to James McHenry, 15 Sept. 1797, James McHenry Papers (LC); Timothy Pickering to Judge John Sitgreaves, 1 Aug. 1797, same to President John Adams, 3 Aug. 1797, same to the governors of N.C., S.C., and Ga., 3 Aug. 1797, copies, Pickering Papers (MHS); Timothy Pickering to the federal attorneys for N.C., S.C., and Ga., 3 Aug. 1797, same to James McHenry, 30 Sept. 1797, copies, State Department Domestic Letters (NA); proclamation of the governor of S.C., 24 Aug. 1797, and President John Adams to Timothy Pickering, 25 Aug. 1797, State Department Miscellaneous Letters (NA); Governor Samuel Ashe to Judge John Sitgreaves, 14 Aug. 1797, copy, same to Major Gen. Robert Smith, 18 Aug. 1797, copy, and minutes of the governor's council, 30 Aug. 1797, all in Governors' Letter Book and Journal of the Council of State, 1795-1855 (NCDAH); Halifax *North Carolina Journal*, 18, 25 Sept. 1797; J. G. M. Ramsey, *The Annals of Tennessee to the End of the Eighteenth Century* . . . (Charleston, 1853), 690.

41 Deposition of James Wallis, quoted in Timothy Pickering to the governors of N.C., S.C., and Ga., 3 Aug. 1797, copies, State Department Domestic Letters.

posing a proclamation to "warn the people of their danger." The same day Pickering called on the governors and federal district attorneys in the three southernmost states to take all necessary steps to stop this ominous enterprise, which, he emphasized, seemed to have some ulterior object. In response to his appeal, the public was warned through the newspapers; the governor of South Carolina offered a $1,000 reward for aid in bringing the principals to justice; and in North Carolina Governor Ashe called an emergency meeting of his council, issued a proclamation for the arrest of Polk and Johnson, and ordered the militia out in pursuit. By this time the adventurers had long since made their escape.

As for dark purposes, Colonel William Polk was reassuring. "It is a mere land speculation," Ezekiel's Federalist nephew informed the authorities, "without any expectation at least by E.P. of seeing or experiencing danger." "I know his weak nerves too well," the nettled colonel added, "to believe he would hazard himself where there would be the most distant idea that blood would be spilt. Mr. Polk is a man charged with impatience, has no fortitude, fickle in the extreme, a lover of home, and never saw blood but from a lancet or his nose in his life; from such a leader I fear nothing."[42]

The whole affair ended in fiasco. Cox did not appear at the appointed rendezvous when the Mecklenburgers reached East Tennessee, and some of them became discouraged and returned home. Most of the rest probably followed shortly after, when they learned that the army detachment near Knoxville, under direct orders from the secretary of war, had constructed a howitzer battery on a narrow section of the Tennessee to blow Cox's heavily armed inland ship out of the water if it tried to descend the river. Cox eventually led the remnants of his band overland to the mouth of the Cumberland and then, for unknown purposes, down the Mississippi, but it is unlikely that Ezekiel pursued the chimera farther than East Tennessee.

The collapse of the Cox adventure did not prevent Ezekiel from renewing the religious controversy on his return home, and the battle raged for some years more. Ezra Alexander's death in 1800 encouraged the orthodox, and the clergy kept up such a drumfire that in 1802 they succeeded in setting off the greatest religious revival Mecklenburg had ever experienced. At one mammoth camp meeting in the Providence section, said to have been attended by five or six

[42] Col. William Polk to Gen. W. R. Davie, 9 Aug. 1797, photostat, McHenry Papers.

thousand people, the wave of enthusiasm swept away some of Ezekiel's staunchest supporters. The contest ended the next year when Ezekiel quit Mecklenburg for good, taking his unsettling library with him.[43]

The Jeffersonian victory of 1800, the gradual cessation of religious controversy, and Ezekiel's departure brought relative peace to Sam Polk's cabin on Little Sugar Creek. Sam continued to prosper and to win the esteem of his neighbors. By 1799 he was a captain in the militia, and within a few years more a major and a justice of the peace. As a man of some substance, he saw to it that young Jimmy was at least taught to read and write, probably at spasmodic sessions of an "old field school." A neighbor recalled years later that "Little Jimmy Polk used to pass along this road often to school, barefooted, with his breeches rolled up to his knees. He was a mighty bashful little fellow."[44] But this placid life in the North Carolina upcountry was soon interrupted.

IX

When Ezekiel shook the dust of Mecklenburg from his heels in 1803, it was to return at last to his short-lived home in the Red River country of Middle Tennessee. This time he went at the head of a sizeable clan, for he had persuaded his married daughter and three of his married sons, all with growing families of their own, to accompany him. Ezekiel gave all of them lands adjacent to his plantation, and for the next few years the Polks settled down to the cultivation of tobacco and then cotton. Only Sam refused to leave Mecklenburg, or more probably it was Jenny who refused to leave her mother and friends for a distant country with its unknown perils and hardships.[45]

---

[43] Foote, *Sketches of N.C.*, 249-250. Ezra Alexander is buried in the Polk Graveyard. When Ezekiel Polk died many years later, he left behind a library of seventy-nine volumes, including works by Gibbon and Hume and others of unspecified title. This was doubtless the deistic library that Foote says was carried to Tennessee. Hardeman County, Tenn., Wills and Inventories, Bk. 1, 14.

[44] Alexander, *History of Mecklenburg*, 50-51; Mecklenburg Court Minutes, 1796-1808, appointment of jurors, Jan. Term, 1799. "List of Justices of the Peace and Militia Officers," from the files of the governor's office (NCDAH) shows Sam Polk as first major of the second regiment of Mecklenburg militia in 1803 and justice of the peace in 1805.

[45] Ezekiel Polk was still a resident of Mecklenburg in Sept. 1803, when he made deeds disposing of his lands there. Mecklenburg Deeds, Second Series, Bk. 18, pp. 36, 39, 51, 59. The first record of Ezekiel in the Red River country is of 7 Feb. 1804. Robertson County, Tenn., Minutes of County Court, 1796-1807, p. 176. There are

Only three years elapsed, however, before a new turn in the history of the Great Speculation intensified the pull to the West. Up to this time most of the lands preempted by the Polks in the 1780's had been closed to occupation as Indian territory. Not until 1805 was the federal government, under steady pressure from Colonel William Polk and other large speculators, able to cajole the Cherokees into surrendering their claim to most of Middle Tennessee; the Chickasaw rights were extinguished by a similar treaty the next year.

Back in '83, while on the military boundary survey, Ezekiel had located for his brother Thomas a number of 5,000-acre tracts just south of the military line, in what was to become Maury County. "Such lands as you never saw," one envious settler had described the tracts, and Ezekiel had gotten several thousand acres of these valuable lands for his services as locator. Naturally he was in the vanguard of the stream of settlers that poured over the military line as soon as the Indian titles were extinguished in 1805-1806.[46] At last, thought the Polks, they had reached a promised land in which they could rest content.

Ezekiel's new home was some ten miles north of the westward-flowing Duck River in the fertile valley formed by one of its principal tributaries, Carter's Creek. Around him settled once more a goodly company of children and grandchildren. One of Ezekiel's sons had died in the Red River country the previous year, and another son had apparently refused to emigrate again. Nevertheless he had with him Matilda and her husband, John Campbell; William and his wife; Clarissa and her new husband, Thomas McNeal; and at least nine grandchildren. In addition two unmarried daughters were still under the parental roof.[47]

Back in Mecklenburg the emigration fever was spreading, and Sam Polk began to weigh more seriously his father's arguments for removal to the West. With the new country opening up, there would be great opportunities for Sam as a surveyor. Besides, upcountry

numerous references to the Polk connection in the indexed typescripts of the Robertson County records in the Tennessee State Library.

[46] Elisha Williams to Joseph Williams, 2 Aug. 1807, Polk Papers (NCDAH; hereafter cited as W. H. Polk Papers); indenture between Charles Polk and William Polk, 10 Sept. 1806, Polk-Yeatman Papers; land grants, Middle District of Tennessee, File No. 91 (NCSS).

[47] Maury County, General Index to Deeds, Bargainor, Vol. 1, 199; Maury County, Minutes of County Court, Bk. 1, pp. 5, 28; Maury County, Wills and Minutes of County Court, Vol. 1, Bk. B, 7; Rogers, "Ezekiel Polk," 15-98.

North Carolina was drifting into a state of stagnation, and his boys would have a better chance to get ahead in the dynamic frontier society of Middle Tennessee. During the summer of 1806 he made up his mind, and when the crops were in, the family prepared to set out on the long, hard journey.

The Polks, if they were like other emigrants of the period, never forgot the day when they "bade adieu to their friends and relatives, the scenes of their early life, the graves of their fathers, and many objects besides around which memory loves to linger, and turned their faces to the setting sun."[48] People came from all over the county for farewells with Sam and his family, and "much tenderness of feeling" was shown; they "parted much as do those who part at the grave," for Tennessee seemed so far away that they never expected to see each other again. "Many, in taking leave, would not venture to speak; a tender embrace, a silent tear, and a pressure of the hand" were all. Only the children, excited by visions of the wonderful new world across the mountains, kept up their spirits.

Early in the morning of the appointed day, the last of the family's belongings were piled into the wagon, and the little caravan started up the road through Charlotte and on northward and then westward toward Morganton, the last village nestling at the foot of the mountains on the upper reaches of the Catawba. There was doubtless a horse or two for Sam and perhaps Jimmy to ride occasionally; four-year-old Franklin and baby Marshall, just one and a half, had to ride; and the little girls, Jane, six, and Eliza, eight, were allowed in the wagon when they tired; but for the most part the family and the slaves had to walk. Traveling in this fashion, they could not hope to cover more than twenty miles in a day, even on the best roads.

The roads, however, were rutted gullies and quagmires, softened by the autumn rains and cut to pieces by the hundreds of families who were migrating that fall. Upon reaching the single road over the mountains, the Polks found themselves in a long line of slowly moving wagons. These migrant families fell quickly and naturally into companies that traveled and camped together, for only through cooperation could they get their heavy wagons over the mountains

[48] The following account is taken from James Ross, *Life and Times of Elder Reuben Ross* (Philadephia, n.d.), 91-105, which describes the experiences of another North Carolina family migrating to Middle Tennessee in the spring of 1807. For additional comments on this journey, see Elisha Williams to Joseph Williams, 29 Nov. 1805, and Sarah Williams to Sally Williams, 29 Mar. 1807, W. H. Polk Papers.

and rivers or protect themselves from the Indians and bandits who still lurked in the desolate areas they had to traverse.

The travelers would have caught their first sight of the Blue Ridge the day before reaching Morganton. A serene blue cloud low on the horizon it appeared at first, but day by day it rose higher and became more forbidding. At length, after toiling up a narrow valley, bounded on either side by forests climbing steeply around vast, jutting masses of solid rock, the company camped at the foot of a virtually perpendicular escarpment. The next day was spent hauling the wagons one by one to the top. Here, "on these lofty heights the emigrant might take his stand," as one of these migrating North Carolinians later recalled, "and turning his face to the east, gaze for the last time on his native State and bid it a final adieu. First and last, how many sorrowful hearts, young and old, have performed this sad rite!"

There was little time for such musing, however, since the most grueling part of the journey had only begun. From here the road crawled across a rugged plateau and along torrential streams that cut a tortuous path through mountain barriers more formidable than the Blue Ridge, before descending into the valleys of East Tennessee. Cabins and fields began to reappear as the valleys broadened, and the company quickened its pace as it neared Knoxville, the center of Tennessee's social, political, and economic life. In the state capital's hospitable tavern Sam and his family were able to enjoy briefly the comforts they had left behind.

All too soon they were on the road again, their ears filled with warnings of a "howling wilderness" forty miles ahead. There were still more than 200 miles to go, and over half this distance lay across the Cumberland Mountain, a barren plateau that isolated the infant communities in Middle Tennessee from the longer-settled eastern section of the state. Forewarned, the Polks loaded their wagon with enough food to last several weeks before venturing into this inhospitable country. Only ten years earlier Indian hostility had made it unsafe to cross the Cumberland plateau without a military guard; and though large-scale attacks no longer occurred, one could never feel secure from wandering Indian bands or white outlaw gangs. Indeed the travelers had reason to be apprehensive of the occasional self-styled "good Injun" who appeared along the road to sell venison, since one could never be sure that he was not reconnoitering for a nearby hostile band.

With a mixture of relief and anticipation the Polks' company plunged down the final steep descent and found themselves at last among the verdant, gently rolling hills of Middle Tennessee. Shortly after reaching the wide Caney Fork, the Polks turned off the main Nashville road to the south, and within another three or four days they were approaching Ezekiel's settlement on Carter's Creek. When the little caravan finally pulled up at Ezekiel's cabin, the joy of reunion was hardly greater for these weary travelers than their happiness at the prospect of warm fires and soft beds. And small wonder; in something like a month and a half they had walked nearly 500 miles across the roughest terrain in eastern North America.

Jane Knox Polk

Colonel William Polk

The University of North Carolina

. . . YOUTH

Felix Grundy

Sam Polk House

Polk's Law Office

. . . BEGINNINGS

Andrew Jackson

Hugh Lawson White

William Carroll

Cave Johnson

. . . TRUE REPUBLICANS

James Knox Polk

Sarah Childress Polk

The Old House of Representatives

John Bell

Richard M. Johnson

POLK'S RIVALS FOR NATIONAL PROMINENCE

The City of Washington, 1833

Ephraim H. Foster

James C. Jones

. . . RIVALS FOR CONTROL OF TENNESSEE

The Courthouse at Nashville, Meeting Place of the Tennessee Legislature

Polk as Governor

"...Henceforth His Career Will Be Downwards"?

2

GROWING UP WITH THE WEST

EZEKIEL POLK had need of all his persuasive eloquence in the first few weeks after his son's family arrived, for the Duck River country presented a dismaying contrast to the serenity and comfort of Old Mecklenburg. Indeed, "the wild and lonely appearance of the country, and the constant dread of Indians" were driving many newcomers back to more settled areas. The inevitable buzzard, wheeling on motionless wings high overhead, looked down on a jumble of forested hills, deeply gashed at regular intervals by the creeks that flowed south to the river. In these narrow, cane-choked valleys the cabins of the first settlers were going up. The impenetrable canebrakes, half as high as the tallest trees, shut out even the noonday sun; they formed a solid wall around the clearings and grew so thick "that a bear, or Indian, could not have been seen at the distance of a few yards."[1]

Yet this same lushness testified to the fertility of these bottom lands, a testimony soon confirmed by the prodigious growth of the pioneer's first corn crop. Sam Polk was more than satisfied to accept a section of his father's domain; the tract he picked lay just south of Ezekiel's place on a trail that would shortly be the main road from the Duck River north to the nearest town, Franklin, and on to Nashville.[2]

These were busy days for the Polks. Eleven-year-old Jim was later to recall proudly that he had been "here cutting the cane a third of a century ago";[3] for this literal carving out of a place in the wilderness was the first step in Tennessee pioneering, and frontier lads retained a vivid memory of the pistol-like explosions of the dry cane as it was heaped on roaring fires. When enough trees had been chopped down and the logs hewn to a proper size, the neighbors all came in for the house raising. A little later, after a few acres had been cleared, they returned just as cheerfully for the logrolling. This

---

[1] James Ross, *Life and Times of Elder Reuben Ross* (Philadelphia, n.d.), 106.
[2] Albert V. Goodpasture, "The Boyhood of President Polk," *Tennessee Historical Magazine*, VII (Apr. 1921), 44; Maury County, Minutes of County Court Bk. I, 28, 46.
[3] Nashville *Union*, 8 Apr. 1841.

POLK'S TENNESSEE

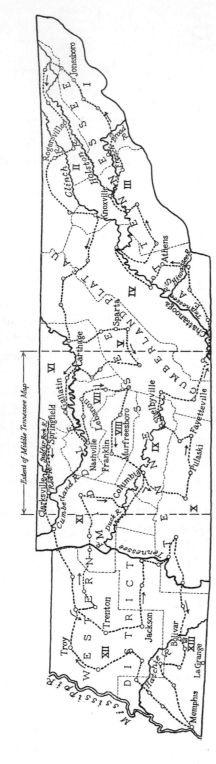

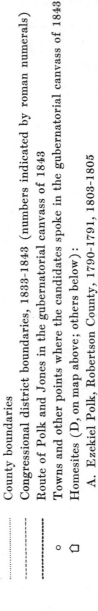

Based on *Mitchell's Reference & Distance Map of the United States* (Philadelphia: S. Augustus Mitchell, 1836).

.... County boundaries

———— Congressional district boundaries, 1833–1843 (numbers indicated by roman numerals)

– – – – Route of Polk and Jones in the gubernatorial canvass of 1843

o Towns and other points where the candidates spoke in the gubernatorial canvass of 1843

⌂ Homesites (D, on map above; others below):

    A. Ezekiel Polk, Robertson County, 1790–1791, 1803–1805
    B. Ezekiel Polk, Maury County, 1805–1821
    C. Sam Polk, Maury County, 1806–1815
    D. Ezekiel Polk's "Mecklen," Hardeman County
    E. Andrew Jackson's "Hermitage," Davidson County

MIDDLE TENNESSEE

Congressmen by districts, 1833-1843 (White men and Whigs italicized):

I   1833, John Blair; 1835, *William B. Carter;* 1841, *Thomas D. Arnold*

II   1833, *Samuel Bunch;* 1837, Abraham McClellan

III   1833, *Luke Lea;* 1837, *Joseph L. Williams*

IV   1833, *James Standifer;* 1837, *William Stone;* 1839, *Julius W. Blackwell;* 1841, Thomas J. Campbell

V   1833, *John B. Forester;* 1837, Hopkins L. Turney

VI   1833, *Balie Peyton;* 1837, *William B. Campbell*

VII   1833, John Bell; 1841, *Robert L. Caruthers*

VIII   1833, *David W. Dickinson;* 1835, *Abram P. Maury;* 1839, *Meredith P. Gentry*

IX   1833, James K. Polk; 1839, *Harvey M. Watterson*

X   1833, *William M. Inge;* 1835, *Ebenezer J. Shields;* 1839, Aaron V. Brown

XI   1833, Cave Johnson; 1837, *Richard Cheatham;* 1839, Cave Johnson

XII   1833, *David Crockett;* 1835, Adam Huntsman; 1837, John W. Crockett; 1841, Milton Brown

XIII   1833, *William C. Dunlap;* 1837, *Christopher H. Williams*

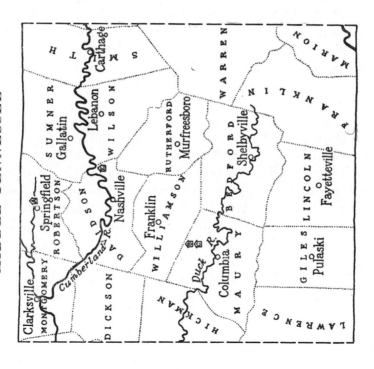

"grand affair—six or eight strong men on each side of a heavy log, carrying it along with measured tread to the heap where it was to be burned"—was another recollection pioneer boys were unlikely to lose. Least of all were they likely to forget the tradition of neighborly helpfulness that underlay all these memories and lived on into more comfortable days through such institutions as corn shuckings and quilting parties.

Even after the extreme hardships of the first years had passed, life was not easy in the Duck River country. Some tobacco was grown to obtain cash for sugar, salt, iron for tools, and occasional luxuries; but by and large the Polks produced everything they ate, wore, or otherwise used, and the energies of every member of the family were needed for this perpetual task. Corn was the main staple, being ground up at a neighborhood grist mill and then worked into many varieties of cornbread, hoecake, and johnnycake. Whisky, too, was a frontier staple, and the still house, that "never-failing sign of a dawning civilization," appeared as soon as the grist mill.

Every settler had his little cotton or flax patch, usually both. Cotton provided dresses for the women, while most of the men's summer clothing was made of linen, spun and woven from the flax. Jim Polk was probably one of the more fortunate frontier boys who had a warm suit of dressed buckskin to wear through the winter. Buckskin was soft and velvety and had a rich buff color when new, but it was extraordinarily durable, and "the young fellow with hunting shirt and trousers made of it was considered as provided for in the way of clothes for an indefinite period of time." After several years of hard use it became blackish and "almost as slick as glass," so that "if a boy on a cold frosty morning put on a pair of these trousers in this state without drawers, as was often the case for the best of reasons, a considerable chattering might be heard."

The varied family enterprises furnished a multitude of tasks for every hand, and "boys were kept pretty well to business during the week." Sunday was a day of rest in a very real sense, and then the youngsters "literally ran wild." If they tired of athletic contests, ball games, and marbles, there were expeditions to the creek to shoot fish with bow and arrow and splash about naked in the water, or excursions through the forest in search of nuts, wild grapes, and persimmons. The frontier had outrun the Presbyterian Sabbath in these first years, and for the moment Jane Polk's remonstrances were unavailing.[4]

[4] Ross, *Reuben Ross*, 173-190.

II

The Polks were leaders in the Duck River country from the beginning. The settlements lay in Williamson County, but it was a whole day's trip to the county seat at Franklin; besides, the county offices were already filled, leaving the new men little chance to play a part in county affairs. Consequently in the summer of 1807 Sam Polk, his brother William, his brother-in-law Thomas McNeal, and over a hundred others petitioned for creation of a new county. The legislature, itself composed of pioneers, was sympathetic to their request; Maury County was organized in December; and Sam Polk and John Campbell, another brother-in-law, were among the jurors summoned to the first county court. The new magistrates promptly provided for a county seat, the town of Columbia being laid off on the south bank of the Duck, six miles down the road from Sam's farm. A rude log courthouse was constructed, and a pen for stray horses was built in a muddy clearing grandly designated the "public square."[5]

Ezekiel, a patriarch at sixty, was beginning to be overshadowed by the vigorous younger men of the clan, and their influence and prosperity kept pace with the growth of the new country. Within two years Sam was a county magistrate, and he was shortly joined on the bench by his brother William. Both William Polk and Thomas McNeal were militia captains by the time the War of 1812 broke out, though McNeal had to enter Andrew Jackson's volunteer army as a private when his company's prejudice "against men of wealth and tallents" prevented his expected election as captain. But Ezekiel was not one to be overshadowed completely by even the most energetic sons. It was he who was selected to appeal to his old friend General Andrew Jackson when the Maury volunteers suffered the supreme indignity of the frontier soldier—being placed under command of an officer from another county, whom they had no voice in choosing.[6]

The prosperity of the Polk connection may be indicated roughly by the case of John Campbell, who died in 1816 leaving a large farm, 9 slaves, 9 horses, 30 cattle, and 109 hogs—a substantial estate for

---

[5] Flournoy Rivers, "The Beginnings of Maury County," *American Historical Magazine* (Nashville), III (Apr. 1898), 140-144; Maury Court Minutes 1, 4, 15, 27, 72.

[6] Dr. Horace Depriest to Gen. John Coffee, 20 Dec. 1813, Andrew Jackson Papers (LC); Mrs. John Trotwood Moore, comp., "Record of Commissions of Officers in the Tennessee Militia," *Tennessee Historical Quarterly*, III (1944), 90, v (1946), 279; Maury County, Wills and Minutes of County Court, Vol. I, Bk. B, 262; Maury Court Minutes, 70, 76; Ezekiel Polk to Andrew Jackson, 2 Sept. 1813, Jackson Papers.

a raw frontier. It was Sam, however, who proved to have the largest share of the Polk talent for land speculation, and he eventually became the wealthiest member of the clan. Sam was ostensibly a farmer, but like many another frontier figure he had done some surveying on the side, and gradually the land business came to be his main interest. Colonel William Polk of North Carolina, having inherited the bulk of Uncle Thomas Polk's lands, had become one of the largest holders of Tennessee acreage. Many of his best tracts were in Maury and the surrounding counties, and Sam became his agent to sell or rent them. Through Cousin William, Sam also secured the agency for the valuable Tennessee lands belonging to the University of North Carolina. Another important kind of business was locating, surveying, dividing, and selling tracts on the old warrants of 1783-1784. All of this business was lucrative, the compensation frequently being a substantial portion of the lands surveyed; and Sam was soon able to deal extensively in real estate on his own account.[7]

Sam's growing affluence reflected the steady influx of settlers into the Duck River country. Within a few years of its establishment, Maury County was to all appearances becoming a settled, peaceful agricultural community. But appearances were somewhat deceptive. The gunshots of Creek hunting parties were still heard occasionally from the forests bordering the newly cleared fields, and no one could say how long the Indians would remain friendly. Men kept their rifles oiled, and the whole county gathered periodically for the exercises in "advancing, bush fighting, retreating, men falling, tomahawking, escalping &c." put on by the "military school" at Columbia. This was in addition to the regular musters of the militia organization, in which all adult males had to serve.[8]

The value of preparedness was proved in the spring of 1812, when a party of marauding Creeks massacred a family on the lower Duck. The militia turned out at once for what proved to be only the prelude

[7] Maury Wills and Minutes, 7, 132; Maury Court Minutes, 62, 76, 83; Goodpasture, "Boyhood of Polk," loc.cit., 43; agreement between William Polk and Samuel Polk, 8 Nov. 1815, James K. Polk Papers (LC; herein cited as Polk Papers, which refers to First Series unless otherwise noted); William Polk to [Mrs. William Polk], 10 Oct. 1818, Lucius J. Polk Papers (SHC); Samuel Polk to William Polk, 9 Sept. 1821, 25 July 1822, Polk-Yeatman Papers (SHC); power of attorney, Trustees of the University of N.C. to Samuel Polk, 31 Jan. 1815, University of North Carolina Papers (SHC); Elisha Williams to Joseph Williams, Aug. 1807, Polk Papers (NCDAH; hereafter cited as W. H. Polk Papers); Nashville Review, 27 Apr. 1810. Maury County, Index to Deeds, Bargainor, Vol. I, 1807-1843, and Bargainee, Vol. I, 1807-1843, lists 120 real estate transactions by Sam Polk in this county alone.

[8] Nashville Democratic Clarion and Tennessee Gazette, 10 Aug. 1810.

to a general war against the Indians and their British allies. A few months later Maury helped furnish the 2,500 men who answered General Andrew Jackson's call for volunteers to occupy West Florida. This expedition accomplished little, but by the time it marched back up the long trail from the lower Mississippi to be discharged at Columbia in April 1813, Old Hickory was on his way to becoming a popular hero. The next two years were to witness his implacable campaign against the hated Creeks and his spectacular victory over the British invaders at New Orleans, exploits that would give him an enduring hold on the loyalty of Tennesseans.[9]

III

Of all General Jackson's Tennessee admirers none was more ardent and none would prove more faithful than Sam Polk's oldest son. Seventeen-year-old Jim Polk would certainly have been in the crowd that gathered at Columbia to welcome the West Florida expedition and its illustrious commander back to Tennessee. He may also have helped entertain the general at his father's house, for Jackson and Sam Polk were well acquainted. Wherever the general first saw the boy, he could not have been greatly impressed, for Jim was not the kind of son in whom frontier fathers take pride.

Small for his age and sickly, he lagged at the numerous tasks imposed on boys around the house and in the fields. When Sam, hoping that his son might one day follow in his own footsteps, took him on surveying trips into the wilderness, the boy usually had to be left in camp to care for the horses and prepare the evening meal, while the rest of the party was out running lines through the tangled forests. Worst of all for Jim was his inability to hold his own in the vigorous outdoor sports of the neighboring farm boys—wrestling, running, jumping, swimming, or simply rough horseplay; and hence he could not escape being branded as a weakling by a frontier community where physical prowess and the arts of field and forest were major virtues.

Jim's difficulties, however, had specific physical causes. More and more frequently he suffered grinding abdominal pains that reduced him to pallid listlessness. The trouble was finally diagnosed as gallstone. Abdominal surgery was still in its pioneer days, and every

---

[9] *ibid.*, 9 June 1812; "Roberts Papers," *American Historical Magazine*, VII (Oct. 1902), 349; Samuel Gordon Heiskell, *Andrew Jackson and Early Tennessee History* (3 vols., Nashville, 1920-1921), III, 138.

successful gallstone removal was reported far and wide in the western press. It was in this way that the Polks heard of the remarkable achievements of a Doctor Ephraim McDowell, who had returned from a brief period of medical training in Scotland to practice at his home in Danville, Kentucky. McDowell's daring career of surgical pioneering, capped by the first successful removal of a tumorous ovary, was attracting attention all over the West and would eventually lead to his enshrinement in the national Capitol's Statuary Hall. Sam Polk decided that the best was none too good for his son; so in the fall of 1812 he and Jim mounted horseback for the 230-mile trip to Danville.

When they finally drew rein before the unpretentious white house that served as McDowell's residence, office, and hospital, Jim was so weak and emaciated that the doctor decreed several weeks of rest before undertaking the operation. McDowell was as considerate as he knew how to be; but anesthesia and antisepsis were still unknown, and all the doctor's kindliness could mitigate only slightly the agony of the surgical ordeal. Fortified with brandy, Jim was strapped on to a plain wooden table and held down by the surgeon's assistants while the incision was being made. How patients survived at all is hard to understand; but Jim was in the hands of a native genius, and the operation succeeded. He began to feel better almost at once. By the time he reached home again, he was in high spirits, jubilantly displaying the offending stone to his family and other admirers.[10]

There can be little doubt that Jim's poor health and his resulting sense of inadequacy in these formative years had a profound influence on the kind of man he eventually became. It was his mother's unyielding Presbyterianism, with its corollaries of duty, self-reliance, and personal achievement, that provided the moral and psychological context in which the boy waged his struggle against pain and lassitude. Jim was never robust, even after the operation, but he had developed a dogged determination and toughness of character that led him to squeeze the last ounce of energy from his frail constitution. In the same fashion, though he was merely intelligent, rather than intellectually brilliant or highly original, he made such

10 John S. Jenkins, *The Life of James Knox Polk, Late President of the United States* (Auburn, N.Y., 1850), 37-38; Samuel D. Gross, *Lives of Eminent American Physicians and Surgeons of the Nineteenth Century* (Philadelphia, 1861), 210-211, 221, 223, 229; Mary Young Ridenbaugh, *The Biography of Ephraim McDowell, M.D., "The Father of Ovariotomy"* (New York, 1890), 76-78; Archibald H. Barkley, *Kentucky's Pioneer Lithotomists* (Cincinnati, 1913), 38.

thorough and effective use of his mental abilities that he outshone men of superior native endowment. The feverish drive of his later years, his intense ambition, his passionate resolution not only to equal but to excel those about him, must have arisen from his early physical inferiority and the frustration of his boyish aspirations, conditioned as he was by his mother's stern gospel of duty.

At any rate Jim's returning vitality brought with it a rush of energies that none had suspected of lying dormant in the unpromising youth. Thinking that merchandising would be a good career for this boy who would never be altogether strong, Sam arranged for his son to learn the business by working in a Columbia store. But this was little to Jim's liking. Already he had visions of the alluring life of a professional man, and measuring out salt and calico for farmers' wives did not suit his ambitions. After a few weeks of store-keeping, Sam yielded to the boy's entreaties, and Jim prepared joyfully to go to school.[11]

IV

Stretching south from Columbia were the lands of the Frierson community, a Presbyterian congregation that had moved in a body from South Carolina to establish one of the earliest settlements in Maury. In good Presbyterian fashion they had set up an academy in their little Zion Church several miles from town, and here in July 1813 Jim Polk enrolled as a student. The school was taught at this time by Middle Tennessee's far-ranging representative of Presbyterianism, the Reverend Robert Henderson. An impressive figure of a man, Henderson combined a classical education and spellbinding oratory with a blunt frontier courage, most memorably demonstrated by a bristling sermon against cockfighting preached to General Andrew Jackson and other prominent men assembled for a weekend of sport with the game chickens. It was a fortunate coincidence that put a teacher so well qualified to meet Jim's needs so close at hand just at this time.[12]

Jim had a good mind, but he had reached the age of eighteen with no more than rudimentary training, so that he spelled poorly and

[11] [J. L. Martin,] "Political Portraits with Pen and Pencil. (No. VI): James K. Polk," *United States Magazine and Democratic Review*, II (May 1838), 199-200.

[12] Mrs. Mary Wagner Highsaw, "A History of Zion Community in Maury County," *Tennessee Historical Quarterly*, V (1946), 113; Heiskell, *Jackson*, III, 681-683; Milo M. Quaife, ed., *The Diary of James K. Polk during His Presidency, 1845-1849* (4 vols., Chicago, 1910), IV, 160.

wrote crudely. Now he was suddenly introduced to fashionable classical education. The zeal with which he attacked "the usual course of latin authors, part of [the] greek testament and a few of the dialogues of Lucian,"[13] however, left no doubt of his latent ability or determination. The whole experience had a tonic effect on the boy. Older than most of the scholars, he worked indefatigably to make up for lost time. The teacher was forbidden to administer corporal punishment, but once a week "Uncle Sam" Frierson, the community patriarch, came to the school, took wrongdoers down to the spring, "talked over their sins with them, and when necessary vigorously applied a birch from a nearby thicket." If this were not sufficiently corrective, "Uncle Sam" would proceed to pray long and loudly over the malefactor, "something much more to be dreaded than three hard whippings." Jim Polk, of course, required no attention from "Uncle Sam," for Parson Henderson found "his moral conduct unexceptionable & exemplary."[14]

Sam Polk was so pleased with his son's progress that after a year he agreed to send him to a larger and more distinguished academy conducted near the new town of Murfreesborough, some fifty miles northeast of Columbia, by another Presbyterian, Samuel P. Black. Shortly after Jim's arrival the school moved to a large log building in the town, and he boarded with a nearby family. Though still slight of figure, he was beginning to develop into an attractive young man. Under Parson Henderson's tutelage he had lost much of his rusticity and awkwardness, and the townspeople noted that he "was neat in appearance." Their daughters—one of whom was destined to become Mrs. James K. Polk—would have been more interested in his "fine eyes" and his hair, which was "much fairer and of lighter growth than it was afterward."[15]

The Murfreesborough curriculum was more varied than that at Zion Church, including, besides the conventional Greek and Latin, mathematics, geography, natural and moral philosophy, astronomy, "Belles-letters," logic, and "such other useful and ornamental

---

[13] Certificate by Robert Henderson, 3 Dec. 1814, Miscellaneous MSS (THS); Gross, *Physicians and Surgeons*, 221.

[14] Highsaw, "Zion Community," *loc.cit.*, 113; certificate by Robert Henderson, 3 Dec. 1814, Miscellaneous MSS (THS).

[15] Samuel H. Laughlin, "Sketches of Notable Men," *Tennessee Historical Magazine*, IV (Mar. 1918), 77-78; Thomas B. Wilson, "Reminiscences of the Civil War," *Tennessee Historical Quarterly*, V (Mar. 1946), 93-94; C. C. Henderson, *The Story of Murfreesboro* (Murfreesboro, Tenn., 1929), 27-29; certificate by Samuel P. Black, 5 Oct. 1815, Miscellaneous MSS (THS).

branches of literature."[16] Jim worked hard again, and at the October exhibition that concluded the work for the year 1815 he stood out as "much the most promising young man in the school." His particularly impressive oration showed that he had learned more than Latin grammar from Parson Henderson.[17]

In two short years Jim had made giant strides. Suddenly finding himself after a boyhood of frustration and hardship, he had been hoarding knowledge with the avidity of a miser in a gold mine. Indeed, with a little encouragement from Black, he was now confident of his ability to move on to college; and Sam, increasingly prosperous and impressed anew by his son's achievements, agreed. North Carolina's state university at Chapel Hill was a natural choice, for Sam's cousin and patron, Colonel William Polk, was one of its most active trustees. After a short visit at home, Jim set out for his native state, pausing in Old Mecklenburg for a visit with relatives and old family friends.

He arrived at Chapel Hill in considerable trepidation, for here he must face a severe academic test. How could his brief exposure to learning in the rural schools of frontier Tennessee, he must have asked himself, possibly have prepared him to pass an entrance examination before an august university faculty? But pass it he did, and with flying colors. After probing closely into his ability to handle English grammar, Latin (Caesar's Commentaries, Sallust, and Virgil), and Greek (Saint John's Gospel), the professors concluded that James K. Polk was qualified for admission to the sophomore class at the beginning of the second term in January 1816. There could have been no more impressive vindication of Jim's teachers or of the intelligence and assiduity with which he had pursued his studies in the two short years since he had first presented himself, an uncouth farm boy, to Parson Henderson.[18]

V

The University of North Carolina had, like Jim himself, passed through an unpromising youth and just reached the age of twenty-one. In 1816 the faculty still numbered only an inept president, the Reverend Robert Chapman; a single professor; a senior tutor; and

[16] Nashville *Whig*, 25 Oct. 1814.
[17] Laughlin, "Sketches of Notable Men," *loc.cit.*, 77-78.
[18] *Polk Diary*, ii, 152-153; *The Laws of the University of North-Carolina. As Revised in 1813* (Hillsborough, N.C., 1822), 5.

two other tutors, recently graduated students who tried to keep order in the dormitories and taught the lower classes.

However poor in faculty and other vital respects, the university was magnificently located on a great ridge, from whose eastern promontory one could look out across the forested hills of Piedmont North Carolina almost as far as Raleigh, the state capital, some thirty miles away. At the highest point on the gently rolling plain that formed the top of the ridge stood the recently completed New College (later called South Building), a three-story structure of simple Georgian lines, surmounted by a cupola, and containing recitation rooms, library, society rooms, and dormitory rooms. New College faced northward on the "Grand Avenue," a broad park of oaks and hickories with natural undergrowth. At right angles to New College and fronting on the park from the east stood the original university building, Old East, a plain two-story structure now used as a dormitory. A simple chapel faced Old East from the west side of the park, while in the opposite direction stood a large frame house called Steward's Hall, where many of the students took their meals. Along a dusty road at the far end of the "Grand Avenue," some 300 yards from the university buildings, straggled the thirteen houses, two stores, and tavern that comprised the village of Chapel Hill.[19]

From its earliest days the university had tried to model itself on the Presbyterians' College of New Jersey, and the fact that both the president and the single professor were Presbyterian ministers indicated a settled determination to carry on instruction under the influence of that resolute faith. Religious indoctrination was assured by a rigorous daily schedule of devotions and study. The students were awakened by the New College bell at six in the morning and fifteen minutes later were summoned to the chapel for morning prayers; prayers were held again at five in the afternoon; and on the Sabbath the whole college community donned black gowns to attend public worship. Each student was examined periodically on the Bible, and any student so daring as to deny the being of God or the divine authority of the Christian religion was dismissed summarily.

Lectures and recitations occupied most of the morning and after-

[19] Archibald Henderson, *The Campus of the First State University* (Chapel Hill, 1949), 15, 25n., 42-43, 45, 60, 65; William D. Moseley to Prof. Elisha Mitchell, 15 Aug. 1853, University of North Carolina, Letters, 1796-1835, ms vol. (NCC).

noon hours. Late in the afternoon and again following the evening meal there was some time for recreation, but a bell at eight in the winter and at nine in the summer sent the boys to their rooms for study until bedtime. The two terms each year were separated by a one-month vacation during December, and there was a six-week recess in the summer. Each term was concluded by a public examination, the one in November being conducted by the faculty, and the other at commencement in June by a committee of the trustees. Besides their regular work, the students were required to give orations following evening prayers, two or more each evening as their names came up alphabetically; and during the senior year each man was called on for two original orations, one of them being delivered at commencement. Tuition was ten, later fifteen, dollars a term, and rooms rented for one dollar.[20]

VI

Though Jim's health was still feeble, he threw himself into his studies with the same energy that had impressed Parson Henderson and Samuel Black. The Chapel Hill curriculum was not extremely varied, but it was solid. Barring occasional ephemerae, such as geography and Biblical and classical history, it consisted mainly of Greek and Roman literature in the first two years, mathematics in junior year, and natural and moral philosophy in senior year. Alongside these studies there was constant drilling in English grammar, from which Jim acquired an excessively meticulous prose style that never left him.

The sophomore classical work was given by the senior tutor, William Hooper, and not until July, when he began the junior program, did Jim come under the influence of the university's real leader, Doctor Joseph Caldwell, the professor of mathematics. Partly because of Caldwell's magnetism and partly from the strongly logical bent of his own mind, Jim became "passionately fond" of this subject. Caldwell had composed his own geometry text, which was then copied in manuscript by the students. The copies were naturally filled with errors, but this had advantages. When corrected by Caldwell a student was always able to say, "Well, that was what I thought myself, but it ain't so in the book, and I thought you knew

---

[20] *U.N.C. Laws*, 4, 7-8, 10, 16-18; Reports from the Faculty to the Trustees, MS vol. (NCC), entry for 6 Dec. 1816; Minutes of the Trustees, 1811-1822, MS vol. (NCC), 131-132, 154.

better than I." Whether or not Jim ever resorted to this *argumentum ad hominem*, he was clearly challenged to his best efforts by Caldwell's teaching, and at the November examination he and his roommate, William Moseley, were judged the best scholars in the class.[21]

The senior work in natural philosophy corresponded roughly to the modern natural sciences, though the emphasis was more on illustrating a priori principles (e.g. the order and harmony of creation) by natural phenomena than on empirical observation and experiment. It was moral philosophy, however, that stood at the apex of the curriculum, for here the instruction in philosophy, ethics, and religion was summarized and systematized. Doctor Caldwell, to whom this all-important subject was entrusted, had been a disciple of the great John Witherspoon at the College of New Jersey, and like many another Presbyterian schoolmaster he had carried away from Nassau Hall a thumb-worn syllabus of Witherspoon's lectures, which became the basis for his own teaching. Like his mentor, Caldwell used the "common sense" approach of the Scottish realists, who had tried to strip John Locke's sensationalist philosophy of its radical implications and to harness it to the defense of a rational religious orthodoxy.

Jim seems to have found the Witherspoon-Caldwell system convincing; at any rate he never betrayed a sign of dissent from the orthodoxy it expounded. Yet the common sense philosophy seems to have had the effect of discouraging personal religious commitment, even while it was indoctrinating against heretical ideas. Answering questions and quieting doubts on the intellectual plane, its net result was often to file the concerns of religion and philosophy away into that area of consciousness reserved for problems settled and closed. Caldwell himself was suspected by his ministerial brethren of a loss of genuine piety, while his young student from Tennessee, though to outward appearance scrupulously orthodox, would never feel himself strongly enough "convicted" to join a church.

In the last half of his senior year Jim got just a taste of the broadened scientific curriculum and enlarged faculty that were to bring the university distinction in coming years. Under Elisha Mitchell, fresh from Yale as the new professor of mathematics, Jim's class was the first to study such advanced geometry as conic sections.

---

[21] William Hooper, *Fifty Years Since: An Address . . . on the 7th of June, 1859 . . .* (Raleigh, 1859), 23; John Y. Mason, *Address before the Alumni Association of the University of North Carolina, . . . June 2, 1847 . . .* (Washington, 1847), 7; *U.N.C. Laws,* 5; Faculty Reports, 5 Dec. 1816.

But Jim missed the teaching of another Yale man, Denison Olmstead, who had been hired along with Mitchell to teach chemistry but who had stayed in New Haven for an additional year of study with the distinguished scientist Benjamin Silliman.[22]

VII

Some of the most important training in these early American colleges was received outside the classroom through the "literary societies." Most students at Chapel Hill were members of either the Dialectic Society or its keen rival, the Philanthropic Society. Jim joined the former during his first term. Each society had its own hall in New College, and here it met each week to debate a prearranged topic. Members were required to participate in these debates every other week and to present written compositions at the alternate meetings, the best essays being filed in the society archives. Eight of Jim's were so honored, and two of them are still extant.[23]

The first, written in 1817, is an argument against "The Admission of Foreigners into Office in the United States."[24] The patriotic young author feared that foreign influence would "insinuate itself into the favor of a credulous populace" and introduce the Old World's monarchial and aristocratic heresies, along with "faction, that destroyer [of] social happiness and good order in society, that monster that has sunk nations into the vortex of destruction." Yet despite his sophomoric distrust of "a credulous populace" and "faction," Jim could not be accounted a conservative. Alexander Hamilton, "a friend to aristocracy," furnished his prime example of the danger of giving power to "those who have been accustomed to cringe to the despots of Europe." He spoke much of equality and rejoiced that Americans did not consent to "a tedious enumeration of noble ancestors." He exulted in "men drawn as if by some magic impulse from the recesses of the western forest that could abash the veterans of Wellington." Liberty was the unique American virtue that he would defend against European subversion.

Jim's second composition, an effusion of schoolboy enthusiasm on

[22] W. D. Moseley to Prof. Elisha Mitchell, 15 Aug. 1853, U.N.C. Letters.

[23] Dialectic Society, Minute Book, 1812-1818, ms vol. (NCC), 25 Jan. 1816; "List of Compositions and Addresses Now in the Archives of the Dialectic Society," in Dialectic Society, Temporary Laws, Etc., 1818, ms vol. (NCC).

[24] "Composition of James K. Polk," ms in Addresses of the Dialectic Society, First Series, ms Vol. IV (NCC).

"The Powers of Invention,"[25] reflected all the winds of thought that circulated through American colleges in the early nineteenth century. Based on Locke's psychology and doing special homage to Newton's "gigantic genius," the essay celebrated the glories of human progress through reason with an extravagance that few eighteenth century *philosophes* ever matched. Yet incongruously mixed with Jim's paeans to reason were reminders of his mother's Presbyterianism and Doctor Caldwell's lectures. "Ambition, that fell destroyer that rankles in the breast of unregenerated man," he admitted, had on occasion perverted reason to wicked purposes; the noble faculty had even been "basely used by a Paine a Hume and a Bolinbroke [*sic*] as the harbinger of infidelity." And he added a final, saving caveat: "But in these speculations it were sacrilegious indeed to attribute the present elevation of our spirits exclusively to human exertion."

Rationalism and dogmatic Christianity were not the only ingredients of the intellectual potpourri that Jim was acquiring at Chapel Hill, for his conclusions were couched in the rhetoric of romanticism. "Spontaneous eloquence" was his object, and however far short he fell, his bombast and exaggerated figures indicated an appeal to heart as well as head. He daringly cited the lawless romantic genius, in the person of the "immortal Faustus," as the highest manifestation of the powers of reason; and unembarrassed by Napoleon's egomania, he declared that "St. Helena blooms with nature's richest production wafted to her shore by the winds of adversity and though fallen yet noble, debased yet acting with philosophic composure." But this was a passing phase. Jim soon adopted radically different rhetorical and philosophical principles, on which he acted for the rest of his life.

A more persistent strain in Jim's thought was the intense nationalism that pervaded all his writings from this period. Only under a free government, he argued, "where genius in rags can aspire to promotion," could reason reach its highest potentialities. Only America could produce such figures as Benjamin Franklin, Benjamin West—"the spontaneous production of America's soil unassisted by the polishing hand of art"—and Robert Fulton. It is easy enough to see inconsistency and juvenility in this product of the young Tennessean's thinking, but they should not obscure the intellectual

[25] Ten-page MS in Polk's hand, in Addresses of the Dialectic Society, First Series, MS Vol. IV.

vigor and the earnest pursuit of some kind of faith that are also shown. The big questions raised by Doctor Caldwell's lectures had obviously had a galvanic effect on a mind that was ordinarily practical and meticulous.

The Dialectic Society enforced its rules strictly, and Jim was fined a half-dozen times for absence, occasionally for "irregularity," and once for "gross irregularity," perhaps for keeping library books too long, spitting tobacco juice on the floor, or some equally heinous impropriety. The society debates were often hotly contested, and one evening Jim and another member were fined ten cents each for exchanging threatening language.

Many of the debates were over questions that would confront Jim later. Unfortunately the minutes for the evening he joined the society do not show which side he took on the question, "Would an extension of territory be an advantage to the U.S.?" A majority of the members voted no. Another evening, after "warm and animated debate," it was decided that the practice of law *is* congenial to the pure precepts of Christianity. Polk's subsequent views triumphed in the debate over, "Ought a representative to exercise his own judgment or act according to the directions of his constituents?" when the verdict was for the second alternative. These aspiring politicians also concluded that the life of a statesman was preferable to that of a warrior. But not all questions were so serious, as witness, "Is an occasional resort to female company beneficial to students?" the result of which was a foregone conclusion.[26]

Both societies had libraries that were superior to the university's meager stock of books. Jim's contributions to the Dialectic collection —a set of Edward Gibbon's *Decline and Fall of the Roman Empire,* Anna Seward's *Memoirs of the Life of Dr.* [*Erasmus*] *Darwin,* Joseph Addison's *Evidences of the Christian Religion,* one of Helen Maria Williams' volumes on the French Revolution, and John H. Eaton's biography of General Jackson—indicated a strong interest in history. The same interest is shown by the fragmentary record of books taken from the university library, Jim being listed as a borrower of Gibbon's *Decline and Fall* and one of the pioneering works on the American Revolution by the South Carolina historian David Ramsay. Ramsay's emphasis on the revolutionary struggle in the Carolina upcountry elicited an enthusiastic response from this

26 Dialectic Minute Book, entries for period 25 Jan. 1816–20 May 1818; Dialectic Society, Committee Minutes, 1816-1824, ms vol. (NCC), 24 Feb. 1817.

young son of Old Mecklenburg. Ramsay was "the Tacitus of this western hemisphere," Jim declared, raised up "to transmit to posterity in the unpolished language of truth, the spirit of liberty which actuated the first founders of our republic."[27]

Jim was an active leader in the "Di." At the end of his junior year, after serving frequently as treasurer, secretary, and chairman of the executive committee, he was elected to the presidency. A precedent was broken when he was elected for a second term the next year. This mark of confidence resulted perhaps from Jim's zealous effort to preserve the society's "bleeding reputation" by prosecuting a member who, besides stealing a shovel from a fellow student, had committed such villainies as letting himself "be publicly kicked in one of the passages of the main building . . . without making any honorable resistance," and claiming to be wealthy with the intention "of imposing himself upon some too credulous one of the female sex." Jim had worked up an airtight case; all the charges were sustained, and the miscreant was expelled from the society by unanimous vote.[28]

"Eloquence" was the subject Jim took for his second inaugural address,[29] and his remarks show that he already had an eye to politics. "You may be called upon," he told his listeners, "to succeed those who now stand up the representatives of the people, to wield by the thunder of your eloquence the council of a great nation and to retain by your prudent measures that liberty for which our fathers bled." And in any case, he continued, "your proficiency in extemporaneous debating will furnish you with that fluency of language, that connexion of ideas and boldness of delivery that will be equally serviceable in the *council*, in the *pulpit* and at the *bar*."

His address was full of the same spread-eagle American patriotism that had pervaded his previous compositions, but now it was expounded in a more sober, argumentative fashion. Jim was, in fact, working his way toward a forensic style that repudiated his earlier

27 Polk's composition on "The Admission of Foreigners into Office in the United States"; *Catalogue of Books Belonging to the Dialectic Society, Chapel Hill, February, 1821* (Hillsborough, N.C., 1821), 4; Dialectic Minute Book, 16 Oct. 1816; "Library Books Borrowed, August 26, 1817–March 25, 1819," MS bound with University Demerit Roll, October 26, 1838–September 18, 1840, MS vol. (NCC).

28 "James H. Simeson's Impeachment & Expulsion, January 21st 1818," MS in Dialectic Society Papers (SHC); Hardy L. Holmes to Polk, 12 Nov. 1817, *ibid.*; Dialectic Committee Minutes, entries for period August 1816–March 1818; Dialectic Minute Book, 8 May 1817, 29 Apr. 1818.

29 MS in Addresses of the Dialectic Society, First Series, MS Vol. IV.

romantic tendencies. This was most evident in the advice which, as an elder statesman, he felt called upon to give the younger Di members. Two faults stood out, he said, in the society's debates.

The one is looseness of preperation [*sic*] before assembling in this Hall. The other is writing and memorizing your exhibitions in which there is often too much attention paid to the elegance of language and too little to the ideas conveyed by it. The former so far from making you fluent and bold, will only tend to corrupt language and embarrass your address. The latter will make you timorous and unprepared to engage in an unforeseen discussion. A due degree of attention should be given to the subject under consideration. The several heads upon [which] you mean to touch should be distinctly arranged in the memory, but the language in which your ideas are expressed should not be elaborate, but that which is suggested at the moment of delivery when the mind is entirely engrossed by the subject which it is considering. The attention of your hearers will not then be diverted from the merits of the question by the studied metaphors and flowers of language.

This young man had grown greatly in wisdom since writing his discourse on "The Powers of Invention," for his latest address was the product of a mature mind, a mind that had measured its strengths and limitations, that knew where it was going and the methods by which its goals might be reached. Much of this self-knowledge Jim doubtless owed to Doctor Caldwell, but even more he had learned for himself in the give and take with his fellow members of the Dialectic. In these same debates he had perfected the techniques that were to make him a "Napoleon of the stump" in the rough and tumble of Tennessee politics and a formidable foe in the Congress of the United States. As a school for statesmanship the Dialectic Society would have been hard to excel.

Many of Jim's fellow students did indeed rise to eminence. His roommate, William D. Moseley, was later governor of Florida; in after years the two friends reminisced about the "many tedious and laborious hours" they had spent in their room on the third floor of New College, "attempting to discover the beauties of Cicero and Homer and the less interesting amusements of quadratic equations and conic sections." Among the other boys at Chapel Hill in Jim's time were a future Cabinet member, a future senator, a future governor, several budding congressmen and state legislators, a future bishop, and a future college president.[30]

[30] W. D. Moseley to Polk, 29 Nov. 1832, Polk Papers; W. D. Moseley to Prof. Elisha Mitchell, 15 Aug. 1853, U.N.C. Letters; "Catalogue of Students (copied by

VIII

Life at "the Hill" was not all serious. The boys spent much of their time in sports, rambles through the surrounding forests, or plain and fancy deviltry. Youthful energy occasionally got completely out of hand, as in 1817 when the trustees were so infuriated by "the late outrages on the buildings of the University & grove" that they ordered the faculty to prosecute the offenders at law. Jim's uncertain health kept him out of the more strenuous diversions, but he got abundant exercise in the mile walk down a long, steep hill to the farmhouse where he took his meals for a time. There were also vacation excursions with Moseley to Raleigh, when the boys stayed at the fine house of Jim's distinguished cousin William, and doubtless also, visits to the homes of classmates during the long summer recess.[31]

The most exciting occurrence during Jim's stay at Chapel Hill was the rebellion of 1816. Warfare, open or covert, between students and faculty, was a normal condition of college life in the early nineteenth century. Faculties maintained as rigid a discipline as possible, and this accentuated the normal student tendency to close ranks in support of myriad seditious enterprises, large and small. Even such a faculty favorite as Jim Polk had advised the Di members to "stoop not from the true principles of honor to gain the favour of the Faculty and thus succeed in your views of promotion."[32] Friction between the two camps was always accumulating out of constant irritations, and every college sooner or later experienced the inevitable explosion.

The most riotous student rebellion in Chapel Hill history was set off one evening in September 1816, when one of the students, William B. Shepard, defied President Chapman's order to delete some controversial passages from his chapel oration. The chapel meeting broke up in pandemonium, and all night long the dormitories were in tumult. The next morning twenty-seven students,

---

Wm. D. Moseley)," ms in *ibid.*; *Catalogus Universitatis Carolinae Septentrionalis* (Raleigh, 1817), 14-16; Kemp Plummer Battle, *History of the University of North Carolina* (2 vols., Raleigh, 1907, 1912), I, 258-259.

31 Resolutions of the Trustees, n.d. [Dec. 1817], and 6 Dec. 1817, U.N.C. Papers; W. D. Moseley to Prof. Elisha Mitchell, 15 Aug. 1853, U.N.C. Letters; Henderson, *Campus*, 27, 57, 110; Hooper, *Fifty Years Since*, 25-31; Battle, *History of U.N.C.*, I, 29, 274; William Hillyard to John Haywood and others, 6 Dec. 1816, U.N.C. Papers; John D. Hawkins to John Y. Mason, 17 Apr. 1847, photostatic copy (NCC).

32 J. K. Polk, "Eloquence," ms in Addresses of the Dialectic Society, First Series, ms Vol. IV.

mostly Shepard's fellow members of the Philanthropic, met to organize for the expected counterattack by the authorities. The faculty, irate and unnerved, was already moving, swiftly and severely. Shepard and all the participants in the defense meeting, except those who would sign an abject recantation, were summarily suspended.

Since President Chapman was a Federalist, the episode quickly became a political issue in overwhelmingly Republican North Carolina, and for a time the university was completely demoralized. The students were sullen and resentful, and a homemade bomb was exploded in front of one tutor's door. They even fell out among themselves. Phi men had furnished the bulk of Shepard's support; that society had been reduced to thirteen members by the suspensions, and the survivors now bitterly accused the Di's of promising to attend the defense meeting and then failing to appear. These charges the Di hotly resented, and Jim was on the committee that tried to make the Phi retract its accusations.

Eventually, however, the students won a partial triumph. Public opinion had been aroused, several of the suspended students were sons of prominent Republican politicians, and tremendous pressure was brought to bear on the board of trustees. In the end President Chapman was forced out and replaced by Caldwell, though in the interest of future discipline Shepard and the organizer of the defense meeting, George Dromgoole, both future congressmen, were expelled.[33]

Caldwell was a great improvement over the inept Chapman, and he set vigorously to work to broaden the curriculum and improve the quality of instruction. William Hooper was promoted to professor of languages, and the two Yale men, Mitchell and Olmstead, were obtained to give the instruction in science and mathematics. Though the rebellion had seemed at first to endanger the university's very existence, it turned out to be just what was needed to shock the institution out of its lethargy, to broaden and liberalize it, and to set it on a course of great prosperity and usefulness in the forty years that followed.

[33] Battle, *History of U.N.C.*, I, 231, 235-239; John Patterson to T. T. Armstrong, 24 Sept. 1816, typed copy, and W. M. Green to M. W. B. Armstrong, 17 Oct. 1816, typed copy, bound with Faculty Reports; Raleigh *Minerva*, 18 Oct. 1816; Raleigh *Register and North-Carolina Gazette*, 4 Oct. 1816; Thomas B. Slade to A. M. Slade, 9 Oct. 1816, U.N.C. Papers; William Hooper to Walter Alves, 6 Mar. 1817, copy, J. C. Norwood Papers (SHC); Trustee Minutes, 122, 133, 136.

IX

A committee of twelve trustees arrived at Chapel Hill on the last Wednesday in May 1818 and spent the following week examining the students preparatory to commencement. This annual event was the state's outstanding social occasion, crowding all available rooms in the tiny village and the surrounding farmhouses with trustees, alumni, politicians, and parents and friends of the students. Young ladies attired in all their finery were much in evidence, for without them there could have been no commencement ball. To seniors the ball took on a large significance, marking as it did their social transition from boyhood to manhood, and they took pains to present themselves in the big dining room of the Steward's Hall arrayed in all the elegance that a lingering eighteenth century tradition authorized. Though none of the North Carolina belles had had sufficient charms to deflect Jim Polk from his serious purposes, he enjoyed feminine companionship as much as any of his classmates and doubtless did his duty by the occasion. This required some doing, since a typical costume consisted of a sea-green coat with high velvet collar and silver buttons; a white damask vest showing the edge of a blue undervest; bosom ruffles; a layer of three-cornered cravats and a cambric stock around the neck; short, white crepe pantaloons lined with pink muslin so as to show a peach blossom tint; flesh-colored silk stockings; and low-cut pumps with silver buckles. The boys completed the effect they made on their dancing partners by wearing their hair long and queued.

The climax of the festivities came on the last day, when each of the seniors in turn took the platform to deliver his original oration. Jim had been adjudged the first scholar in the class and was accordingly assigned the Latin Salutatory, but unfortunately no scrap of evidence has survived to indicate what he said or how it was received. In any case commencement was a proud occasion for this Tennessee farm boy, who only five years before had entered the little academy at Zion Church to learn the elements of grammar and make his first acquaintance with classical education. But the joy and pride of commencement were mixed also with the sadness of suspending the intimate friendships and pleasant associations of college life. Mementos were exchanged during the final days, and

William Moseley would cherish for the rest of his life the breast pin given him by his roommate, Jim Polk.[34]

The hard work of the senior year had brought Jim's frail constitution close to collapse, and he was not able to set out immediately on the exhausting trip to Tennessee. When his father came east for him late in July, he was still in no condition for sustained travel, and Sam had to return home leaving Jim for further rest and visiting with his North Carolina friends. He was doubtless in Chapel Hill for the wedding of one of his classmates two weeks after commencement and was back again in August, when he drew some books from the university library. Not until October was he well enough to begin the journey home.[35]

The two and a half years at Chapel Hill had made a great difference in Jim. The change was not in outlook, for his thinking would always run in conventional channels; Doctor Caldwell's lectures had merely translated the received opinions of the day into settled convictions from which Jim never after deviated significantly. But Jim had a keen mind, and his native aptitude for logical analysis had been whetted by broad and systematic training into a keen instrument which would carry him far.

Most important of all, he had found himself. Now he knew exactly what he wanted to do, and the Dialectic Society had given him a splendid professional preparation for the political career on which he had set his heart. It was a confident and self-assured young man, therefore, who rode along the dusty roads of Piedmont North Carolina that autumn and up the steep mountain trails that led to Tennessee. But his most sanguine mood would not have suggested that when he next returned to his alma mater thirty years hence, as the central figure in dedicating a memorial to his old teacher, Doctor Caldwell, the inscription would proudly inform posterity that "THE PRESIDENT OF THE UNITED STATES . . . AND OTHER ALUMNI HAVE RAISED THIS MONUMENT."[36]

[34] Raleigh *Register and North-Carolina Gazette,* 1 May 1818; *Memoirs of Edward J. Mallett, a Birthday Gift for Each of His Children* (n.p., n.d.), 38-39; Battle, *History of U.N.C.,* I, 258; W. D. Moseley to Polk, 1 Dec. 1830, Polk Papers.

[35] William Polk to Mrs. William Polk, 27 July 1818, G. W. Polk Papers (SHC); Raleigh *Register and North-Carolina Gazette,* 19 June 1818; "U.N.C. Library Books Borrowed," entries for 15, 25 Aug. 1818; Goodpasture, "Boyhood of Polk," *loc.cit.,* 48-49.

[36] Monument to Dr. Joseph Caldwell, campus of the University of North Carolina.

X

If Jim Polk had changed in his three years at Chapel Hill, the countryside he traversed on his homeward journey in the fall of 1818 had changed even more. During his absence Tennessee had been miraculously transformed. The look of a raw, undeveloped frontier was almost gone, and everywhere people who but yesterday worried about bare survival were dreaming of wealth and greatness. Along the road Jim saw fields being cleared, fine houses going up, and brown cotton stalks standing on countless acres previously devoted to corn, pasturage, or forest. Every town had its new store buildings filled with fine imported goods. There were few loafers around the courthouse squares, and in the tavern barrooms at night Jim heard feverish talk of fortunes to be made in new towns, new cotton lands, steamboats, banks, and innumerable other enterprises.

Jackson's victories had eliminated the Indian menace for good, the Chickasaws had just surrendered the last great segment of the state to be opened for settlement, and unprecedented numbers of immigrants were crowding all roads west. The golden flood of banknotes poured into the state for war purposes had been such an exhilarating stimulant that the Tennessee banks had kept their printing presses going ever since, and almost anyone could have a fistful of money for the asking. Cotton was bringing fancy prices at New Orleans, and steamboats were pushing up Tennessee's rivers and creeks to take on fleecy bales in remote areas that a few years before had known only the pioneer's subsistence farming. This heady atmosphere was bound to be intensely challenging to a young man returning from college to make his way in the West.

No better example of the postwar entrepreneurial spirit could be found than Jim's own father. Sam Polk had entered into partnership with James Walker, a shrewd young Kentuckian who had arrived penniless in Columbia just before the war to establish the town's first newspaper, and the two of them were engaged in all sorts of enterprises. At their store on the public square they took in cotton and tobacco from all the surrounding countryside for consignment to New Orleans, supplying the farmers in return with a wide variety of merchandise imported from the eastern cities. As contractors for the War Department, Polk and Walker furnished provisions to the defeated Indians of the Southwest, whose dependence on the federal government was making them amenable to the land cessions constantly demanded of them. As contractors for the Post Office Department, the partners carried the federal mail from Nashville southwest into the Chickasaw country on its way to Natchez and New Orleans. At the same time Walker continued to publish his Columbia newspaper, while Sam's land business was bigger than ever.[37]

A year before Jim's return, Sam had signalized his growing affluence by moving his family from the humble farmhouse on the Nashville road to a splendid two-story brick dwelling on the best street in Columbia. The only house in town that rivaled Sam's was James Walker's next door. Walker had astutely married Jim's sister Jane, and the union had already been blessed by three children, with eight more still to come. A second sister, Lydia, had married another prominent townsman, Dr. Silas E. Caldwell. Still at home with Sam and Jane were two little girls, Naomi and Ophelia, aged ten and six, and five boys, ranging from sixteen-year-old Franklin, through Marshall and John, to three-year-old William and baby Samuel, a year old.[38]

Though Columbia's population barely exceeded 300, the townspeople envisioned a great future. They were inordinately proud of their new brick courthouse, and James Walker was raising money for a handsome Masonic Hall. The town's first bank had been chartered, with Walker as president and Sam a director, and plans were being drawn for a brick bank building that would be more elegant than anything yet seen south of Nashville. Simultaneously the two entrepreneurs were busy organizing a company to build a road from Columbia to the Tennessee River and to operate a steamboat from there to New Orleans.[39]

Despite his debilitated condition, Jim did not tarry long to enjoy the felicities of the reunited family circle. With Tennessee booming

---

37 W. S. Fleming, *A Historical Sketch of Maury County, Read at the Centennial Celebration in Columbia, Tennessee, July 4th, 1876* (Columbia, 1876), 32; Nashville *Clarion*, 9 June 1818; Nashville *Gazette*, 7 July 1819; Capt. John Hutchings to Andrew Jackson, 9 July 1815, Jackson Papers; Sam Polk to Jackson, 17 Aug. 1815, *ibid.*; Jackson to Sam Polk, 19 Aug. 1815, *ibid.*; Polk and Walker to Jackson, 15 Aug. 1816, *ibid.*; Sam Polk to Robert Butler, 22 Aug. 1816, *ibid.*

38 Sam Polk to [John Overton], 31 Jan. 1817, John Overton Papers, Claybrooke Collection (THS). Birth, marriage, and death records for Sam Polk's family are in the family Bible on display in the Sam Polk House, Columbia.

39 Goodpasture, "Boyhood of Polk," *loc.cit.*, 44-45; *Century Review, 1805-1905, Maury County, Tennessee* (Columbia, 1905), 14; Fleming, *Maury County*, 35; Columbia *Chronicle*, 1 Aug. 1816.

and opportunities for ambitious young men opening on every side, he was impatient to complete his preparation and enter the fray. The bar was already becoming the obvious avenue to a political career, but legal education was still a rather hit-or-miss affair. Would-be lawyers generally sought admission to some established attorney's office, where they made themselves useful by building fires, running errands, and copying documents, in return for the privilege of reading the law books and having knotty points explained to them. That Jim chose Nashville's celebrated Felix Grundy for his mentor told much about his ultimate ambitions.

A superb orator, Grundy had been one of the leading War Hawks in Congress some years before, but he had given up politics temporarily for the more lucrative career of criminal lawyer par excellence. It was Grundy whom Andrew Jackson had in mind when he explained why he had sent his nephew to Kentucky for legal training. Nashville, complained the general, had "no legal character of sufficient standing in morality and law knowledge," adding testily that "I hate a quack of any kind." But this was not quite fair. Grundy made no pretense of being a great legal expert; he was instead a master manipulator of human emotions, who could do almost anything with a jury. Though he was engaged to defend the most notorious criminals, the legend was already spreading through the West that he had lost but one capital case. From such a teacher Jim Polk would learn more than legal principles.[40]

Nashville was the most impressive metropolis Jim had ever seen. Boasting over 3,000 inhabitants, paved streets, an array of two- and even three-story buildings, a college, two bookstores, and three newspapers, it was already the commercial center of Middle Tennessee and was rapidly becoming the political center of the whole state. Still other features might have attracted the attention of a young man in the city for the first time—the numerous taverns, the nearby race track, or the theater, which was currently presenting such delectable attractions as "the favorite Farce in 2 Acts, translated from a French piece entitled La Jeune Femme Coliere, called the Day after the Wedding Or, A Wife's First Lesson."[41]

Whatever his extramural activities, Jim applied himself indus-

[40] Jackson to A. J. Donelson, 26 Apr. 1822, John Spencer Bassett, ed., *Correspondence of Andrew Jackson* (7 vols., Washington, 1926-1935), III, 159; Joseph Howard Parks, *Felix Grundy, Champion of Democracy* (University, La., 1940), 91-102.

[41] Nashville *Whig*, 13 Mar. 1819.

triously to the ponderous volumes in Grundy's office, and before long other young attorneys, that dashing madcap Sam Houston, for instance, were seeking his advice on legal matters. Despite his conscientious and generally successful efforts to master the law, however, Jim soon had a chance to show that his real interests lay elsewhere. He shared Grundy's office with another young man, Francis B. Fogg, who had come to Nashville in search of legal training about the same time. By contrast with Jim, Fogg was a lawyer's lawyer. The subtleties of judicial precedents and juridical principles were his passion, and his legal erudition would eventually make him Nashville's most expert attorney. As the two were working away one hot day in the summer of 1819, Grundy came in and suggested to Fogg that he go to Murfreesborough, where the legislature was about to meet, and seek election as clerk of the senate. Grundy had just been elected to the legislature himself, and he thought he had enough influence to get the position for Fogg if he wanted it. It would be a great advantage for a young lawyer, Grundy went on, because it would bring him in contact with most of the state's leading men. Fogg thought the proposition over a few minutes, but finally said that he would rather stay and perfect his legal knowledge, even if he got no cases.

Jim had listened to this conversation enviously and heard Fogg's decision with amazement. Here was an opportunity he would give his eyeteeth for, and he resolved not to let it get away from him. "Well, Fogg," he said, as soon as Grundy was out of earshot, "as you have refused Mr. Grundy's offer, I would be glad if you would tell him that I would like to have the place myself, if he will assist me to get it." Grundy proved cooperative and wrote the necessary letters to key senators, while Jim enlisted the backing of the member from Maury; and when the legislature assembled on September 20, Jim was elected over his single competitor.[42]

The little town of Murfreesborough was only seven years old in 1819, but the boom years had given it big ideas. Arguing that their town was more easily reached from East Tennessee than any other in the middle part of the state, its citizens had begun a campaign to make it the state capital. Having levied a special tax to recondition the little courthouse on the public square, they had now induced the legislature to meet there for the first time. The members

42 [John Wooldridge, ed.,] *History of Nashville, Tenn.* . . . (Nashville, 1890), 517; Tenn. *Senate Journal,* 1819, p. 4.

of the lower house convened in the courtroom on the first floor, and the twenty senators occupied a room upstairs. There were several taverns around the square to accommodate the legislators, while beyond the square stood a public warehouse for cotton and tobacco and a huddle of unpretentious houses. Except for a single brick house and a handsome little church that the energetic Presbyterians were building under the prodding of Jim's old teacher, Parson Henderson, there was little to distinguish Murfreesborough from any other village just emerging from its frontier phase.[43]

This crude setting did not strike the lawmakers as incongruous. Though a meeting of the legislature, the supreme political authority of a sovereign state, was a solemn event, Tennessee's leaders were roughhewn men with quids of tobacco in their cheeks and raw corn whisky on their breath. With unconscious dignity they observed the rules of decorum that had descended to them through an ancient parliamentary tradition, coming in or standing to speak uncovered but replacing their hats when they sat down.

Jim's position carried considerable responsibility. His most important task was to keep an accurate senate journal, but the smooth operation of the whole legislative process depended on his making sure that the endless stream of bills, resolutions, joint resolutions, and committee reports moved in proper order day by day from floor to committee, from committee back to floor, from senate to house, and finally on to the governor. For these services he was paid the handsome sum of six dollars a day, which compared very well with the four dollars per diem received by the members. The young clerk's careful, businesslike habits stood him in good stead, and he served to such satisfaction that he was reelected without opposition when the next legislature convened in 1821; he also served, of course, during the special sessions that met in 1820 and 1822.[44]

XI

The legislature rarely sat longer than a month, so Jim was able to spend the greater part of each year building up his law practice and personal popularity in Maury County. He had gone back to Nashville in the autumn of 1819 to complete his studies with Grundy, and by spring he was ready to appear before the state supreme court to be examined for a license. This perfunctory test he passed

[43] Henderson, *Murfreesboro*, 30, 41, 101-102, 133.
[44] Tenn. *Senate Journal*, 1819, p. 17, 1820, p. 175, 1821, p. 4.

without much difficulty, and when the June term of the circuit court convened at Columbia, he was admitted to the bar. The brief ceremony looked routine and trivial to the spectators in Judge Harris's courtroom, but for Jim it was a momentous occasion. He was now on his own, and henceforth, his brothers and sisters were informed, they might, if they pleased, address him as James.

Sam Polk obligingly got himself indicted for affray on James's first day in business, and the newly launched attorney enabled his father to escape with a fine of one dollar plus court costs. Sam did more for his son, paying $220 for construction of a little one-room law office on a lot James had rented on the south side of the public square, and laying out $140 to buy part of the law library of one of the older attorneys in town. James demonstrated his seriousness about the law by himself spending $660 for additional law books the next year, and by subscribing to Carey and Lea's erudite *Journal of Jurisprudence*.[45]

Tennessee was full of struggling young lawyers, many of them having but poor pretensions to the title. The confused land situation, however, had made litigation rife, and it was followed closely by a public that had few other means of entertainment. With large and critical audiences in the courts, young attorneys were anxious to make a reputation by their declamations to the jury, so that even in minor cases the long-suffering jurors would be harangued by as many as six lawyers on each side. Forensic technique, of course, outweighed legal knowledge, and James had no reason to regret his training under Grundy, though he found it necessary to prepare his cases more carefully than his eloquent preceptor ever had to do.

The Maury bar handled most business before the farmer-justices who composed the county court, but when the circuit judge arrived in town to hold superior court, lawyers from adjoining counties and even from Nashville were attracted. The Columbia attorneys also followed the superior court in its circuit through the neighboring counties of Bedford, Lincoln, Giles, and Lawrence. On his travels from one county seat to another the judge would be accompanied by a whole host of lawyers, riding horseback, putting up six to a room in the rough county seat taverns, gathering around the long tavern tables after court adjourned for simple but hearty meals,

45 Maury County, Circuit Court Minute Book, 1817-1821, pp. 119, 246, 355; articles of agreement, 29 Apr. 1820, Polk Papers; receipt, 30 Dec. 1822, *ibid.*; Polk to James Walker, 1 Jan. 1828, *ibid.*; Polk to Carey and Lea, 4 Nov. 1822, Lea and Febriger Papers (HSP).

and collecting in the barrooms late at night for whisky, stories, and horseplay.[46]

A few months after he began to practice, James formed a partnership with another young lawyer, Madison L. Caruthers. Most of their business at first was in Maury County, collecting debts or small damages for five- and ten-dollar fees, though James's father and Colonel William Polk were giving them some more lucrative land cases. Their total income for the last four months of 1820 was just over $250, with the biggest fee, $75, coming from Sam Polk. But their affairs improved steadily. "$813 each!" James noted enthusiastically on the account book when he added up the fees for 1821. While this amount seems modest enough, it constituted a considerable degree of professional success for two beginning lawyers; and the next year the partnership did $2,305 worth of business.[47]

It was soon apparent that James, because of his family connections and his ability and energy, was carrying more than his due weight in the partnership. In November 1822 he broke his connection with Caruthers and formed a new partnership with Aaron V. Brown, a rising young lawyer who as state senator from Giles County might be expected to bring the firm a large amount of business. Brown had been at Chapel Hill just before James, and with this common interest they had formed a lifelong friendship when thrown together at the legislative sessions. The partners announced that they would attend all the courts in the circuit, but actually they practiced mainly in Maury, which meant that James was doing most of the work. At any rate the partnership collected only $2,732.50 in its fifteen months of existence, with $2,300 of the total coming from Maury alone. After March 1824 Polk practiced on his own, collecting fees of $2,659 by himself in the remaining months of that year. This was his peak period as a lawyer, for politics would soon be taking most of his time.[48]

XII

James's prosperity coincided with the opening of the westernmost

[46] Edmund Dillahunty to R. L. Caruthers, 3 July 1824, Robert L. Caruthers Papers (SHC).

[47] Partnership Book of Caruthers and Polk, MS vol., Polk Papers; Col. William Polk to J. K. Polk, 17 Feb. 1821, *ibid.*; J. K. Polk to Col. William Polk, 24 Sept. 1822, Polk-Yeatman Papers.

[48] Nashville *Whig*, 11 Dec. 1822; Partnership Book of Polk and Brown, MS vol., Polk Papers. This volume also records cases handled by Polk alone through 1833.

quarter of Tennessee to holders of the old land warrants of 1783-1784, and the young attorney did not shrink from the opportunity to multiply his legal earnings in this last great burst of speculation. The state was scoured for any old warrants that might still be outstanding, while locators and surveyors swarmed into the Western District to pick off the choice tracts. "How I have overlooked my Chance here of making a Princely Fortune!" exclaimed a visiting North Carolinian. "Had I known a few Months Ago what I know now, I would have been rich before this. . . . The Truth is, the Rich Spoil has been divided among a few, *very few*; It is all a Mystery even to the People of Nashville."[49]

The Polks, of course, were among the insiders. Sam Polk and another man formed one of the most active locating and surveying companies, receiving as much as half of each tract for their services and building up a handsome domain of their own. Much of their business came from Colonel William Polk, who was the most princely of the warrant holders.[50]

Sam took James as his partner in still another company, which sent an agent to North Carolina to buy warrants. They raised $5,000 for the initial payments, with James making his contribution partly in legal services. Meanwhile both men were steadily buying and selling lands on their own account. Promoting new towns was one of the most popular speculative activities, and James bought some lots in Jackson, which vindicated his judgment by becoming the capital of the Western District's richest cotton-raising region. Sam, of course, was a more extensive operator than his son could be, but there is no way of determining accurately how many acres passed through his hands in these years. Four years after his death 67,000 acres of the lands he had devised to his sons remained unsold.[51]

The Polks were especially interested in lands on the Big Hatchie

49 William Henry Hoyt, ed., *The Papers of Archibald D. Murphey* (2 vols., Raleigh, 1914), I, 248; Thomas P. Abernethy, *From Frontier to Plantation in Tennessee: A Study in Frontier Democracy* (Chapel Hill, 1932), 250-251.

50 Nashville *Gazette*, 20 Sept. 1820; Goodpasture, "Boyhood of Polk," *loc.cit.*, 44-45; Hardeman County, Tenn., Wills and Inventories, Bk. I, 1823-1835, p. 26; indenture, 29 Nov. 1823, Polk Papers; Col. William Polk to J. K. Polk [answered 26 Aug. 1830], *ibid.*; receipt, 10 Oct. 1831, *ibid.*

51 Articles of agreement, 2 May 1820, Polk Papers; numerous land grants and indentures to J. K. Polk, 1822-1824, *ibid.*; entry for 7 Apr. 1831 in Sam Polk Account Book, MS vol. in *ibid.*; Samuel Cole Williams, *Beginnings of West Tennessee: In the Land of the Chickasaws 1541-1841* (Johnson City, Tenn., 1930), 136.

River in what is now Hardeman County; and in 1821 Sam sent some of his slaves there to clear a plantation, though he never moved his family to the new country. The actual migration of Polks to the Hatchie was led, as previous Polk migrations had been, by old Colonel Ezekiel himself. Ezekiel's plantation in northern Maury had remained the hub of a widely ramifying network of kin. In 1811, after the death of his second wife, Ezekiel had married a "young, handsome & Agreeable" widow, by whom this irrepressible patriarch had proceeded to have four more children, the last of them when he was seventy-one years of age. In the course of a long life he had fathered at least 14 children, who would in turn, by conservative computation, be the progenitors of 92 children and 307 grandchildren.[52]

Ezekiel was in his seventy-fourth year in the autumn of 1821, when the opening of the Western District inspired his last pioneering venture. Taking a gang of slaves out to the Hatchie country, he cleared land and put up cabins, and early in the winter moved his family once more to a rough pioneer home. Sam Polk never ceased to marvel at his father. *"Is he not a strange old man!!!"* was the only comment he could muster.[53]

Ezekiel's clearing was the first important settlement in that part of West Tennessee, and the pioneering pattern always associated with Ezekiel soon repeated itself. Within a few years he was joined by the families of his son William, his son-in-law Thomas McNeal, and his newest son-in-law, Thomas J. Hardeman. The richness of the cotton lands and the navigability of the Hatchie caused the community to grow rapidly. In 1823 a new county was laid off and named for Hardeman's father; the first county court was held at Thomas McNeal's house and presided over by William Polk; Sam Polk built the first mill in the county, and the county seat was located on lands given by him and another man. It is not wholly fanciful to suppose that Ezekiel dictated the naming of the new town for the most conspicuous revolutionary of the day, Bolivar.[54]

For the last time Ezekiel settled down to watch the frontier pass

[52] Alice B. Keith, ed., "William Maclean's Travel Journal from Lincolnton, North Carolina, to Nashville, Tennessee, May-June, 1811," *North Carolina Historical Review*, xv (Oct. 1938), 384. The computation is from Wilmot Polk Rogers, "Ezekiel Polk and His Descendants" (San Francisco, 1939), typescript copies (LC and THS), and is incomplete.

[53] Sam Polk to Col. William Polk, 9 Sept. 1821, Polk-Yeatman Papers.

[54] Warner W. Clifft, "Early History of Hardeman County, Tennessee," M.A. thesis, George Peabody College for Teachers (1930), 9-11, 16; Williams, *West Tenn.*, 147-149.

beyond him, to consolidate the gains of another pioneering venture, and to oversee the affairs of a vigorous clan. He continued to accumulate property and began to plan his pretentious, white-pillared "Mecklen." Dying on August 31, 1824, before this monument to his metamorphosis from pioneer to southern gentleman was completed, he left a large estate, including thousands of acres, 24 slaves, 9 horses, 123 hogs, 36 cattle, 22 sheep, and a library of 70 volumes.[55]

Ezekiel was characteristically jealous of his fame. Shortly before leaving Maury he had tried to insure a just picture of himself for posterity by composing his own epitaph, which he left at death with specific instructions: "As there is no rock in this country fit for grave stones, let it be done on durable wood, well painted and placed upright at my head, and a weeping willow planted at my feet." It is only just to the old colonel to give the inscription in full.

> Here lies the dust of old E.P.
> One instance of mortality;
> Pennsylvania born, Carolina bred,
> In Tennessee died on his bed.
> His youthful days he spent in pleasure,
> His latter days in gathering treasure;
> From superstition liv'd quite free,
> And practised strict morality.
> To holy cheats was never willing
> To give one solitary shilling.
> He can foresee, (and for foreseeing
> He equals most of men in being,)
> That church and state will join their power,
> And misery on this country shower;
> The Methodists with their camp bawling,
> Will be the cause of this down falling;
>   An error not destin'd to see
>   He wails for poor posterity,
> First fruits and tenths are odious things,
> And so are Bishops, Tithes and Kings.[56]

James K. Polk, perhaps unfortunately, inherited few of his doughty grandfather's singular characteristics. But Ezekiel did bequeath to his grandson a zealous Jeffersonianism and enough kin to make Hardeman County his one political stronghold in that section of Tennessee.

[55] Hardeman Wills and Inventories, 9-14. "Mecklen" was completed after Ezekiel's death, and in 1950 was still standing in a greatly dilapidated condition a short distance west of Bolivar.

[56] This version is taken from the Jackson *Gazette*, 13 Sept. 1824, which printed it two weeks after Ezekiel's death, from a manuscript in his own hand.

3

THE POLITICS OF DEMOCRACY

POLITICS WAS YOUNG POLK'S REAL PASSION during these first years back in Tennessee, and everything he did pointed toward a political career. Circuit riding with lawyers and judges afforded intimate association with the leading men of Middle Tennessee; constant speaking in crowded courtrooms brought him before the voters; legal fees and land profits gave him a measure of financial independence and made him less vulnerable to the uncertainties of public life; while the annual meetings of the legislature introduced this ambitious young man into the centers of political power.

Polk would have been tempted by the political excitement of that first summer with Grundy in Nashville even if he had had no political ambitions, for 1819 was a year of political revolution, and Grundy was its master spirit. This was the year when the postwar boom collapsed in America's first great financial panic, a catastrophe that sent cotton prices tumbling, dried up credit, plunged merchants and planters into bankruptcy, and spread suffering through all levels of society. The panic had even more momentous political consequences. Out of its hardships stemmed debtor discontent, workingmen's parties, bitter sectional conflict over tariffs and slavery, and, arising from and comprehending all these developments, the country's first powerful movement for thoroughgoing political democracy. This democratic groundswell would sweep through the states in the 1820's before it finally inundated the federal government in the guise of Jacksonian Democracy.

Polk had been in Nashville only a few months when, in early May 1819, the cotton market broke sharply and the heady prosperity of the last few years fell apart with dismaying suddenness. By the middle of the month panic had spread through Middle Tennessee, as gold and silver drained out of Tennessee banks to satisfy eastern and European creditors; the banks called in their loans; the Nashville merchants dunned the country merchants; the country merchants dunned their customers; and everywhere men scrambled for cash to meet their obligations and save their property from forced sale. But hard money seemed to disappear. The whole fantastic web of credit had been woven out of bank notes supposedly redeemable in gold or silver, and the Tennessee banks now found themselves with only a small stock of the precious metals to cover nearly five million dollars in obligations.

Banks were a relatively new phenomenon on the American scene. In the early days of the republic the only recognized money had been gold and silver coin, and these precious metals were still the only legal tender, or money that a creditor had to accept in payment of debts. But around the turn of the century state legislatures had begun issuing limited-liability charters to banking corporations, which promptly supplied a new form of currency. These banks, like their modern counterparts, made profits by loaning money; but unlike modern banks they made loans in the form of their own bank notes. Bank notes were simply certificates bearing a promise by the issuing bank to pay on demand a designated amount in gold or silver, and they generally supplanted coin as the circulating medium. So long as people had confidence in a bank's ability to redeem its notes in coin ("specie" was the more common term), they were seldom returned for redemption. This enabled the banks to multiply their profits by multiplying their loans and thus expanding their note issues many times beyond their specie reserves. It was this fantastic proliferation of credit through such bank notes that had largely sustained the postwar boom and ultimately brought on the crash.

Down in Columbia, Sam Polk and James Walker foolishly went ahead with their steamboat project, paying $40,000 to have a boat built at Pittsburgh; after three unprofitable seasons they would be glad to sell it for $7,000. By July over 500 suits for debt had been instituted in the county court at Nashville, the wealthiest businessmen were going under, and every day additional unfortunates saw their property sold under the sheriff's hammer for less than half its worth a few months earlier.

Was the ruin to be universal? Was there no way out? With one voice Nashville demanded that the banks suspend specie payment on their notes, so as to relieve the intolerable pressure on their debtors, and the harassed bank directors were only too glad to comply. Yet this merely created new problems. With confidence in the banks shattered, their notes depreciated steadily; and with specie unavailable, debtors were at the mercy of creditors who refused to take the discredited bank notes in place of gold and silver. In desperation the people turned to the legislature.[1]

Since the great referendum that vanquished Federalism in 1800, Tennesseans, like most of their countrymen, had been content to leave the affairs of government in the hands of their "natural leaders," those aggressive and generally well-to-do men who had something to gain from political control. This had meant fairly continuous domination of the state by the group of land-speculating frontier gentry that traced its origins back to William Blount and his allies.[2]

The real leader of this loose factional grouping in 1819 was John Overton, a lawyer, planter, bank president, and land speculator from the neighborhood of Nashville, who was reputed to be the wealthiest man in Tennessee. In the eastern end of the state the Blount-Overton coterie was led by Overton's brother-in-law, Hugh Lawson White of Knoxville, while its interests were represented in the state executive department by Governor Joseph McMinn and in the United States Senate by John H. Eaton. Andrew Jackson had been long and intimately associated with all these men. Since none of them were in the state legislature, floor leadership for their group was exercised by Abram Maury of Middle Tennessee and Pleasant M. Miller, a son-in-law of William Blount from Knoxville.

The Blount-Overton men had demonstrated their enterprising qualities in land dealings from the first, and during the postwar boom they had been quick to recognize the new possibilities in banking. It was they who had established the state's two banks, with headquarters at Knoxville and Nashville. Each bank had branches in several other towns, the Columbia bank in which Sam Polk and James Walker were the guiding spirits being a branch of the Knoxville Bank. This institution was headed by Hugh Lawson White, while Overton himself was president of its Nashville branch. The president of the Nashville Bank was an Overton ally, and its directorate included such Overton stalwarts as Senator Eaton and Jackson's crony, Major William B. Lewis.

[1] Joseph Howard Parks, *Felix Grundy, Champion of Democracy* (University, La., 1940), 103-105; *Century Review, 1805-1905, Maury County, Tennessee* (Columbia, 1905), 14; Nashville *Whig*, 17, 29 May, 19, 26, 29 June, 3 July 1819; Nashville *Clarion*, 8, 22, 29 June, 13 July 1819.

[2] The following account of Tennessee politics in the early 1820's is based on Charles G. Sellers, Jr., "Banking and Politics in Jackson's Tennessee, 1817-1827," *Mississippi Valley Historical Review*, XLI (June 1954), 62-74.

The enemies of the Overton group, however, were strong and aggressive. The most conspicuous figures among them were United States Senator John Williams of Knoxville and Congressman Newton Cannon of Middle Tennessee, but the real opposition leader was a state representative, Andrew Erwin, a planter and land speculator from Bedford County, which adjoined Maury County on the east. Erwin's principal supporters in the state senate were Theoderick F. Bradford of Bedford County and Senator Williams' brother, Thomas L. Williams, who had just defeated Hugh L. White for the seat from the Knoxville district. There had been little difference on issues between these two factions. Like the Blount-Overton men, the Erwin faction was held together mainly by personal friendships and common enmities, nearly every member of this group having quarreled violently with Andrew Jackson.

Felix Grundy was the only important Tennessee politician who stood aloof from both factions. When the panic struck, he was the first to sense that popular discontent would impose a new pattern on politics, and the first to stake his political future on the novel technique of appealing explicitly to popular demands and prejudices. Announcing for the lower house of the legislature on a platform promising relief to debtors, he won out over the bitter opposition of the creditor and banking interests.

James Polk had arrived in Nashville just in time to witness the birth of the new-style politics at the elbow of its pioneer practitioner. Moving on to Murfreesborough with Grundy when the legislature convened in September, he occupied an ideal vantage point for observing the parliamentary maneuvers by which his wily preceptor converted a popular mandate into public policy and personal advantage. For a budding Jacksonian politician, this was uncommon luck.

At the same time, the situation presented special difficulties for Polk. Previously the task of the aspiring young politician had been to establish the right connections with the right people, and the great advantage of Polk's clerkship was the opportunity it gave him to become well acquainted with the leaders of both factions. But just at this moment it began to appear that he could not expect to rise merely by the traditional method of ingratiating himself with the established leaders. An aroused electorate was beginning to ask how a candidate would vote on vital issues, not who his friends were; and even the established leaders might be overthrown. Under this new state of things the old personal-factional alignments were doomed, as politicians were increasingly forced to choose sides on the basis of issues that concerned the voters. Slowly but painfully over the next decade and a half Tennessee politicians would be forced into the mold of a two-party system, the institutional embodiment of a fundamental political revolution.

II

Popular discontent was channeled in its initial stages by Felix Grundy, who with strong support from the Erwin faction dominated the legislature of 1819-1820. Grundy's radicalism was more apparent than real, however, as became clear when the legislature provided for private appropriation of the newly opened Western District lands. The speculators, who were seeking permission to shift their often dubious claims from less desirable areas to the Chickasaw country, were greatly disquieted by the relief agitation that preceded the legislative elections, fearing that "no confidence is to be placed in these popularity hunting democrats."[3] But Grundy proved to be a strong champion of the speculating interests, and the legislation passed under his guidance expedited the satisfaction of every valid claim.

Even on the debtor relief question Grundy seemed more interested in quieting the popular clamor than in winning a clear-cut victory over the banking and speculating interests of the Overton faction. The legislation he pushed through in 1819 actually maintained the currency of the depreciated bank notes by delaying execution on a debt only if the creditor refused to receive them in payment. And although public opinion and Erwinite agitation later induced him to sponsor a more radical scheme for a state "bank" that would loan state-backed paper money in small amounts to debtors, Grundy saw to it that this "bank" was put in the hands of conservative directors, who restricted its operations as much as possible.

Meanwhile conditions were not improving, and the voters were now too aroused to be satisfied with anything short of a complete change in the state's political leadership at the election of 1821. In its candidate for governor, General William Carroll, the Erwin faction had at last found a champion more reliable than Grundy but his equal in popular appeal. Carroll had come out of the Battle of

3 Alfred Balch to Col. William Polk, 1 Mar. 1819, Polk-Yeatman Papers (SHC).

New Orleans with a military reputation second only to Jackson's; a Nashville merchant during the boom years, he had been ruined by the panic and now ran as a poor man. To oppose Carroll, the Overton men picked Colonel Edward Ward, a wealthy, well-educated planter, who was a longtime neighbor and intimate friend of Andrew Jackson.

The Overton-controlled banks were in the middle of this political battle. Their ability to pay ample dividends while refusing to redeem their notes, their severity toward their debtors, the apparent immunity of their directors and friends to the general distress, and their efforts to crush Grundy's state bank had brought down on their heads a storm of public fury. Ward was regarded as the candidate of the "old bank directors & the rich generally," and he attacked the new state bank directly.[4]

Carroll, on the other hand, blamed the depression on the banks and said he wished he "had never seen one in the state." He would favor abolishing them all if it were not that their "*sudden* downfall" would involve the community in a new train of economic disasters. The best that could be done was to watch them closely and force them to resume specie payments. About Grundy's state bank he said nothing specific, but he was generally supported by its friends.[5]

Carroll's views were heartily approved by the voters, who gave him a majority in all but two counties, and a total of 41,244 votes to 11,171 for his opponent.[6] During the next fourteen years he would be politically invincible in Tennessee, serving continuously as governor, except for a two year interim required by the state constitution.

The political revolution that swept Carroll into office was achieved by a union of two forces: those who believed that banking abuses could be overcome by public banking, and "hard-money" men, who opposed any kind of paper system, public or private. Carroll was actually closer to the latter group, and he argued eloquently that a depreciated currency injured farmers and laborers more than anyone else. The governor's experience as a merchant, however, made him sympathetic to the need for sound commercial credit, and he did not go so far as those who wanted to see all banks abolished, leaving only gold and silver coin as the circulating medium.

Carroll's moderate hard-money ideas found strong support when the legislature convened following his election. His backers promptly

---

[4] Nashville *Whig*, 18 July 1821.   [5] *ibid.*, 4 July 1821.
[6] *ibid.*, 6, 22 Aug. 1821.

introduced measures to force the banks to pay specie on their notes, and a last ditch struggle ensued. The outcome was a compromise act requiring resumption of specie payments by April 1824. The foes of the banks failed in their attempt to prohibit payment of bank dividends until resumption had taken place, but they felt that they had achieved enough to be able to look "forward to the day when the present *paper system* will give place to a sound and healthy *metallic currency.*"[7]

James Polk unquestionably followed this momentous contest with the keenest interest from his vantage point at the clerk's table, but he astutely avoided committing himself prematurely and continued to cultivate good relations with the leaders on both sides. Indeed this unprecedented situation presented peculiar difficulties for a young man bent on a political career. It was probably for this reason that in 1821, instead of offering himself to the voters as a candidate for public office, he sought reelection to the clerkship, for which he received the unanimous support of both factions.[8]

III

Life was more than business and politics, even for a young man of James Polk's seriousness. Like the other swains around Columbia, he took no little interest in the local belles and the shifting alliances between them and various friends. Nor was he immune to these involvements himself, for a letter from one of his cronies contains a tantalizing reference to a certain Catherine, "the greatest imaginable plenitude of perfection in every respect," who walks gracefully—talks pleasantly, prettily & fluently, laughs loudly, humourously &c; And says *James* with her wonted sweetness." Indeed, James's irreverent informant continued, "If you could but know how many pretty things she speaks of you, it would wring sighs from you—nay you would belch them out from the bottom of your belly—alias the inmost recesses of the heart."[9]

The young attorney was now living at home, and much of his life centered around the family. Franklin and then Marshall, like their older brother, had gone off to Chapel Hill. Frank was already show-

[7] "Circular of Aaron V. Brown," 25 Aug. 1822, broadside, John Overton Papers, Claybrooke Collection (THS).

[8] Tenn. *Senate Journal*, 1821, p. 4.

[9] J. W. Egnew to Polk, June 1820, James K. Polk Papers (LC; herein cited as Polk Papers, which refers to First Series unless otherwise noted).

ing signs of the wildness that would bring him to an early grave, and Sam had to beg Colonel William Polk, who was supervising the boys from Raleigh, to keep him "within the bounds of prudence." The family was overjoyed when the two youngsters came home in 1824 after an absence of several years. Even before their return the house was crowded. The next brother, John, was interested only in being a farmer, and it was the two youngest boys, Bill and Sam, who were the family favorites.[10]

James's older sisters, Jane Walker and Lydia Caldwell, already had families of their own. Sam could now afford to send Naomi off to the fashionable "Female Academy" in Nashville to learn French, needlework, and piano; returning in 1825, she married James Walker's business partner, Adlai O. Harris. This left little Ophelia to contend with her boisterous brothers alone.[11]

Though Sam Polk was just entering his fifties, he was already beginning to feel the effects of the constant exposure to which his land business had subjected him. He fell ill on his trip to the Hatchie country in 1821 and never again recovered his former vigor. Spells of rheumatism confined him at home for months at a time, and he had to admit to his old friend and patron, Colonel William Polk, that "my days of active service are ended."[12]

The equally wearing tasks of motherhood and pioneering on the domestic front had impaired neither the spirit nor the vitality of Sam's wife. Still a pious Presbyterian, Jane Polk herded as many of the family as she could corral to hear Parson Blackburn preach on Sundays. The Presbyterians had to worship in the courthouse at first, but by 1823 they had a church of their own. When the handful of local Episcopalians, not to be outdone, put up a church nearby and furnished it with an organ, Jane was scandalized and sniffed contemptuously that there should be a monkey to go with this heathenish circus instrument. An anxious, devoted wife and mother, she bent all her energies toward keeping her family close together in this world and saving them from damnation in the next.[13]

James was a loyal son and genuinely devoted to his brothers and

[10] Sam Polk to Col. William Polk, 9 Sept. 1821, Polk-Yeatman Papers; Lucius J. Polk to Col. William Polk, 4 July 1824, Polk-Brown-Ewell Papers (SHC).

[11] Nashville *Whig*, 21 June 1824.

[12] Sam Polk to Col. William Polk, 25 July 1822, Polk-Yeatman Papers.

[13] W. S. Fleming, *A Historical Sketch of Maury County, Read at the Centennial Celebration in Columbia, Tennessee, July 4th, 1876* (Columbia, 1876), 35-38; Mrs. Alfred O. P. Nicholson, "Reminiscences of an Octogenarian," typescript copy of a series of articles in the Columbia *Maury Democrat*, 1894 (SHC), 5.

sisters, but he was no "mama's boy." Though he was not naturally warm or outgoing and would never have any really intimate friends, he had trained himself to be affable and cordial. He was popular with the other young men around town, and even as far away as Nashville he had the reputation of being "a fine fellow." The best evidence of his standing was his rapid rise in the elections for militia officers. In 1821 he was chosen a captain in the local cavalry regiment, and before long he was a major.[14]

About 1822 James's friends observed that he was frequently making the fifty-mile trip from Columbia to Murfreesborough, even when the legislature was not in session. The cause of all this traveling, of course, was a young lady, Sarah Childress, one of the reigning belles of the little capital. James was not one to dally when he had made up his mind, and within a year the young people had come to an understanding. During 1823 Sarah was buying lace handkerchiefs, shoes, kid gloves, and yards of black satin, green gauze, plaid silk, "circassion" plaid, and varicolored ribbon, to be manufactured into bridal finery.[15]

Sarah Childress was not a beautiful girl, but she was considered something of a "catch." Her father, Major Joel Childress, had been a wealthy merchant, tavern keeper, planter, and land speculator. Moving to Murfreesborough from Sumner County, he had kept a tavern and store on the public square and become intimate with the state's leading men. The full dress uniform that Andrew Jackson took to New Orleans in 1814, a magnificent outfit costing over $500, had been bought for him in Philadelphia by Joel Childress. The major's own military experience was confined to letting himself be enlisted by one of Jackson's overzealous recruiting agents at a drunken barroom revel. Childress had no recollection of what had happened the next morning, and as a result he was threatened with court martial and compelled to spend some days in camp before finally getting out of the scrape.

By the time Murfreesborough became the state capital, Major Childress had moved his family to a plantation several miles out of town. Here he entertained politicians, lawyers, and judges, when

14 H. Rawlings to R. L. Caruthers, 28 Nov. 1824, Robert L. Caruthers Papers (SHC); commission, 25 Sept. 1821, Polk Papers; J. G. Searcy to Polk, 25 Nov. 1823, *ibid.*

15 Anson and Fanny Nelson, *Memorials of Sarah Childress Polk: Wife of the Eleventh President of the United States* (New York, 1892), 15; bill, 1 Jan. 1824, Polk Papers.

their business brought them to the little capital. Governor McMinn lived with the Childresses for a time, while Grundy, Overton, and other prominent Tennesseans were frequent guests.[16]

The Childress home was splendidly furnished, and the four children were provided with the best in clothing and education. From her earliest recollections, Sarah "had dressed in silks and satins of delicate textures, in beautiful designs and colors, and had never known, even in childhood, what it was to be simply clothed, or to long for splendor of raiment, having always possessed it." Major Childress was a close friend of James Polk's old teacher, Samuel Black, and a trustee of his academy; and when Sarah and her sister Susan had gone as far as they could in the neighborhood common school, they were sent to Black for private lessons after the regular academy classes were over in the afternoon. Sarah's brother Anderson was one of James's classmates at the academy, and it was doubtless here that she first became casually acquainted with her future husband. While James was away at Chapel Hill, the Childress girls went off to a fashionable school at Nashville, where they were taught to play the piano and introduced into the most polished society Middle Tennessee afforded.[17]

A large-scale speculator in Alabama lands during the boom years, Joel Childress was resolved to spare no expense in the education of his daughters. Before Sarah was fourteen they had exhausted Tennessee's educational facilities for girls; so about the time James was completing his studies at Chapel Hill, the young ladies were mounted on horseback and sent off under care of their brother Anderson to enter the best girls' school in the South, the Female Academy conducted by the Moravians at Salem, North Carolina. Tennessee editors railed at parents who, instead of patronizing local schools, sent their daughters to Salem, whence they returned "tipped over with the German *bon ton*, unfitted for the society in which they move." The polite arts of fancy needlework, music, and drawing did receive much attention at Salem, but the emphasis was on such practical subjects as reading, writing, grammar, arithmetic, history, and

---

[16] Nashville *Tennessee Gazette*, 31 July 1805; Samuel H. Laughlin, "Sketches of Notable Men," *Tennessee Historical Magazine*, IV (Mar. 1918), 77; Nashville *Gazette*, 18 Aug. 1819; Nashville *Whig*, 16 Nov. 1814; memorandum, 29 June 1814, Andrew Jackson Papers (LC); James Dickson to Jackson, 29 Dec. 1814, *ibid.*; "Correspondence of Gov. Jos. McMinn," *American Historical Magazine* (Nashville), IV (Oct. 1899), 322-328; Nelson, *Sarah Polk*, 2-3.

[17] Nelson, *Sarah Polk*, 4-5; Nashville *Whig*, 25 Oct. 1814; will of Joel Childress, 10 Aug. 1819, Polk Papers.

geography. Classical education was not considered suitable for young ladies. The Moravian academy was noted for its familylike living arrangements and religious atmosphere, and since the enrollment was small, great care could be taken with each pupil. The Childress girls did not stay at Salem long enough, however, to become altogether spoiled for life in the rude West, for in 1819, after only a year, they were called home by the illness and death of their father.[18]

Major Childress left his family what appeared to be a munificent estate, including thirty slaves and extensive land holdings in Tennessee and Alabama. Soon after his death Susan married Doctor William R. Rucker, and Anderson reached his majority. Left with an eligible daughter and a small boy, John, on her hands, Mrs. Childress doubtless encouraged the calls of the promising young man from Maury County.[19]

IV

Polk's ambition required little spur, but the Murfreesborough belle increased his dissatisfaction with the lowly position of senate clerk, and the special session of 1822 was barely over when he announced his candidacy for the lower house of the legislature in the coming year's election. Polk would need all his popularity and widespread family connections in Maury, for his opponent was a veteran incumbent, who had built up a strong following. Since most of the voters were farmers living widely dispersed over the county, the challenger also needed a large amount of energy and determination. These qualities Polk had in abundance, and he spent much of the year preceding the election riding up and down the creeks of Maury, winning the confidence of neighborhood squires and convincing the voters generally that he was a "regular fellow."

The public would have been greatly interested in this election in any case, coming as it did at the peak of the political revolution in Tennessee. But Polk's incessant campaigning, which steadily narrowed the gap between him and his more experienced opponent, inspired unusual fervor on both sides. As the close race moved down

[18] Nashville *Whig*, 6 Oct. 1823; Nelson, *Sarah Polk*, 7-12; Adelaide L. Fries, *Historical Sketch of Salem Female Academy* (Salem, N.C., 1902), 3-11.

[19] Inventory of Joel Childress estate, 12 Apr. 1820, Polk Papers; William H. Whitsitt, "Annals of a Scotch-Irish Family: The Whitsitts of Nashville, Tenn.," *American Historical Magazine*, ix (1904), 240.

to the wire, the rivals redoubled their efforts, saving only enough energy for the final drive to get their respective supporters to the polls. The election itself took two days, with each voter marching up to the polling place and declaring his choice publicly, while candidates and campaigners crowded around, using all the arts of flattery, cajolery, persuasion, and intimidation in eleventh hour efforts to influence the outcome. Excitement mounted as the lead shifted from side to side, and with liquor flowing freely—Polk paid for twenty-three gallons of cider, brandy, and whisky in one election district alone—the second day of voting was punctuated by fights between the inflamed partisans. When the poll books were finally closed and the results announced, a shout went up from Polk's friends. Well tutored by a master of the new-style democratic politics, he had made good use of all the rough arts of frontier electioneering and had been elected by a comfortable majority.[20]

The third week of September 1823 found the usually sleepy little town of Murfreesborough buzzing with activity. The legislature was assembling for its biennial session, and each arriving coach discharged its complement of travel-weary lawmakers. The public square was crowded with elegantly attired lawyers from Nashville and Knoxville, lean-visaged farmers from the valleys of East Tennessee, plain-mannered planters from the rich cotton counties in the middle part of the state, and ambitious younger men, mostly lawyers, from all quarters. But it was the newly settled Western District that sent the most picturesque representative, the redoubtable coon catcher and bear killer, Colonel Davy Crockett. Crockett was already making a name for himself as champion of the poor squatters whose cabins were being pushed ever deeper into the canebrakes by the advancing cotton kingdom, and for the conservative leaders of the Overton faction his presence was a disturbing reminder of the political revolution that had broken their grip on the state government during the last four years.

The Overton men were far from demoralized, however, and though they had not dared oppose Governor Carroll for reelection, they had organized a powerful counterattack for this session of the legislature. Most important, they had built up a strong movement to repeal the specie resumption act of 1821. In addition the perennial land ques-

[20] Nelson, *Sarah Polk*, 16; J. K. Polk to Col. William Polk, 24 Sept. 1822, Polk-Yeatman Papers; Nashville *Gazette*, 11 Aug. 1819; Nashville *Clarion*, 8 Aug. 1821; receipts, 7-9 Aug. 1823, Polk Papers; John S. Jenkins, *The Life of James Knox Polk, Late President of the United States* (Auburn, N.Y., 1850), 52.

tion was again up for consideration, with lines drawn between the speculators and the squatters and others traditionally opposed to the Blount-Overton land policy. Moreover Grundy was now solidly back in the conservative camp and had joined Overton and Eaton in bringing out Andrew Jackson as a candidate for president. It was generally expected that Jackson's great popularity would be used to defeat Senator Williams, a Carroll supporter and an avowed enemy of Old Hickory, for reelection at this session.

With a showdown battle impending, the leaders on both sides took great interest in the position of the brisk, genial young man who was embarking on his first elective office as representative from Maury County. Polk was one of the few college men in public life. His campaign for the legislature had established him as an effective vote getter, and he had already impressed the veterans with his shrewdness and capacity for work. With the lines drawn as closely as they were in 1823, he was surely watched intently by both sides.

It would have been natural for Polk, his background and connections being what they were, to cast his lot with the conservative Overton faction. The whole political history of the state suggested that opposition to these powerful and wealthy men could not long prevail, while a young man of Polk's advantages might expect to advance rapidly to a position of prominence under their sponsorship. But this was not the course he chose. When the house had organized, it was Polk who moved that special committees be appointed to insure adequate consideration for the progressive proposals in Governor Carroll's message. Before many days had gone by, it was clear that this freshman member was leading the governor's supporters in the fight against the banks and for the Carroll reform program.[21]

The Tennessee legislature was no place for a political neophyte. "*Every thing* here is done by Management," reported one shrewd observer. "Intrigue and bargaining (they call it Log-Rolling here) are at the bottom of every thing."[22] But four years of observation from the speaker's desk in the senate and of riding the circuit with Grundy and the other lawyer-politicians of Middle Tennessee had given Polk a liberal education in practical politics. Andrew Erwin, the only supporter of the governor who was a match for Grundy,

21 Tenn. *House Journal*, 1823, p. 16.
22 William Henry Hoyt, ed., *The Papers of Archibald D. Murphey* (2 vols., Raleigh, 1914), I, 251.

was no longer in the house, and the Carroll men gladly recognized Polk's abilities and followed his leadership.

Since Murfreesborough's handsome courthouse had burned the year before—all Murfreesborough swore the catastrophe was the work of incendiaries from Nashville or Sparta, its rivals for the privilege of playing host to the lawmakers—the legislature was meeting in the Presbyterian church. The opposing forces were not slow in squaring off. Debate in the house quickly became heated, and the proceedings of the senate, sitting in the gallery, were disturbed frequently by the din rising from what was now literally the lower chamber on the main floor.[23]

V

The hardest fight was over the banking question. When the bank men began complaining that the banks could not resume without calling in so many of their loans that a host of debtors would be ruined, Polk, Crockett, and the other Carroll supporters replied vehemently. Polk contented himself at first with urging the house to defer action until a committee appointed to ascertain the banks' condition should report. But Davy Crockett with characteristic bluntness and impatience wasted no time in making it plain that he "considered the whole Banking system a species of swindling on a large scale."[24]

The investigating committee no sooner reported that the banks were perfectly able to resume than the bank men introduced a bill to amend the specie resumption act by substituting an elaborate recital of the ineffectual penalties for a refusal to pay specie already prescribed by the bank charters and the common law. The newspapers reported that Grundy was "the reputed father of this strange production," and pointed out that for all its "ambiguous manner and studied phraseology," its effect would be to repeal the specie resumption act.[25]

If Grundy hoped to rush this measure through before its meaning was understood by the farmer-legislators, he underestimated the vigilance of his former protégé. Polk jumped to his feet and moved that it be laid on the table for three days, after which a full discussion might be had. When Grundy protested that bills were usually

---

[23] Nashville *Whig*, 24 July 1822; C. C. Henderson, *The Story of Murfreesboro* (Murfreesboro, Tenn., 1929), 41.

[24] Nashville *Whig*, 13 Oct. 1823; *ibid.*, 29 Sept. 1823.

[25] Nashville *Gazette*, quoted in Clarksville *Tennessee Watchman*, 7 Nov. 1823.

permitted to pass their first reading without opposition, Polk rejoined that he "was aware that this bill was the favorite child of the gentleman from Davidson [Grundy], that he fostered and nourished it, and hoped ere long to raise it to manhood." But, said Polk, this measure would repeal the resumption law, and he wanted it "arrested at the threshold." A further suspension of specie payments, he thought, would cause an unheard-of depreciation in bank notes, the only currency the state had.

Thus alerted, the house approved Polk's motion to table, and the stage was set for a protracted debate, mainly between Polk and Grundy. Grundy painted a dire picture of the poverty and suffering that would follow forced resumption. But his main argument was the one laid down by Chief Justice John Marshall in the Dartmouth College case: that "rights vested in corporations cannot be afterwards affected by legislative authority." The banks, he said, "if they had sense," would refuse to obey the resumption act, and the state would be defeated in the ensuing legal contest. Even if the state had the power, Grundy concluded, it would be bad policy to force resumption, because all the specie would be carried out of the state, and the remaining bank notes would depreciate to nothing.

In reply Polk cited various acts of the British Parliament as precedents for voiding corporation charters and then went on to argue for the benefits to be expected from resumption. If the resumption act "was such a nullity," he said, "it would do no harm, and therefore it was unnecessary to repeal it." But he did not think it was a nullity, and repeal "would destroy the confidence of the community, and produce a further depreciation, which would be calamitous to the people." Just in case the resumption act should turn out to be a nullity, Polk proposed a substitute for Grundy's bill enabling note holders to secure speedy execution on the property of any bank that refused to pay specie.

This proposal provoked one of those scathing rejoinders for which Grundy was famous. First of all, he said, he did not think Tennessee should follow British precedents; besides, he did not believe Parliament had ever taken the actions Polk ascribed to it. Polk's substitute, he went on, "had nothing in it." It purported, said Grundy, to give a man speedy recovery on a bank note by waiting for a circuit court, giving ten days' notice, and getting a motion, "and this was called a speedy recovery." As for himself, he wanted no such speedy recovery, for the laws already provided that, without waiting for a court, he could apply to a justice of the peace for a judgment for any amount up to $100 due by note and get it in ten minutes. Grundy did not add, of course, that no justice had ever dared test his jurisdiction against one of the powerful banking corporations.[26]

Polk devoted many hours to refuting Grundy's arguments, but as the debate dragged on the bank men succeeded in raising a furor over the disastrous consequences of immediate resumption. Recognizing that some concession was unavoidable, Polk astutely withdrew his first substitute and proposed another whereby the banks were to resume specie payments gradually over a two-year period, and in this form the bill became law. The banks did resume fully when the mandatory date arrived in 1826, but even with two extra years to prepare, they were unable to survive the financial contraction of that year, and within a few months were forced to close their doors and wind up their business. Grundy and his banking cohorts of the Overton faction had been able to delay the execution of Carroll's hard-money policy, but thanks largely to Polk, they had been unable to prevent it.[27]

VI

Hardly less important than banking was the land question, which was becoming involved with the new issue of public education. Governor Carroll wanted to put a stop to dubious claims backed by the speculators and use the remaining ungranted lands to endow a common school system. Here again Polk's support of the governor's position brought him into conflict with Grundy and the Blount-Overton speculating group, and also with his alma mater, the University of North Carolina.

Most of the outstanding North Carolina warrants had been satisfied in the scramble for Western District lands. But just as the speculative fever seemed about to subside, it had been revived by a new flood of warrants. Taking advantage of Tennessee's obligation to satisfy all Revolutionary military bounty warrants, North Carolina had recently declared all unclaimed soldier land rights escheated to her state university. When the university presented the first of these warrants in 1822, Grundy had tricked the hostile Tennessee legislature into referring them to a special committee for adjudica-

---

[26] Nashville *Gazette*, quoted in Knoxville *Register*, 14 Nov. 1823; Nashville *Whig*, 3 Nov. 1823.

[27] Tenn. *House Journal*, 1823, pp. 229, 321-322, 330; Sellers, "Banking and Politics," *loc.cit.*, 74.

tion. Here, by prearrangement between Grundy and the university's agents, they had been validated and divided among the university, Cumberland College at Nashville (of which Grundy was a trustee), and East Tennessee College. These warrants passed quickly into the hands of the speculators and gave their operations a new lease on life.[28]

When the university presented still more warrants to the 1823 legislature, Grundy argued that Tennessee was honor-bound to satisfy them. Polk objected strenuously that Tennessee was not obliged to go on indefinitely recognizing forty-year-old North Carolina claims. He wanted the Western District lands saved as the foundation for a common school fund, and he was ably seconded by Davy Crockett, who demanded that the poor "occupants" in the Western District be given first chance at the lands on which they were living. On a close vote Grundy and the university were defeated.[29]

But Polk was not content with merely opposing private appropriation of these lands. The federal government held title to all Western District acreage not needed to satisfy North Carolina claims, and the next step was to ask Congress to cede the remaining lands as an endowment for Tennessee's schools. Accordingly Polk got himself appointed chairman of a committee to draft a memorial to Congress.[30]

When the legislature approved Polk's memorial, the outraged Overton men demonstrated their loyalty to the bistate speculating fraternity by trying to defeat their own state's interests. The Tennessee secretary of state, an Overton ally, promptly sent a copy of the memorial to Polk's cousin William, who was both the leading speculator and the leading trustee of the university. "I do hope," wrote this Tennessee official, "that you will take such steps as will lead us into a knowledge of our interests—you must bring the question before Congress in such a way as to elicit an expression of their determination, for until we are brought to know the impossibility of laying our hands on the vacant land in the west we will treat your

28 Thomas P. Abernethy, *From Frontier to Plantation in Tennessee: A Study in Frontier Democracy* (Chapel Hill, 1932), 250-261; Parks, *Grundy*, 159-164.

29 Tenn. *House Journal*, 1823, pp. 50, 89-90, 275; Nashville *Whig*, 29 Sept. 1823.

30 The MS report, in Polk's hand, is in Legislative Reports, Box 129, Tennessee Archives, Nashville. It is printed in Tenn. *House Journal*, 1823, pp. 325-329, and reprinted in Robert H. White, ed., *Messages of the Governors of Tennessee* (Nashville, 1952-), II, 55-57. See also Tenn. *House Journal*, 1823, pp. 23, 33.

unsatisfied claims with unkindness." Colonel Polk was quick to act on this friendly suggestion. The North Carolina legislature promptly dispatched a memorial to Congress complaining of Tennessee's refusal to provide for the university land warrants, and these objections prevented favorable action on the memorial drafted by the colonel's Tennessee kinsman.[31]

Meanwhile the controversy was exacerbated in Tennessee by a court order allowing the university claims that the legislature had rejected. When the legislature was called into special session in 1824, Polk joined Davy Crockett and five other members in a futile effort to secure an investigation of this "illegal" proceeding. The university at this session presented claims for an additional hundred thousand acres, offering to divide them as before with the Tennessee colleges. "Tennessee," wheedled the university's memorial, "has now an opportunity of endowing her Colleges out of the public property of the nation; and will she forego the opportunity?"[32] Polk almost carried a vote against hearing the university agents, and after they spoke their pleas were summarily rejected. The university forces finally offered to devote half the warrants to a fund for Tennessee's common schools. Grundy was "peculiarly eloquent and impressive" in portraying "the advantages which the state and people would derive from the promotion of schools, academies and colleges, and the diffusion of knowledge emanating therefrom." But Polk "cautioned the house against the charm of Mr. Grundy's eloquence," and the antiwarrant men voted down the proposal.[33]

Polk, Crockett, and company were not so successful, however, in halting the continued appropriation of Western District lands through the transfer of old warrants held by Tennesseans. In the session of 1823 they were overcome by such strong majorities as 28 to 12, 26 to 8, and 25 to 11, though they did manage to obtain for the occupants first right to purchase lands they had improved. At the special session of 1824 Crockett complained bitterly that speculators had been allowed to locate fraudulent claims in the District and that the occupants had not been given the easy terms they were promised. "The speculators," he charged, had

[31] Daniel Graham to Col. William Polk, 1 Dec. 1823, Polk Family of North Carolina Papers (LC); *Murphey Papers*, II, 323-328.

[32] *Murphey Papers*, II, 331; Tenn. *House Journal*, 1824, pp. 41, 55; Albert Lincoln Bramlett, "North Carolina's Western Lands," Ph.D. dissertation, University of North Carolina (1928), 200.

[33] Nashville *Whig*, 11 Oct. 1824; Tenn. *House Journal*, 1824, pp. 42-43, 92-93, 182; *Murphey Papers*, I, 302-303.

pretended to be great friends to the people in saving their land, had gone up one side of a creek and down another, like a coon, and pretended to grant the poor people great favors in securing their occupant claims—they gave them a credit of a year and promised to take cows, horses &c in payment. But when the year came around, the notes were in the hands of others; the people were sued, cows and horses not being sufficient to pay; the land itself went to pay for securing it.

Crockett and Polk were unable to secure redress, and the house again voted to continue granting Western District lands on old warrants, though this time the speculators' majority was reduced to 2 votes.[34]

Another land problem involved the Cherokee country in the southeastern corner of the state, which had been closed to North Carolina warrants. The speculator-controlled legislatures had for years been indulging the squatters in this area, allowing them to buy their lands on credit and then regularly postponing the collection of both principal and interest. In exchange, the representatives from this section had been helping to pass the speculators' legislation for disposing of lands in the rest of the state.

When the usual proposal for further relief to purchasers of the Cherokee lands came up in the 1823 legislature, Polk led the opposition, objecting to "any species of relief," except, perhaps, a remission of the interest due. But as one observer noted, this issue was "a handmaid to the success or defeat of all projects," and Polk could get only eleven other members to stand with him against this legislative horse trading. He was again overridden on his proposal to have the proceeds from the lands set apart for education in this area used for common schools instead of colleges and academies.[35]

On the land question as on banking Polk had stood out against the selfish plans of the state's most influential men. Though he had not been completely successful, the strong stand of the antispeculating forces had insured an early end to private appropriation of the remaining Western District lands. In addition, he had given powerful impetus to an ultimately successful movement to vest the proceeds of these and other lands in a common school fund. But title to this potential school endowment was still held by Congress. The

---

34 Nashville *Whig*, 27 Sept. 1824; Tenn. *House Journal*, 1823, pp. 50, 57, 90, 148-149, 157; *ibid.*, 1824, pp. 190-191, 199; Tenn. *Acts*, 1823, pp. 42-45; *ibid.*, 1824, p. 15.

35 Clarksville *Tennessee Watchman*, 7 Nov. 1823; Tenn. *House Journal*, 1823, pp. 188-189; Tenn. *Acts*, 1823, pp. 33-39. For Polk's position on several related land questions, see Charles G. Sellers, Jr., "James K. Polk's Political Apprenticeship," East Tennessee Historical Society, *Publications*, No. 25 (1953), 47-48.

campaign for schools for the people was transferred to the national legislature, where it would again be led by James K. Polk.

VII

Carroll's program was more than a negative attack on the privileges of the past; the governor called for a whole series of reforms reflecting the democratic stirrings of the period. He wanted a common school system, an extensive network of internal improvements by the state, reform of the penal laws, establishment of a penitentiary and an insane asylum, abolition of imprisonment for debt, and democratization of the state constitution.

Though Polk led the Carroll forces in the house, he was not a slavish follower of the governor or anyone else. Always careful of the taxpayers' money, he fought the penitentiary bill at every stage. On internal improvements his record was more mixed. He was strongly opposed to a measure affecting his own constituents, a proposal to charter a company to build and operate a toll turnpike from Nashville to Columbia. Polk's main objection was that Nashville would get most of the benefit of the road, but he also thought the state should not force his constituents to pay tolls to a private corporation.

In the course of his remarks on the turnpike bill, Polk discussed rather ambiguously the general policy of internal improvements by the state and federal governments. Noting that the constitutionality of federal improvements had long been questioned, he asserted that the matter had been settled conclusively by the recent congressional approval of the General Survey Bill. This measure had aroused great excitement in Tennessee by authorizing the survey of a national road from Buffalo to New Orleans by way of Washington. Polk referred to the project approvingly and was on the committee appointed a few weeks later to petition Congress to route the road through Tennessee. It would seem that hostility at home to the Nashville toll road had turned him against private turnpike companies, while enthusiasm for the proposed national road was leading him into a cautious approval of federal projects. Here again, as on almost every issue, Polk and Grundy crossed swords as leaders of the opposing forces.[36]

[36] Nashville *Whig*, 27 Sept. 1824: Tenn. *House Journal*, 1823, pp. 16, 49, 94; *ibid.*, 1824, pp. 158, 171; Stanley J. Folmsbee, *Sectionalism and Internal Improvements in Tennessee, 1796-1845* (Knoxville, 1939), 52-53.

On still another question the young lawmaker seems to have been guided by the demands of political expediency. The legislature had battled for some years over the quorum court system, a sensible scheme to improve the county courts by designating a small number of justices as a permanent panel to try cases, rather than having all the justices present sit in judgment. The Maury squires seem to have been up in arms over the proposal, a former Maury representative who supported it having lost his seat to a strong critic of this constructive reform. Polk read the handwriting on the wall and voted uniformly against allowing his or any other county to adopt the quorum court system.[37]

Despite these vacillations, Polk's record leaves no doubt that he was in accord with the democratic tendencies represented by Governor Carroll. He showed this indirectly when Crockett introduced a resolution that the legislature grant no divorces at the current session. Polk made a long speech in opposition to the practice of granting divorces only by special act of the legislature. He endorsed Crockett's suggestion that the public prosecutors be directed to handle divorce cases for indigent persons, though he thought the state had better give the prosecutors special compensation for this business, if justice were to be obtained.[38]

This concern for the poorer members of society is even more evident in Polk's views on taxation. The state derived its revenue largely from levies on lands and polls. When the perennial tax reduction bill was introduced in 1823, Polk supported a reduction on white polls but argued against reducing the land tax. The poll tax, he thought, was too high in proportion to the land tax. Much of the state's land was owned by out-of-state speculators, who withheld it from sale and rented it to poor farmers who were unable to buy it. "We ought to do everything in our power," Polk declared, "to produce as nearly as practicable an equal distribution of lands, to induce foreigners to sell out their lands, so that they might be settled by independent free-holders, who would feel an interest in the soil, and become endeared to the government."[39]

A more serious inequity in the tax system, the requirement that all land be taxed at the same rate per acre, regardless of value, was imbedded in the state constitution. This, together with the undemo-

---

37 Nashville *Gazette*, 13 Nov. 1819; Nashville *Whig*, 29 Sept. 1823; Tenn. *House Journal*, 1823, pp. 225-226; *ibid.*, 1824, p. 133.
38 Tenn. *House Journal*, 1823, pp. 29, 38; Nashville *Whig*, 22 Sept. 1823.
39 Nashville *Whig*, 24 Nov. 1823.

cratic structure of local government, was the cause of the powerful movement for a constitutional convention in the 1820's. A convention could be called only by a two-thirds vote of the legislature followed by a favorable referendum, and this difficult procedure frustrated repeated attempts by the reform party. In 1823 the convention resolution got a 33-to-25 majority, but this was 6 votes short of the necessary two thirds. Polk was for the convention, of course, and took such an active part in the fight that he was designated to introduce the convention resolution at the special session of 1824. This time the reformers rounded up 36 votes, to 24 opposed, still 4 short.[40] Not until 1833-1834 would Tennesseans be able to clear the hurdles set up by their constitution and remodel their government along more democratic lines.

VIII

Only one other major question came before the legislature during Polk's term, but his decision on it would have a profound bearing on his future political career. Andrew Jackson's candidacy for president posed a problem of peculiar difficulty for Governor Carroll's able lieutenant. The general was on intimate terms with Colonel William Polk, he was a longtime friend of Sam Polk, and he had known James himself since he was a boy.[41] It would have been natural for the young legislator to go along with the Jackson movement, just as it would have been natural for him to side with Grundy, the speculators, the banks, and the university. But Polk had refused to follow the path of least resistance on legislative questions, and in so doing had aligned himself with men who were cool to Jackson.

The question of who should succeed President James Monroe when his second term expired, in 1825, had begun to be agitated in Tennessee as early as 1818, and it quickly became involved in the struggle between the Overton and Erwin factions. Jackson and most of his friends among the Overton faction were supporters of the national administration and friendly to the aspirations of Secretary of State John Quincy Adams, with Secretary of War John C. Calhoun as a second choice. Their Tennessee opponents, on the other hand, were backing the secretary of the treasury, William H.

---

[40] *ibid.*, 1 May 1819; Nashville *Clarion*, 8 June 1819; Tenn. *House Journal*, 1823, pp. 115-116; Tenn. *Senate Journal*, 1824, Appendix, i-iv.

[41] [Tennessee Democratic Central Committee, comp.,] *Vindication of the Revolutionary Character and Services of the Late Col. Ezekiel Polk, of Mecklenburg, N.C.* (Nashville [1844]), 16.

Crawford, who, as the choice of the old-line Republican leaders, was expected to get the support of the regular congressional caucus. The quarrel became particularly sharp in Tennessee when the Crawford men in Congress, including Senator John Williams and Congressmen John Cocke and Newton Cannon of Tennessee, attacked Jackson's conduct on the Seminole expedition.

It was 1821-1822, however, before the politicians began to make serious plans to influence the outcome of the national election. By this time the emergence of Henry Clay as a western candidate and as the favorite of such diverse individuals as Grundy, Carroll, and Overton had seriously confused the situation. Even more important in its effect on the final result was Carroll's victory over the Overton faction in the state election of 1821. It was this event that led directly to the introduction of Andrew Jackson as a contender for the presidency in the early months of 1822.

The man who seems to have given the initial impetus to Jackson's nomination was Overton's East Tennessee ally, Pleasant M. Miller. Miller had hoped to succeed his bitter enemy John Williams in the federal Senate on the expiration of his term in 1823, but the political revolution of 1821 had dashed the aspirations of all the Overton men. This canny politician perceived, however, that if Old Hickory were a candidate for president, his great popularity might be used to send one of his friends to the Senate in place of the hostile Williams and to restore the Overton men to power in the state. After some initial skepticism about Miller's plan, Overton finally gave up his preference for Henry Clay, and through the winter and spring of 1822 the two schemers busily made preparations to nominate Jackson at the forthcoming special session of the legislature. Grundy had just broken with the Erwin-Carroll party and was now ready to hop aboard any bandwagon that might happen along; so he, too, abandoned Clay and fell in with the plans of Miller and Overton.[42]

It was Grundy who introduced the nominating resolutions at the special session of 1822. Since the Carroll party did not dare offend

[42] P. M. Miller to John Overton, 27 Jan., 8, 25 June 1822, Overton Papers; John Overton to his nephew, 23 Feb. 1824, newspaper clipping in the John Overton Papers, microfilm (JUL; not to be confused with the Overton Papers in the THS, cited elsewhere); John Overton to Henry Clay, 16 Jan. 1822, Henry Clay Papers (LC; hereafter cited as Clay Papers); Andrew Hynes to Clay, 30 June, 31 July 1822, *ibid.*; G. C. Thompson to Clay, 12 Aug. 1822, *ibid.*; Grundy to Jackson, 27 June 1822, Jackson Papers; Nashville *Constitutional Advocate*, 17 Sept. 1822.

state pride by opposing Tennessee's hero, they passed unanimously. There is every indication that the leading proponents of the nomination had little serious hope or intention of electing Old Hickory to the presidency. "They have no more notion of trying to make him President than of making me," snorted Jackson's old friend Hugh Lawson White, and he refused to have anything to do with what he considered a maneuver for local political advantage. Most of the Jackson leaders really preferred Henry Clay or John Quincy Adams. Some of them continued to assure Clay that he would ultimately get Tennessee's votes, while more than one suspicious observer charged that the whole movement was designed to divide the western vote, so as to increase John Quincy Adams' chances.[43]

Miller and company used the Jackson question for all it was worth in the state elections of 1823. They organized Jackson meetings all over the state and put up legislative candidates pledged to vote against Senator Williams wherever they could. But their only notable success was to defeat Andrew Erwin for Congress in the Bedford-Maury district. Senator Williams' brother beat the Miller-Jackson candidate for the legislature in the Knoxville district, and when the senator himself toured the state to line up his supporters on the eve of the session, he found himself with a comfortable majority over the announced opposition.[44]

Much of Williams' advantage arose from the fact that Miller was not the only Jackson man who wanted to go to the Senate. William G. Blount, son of the great speculator and a former congressman from East Tennessee, threatened to enter the race; while Jackson's old crony, the veteran East Tennessee politician John Rhea, actually abandoned his seat in Congress to offer as a candidate. When the legislature met, both Miller and Rhea were in the field, and Jackson's supporters were forced into desperate efforts to stave off the election to give them time to unite their strength on one of their two candidates. The least division would ensure the election of Jackson's notorious enemy and almost certainly destroy his presidential prospects.[45]

[43] H. L. White to Overton, 30 Jan. 1823, Overton Papers; White to David Campbell, 19 June 1823, David Campbell Papers (DU); Carroll to Clay, 1 Feb. 1823, Clay Papers; Thomas Hart Benton to Clay, 23 July 1823, *ibid.*

[44] Samuel Martin to Jackson, 17 June 1823, Jackson Papers; James Campbell to David Campbell, 15 Sept. 1823, Campbell Papers; John Williams to Rufus King, 19 Nov. 1823, Rufus King Papers (NYHS); Nashville *Constitutional Advocate*, 24 June 1823.

[45] John Rhea to Jackson, 18 June 1823, *Jackson Papers*; R. G. Dunlap to Jackson,

There are strong indications that this was exactly what some of the Overton men desired. Grundy, strangely, was leading the fight to bring on the election at once; Hugh Lawson White was in Murfreesborough surreptitiously working for Williams; and there were indications that even Overton was supporting the incumbent. Only Miller, who had a personal stake in the matter, and Jackson's close friends Senator Eaton and William B. Lewis seemed to take his candidacy seriously and continued to struggle for Williams' defeat.[46]

Were Overton and his associates beginning to sense dangers in the Jackson boom they had so heedlessly launched the year before? A dismaying enthusiasm for Old Hickory was already beginning to erupt from sources that these old-fashioned politicians were learning to regard with apprehension—Mississippi frontiersmen, the unwashed denizens of Philadelphia, and the dangerously democratic farmers of interior Pennsylvania and North Carolina. Jackson himself was becoming disturbingly doctrinaire and independent. Though the Overton leaders were his oldest friends from Tennessee's territorial days, he had grown increasingly critical of their banking and speculative activities. He had told Lewis a few years before that all banks were unconstitutional, and that very summer he had thrown his influence behind a hardly respectable Nashville editor who was the scourge of Tennessee land speculators and bankers. Adding insult to injury, Jackson had even backed his journalistic friend against the regular Overton ticket for the legislature. The Overton men might well have been disturbed, for Jackson was in fact discovering that personal friendship was no longer an adequate basis for political alliance.[47]

At any rate the situation in Murfreesborough as Governor Carroll reported to Henry Clay, was extremely "strange and uncertain." Both sides were sending out urgent summons to prominent men all over the state to come and put pressure on doubtful members. Polk must have been the target of much of this pressure. He had witnessed at close hand Erwin's defeat for Congress on the

2 July 1823, *ibid.*; S. Williams to Jackson, 4 Sept. 1823, *ibid.*; Tenn. *House Journal*, 1823, p. 20; Nashville *Whig*, 22 Sept. 1823.

46 Nashville *Whig*, 22 Sept. 1823; J. G. M. Ramsey to F. P. Blair, 5 Oct. 1835, Blair-Lee Papers (PU); Nashville *Union*, 22, 25 Sept. 1835; John Williams to Overton, 14 Jan. 1823, Overton Papers; Thomas L. Williams to Overton, 20 Sept. 1823, *ibid.*; Overton to White, 11 Feb. 1823, Overton Papers (JUL); William Brady and Thomas Williamson to Jackson, 20 Sept. 1823, Jackson Papers; Jackson to [Brady and Williamson], 27 Sept. 1823, draft copy, *ibid.*

47 Sellers, "Banking and Politics," *loc.cit.*, 75-81.

Jackson issue. Should he stick with Governor Carroll and John Williams; or, in order to support Jackson, should he side with the men whose legislative program he had been opposing so staunchly? When the preliminary maneuvering over the time of the senatorial election took place, Polk voted with the Jackson men.[48]

It soon developed that Miller had so many personal enemies that he could not unite the Jackson forces. Then the Jackson men procured an endorsement of Rhea by the general himself, but even this left them three votes short of a majority. Their only hope was to bring Jackson to Murfreesborough to convert members who had already pledged their votes to Williams. But the general would not come, and the election could be staved off no longer.

Finally, in desperation, Eaton and Lewis had Jackson's name placed before the legislature as Williams' competitor. When the messenger bearing this news reached the Hermitage, Jackson mounted up and left posthaste for Murfreesborough, arriving there in the middle of the night preceding the election. Even with Jackson as the candidate and with Jackson present, Williams was beaten by a vote of only thirty-five to twenty-five. Polk voted for the general, but Crockett and the bulk of the Carroll party stood by Williams.[49]

Polk's support of Jackson may have been decisive. The general's friends had been none too sure that even he could defeat Williams, and had he failed to do so, his presidential prospects would have been destroyed. Under these circumstances the support of so influential a leader of the Carroll forces as Polk was important indeed.

How is Polk's legislative record to be explained? Why did he turn his back on his family's interests and friends, his old preceptor and benefactor Grundy, and his alma mater, to side with Carroll and the democratic reform party? And then why did he diverge from Carroll on the presidential question, to ally himself with the men he had been fighting on almost every other matter before the legislature? The only answer that seems to fit all the facts is that Polk was a doctrinaire champion of political democracy and Jeffersonian

[48] Carroll to Clay, 1 Oct. 1823, Clay Papers; Tenn. *House Journal*, 1823, p. 20; Nashville *Whig*, 22 Sept. 1823.

[49] [William B. Lewis] to Gov. Lewis Cass, n.d. (HEH); Carroll to Clay, 1 Oct. 1823, Clay Papers; John Spencer Bassett, ed., *Correspondence of Andrew Jackson* (7 vols., Washington, 1926-1935), III, 210-211; Jackson to [?], 4 Oct. 1823, Jackson Papers, Second Series; John Williams to Rufus King, 19 Nov. 1823, King Papers; Tenn. *House Journal*, 1823, pp. 76-77.

principles. The context of his political thought was the image of Old Mecklenburg, where men lived simply on the fruits of their own labor without expectations of easy wealth and dealt honestly with each other on a basis of rough equality and mutual respect. It was this image that made meaningful the Republican dogmas he had heard from his father and grandfather, and when his views were taking their final shape in the early 1820's, it was this image that made the land and banking speculations of the Overton oligarchs repugnant and prepared him to accept the new dogma of popular sovereignty. His ideology was virtually complete when he took his seat in the legislature, and from it he would never deviate in the course of a long political career. Though he may fairly be accused of inflexibility and lack of imagination, this very dogmatism was to save him from the politics of expediency practiced by men like Felix Grundy.

To be sure, Polk was enough of a practical politician to recognize when yielding was unavoidable, as his course on the quorum court and internal improvement issues demonstrated; otherwise he could not have remained so long in public life. It should be added, also, that he had absorbed some of Grundy's keen sensitivity to currents of opinion, and this doubtless helped to push his thinking in the direction of the democratic revolution that dominated his first, formative years in politics.

Given this ideological bent, Polk's support of Carroll on state issues becomes perfectly consistent with his support of Jackson in the presidential election. Jackson's own opinions on public policy, it must be remembered, were closer to Carroll's than to those of the Overton group. Moreover Old Hickory's position as the western, anticaucus, popular-hero candidate tended to make him the focal point for the democratic movement as it began to manifest itself in national politics. These things made it easy for a man of Polk's convictions to back the general, regardless of the local circumstances that led to his candidacy. Whatever the reasons for it, Polk's decision was to have momentous consequences, not only for his own career, but for the Jackson movement generally.

IX

Neither the excitement of campaigning nor preoccupation with legislative duties had prevented the rapid progress of James Polk's courtship of Sarah Childress. The wedding was set for New Year's

Day, 1824. Polk engaged as "waiters" his law partner, Aaron Brown, and his distant cousin, Colonel William Polk's son Lucius, who had just moved to Maury to manage his father's land business. Sarah had four attendants. It was a large country wedding, held on a Thursday evening at the Childress plantation house. Parson Henderson performed the ceremony.

A Polk-Childress wedding was a major social event in Middle Tennessee, and friends of the young couple, including Andrew Jackson Donelson, the orphaned nephew to whom the childless General Jackson had become a father, came from as far as Nashville and Columbia for the festive occasion. The parties continued through the Monday following the ceremony, and James and his bride had to decline a dinner on Tuesday to get back to Columbia for the entertainment planned there. Lucius wrote to his sister that his time was "not very agreeably spent," since "our Tennessee girls are not of the first order either in accomplishments or beauty."[50] But Lucius himself was "the most anxious man to get married," and eventually did find a Tennessee belle who met his discriminating requirements.[51]

It was nearly a week after the wedding when James and Sarah finally reached Columbia. On the evening of their arrival Sam and Jane Polk gave a large party to introduce Sarah to the Columbia kin and their friends. Despite her plainness the curious neighbors found James's twenty-year-old bride an attractive girl. Full of a youthful vivacity that never left her, Sarah was at her best in social gatherings. She wore her fine clothes with a flourish, her careful training had given her a charming social manner, and her intelligence made her an animated conversationalist. Indeed some may have felt that she displayed more independence of judgment than was fitting in a woman; and one of the townsmen proved himself a perceptive judge of character when he noted that "her eyes looked as if she had a great deal of spice."

The couple settled down to housekeeping in a cottage James had rented for the year. Shortly after they moved in, a little Negro boy, astride a large water barrel mounted on a gleaming new cart, rode up to the door and informed Sarah that "Old Marster" had sent

---

50 Lucius J. Polk to Mary B. Polk, 27 Feb. 1824, Polk-Yeatman Papers; Anderson Childress to A. J. Donelson, 25 Dec. 1823, Jackson Papers; Lucius J. Polk to David L. Swain, 20 Dec. 1823, Epistolary Correspondence of David L. Swain, MS Vol. I (NCC); Nelson, *Sarah Polk*, 17-18.

51 Jessie Clay Connors, "The Years Are Kind," Nashville *Tennessean Magazine*, 10 July 1949, p. 8.

him. The townspeople had to haul their water from the spring, and this was Sam Polk's wedding present, a water cart complete with barrel and driver. The Negro boy, Elias, was to be James's personal servant for many years.[52]

After a year of renting James and Sarah moved into a house of their own across the street from Sam Polk's and James Walker's. It was a modest structure with an unfinished second floor and a separate kitchen and smokehouse standing in the backyard. Like most of the Polk women, Sarah had been raised by her mother to be a faithful Presbyterian, and her young husband promptly purchased a pew in Columbia's new Presbyterian church, where he was to be seen every Sunday that he was in town, in company with his wife and mother and such other menfolk as these two determined ladies could bring with them.[53]

Though James was often away from home on legal or political business, the constantly growing Polk-Walker-Caldwell-Harris clan provided Sarah with plenty of company. She quickly became a great favorite with Jane Polk, and she was equally dutiful to her own mother. James had bought his wife a carriage, in which they frequently made the fifty-mile journey over muddy roads and through often-swollen streams to Murfreesborough. The great social event of these years, however, was their trip to Nashville for the celebration honoring the visiting Lafayette in May 1825. Twenty-five thousand people from all over Tennessee congregated for this event. The Polks stayed with Judge John Catron of the state supreme court, and the company-loving Sarah was thrilled and exhausted by the continuous round of oratory, parades, military reviews, balls, and dinners.[54]

As a matter of fact, Sarah saw precious little of her young husband during their first two years of marriage. His outstanding record in the legislature had made him a marked man, and he had no disposition to resist the political allurements held out to him. Carroll had rewarded his legislative services with a commission as colonel on the governor's staff, and the Jackson men had even bigger plans for him. Polk had been in the legislature only two weeks when some began to speculate that he would be a strong contender for

---

[52] Nicholson, "Reminiscences," 16; rental agreement, 30 Dec. 1823, Polk Papers.

[53] Receipt, 20 Aug. 1825, Polk Papers; indenture, 12 Nov. 1824, *ibid.*

[54] Nelson, *Sarah Polk*, 20-22, 256; Josephus C. Guild, *Old Times in Tennessee, with Historical, Personal, and Political Scraps and Sketches* (Nashville, 1878), 57-58, 111-112, 445-447; Nashville *Banner*, 22, 26 Jan. 1830.

Congress, and at the close of the 1823 session Lucius Polk reported to the North Carolina kin that "James is one of the first young men in the state." He could, predicted Lucius, be elected to the national legislature with ease.[55]

Events in Pennsylvania and elsewhere during the winter of 1823-1824 convinced even Overton and Grundy that Jackson's candidacy was to be taken seriously. A movement started by obscure Tennessee politicians for their own local purposes had unexpectedly been caught up by a deep ground swell of democratic aspiration, and the original Jackson promoters found themselves, perforce, riding a whirlwind of their own devising. As they at last threw themselves wholeheartedly into the task of making Jackson president, they gave top priority to rooting out the anti-Jackson elements in Tennessee.

John Williams' retirement from political life had left Andrew Erwin as the principal thorn in the sides of the Jackson leaders, and there was a real danger that Erwin would get himself into Congress, where he could do incalculable damage to the Jackson cause. The sixth congressional district, which included Maury, Erwin's home county of Bedford to the east, and the less populous counties of Lincoln and Giles to the south on the Alabama border, had been laid off by the Carroll-dominated legislature of 1822 for the express purpose of sending Erwin to Congress. The extraordinary Jackson excitement in the election of 1823 had enabled Colonel James T. Sandford, a well-to-do Maury planter, to defeat the anti-Jackson leader. But Erwin still retained most of his strength in Bedford, which was the largest county in the district, and Sandford had been none too effective a congressman. So a strong candidate would be needed to prevent an Erwin comeback. During the summer of 1824 there were frequent letters and conferences between Polk, Grundy, and Judge Alfred Harris of Lincoln County, who had been the original Jackson candidate against Erwin two years before. By August Polk's hat was in the ring.[56]

The main problem for the Jackson men was a plethora of candidates. Erwin cannily encouraged division among his enemies by refusing to say whether he would run, and by the end of the year there

[55] Quoted in Connors, "The Years Are Kind," *loc.cit.*, 8; Nashville *Whig*, 17 Nov. 1823.

[56] Polk to Grundy, 18 July 1824, Felix Grundy Papers (SHC); Nashville *Republican*, 21 Aug. 1824; *Biographical Directory of the American Congress 1774-1927*, 64th Cong., 2nd Sess., H.D. No. 783 (Washington, 1928), 1493.

were five avowed Jackson men in the field. Sandford had been greatly weakened since the previous election, but another Maury candidate, Colonel Francis Willis, had been entered to take votes away from Polk in his home county. The three really formidable contenders were Polk; Lunsford M. Bramlett, a popular lawyer from Giles County; and Colonel Jonathan Webster, who had helped organize the 1823 rebellion against Erwin in Bedford and had defeated Erwin's lieutenant, Theoderick F. Bradford, for the state senate. When Erwin finally announced as a candidate in the spring of 1825, Webster was persuaded to withdraw, leaving Polk and Bramlett to fight it out for the bulk of the pro-Jackson votes.[57]

Meanwhile the presidential election had taken place. Though Jackson received the most votes, he did not have a majority, and under the constitutional provision for such cases the election had been shifted to the House of Representatives for a choice between the three highest contenders, Jackson, Adams, and Crawford. The fourth candidate, Henry Clay, had been eliminated as the lowest man in the electoral college, while Crawford was soon put out of the running by a paralytic stroke. With the choice thus narrowed to Jackson and Adams, Clay was in a position to determine the outcome through his strong following in the House. When the House barely elected Adams and Adams appointed Clay as his secretary of state, the Jackson men began to cry "bargain and corruption." All of this was damaging to Erwin's chances in the congressional race, for his son's marriage to one of Clay's daughters had brought the Erwin men into the camp of the suddenly unpopular Kentuckian.[58]

The current excitement over internal improvements, however, enabled the resourceful Erwin to convert his disadvantage into an asset. Up and down the district he went, telling the voters that "the constructing of roads and canals through their country is of more importance to them than the presidency of the U S for 100 years." If, he said, you want the great national road to New Orleans routed through Tennessee, you will do better to elect a man "who can have influence with Mr Clay the champion of internal improvements," than to elect one of these Jackson men, who wish only "to gratify a personal pique & in doing so would let the Carolinians have the national road." At the same time Erwin's supporters in Maury County

---

[57] Nashville *Whig*, 18 Oct., 6 Dec. 1824, 23 Apr., 30 July 1825.
[58] *ibid.*, 3 Nov. 1823.

began agitating for the turnpike to Nashville, which Polk had blocked in the legislature.[59]

Erwin used the internal improvements issue with such effect that Polk was compelled to issue a circular reassuring the voters about his position. Admitting that there had been serious doubts about the constitutionality of federal improvements, he repeated the argument he had made in the legislature the previous autumn: that the question had been settled by the recent action of all branches of the government in approving the General Survey Bill. "The establishment of mail routes," he went on, "the construction of roads and canals, the removing of the obstructions in our navigable watercourses, thereby connecting together distant points of the Union, by an easy and speedy communication, so as to afford facilities in times of invasion for the speedy transportation of troops and the munitions of war, are powers believed to be within the pale of the Federal Constitution." "But," he added in caveat, "with the assent of the state, within which the contemplated improvement is to be made." This assent for the national road, he argued, had already been given by the Tennessee legislature at its last session. So much for the constitutional issue.

"The *expediency* of making Internal Improvements," Polk maintained,

is unquestioned; it is only upon the question of POWER that doubt has arisen. They are calculated to promote the agricultural, commercial and manufacturing interest of the country; they add to the wealth, prosperity and convenience, of the great body of the people, by diminishing the expenses, and improving the facilities for the transportation of our surplus products to market, and furnishing an easy and cheap return of those necessaries required for our consumption.

"A judicious system of Internal Improvements, within the powers delegated to the General Government," he concluded, "I therefore approve."[60]

This was the most serious departure from Old Republican orthodoxy of Polk's entire career, and it would rise to haunt him later. But he was following a distinguished example. During Jackson's brief senatorial service, Eaton's influence and the need to reassure his supporters in Pennsylvania and the Northwest had drawn the

[59] James Campbell to David Campbell, 18 May 1825, Campbell Papers; Nashville *Republican*, 29 Jan. 1825; Nashville *Whig*, 14 Feb. 1825.
[60] Nashville *Republican Banner*, 10 July 1839.

general into a reluctant support of various internal improvement measures on the ground of military necessity. Had Polk not taken a similar position, he probably could not have been elected. After all, he may have rationalized, a congressman's duty is to represent his constituents' views, not to impose his own views on them.

Erwin was not Polk's only worry. Lunsford Bramlett had been practicing law six years longer than Polk and, though a poor speaker, had built up a devoted following, especially in Giles County. To attract the bulk of the anti-Erwin vote, Polk would have to create the impression that he was the strongest of the Jackson candidates. All candidates were expected to "live on their horses for about six months previous to the election," but in this campaign Polk set a new standard. As he rode constantly up and down the district, his friends were inspired to redouble their efforts, while his opponents grew worried.[61] Their fears were confirmed by the election returns. Out of a total of 10,440 ballots cast, Polk had 3,669, Erwin 2,748, Bramlett 2,347, Sandford 1,512, and Willis 115.

Polk had won by carrying 54 per cent of the big vote in Maury County and, with the aid of Judge Harris, 43 per cent of Lincoln. Erwin, of course, was far ahead in Bedford, but here Polk's friends Jonathan Webster and Archibald Yell helped him break even with Bramlett for the rest of the vote. Sixty-three per cent of the Giles vote went to Bramlett, but this was the smallest of the counties, and even here, through Aaron Brown's influence, Polk received 250 votes. Sandford and Willis picked up only negligible support outside Maury.[62]

In the seven years since Polk's graduation at Chapel Hill, he had become one of the most successful young lawyers in Tennessee, a colonel of the militia, an intimate of the state's most prominent men, and the leader of Governor Carroll's democratic forces in the state legislature. Now he had vanquished Andrew Jackson's most dangerous enemy and was going on to Congress to help direct the national campaign to vindicate Tennessee's hero and place him triumphantly in the presidency.

The same seven years had seen momentous changes in the political behavior of the American people. Crusty old Judge Thomas Em-

61 James Campbell to David Campbell, 18 May 1825, Campbell Papers; James McCallum, *A Brief Sketch of the Settlement and Early History of Giles County, Tennessee* (reprint edn., Pulaski, Tenn., 1928), 115-116; Nelson, *Sarah Polk*, 25-27; James Walker to Polk, 15 Jan. 1827, Polk Papers.
62 Nashville *Whig*, 13 Aug. 1825.

merson, retired in disgust from the Tennessee supreme court, spoke for the old-school politicians when he wrote to a friend shortly after Polk's victory: "Had I the power no exertion of which I was capable should be wanting to arrest the progress of that wild & furious democracy which has long threatened to overwhelm our Country at no distant day in the Vortex of Anarchy."[63] Old men—if we except an Andrew Jackson—could not understand new ways. The field would be left to the young.

Governor Carroll, more than anyone else the symbol of the new democratic order in Tennessee, was still smarting from old antagonisms and found himself unable to share Polk's conviction that Andrew Jackson could lead the democratic forces to a national triumph. The governor viewed the outcome of the sixth district congressional election with mixed feelings. "Colo. Polk," he grudgingly admitted to Henry Clay, ". . . is a young man of sprightly talents, and will probably remain several years in congress; and may hereafter have a show of influence in the political concerns of the State."[64] The governor was growing no younger.

[63] Thomas Emmerson to Overton, 9 Sept. 1825, Overton Papers.
[64] Carroll to Clay, 4 Oct. 1825, Clay Papers.

4

THE FACTIOUS OPPOSITION

IN THE AUTUMN OF 1825 the congressman-elect left his young wife in the Columbia cottage and set out on horseback for Washington. At Nashville he was joined by several other Tennessee members, whose company lightened the tedium of the journey up across Kentucky and eastward through the mountains. From southern Ohio, where these hardy western politicians turned on to the smooth surface of the National Road, the going was easy all the way to Baltimore. Here they left their horses and boarded a stage for the capital city.[1]

The approach to Washington was not impressive. The bumpy dirt road traversed a desolate country almost to the District of Columbia line, and scattered houses had hardly begun to appear when suddenly the bowl-shaped dome of the Capitol loomed through the trees ahead. Without pausing to let the Tennesseans scan this massive stone edifice, the driver whipped his tired team to a gallop. Across the square swept the coach, down the hill, through the muddy Tiber, and up the broad surface of Pennsylvania Avenue to the hotel. Stiff and weary, Polk crawled out to take his first look at the city where he would spend a large part of the next fourteen years.[2]

Finding a place to live was the most immediate problem. Few lawmakers brought their wives and families to Washington, and fewer still could afford to maintain a house in the city. The common practice was for a group of congenial congressmen to organize a "mess" in one of the numerous boardinghouses or hotels. Each man had a room to himself, where he slept, received visitors, and carried on the heavy correspondence essential to reelection. But they all took their meals at the long dining room table, and often whiled away the evenings together with cards or talk in the parlor. The

[1] Anson and Fanny Nelson, *Memorials of Sarah Childress Polk: Wife of the Eleventh President of the United States* (New York, 1892), 27-28.

[2] For descriptions of Washington and the Capitol about this time, see Nashville *Republican*, 15 Jan. 1825, 30 Jan. 1829; Jonathan Elliot, *Historical Sketches of the Ten Mile Square Forming the District of Columbia* . . . (Washington, 1830).

five members from Middle Tennessee joined a large mess at Captain Benjamin Burch's house on Capitol Hill.[3]

His living arrangements settled, Polk spent the remaining days before the session opened seeing the city. Actually there was not much to see. Foreigners still called Washington "the city of magnificent distances" in derision. Major L'Enfant's design had been grand enough, but as yet there were too few buildings to fill the sweeping avenues and broad squares. Only the mile-and-three-quarter stretch of Pennsylvania Avenue between the Capitol and the President's House was built up with any regularity, and even here there were frequent gaps in the rows of boardinghouses, stables, hotels, gambling dens, and shops. The avenue had been enhanced by four bordering rows of poplars, but in winter it was usually knee-deep in mud, while swirling clouds of dust made walking almost as unpleasant in drier seasons.

Only the public buildings gave the city some air of distinction. At the western end of the avenue, the plain but handsome President's House, not yet generally called the White House, looked down a gentle slope to the marshes and shallows of the Potomac. Flanking it was a group of unpretentious brick structures where the executive departments were housed.

The main object of civic pride was the Capitol, dominating the city from its eminence at the other end of the avenue. Here members of Congress hastened as soon as they arrived to claim choice seats in their respective chambers. Polk would not have been many hours in Washington before making his way to the large square at the eastern front of the imposing structure. He found the area piled high with stone and other building materials, for British destructiveness had made it necessary to rebuild the northern and southern wings before the massive, domed central section was even begun; and after thirty years of work the Capitol was only now nearing completion. The heavy columns of the portico were just being swung into place, but there were still no stairs from the square to the main floor.

Entering the basement floor at ground level and ignoring for the moment the cramped room off to the right where John Marshall presided over his Supreme Court, Polk would have ascended a stairway directly to the awesome rotunda. Though unheated as yet, the vast floor was crowded during sessions of Congress with hawkers,

[3] *Congressional Directory*: 19th Cong.: 1st Sess., 41; Nelson, *Sarah Polk*, 30-31.

office seekers, newspaper reporters, lobbyists, and curious rustics on their first visit to the metropolis.

The wings where the two houses of Congress sat opened into the rotunda from the north and south. Taking the northern corridor and turning off to the right, one came into the semicircular chamber occupied by the forty-eight members of the Senate. Impressively designed in the classic mode, the room was just large enough to permit nineteenth century spellbinding without being too large to dispel the air of intimacy and informality in which the senators liked to conduct their business. Tucked into odd corners of this as of the other wing were offices and committee rooms, not to mention refreshment rooms, where congressmen and citizens alike helped maintain the early republic's fabulous reputation for liquor consumption.

The showplace of the Capitol was the Hall of the House of Representatives (the later Statuary Hall), which took up nearly the whole southern wing. Semicircular like the Senate chamber, it was much larger, its arching half-dome ceiling rising to a cupola sixty feet above the floor. The main entrance, in the middle of the semicircle, opened directly across from the elevated speaker's desk, toward which the members' desks faced in concentric rows. Around the walls a screen of lofty pillars of variegated Potomac marble supported galleries for visitors. The only heat came from blazing fireplaces on either side of the speaker's desk.

There was just one real trouble with the House chamber: it was poorly designed for oratory. A speaker's words either got lost in the spacious dome overhead or bounced around on the curving walls so as to be barely audible several aisles away and almost indistinguishable in the gallery. Complaints about this never ended, and all kinds of expedients were tried. The height and slope of the floor were varied, recesses were let into the ceiling, draperies were hung between the columns, and the seating plan was reversed, all without effect. The only remedy that would have been a solution—construction of a flat ceiling just above the gallery—would have destroyed the effect of the dome, and this the members could never bring themselves to approve.

II

The session began on December 5, 1825, with the well-organized forces of the Adams administration in firm control of both Senate and House of Representatives. The political situation was badly confused. The president's appointment of Clay as secretary of state had united the followers of both men, mainly from the Northeast and Northwest, behind an administration that was expected to champion tariffs and internal improvements at home and a vigorous foreign policy abroad. With the Virginia Dynasty in eclipse, with Adams in the White House, with Marshall's Supreme Court asserting the federal powers more sweepingly every year, and with the Adams-Clay men in command of Congress, the nationalizing tendencies of the postwar period seemed to have reached their peak.

Beneath the surface, however, countercurrents were running strong. The postwar period's mood of generous nationalism had been nurtured by prosperity, and with the Panic of 1819 had come a resurgence of hostility and suspicion among sections and classes. The national bank was under attack in state after state. Virginia was up in arms against Marshall's constitutional dicta. Southern planters were blaming their troubles on the tariff and showing less and less enthusiasm for federal road and canal projects. Urban workingmen were developing a spirit of grievance and beginning to organize for political and economic action. Everywhere a vague but powerful feeling was spreading that bank charters and tariffs and toll roads were special privileges granted to the few at the expense of the many.

John Quincy Adams was too inclined to view his election as providential and his mission as divinely ordained to take seriously such diffuse signs of a shift in national mood, and his annual message, read to Congress on the second day of the session, was the manifesto of nationalism at high tide. "The spirit of improvement is abroad upon the earth," announced the president. When foreign nations were "advancing with gigantic strides in the career of public improvement," he went on, it would be disgraceful for the United States to stand still. "Liberty is power," Adams lectured the lawmakers, and "the tenure of power by man is, in the moral purposes of his Creator, upon condition that it shall be exercised to ends of beneficence, to improve the condition of himself and his fellow-men."

The president then called on Congress to exercise its power by encouraging commerce; appropriating funds to send ministers to the projected Panama Congress of the new republics of Hispanic America; invigorating the militia; underwriting an ambitious system of roads, canals, fortifications, and harbor improvements; expanding the navy and creating a naval academy; establishing a national university and "light-houses of the skies," Adams' unfortunately fanciful term for astronomical observatories; and supporting a series of exploring expeditions. As if all this were not enough, Adams concluded by cautioning the congressmen against being "palsied by the will of our constituents."[4]

This was at the same time one of the most courageous and one of the most ill-advised messages in the history of the presidency. Nothing could have been better designed to unite Adams' disorganized opponents and doom his administration to defeat. Since the War of 1812 and the death of the Federalist party, national politics had shown the same pattern of personal-factional alignments that had characterized Tennessee politics. Most recently politicians had been grouped according to whether they preferred Adams, Clay, Crawford, Calhoun, or Jackson for president, their preferences being determined only slightly by differences on public policy. But the latter half of the twenties would witness the same shift away from the personal-factional pattern that had already begun in Tennessee. By taking a strong position on policies in which the voters were increasingly interested, Adams facilitated this shift, a development that would be disastrous for him, since he had taken the unpopular side.

At the beginning of the session the avowed Jackson men, a relatively small group made up mainly of Tennesseans, were the only congressmen openly hostile to the administration. The Adams and Clay factions, of course, were just as openly in support of the president, but the numerous friends of Crawford and Calhoun were uncommitted. The Tennessee legislature had renominated Jackson for president in October, while Polk was in Nashville on his way to Washington, and the general had seized upon this excuse to resign from the Senate, being replaced by Hugh Lawson White. The Tennesseans had then descended on the capital determined to launch a four-year fight for the vindication of Jackson and the popular will.

All hope of creating a formidable opposition to the Adams administration depended on enlisting the experienced politicians who had previously supported Crawford and Calhoun. The early days of December, therefore, found the Tennesseans in frequent consultation with the Crawford leaders. Crawford himself had been

4 *House Journal*: 19th Cong.: 1st Sess., 10-27.

eliminated as a factor by physical prostration, and Senator Martin Van Buren, the astute chieftain of the Bucktail faction in New York politics, now called the turns for the Crawford group. Van Buren and his friends recognized early that Jackson was the only candidate who could defeat the Adams-Clay coalition in 1828, but the exigencies of New York politics kept them from taking a conspicuous part in the opposition at first.

The Tennesseans had better luck with Vice President Calhoun and his friends. Calhoun had withdrawn from the 1824 presidential race at the last moment and gone into the second office unopposed. As soon as Henry Clay was designated Adams' heir apparent, Calhoun saw that his road to the White House was blocked indefinitely unless the administration could be defeated. Consequently his friends entered heartily into support of Jackson, who had declared that a president should serve only a single term. Robert Y. Hayne of South Carolina brought to the opposition in the Senate an experienced leadership that the Jackson men themselves could not have supplied, while the same service was performed in the House by two other South Carolinians, James Hamilton, Jr., and the fiery George McDuffie. Their cooperation with the Jackson men was facilitated when Hayne and Hamilton joined a mess with Jackson's successor in the Senate, Hugh Lawson White.

The ultranationalism of Adams' message helped these divergent elements unite on a platform of resistance to the revival of Federalist heresies. Before Congress had been in session a week, John Quincy Adams was confronted with an opposition more implacable, formidable, and irresponsible than would harass any other American president until the time of Andrew Johnson.

Imbued as he was with Jeffersonian dogmas, Congressman Polk seems to have been genuinely shocked by the Adams-Clay philosophy. As he saw it, the old struggle between Republicans and Federalists had been renewed. The issue, he told his constituents, "is in fact joined between the people in vindication of their rights, on the one side, and the power and patronage of public rulers on the other." He had no doubt that the "present dynasty" aimed "to accumulate in the Federal Head all possible power; to stretch and construe away the most salutary provisions of the Constitution, so as to enable them, by dispensing a more extensive patronage, to perpetuate their power." The Jacksonians, on the other hand, "regard the Constitution as a charter of limited powers; as containing certain enumerated and specific grants of power; and reserving to the States and to the people all power, not thus delegated; and wisely intended to operate as salutary checks upon the General Government, and a security for the people against the ambitious and unjust claims of their rulers." "In this crisis," he concluded, "the people of the U. States are emphatically called on to decide the great issue; and upon their decision depends, in my opinion, not only the purity but the perpetuity of our free institutions. . . . A political struggle, worse than that of 1798 has ensued, and we must 'fight the battle o'er again.' "[5]

III

The nineteenth Congress was only four days old when McDuffie launched the opposition's offensive by calling for a constitutional amendment to prevent the presidential election from devolving on Congress. His purpose, of course, was to revive the "bargain and corruption" charges against Adams and Clay, and the debate was long and bitter. McDuffie himself charged Clay with organizing a "bold and daring, and shameless coalition, setting at defiance the will of the nation, and neglecting even the external decencies of political morality." When an administration man replied in like terms, the South Carolina hotspur retorted that since Clay was "the skulking manager who moves the wires of this whole concerted operation," he would not notice the "*minions* and *tools* and *understrappers*" the secretary had sent "to utter insolence and scurrility on this floor." The House was thrown into an uproar, and a duel was barely averted when McDuffie's second refused to recognize rifles as proper weapons.[6]

Polk's first major speech was delivered in this seething atmosphere. Opening with the vehement declaration that "*this is a Government based upon the will of the People; that all the power emanates from them; and that a majority should rule*," he went on to describe the influences that could corrupt the Congress and defeat the people's will. His mother's Presbyterian precepts had left him with no exalted view of human nature. "From my earliest infancy," he recalled, "I have been taught to believe, that, from the fall of our

[5] J. K. Polk, *Circular . . . March 4, 1827*, handbill bound in vol. of speeches, James K. Polk Papers (LC; herein cited as Polk Papers, which refers to First Series unless otherwise noted).

[6] *Register of Debates*: 19th Cong.: 1st Sess., 1931-1988; Charles M. Wiltse, *John C. Calhoun* (3 vols., Indianapolis, 1944-1951), I, 330-331.

first great parent until the present hour, man has been depraved, frail, and impure." It followed that members of Congress were no more immune to corruption than other men. Polk proposed that the electoral college be abolished, so that the people could vote directly for president.

His long speech touched on many collateral subjects that had come up in the debate. Carrying his devotion to popular rule to its logical conclusion, he argued that on questions of expediency a representative was bound to follow the known wishes of his constituents, rather than his personal judgment. He was unquestionably following the wishes of his own constituents when he defended Jackson against the covert allusion of a New England member who feared the government might be destroyed by the election of some "military chieftain." "Yes sir," the young Tennessean declared hotly, "by some '*military chieftain*,' whose only crime it was to have served his country faithfully at a period when that country needed and realized the value of his services." Some politicians, said Polk, were continually in alarm lest "the People"—Polk usually capitalized the word —should destroy the government. Actually, he declared, if the government were ever destroyed, it would be by "the encroachments and abuse of power, and by the alluring and corrupting influence of Executive patronage." There would be infinitely more danger from an administration that lacked "the People's" support than from "all the ideal dangers which the gentlemen seem to apprehend are covertly lurking among the great body of the people of this Union."

It was altogether fitting for Polk to make his debut on the national stage as a radical champion of popular sovereignty. It was also ironically fitting that he was compelled to grapple with the subject of slavery. Democracy and slavery were the horns of the dilemma that would baffle him at the end of his political career. But he was never to change his view of the problem, this maiden speech expressing it as well as any he would ever give. It was a question of "peculiar delicacy," and he regretted that this "unfortunate subject" was already being brought into the discussion of almost any topic. Slaves, he admitted, differed from all other kinds of property in that "they were rational; they were human beings." Slavery seemed to this young Tennessean, in fact, a common evil, affecting both the slave states and those that had gotten rid of it. But as a practical man—and here Polk echoed his patron saint, Jefferson—he was acutely aware of the difficulties of uprooting the institution. Slaves were already in our midst when the country became independent, he pointed out, having been "entailed upon us by our ancestors," and the country would just have to make the best of the situation.

This being the case, Polk had no compunctions about defending the interests of the section he represented. If slave population was to be counted in apportioning direct taxes, he argued in this debate, it should also be counted in allotting representation and electoral votes. In short, he saw slavery as unfortunate but irremediable. Most of all it was a dangerous subject that should be let alone. Polk never defended the South's "peculiar institution" in principle, but he opposed every attempt to interfere with it.[7]

General Jackson sent the young congressman hearty congratulations on his speech, while a Western District newspaper commented that Polk "promises to become a statesman of the highest order." But the proposal for electoral reform did not get far in the administration-controlled House. Polk was on the special committee to which it was referred, but the committee was loaded with Adams men, and there it died. The Jacksonians were not disappointed. Just now political capital was more important than constitutional change, and already their printed speeches were flying through the country.[8]

IV

While the House was debating electoral reform, the opposition senators had been assailing the president's intention of sending representatives to the Panama Conference of the revolutionary republics of Latin America. Clay had long advocated close ties with the new commonwealths to the south, while two years before, Adams had helped frame President Monroe's famous declaration that the United States would resist any interference with the fledgling states. Adams was now careful to disclaim any departure from traditional American neutrality, but the Jacksonians nevertheless seized on the issue as an ideal weapon for demagogic forays against the administration.

Though appointment and confirmation of diplomats were functions of the president and Senate, this question, too, got into the House when the opposition leaders tried to block appropriations for the mission. In a parade of inflammatory speeches the Jackson men again sought to alarm the country with visions of deep-laid plots

[7] *Reg. Deb.*:19:1, pp. 1633-1653.
[8] Jackson *Gazette*, 22 Apr. 1826; Jackson to Polk, 3 May 1826, Polk Papers; *House Journal*:19:1, pp. 401-406; *Reg. Deb.*:19:1, p. 2659.

committing the United States to military alliances and involving the country in wars for South American independence.

The extreme anti-Panama men were in a minority, but Polk stated their position for the record in a series of resolutions declaring that the mission would probably "involve the nation in *'entangling alliances,'* " and that the House had not only a right but a duty to judge the expediency of foreign missions before appropriating for them. In presenting his resolutions Polk ridiculed the notion that House members were "mere passive agents, to record the decrees of the President and the Senate." When "the People's" representatives were called upon to appropriate "the People's" money, he declared, they should exercise their own sound judgment.[9]

Meanwhile the Foreign Affairs Committee had reported in favor of an unrestricted appropriation. It was soon apparent, however, that the balance of power rested with a group of moderate opposition men interested in inter-American trade, who proposed to amend the committee's resolution by adding that the mission was not authorized to commit the United States to aid the South American republics. Polk supported this amendment but promptly announced that he would vote against the amended resolution. All our sympathies, he said, were with the new republics of the South, "but self-preservation is the first law of nature and of nations." In view of his later expansion of the Monroe Doctrine, it is interesting to find him asserting in this debate that President Monroe "had no power to bind the nation by such a pledge."[10] "For however great our sympathies may be," he later told his constituents, "in behalf of those struggling for liberty in every portion of the Globe (and I confess, mine are great) yet to avoid the disastrous calamities of war, and to preserve the peace and tranquility of our own country, are paramount considerations with an American politician."[11]

In the end the moderates joined the pro-Panama men to pass the appropriation over Polk and his allies, 134 to 60, but the whole loud affair came to nothing. The speech making and parliamentary harassment delayed the mission's departure, one of the ministers died on his way to Panama, and the other did not reach there until after the conference had adjourned.[12]

The Jacksonian opposition by no means reserved its fire for such

9 *Reg. Deb.*:19:1, p. 2166.   10 *ibid.*, 2489.
11 Polk, *Circular, 1827.*
12 *House Journal*:19:1, pp. 452, 457, 469; *Reg. Deb.*:19:1, p. 2551.

major forays as those on electoral reform and the Panama mission. Throughout the four years of Adams' presidency, no opportunity for sniping was let pass. Polk was not active in this guerrilla warfare, but when such questions came to a vote, he was always found on the Jackson side. He did join the attack on Clay for distributing the public printing exclusively to administration newspapers, but only to express his resentment at the administration forces for denouncing the Jacksonians as "factious oppositionists." The same language, Polk declared, had been used against the Jeffersonians of '98, when they were contending for the same principles.[13]

V

Polk had more to worry about than the derelictions of Adams and Clay, for as long as the Erwin faction remained powerful in Bedford County, his political future was precarious. He hastened home when Congress adjourned in the late spring of 1826 and spent the summer mending his fences and listening for signs of opposition. It may be assumed that few militia musters and court sessions were held that summer without the presence of Congressman Polk.

Polk took a prominent part in the festivities at his own regiment's muster in September, when Governor Carroll was honored with a review and dinner. Beginning at two in the afternoon, the dinner was climaxed, as was customary on such occasions, with a series of toasts prepared by the arrangements committee, after which the various diners offered volunteer toasts of their own. As the most distinguished member of the regiment, Polk was recognized for the first volunteer toast, and he made it a ringing call to arms:

The present crisis of affairs: The issue is joined between the power of executive patronage and the rights of the people. May the constitution survive the shock in its original republican simplicity & purity and may the triumph, of the people in elevating to the Chief Magistracy of the Union the man of their choice, be as signal in 1829, as it was glorious in 1801, on the ascension of that venerable patriot Thomas Jefferson to the Presidential chair.

After drinking to an interminable number of similar sentiments, the company spent the evening, naturally enough, "in the utmost hilarity and harmony."[14]

The summer and autumn passed all too quickly. Soon it was

---

13 *Reg. Deb.*:19:2, pp. 991-992.   14 Nashville *Banner*, 17 Oct. 1826.

November and time to return to Washington for the second or short session of Congress. Congress always met on the first Monday of December; but the first session of each Congress, beginning in odd-numbered years, lasted into late spring or early summer, while the second session, beginning in even-numbered years, had to end by March 4.

Having complained to General Jackson about her husband's long absence the previous winter, Sarah Polk now announced her determination to accompany him to the capital. To escape the aches and perils of a stagecoach journey over the rocky roads of eastern Tennessee and western Virginia, they went in their own carriage, taking two of the slaves, a maid and a manservant. At Nashville they were joined by that mercurial dandy, General Sam Houston, and at Knoxville Senator White completed the party. The little company traveled at a leisurely pace, spending the nights at taverns or farmhouses along the way. On reaching Washington, James and Sarah put up for a few days at Williamson's Hotel, while they looked for a mess. With his wife along James could not rejoin the bachelor Tennesseans, but quarters were finally found with a motley assortment of members from eight states in a house on Pennsylvania Avenue.

By now the Polks were resigned to childlessness, and Sarah, barred from the career almost universally followed by the women of her day, had to make a life for herself. She tried resuming her piano lessons, but before long the capital's whirl of parties, dinners, and balls forced her to abandon music. Responding eagerly to Washington's fervid preoccupation with politics, she became an expert on the subjects being debated in Congress and on the shifting lines of partisan allegiance. When James was to address the House, Sarah was sure to be in the ladies' gallery. But she was too much the nineteenth century woman to bring politics into the drawing room, preferring instead to impress her husband's friends with a display of the more conventional feminine graces. Though she delighted in her active social life, Sarah was not altogether frivolous. On most Sundays she might be seen, with Mr. Polk in tow, on her way to the First Presbyterian Church on Four-and-a-Half Street.[15]

The Polks were hardly settled in their new quarters when word arrived from home that Lunsford M. Bramlett would oppose Polk at the coming August election. The congressman's friends were plainly

15 Nelson, *Sarah Polk*, 28-32, 44, 51, 161; *Cong. Directory*:19:2, p. 41.

worried by Bramlett's industrious electioneering. The challenger was reported to have spent the entire month of January at the Maury circuit court and to have won favor with the citizens of Lincoln County by lending them two colts to run in a race at Fayetteville. Worse still, Bramlett seemed likely to get the Erwin faction's blessing in Bedford County, which, combined with his own strength in Giles, would make him a dangerous competitor. One of Polk's Bedford supporters was ready to concede the county and advised the congressman to look well to his course in the House. "When Hayne's Bankrupt bill comes before your body . . .," he wrote "go against it might and main. Make a speech, a thundering speech against it. I do not know what your sentiments are on this subject but I think I know what your interest is, and that is something which in all doings we are not to forget entirely."[16]

Polk, however, radiated confidence. Reaching home soon after Congress adjourned on March 4, he informed his friends that he felt no danger. "I shall enter the contest as usual," he announced, "and will be found at my post."[17] On the stump once more, he assailed President Adams' assertion that "Liberty is power." This doctrine destroyed "all the great barriers of the Constitution," Polk warned, and would lead "not only to consolidation, but to despotism itself." Polk's own brand of democracy was a conjuring up of the plain republicanism of Old Mecklenburg. "Splendid national universities," he snorted; "light-houses of the skies; military and naval schools; expensive and unnecessary foreign missions; a profuse expenditure of the money; and 'all the pomp and pageantry, and show' of European etiquette, all mark the departure from that republican simplicity and purity in which the venerable Jefferson administered the Government."

How powerfully the stirring political events of his boyhood Mecklenburg influenced his political thinking was evident in his repeated insistence that this was a crisis like that of 1798-1800. With liberty itself threatened, he argued, there could be no neutrals: "Those who are not for the People, and for popular rights, are against them." But he had no doubt that "the great body of the People, the uncorrupted and the incorruptible source of all power," would rescue the

16 Jim R. White to Polk, 30 Dec. 1826, Polk Papers; *id.* to *id.*, 8 Feb. 1827, *ibid.*; James Walker to Polk, 16 Dec. 1826, 15 Jan. 1827, *ibid.*; C. W. Webber to Polk, 23 Jan. 1827, *ibid.*; Henry Robertson to Polk, 4 Feb. 1827, *ibid.*

17 Polk to Dr. Alfred Flournoy, 20 Mar. 1827, typed copy, Polk-Flournoy Letters, a special section of Polk Papers.

republic. "In the contest of 1798," he proclaimed, "we prevailed, and if we are true to ourselves in 1828, the same redeeming spirit will be found in the community."[18]

Only this doctrinaire quality, this passionate faith in the rightness of his cause and its ultimate victory could have sustained the incredible exertions of Polk's long political career. Again and again he was to sound this note. Somehow his religious impulses, his political principles, and his ambitions had all been fused together into a religion of democracy that he identified with the personal fortunes of James K. Polk. For the moment this faith made him confident of success against Bramlett.

Impartial observers were not so sure. Through the spring and summer the two candidates rode tirelessly through the district, seeking out voters wherever they assembled, especially at courts and militia musters. And though Polk rang all the changes on the "coalition" of Adams and Clay and the parallel "coalition" of Erwin and Bramlett, the outcome still seemed doubtful. Two weeks before the election Erwin's son reported to Henry Clay that "we think we will be able to beat Polk even." Bramlett would not be a great improvement, young Erwin admitted, but at least he would not "like Polk make it a business to ride thro his Dist[rict] relating falsehood unsparingly."[19]

The results, however, confirmed Polk's optimism. He received 6,350 votes to Bramlett's 4,846, carrying even Bedford by over 300 votes. Bramlett had a majority only in his home county of Giles. The returns made it clear, moreover, that Polk had not ridden to victory on Andrew Jackson's coat tails. Governor Carroll had served out the three terms allowed him by the state constitution, and at this same election the anti-Jackson men were backing Newton Cannon for governor against Sam Houston. While Polk carried Maury by 1,472 votes and Bedford by 360, Cannon defeated Houston in these counties by majorities of 599 and 1,890. Houston, however, had a majority in the state as a whole.[20]

VI

During the summer of strenuous campaigning, Congressman

18 Polk, *Circular, 1827.*

19 James Erwin to Henry Clay, 17 July 1827, Henry Clay Papers (THS; herein cited as Tenn. Clay Papers).

20 Franklin *Western Balance,* 10 Aug. 1827; Nashville *Banner,* 11 Aug. 1827.

Polk had still another worry than the outcome of the election. Sam Polk's health had gone from bad to worse. His trouble seemed to be as much mental as physical, and his friends thought that "his consent only is [want]ing to his recovery."[21] By the time James and Sarah got home from Washington, Sam's condition had become so alarming that he finally "embraced religion to the great joy of the whole family."[22] His mind began to wander, and he had to be dosed with laudanum. By autumn the family had given up all hope of recovery, and the end came in November, just as James was preparing to return to Washington. The handsome vault erected over Sam's remains proclaimed with singular aptness the central motif in the life of this typical figure of the Old West. "Men of enterprise," ran the inscription, "here Moulder the Mortal Remains of a kindred Spirit."[23]

Sam Polk's death imposed on James, as the oldest son and coexecutor with James Walker, heavy responsibilities for the involved estate and the minor children. His task was not made any easier by his relatives' proneness to quarrel over wills. Already he was engaged in a vexatious litigation with his brother-in-law Anderson Childress, by whose careless administration Joel Childress's estate had been wasted. Besides, when Ezekiel Polk died in 1824, a dispute had arisen between his heirs and Sam Polk over amounts of money alleged to be owed to each by the other. As Sam's executor, James now inherited this controversy. The courts eventually decided that Sam's estate owed Ezekiel's $1,770.38, while Ezekiel's owed Sam's $1,740.44¼, the petty award of $29.93¾ being far less than the legal and court costs.[24]

Sam left a large estate, including over fifty slaves and thousands of acres of land, and it, too, caused a dispute among these contentious and property-conscious Polks. He was hardly cold in his grave before the married daughters and their husbands tried to break his will, complaining that the younger children had received an unfair share. This quarrel developed just as James was starting for Washington, but before he left he promised his younger brothers and

[21] Leonidas Polk to Col. William Polk, 23 Oct. 1827, Leonidas Polk Papers (SHC).
[22] Lucius J. Polk to Col. William Polk, 8 May 1827, Polk-Brown-Ewell Papers (SHC).
[23] Samuel Polk vault, Greenwood Cemetery, Columbia.
[24] Various legal documents dated 23, 28, 29 Aug., 3 Sept., n.d. [Aug.] 1828, Polk Papers; Maury County, Chancery Court Minutes, 1823-1829, pp. 84-93 (wherever Tennessee county records are cited herein, the typescript copies in the State Library at Nashville have been used).

sisters that he would protect their rights. Consequently the older children's ire was turned on him. Lydia's husband, Doctor Caldwell, threatened to spend a considerable part of what he was worth to get a fair portion for his wife. If James interfered, he added, he would spend the rest of it to beat him at the next election. The matter was finally compromised and friendly relations were restored, but settling the complicated affairs of the estate continued to take much of James's time when he was at home.[25]

James now had to stand as a father to the younger children, and some of them were problems. Fifteen-year-old Ophelia as yet gave no cause for special concern, while Marshall had just married an attractive North Carolina girl and brought her home to Tennessee. But among the other brothers—Franklin, John, Samuel (known to the family by his middle name, Washington), and William—only one ever married, and all of them were to cause their mother and elder brother great anxiety. Frank was already such an alcoholic that Sam's will had ordered his bequest held in trust until the executors decided he could manage it wisely.

This whole situation was extremely hard on Jane Polk, who was distraught with grief over Sam's passing, despite the consolation of seeing him received into the church before it was too late. "I never saw any person take trouble to heart as she does," reported Maria Walker.[26] But she bore her tribulations courageously. One of her letters to James and Sarah tells much about this pioneer woman, who raised ten children and outlived both her husband and her distinguished son:

My Dear Children

I received your letter of the 12 of December, one from Sarah a few days before. Your kind and friendly advise [about the will controversy] will be attended to on my part as nothing would be so distressing to me as family disturbance. I suppose you have heard before this time how your brothers and brotherinlaws have fixed the business. Whether it is best or not, I do believe they acted from the purest motives to preserve peace and save your father's name from being canceled in court, as you know many things would have been said about his mind not being rite and every little action exposed that he done when under the influence of the lodnam. The very thought of such a thing appea[re]d as it would have been more than I could a borne up under. I long to hear what you think about the matter.

25 Will of Sam Polk, 13 Dec. 1826, copy, Polk Papers; James Walker to Polk, 21 Nov., 7 Dec. 1827, *ibid.*; Franklin E. Polk to J. K. Polk, 12 Dec. 1827, *ibid.*; Polk to Walker, 11 Dec. 1827, *ibid.*
26 Maria Walker to Sarah Polk, 17 Feb. 1828, Polk Papers.

Your brother Marshall and sister Laura is living with me. I think Laura is a very fine agreeable girl. She is kind and good to me. She is none of your high dashers, she is mild and modest, converses sencibly and loves to go to Church. . . . Your brother Jack . . . is now preparing for farming. I do hope he will do well, he seems so intent upon it. He has just come home this evening. It does me good to see him so steady. Franklin is now gone to the western district to view his lands and rent some of it out. I feel great uneasiness about him as he has had a spell of drinking since you went away which had like to a killed him. He was worse than ever he was before. He was very much alarmed about himself. He promised me he would not drink any while gone. William and Washington are going to school.

We live much retired. Just visit in the family circle. Our neighbours have been kind and attentive to us but still my dear children there is such a vacancy which no one can supply. But when we consider the hand that done it we must say surely it is the lord, let him do whatsoever he will. Holy Just and true art thou O god. It is thou that has a rite to every Creature thou hast made. It is the Lord that can raise our comforts high or sink them in the grave as he pleases. Be still then my soul. Let not a murmering sigh arise. I trust this close visitation of providence will not soon be forgotten. May it please the almity out of his mere goodness to sanctify it to myself and all my dear children. It is a loud call to prepare for death. . . .

It is now ten oclock at night. My three youngest children are now sleeping [in] the room by my side. Laura and Ophelia join with me in sending their love to you & Sarah. Ophelia says she will write to Sarah soon. She has made several attempts but always failed as usual. Nothing more at present but remains your affectionate

Mother until death
JANE POLK[27]

VII

On their trip through Kentucky and up the Ohio River to Washington in the fall of 1827, James and Sarah had the company of two new members of Congress, John Bell, who had just defeated Felix Grundy in the Nashville district, and Robert Desha. This session the Polks were able to get into a congenial and distinguished mess. Senator White had been living in the Pennsylvania Avenue boarding house of the amiable widow Mrs. Ann Peyton, and here the Polks now joined him. This mess had already become the headquarters of the Calhoun coterie that had been leading the Jackson forces in Congress. The vice president himself was one of the company, as were two of his principal lieutenants, Senators Littleton W. Taze-

---

27 Jane Polk to J. K. and Sarah Polk, 5 Jan. 1828, Polk Papers. A minimum of capitalization, punctuation, and paragraphing has been supplied; otherwise the copy is exact.

well of Virginia and Levi Woodbury of New Hampshire. In addition the mess included Senators Mahlon Dickerson of New Jersey and Powhatan Ellis of Mississippi; Congressman William Haile of Mississippi; Gulian C. Verplanck, the scholarly representative of the New York City mercantile interests; another New Yorker, the ebullient Rudolph Bunner; and two other Tennesseans, Pryor Lea, Senator White's protégé from the Knoxville district, and John Bell. Several of the members had brought their wives, so Sarah was at no loss for company.[28]

The congressional elections had testified to the nationwide popularity of Andrew Jackson, and when the twentieth Congress convened, the Adams administration found its supporters outnumbered in both houses. The Jacksonians promptly elected Andrew Stevenson of Virginia to the speakership of the House of Representatives, and the Jackson men were duly rewarded with choice committee assignments. Here Polk's connections with the leaders stood him in good stead. In the previous Congress he had been denied any committee assignment until the second session, when he was placed on the insignificant Committee on Public Expenditures. But now he was appointed to the Foreign Affairs Committee, which was second in importance only to the Ways and Means Committee and second in prestige to none. Actually the Foreign Affairs Committee considered little important business during the twentieth Congress, spending most of its time tediously examining claims against the government.[29]

The one major foreign affairs issue that arose during this period was the Oregon question, which Polk would settle conclusively twenty years later. Some of the Jacksonians wanted to make political capital out of the Adams administration's decision to extend indefinitely the agreement with Great Britain for joint occupation of this little-known territory in the Pacific Northwest. Demanding more aggressive support of American claims to the disputed country, they introduced a bill to erect fortifications, sell lands, and establish a territorial government in the area.

Polk was unwilling to take partisan advantage of this situation and advocated a cautious policy. He agreed that the United States had the best title to the entire territory, but he pointed out that the Oregon bill proposed clear violations of the recent solemn agreement

28 Polk to Dr. Alfred Flournoy, 11 Oct. 1827, Polk-Flournoy Letters; *Cong. Directory*:20:1, p. 48.
29 Edward Everett, Diary (MHS), 10 Dec. 1827; *House Journal*:19:2, p. 23; *ibid.*:20:1, p. 25.

with the British. He thought it would be well to extend the jurisdiction of the Michigan territorial courts over American citizens in the area and to send out exploring parties, but constructing forts and selling lands would only invite hostilities. These arguments were so persuasive that the bill was withdrawn and modified in line with Polk's suggestions. But it came to a vote still providing for forts, and Polk voted with the majority against it.[30]

The hottest battles in the twentieth Congress raged around the tariff and internal improvement issues, and here Polk took the position of a doctrinaire Jeffersonian defender of state rights and strict construction. The tariff he opposed in every shape. When the woolens manufacturers had tried to get increased protection from the previous Congress, Polk had voted for every weakening amendment and delaying motion and had stood with the minority when the bill passed the House, only to be killed in the evenly divided Senate by Vice President Calhoun's casting vote. To be sure, Polk had voted for an amendment raising the duty on foreign distilled spirits, which may have represented either a wavering in favor of western whisky makers, or a desire to make the bill less palatable to its eastern sponsors.[31]

The tariff men were now back with a powerful lobby, pushing a general upward revision of import duties. Running into a tangled parliamentary situation, this movement eventually produced the famous "Tariff of Abominations." The committee that drew the original bill was dominated by northern and western Jacksonians, men interested in greater protection for farm products, especially raw wool. Accordingly they gave much larger increases to wool and other raw materials than to woolens and other manufactured goods. The tariff men, mostly New Englanders and Adams supporters, objected of course, while the antitariff men, mostly from the South, tried to push the raw material duties still higher, in order to make the whole measure so unacceptable to New England that the representatives of manufacturing districts would join the southerners to defeat it.

As a consistent antitariff man, Polk had little sympathy for this questionable strategy. On one occasion he did vote to retain a high duty on the molasses that New England imported for rum making, when a South Carolina member explained that "keeping it in the

[30] *Reg. Deb.*:20:2, pp. 129-132, 143-144; *House Journal*:20:2, pp. 140-141.
[31] *House Journal*:19:2, pp. 249, 254, 258, 261, 263, 269-272.

bill would get votes against the final passage of the bill." But on almost every other occasion Polk opposed higher duties, whether on manufactured goods or on farm products and raw materials. This time he voted against all efforts to raise the duty on distilled spirits, as well as being the only Tennessean to oppose greater protection for indigo, another western product.[32] In the end the unhappy New Englanders gave the bill enough votes to pass, though one of them bitterly moved to amend its title by adding, "and to transfer the capital and industry of the New England States to the other States in the Union."[33]

Polk had announced his opposition to a protective tariff when he first ran for Congress, and he elaborated his arguments against it in a circular to his constituents in 1829. Pointing out that his district was an agricultural one, he declared that the tariff unfairly protected the manufacturers of one section at the expense of the agriculturists of another. "It must ever be unjust," he said, "to tax the labor of one class of society to support and fatten another." Polk admitted that the tariff had fallen most heavily on the planters of the South, while Tennesseans were more fortunately situated, "our lands being fresh and fertile, theirs sterile and far exhausted by long cultivation; ours being adapted to the culture of some articles, other than cotton, which theirs will not produce." Yet, he argued, it is "clearly our interest not to support any tariff or system of duties, with a view either to prohibition or protection, or for any other than the legitimate purpose of raising a revenue to pay the debt and expenses of this government." Polk did concede, though, that a revenue tariff might be regulated so as to enable the country to produce the "very few articles absolutely necessary" for national defense.[34]

On the issue of internal improvements, Polk was painfully embarrassed by his constituents' enthusiasm for the proposed national road from Buffalo to New Orleans by way of Washington. This was the project he had endorsed in the legislature, and its popularity had been responsible for his equivocal position on the whole question of internal improvements in his first campaign for Congress. Three routes had been suggested: one leading through the principal towns

---

[32] *Reg. Deb.*:20:1, p. 2011; *House Journal*:20:1, pp. 487-609, 761-763; John A. Garraty, *Silas Wright* (New York, 1949), 52-67.

[33] *House Journal*:20:1, p. 609.

[34] *Circular Letter of James K. Polk to His Constituents: February 28th, 1829*, pamphlet (Washington, 1829).

on the Atlantic and Gulf coasts, one taking a middle course through the upcountry just east of the mountains, and a third following the great valleys of Virginia and East Tennessee into northern Alabama. The army engineers had just reached Tennessee on their survey of the third route when Polk left home for his first session in Congress.

There was some disagreement in the Tennessee delegation over the road, since the Middle Tennesseans wanted it brought across the Cumberland plateau and routed through their section on to New Orleans. One of Polk's first acts in Washington was to join the other Middle Tennessee congressmen in requesting the secretary of war to have this route inspected also. Despite the secretary's promise to issue the necessary instructions, the engineers returned to Washington in March 1827 without having made the additional survey; and Congress turned a deaf ear to Polk and his Middle Tennessee allies when they tried to get this failure investigated.[35]

Meanwhile the Middle Tennesseans had patched up their quarrel with East Tennessee. Landlocked East Tennessee was anxious for two other improvement projects, one a canal connecting the Tennessee River with the Alabama rivers that emptied into the Gulf of Mexico, and the other a canal around Muscle Shoals on the Tennessee in northern Alabama, which would make it possible for large vessels to ascend the river as far as Knoxville. The Middle Tennesseans backed these projects in return for East Tennessee support of the Middle Tennessee road route. The same day that Polk voted for the Muscle Shoals bill, which gave Alabama 400,000 acres of public land to finance the project, he also supported a similar land grant to Ohio for canal purposes. This method, he argued, steered clear of the constitutional objection, since Congress had an undoubted power to dispose of the public lands.[36]

The episode, however, brought home the horse-trading principle underlying internal improvement legislation; a man who wanted a single project found himself drawn into support of the whole system. From this time on Polk rapidly lost his enthusiasm for the New Orleans road in particular and for internal improvements in general. Even if the policy had not violated his Republican orthodoxy, the

---

35 Nashville *Whig*, 28 Nov., 5 Dec. 1825; Nashville *Banner*, 13 Jan. 1826; Nashville *Republican*, 14 Jan. 1826; Robert Allen to [R. L. Caruthers], 21 Dec. 1825, Robert L. Caruthers Papers (SHC); *Reg. Deb.*:19:1, pp. 1860-1861.

36 James Campbell to David Campbell, 9 Jan. 1825 [1826], David Campbell Papers (DU); *House Journal*:19:2, pp. 786-790.

Adams administration's enthusiasm for it would have made a good Jacksonian suspicious. The Columbia newspaper, which was edited by one of Polk's friends, had denounced "these long roads extending through an half dozen states" as "intended to bribe those States out of State Rights," and censured the Tennessee congressmen for "taking the bait." If the road were to be built somewhere anyhow, said the editor, it would be all right to ask that Middle Tennessee be considered. But, he went on, Polk and his colleagues should have declared first that the project was both unconstitutional and inexpedient.[37]

Polk was already beginning to qualify his position. "He did not wish to be understood, in the remarks he had made," he told the House, "as committing himself on the broad question of power in the General Government to make Internal Improvements." If a proper occasion arose, he "might give his views to the House upon that subject." For the present he would only say that "he was not prepared to go to the length that some gentlemen had done. . . . The road, as we are informed, was to be made, at all events, *in some direction*; and, if so, we wished our section of country examined and surveyed as well as others."[38]

In the campaign of 1827 Polk defended his votes for the projects mentioned on the ground that the states involved had approved them. But as to the general policy of internal improvements, he confessed grave doubts. Tennessee projects might be all right, he said, but when they were completed, "It will be a question of serious consideration whether the means of the Government (if all Constitutional difficulties are removed), are, at this time, adequate to the undertaking, without imposing new burthens on the community, by additional taxation, or retarding the payment of the National Debt —neither of which ought, as I conceive, on any account short of absolute necessity, to be sanctioned." Indeed projects in which other states were interested got short shrift from Congressman Polk. With the exceptions already noted, he opposed all the scores of other improvement measures that appeared in Congress, voting even against repair or extension of Thomas Jefferson's National Road.[39]

[37] *Columbian,* quoted in Jackson *Gazette,* 11 Feb. 1826; Nashville *Whig,* 11 Feb. 1826.

[38] *Reg. Deb.*:19:1, p. 1861.

[39] Polk, *Circular, 1827*; *House Journal*:19:1, pp. 575, 599; *ibid.*:19:2, pp. 314-315, 318, 331, 335, 349-351; *ibid.*:20:1, pp. 388-391, 393-395; *ibid.*:20:2, pp. 182-183, 301-303, 308-309, 368-370, 377-379.

On no other question did Polk deviate one jot from the gospel of simplicity, economy, and localism. He took Georgia's side in its dispute with the Adams administration over the Indian question. He was one of the most zealous critics of unessential expenditures to be found in Congress. He was particularly averse to the congressional habit of voting public documents to members, and his opposition extended to a wide variety of other propositions, ranging from relief for victims of a disastrous fire in Alexandria to establishment of a naval academy.[40]

Polk's penchant for economy in granting pensions to Revolutionary soldiers gave his enemies a weapon they would later use against him. The Revolutionary veteran was a venerated figure in early nineteenth century America, and Polk was by no means opposed to the pension principle itself. In fact he favored extending the system to include all who had fought at least six months, in whatever capacity. But he could see no reason for governmental assistance to men who did not need it. It was ridiculous, he argued, to pension his kinsman, Colonel William Polk, one of the wealthiest men in North Carolina; and he voted against the pension bill because it did not contain such a limitation.[41]

The road mania had stretched Polk's Jeffersonian scruples dangerously. For a time he wavered, but in the end he would come out a firmer champion than ever of the nostalgic America that looked back longingly to countless Old Mecklenburgs.

VIII

Polk's chief project during his first four years in Congress was trying to get the United States to cede Tennessee the unappropriated Western District lands as an endowment for education. The dispute with North Carolina over the university warrants had prevented the eighteenth Congress from acting favorably on the memorial Polk had drafted for the Tennessee legislature in 1823. By the time Polk entered the House, in 1825, however, this controversy had been compromised, and there was reason to hope that the nineteenth Congress would grant Tennessee's request.

Polk promptly secured the support of the North Carolina mem-

---

40 *House Journal*:19:2, pp. 273-274, 279-282, 292-294; *Reg. Deb.*:19:2, pp. 358-359, 773; *ibid.*:20:1, pp. 2729-2730.

41 Columbia *Western Mercury*, extra, 17 June 1833; *House Journal*:19:1, pp. 500, 504; *ibid.*:19:2, pp. 152, 163; *ibid.*:20:1, pp. 739-741; *ibid.*:20:2, pp. 330-332, 336-338; *Reg. Deb.*:20:2, pp. 378-379.

bers and got another Tennessee memorial on the subject referred to a friendly special committee of which he was chairman. Within a few weeks he was ready with an elaborate report supporting the Tennessee claims and a bill ceding the lands. But the administration majority never permitted the subject to come up for consideration. At the second session Polk finally got his bill to the floor, but not until so late in the session that, when strong opposition developed, it had to be tabled for lack of time.[42]

So the whole process—reference to a special committee, preparation of a report, and introduction of a bill—had to be repeated in the twentieth Congress. But this time, with a Jacksonian majority, the prospects were brighter. Polk again headed the committee, which was composed of another Tennessean, a North Carolinian, and an Alabaman, all favoring Tennessee's claims, and three New Englanders opposed. For a time it seemed that Polk would have as much trouble with his fellow Tennessean as with the New Englanders. Colonel Davy Crockett had come to Congress boasting that he could "wade the Mississippi, carry a steam-boat on his back, and whip his weight in wild cats," by way of preface to declaring that he was not afraid to address the House, since he could "whip any man in it." Crockett had been elected on the strength of his reputation as champion of the Western District's poor squatters. He was, of course, extremely interested in the land bill and was an inevitable choice for Polk's committee.[43]

Through long and bitter experience West Tennessee had learned not to rely on the state legislature to protect its interests in land matters, and its distrust had been excited anew by a campaign John Bell was waging to have a large part of the unappropriated lands set apart as an endowment for Nashville's Cumberland College. This was the same institution that had shared in the University of North Carolina warrants, by which many of the Western District occupants had lost their homes.

Crockett had run for Congress as the "poor man's friend," declaring that colleges would be of no help to the poor people of the Western District. If, he said, "we can only get a common country, or as College Graduates sometimes deridingly call it, a B-a school,

---

[42] W. P. Mangum to Col. William Polk, 23 Jan. 1826, William Polk Papers (NCDAH); *Reg. Deb.*:19:1, pp. 1075-1077; *House Committee Reports*:19:1, No. 68; *House Journal*:19:2, p. 352; Polk, *Circular, 1827.*

[43] Nashville *Republican*, 18 Mar. 1828; *House Journal*:20:1, p. 33; Jackson *Gazette*, 31 Dec. 1825.

convenient enough to send our Big Boys in the winter and our little ones all the year, we think ourselves fortunate, especially if we can raise enough Coon-Skins and one little thing or other to pay up the teacher at the end of every quarter."[44] On his way to Washington, Crockett had met Andrew Erwin's son in Nashville, and the latter reported to Henry Clay that the new representative was "not only illiterate but he is rough & uncouth, talks much & badly, and is by far, more in his proper place, when hunting a Bear in a cane Brake, than he will be in the Capital." However, young Erwin added, Crockett was fiercely independent, as he proved by voting against Jackson for the Senate, and would thus be a likely convert for the administration party.[45]

Crockett entered the House, therefore, full of suspicions about what the Tennessee legislature would do with the Western District lands, if it got its hands on them. He feared particularly that the proceeds would be used for colleges, and even more that the speculator group would block any provision enabling the squatters to get title to the lands they occupied. When Polk's committee met, Crockett insisted that Congress require the Tennessee legislature to devote all the proceeds to the benefit of the Western District. In dealing with the doughty colonel, Polk was greatly aided by the fact that the two had previously stood together against the speculators and university warrants in the legislature, but he still needed all the tact he could muster. Finally he convinced Crockett that no bill could pass unless the entire Tennessee delegation united on a general relinquishment to the state. He then helped Crockett persuade the committee to reject the Cumberland College petition and to insert a requirement that the land proceeds be used only for common schools.[46]

With Crockett pacified, Polk forced his bill through the committee over the New Englanders' objections and reported it to the House on December 24. But the long tariff debate intervened, and not until April 24 was the Tennessee land question first discussed.[47]

Polk's speech was like a lawyer's brief in its detailed, methodical presentation of the case for his state. Describing the tangled history of the Tennessee land question, Polk based his argument mainly on

[44] Jackson *Gazette*, 5 May 1827, 21 June, 27 Dec. 1828; *House Documents*:19:1, No. 160.

[45] James Erwin to Clay, 30 Sept. 1827, Tenn. Clay Papers.

[46] Jackson *Gazette*, 12, 16 Feb., 2 Apr. 1828; Nashville *Banner*, 16 Feb. 1828.

[47] *House Journal*:20:1, pp. 87, 160, 170, 627; *House Reports*:20:1, No. 32.

the fact that Congress had intended to have Tennessee receive as school lands 640 acres out of each six-mile square in the older two thirds of the state, but that the multiplicity of North Carolina warrants had prevented the state from realizing more than 22,000 of the expected 444,000 acres. Hence the deficiency should be made up from the Western District lands. Contending that even here the good lands had all been appropriated, he argued that the federal government would never be able to realize enough on the remainder to cover the cost of setting up land offices. But Tennessee, with land offices already established, could dispose of the unsold scraps of land to the benefit of her school fund.[48]

When the debate was resumed five days later, John Locke of Massachusetts, who had already given Polk trouble in committee, revealed the source of the opposition that had bottled up the Tennessee land bill in the previous Congress. Eastern members, apprehensive of the rising political power of the West, were growing hostile to the generous grants of public lands that the new states were receiving for education and internal improvements. Still distrustful of the information Congress had about the Tennessee lands, Locke charged that they were more extensive and valuable than had been reported.

Davy Crockett now came loyally to the defense of Polk's bill. As a resident of the Western District, he supported Polk's claim that the lands were mostly worthless. But he advocated the bill on another ground, that it would enable the poor occupants to get title to their farms. Not only would the bill "make glad the hearts of the poor" by securing their land, but it would also educate the poor man's child. Apologizing for his "plain and unvarnished" manner, Crockett admitted that he had never set foot in a school and lacked the advantages of education. But, he said, "I thank heaven I know their worth, from having experienced the want of them, and on that account, I am the more anxious to extend them to those who will come after me."[49]

The next day it became clear that the New Englanders had succeeded in raising doubts about the validity of Polk's case. Many of Tennessee's original supporters were taken aback when it developed that some three or four million acres, about half the Western District, were involved. Critics also pointed out that Tennessee had

---

[48] *Reg. Deb.*:20:1, pp. 2496-2500.
[49] *ibid.*, 2514-2549.

previously received full title to the valuable Cherokee lands in the eastern part of the state. Furthermore it was the state's own fault that only 22,000 acres of school lands had been reserved. Speculators had controlled the legislature, and the interest of schools had been sacrificed to the interests of warrant holders.

As the opposition pressed home these points, the debate took on a tone of bitterness indicative of the more than local application of the question. The House soon tired of the whole business and ordered the speech making ended and a vote taken. Realizing that the tide had turned against him, Polk reluctantly accepted an amendment limiting the cession to just enough acreage to make up the deficiency in school lands. But even this did not save the bill. Jackson men and Adams men alike supported a motion to table, which carried by a vote of 113 to 63. Crockett immediately revealed his real object by introducing a resolution for a direct federal donation of 160 acres to each actual settler.[50]

The vote was hardly a clear expression of congressional opinion on the Tennessee land bill, for the opposition had simply talked it to death. At the short second session (1828-1829), Polk hoped to pass the bill by making it a party measure and securing the support of the Jacksonian majority. But Crockett's resolution had presaged a dangerous split in the Tennessee delegation, made even more certain when the leading anti-Crockett newspaper in the Western District endorsed his suggestion of a direct donation to occupants and proposed in addition that the proceeds from the remaining lands be spent for education and internal improvements in the Western District only. Crockett came back to Washington announcing that, while his colleagues might obey the legislature, he would obey his constituents.[51]

When Polk got his bill of the previous session taken from the table early in January 1829, Crockett promptly offered an amendment providing a direct federal donation of 160 acres to each occupant. He had supported Polk's bill at the previous session, he said, in the hope that when it failed, his colleagues would aid his measure. But the other Tennesseans refused to accept his amendment, whereupon he declared hotly that he would prefer to see the whole bill killed.

---

[50] *ibid.*, pp. 2549-2550; *House Journal*:20:1, pp. 653, 659-660, 721; *House Executive Documents*:20:1, Nos. 76, 232; *Speech of Mr. Polk, of Tennessee, Delivered in Committee of the Whole, April 30th, 1828* . . . , pamphlet (Washington, 1828).

[51] Jackson *Gazette*, 21 June 1828, 3 Jan. 1829.

Polk then agreed to an amendment requiring the Tennessee legislature to give occupants priority of entry for 160 acres; but this did
not satisfy Crockett, who charged that the legislature would force
his constituents to pay high prices for their lands and then spend
the proceeds for things that were of no benefit to the Western District. The poor people in his district, he went on, had already been
victimized by the university warrants, and "if their little all is to be
wrested from them, for the purposes of State speculation; if a
swindling machine is to be set up to strip them of what little the
surveyors, and the colleges, and the warrant holders, have left them,
it shall never be said that I sat by in silence, and refused, however
humbly, to advocate their cause."

The Adams-Clay men greeted this split in the Tennessee delegation with delight and did everything they could to encourage the
rebellious Colonel Crockett, rallying to his amendment and doctoring
his speeches for publication. Reports circulated that Crockett was
promising to support any measure of any member who would support his amendment, and he did vote with the administration forces
against the Jackson party's proposal for viva-voce election of House
officers. The land bill, of course, was doomed by Crockett's apostasy.
After three days of rancorous debate, a motion to table carried, 103
to 63.[52]

Enraged, the other Tennessee members began a campaign against
Crockett in the newspapers at home. When Crockett discovered that
Pryor Lea had written one of the articles attacking him, he denounced Lea in the Washington press as "a poltroon and puppy,"
but this did not discourage Polk from bringing the Columbia paper
into the hue and cry against Crockett, or from furnishing ammunition to Crockett's opponent in the congressional election of 1829.
The net effect of all this agitation was to transfer Crockett to the
anti-Jackson ranks without displacing him from Congress. The people of the Western District were delighted with their homespun
representative and reelected him by a large majority.[53]

Polk made his final effort for the Tennessee land bill at the first
session of the twenty-first Congress (1829-1830). This time he had

[52] *Reg. Deb.*:20:2, p. 163; *ibid.*, 161-168; Polk to P. M. Miller, 16 Jan. 1829, copy,
Polk Papers; Polk to Pryor Lea, 17 Feb. 1829, copy, *ibid.*; H. L. White to Pryor
Lea, 17 Feb. 1829, *ibid.*
[53] Nashville *Republican*, 19 Feb., 3 Mar., 7 Apr. 1829; Jackson *Gazette*, 21, 28
Mar. 1829; Polk to A. R. Alexander, 1 May 1829, Polk Papers; "Col. Crockett & his
course in Congress," 5-p. MS in Polk's hand, *ibid.*, Vol. LXXX, Nos. 8484-8504.

the state's memorial referred to the regular Committee on Public Lands, but he could not prevent Crockett from securing the appointment of a special committee under his chairmanship to consider the whole question. A week later, despite all Polk could do, his wily antagonist got the Tennessee memorial transferred from the Public Lands Committee to his special committee, of which Polk was also a member.

Compromise was now unavoidable, and the committee's bill was a reasonable reconciliation of the various points of view. Tennessee was to receive enough land to make up the deficiency in school lands, none of it to be sold for less than twelve and one half cents an acre, and all the proceeds were to go to the common school fund. Occupants were to have preference of entry for 160 acres at twelve and one half cents with a year to pay. The committee voiced the opinion that Tennessee was entitled to all the vacant Western District lands, but it refrained from recommending a complete cession out of deference to eastern fears that this might be a precedent for a general relinquishment of the public lands to the western states.

Though most of the Tennessee congressmen gave their grudging support to this measure, it failed by a vote of 90 to 69. At the second session of this Congress, Polk and his allies opposed a motion to reconsider the compromise bill because they knew that Crockett had abandoned it. Anxious for passage of any measure by which his occupants could get title to their farms, Crockett had prepared a substitute bill allotting the land proceeds to the federal treasury. Such a proposition would have been so dangerously attractive to Congress that the other Tennesseans decided to keep the whole subject off the floor, and here the matter rested. Not until 1846 would the vexed question of the vacant Western District lands be settled finally.[54]

IX

Though the Tennessee land bill received more of Polk's time and attention than any other measure during his early years in Congress, it still was not his primary concern. Legislation played second fiddle to president making in the four sessions of Congress that met,

[54] *Reg. Deb.*:21:1, pp. 474, 480-481; *House Journal*:21:1, pp. 44, 227, 511, 600-601, 605; *ibid.*:21:2, p. 152; *House Reports*:21:1, No. 137; Nashville *Republican*, 23 Feb. 1830; *David Crockett's Circular*, pamphlet dated 28 Feb. 1831, pp. 6-7, 12-15; Albert Lincoln Bramlett, "North Carolina's Western Lands," Ph.D. dissertation, University of North Carolina (1928), 222-225.

squabbled, and adjourned during the presidency of John Quincy Adams; and no one was more devoted to the success of Andrew Jackson than the methodical young man from Columbia, Tennessee.

Probably because of his services to the Carroll party, Polk never got on well with Senator Eaton, who was Jackson's personal campaign manager at Washington. Consequently he was allowed only a minor role in the Jackson party at first, though he early impressed one observer as "the cleverest man in the delegation." Eaton did use him when he needed financial backing for the Jackson newspaper at Washington in the spring of 1826. The newly launched *United States Telegraph* was faltering under an inept editor. Eaton was anxious to transfer it to Duff Green, a hard-hitting Calhounite from Missouri, but financial problems stood in the way. The transfer was finally effected when Polk and others endorsed the notes that enabled Green to get control.[55]

Gradually, however, Polk gained the confidence of the Calhoun-Jackson men, and he quickly became a favorite with Senator White. After he moved into the same mess with White and the leading Calhounites in 1827, he became one of Jackson's chief defenders against the attacks that were making this presidential campaign unprecedented for scurrility. When the administration ransacked the War Department files for what President Adams called Jackson's "victories over the grammar and spelling-book," it was Polk and White who came to the general's defense.[56]

This line of attack hardly called for a defense before the voters who counted in 1828, but other assaults were less innocuous. Refutation of the slander that Jackson and his wife had lived in adultery before their marriage was left to the general's friends around Nashville, while Polk took up the cudgels against another attack almost as unscrupulous. This was the famous "Six Militia Men" case, which worried the Jackson managers more than any other charge leveled.

During the War of 1812 Jackson had approved a court martial verdict sentencing six deserters to be shot. The soldiers had left camp in defiance of their officers, maintaining erroneously that they

[55] Willie P. Mangum to Col. William Polk, 23 Jan. 1826, William Polk Papers; memorandum, 20 May 1826, Polk Papers; agreement between Duff Green and John S. Meehan, 5 June 1826, Duff Green Papers (in possession of Prof. Fletcher M. Green, Chapel Hill, N.C.); S. D. Ingham to Green, 5 June 1826, *ibid.*; Green to Meehan, 28 May 1833, *ibid.*; Wiltse, *Calhoun*, I, 349.

[56] Charles Francis Adams, ed., *Memoirs of John Quincy Adams, Comprising Portions of His Diary from 1795 to 1848* (12 vols., Philadelphia, 1874-1877), VII, 478-480, 489; White to Jackson, 22 Feb. 1828, Andrew Jackson Papers (LC).

were obligated for only three months' service, and Jackson's army would have melted away if their claim had been admitted. Digging up the case as the election year opened, the Adams forces began indicting Jackson as a military autocrat and murderer and flooded the country with the notorious "Coffin Handbill," a grisly memento of the executed soldiers. This was political dynamite, and the Jacksonians knew it.

Polk feverishly collected statements from high military officers and other witnesses and pried suppressed evidence out of the War Department, and all this went into an exhaustive report exonerating the general issued by the House Military Affairs Committee. But this cumbrous document was poorly calculated to overtake the flying slanders already loose in the country. We must "carry the War into Africa," Polk wrote to Jackson, and he promptly suited his actions to his words, filling the newspapers with communications and further evidence on the subject. Polk's concise account of the case for the Baltimore *Republican* was widely circulated and copied, catching many more eyes than the bulky committee report.[57]

The factor that contributed most to Polk's growing prominence in the Jackson ranks, however, was his friendship with Old Hickory. Jackson had been greatly impressed by Polk's victory over Andrew Erwin in 1825, and visiting Columbia shortly afterward, he had identified himself with the youthful congressman-elect by toasting the "heroic Mecklenburg revolutionists." Having no children of his own, the general took a warm fatherly interest not only in his nephews, but also in his younger political supporters. Sam Houston was Jackson's favorite at first, but in writing to him the general soon began to single out "Major Polk & Lady" for special greetings. When Houston left Congress in 1827 to run for governor, Polk replaced him as the general's confidant in the lower house. Polk dispatched long reports of congressional affairs to the Hermitage, while Jackson took pains to call on Polk's family when he passed through Columbia, sending the congressman news from home and expressing hearty approval of his actions in Washington.[58]

Jackson's managers worried continually lest he lose his patience

57 Polk to Jackson, 13 Apr. 1828, Jackson Papers; Jackson to Polk, 23 Mar., 3 May 1828, Polk Papers; *Reg. Deb.*:20:1, pp. 975-976, 1031-1038, 1048, 1252, 1486-1490; Adams, *Diary*, VII, 527.

58 Leonidas Polk to Lucius Polk, 18 Oct. 1825, Leonidas Polk Papers; Jackson to Sam Houston, 22 Nov. 1826, Jackson Papers; Jackson to Polk, 3 May 1826, Polk Papers.

and publish an indiscreet reply to his enemies. As early as 1826 Polk had warned the general against an anticipated attempt to elicit his opinions on internal improvements. "Without great care in the phraseology employed to convey our ideas," Polk cautioned, "you know the plainest sentiment in the English language may be perverted." Jackson might have taken offense at this presumptuous advice from a younger man; instead he replied warmly, saying he would welcome frequent letters.[59] By the end of the campaign he had the highest confidence in Polk's judgment. "The reasons contained," Jackson replied to one of Polk's letters of advice, "leaves no room to doubt the correctness of your conclusions"; and he filed Polk's letter away with the notation: "My friend Col. Polk's letter to be kept as a token of his real friendship."[60]

X

Polk spent a busy summer in Tennessee just before the election, for such anti-Jackson sentiment as existed in the state was concentrated in his district, where Andrew Erwin and Theoderick Bradford still wielded great influence. But Polk and his friends in Bedford County soon built up a formidable Jackson organization, which, among other things, inflicted corporal punishment on an Erwin lieutenant who had attacked Jackson in the newspapers.[61]

Besides campaigning, Polk had to nurse Sarah through a severe attack of measles in August, and he spent most of October riding through the Western District, seeing to the lands that his father had left. He was back home in time for the election, and as soon as Jackson's victory was certain, prepared to return to Washington.

Sister Ophelia, now a much sought-after belle of sixteen, went along with James and Sarah this year to spend the winter at the capital. In Nashville they were joined for a visit to the Hermitage by Governor Sam Houston, who was much impressed with Ophelia. "Miss Polk is not only a fine young lady—" reported the bachelor governor, "but has the *'Quills'* to the amount of many thousands— say $40,000." Fortunately for Ophelia, Houston's heart was already set on another rich young lady.[62]

59 Polk to Jackson, 4 Dec. 1826, Jackson Papers; Jackson to Polk, 4 Dec. 1826 [misdated], Polk Papers.

60 Polk to Jackson, 8 Sept. 1828, photostat (Sam Polk House); Jackson to Polk, 16 Sept. 1828, Polk Papers.

61 Archibald Yell to Polk, 20 Jan., 10 Feb., 2 Mar. 1828, Polk Papers; Nashville *Banner*, 3 May, 27 June 1828.

62 Amelia W. Williams and Eugene C. Barker, eds., *The Writings of Sam Houston,*

Reaching Washington, the exultant Jacksonians prepared for a gay winter. Sarah was still so wan from her illness, Senator Woodbury observed, that she "looks as if grown 45 years older and seems awkward and *distrait*." But Woodbury was a somewhat jaundiced witness, his family having just been barred from the jovial circle at Mrs. Peyton's because he had a clergyman in his party. As a matter of fact Sarah rapidly regained the vitality and good spirits that made her the favorite of the whole group and the special favorite of the courtly New York widower Gulian Verplanck. It was Verplanck who escorted Sarah and Ophelia to a reception at the President's House, where they gloated unkindly over the sour visage of John Quincy Adams.[63]

Meanwhile Polk was handling the arrangements for the president-elect's journey to Washington.[64] Congress marked time pending his arrival, while the growing crowd of politicians at the capital schemed and maneuvered for advantage under the incoming administration. By March 4 the city was jammed, and the whole multitude turned out for the most exciting inaugural ceremony in years.

As Andrew Jackson emerged from the Capitol rotunda, a great shout of acclaim rose from the packed square below. Polk and his fellow congressmen, crowding behind the spare, erect figure of the president-elect on to the east portico, were at no loss to interpret the frenzied cheering. The people's will had been vindicated, and from every quarter of the Union the people had gathered to celebrate their triumph. In this young nation, farmers and shoemakers, laborers and shopkeepers were sovereign.

No one in the vast throng rejoiced more heartily than the youthful politician from Tennessee, for Representative Polk was a product of this democratic awakening and already a veteran of its battles. If his expression, ordinarily so carefully controlled, betrayed jubilation on this momentous occasion, it also concealed some sobering thoughts. What kind of government was a people's government? What policies would a people's administration follow?

1813-1863 (8 vols., Austin, 1938-1943), ii, 10-11; Polk to Dr. W. R. Rucker, 4 Sept. 1828, Polk Papers; entry for Oct. 1828, under "Estate of Samuel Polk," in Partnership Book of A. V. Brown and J. K. Polk, *ibid.*

[63] Levi Woodbury to Mrs. Woodbury, n.d. (placed 3 Dec. 1828), Levi Woodbury Papers, First Series (LC); G. W. Olney to Woodbury, 6 Dec. 1828, *ibid.*; G. C. Verplanck to W. C. Bryant, 1 Jan. 1829, Bryant-Godwin Papers (NYPL).

[64] Polk to Jackson, 1, 4, 5 Dec. 1828, Jackson Papers; Eaton to Jackson, 8 Dec. [1828; misplaced 1820], *ibid.*

Polk never doubted that Jackson was an old-fashioned Jeffersonian like himself, or that he would strive to bring the government back to Republican economy and simplicity. The president's brief inaugural address referred reassuringly to the rights of the sovereign states, the danger of standing armies, the need for reforming the bureaucracy, and, most promisingly of all, the importance of extinguishing the national debt by "a strict and faithful economy."

But the situation, as Polk knew, was not quite so simple. Many of Jackson's supporters, especially in the Northwest, had been able to campaign for him wholeheartedly only because he had supported internal improvements during his short service in the Senate. More than a few Jacksonian congressmen, especially the New Yorkers and Pennsylvanians, came from districts that demanded protection for American manufacturers, and still others upheld the national bank. Thus Jackson's ambiguous references to protection for any products "essential to our national independence" and to the utility of internal improvements, "so far as they can be promoted by the constitutional acts of the Federal Government," were not wholly unexpected.[65] The president could not take a forthright position without antagonizing some part of his heterogeneous following. Shrewd and realistic, Polk must have foreseen the years of intraparty pulling and hauling that would be necessary to force various groups into line or out of the party on various issues, before it would be clear just what constituted loyal Jacksonianism.

The moment of victory brought a disillusioning lesson in the nature of democratic politics that Polk had somehow failed to learn before. Whatever Jackson's election promised ultimately for the country, its most immediate effect had been to fill Washington with swarms of professed Jacksonians loudly asserting their claims to preferment by the new administration. It was only too clear that many of these men cared less for policies and principles than for securing patronage, building up political organizations, and advancing the pretensions of this or that aspirant for the presidency.

By Inauguration Day the deep division within the party over who should succeed Jackson in the White House was already an open scandal, and events promised to take a direction that an ideological politician of the state rights, strict construction school could neither approve nor profit by. In the developing internal struggle for power,

[65] James D. Richardson, comp., *A Compilation of the Messages and Papers of the Presidents 1789-1902* (10 vols., Washington, 1905), II, 436-438.

the question of whether tariffs, banks, and federal roads should be voted up or down would be intimately tied to the question of whether John C. Calhoun or Martin Van Buren should hold the ascendancy. Shocked and discouraged, Polk began telling friends that he would probably abandon politics as soon as Jackson's term was up.[66]

[66] William Mecklenburg Polk, *Leonidas Polk: Bishop and General* (2 vols., New York, 1893), I, 93.

5

DEFINING DEMOCRATIC REPUBLICANISM

A BITTER STRUGGLE over the presidential succession had become inevitable as soon as the Jacksonian coalition was organized in the wake of the election of 1824. The Calhoun men had seemed to win the early rounds, especially with Duff Green's installation in the editorial chair of the *United States Telegraph*, and they furnished the leadership for the prolonged assault on Adams and Clay in the nineteenth and twentieth Congresses. Until two weeks before Jackson's inauguration the optimism of Calhoun's partisans had continued unabated. The announcement of the Cabinet list fell on them like a thunderbolt.

The first Cabinet position, the secretaryship of state, went to Van Buren himself. John H. Eaton, a Van Buren supporter, was given the War Department, and two of Eaton's friends, John Branch of North Carolina and John M. Berrien of Georgia, were appointed secretary of the navy and attorney general. Only two Calhoun men, Postmaster General John McLean and Secretary of the Treasury Samuel D. Ingham, were included at all, and the former was quickly kicked upstairs to the Supreme Court, to be replaced by another Van Buren adherent, William T. Barry of Kentucky.

Not only had the distinguished Calhoun leaders been passed over, but the men chosen, with the exception of Van Buren and possibly Berrien, were undeniably mediocre. Furthermore in the cases of Eaton, Ingham, and Branch, Jackson had violated his own dictum that members of Congress should not be appointed to office. Disappointment was the general reaction among the Jacksonians, but the loudest of the lamentations that reverberated through congressional boardinghouses rose from the Calhoun men, who were completely demoralized by the suddenness of the coup that seemed to set Van Buren on the road to the White House. How had this abrupt reversal been accomplished? Part of the answer lies in certain obscure maneuverings in Tennessee.

Only the Jackson campaign had saved the old Overton faction from eclipse in the president's home state. The Jackson party was in their hands, and to all appearances the state was unanimously for Jackson. But this apparent unanimity concealed the continuing vitality of the anti-Overton group led by Andrew Erwin, Governor Carroll, John Williams, and Newton Cannon. Governor Carroll's popularity with the voters was undiminished, he retained great influence with the legislature, and the state patronage he controlled for most of this period was a potent political weapon.

Time and again during the later 1820's this opposition group had caused trouble. In 1825 the Overton leaders had been compelled to accept the independent-minded Hugh Lawson White as Jackson's successor in the Senate, because he was the only candidate who could get enough opposition votes to defeat John Williams. Another scare was thrown into the Overton ranks the next year, when Carroll threatened to contest Eaton's reelection to the Senate. Though the Jackson question was finally brought to bear with enough force to save Eaton, he squeaked through by only nine votes. When Carroll's third term as governor expired in 1827, Sam Houston, the popular Overton-Jackson candidate to succeed him, could garner only 56 per cent of the vote against Newton Cannon. At the same election, John Bell, Carroll's choice for Congress from the Nashville district, had defeated Felix Grundy, the Overton-Jackson candidate, by more than a thousand votes; Davy Crockett had displaced an Overton congressman in the Western District; John Williams had outpolled an Overton-Jackson-White candidate for the state senate from Knoxville; and Thomas D. Arnold, a rancorous anti-Jackson man, had come within 300 votes of ousting Senator White's protégé, Pryor Lea, from Congress.[1]

Even Carroll and Crockett declared for Jackson's presidential candidacy in 1828, but by Inauguration Day the Tennessee situation again looked ominous. After one term out of office, Carroll was again eligible and anxious to run for governor. Sam Houston, however, had found the gubernatorial chair to his liking—so much so

[1] Henry S. Foote, *The Bench and Bar of the South and Southwest* (St. Louis, 1876), 136; Carroll to Clay, 25 Nov. 1825, Henry Clay Papers (LC; herein cited as Clay Papers); James Erwin to Clay, 12 Dec. 1825, *ibid.*; John P. Erwin to Clay, 12 Aug. 1827, *ibid.*; James Erwin to Clay, 17 July 1827, Henry Clay Papers (THS; herein cited as Tenn. Clay Papers); F. W. Armstrong to Jackson, 7 May 1826, Andrew Jackson Papers (LC); Eaton to W. J. Hamilton, 3 Sept. 1826, Personal Papers, Miscellaneous (LC); Eaton to Overton, 25 Sept. 1826, John Overton Papers, Claybrooke Collection (THS); Jackson *Gazette*, 19 Aug. 1826; Nashville *Republican*, 30 Sept., 4 Nov., 2 Dec. 1826; Robert H. White, ed., *Messages of the Governors of Tennessee* (Nashville, 1952-), II, 176-200, 222n.; Joseph Howard Parks, *Felix Grundy, Champion of Democracy* (University, La., 1940), 173.

that he had at last succumbed to matrimony—and he did not propose to relinquish it without a fight. A Senate seat was also open as a result of Eaton's elevation to the Cabinet, and Felix Grundy was Jackson's choice to fill it. When Houston's friends began to despair of overcoming Carroll's popularity, they threatened Jackson's plans for the senatorship by a movement to award the post to the unsuccessful gubernatorial candidate. All of this coincided with signs of an even more ominous split among the Tennessee Jackson men.[2]

The main cause of discontent in the Tennessee Jackson party was the influence that the old Overton leaders had over the president. Senator Eaton and Major William B. Lewis were particularly disliked by many Tennessee politicians. Eaton, who had gone to the Senate in 1817 as the hand-picked choice of Jackson and Overton, had never been popular in the state, while Lewis had gained prominence only as a longtime crony of the president. Though Lewis had considerable aptitude for intrigue, neither was a man of outstanding ability. Grundy's alliance with Eaton and Lewis had been strictly a *mariage de convenance*, neither party to which trusted the other, while Polk and a large body of recruits to the Jackson ranks had recently been their bitter opponents on state issues. The announcement of Jackson's Cabinet was the signal for these intraparty antagonisms to burst into the open, for the Cabinet list was largely the work of the Overton-Eaton-Lewis clique.

Following the election of 1824, Senator Eaton, as Jackson's Washington manager, had eagerly welcomed the aid of the Calhoun men and had been instrumental in placing Duff Green in charge of the *Telegraph*. Just when and how he and the rest of the Overton faction were weaned away from Calhoun and over to Van Buren's side is not altogether clear, but the scanty evidence suggests that an important role was played by an obscure Nashville lawyer, Alfred Balch. Balch had become a devoted disciple of William H. Crawford while a law student in Washington; but after the election of 1824 he had switched his allegiance to Van Buren and gone to work to recruit a Van Buren party in Tennessee. Though personally inconsequential, Balch knew most of the prominent Tennessee politicians, and he was tireless and persuasive in the cause of his new-found hero. Sam Houston, who had his own reasons for disliking Calhoun, was

2 Daniel Graham to A. J. Donelson, 2 Feb. 1829, Andrew Jackson Donelson Papers (LC); John C. McLemore to Donelson, 5 Apr. 1829, *ibid.*; R. L. Caruthers to Donelson, 8 Apr. 1829, *ibid.*

probably Balch's first important convert, and other Overton leaders around Nashville soon began to be impressed with his arguments also.[3]

The seeds sown by Balch were cultivated with great success by Major James A. Hamilton, who was sent by Van Buren's New York Republican party to accompany Jackson to New Orleans for an anniversary celebration of his victory over the British in January 1828. While at the Hermitage and on the steamboat trip down the Mississippi, Hamilton plied Major Lewis and the other Overton leaders with insinuations against Calhoun's loyalty to Jackson. Soon, as one member of the party informed the general, "Major Lewis's mind seemed to be filled with suspicions and projected injuries awaiting your fate."[4]

Balch and Hamilton owed their persuasiveness mainly to possession of a secret weapon, which, as they assured the Tennessee politicians, made Calhoun's downfall inevitable. This was the knowledge that William H. Crawford, who cherished in his Georgia retirement an abiding hatred for Calhoun, was ready to testify that back in 1818 Calhoun, as secretary of war, had advocated punishing Jackson for his invasion of Florida. Balch and Houston had already dug up some evidence of this, and on his way back to New York from the New Orleans celebration, Major Hamilton stopped in Georgia to see Crawford and complete preparations for playing this trump card when the time was ripe. Meanwhile Balch continued to assail Tennessee politicians with confident predictions that "the little Dutchman will outwit the Southron." The Overton-Eaton-Lewis group had no strong predilection toward either Van Buren or Calhoun, but they had demonstrated abundantly that they had a keen eye for the main chance. Thus it happened that even before Jackson got to Washington, his most trusted advisers were committed to Van Buren's plans.[5]

There were still other and more surprising recruits. Governor Carroll, like every other prominent Tennessean, had been a target for Balch's arguments, and on a trip to the North during his term

[3] Alfred Balch to Martin Van Buren, 27 Nov. 1828, Martin Van Buren Papers (LC); Balch to John McLean, 20 Jan. 1833, John McLean Papers (LC); Marquis James, *The Raven: A Biography of Sam Houston* (reprint edn., New York, 1949), 44-45, 50-52, 58-60.

[4] R. G. Dunlap to Jackson, 10 Aug. 1831, Jackson Papers.

[5] Balch to Col. William Polk, 3 Dec. 1828, Polk-Yeatman Papers (SHC); Charles M. Wiltse, *John C. Calhoun* (3 vols., Indianapolis, 1944-1951), I, 362-364, II, 76-79.

out of office he had met Van Buren. The New Yorker must have exercised all his charms on the bluff Tennessean, for Carroll came home a convert to the Van Buren cause. An extremely astute political observer, he seems to have perceived that Van Buren would shortly be the key figure in the Jackson party. Carroll was a poor man with a large family, and from this time forward he was a persistent applicant to Jackson and Van Buren for a federal office. He was also henceforward a generally faithful tool of the Overton-Eaton-Lewis clique, so long as they remained loyal to Van Buren. Carroll's protégé, Congressman John Bell, seems to have gone over to the Van Buren camp about the same time.[6]

Carroll's conversion made it even more urgent to take care of him in some way. How could this be done if Houston were to be reelected governor and Grundy sent to the Senate? This problem had to be solved, for it arose simultaneously with the threatened revolt by a large part of the Tennessee Jackson party over the Cabinet question. It was not just Eaton's secretaryship that irritated so many Tennessee politicians, or even Major Lewis's appointment to a Treasury job and installation in the White House family circle as the president's confidant. When a number of Tennessee congressmen protested to Jackson himself against the Cabinet list, that canny observer, Van Buren, perceived that what really bothered them was not the appointees themselves, but the influence of the Overton-Eaton-Lewis clique in making the selections. "Their *amor proprius* was offended," the New Yorker concluded, by what seemed to be "an undeserved preference."[7]

Back in Tennessee, Pleasant M. Miller, who was running for Congress as the Jackson candidate against Davy Crockett, withdrew from the race, publishing a blistering attack on the president for appointing members of Congress to office. Senator White, whom Eaton had cleverly maneuvered out of the secretaryship of war, complained that the major appointments had been arranged, on the advice of Overton, Lewis, and company, before the president ever left the Hermitage. The general's other friends, he said, "feel hurt, that a limited number and those not all of the first order of men, should have his confidence exclusively; and that others are to be used

---

[6] Van Buren to Carroll, 7 May 1829, draft copy, Van Buren Papers; Carroll to Van Buren, 4 Aug. 1829, *ibid.*; Carroll to Jackson, 20 Feb. 1832, typed copy, Jackson Papers, Second Series.

[7] John C. Fitzpatrick, ed., *The Autobiography of Martin Van Buren,* American Historical Association, *Annual Report,* 1918, II (Washington, 1920), 341.

as mere drudges to give effect to their measures, or what oftener happens, to rid up difficulties which the foolish advice of small men have involved him in." So disgruntled was White that he refused to help Jackson get Grundy sent to the Senate.[8]

All this dissatisfaction gave the Erwin faction a golden opportunity to build up Carroll's campaign against Houston for governor. The cry was raised that Eaton and Lewis were "to get the fat offices," while the president was neglecting the faithful and needy Carroll, "who fought side by side with him and was his companion in the dangers & glories which raised him to his present elevation." Knowing that this argument would be conclusive with the voters, the Overton leaders feared that Carroll would rally around him both the old opposition faction and the discontented Jackson men, a combination that would sweep all before it. In their alarm they beseeched the president to offer Carroll either a generalship in the army or the ministry to Mexico. With Carroll out of the way, Houston could continue as governor, and Grundy could go to the Senate as planned. Jackson, however, was not amenable to this plan. Carroll's popularity and independence were not calculated to allay Old Hickory's long-standing animosity, and only when the frightened politicians insisted did the president consent to make Carroll chargé d'affaires to some South American country.

Just at this moment and before news of Jackson's offer reached Nashville, the threatening political skies were suddenly cleared by an explosion in the household of Governor Sam Houston. Without a word of warning or explanation, Houston sent his bride of three months home to her family, resigned the governorship, and departed for the West to live among the Indians. This peculiar episode in Houston's life will probably never be understood fully, but it did serve to ease the political situation. Carroll went into the governorship unopposed, haughtily declining an appointment he considered beneath his dignity, while the legislature duly chose Grundy to succeed Eaton in the Senate.[9]

This fortuitous turn of events only slowed the progress of division within the Tennessee Jackson party. So far, hostility to the Overton-Eaton-Lewis group had been the root of the discontent, but the winter of 1828-1829 saw the factional bickering among the Ten-

8 White to Overton, 28 June 1829, Overton Papers; Nashville *Republican*, 7 Apr. 1829.

9 McLemore to Donelson, 5 Apr. 1829, Donelson Papers; Jackson to [McLemore], 26 Apr. 1829, draft copy, Jackson Papers; Carroll to [Grundy], 21 May 1829, *ibid.*

nessee Jacksonians merged into the epic battle between Van Burenism and Calhounism for control of the potent political instrument
that had been molded out of Andrew Jackson's popularity. The
catalyst that worked the change was a woman, and none too respectable a woman at that.

Peggy O'Neale, the daughter of a Washington tavern keeper, was
an attractive, vivacious girl of free and easy ways. She had married
a Lieutenant Timberlake of the navy, but since her husband was
often at sea for long periods, Peggy continued to live at her parents'
tavern. For years Jackson's bachelor friend Senator Eaton had been
the only regular congressional boarder at the O'Neale tavern, and
rumor had it that Eaton and Peggy were friendlier than they
should have been. When, during the last weeks of the presidential
campaign, the scandalous reports were given fresh life by news that
Timberlake had cut his throat in a distant Mediterranean port,
Jackson ordered Eaton to marry Peggy "forthwith." The wedding
took place on New Year's Day, 1829.

Eaton's elevation to the Cabinet a few months later created a
social crisis, for the good ladies of the capital's best circles were
determined to have nothing to do with Mrs. Secretary Eaton. Jackson reached Washington bowed down with grief over the recent death
of his beloved Rachel, who had been pursued to her grave by the
scandalous charges of his political opponents. His generous instincts
were instantly aroused in defense of Mrs. Eaton, and he interpreted
the whole affair as a plot by Henry Clay to discredit his administration. But events soon took a different turn.

Unfortunately for the vice president, Mrs. Calhoun was one of the
ladies who refused to countenance Peggy's social pretensions. The
womenfolk of three Cabinet members, Branch, Berrien, and Ingham,
took the same position. Jackson's nephew, Andrew Jackson Donelson, had come to Washington as the president's private secretary,
and even his wife, who was serving as White House hostess, refused
to obey the presidential edict that Mrs. Eaton be accepted. Van
Buren, however, was a widower, and he advanced immeasurably in
Jackson's esteem by his marked attentions to the Eatons. Moreover
Van Buren's friend Postmaster General Barry had left his family
at home and was able to take up residence in the Eaton household.

Eaton lost no time in holding his Cabinet colleagues responsible
when their families snubbed his wife, and tempers were soon running
so high within the Cabinet that the president turned more and more

for advice to an unofficial "Kitchen Cabinet," composed of Van Buren's friends Isaac Hill, Amos Kendall, and Major Lewis. The ultimate effect of these developments was to make Van Buren the president's favorite, while Calhoun replaced Clay as the villain of the affair. By the time Congress returned to Washington in December 1829, Major Lewis had persuaded Jackson that Van Buren should be his successor.[10]

II

These disruptive eddies, already running strong by Inauguration Day, bulked large in Congressman Polk's concern about the future. Before Old Hickory's election, it had been enough to be a loyal Jackson man. Now much seemed to depend on what kind of Jackson man one decided to become. Like most of his Tennessee colleagues, Polk had little use for Lewis and Eaton. Did this mean that he must avow himself a Calhoun partisan?

Other Tennesseans, disgusted by the undercover campaign against Calhoun, had begun to take the vice president's side even before the election. Three members of Jackson's party on the New Orleans excursion had been so outraged by Major Hamilton's intriguing with Lewis that they were barely prevented from going ashore and returning home. Grundy had been devoted to Calhoun since their War Hawk days together in Congress, and after the victory of the Jackson electors at the polls, he was instrumental in scotching a fantastic scheme to drop Calhoun as Jackson's running mate in the electoral college. In the days following the election Calhoun had other friends around Nashville who knew of the Cabinet negotiations at the Hermitage and tried to influence Jackson in favor of the vice president's friends. Polk himself, along with Senator White and Representatives Lea and Desha, had been living on the friendliest terms with Calhoun and his associates in Mrs. Peyton's congenial Washington mess.[11]

Whatever his inclinations, Polk was more cautious than some of his colleagues. He was not among the Tennessee congressmen who incurred the president's wrath by calling on him in person to protest the Cabinet appointments. Nor was Polk so rash as those friends of Jackson who tried to convince him that the scandalous charges

[10] Wiltse, *Calhoun*, II, 26-28.
[11] R. G. Dunlap to Jackson, 10 Aug. 1831, Jackson Papers; Grundy to Jackson, 20 Nov. 1828, *ibid.*; Balch to Van Buren, 27 Nov. 1828, Van Buren Papers.

against the Eatons were true. Fortunately the adjournment of Congress enabled the Polks to get away from Washington and its vexing problems immediately after the inauguration.

The summer of 1829 at home in Tennessee was the most restful Polk had enjoyed in years. His convincing victory over Bramlett two years before had demoralized the opposition in his district, and he did not have to campaign to insure his reelection. But November soon arrived, and with it the necessity of returning to the capital, now more distracted than ever by the intraparty feud. This time the Polks took the Ohio river steamboats, reaching Baltimore in such good time that they were able to make a steamboat excursion down Chesapeake Bay to Norfolk before going on to Washington. The additional traveling, however, was too much for Sarah. She arrived at Mrs. Peyton's familiar establishment "much indisposed," though not, as sharp-eyed Levi Woodbury reported to his wife, "with those complaints, that are due to terminate within a given number of months."[12]

This was to be one of the most trying winters Polk would ever spend in Washington, as he tried to walk the tightrope between his dislike of Eaton and Lewis on the one hand and his loyalty to Jackson on the other. Sarah did not make things easier for him by joining the embattled Washington ladies who ostracized Mrs. Secretary Eaton. Once Sarah made up her mind, she could not be moved, at least not by a mere husband. The gossipy Senator Woodbury had calculated earlier that only one member of Congress was more henpecked than Polk, and now another colleague observed that Mrs. Polk "would sooner suffer Randolphs Black John to set at Table with her than be [on] any familiarity with a Lady whose only fault is that the Secretary has made her honest—instead of finding her ready made."[13]

When Congress got down to business and the legislative strategies of the two wings of the party began to be developed, Polk found himself closer to the Calhoun men than to the Van Burenites on policy questions. All factions expected the Jackson party to oppose in some fashion the nationalizing tendencies of the Adams-Clay group, for Henry Clay hoped to rise again to power through an

[12] Levi Woodbury to Mrs. Woodbury, 6 Dec. 1829, Gist Blair Papers (LC); *id.* to *id.*, 29 Nov. 1829, *ibid.*

[13] Rudolph Bunner to G. C. Verplanck, 9 Jan. 1830, Gulian C. Verplanck Papers (NYHS); Woodbury to Mrs. Woodbury, n.d. (placed 3 Dec. 1828), Levi Woodbury Papers (LC).

alliance of the West and Northeast based on his American System—
internal improvements for the West, protective tariffs for the Northeast, both implemented through a system of distributing federal
surpluses to the states, and a sound national banking system for
businessmen in both sections. The Jacksonians must necessarily oppose the American System in part, but the nature of that opposition
would depend on whether Calhoun or Van Buren won ascendancy.

The protective tariff, which Polk had just been castigating in a
circular to his constituents, was the crucial issue. Van Buren staked
his political future on a union between southern planters and northern "plain republicans," an extension of the old alliance of the South
with New York and Pennsylvania on which the Virginia Dynasty
had built its power. He could afford to come out strongly against
internal improvements and the national bank, but the tariff issue was
highly embarrassing to his plans, since his potential supporters,
north and south, disagreed violently over it. Consequently it was
Van Buren's object in the early years of the Jackson administration
to avoid agitation of the tariff question at all costs.

Calhoun, on the other hand, hoped to orient the Jackson party
toward a South-West alliance, which would provide a low tariff for
the South and a liberal land policy for the West. The great obstacle
here was the disagreement between southerners and westerners over
internal improvements, while even Calhoun's southern following was
split on the bank question. He naturally sought to avoid these issues
while he pushed tariff reform and low land prices. The vice president
had only recently, in the wake of increasingly intransigent South
Carolina opinion, moved to an uncompromising antitariff stand. A
year before, in 1828, when he anonymously drafted the "South Carolina Exposition and Protest" against the Tariff of Abominations,
only the hope that Jackson would strike down the protective system
had kept the South Carolinians from more radical action. But now
Jackson met his first Congress with a declaration that "The operation of the tariff has not proved so injurious . . . or so beneficial . . .
as was anticipated." The President urged "utmost caution" in re-
vising the duties, and his only specific recommendation was for a
reduction on tea and coffee.[14]

One did not have to be a Calhounite to see behind this passage the
influence of Martin Van Buren. Antitariff men, cheap land men, and
Calhoun men alike joined forces in a desperate effort to thwart the

[14] *Messages of the Presidents*, II, 449-450.

New Yorker and commit the Jackson party to the southern-western position. With this effort Polk cooperated.

The South-West campaign was launched in the Senate. Replying to an innocuous resolution for a temporary limitation of land sales, offered by Senator Samuel A. Foot of Connecticut, Thomas Hart Benton of Missouri took the opportunity to denounce the Northeast as an enemy to western development and to suggest that its tariff and illiberal land policies were designed to enslave the South and West. Benton's tacit proposal for cooperative action by the South and West was accepted for the South by Calhoun's spokesman on the Senate floor, Robert Y. Hayne of South Carolina. Hayne made it clear that southerners would support a liberal land policy, implying that they would expect the West to aid them in reducing the tariff.

The alarmed New Englanders pressed forward their ablest orator, Daniel Webster, to answer the charges against their section and to throw some kind of stumbling block in the path of the antitariff coalition that seemed to be taking shape before their eyes. Webster succeeded magnificently by adroitly shifting the course of the debate.

In drawing up the "South Carolina Exposition" the previous year, Calhoun had worked out briefly the argument that essential sovereignty in the American Union remained with the states, and that a state could suspend the operation of federal laws it deemed unconstitutional. This doctrine of nullification had attracted little attention at first, but Webster now seized upon it to charge the South, in effect, with treasonable designs against the Union. Picking up Webster's bait readily, Hayne replied with a sweeping elaboration and defense of the nullification theory. Thus Webster was enabled to turn the argument from the tariff to constitutional interpretation, and in his famous second reply to Hayne to appeal to the patriotic nationalism of the vast majority of Americans.

The capital and the country were electrified by what the newspapers were soon calling the Great Debate. Nationalism versus state rights became the absorbing topic of the day, and before the session was over almost every senator and many members of the House had expatiated at large on the subject. Polk cautiously refrained from a direct expression of his views, but he clearly sympathized with the South Carolinians. At any rate he never denied the charge that he endorsed Grundy's speech defending nullification and that he dissented from a denunciation of nullification by one of his more nationalistic Tennessee colleagues in the House.

Polk seems to have been, like Grundy, originally sympathetic with nullification in theory, as a logical extension of the Old Republican doctrines expounded by the Virginia and Kentucky Resolutions of 1798-1799. Even in 1830 no one imagined that nullification would ever actually be put into practice, and in fact Grundy's speech was highly popular in Tennessee. But again like Grundy, Polk lost his enthusiasm for Calhoun's ideas as soon as South Carolina threatened to act on them. "Consolidation on the one hand, and nullification on the other," he denounced at a dinner in his honor at Knoxville in the autumn of 1831, "as extremes equally dangerous, and equally to be avoided." President Jackson, he said, could be counted on to "trim the vessel of State so as to escape those dangerous passes, and safely navigate her to a secure haven."[15]

Despite his caution, Polk almost got into trouble with the president by associating with an overt movement against Van Buren's domination of the Cabinet. Some time after the middle of March 1830, Representative Charles A. Wickliffe and two other Kentucky Jacksonians who later sided openly with Calhoun conceived the idea that a show of strength by anti-Van Buren congressmen might induce the president to change his course. Wickliffe's first move was to enlist those members from Tennessee who were likely to be sympathetic. Accordingly Senators White and Grundy and Representatives Polk, Cave Johnson, and Robert Desha were invited to a strategy meeting. Grundy's friendship for Calhoun was well known; Johnson, a new member who was to become one of Polk's closest political associates, had come to Washington under Grundy's influence; and Desha was Calhoun's most outspoken supporter in the Tennessee delegation, a fact that would soon lead him into a violent break with Jackson. Senator White, though cool to Van Buren's ascendancy, was reluctant to attend and had to be persuaded by Polk.

To Wickliffe's disappointment, the Tennesseans were too timid for the bold course he had in mind. White objected even to discussing a proposal that Jackson be urged to remove Eaton, and Wickliffe finally had to settle for a declaration that the president should resume holding Cabinet meetings, now virtually discontinued because of the bad feeling between Eaton and the secretaries whose families

---

[15] Nashville *Republican*, 22 Nov. 1831; E. J. Frierson to Polk, 23 Sept. 1836, James K. Polk Papers (LC; herein cited as Polk Papers, which refers to First Series unless otherwise noted); Parks, *Grundy*, 184-186.

were snubbing his wife. Jackson soon heard a distorted account of the affair emphasizing the original designs against Eaton. "Let them come on," he shouted to his informant. "I would resign the Presidency or lose my life sooner than I would desert my friend Eaton." So Senator Bibb of Kentucky received scant encouragement when he arrived with the group's advice.

Fortunately for Polk, the president did not learn at the time who had attended the meeting, though Major Lewis did his best to find out. Later, when the history of the affair was unexpectedly exposed, Polk and his fellow Tennesseans refused to say anything about it, phrasing their refusal so as to throw all the onus on Wickliffe. Wickliffe had, to be sure, initiated the business, and the Tennesseans had been cautious. But it is hard to believe that they had attended such a meeting without some idea of its objects. And it is harder still to absolve Polk of complicity, in view of his strenuous efforts to get Senator White to participate.[16]

Less than a month after the Wickliffe meeting, the efforts to forge a South-West coalition and to commit the Jackson party to a low tariff–cheap lands–strict constructionist position culminated in the celebrated Jefferson Birthday Dinner of April 13, 1830. Its promoters had planned a brilliant affair, but the results were bitterly disappointing. The honor guest, President Jackson, had been increasingly disturbed by the nullification talk that emanated from the Great Debate, and Van Buren, Eaton, and Lewis had done all they could to feed his suspicions. By his own account Jackson was "unsuspecting until I sat down to the dinner table, having been assured by the committee who waited upon me, that nothing of politics was to be included in it." But on reading the prepared toasts he "saw the whole plot,"[17] and when called on for the first of the volunteer toasts, he seized the opportunity to declare his position. *"Our Federal Union,"* Old Hickory's penetrating western twang cut

[16] S. F. Bradford to W. B. Lewis, 28 Feb. 1832, Jackson Papers; John Coffee to Jackson, 28 Apr. 1831, *ibid.*; Grundy to Jackson, 30 Sept. 1831, *ibid.*; Charles A. Wickliffe to White and others, 24 Dec. 1831, Polk Papers; Wickliffe to White and Polk, 21 Jan. 1832, *ibid.*; Wickliffe to White, Grundy, and Polk, 29 Jan. 1832, *ibid.*; White to Wickliffe, 30 Jan. 1832, copy, *ibid.*; Polk to Wickliffe, 31 Jan. 1832, copy, *ibid.*; 6-p. MS in Polk's hand placed at end of 1836, *ibid.*; Henry Daniel to Wickliffe, 26 Dec. 1831, copy, Blair-Lee Papers (PU); W. H. Overton to Wickliffe, 5 Jan. 1832, copy, *ibid.*; G. M. Bibb to Wickliffe, 22 Jan. 1831 [1832], copy, *ibid.*; F. P. Blair to White, Grundy, and Polk, 21 Feb. 1832, *ibid.*; Nashville *Republican*, 27, 29 Sept. 1831; Washington *National Intelligencer*, 20 Feb. 1832.

[17] Jackson to Samuel J. Hays, 23 Apr. 1831 (typed copy in possession of Mr. A. J. Hays, Memphis, Tenn.).

through the large room, *"It must be preserved."*[18] In seven emphatic words the president condemned the direction in which a majority of his followers were trying to push their party. Behind the whole affair he saw, or thought he saw, the specter of nullification.

Jackson's declaration, chortled the Kitchen Cabinet, "operated as a powerful damper upon some of the Hotspurs, all of whom know that Old Hickory *means what he says.*"[19] But the assembled politicians had already drunk to twenty-four prepared toasts before the president spoke, and the full significance of his challenge did not sink in at once. Vice President Calhoun followed him, more doggedly than defiantly, with the sentiment: "The Union: Next to our liberty, the most dear; may we all remember, that it can only be preserved by respecting the rights of the States, and distributing equally the benefits and burdens of the Union." And the other guests, nearly a hundred of them, carried through with their toasts extolling "The reserved Rights of the People!!" "the sovereignty of the States," and "low taxes in peace." The president had left before Polk got the floor to offer a conventional version of the Jeffersonian constitutional doctrine: "Public opinion: May it always perform one of its appropriate offices, by teaching the public functionaries of the State and of the Federal Government, that neither shall assume the exercise of powers entrusted by the Constitution to the other."[20]

Like other Jacksonians of a state rights cast, Polk must have waked the next morning to sober second thoughts. If his mind, fogged by the late hours and innumerable toasts, still missed the import of the previous evening's events, he would not remain in doubt much longer; for matters were moving toward a dénouement under the guiding hand of a master politician. "Van Buren glides along as smoothly as oil and as silently as a cat," reported one of his admiring lieutenants shortly after the dinner. "If he is managing at all, it is so adroitly that nobody perceives it. . . . He has the entire confidence of the President and all his personal friends, while Calhoun is fast losing it."[21]

Eighteen days after these words were written, the president addressed an abrupt note to the vice president, demanding to know whether Calhoun had, in fact, advocated disciplining Jackson for his

18 Nashville *Banner*, 11 May 1830.
19 Amos Kendall to [F. P. Blair], 25 Apr. 1830, Blair-Lee Papers.
20 Nashville *Banner*, 11 May 1830.
21 Kendall to [Blair], 25 Apr. 1830, Blair-Lee Papers.

activities in Florida in 1818. Major Lewis had chosen this strategic moment for the explosion he and Major Hamilton had planned on the way to New Orleans over two years before. Through the summer a stream of increasingly angry letters shuttled back and forth between the two chief officers of the government. Long before the break became public, Jacksonian politicians realized that they must soon take their stand either for Calhoun, or for Old Hickory and Van Buren. There would be no middle ground.

When Congress adjourned in May 1830, the Polks escaped Washington's tense atmosphere for an excursion to New York City, then up the Hudson and along the Erie Canal to Niagara Falls, and finally home by way of Ohio and Kentucky. On numerous horseback trips through his district during the summer, Polk found that he had never been more popular. Even his old rival, Lunsford M. Bramlett, acknowledged his political strength and presided at a dinner in his honor at Pulaski in the lower end of the district. Here, as elsewhere, Polk argued for Jeffersonian orthodoxy, concluding his speech with a toast that brought his hearers to their feet cheering: "*The true American System*—Labour untrammelled by Legislation; equal and impartial protection to Agriculture, Commerce and Manufactures; free trade with all the world; sell what we have to spare in the market where we can sell for the best price; buy what we need in the market where we can buy cheapest."

Jackson was in Tennessee that summer to negotiate an Indian treaty, and Polk took his youngest brother, Sam, up to Franklin to see the conclave. The president continued to treat Polk with undiminished confidence, declining his invitation to visit Columbia with sincere regret. At the same time, however, he sent Polk an enthusiastic account of the administration's diplomacy that amounted to a lecture on the merits of Secretary of State Van Buren.[22]

His chief's cordiality Polk was determined to preserve at all costs, and with the Eaton affair nearing its climax, Sarah was told that she would have to remain at home when it was time to return to Washington in November. She was staying behind, she jokingly told her friends, "to save money to make a display on next winter."[23] But

[22] Nashville *Republican*, 21 Aug. 1830; J. K. Polk to Col. William Polk, 1 May 1830, Lucius J. Polk Papers (SHC); Polk to Jackson, 14 Aug. 1830, copy, Polk Papers; Jackson to Polk, 18 Aug. 1830, *ibid.*

[23] Anson and Fanny Nelson, *Memorials of Sarah Childress Polk: Wife of the Eleventh President of the United States* (New York, 1892), 34.

even Columbia was a fair field for a display, and Mr. Polk set out for Washington with explicit instructions:

A handsome black silk dress made up and sent by the first opportunity. 1 spring dress of fashionable material and bring with you selected by Mrs Pleasanton or Mrs Overton. If there is any thing new or pretty in the bonnet way for the spring you can get one but leave that to the *Ladies* If Mrs O. says there is any thing new since I was there in the cape way get one if it does not cost more than $5

Any little fashionable article of dress that does not cost much buy for me if it [is] entirely new and out of the way that is if you think we have not got it *here*.

And all this, the dutiful husband was told, "with the '*strictest eye to economy.*' "[24] Sarah was going to dazzle someone, Peggy or no Peggy.

Polk's precaution proved to be wise. He arrived in Washington to find that the Van Burenites had established a new Jackson newspaper, Francis P. Blair's *Globe*, to compete with Duff Green's *Telegraph*. Calhoun's absence from White House functions was conspicuous, and no one doubted that a complete break with the president had finally come. In January the *Globe* announced that Jackson would accept a second term. In February the vice president made public his estrangement from Jackson by publishing the long, angry correspondence the two men had commenced the previous spring. Two months later Eaton and Van Buren resigned from the Cabinet, permitting Jackson to eradicate the last shred of Calhoun influence from his administration by demanding the resignations of Ingham, Berrien, and Branch.

Through all these events Polk kept strictly to himself any sympathies he may have had with Calhoun. "I have written you my opinions freely," complained one of his friends at home, ". . . but I must acknowledge that you have been more prudent with yours for I am not able to even conjecture how your feelings are after all your long letters." Polk might have replied in the words of his friend Grundy. "My own course is fixed," wrote Grundy in response to a similar inquiry. "If Calhoun runs, I am for running Jackson with him, if Van-Buren runs, I am for running Jackson with him and so on to the end of the chapter—this I believe the prudent and wise

[24] Memorandum in Congressional Memo Book for 1830-1832, Polk Papers.

course."[25] Above all, these Tennessee strict constructionists were resolved not to break with the president.

This was not just political cowardice. The Calhoun-Jackson feud was primarily a matter of personalities, and issues and philosophy were involved only incidentally. Polk did not desert Calhoun, for Calhoun's promotion had never been his object. The attempt to ally South and West had been supported by several sections of the Jackson party for several different reasons. Calhoun's most ardent supporters, including Wickliffe, Desha, and the South Carolinians, undoubtedly hoped that it would make him president. But to many others who cooperated in the attempted bargain on land prices and tariff reform, in Wickliffe's plot against Eaton, and in the Jefferson Birthday Dinner, Calhoun's aspirations counted for nothing. Benton, who first proposed the South-West alliance and who, with Desha, planned the dinner, was plainly interested in cheap land for the West and little more. Before long he would be recognized as Van Buren's heir apparent. Another promoter of the dinner and a member of the invitations committee was Congressman Churchill C. Cambreleng. A loyal member of the New York Republican organization and one of Van Buren's most trusted aides, Cambreleng would have had no part in any scheme to advance Calhoun. As representative of a New York City commercial constituency, though, Cambreleng advocated a radical free trade policy and was willing to cooperate with other groups to achieve tariff reform.[26]

Polk belonged to none of these categories. He was not a Calhoun man. He was not preoccupied with a desire for cheap lands. He was not even exclusively concerned about lower tariffs, though he obviously considered tariff reform important. Instead he belonged to a group that wanted to bring the government in all its policies back to the republican simplicity of the Jeffersonian order. Polk might have complained with Senator White that, "I shall never have my exertions applauded in the *Telegraph,* nor in any other paper published here," because "I have not, nor will I commit myself to support any pretender after Jackson is off the stage."[27] He could cooperate with Calhounites on some issues and with Van Burenites on others, but he could not commit himself wholly to the legislative

[25] Archibald Yell to Polk, 13 Mar. 1831, Polk Papers; Grundy to Daniel Graham, 24 Jan. 1831, Felix Grundy Papers (SHC).
[26] Wiltse, *Calhoun,* II, 424, note 1.
[27] Nancy N. Scott, *A Memoir of Hugh Lawson White* . . . (Philadelphia, 1856), 270.

strategy of either faction without compromising his Jeffersonian principles on some issue or another.

Polk and his fellow ideologues were compelled, therefore, to fight doggedly on, resisting the heavy pressures driving them toward the Van Buren camp or the Calhoun camp, opposing now one group and now the other, and occasionally coming into unavoidable conflict with the president himself. Polk was able to follow this difficult course only because he never lost confidence that he was right and that Jackson at heart agreed with him. If the baleful influence of Eaton and Lewis could only be eliminated, the administration might be brought back to Jeffersonian first principles.

III

Polk's position was simply that the American System should be opposed in its entirety—tariffs, internal improvements, high land prices, distribution, national bank, and everything connected with them. The American System, "as it is falsely called," he announced to Jackson's first Congress, was "a stool that stands upon three legs." The first leg was high land prices, which were designed to restrict westward emigration, and thereby to "retain a population of paupers in the East, who may, of necessity, be driven into manufactories, to labor at low wages for their daily bread." The protective tariff, the second leg of the stool, had the double purpose of enabling the manufacturer to sell his products at higher prices and of producing a federal surplus to sustain the third leg, the internal improvements program. All of them together, said Polk, constituted the "splendid system," to support which the people of the Union were to be "oppressively taxed, in all time to come, unless the policy is changed."

Polk left no doubt about what policy he proposed:

I would sell out the public lands at low prices—at much lower prices than they ever have been sold. I would have them speedily settled by a hardy race of enterprising freemen, who would feel that they had a stake in the Government. I would impose no unnecessary taxation upon them, to support any particular interest. I would relieve the burdens of the whole community, as far as possible, by reducing the taxes. I would keep as much money in the treasury as the safety of the Government required, and no more. I would keep no surplus revenue there to scramble for, either for internal improvements, or for any thing else. I would bring the Government back to what it was intended to be—a plain economical Government.

Here in a single paragraph Polk summed up his whole political philosophy. Here are the objectives to which he devoted his respectable abilities and his remarkable energy during his nine remaining years in Congress. And here are echoes of that nostalgia for the plain republican order of Old Mecklenburg—"a hardy race of enterprising freemen" under "a plain economical Government"—that was the emotional wellspring of his neo-Jeffersonian faith.[28]

This was more than a routine mouthing of shibboleths. Polk spoke with unusual earnestness, for this confession of political faith came during a debate over the only issue that had ever caused him to stray far from the straight and narrow path of Jeffersonian orthodoxy, the Buffalo-to-New Orleans road. This project had been delayed from session to session by contention over which route the road should follow. Five main routes and sixteen subordinate ones had been surveyed by the time the perennial bill came up again in 1830. The strategy of its sponsors was to push an appropriation of two and a quarter million dollars for the road without specifying a route, so as to attract the support of advocates of all the routes.

This was the first major internal improvements measure to come before Congress since Jackson's inauguration. His inaugural address of the previous March had been highly ambiguous on the subject, but over the summer Martin Van Buren had been in Washington, and Jackson had become convinced that the internal improvement policy threatened his cherished object of paying off the public debt. Consequently he brought pressure on his friends in Congress to vote against the Buffalo–New Orleans project, letting it be known that he would not sign the bill if it should pass.[29] Having begun to regret his endorsement of this project as early as 1827, Polk took this occasion to combine an avowal of his political philosophy with a flat renunciation of his former views on internal improvements.

No member of the House, he said, had experienced the lure of such a great national project at closer range than himself. He recalled that when this same road was first proposed, the people in his district "seemed to be carried away with the prospect of having millions of public money expended among them. We were to have a main route and cross routes intersecting the district in every direction. It was to run down every creek, and pass through almost every neighborhood in the district." But fortunately "the delusion passed

28 *Register of Debates*: 21st Cong.: 1st Sess., 692-700.
29 Elisha Whittlesey to John McLean, 23 May 1830, McLean Papers.

off," as the people began to appreciate the tendency of such projects to "accumulate power in the federal head" and to "build up here a splendid Government, differing, if this tendency shall continue, only in name from a consolidated empire." From this time on, Polk voted against every federal improvement measure, including appropriations for improving navigation on the Cumberland and Tennessee rivers in his own state.[30]

The New Orleans road bill was finally defeated by disagreement over the route, and the real test of the internal improvement policy came on a proposal that the federal government buy stock in a company building a road from Maysville to Lexington in Kentucky. That Polk was assigned to lead the fight against this measure was evidence of both his growing prestige in Congress and his standing with the administration. At the same time the administration strategists were astute in entrusting their cause to a man who stood outside the circle of Van Buren's lieutenants and who had many friends among those disgruntled with Van Buren's ascendancy.

Polk grounded his argument against the Maysville road on the fact that it was not a national project. "Anything is national," he complained, "which gentlemen may deem proper to think expedient." A host of really local projects passed Congress, he went on to show, because, "All the friends of the system vote for every project, so that they may get their own projects carried." The accuracy of this analysis was proved by the result, since the supporters of all the pending projects united to push this test measure through both houses.[31]

For two weeks the capital buzzed with speculation over what Jackson would do with the bill. Van Buren's desire that the administration take a stand against the improvement policy was well known, and the president had voiced substantial doubt about the constitutionality of federal roads in his message at the convening of Congress. On the other hand, a veto might be disastrous to the Jackson cause in the West.

The decision was never really in doubt. Jackson's Maysville Veto not only condemned the immediate project as local rather than national, but also went on to expound the president's position on the whole question. Again avowing his doubts about the constitutionality of congressional appropriations even for clearly national undertak-

[30] *Reg. Deb.*:21:1, pp. 692-700; *House Journal*:21:1, pp. 362, 486, 708.
[31] *Reg. Deb.*:21:1, pp. 831-833.

ings, Jackson suggested that a constitutional amendment would be necessary to settle the matter. He was firmly convinced, moreover, that such expenditures, even if constitutional, would be inexpedient until the national debt was paid. Even should the debt be paid and the constitutional difficulties overcome, the president was still fearful of the rivalries and logrolling among various local interests that an internal improvement policy would entail. To avoid this difficulty, he repeated the proposal of his annual message: that Congress confine itself to distributing any future surplus to the states, who could spend it for improvements if they wished.

The rage of the western Jacksonians was expressed in the House by William Stanberry of Ohio, who was so carried away as to denounce Jackson himself for this "low, undignified, electioneering paper." "The hand of the magician [Van Buren]," he surmised correctly, "is to be seen in every line of it." Having been coached at the White House to defend the president's handiwork, Polk promptly "undertook to state" that the veto message was "emphatically his [Jackson's] own and the views presented for the rejection of this bill, were the result of the honest convictions of his own deliberate reflection." Then Polk launched into a scathing attack on the apostate Stanberry, ending with an apostrophe to the wisdom, patriotism, and courage of the president's action. A majority of the House voted to override, but the improvement forces fell far short of the necessary two thirds. The vote revealed a deep split between the South and the West, and the South-West alliance died along with the improvement policy.[32]

That Polk led the administration forces in this decisive battle over internal improvements at the very moment when the scheme for a South-West alliance was being pushed indicates that he was no tool of the Calhounites. But neither, despite his unbounded admiration for Jackson, was he a slavish follower of the president. At the same time he was opposing the New Orleans road and defending the Maysville Veto, he was also opposing Jackson's distribution proposal.

In the debate on the New Orleans road Polk had explicitly refused to commit himself on the merits of distribution, though he admitted it would be better than the current method of piecemeal appropriations for improvement projects. When the president returned to the

---

[32] *ibid.*, 1141-1142; *Messages of the Presidents*, II, 483-493; *House Journal*:21:1, p. 763.

proposal in his second annual message of December 1830, Polk got the matter referred to a special House committee under his chairmanship. The report which Polk drafted and which the committee accepted took sharp issue with the president's views. He began by agreeing with Jackson that no money should be either appropriated directly or distributed to the states for internal improvements until the debt was paid. But when the debt was retired, Polk said, the government should reduce taxes rather than accumulate a surplus for distribution. Since the bulk of federal income came from custom duties, he was appealing here for tariff reform, though he did not wholly repudiate the protective system. Duties should be eliminated first, he thought, on articles not produced in the United States, and "upon such as may be considered necessaries of life, consumed by the poor as well as the rich."[33]

IV

Distribution and internal improvements were obviously bound up with the tariff issue, and the tariff issue was moving toward a crisis. By 1831 Polk was telling his constituents that the national debt would soon be paid and that Congress must then either reduce the duties or "gravely set about to devise ways and means to squander the money." It was for the latter purpose, he explained, that the internal improvements program had been brought forward.[34]

An effort to remedy the worst excesses of the Tariff of Abominations had been made at the session of 1829-1830. Polk had supported an attempt to reduce most duties to the pre-1824 level, and when that failed, he voted for an equally unsuccessful proposal to return them to where they had been before 1828. But in the end the bill was so disappointing that he and forty other antitariff extremists voted against it.[35] In South Carolina the following autumn, the nullifying party had won a majority in the legislature, but not the two thirds necessary for calling a state convention to nullify the tariff.

Calhoun's conservative influence had checked the hotter spirits in South Carolina up to this time, but when Congress again failed to provide real relief at its session of 1830-1831, matters began to get out of hand. In a desperate effort to regain control over the situation, Calhoun openly took his place at the head of the nullifying

[33] *House Committee Reports*:21:2, No. 51; *House Journal*:21:2, pp. 36, 38.
[34] Draft of a circular, 22 Feb. 1831, Polk Papers.
[35] *House Journal*:21:1, pp. 626-630, 639, 641, 645.

group. His Fort Hill Address of July 1831 was a temperate statement of the nullifiers' position. The question of tariff reform, with nullification as the alternative, was thus placed squarely in the lap of Congress when it reassembled in December 1831. But with a national election impending, both Clay's followers and the northern Jacksonians refused to make any substantial concessions. Polk voted for every amendment to lower duties and against every amendment to raise them, but the tariff reform bill that resulted was an ambiguous document of doubtful effect. Calhoun's followers found it such a sham that they voted against it, though Polk and most of the anti-tariff Jacksonians supported it as the best that could be obtained.[36]

Events now moved rapidly. At the October 1832 election in South Carolina, the nullifiers won an overwhelming legislative majority, a special session was promptly convened, a convention was authorized and assembled, and on November 24 South Carolina solemnly declared the tariff acts of 1828 and 1832 null and forbade collection of duties under them within her borders. Thus, when the second session of the twenty-second Congress met, on December 3, 1832, South Carolina and the United States stood poised against each other.

If the president's message held out a prospect of compromise by advocating tariff reduction, his Nullification Proclamation of a week later served notice that the settlement would have to be on his own terms. This bristling document, moreover, put Polk and the other state rights Jackson men in an extremely uncomfortable position, for Old Hickory defined the Union in the language of John Marshall and Daniel Webster. Any hope that the politicians could avoid taking a public position either for the radical state rights doctrine of South Carolina, or for the nationalistic doctrine of the Nullification Proclamation, evaporated when Jackson demanded that Congress authorize him to collect the revenues by force. "*Subrosa* what will you state right sticklers do now?" jibed Polk's friend Aaron Brown.[37] And peppery old John Quincy Adams, now back in the House, had his joke too. "I received this morning," the ex-president gleefully noted in his diary, "from A. Fitch a copy of Governor Robert Y. Hayne of South Carolina's counter-proclamation to that of the President of the United States. It is dated the 20th, and is full of very bitter words. I sent it to Polk, of Tennessee."[38]

[36] *House Journal*:22:1, pp. 915-1012.
[37] A. V. Brown to Polk, 20 Jan. 1833, Polk Papers.
[38] Charles Francis Adams, ed., *Memoirs of John Quincy Adams, Comprising Portions of His Diary from 1795 to 1848* (12 vols., Philadelphia, 1874-1877), VIII, 512.

The administration strategy was clear: to isolate Calhoun by taking credit for tariff reduction, while discrediting nullification as a revolutionary assault on the Union. Over in the Senate, Felix Grundy made his choice quickly and, though it cost him some discomfiture, led the fight for Jackson's Force Bill. But tariff bills had to originate in the House, and here the administration was counting heavily on Polk. Fortunately for the Jackson men, George McDuffie of South Carolina, long chairman of the powerful, tariff-writing Ways and Means Committee, did not reach Washington in time for the opening of Congress. This enabled Speaker Andrew Stevenson to shove Polk's messmate Verplanck, a Van Buren disciple, up to the chairmanship. This in turn permitted him to transfer Polk from the Foreign Affairs Committee, where he had been of little benefit to the administration forces, to Ways and Means, where his analytical ability and methodical industry would be invaluable in this crisis.[39]

The committee got down to work without delay, and both Polk and Verplanck were in frequent consultation at the White House and with Secretary of the Treasury Louis McLane, who appears to have played an important part in drafting the bill. There was no trouble deciding what should be done, for the committee contained only two staunch protectionists, and one of them was so frightened by South Carolina's threats that he was ready to accept substantial tariff reform. Probably in accordance with the wishes of Secretary McLane and other administration leaders, the committee decided to roll duties generally back to the level of the act of 1816, the first of the markedly protective tariffs.

Drawing the actual bill required a great deal of labor. Many exceptions and special cases had to be provided for, and the committee wished to accompany its bill with a report giving an elaborate analysis of the revenues that might be expected under both the current rates and the proposed modifications. The work was done under pressure, for this was the short session of Congress, and the bill would have to be ready long before the mandatory adjournment date, March 3, to have any prospect of passage.

Much of the labor undoubtedly fell to Polk, and he and the rest of the committee were ready with their bill and report in less than three weeks. Not until the eighth of January, however, could the House be induced to take up this, the most important question before it. In

[39] Parks, *Grundy*, 194-204; Michael Hoffman to Van Buren, 9 Dec. 1832, Van Buren Papers.

presenting the bill Verplanck contented himself with a brief statement of the necessity for reducing the federal revenues and urged the House, in view of the shortness of time, to avoid a debate on the general merits of protection and get down to the details of the bill at once. But this was precisely what the protectionists did not propose to do.

Van Buren had the New York Jacksonians fairly well in hand, and most of the other protectionist Jacksonians could be got to support some measure of reduction; but the anti-Jackson protectionists quickly made it clear that they opposed the slightest concession to the treasonable South Carolinians. Day after day they consumed precious hours with long speeches prophesying the ruin of American manufacturers and the dismemberment of the Union. Verplanck and Polk tried to conserve the time left by refraining from reply, but when two weeks passed with no sign that the flow of words was diminishing, Verplanck undertook to answer some of the protectionist criticisms. It was left to Polk, however, to close the debate for the committee with a convincing argument, based on data gathered by the Treasury Department, that the proposed duties would not substantially injure any American manufacturers. Polk's facts and figures impressed the House and, according to a protectionist observer, "made members flutter who were round him," but unfortunately they also provided fresh material for further speeches by the opposition.[40]

As the prospects for Jacksonian tariff reform grew darker, it was Polk, rather than the able but torpid Verplanck, who aggressively pushed the fight for the administration bill. Almost every day saw a parliamentary battle, as Polk tried to hasten the bill's progress by holding the House in session later than the usual hour of adjournment. Continually he goaded his colleagues with reminders that delay would be fatal to settlement of a controversy that might have disastrous consequences. It was the end of January before the House began to heed his exhortations and got down to particulars.

The action on specific provisions, however, proved more discouraging than the long debate. Again and again the anti-Jackson protectionists secured enough support from wavering Jackson men to raise particular duties. Gradually but inexorably the committee bill was becoming a travesty of tariff reform, like the act of the previous session. Meanwhile the interminable process of roll call and parlia-

[40] *Reg. Deb.*:22:2, pp. 1162-1175, 1225 and ff.

mentary maneuver was bringing Congress closer and closer to adjournment. Even if the bill were not ruined by amendment, it would be nip and tuck to get it through the House in time for the Senate to act before March 3.

Suddenly, on February 12, the initiative was snatched from Polk, Verplanck, and the House of Representatives. In a dramatic speech to the Senate, Henry Clay, previously the high priest of protectionism, proposed that all tariff rates be reduced to a uniform level of 20 per cent, the reduction to be accomplished gradually over a ten-year period. Calhoun's prompt endorsement of Clay's proposal revealed that Jackson's two most dangerous foes had joined forces in a brilliant maneuver to rob the administration of credit for tariff reform. Clay's proposal was even more radical than the Verplanck bill, but its immediate impact would not be so great, and Clay was confident he could get enough votes from moderate protectionists to pass it.

This abrupt turn of events made Polk's task almost hopeless, since he had to combat not only a coalition of anti-Jackson men with protariff Jacksonians, but also a threatening new coalition of Calhounites and Clayites. He struggled on, however, until February 25, when, a few minutes before adjournment for the day, Robert P. Letcher, the Clay spokesman in the House, moved that Clay's proposal be substituted for the committee bill. By this time the Clay measure was the only hope for real tariff reform, so Polk threw in the sponge and voted for Letcher's motion. With a whoop of relief, the House members delayed their suppers long enough to rush the new bill to a third reading. Final passage was a mere formality the next day.[41] Thus was born the famous Compromise Tariff of 1833. Though the administration lost credit for tariff reform, Jackson–Van Buren men breathed sighs of relief. Not only had the dangerous shoals of nullification been navigated safely, but the issue most dangerous to preservation of the Jacksonian coalition had been well-nigh removed from the sphere of political contention.

Jackson was now more insistent than ever that the Force Bill be passed along with tariff reduction. Though Polk had lost whatever sympathy for nullification he may have had, his Old Republican prejudices must have been outraged by the extreme nationalism of the Nullification Proclamation and even more by the president's demand for authority to coerce a sovereign state. But like Grundy in

[41] *House Journal*:22:2, p. 415.

the Senate, Polk yielded to Jackson's wishes and helped pass the Force Bill. He seems to have been somewhat shamed when his fellow Tennessean Cave Johnson and his messmate Clement C. Clay of Alabama joined the little band of Calhoun men to vote against the president's measure. At any rate, on the next to the last day of the session, Polk was found lending his support to McDuffie's facetious motion for amending the bill's title to read: "An act to subvert the sovereignty of the States of the Union; to establish a consolidated government without limitation of powers, and to make the civil subordinate to the military power."[42]

Polk's vote for the Force Bill was contradicted by his steady adherence to state rights, limited-government principles on nearly every other issue that came before Congress during Jackson's first administration. When Georgia, abetted by Jackson, defied a Supreme Court order dealing with the Indians within its borders, Polk opposed all efforts to impugn its course. The South Carolinians promptly sought an alliance with the Georgians by proposing to repeal the famous twenty-fifth section of the Judiciary Act of 1789, which permitted the Supreme Court to review decisions of the state courts. Polk was among the fifty-one members of the House—half of them from South Carolina, Georgia, and Virginia—who supported this radical attack on the supremacy of federal law.[43]

Polk continued to be one of the most uncompromising foes of what he regarded as unnecessary expenditures and was found in opposition to most bills for relief of private individuals. He voted against appropriations for the military academy at West Point and saw a far-reaching and sinister principle in a proposal to donate some of Congress's firewood to the suffering poor of Georgetown during the severe winter of 1830-1831. On one of the rare occasions when Polk favored a private relief bill—the case of Susan Decatur, in which Jackson was greatly interested—old John Quincy Adams, himself always generous with the public funds, had another chuckle at the expense of his penny-pinching Tennessee colleague. "The vote was carried by tellers," he reported, "and I went through arm-in-arm with Polk, much to the amusement of the House."[44]

As a westerner Polk opposed the scheme to distribute the proceeds

[42] *ibid.*, 204, 410, 453-454.
[43] *House Journal*:21:1, pp. 351, 354; *ibid.*:21:2, pp. 86, 213, 227; *Reg. Deb.*:21:1, p. 595.
[44] Adams, *Diary*, IX, 134; *Reg. Deb.*:21:2, pp. 558-559; *House Journal*:23:1, p. 860.

of land sales among all the states and supported preemption and graduation measures, which were designed to lower land prices and to give preference to actual settlers. He likewise upheld the administration policy of removing the Indians to reservations west of the Mississippi and worked hard for the perennial and much-needed bill to extend the benefits of the federal court system fully to the western states.[45]

V

Through all of Jackson's first term Polk retained the president's complete confidence. In addition to his activity on major issues, he served the administration on many lesser questions and slowly but surely came to be recognized as one of the leading Jacksonians in the House.

At the 1829-1830 session Polk almost got involved in a duel over one of these minor matters. Pryor Lea had barely beaten the rancorous anti-Jackson man Thomas D. Arnold for Congress in the Knoxville district, and Arnold had followed him to Washington to contest the election. In pleading his case before the committee of the whole house, Arnold charged that Hugh Lawson White had bribed a member of the legislature that elected him to the Senate. Polk was infuriated by this vicious and completely unfounded attack on his friend and patron. Arnold's insinuations, he told the House, "*are* base calumnies, and, when examined the whole world will know them to be so, and will properly appreciate the unworthy motive which has induced the petitioner to utter them in this public manner."[46]

Having been called a liar, Arnold retaliated by publishing in the widely circulated Washington *National Intelligencer* a purposely insulting denunciation of Polk as a "shivering dastard," to which he appended the following "card": "I pronounce James K. Polk, of Tennessee, to be a coward, a puppy, a liar, and a scoundrel generally." Even as a conventional invitation to a duel, this was excessively scurrilous. It was to Polk's credit that he ignored Arnold's insults, and the House eventually seated Lea.[47]

Two years later Polk was involved in an incident even more spec-

[45] *House Journal*:21:1, pp. 180-185, 337, 621, 705, 779; *ibid.*:22:2, p. 460; *Reg. Deb.*:21:1, pp. 489, 546-551.
[46] Washington *United States Telegraph*, 1 Jan. 1830; *ibid.*, 8 Jan. 1830; *House Journal*:21:1, pp. 155, 159-160.
[47] Nashville *Banner*, 2 Feb. 1830.

tacular than the Arnold-Lea dispute. In the spring of 1832 the bizarre figure of Sam Houston suddenly emerged from the Indian country and appeared in the lobby of the House just as Representative William Stanberry of Ohio accused him of fraud in connection with a government contract for supplying rations to the Indians. The fiery Houston bounded out on the floor and would have settled the matter then and there, if Polk had not hustled his friend out into fresh air before serious damage was done. Some days later, however, Houston accidentally encountered Stanberry on Pennsylvania Avenue, leaped on him like a wildcat, and beat the unfortunate congressman black and blue with a hickory cane.

The next day Stanberry, in bed with aches and bruises, sent the speaker a complaint, and his friends demanded that Houston be arrested for contempt of the House. Polk objected strenuously, arguing that the House had no right to punish an action committed out of its presence and that to do so would set a dangerous precedent for invading the liberties of individual citizens. But the members were so shocked by the episode that they ordered Houston taken into custody and proceeded to try him. Meanwhile the opposition newspapers told the country that the capital was filled with assassins, hired by the president to intimidate any congressman who dared oppose his imperial will.

Polk took charge of Houston's defense when the case came before the House for decision. Pitching his argument on broad constitutional grounds, he maintained that the sacred right to trial by jury was being violated. The House was copying—shocking but true—the procedure of the British House of Commons! It was claiming the identical power it had tried to assume with the Alien and Sedition Acts. Announcing that he would vote for acquittal, Polk concluded: "I regard it as amongst the proudest votes of my public life; as a vote in behalf of liberty of the citizen against lawless power; as a vote against an attempted violation of the constitution of my country by this House." This was lofty rhetoric, probably inappropriately lofty, but the defense was hard put to divert the members' attention from the air of noble suffering in which Stanberry contrived to wrap his painful body.[48]

The trial at the bar of the House dragged on for several weeks. On the night before Houston was to close his own defense, Polk,

[48] *Reg. Deb.*:22:1, pp. 2822-2839; *ibid.*, 2512-2513; James, *The Raven*, 133-135, 163-170.

Grundy, Speaker Stevenson, and a few other friends dropped into his room at Brown's Hotel. Bottles were produced, and the gathering grew hilarious. Polk, as Houston ruefully recalled, "rarely indulged," and this sort of thing was not to his taste, much less to Sarah's. By midnight the speaker was snoring loudly on the sofa, and the usually eloquent Grundy had lapsed into a rambling monologue, but Polk had long since departed.

Though Houston was still a bit tipsy when he spoke the next day, he made such a stirring appeal against legislative persecution of individuals that the House let him off as lightly as possible. The speaker was instructed to inflict a reprimand on the impenitent offender, which order Stevenson executed with his tongue very much in his cheek. Polk could not resist venting his sarcasm on the House at this ludicrous outcome. His colleagues dared not deprive Houston of his liberty, he charged, for this would have brought a real test of their powers. Instead, they "had wisely preferred to play the schoolmaster and reprimand the accused like a naughty boy; telling him, in effect, that if he did so again, and beat another member, he should be reprimanded again; and if he beat a third, he would again be reprimanded."[49]

While these episodes were endearing Polk still more to President Jackson, his conscientiousness and parliamentary ability were making him one of the recognized leaders of the House. In conjunction with an equally conscientious opposition member, he organized a "business party" to cut down irrelevant debate and help the sluggish body get through its calendar. Soon the anti-Jackson members were directing their probing inquiries at him, because he "was said to be very intimate at the White House."[50]

The first formal recognition of Polk's growing prestige came at the opening of the twenty-second Congress in December 1831, when he was made chairman of the committee to draft a bill reapportioning the House seats among the states on the basis of the recent decennial census. This was a strategic post. Since any ratio of representation adopted would leave the states with varying unrepresented fractions of population, certain states and sections would inevitably be favored at the expense of others. With sectional jealousies at fever pitch, with some states in danger of having their representation reduced, with the new ratio slated for use in the imminent presiden-

49 *Reg. Deb.*:22:1, p. 3034; James, *The Raven*, 167.
50 *Reg. Deb.*:22:1, p. 3027; *ibid.*:22:2, p. 865.

tial election, and with every member's district likely to be affected by the ratio adopted, the apportionment bill was the center of the most intense interest.

Finding the ratio best suited to Polk's purposes was a complicated task, and his personal papers contain many pages of tables showing the effects of various possible ratios, as well as calculations of the counties that might be included in his own district under various figures. By January 10 he was ready with a bill proposing a ratio of one representative for every 48,000 of federal population. This measure was ingeniously drawn from a Jacksonian viewpoint, being especially favorable to the western states, with the exception of Henry Clay's Kentucky. In the South, Georgia and treasonable South Carolina would have large unrepresented fractions, South Carolina's being the largest of any state; but New England was the section hit hardest.

Polk's bill provoked a perfect storm of debate. Four months were consumed by the unremitting efforts of various delegations to shift the ratio to a figure more favorable to their respective states. John Quincy Adams was more upset by this bill than any other measure that had arisen since his return to Congress. "The iniquity of the Apportionment bill, and the disreputable means by which so partial and unjust a distribution of the representation had been effected" cost him many a sleepless night, spent "meditating in search of some device, if it were possible, to avert the heavy blow from the State of Massachusetts and from New England."

Early in February the disgruntled states finally got together enough votes to change the ratio to 44,300. But Polk rallied his forces overnight and asked for one more ballot on a motion to recommit the bill with instructions to insert the figure 47,700. If he were outvoted on this proposition, Polk promised to submit. His new ratio would give an additional member each to Georgia, Kentucky, and New York, and these states provided enough votes to put it over. "It has been settled out-of-doors, like everything else upon this bill," Adams fumed, but he and his friends were powerless to dent the coalition Polk had assembled. When the bill passed the House, the ex-president could only wail, "I hung my harp upon the willow." Adams' allies in the Senate resorted to a different strategy, sending the bill back to the House with a novel plan whereby major fractions would be represented. But Polk now had his votes so well in hand that the Senate was finally compelled to accept the original House version.[51]

VI

Though the heterogeneous composition of Jackson's following had given an air of vacillation to his first administration, Old Hickory's forces were gradually coming over to the position that Polk had occupied all along. Internal improvements had been checked; distribution had been repudiated and a liberal land policy endorsed; and with passage of the Compromise Tariff, the troublesome issue of protection had been settled along lines acceptable to antitariff men. Jacksonian Democracy was well on its way to being defined in terms of Polk's Old Republican orthodoxy; and the Jacksonian coalition of miscellaneous factions was becoming a real political party with a set of policies that its members were under pressure to support.

Clay's followers, united behind his boldly conceived American System, had taken on the characteristics of a political party even more rapidly. Both groups had originally claimed to be Republicans, and old-fashioned Jackson men like Polk continued to call themselves by that name. But gradually the bulk of the Jackson party adopted the name Democratic Republicans, or simply Democrats. The Clay men, after a short period as National Republicans, would soon be known as Whigs. Each group contained discordant elements, of course, most notably Calhoun's devoted little band of State Rights Whigs, but by the presidential election of 1832 the country again had a well-developed two-party system on a national scale.

A careful student of the two parties' leadership in the election year of 1832 might have missed Congressman Polk entirely. Yet during the past four years his hard work, his ability to learn, his dogged adherence to his principles, and the president's friendship had brought him safely past that critical point where a man's career either levels off toward mediocrity or mounts the threshold of continuing achievement. Polk had learned much since his failure with the Tennessee land bill, and the parliamentary leadership he displayed in the apportionment fight of 1831-1832 made him a figure to watch among the Jacksonians. It was at the very next session that he was transferred to the Ways and Means Committee and

[51] Adams, *Diary*, VIII, 471-472; MSS relating to the apportionment bill, placed 4 Jan. 1832, Polk Papers; *Reg. Deb.*:22:1, pp. 1531-1534, 1542-1546, 1562-1568, 1589-1595, 1649-1662, 1709-1726, 1812-1815; *House Journal*:22:1, pp. 305, 314, 344, 352-361, 368, 664, 697, 712, 744, 754, 767.

given a major share of responsibility for the administration's tariff reform program. But it was not on account of tariff reform alone that the administration wanted Polk in this strategic post, for an even more crucial battle was taking shape.

On one issue the party lines were still undrawn, but the bitter struggle over this question of banking and financial policy would shortly usher in one of the stormiest decades in American political history. And in this struggle, which more than any other would reveal the real meaning of Jacksonian Democracy, few politicians would play a greater role than James K. Polk.

6

THE DEMOCRACY AND THE MONEY POWER

ON THE NIGHT OF JULY 8, 1832, Martin Van Buren, returning from England after the Senate had rejected his nomination as American minister, reached Washington. Hastening to the White House, he found the president stretched out on a sick bed, "a spectre in physical appearance but as always a hero in spirit." Grasping Van Buren's hand, Jackson came straight to the point. The Bank "is trying to kill me," he announced with calm conviction, *"but I will kill it!"*[1] Two days later he declared war with his celebrated Bank Veto.

The Bank's chief executive took up the gage of battle in similar spirit. The Veto "has all the fury of a chained panther, biting the bars of his cage," wrote Nicholas Biddle to Henry Clay. "It is really a manifesto of anarchy, such as Marat or Robespierre might have issued to the mob of the Faubourg St. Antoine; and my hope is, that it will contribute to relieve the country from the dominion of these miserable people." "You," Biddle told Clay, "are destined to be the instrument of that deliverance."[2] And so began the epic struggle between the most powerful financial institution the country had ever known, backed by the business elite and a phalanx of lawyers, editors, and politicians, on the one hand, and on the other "these miserable people," the Jacksonians, voicing the inchoate democratic aspirations of countless Americans.

Chartered by Congress in 1816 for twenty years, the Second Bank of the United States was modeled on the earlier national bank fathered by Alexander Hamilton. With a capital of thirty-five million dollars and with power to open branches anywhere, this Philadelphia corporation dominated credit and exchange transactions throughout the country. Its resources augmented by the federal funds deposited without interest in its vaults, it was permitted to issue as many bank notes as its president and cashier could sign. The federal government's promise to receive these notes helped in-

[1] John C. Fitzpatrick, ed., *The Autobiography of Martin Van Buren*, American Historical Association, *Annual Report*, 1918, II (Washington, 1920), 625.

[2] Calvin Colton, ed., *The Private Correspondence of Henry Clay* (Boston, 1856), 341.

sure their circulation at or near par in every section. In return for its privileges the Bank had agreed to pay the government a bonus of $1,500,000 and to receive, transfer, and disburse federal funds without charge.

Because it accumulated masses of the notes of state-chartered banks in federal deposits and in the ordinary course of business, the Bank had an almost life and death power over these local institutions. By returning their notes promptly for redemption in specie, it could force the state banks to restrain their issues so as to have ample specie reserves on hand. By extending or restricting its own issues, it could encourage the state banks to follow suit, thus regulating the expansion and contraction of credit and producing inflation or deflation. When properly managed, the Bank served as a balance wheel for the entire economy, restraining the state banks in times of inflationary pressure and coming to their aid in periods of stringency.

Yet this puissant institution was essentially a private, profit-making enterprise, four-fifths owned by private stockholders, who chose twenty of the twenty-five directors. The government's only check on the Bank, aside from the five directors appointed by the president, was the secretary of the treasury's power to remove the government deposits from its vaults.

The Bank had been poorly managed in its early years, but it began to prosper in 1823, when Nicholas Biddle moved into the president's room of its imposing Grecian temple on Philadelphia's Chestnut Street. This brilliant financier had perceived the Bank's potentialities as a central banking institution, and his administration had proven both profitable to the stockholders and beneficial to the national economy. Justly proud of his accomplishments, Biddle was understandably contemptuous of the financial abilities of politicians. Jackson's election worried Biddle, for the Bank was becoming concerned over a renewal of its charter, which would expire in 1836. Biddle, like Jackson, was a man of decided opinions and accustomed to having his way. With two such leaders and with substantial economic and political interests at stake, the recharter question was full of explosive possibilities.

II

Old Republicans had always been suspicious of banks in general and national banks in particular. Jefferson himself had thought that "banking establishments are more dangerous than standing armies," while the Virginia philosopher of Jeffersonianism, John Taylor of Caroline, had flayed the "paper system" in book after book as a fraud whereby wealth was transferred from the laboring and productive many to a privileged, parasitic few. The "artificial" or "fictitious" type of property represented by bank stock and bank notes, Taylor argued, was plundering the people, destroying the old agrarian America, and raising up a financial aristocracy.[3]

The strident protests of the Old Republicans had fallen with little effect on the exuberantly nationalistic America of the years after the War of 1812. But when the Panic of 1819 engendered a ground swell of opposition to the probusiness American System, a reborn Republicanism found itself indebted to the little group that had preserved its philosophy. Taylor's disciples, the brilliant but half-mad Virginian John Randolph and the aged Nathaniel Macon of North Carolina, the archetype of plain republicanism, were still in Congress in the mid-1820's to provide inspiration and ideology for Polk and other young men bent on resurrecting the Jeffersonian faith.

The Bank would have had little to fear had its opposition arisen from this ideological source alone. But down in Tennessee Governor Carroll spoke for farmers who had been taught by hard times that banks were inimical to their interests; and eastern workingmen were coupling their campaigns for free public schools and against imprisonment for debt with demands that "the present system of banking and paper money" be curbed, lest "the great body of the working people must give over all hopes of ever acquiring any property."[4] Thus several important groups of "hard-money" men—Old Republicans and hard-pressed farmers and workingmen—were becoming hostile to all banks, state or national.

Still other attacks on the Bank came from a quite different source. The postwar boom had tended to break down the Hamiltonian conception of an exclusive business elite. Farmers and country storekeepers, as well as Boston merchants and Philadelphia financiers, had had visions of quickly won riches and had set up a cry for the abundant credit without which none of these visions could come true.

[3] Sister M. Grace Madeleine, *Monetary and Banking Theories of Jacksonian Democracy* (Philadelphia, 1943), 20; Eugene Tenbroeck Mudge, *The Social Philosophy of John Taylor of Caroline* (New York, 1939), 172-180.

[4] Philadelphia *Free Trade Advocate*, 16 May 1829.

Compliant legislatures responded by chartering hordes of local banks, and these petty institutions, often with no real capital, promptly began to flood the country with their notes. These poorly backed notes depreciated, of course, and soon there were a hundred different currencies, each depreciated at a different rate.

It was partly to meet this situation that the Second Bank of the United States had been chartered in 1816. When the national bank forced the local banks to resume redeeming their notes in specie, thus curtailing their note issues and profits, it became highly unpopular with a whole class of new men on the make, who looked to the local banks for credit. Several states promptly inserted prohibitions against banks not chartered by themselves in their constitutions, and six other states levied prohibitive taxes on banks chartered outside their borders. Feeling against the national bank reached a peak when the Bank overextended itself so recklessly that it was able to survive the Panic of 1819 only by a severe contraction that was disastrous to scores of equally overextended local banks, their thousands of incautious borrowers, and the hundreds of thousands in whose hands their bank notes depreciated. Only Chief Justice Marshall's decisions in McCulloch *v.* Maryland and Osborn *v.* Bank of the United States saved the Bank from destruction at the hands of vengeful state legislatures.

The whole situation was symptomatic of a fundamental revolution in American life. Entrepreneurship was being democratized. To nascent capitalists in every village of the land, democracy was coming to mean equal opportunity for exploiting the boundless wealth of an expanding economy. Such men insisted that the Hamiltonian alliance between government and a favored few must be destroyed, so that the largesse could be opened to all the enterprising. This spirit of entrepreneurial democracy was of a very different quality from neo-Jeffersonianism, though both attitudes were often found incongruously mixed in the same individual. Just as the two impulses had united in the attack on the national banking monopoly in 1819, so they united nine years later to put Andrew Jackson in the White House. Nicholas Biddle had good reason to be worried; he would have been even more worried had he known as much as Congressman Polk knew about Andrew Jackson and his views on banks.

III

The national bank question was by no means new to Polk, Jackson, or any other prominent Tennessean. Back in 1817, when the national bank was just going into operation, William Carroll and other leading Nashville merchants, desiring sound commercial credit and disgusted with the speculative policies of the state-chartered Knoxville and Nashville banks and with the political machinations of the Overton faction, had enlisted Felix Grundy's aid in an effort to get a branch of the new institution for Tennessee. The Overton men, under the leadership of Hugh Lawson White, then president of the Knoxville Bank, had promptly induced the legislature to lay a prohibitive $50,000 tax on any bank chartered outside the state and to charter ten new village banks, one of them being the Columbia bank in which Sam Polk and James Walker were moving spirits. All of these petty institutions quickly became branches of the two older banks, and their supporters were thus tied in with the powerful state banking interest and the Overton faction. Carroll and the Nashville merchants, on the other hand, were thrown into the arms of the Erwin faction, and it was in this way that Carroll became the anti-Overton, anti-state-bank candidate for governor in 1821.[5]

Jackson, like Overton and White, had opposed this effort to secure a branch of the national bank for Tennessee, regarding it as a movement of "the arristocratic few in Nashville."[6] But unlike the Overton men, he opposed the national bank on Old Republican, hard-money, strict constructionist grounds, which made him equally inimical to state banks. "Every one that knows me," he later told Polk, "does know that I have been always opposed to the U. States Bank, nay all Banks."[7] In 1820, when Grundy's plan for a state-operated bank was pending, Jackson wrote to Major Lewis that "the constitution of our State, as well as the constitution of the United States prohibits the establishment of Banks in every State."[8] Under Grundy's scheme, he argued, "the imprudent speculator may be enabled to extricate himself from his pecuniary embarrassments but the burthen must ultimately fall upon the honest farmer and industrious tradesman."[9]

The collapse of the old banks in 1826-1827, as soon as they were

[5] Charles G. Sellers, Jr., "Banking and Politics in Jackson's Tennessee, 1817-1827," *Mississippi Valley Historical Review*, xli (June 1954), 65-66.

[6] Jackson to T. H. Benton, n.d., draft, Andrew Jackson Papers (LC), Vol. cxvii, No. 132.

[7] Jackson to Polk, 23 Dec. 1833, James K. Polk Papers (LC; herein cited as Polk Papers, which refers to First Series unless otherwise noted).

[8] Jackson to W. B. Lewis, 16 July 1820, Ford Collection (NYPL).

[9] Nashville *Whig*, 26 July 1820.

forced to resume specie payments, brought a renewed effort to secure a Tennessee branch of the national bank. Very quietly the Nashville merchants launched a campaign to induce the legislature to repeal the $50,000 tax on foreign banks. Jackson rushed to Nashville as soon as he got wind of this "secrete and combined movement of the arristocracy," but he found the bill had already passed the lower house. Despite his expostulations with members of the senate, it squeaked through its final reading by the margin of a single vote. Shortly thereafter, on petition of Carroll and his allies, the Bank opened a branch at Nashville and was soon financing most of the crop and commercial transactions of Middle Tennessee. When Van Buren's emissary, Major Hamilton, visited the Hermitage some months later, Jackson was still fulminating against the Bank.[10]

The organization of the Nashville branch saw the beginning of a *rapprochement* between the Overton men and their old antagonists, the Nashville merchants of the Erwin-Carroll faction. Overton's newspaper organ, the Nashville *Republican,* had advocated repeal of the foreign bank tax, and his friends joined the Carroll men in managing the new institution. Nicholas Biddle had consulted Eaton and Lewis about the branch directors, and among those appointed were Overton himself and Polk's brother-in-law James Walker, while the cashier of the defunct Nashville branch of White's Knoxville Bank became cashier of the new branch of the national bank.[11]

Jackson was not mollified by these favors to his associates. The presidential election was hardly over before he began planning his campaign against the Bank. He wanted to include the subject in his inaugural address, but Overton and Lewis persuaded him to defer it until his first annual message. The Bank question did not lie completely dormant, however. While Jackson was still planning his inaugural address, a Western District newspaper, the Jackson *Gazette,* began an editorial assault on the national bank and the whole credit system. Nashville interests were responsible for introducing the Bank into Tennessee, charged the *Gazette,* with the result that "the people are oppressed, and a monied aristocracy is about to rise up in our state, which will control its financial concerns." Candidates

---

[10] Jackson to Benton, n.d., draft, Jackson Papers, cxvii, No. 132; Sellers, "Banking and Politics," *loc.cit.,* 78; *Reminiscences of James A. Hamilton . . .* (New York, 1869), 69.

[11] Nashville *Republican,* 25 Nov. 1826, 19 July 1830; Ralph C. H. Catterall, *The Second Bank of the United States* (Chicago, 1903), 246-247.

for Congress, the editor declared, should be forced to say whether they favored recharter.[12]

The same line of attack was taken up a few months later by an old friend of the Polks, Judge John Catron of the state supreme court. A poor, self-educated farm boy from the mountains, Catron had risen to eminence at the bar and would later become a justice of the United States Supreme Court. He now addressed himself through the Nashville newspapers "TO THE CULTIVATORS OF THE SOIL, AND LABORING PEOPLE OF TENNESSEE," on the subject of the credit system and the national bank.

The judge was alarmed by the tremendous expansion of credit that had occurred since the Nashville branch opened. The national bank, he charged, had encouraged the people to borrow beyond all bounds of prudence and was making usurious interest on its loans, so that tremendous profits were being drained out of the state, while the people were going ever deeper into debt. This ruinous expansion of credit might be checked, Catron suggested, by a law barring loans on personal security of debtors and their endorsers; but more important, recharter of Mr. Biddle's bank must be prevented. If there had to be a national bank, Catron argued, let it be truly national. Let the president appoint the directors. Let branches be established only on petition of legislatures, and let the legislatures appoint the branch directors. Let a branch's capital be limited to the amount of stock owned within its state, and make the stock subject to state and federal taxation.[13]

Catron's campaign against the Bank opened just two months before Tennesseans went to the polls to elect the legislature that would choose Eaton's successor in the Senate. Shortly after the judge's original communication appeared, the newspapers began to carry anonymous notices demanding that legislative candidates take a position on the issues he had raised. Soon critics were charging that Catron's whole purpose was to affect the legislative and senatorial elections.

Jackson's choice to fill the senatorial vacancy was Felix Grundy, but at the time Catron opened his anti-Bank campaign it appeared that Grundy might be defeated. Just three weeks earlier Jackson

[12] Polk to Jackson, 23 Dec. 1833, Polk Papers; Jackson to Polk, 23 Dec. 1833 (on the same sheet as the preceding), *ibid.*; Jackson *Gazette*, 13 Dec. 1828, 17, 31 Jan. 1829.

[13] Nashville *Republican*, 12, 26, 30 June, 3, 7 July 1829.

had written asking Grundy's advice about some such federal fiscal agency as Catron had in mind. When the legislature met, it instructed Tennessee's senators to vote against recharter, and Grundy won the senatorial election. Immediately thereafter Grundy replied to Jackson, outlining a plan of his own, which differed from Catron's only in minor details. It seems likely that Catron's campaign was undertaken in concert with Jackson and for the purpose of either forcing Grundy into line with the president's position on the Bank, or electing to the Senate some more amenable politician, probably Catron's friend Judge William E. Anderson.[14]

There is still another possible explanation. It seems significant that Catron was numbered with Alfred Balch and William Carroll among the earliest and most enthusiastic champions of Martin Van Buren in Tennessee. Did this affair have some connection with the little coterie of Van Buren supporters Balch claimed to have been recruiting? Van Buren had declared his opposition to the Bank as early as 1826, and Balch, who was in the New Yorker's confidence, dated his organizing activities from about the same period. In one of his anti-Bank articles, Catron revealed that he had always been opposed to the national bank, that he had been mulling over the defects of the paper credit system for a decade, and that "some of us" had "for years been pledged to stand together boldly and firmly when the day should arrive for the execution of a policy new in these states, & which is to be great in effect."[15] Catron, Balch, and Carroll were still working together as late as 1835, when the first two pushed Carroll for the Democratic vice presidential nomination. And it was Van Buren who elevated Catron to the federal Supreme Court.

Were these Tennessee politicians, perhaps on the basis of hints from Van Buren, trying at the outset of Jackson's administration to make Jacksonism synonymous with Van Burenism, and Jackson–Van Burenism synonymous with anti-Bankism? At any rate Catron, Balch, and Carroll would all remain steadfastly anti-Bank and pro–Van Buren, while most of the Overton-Eaton-Lewis group was going over to the Whigs.

14 *ibid.*, 19 June, 24 July 1829; Jackson *Gazette*, 27 June 1829; Nashville *Banner*, 22 Aug. 1829; Grundy to Jackson, 22 May, 22 Oct. 1829, Jackson Papers; Carroll to Jackson, 25 May 1829, *ibid.*; Daniel Graham to A. J. Donelson, 2 Feb. 1829, Andrew Jackson Donelson Papers (LC); Edward Everett, Diary (MHS), 28 May 1829.
15 Nashville *Republican*, 12 June 1829.

IV

We can be sure, in any event, that Catron and his coadjutors reflected Jackson's own position on the Bank question. The president insisted on expressing his views in his first annual message to Congress, in December 1829, and his remarks fell like a thunderbolt on the Bank forces. "Both the constitutionality and the expediency of the law creating this Bank," the President declared, "are well questioned by a large portion of our fellow-citizens; and it must be admitted by all, that it has failed in the great end of establishing a uniform and sound currency." To Jackson, as to other hard-money men, "a uniform and sound currency" was gold and silver coin, or at least notes readily convertible, anytime or anywhere, into the precious metals.

The president did not deny that some kind of national fiscal agency might be deemed essential. But if this were the case, he said, let it be truly national, founded wholly on the credit and revenues of the government, and avoiding the constitutional objections to the existing Bank. Obviously what Jackson had in mind was not a "bank" in any conventional sense. He was not to make a specific proposal for another year, but meanwhile he discovered in Senator Thomas Hart Benton a man congenial to his own radical views on banking. It was Benton who brought to Jackson's attention the similar schemes of John Randolph and the Philadelphia reformer Stephen Simpson for a national exchequer bank, founded on the public funds, forbidden to make loans, but selling bills of exchange to facilitate the transfer of private funds from place to place. As a national institution of large resources it would be able to restrain the state banks and preserve a specie-redeemable currency. This was substantially the plan that Jackson proposed to Congress in his second annual message of December 1830.[16]

The ever sanguine Biddle, however, refused to believe that Jackson meant what he plainly said, and continued to hope that the Bank might be rechartered with slight modifications to meet the presidential objections. This delusion was encouraged by the president's busy and irresponsible friend Major Lewis, and by the cordial disposition of the Cabinet after its reorganization in 1830. The new secretary of the treasury, Louis McLane, campaigned openly for

16 *House Journal*: 21st Cong.: 1st Sess., 27-28; T. H. Benton to A. J. Donelson, 17 Dec. 1829, Jackson Papers; Stephen Simpson to Jackson, 17 Dec. 1829 (on a printed circular), *ibid.*; John Randolph to Benton [17 Dec. 1829], copy, *ibid.*

recharter, and was permitted to argue for the Bank in his report to Congress in 1831.[17]

Andrew Jackson's firm resolution to do his duty as he saw it was the chief obstacle to Biddle's plans, but it was not the only one. The country was entering another boom period in the early thirties. With scores of canals and turnpikes completed or under way, steamboats revolutionizing the western economy, cotton bringing record prices, vast areas coming into cultivation for the first time, and the population growing rapidly, the entrepreneurial democracy, strident and impatient of restraint, was again becoming a major force in American life. Again it was the state banks that were the citadels of the entrepreneurial spirit, and again these local institutions chafed at the restrictions imposed on them by Biddle's policies.

This resentment of the national bank was most acute in New York, and in New York the Democracy was led by Martin Van Buren. Anti-Bankism was one of the main foundations on which Van Buren proposed to build his political power, and before the Jackson administration was a year old, Amos Kendall of the Kitchen Cabinet was reporting that the Bank issue was "a question upon which there will be no compromise." "It will come to this," predicted Kendall, "that whoever is in favor of that Bank will be against Old Hickory."[18]

In addition Jeffersonian state rights ideas were showing renewed vitality in many parts of the country, especially the South, and movements hostile to the Bank were receiving the support of ominously large numbers of state rights congressmen. Jeffersonianism, however, meant more than state rights to men like the ponderous Benton, who startled his senatorial colleagues with the declaration that "Gold and silver is the best currency for a republic; it suits the men of middle property and the working people best; and if I was going to establish a working man's party, it should be on the basis of hard money; a hard money party against a paper party."[19]

Similar sentiments were spreading in the eastern cities. New York merchants, ardent free traders already, were showing an aversion to monopoly in the banking field. In Philadelphia, the editor-economists William M. Gouge and Condy Raguet were fortifying John Taylor's critique of the paper system with principles drawn from

[17] Catterall, *Second Bank*, 186-214.
[18] Amos Kendall to F. P. Blair, 1 Mar. 1830, Blair-Lee Papers (PU).
[19] *Register of Debates*:21:2, pp. 74-75; Catterall, *Second Bank*, 165-167, 205-206.

Adam Smith and from David Ricardo's attack on the Bank of England, finding support for their ideas among intellectuals, philanthropists, the newly organized Workingmen's Association, and even among those who are best described as entrepreneurial democrats. These eastern hard-money men were to play an important role in the later phases of the Bank War, but the brunt of the earlier congressional battles was borne mainly by the Jeffersonian South and West, with powerful backing from the state banking interests.

Polk had first indicated his hostility to the Bank by supporting a resolution for sale of the government's Bank stock in 1827.[20] The Bank question did not arise again in the House until President Jackson made his sensational reference to the subject in his annual message of 1829. The congressional response to the president's remarks indicated that the established congressional leaders of the Jacksonian coalition were not to be counted on in a contest with the big corporation. Both the House Ways and Means Committee and the Senate Finance Committee brought in reports upholding the Bank and politely ridiculing Jackson's suggested substitute.

But other Jacksonians were spoiling for a fight with the Bank. A month after the Ways and Means Committee reported, a radical Jackson man from North Carolina, Robert Potter, introduced a series of resolutions declaring the national bank both unconstitutional and inexpedient. "The paper money, or banking system, generally," ran the resolutions, "is, in its tendency, ruinous to the *interests of labor*, and *dangerous to the liberties of the people*." Polk joined the anti-Bank men in laying these resolutions on the table to be taken up later, but the session ended before they could be brought to the floor.[21] When, in December 1830, Jackson submitted his plan for an alternative national fiscal agency, Polk again joined the anti-Bank men in an unsuccessful attempt to refer this section of the president's message to a special committee, rather than to George McDuffie's pro-Bank Ways and Means Committee.[22]

By the time the twenty-second Congress convened in December 1831, there was strong pressure for immediate recharter, and the Jackson men were deeply divided. The new, pro-Van Buren adminis-

---

20 *House Journal*:20:1, pp. 79-81. Polk actually voted with the other supporters of the resolution to lay it on the table, so it could be debated later. When the pro-Bank majority forced an immediate vote on the resolution, however, he was not willing to side with the nine members who supported it without debate.

21 *House Journal*:21:1, p. 620.

22 *House Journal*:21:2, p. 37; *Reg. Deb.*:21:2, pp. 50-75.

tration organ, Frank Blair's *Globe,* was taking an anti-Bank line, but the two leading members of the reorganized Cabinet, Edward Livingston of the State Department and Louis McLane of the Treasury, were telling Biddle that they could persuade the president to approve a modified charter, if only the question were not pressed until the next session, after the presidential election.

Jackson received additional pressure to permit recharter from some of his Tennessee friends. The fundamentally conservative Overton men were already showing a disposition to ally themselves with the Erwin faction in defense of the Bank. The Nashville *Republican* had deprecated Catron's attack on the Bank and his introduction of the Bank issue into the state elections of 1829, and from time to time it ran articles favorable to the Bank. The pro-Bank forces in the legislature were being led by the former anti-Overton stalwart Theoderick F. Bradford, who had succeeded to the command of the old Erwin organization in Bedford County. At the same time Eaton's kinsman Allen A. Hall, who edited the *Republican,* was supporting Congressman John Bell, the protégé of Governor Carroll and the Nashville merchants. Both Eaton and Lewis were working in Washington to convert the administration to the Bank's position, and Bell, while receiving increasingly favorable notice from the *Republican,* was observed to be on intimate terms with the pro-Bank Secretary McLane.[23]

Even before Congress met, these pro-Bank Jackson men had been alarmed by reports that the president would veto a recharter bill. Eaton had implored Jackson not to attack the Bank in his message. The tariff and internal improvement questions had been settled, he pointed out, and a fight over the Bank was the only remaining threat to the party's harmony and the administration's success. Yielding to this and similar pressure, the president contented himself with calling attention to his previous remarks on the subject. But as the sequel showed, Old Hickory had changed his mind not a bit.[24]

Nicholas Biddle was in great perplexity. If he relied on Livingston and McLane's promises that Jackson would consent to a modified charter after the presidential election, he ran the risk of offending

---

[23] Nashville *Republican,* 24 July 1829, 13 Jan. 1831, 14, 17 Apr. 1832; Nashville *Banner,* 20 July 1836; Catron to A. J. Donelson, 31 Dec. 1829, Donelson Papers; Jonathan Webster to Polk, 23 Apr. 1832, Polk Papers; Joseph Howard Parks, *John Bell of Tennessee* (Baton Rouge, 1950), 140.

[24] Eaton to Jackson, 5 Nov. 1831, Jackson Papers, Remnants; *House Journal*:22:1, p. 21.

Henry Clay, whom the National Republicans had already nominated to run against Jackson. Clay was anxious to have the recharter bill introduced at once, so that if Jackson did not approve it, his veto could be made an issue in the coming campaign. Under steady pressure from Clay, Biddle set his Washington lieutenants to a careful counting of heads in Congress. A safe majority, they found, would vote for recharter, and many others personally favored it, though their actual votes were doubtful. Felix Grundy, for example, opposed recharter at this session but would support it later, while John Bell "will vote with us *if he can*." Finally, in January 1832, apprehensive over Jackson's eventual course and reluctant to alienate the National Republicans, the Bank president made up his mind, and the memorial for a new charter was sent to Congress.[25]

The first test in the House came when McDuffie succeeded, by a vote of 100 to 90 (Bell voting for the motion and Polk against), in getting the Bank's memorial referred to his Ways and Means Committee. Jackson was now fully determined to defeat recharter, and leadership of the anti-Bank forces was given to Senator Benton. At Benton's instance, Representative Augustine S. Clayton, a new member from Georgia, presented on February 23 a list of damaging charges against the Bank and demanded an investigation before a vote was taken. The anti-Bank minority was playing for time. Clayton's charges were based mainly on suspicion, but if incriminating evidence could be uncovered, the Bank's enemies might still defeat the recharter bill. If not, they relied on a veto, in which case the evidence gathered by the investigation would make good ammunition for the presidential campaign.

The Clayton resolution caught the recharter forces off balance, and Polk led the anti-Bank men in a rush to exploit this opening. Reference of the subject to the Ways and Means Committee, he complained, had already indicated a disposition to push the new charter through without adequate consideration. Now, though grave charges had been made, there was great opposition to the request for an investigation. The public would naturally infer, Polk insinuated, "that there might be something 'rotten in the state of Denmark.' "[26]

[25] Reginald C. McGrane, ed., *The Correspondence of Nicholas Biddle Dealing with National Affairs, 1807-1844* (Boston, 1919), 156-157; Catterall, *Second Bank*, 206-224.

[26] *Reg. Deb.*:22:1, pp. 1898-1901; *House Journal*:22:1, p. 168; Catterall, *Second Bank*, 224-230.

Worried by these arguments and confident of his ultimate majority, McDuffie finally conceded the point. Clayton was named chairman and given a committee with an anti-Bank majority to proceed to Philadelphia and investigate his charges. None of the investigators was an expert on financial matters, and the Bank officials, of course, gave them no assistance in examining the corporation's books. Restricted in abilities, scope, and time, they came up with only a mass of undigested information. This was enough to enable the committee majority to assert that the Bank had violated its charter in several instances, but they failed to make out a convincing case in support of the original Benton-Clayton charges.[27]

The unexpected bid for recharter and the Clayton investigation had aroused great excitement throughout the country, and the Bank interests were making strenuous efforts to bring pressure on members of Congress. Polk had announced at once that he opposed recharter and had sent copies of Clayton's speech to his constituents. But his enemies at home were already at work. In Columbia a meeting was organized to pass resolutions favoring recharter, and the Maury County grand jury was induced to take the same position in a set of resolutions ingeniously drawn to appeal to Polk's hard-money convictions. Failure to recharter the Bank would be calamitous, said the jurors, "especially as withdrawal of its notes from circulation would produce a scarcity of money, which would induce the legislature to resort to relief laws and establishment of innumerable local banks with authority to issue notes on a fictitious capital and thus aggravate the situation."[28]

In Bedford County, Polk's old enemy Bradford, who was preparing to oppose him for Congress the following year, was busy circulating petitions for recharter and organizing a pro-Bank meeting at Shelbyville. Polk's friends, however, urged him not to be alarmed. "The Bank suits the merchants and speculators of all parties," he was told, "but once the farmers are led into an understanding of the matter, they will put down the Bank men in this county."[29]

The pro-Bank Jackson men were acutely embarrassed as events in Washington moved rapidly toward a veto and a strenuous presidential campaign on the Bank issue. In March, John Bell took the

---

[27] *Reg. Deb.*:22:1, pp. 2160-2163; Catterall, *Second Bank*, 230.

[28] William Stockard and others to Polk, 28 Apr. 1832, Polk Papers; Thomas Harney to Polk, 16 Apr. 1832, *ibid.*; A. C. Hays to Polk, 17 Apr. 1832, *ibid.*; C. C. Mayson to Polk, 18 Apr. 1832, *ibid.*; T. H. Cahal to Polk, 4 May 1832, *ibid.*

[29] Jonathan Webster to Polk, 23 Apr., 3 May 1832, Polk Papers.

House floor to explain his position. He considered the Bank "important, if not essential to the safe and economical administration of the public revenues," but he implored the majority to delay the recharter bill until after the election.[30] The Nashville *Republican* was enthusiastic about Bell's speech. The editor could not "well conceive how an impartial mind can resist the force and conclusiveness of the reasons he urges for not acting on that subject this session of Congress." At the same time, the *Republican* went on, some kind of national bank was "absolutely necessary to the preservation of a sound currency throughout the Union."[31]

Neither Bell's entreaties nor the Clayton investigation made any sensible impression on the Bank forces, and their disciplined majorities beat down every delaying tactic. When the bill passed the House by a vote of 107 to 85, it was opposed by all the Tennesseans except Jacob Isacks, who had already broken with Jackson over the internal improvements issue, and Thomas D. Arnold, who had finally gotten into Congress. Bell would probably have supported the Bank had his vote been necessary, but under the circumstances he thought it better to avoid a break with the president.[32]

The bill reached the White House on July 4. Against the wishes of every member of his Cabinet except Attorney General Roger B. Taney, Old Hickory persevered in his determination to disapprove it. On July 10 his celebrated Bank Veto went to Congress. Jackson's case against the Bank laid heavy stress on its exclusive privileges, an approach calculated to appeal to the rising spirit of entrepreneurial democracy. This was supplemented with a persuasive constitutional argument contributed by Attorney General Taney. Denying that the president must be guided in his constitutional opinions by the Supreme Court, the message attacked Marshall's famous decision in McCulloch *v.* Maryland and pronounced the Bank unconstitutional. A denunciation of the foreign ownership of much of the Bank's stock was also included, in deference to the prejudices of that segment of the population not susceptible to constitutional reasonings.

The hard-money convictions that underlay the objections of the Veto's authors—Jackson himself, Taney, and Amos Kendall—were only hinted at. The president did assert that gold and silver coin

[30] Nashville *Republican*, 14 Apr. 1832.   [31] *ibid.*, 17 Apr. 1832.
[32] *House Journal*:22:1, pp. 877, 1036-1037, 1057, 1069, 1074; C. F. Mercer to Biddle, 27 Jan. 1832, Nicholas Biddle Papers (LC).

"are the only currency known to the Constitution." But to venture beyond this would be to alienate the powerful state banking interests, whose aid was needed to win the impending election. After that, there would be time enough for further reform.

The real heart of the message was the eloquent paragraph expounding the social philosophy behind the whole Jacksonian program:

> It is to be regretted that the rich and powerful too often bend the acts of government to their selfish purposes. Distinctions in society will always exist under every just government. Equality of talents, of education, or of wealth can not be produced by human institutions. In the full enjoyment of the gifts of Heaven and the fruits of superior industry, economy, and virtue, every man is equally entitled to protection by law; but when the laws undertake to add to these natural and just advantages artificial distinctions, to grant titles, gratuities, and exclusive privileges, to make the rich richer and the potent more powerful, the humble members of society—the farmers, mechanics, and laborers—who have neither the time nor the means of securing like favors to themselves, have a right to complain of the injustice of their government. There are no necessary evils in government. Its evils exist only in its abuses. If it would confine itself to equal protection, and, as Heaven does its rains, shower its favors alike on the high and the low, the rich and the poor, it would be an unqualified blessing.[33]

The Bank men fumed for the record, but they did not have the votes to override the veto. Congress went home amid noisy overtures to what both sides announced would be a great national referendum. When the dust of battle settled in November, the results showed 219 electoral votes for Jackson and 40 for Clay.

To a lesser man than Nicholas Biddle this would have been decisive. But in Philadelphia the Bank's president announced: "The bank does not mean to commence any systematic reduction of its loans with a view to winding up its affairs. It does not mean to begin to close its concerns. It means to go on in its general business just as if no such event as the President's negative had ever happened."[34] In supposing he could force the government to change its policy after the people had rendered their verdict, Biddle was making the mistake of his life.

The Bank's decision to continue the struggle only strengthened Jackson's conviction that the "Monster of Chestnut Street" must be destroyed forthwith. But first there would have to be some changes

---

[33] James D. Richardson, comp., *A Compilation of the Messages and Papers of the Presidents, 1789-1902* (10 vols., Washington, 1905), II, 576-591.

[34] *Biddle Correspondence*, 198.

in the president's following. The skirmish over recharter had demonstrated beyond question the Jackson party's need for new leadership in Congress. Representative Polk had played only a minor role in the Bank War so far, but he had established a record of undeviating support for the president's position, and his effective work on other issues had impressed his Democratic colleagues. The next two sessions would make James K. Polk a national figure.

V

The heavy responsibilities that would be thrust upon the Tennessee congressman were still some months away when Congress adjourned in July 1832, hard on the heels of the Bank Veto. Traveling at a leisurely pace in their own carriage, with the faithful Elias on the box, James and Sarah had a pleasant trip home. Legislative duties, strenuous though they were, actually occupied less than half of James's time, for even the long sessions in alternate years rarely sat later than July. But there was much to do at home in the summers and autumns.

The family continued to be a heavy responsibility. Though James professed not to be dissatisfied that he had no children of his own, one of his friends ventured the opinion that "however indifferent *Gentlemen* may *appear* as to this *privation,* their *'better part'* are on this point much more sensitive."[35] The attention that James and Sarah might have bestowed on their own children was largely transferred to his younger brothers and nieces and nephews. The family's losses in these years were heartbreaking, especially to James's widowed mother. Frank, the second brother, died an alcoholic in January 1831 at the age of twenty-eight. Marshall, who had taken his young wife back to North Carolina and established himself as a lawyer in Charlotte, died four months later, leaving two small children and an encumbered estate. The death of still a third brother, John, the bachelor farmer, came also in the same year. James assumed responsibility for the three estates and for Marshall's little family.[36]

The last of his sisters had married in 1829, when seventeen-year-old Ophelia became the wife of a Columbia physician, Doctor John B. Hays. Abundantly endowed with the hotheadedness and instability that cropped out so frequently among the Polks, Ophelia

[35] W. D. Moseley to Polk, 1 Dec. 1830, Polk Papers.
[36] Family Bible, Sam Polk House; James Walker to Polk, 20 Nov. 1832, Polk Papers.

promptly proceeded to make life miserable for her husband, her servants, and her relations. Her tantrums were endangering her marriage, and James was continually being called in to untangle unpleasant situations. Ophelia was so clearly to blame that her own family sided against her, one of the brothers-in-law hoping that Doctor Hays could be persuaded "to lock her up and conquer her by force if nothing else will do."[37]

Jane Polk was now left with only the two boys, Bill and Sam, aged sixteen and fourteen. All her hopes were pinned on them, and James took special interest in their welfare. It was decided that Bill should follow the older brothers to the University of North Carolina, and in 1832 he was sent for preparatory training to the excellent Bingham School at Hillsborough, near Chapel Hill. Bill, too, had the temperamental wildness of most of his brothers, and James entreated old Colonel William Polk, who had agreed to supervise the boy, to "controul him whilst at school precisely as you would your own son."[38] But when Bill got to Chapel Hill, all the precautions went for naught, and he quickly ran into debt. "It is painful to perceive," his guardians, Polk and James Walker, were soon writing in familiar strain, "that your whole mind seems to be ingrossed to effect the object of getting money," and they laid down the law as to how much would be allowed him.[39] Only Sam, the baby of the family, as yet caused his mother and brother no great worry. His winning disposition made him a universal favorite, and James and Sarah were particularly fond of this youngest brother.

Polk's business interests also demanded much attention. Though he had little time for legal practice, he found it expedient to enter a partnership with a young Columbia lawyer. Polk furnished the prestige and occasional advice and arguments, but the younger man handled most of the business, with profits being split evenly. Besides this, James still had on his hands large amounts of land belonging to the estates of Sam Polk and Major Childress, both of which were still in process of liquidation. And James himself, by inheritance,

[37] A. O. Harris to Polk, 17 Dec. 1833, Polk Papers; James Walker to Polk, 5 Dec. 1830, 14 Dec. 1833, *ibid.*; Ophelia C. Hays to Polk, 14 Dec. [1833], *ibid.*; Sarah Polk to Mary A. Polk, 29 Dec. 1834, Polk-Dillon Papers (SHC).

[38] J. K. Polk to Col. William Polk, 28 Nov. 1832, Polk-Yeatman Papers (SHC).

[39] J. K. Polk and James Walker to W. H. Polk, 16 Apr. 1834, Polk Papers; W. H. Polk to J. K. Polk, 16 Jan. 1834, *ibid.*; J. K. Polk to Col. William Polk, 5 Jan. 1834, Polk Family of North Carolina Papers (LC).

speculation, and purchase, had become the owner of extensive Western District lands requiring management.[40]

It was probably in the winter of 1831-1832 that he began clearing a 970-acre tract in Fayette County, in the southwestern corner of the state, for a cotton plantation. He had fifteen slaves at this time, of whom three were "family Negroes" used as domestics in Columbia and Washington. The rest, probably supplemented with slaves rented from the estates of his deceased brothers, were sent to the new plantation.

The first year of cultivation was not very successful, only fourteen bales of cotton and some corn being produced. The overseer promised that he would be able to cultivate 125 acres of cotton and the same amount of corn the next season, but James Walker advised his brother-in-law that the man was too obstinate to be a good manager, and a new overseer was employed. Wherever the fault lay, sickness was the greatest problem on the plantation, with ten or eleven of the Negroes frequently being ill at once. Walker and another brother-in-law, Doctor Caldwell, who operated a plantation in a neighboring county, acted as Polk's agents when he was away attending Congress.[41]

Though Polk like many other southerners deplored slavery in the abstract, he cannot be classed among the liberal men of the South. He was a realist on most questions, and here his realism meant harshness. When the House was debating a bill to establish a penitentiary for the District of Columbia in 1830, Polk opposed substituting imprisonment for physical punishment so far as slaves were concerned. The question should be decided, in his opinion, wholly on the grounds of what was most expedient for disciplining the slave population. "A slave dreads the punishment of stripes more than he does imprisonment," Polk asserted, "and that description of punishment has, besides, a beneficial effect upon his fellow-slaves." Imprisonment, he thought, did not amount "to such an efficient restraint as was necessary under the peculiar circumstances of such cases."[42]

VI

While Polk's slaves were picking the last meager cotton bolls out

[40] Articles of agreement, 2 Nov. 1830, Polk Papers; Sam Polk Account Book, *ibid.*
[41] Walker to Polk, 24 Jan. 1833, Polk Papers; will of J. K. Polk, 24 Oct. 1831, *ibid.*; John Spencer Bassett, ed., *The Southern Plantation Overseer As Revealed in His Letters* (Northampton, Mass., 1925), 35-51.
[42] *Reg. Deb.*:21:1, p. 824.

of his stump-strewn clearings in West Tennessee in the fall of 1832, a situation was developing in Washington that would catapult their master into leadership of the Jackson forces in the House of Representatives. Andrew Jackson knew his veto had not killed the Bank. Its charter still had three years to run, and the president feared that with its power to bring pressure on the business community, its loans to politicians, and its subsidies of the press, it might yet muster the support of the two thirds of Congress necessary to override a veto. Much of the Bank's continuing financial power rested on its retention of the public deposits, and even before his triumphant reelection Jackson had discussed the idea of transferring the deposits to the state banks. The election returns were still coming in when he called his Cabinet together to consider means of dealing a final blow to the institution.[43]

At this juncture the nullification crisis intervened, and when Congress met in December 1832, the president was preoccupied with measures to crush the Calhounites. But he did not forget his designs against the Bank. His annual message recommended that the government's Bank stock be sold, and went on to describe Biddle's recent maneuvers to avoid paying off the government's bondholders on schedule. The Treasury had already appointed an agent to investigate this apparent inability to furnish the public funds when called for, and he had found the Bank to be perfectly solvent. But the president was obviously dissatisfied with the Treasury report and argued that the Treasury's powers were inadequate to get to the bottom of the Bank's real condition. "The credit which is given throughout the country to many serious charges impeaching its character," Jackson asserted, "may justly excite the apprehension that it is no longer a safe depository for the money of the people." Accordingly he urged Congress to make a full investigation of the Bank and its branches.[44]

It was at this session that Polk was transferred to the Ways and Means Committee. On this, the most powerful committee of the House, formerly headed by the pro-Bank Calhounite George McDuffie, the administration's success at this session largely depended. Not only would it write the tariff bill on which settlement of the nullification crisis hinged, but any Bank investigation would also

---

[43] Duff Green to Calhoun, 23 Oct. 1832, Duff Green Papers (in possession of Prof. Fletcher M. Green, Chapel Hill, N.C.); Green to Milton Gregg, 24 Oct. 1832, *ibid.*; Carl Brent Swisher, *Roger B. Taney* (New York, 1936), 207-285.
[44] *House Journal*:22:2, p. 15.

fall within its province. There was considerable discontent among the Jacksonian congressmen when the New York free trader Verplanck was raised to the chairmanship with a special view to the tariff question. Some members recalled his indignant reaction to the Bank Veto at the previous session, and one of them complained to Frank Blair of the *Globe* that "Col. Polk . . . was the proper person to fill that highly responsible station."[45] Van Buren may well have been responsible for the choice. Content with the Bank Veto and reluctant to see the political waters roiled by needless agitation, the cautious New Yorker was apprehensive of the headstrong president's aggressive plans for further assaults on the Bank.

When Polk did not get the chairmanship, it was a foregone conclusion that he would fill the remaining committee vacancy. With the Clayton fiasco fresh in mind, the administration certainly needed one of its ablest and most reliable supporters on this crucial committee. Polk owed his promotion partly to his standing with his fellow Jacksonians in the House and partly to the president. He had no close friends in the administration's inner circle. Major Lewis and his Kitchen Cabinet associates had no love for Polk. Nor, on the basis of Polk's record to date, could Van Buren have had much enthusiasm for him. The president himself must have finally taken a hand in the matter. He had been in Tennessee during the summer and had undoubtedly discussed political matters with Polk.

Even with Polk, the Ways and Means Committee was far from safe on the Bank issue. Of the six other members only Mark Alexander, a veteran Virginia Jeffersonian, and Nathan Gaither of Kentucky could be relied on. Ranged on the other side of the question were Chairman Verplanck, Ralph I. Ingersoll of Connecticut, and Richard H. Wilde, a Georgia Calhounite. Control of the committee hinged on an inconspicuous Pennsylvania Democrat, John Gilmore, and to this unhappy individual both sides proceeded to apply all the pressures they could command.

Because of this uncertain situation, the administration decided to have the Bank question referred to a special committee, and Polk found himself in the awkward position of opposing reference to the committee of which he was a member. Ridiculing the Treasury report on the delayed payment of the national debt as a mere compendium of the Bank's monthly statements, he insisted that the episode showed

[45] Jesse Speight to F. P. Blair, 22 Mar. 1833, Blair-Lee Papers.

the Bank's inability to continue without the public deposits, a situation that called for thorough investigation.

Biddle's agent in Congress, Representative John G. Watmough of Pennsylvania, did not dare refuse an investigation entirely, but he was finally able to get the matter referred to the Ways and Means Committee, which already had its hands full with the tariff and appropriation bills. Thus, Watmough informed the Bank president, the investigation would be delayed and the investigators would be unable to extend their inquiries to Philadelphia. Best of all, he concluded, "we shew the nation that Congress notwithstanding all the Executive influence was brought to bear on the question, could not be induced to travel out of the ordinary track."[46] In the long run, though, the Bank men had made a serious mistake, for by their action the task of discrediting the Bank was placed mainly on the shoulders of the tenacious and ambitious James K. Polk.

The committee was so preoccupied with preparing and defending its tariff bill that not until January 23 did it get around to Bank matters, and then it proceeded first to the question of selling the government's stock. President Jackson was particularly insistent on this action because it would hasten final payment of the federal debt, but the committee could not agree on the terms of sale. Polk was working closely with Secretary McLane, finally getting him to draw up a bill, which Polk then managed to push through the committee.

When Polk reported the bill to the House on February 13 for its first reading, the alert Bank men objected to its even being considered. Polk's former ally Charles Wickliffe of Kentucky, who had long since gone over to the opposition, charged that the measure was merely a preliminary to a more important one. "The Government deposites are to be withdrawn," he predicted. "They are wanted elsewhere! State banks are to be enlisted as soldiers in the next campaign. The Government deposites are wanted to pay the bounty." Polk could only weakly deny these allegations, and his bill was promptly killed by a nine-vote majority.[47] As Watmough reported the episode to Biddle, Polk "was in hopes to have sneaked the Bill into the House unobserved. Nothing could have exceeded his mod-

---

[46] John G. Watmough to Biddle, 13 Dec. 1832, Biddle Papers; *id.* to *id.*, 15-16 Dec. 1832, *ibid.*; C. A. Wickliffe to Biddle, 13 Dec. 1832, *ibid.*; *House Journal*:22:2, p. 22; *Reg. Deb.*:22:2, pp. 833, 840, 849-851.

[47] *Reg. Deb.*:22:2, p. 1710; *ibid.*, 1707-1722; Louis McLane to Polk, 8, 9 Feb. 1833, n.d. (placed at end of 1833), Polk Papers; Samuel Jaudon to Biddle, 21, 23 Jan. 1833, Biddle Papers.

esty." But, Watmough exulted, "we caught him (*in flagrente delicto*), saw his weakness, pounced upon him, did not give him or his coadjutors a moment even to breathe & ended by entirely rejecting the Bill."[48]

But this was only a side issue. Jackson was impatient for the investigation, which he counted on to give him a pretext for removing the deposits. The session was only two weeks old when the president sent Polk evidence to support his contention that "the hydra of corruption is only *scotched, not dead*," and that Biddle hoped to secure sufficient votes to recharter the Bank despite a veto. "An investigation kills it and its supporters *dead*," said Jackson. "Let this be had—call upon the sec' of the Treasury who must agree with me that an investigation by Congress is absolutely necessary." To these instructions he added a peremptory postscript: "Have Sullivan, a Government director before the committee—attend to this. A.J."[49]

John T. Sullivan had been in Washington for some time complaining to all who would listen that the five directors appointed by the government were barred from the Bank's management, and also making sensational charges about the Bank's corrupt loans to newspapers and members of Congress. Sullivan was not the only anti-Bank lobbyist. Probably the Bank's most dangerous enemy next to Jackson himself was Reuben M. Whitney, a Philadelphia businessman and former director of the Bank, who for some reason had contracted an implacable hatred for Biddle and his institution. Intimate with Amos Kendall, Whitney became a trusted adviser to the president, the Kitchen Cabinet, and the Treasury Department on Bank matters.

The Bank, for its part, was well supplied with lobbyists, two of whom were members of the House. Watmough was deeply indebted to the Bank and served as Biddle's faithful lackey in Congress, reporting to him several times a week and executing all his orders. "I shall live in the hope to repay you the vast debt I owe you," he wrote to Biddle, "both on the score of gratitude & affection & of money, by an ardent exertion of all the energies I possess to that end." A much abler man than Watmough was the distinguished Philadelphia lawyer and counsel to the Bank, Horace Binney, who had been per-

[48] Watmough to Biddle, 13 Feb. 1833, Biddle Papers.
[49] Jackson to Polk, 16 Dec. 1832, Polk Papers.

suaded to come to Congress for the express purpose of defending the institution.[50]

Still a third Bank representative, the cashier of the Philadelphia office, Samuel Jaudon, was sent to reinforce Watmough and Binney when the committee finally embarked on its investigation. Jaudon was selected partly because he had married a daughter of Hugh Lawson White's new wife. Senator White's first wife had died the previous year, and just before Congress met he had married his landlady, Mrs. Ann Peyton, the amiable widow in whose house White and the Polks had passed so many pleasant winters. Biddle now hoped that Mrs. White's son-in-law could induce the senator to take a more favorable view of the Bank, in which case, as the Bank president told Watmough, "the influence of that change on Mr. Polk of your House would probably be effectual."[51] The Whites were still sharing the old quarters on Pennsylvania Avenue with the Polks and some of their other companions of earlier years, but Mrs. White had, of course, risen above the status of landlady, and this was the last season the old mess would spend together.

Jaudon proceeded to White's quarters as soon as he reached Washington on January 18, but he failed to make any impression on the senator, or on Polk, who came in while he was there. It was just a week later that Polk persuaded the Ways and Means Committee to launch its investigation by calling as witnesses the five government directors and General Thomas Cadwalader, the Bank's agent in negotiating postponement of the government debt. At the insistence of other members of the committee, two additional directors representing the stockholders were called.[52]

From January 31 through February 21, the committee met regularly six days a week to interrogate the witnesses. Polk did most of the questioning, with Reuben Whitney serving as his prompter. In addition to drafting long lists of questions for Polk to ask the various witnesses, Whitney advised what lines of investigation would be most damaging to the Bank and suggested particular documents the Bank should be required to produce. Polk was also in regular consultation with Secretary McLane. At one point Whitney urged Polk to get McLane to appoint Amos Kendall a Treasury agent to make a certain investigation at Bank headquarters, but this plan

50 Watmough to Biddle, 28 Nov. 1834, Biddle Papers.
51 Biddle to Watmough, 13 Jan. 1833, Letter Books, Biddle Papers.
52 Jaudon to Biddle, 18, 19, 21, 23, 24 Jan. 1833, Biddle Papers.

did not work out, and Whitney himself shortly departed for Philadelphia. The Bank men now became alarmed and tried to force an immediate report. Only a week of the session remained, but Polk was able to secure a postponement in order to send for the additional evidence Whitney had uncovered.[53]

Before the hearings had progressed very far, it became apparent that the doubtful committeeman, Gilmore, following the lead of the Democratic governor of Pennsylvania, would side with the Bank and give it a majority. Consequently when the committee finally reported on March 1, the next to last day of the session, the majority proposed a resolution that the government deposits might safely be continued in the Bank. This recommendation was accompanied by a five-page report emphasizing that the Bank's assets far exceeded its liabilities, and asserting, on the authority of the directors, that the debts due it were sound. The majority almost completely ignored the postponement of the federal debt, arguing that most of the bonds had eventually been paid and the matter called for no further action.[54]

Polk, however, submitted a thirty-five page minority report, signed also by Alexander and Gaither, and the next day he offered a seven-page supplement, based on the documents received from Philadelphia too late for discussion in his earlier report. In addition the minority appended 134 pages of supporting testimony and documents. Polk could not have had more than a week after the conclusion of testimony to prepare his report. The committee had denied him an extra day to complete the task, and he had been able to do so only because Verplanck had accidentally left the majority report at home on the day he planned to submit it. Working under far greater handicaps than the abortive Clayton committee of the previous session, Polk accomplished his assignment magnificently, furnishing abundant materials for the anti-Bank agitation of the coming months and effectively paving the way for the president's removal of the government deposits.

Polk's report was an exhaustive examination of the Bank's attempt to postpone liquidation of the federal debt and the reasons for it. During 1831 and the first half of 1832, the rapidly mounting federal surplus deposited with the Bank had induced it to expand

[53] Reuben M. Whitney to Polk, 27 Jan. [1833; misplaced 1832], 9, 11 Feb. 1833, Polk Papers; Louis McLane to Polk, 4 Feb. 1833, *ibid.*
[54] *House Committee Reports*:22:2, No. 121, pp. 1-5.

its loans to such an extent that only by a severe contraction, if at all, would it be able to meet a sudden demand for a large amount. When in March 1832 the Treasury informed a startled Biddle that it would discharge six or seven millions of the federal debt in a little more than three months, he had rushed to Washington and persuaded Secretary McLane to postpone payment until October, agreeing that the Bank should pay the interest on the bonds during the period of extension. Meanwhile he was doing everything in his power to raise the necessary funds by calling in the Bank's loans. But these measures were insufficient, especially after the Treasury informed him in July 1832 that most of the remaining federal debt, some $13,000,000, would be paid off in October and January.

It was at this point that the desperate Bank president dispatched General Cadwalader to Europe to persuade the foreign holders of a large part of this debt not to submit their bonds for redemption, the Bank agreeing to pay the interest on them for three, six, or nine months longer. Unable to arrange for enough of the debt in this manner, Cadwalader finally entered into an agreement whereby the British financial firm of Barings was to buy up the bonds for the Bank and hold them. Aside from obstructing the government's financial plans, such a purchase of federal bonds by the Bank was expressly forbidden under its charter. When news of this arrangement found its way into a New York newspaper, Biddle tardily disavowed the Cadwalader contract, and the Bank was forced to secure a loan from Barings at a substantial rate of interest to pay the debt on schedule. Many bonds, however, were still withheld under Cadwalader's original plan, so that complete retirement of the federal debt was actually delayed until well into 1833.

Polk's minority report thoroughly exposed these irresponsible actions and expertly disposed of Biddle's flimsy excuses. But the heart of the report was its revelation of the shaky financial position that had forced the Bank into such transactions. The real trouble, as Polk demonstrated beyond all doubt, was the foolish extension of the Bank's loans at its western branches, particularly through bills of exchange based on the cotton crop. A planter was able to obtain the proceeds from his crop as soon as it was harvested by selling the Bank such a bill (an order to his agent in New Orleans to pay the face amount to the Bank at a future date), the Bank cashing the bill six months later when the cotton was sold in New Orleans, having deducted interest for this period from the amount paid the planter.

But both 1831 and 1832 had been years of poor yield, and there had not been enough funds at New Orleans to meet the bills when they fell due. Rather than suing its debtors, the Bank had generally met this situation by permitting them to draw new bills on other points, charging them a second time with interest and commissions. After a careful analysis of these operations at the Nashville branch, Polk's report concluded:

Upon the supposition that [the ten million dollars of western Bank debt] is all in the same condition as the bill debt at Nashville, at least *seven* out of the *ten* millions is secured by paper called *race-horse bills*, which is running from branch to branch, waiting for crops to be raised to meet them, and ruining the drawers with interest, exchange, commissions for endorsement and acceptance, and other expenses. . . . In our opinion, no system of banking operations could be invented more desolating and fatal to the trading and planting community of the west than this extension of bank credits and over-trading in domestic exchange.

It was the amount of the Bank's resources tied up in this business that had made it impossible to call in the government's funds when they were demanded.

The minority admitted that the shortness of time had prevented a sufficiently thorough examination to determine the Bank's condition conclusively. "Whether existing facts are sufficient to justify the Executive in taking any step against the Bank, authorized by the charter," they said, "is a matter for the decision of the proper officers, acting upon their own views and responsibility; an opinion by Congress can make it neither more nor less their duty to act." Accordingly the minority simply offered a resolution discharging the committee from further consideration of the subject.[55]

The reports were not debated until Saturday, March 2, the last day of the session. Polk entreated Watmough not to press the majority resolution, since a lengthy debate would endanger the appropriation bills yet to be acted on. The confident Watmough scorned this appeal and challenged Polk "to come out boldly with all he knew." "My confidence," Biddle's man reported, "had a sensible effect upon his nerves from which he did not recover during his whole effort which was indeed a weak one."[56]

Polk's position was unquestionably difficult, for the Bank forces were in a clear majority; and since there had not been time to print

[55] *Ibid.*, 7-42. Polk's supporting documents occupy pp. 43-184.
[56] Watmough to Biddle, 2 Mar. 1833, Biddle Papers.

the reports, there was little prospect that he could present enough of his voluminous evidence orally to impress those members who were still open to conviction. A summary of his evidence and conclusions was all he had time for, and in the end he had to rely on urging the House not to "whitewash the bank" before it had the facts. The disciplined Bank forces allowed only Polk to speak on the anti-Bank side before pressing their resolution to a vote. At this point Bell and many other pro-Bank Jackson men "cleared out," and the Bank was upheld by the convincing majority of 109 to 46. Watmough could not resist crowing over his victory. "Well, Col[.]," he chortled to Polk, "you see we have beaten you again & we can always do it; give us ten days more & we will recharter the Bank in Spite of you." As a result of the Bank debate, the House had to sit through the night winding up its business and did not finally adjourn until five o'clock Sunday morning.[57]

Jackson's inauguration for his second term took place the next day, and the Polks left for home immediately afterward, taking a stage to Pittsburgh and a steamboat down the Ohio, and stopping at Cincinnati to buy some furniture for the house in Columbia, which was being enlarged. At the mouth of the Cumberland the Polks changed to another boat, which took them up to Nashville.

Only fifty miles more and they could relax in the pleasant house on Garden Street. But the troubles of this session were not yet over. Their stage left Nashville about two in the morning, and it was still dark when the driver plunged into the ford of a swift stream. Almost before anyone realized that the stream was flooding, water came pouring into the coach. Neither James nor Sarah could swim, but a quick-witted fellow passenger, catching sight of a horse on the bank, jumped into the water, swam to the animal, and used it to extricate all the passengers without their suffering any more damage than a "genteel wetting." "Since it is all over," Polk reported, "Mrs. Polk seems to consider it the greatest adventure of her life, but would not I judge be willing to try the experiment again."[58]

[57] Watmough to Biddle, 12 Mar. 1833, Biddle Papers; John Connell to Biddle, 2 Mar. 1833, *ibid.*; *Reg. Deb.*:22:2, pp. 1922-1927.

[58] Polk to C. C. Clay, 25 Mar. 1833, Clement C. Clay Papers (DU); James Findlay to Irwin and Findlay, 28 Feb. 1833, Polk Papers; Anson and Fanny Nelson, *Memorials of Sarah Childress Polk: Wife of the Eleventh President of the United States* (New York, 1892), 33-34.

7

"POLK DESERVES A MEDAL"

WHILE POLK WAS WARMLY ENGAGED at Washington with the Monster of Chestnut Street, a second front had opened in his rear, and from the summer of 1833 on he was compelled to fight for political survival in Tennessee. The magic of Old Hickory's name had been regarded as ample guarantee that Tennessee would never stray from the ranks of his party. Few Tennesseans had been unwilling to follow his leadership heretofore, and differences over internal improvements and state rights had ruffled the surface of party harmony only slightly. But the Bank Veto produced real alarm in the influential Nashville mercantile community, with its allied lawyers and newspapers and its counterparts in trading towns throughout the state. A uniform circulating medium, abundant credit, and the nationwide facilities of the national bank seemed indispensable to Tennessee's extensive commercial relations, based on the cotton crop, with New Orleans, the eastern cities, and Europe.

Striking directly at the state's most substantial interests, Jackson's radical ideas on banking were bound to produce a political explosion; but the president's prestige was so great that the first attack on his policies was launched obliquely, with Polk's minority report as the primary target. The day after Polk reached home in the spring of 1833, the Nashville *Republican* came out lamenting "the disastrous effects" that his minority report "must instantly exercise on Western credit."[1] A week later a body of prominent Nashville citizens, under the leadership of John P. Erwin, convened to protest that Tennessee "has been misrepresented, if not grossly calumniated by the minority of the Committee of Ways and Means." And almost immediately Polk's old enemy Theoderick Bradford announced for Congress against him at the August election.[2]

This political activity was not confined to Nashville or to Polk's district. All over the state the political fever was rising, and the summer of 1833 was destined to produce the most intense political

[1] Nashville *Republican*, 22 Mar. 1833.
[2] *ibid.*, 1 Apr. 1833; *ibid.*, 6 May 1833.

excitement Tennessee had known since Billy Carroll overturned the Overton faction back in 1821. Nor would the excitement soon subside, for the next few years were to witness a violent process of realignment among the state's political factions, resulting finally in a genuine two-party system.

Despite the state's surface unanimity for Jackson, Tennessee politicians had continued through his first administration to divide into three major factional groupings. The Eaton-Lewis clique, still guided by John Overton and still circulating its views through the columns of Allen A. Hall's Nashville *Republican*, regarded itself as the exclusive executor of Jackson's political estate in Tennessee. A second group of Jackson men, including Senators White and Grundy, Congressmen Polk and Cave Johnson, and Andrew Jackson Donelson, the president's nephew and private secretary, continued to resent the pretensions of Overton and his friends. The Nashville *Banner*, edited by Samuel H. Laughlin, was more or less sympathetic to their cause.

The third group consisted of the covertly anti-Jackson successors to the former Erwin faction: Crockett in the Western District; Thomas D. Arnold, William B. Carter, and the Williamses at the opposite end of the state; and the Erwins, Theoderick Bradford, Newton Cannon, and a large group of Nashville businessmen and lawyers in Middle Tennessee. Some of these men had the temerity to underwrite a Clay newspaper at Nashville, but most of them refused to take an open position against the president. Governor Carroll retained the support of this group and continued to appoint its members to state offices, despite his recent conversion to the Van Buren cause.

There had been a constantly shifting pattern of alignment among these three groups. In 1829 the Grundy-White faction had threatened to join the Erwin group to elect Carroll over Houston for governor; but ever since the passing of this crisis there had been a growing tendency for the Carroll-Erwin men to side politically with the Overton-Eaton-Lewis men, with whom they were already cooperating in managing the Nashville branch of the national bank. John Bell, for example, had moved so far into the Overton orbit that Major Lewis backed him for one of the Cabinet vacancies in 1831.[3] Both the nullification and Bank issues served to accelerate this de-

---

[3] James Parton, *Life of Andrew Jackson* (3 vols., New York, 1861), III, 383.

veloping alliance, and its progress was most clearly revealed in the maneuvering over Tennessee's two senatorships.

When Eaton resigned from the Cabinet in the reorganization of 1831, Jackson had put heavy pressure on Senator White to accept the secretaryship of war, so that a senatorship would be opened for Eaton. But White stubbornly refused to be used in this way, whereupon Overton's friends resolved to run Eaton against Grundy for the other Senate seat. Though Grundy's term did not expire until March 1833, he perceived the Eaton movement and tried to nip it in the bud by bringing on the senatorial election at the 1831 legislature, before the Eaton forces were prepared to make a fight. At this juncture, however, Ephraim H. Foster entered the race. A wealthy, polished commercial lawyer, Foster was a nominal Jacksonian, but he was most closely identified with Nashville's conservative, anti-Jackson merchants of the Erwin-Carroll faction.

The resulting contest was featured by some significant crossing of factional lines and cooperation between the two anti-Grundy groups. Though Foster was working closely with Bell, Bell's patron, Governor Carroll, was still anxious for the Mexican ministry, which Van Buren kept dangling before his nose, and took the lead for Eaton. Even Andrew Erwin, whose first choice was doubtless Foster, was heard to say that he preferred Eaton to Grundy. All this occurred just after the open break between Jackson and Calhoun, and Grundy's efforts to secure a fair hearing for the vice president gave his two sets of enemies a common argument against him. In the end the Eaton backers and the Foster backers combined forces to postpone the senatorial election.[4]

Meanwhile the Eaton-Lewis faction had been busily promoting Van Buren to succeed to the presidency after Jackson's second term. The Grundy-White men, on the other hand, refused to commit themselves until the Senate rejected Van Buren's nomination as minister to England early in 1832. This created such a strong sentiment

[4] Carroll to Van Buren, 8 Apr. 1831, Andrew Jackson Papers (LC); Jackson to White, 9 Apr. 1831, copy, *ibid.*; White to Jackson, 20 Apr., 15 June 1831, *ibid.*; Balch to Jackson, 14 Sept. 1831, *ibid.*; R. M. Burton to Jackson, 5 Oct. 1831, *ibid.*; Carroll to Jackson, 13 Nov. 1831, *ibid.*, *id.* to *id.*, 27 Sept. 1831, *ibid.*, Second Series; Carroll to Van Buren, 11 Apr. 1831, *ibid.*; Jackson to S. J. Hays, 23 Apr. 1831 (typed copy in possession of Mr. A. J. Hays, Memphis, Tenn.); White to Overton, 15 June 1831, John Overton Papers, Claybrooke Collection (THS); Archibald Lytle to Overton, 19 June 1831, *ibid.*; Boyd McNairy to Henry Clay, 28 Sept. 1831, Henry Clay Papers (LC); H. R. W. Hill to John McLean, 14 Oct., 16 Nov. 1831, John McLean Papers (LC); Nancy N. Scott, *A Memoir of Hugh Lawson White* . . . (Philadelphia, 1856), 247-248.

for vindicating the New Yorker against Jackson's enemies that Grundy and the *Banner* endorsed him for the vice presidential nomination, and Polk's brother-in-law James Walker was a Van Buren delegate to the Democratic national convention, though he was prevented from attending.[5]

On the very eve of the convention a strange thing happened. Eaton and Overton suddenly reversed their political strategy of the past four years and made a last minute effort to have Van Buren dropped as Jackson's running mate. The president put a stop to this scheme before it did any damage, but the episode was revealing. The struggle over rechartering the Bank was just nearing a climax in Congress, and these conservative Tennesseans had apparently begun to realize that the administration's disturbing anti-Bank policy was related to Van Buren's ambitions.[6]

When the senatorial question again came before the legislature in the fall of 1832, Grundy and Foster were still the only avowed candidates. Polk, Johnson, and other friends were pushing hard for Grundy's election, but the *Republican* opened a compaign against him on the ground of his sympathy with nullification. When it became apparent that Grundy would defeat Foster anyhow, the Foster men promised to back Eaton, and he was brought into the contest with Jackson's blessing. The Foster and Eaton men joined forces to postpone the election two weeks, hoping to stir up enough public support for Eaton to wean some of Grundy's votes away from him. In this they had some success, but in the end the Foster men refused to abandon their candidate as promised, and another deadlock resulted. Through thirty ballots Foster and Grundy maintained a total of 19 to 24 votes apiece, Foster usually being a little ahead, while Eaton's total rose from 15 as high as 19 and closed at 18. The election again had to be postponed for another year. The coalition had blocked Grundy, but they had not yet succeeded in effecting a workable union themselves.[7]

[5] Balch to Jackson, 14 Sept. 1831, Jackson Papers; Grundy to Jackson, 4 Feb. 1832, *ibid.*; Carroll to [Jackson], 18 Feb. [misplaced 7 Feb.] 1832, *ibid.*; Eaton to Jackson, 13 Mar. 1832, *ibid.*; Carroll to Jackson, 6 May 1831, 20 Feb. 1832, typed copies, *ibid.*, Second Series; Bell to Overton, 20 Jan. 1832, Overton Papers; James Walker to Overton, 28 Apr. 1832, *ibid.*; Nashville *Banner*, 16 Sept. 1834; Washington *Sun*, 25 Mar. 1835; Nashville *Republican*, 16 Feb., 10 Mar. 1832.

[6] Parton, *Jackson*, III, 421; John C. Fitzpatrick, ed., *The Autobiography of Martin Van Buren*, American Historical Association, *Annual Report*, 1918, II (Washington, 1920), 587-591.

[7] Cave Johnson to Polk, 25 June 1833, James K. Polk Papers (LC; herein cited as

The nullification crisis in the winter of 1832-1833 afforded an opportunity for this incipient coalition of anti-Jackson men with the Eaton-Lewis faction to be more closely cemented. As former supporters of William H. Crawford, the Erwins had never had any use for Calhoun, and they jumped at the chance to join the Eaton-Lewis faction in applauding the president's Nullification Proclamation. The two factions were equally represented in the leadership of a meeting that Governor Carroll called for this purpose in Nashville; and at a Washington's birthday celebration in Bedford County, Andrew Erwin endorsed the Proclamation, while one of his lieutenants declared that "Andrew Jackson was the only man in the United States who should be at the head of affairs." But the Erwinites were not endorsing all Jacksonians. At this same meeting another Erwin man offered as a toast, "May E. H. Foster 'lick' old Felix at the next election."[8]

John Overton's death two months after the Bedford meeting symbolized the passing of the old order in Tennessee politics. Meanwhile Polk's Bank report had provided the two conservative groups with another platform on which they could stand together. The Bank's frantic efforts to reduce its outstanding loans had produced a severe shortage of credit in Tennessee during the winter, and as early as February 1833 Senator White was being blamed for circulating reports that the Nashville branch was in a precarious position. The publication of Polk's report immediately brought all this resentment down on his head. The charge that Polk was damaging western credit originated with the leading businessmen of Nashville, mostly members of the anti-Jackson faction, but the *Republican* defended the president and him only weakly. The Nashville meeting that denounced Polk's minority report was reported to have various objects, "immediate and ulterior," and political considerations were obviously involved. Polk was convinced that the whole movement was designed to help his competitor, Bradford, in the congressional election. Why, he asked, had the Nashville counterreport singled out Maury County in its argument to prove the soundness of western debts? And why were copies of it scattered broadcast over his district,

---

Polk Papers, which refers to First Series, unless otherwise noted); J. C. McLemore to Jackson, 25 Sept. 1832, Jackson Papers; Nashville *Republican*, 18 May, 1 June, 21, 24 Sept., 5, 8, 28 Oct. 1832.

[8] Nashville *Republican*, 6 Mar. 1833; Catron to Jackson, 3 Jan. 1833, Jackson Papers; Carroll to Jackson, 18 Dec. 1833, *ibid.*, Second Series.

instead of being sent to the eastern cities, where its authors claimed that western credit had been so badly damaged?

Furious at "the Bank organs and politicians at Nashville," Polk suspected that the Bank itself was behind the efforts to defeat him.[9] His suspicions were endorsed by no less an authority than Major Lewis, who was visiting in Tennessee. "The Bank people," Lewis reported back to Washington, "are doing all they can against Polk."[10] Even Cave Johnson confessed to Polk his fears that "the bank men with their cunning and money and double-headed game might trouble if not beat you."[11]

Polk did not secure any concrete evidence of the Bank's direct participation against him until the very eve of the election, when his district was flooded with an extra edition of the Washington *National Intelligencer* containing a misleading account of his arguments in the House debate on his minority report. Almost simultaneously Polk learned through Reuben Whitney that the Bank was subsidizing the *Intelligencer* heavily. Shortly afterward Polk discovered that these particular copies of the *Intelligencer* extra had in fact been printed by the Nashville *Banner*, which despite its former friendliness to the Polk-Grundy group had recently been leading the Nashville attack on Polk's minority report.

Though Polk's evidence was incomplete, the truth was in accord with his worst suspicions. This extra edition of the *Intelligencer* had been carefully prepared by Watmough and Biddle, with particular attention to its treatment of Polk. And in Philadelphia, at almost the moment Polk was putting two and two together down in Tennessee, the government directors, at Whitney's urging, were forcing Biddle to reveal the contents of his special account book covering the Bank's dealings with newspapers. The Nashville *Banner*, too, turned out to be in the Bank's employ.[12]

But the Bank was not the only source of Polk's difficulties, for his friend Cave Johnson complained of being "bedevilled enough in the same way,"[13] and he had not been conspicuous enough to attract

[9] *Col. Polk's Speech to His Constituents . . . 15 Apr.* [*1833*] *. . . ,* broadside bound in vol. of speeches, Polk Papers; S. G. Smith to Polk, 18 Feb. 1833, *ibid.*; Nashville *Republican*, 1 Apr. 1833.

[10] Lewis to Jackson, 26 Apr. 1833, Jackson Papers.

[11] Johnson to Polk, 25 June 1833, Polk Papers.

[12] Polk to F. P. Blair, 8 Aug. 1833, Blair-Lee Papers (PU); Whitney to Blair, 14 Aug. 1833, *ibid.*; Watmough to Biddle, 16 Mar. 1833, Nicholas Biddle Papers (LC); Washington *National Intelligencer—Extra*, n.d. (placed 2 Mar. 1833), *ibid.*

[13] Johnson to Polk, 25 June 1833, Polk Papers.

Nicholas Biddle's personal attention. A pro-Bank candidate had been entered against him also, but Johnson went right on denying that Congress had any power to charter a Bank and contending that "a metalic [*sic*] currency is the only one contemplated by the Constitution."[14] Johnson's enemies, with the powerful aid of the Nashville *Republican*, were also taking advantage of his vote against the Force Bill to charge him with being a Nullifier, and Johnson was convinced that these accusations "had their origin from Major Eaton and W. B. L[ewis]."[15] The campaign grew so heated in his district that partisans on both sides attended political meetings "well armed and prepared for any contingency," and "serious apprehensions for weeks were entertained of some bloody affairs taking place."[16]

Polk and Johnson both blamed their troubles on "the *'little knot of politicians'* at Nashville who undertake to control the politics of the State,"[17] but the excitement was not confined to their districts. A new legislature was to be chosen at this election, and it would have to fill Tennessee's vacancy in the Senate. Legislative candidates were running as Grundy men, Eaton men, or Foster men, and the senatorial question was even brought into some congressional contests. In the Murfreesboro congressional district a Polk-Grundy ally, William Brady, was opposed by John Bell's brother-in-law, David Dickinson, who was "making a bold attempt to pull down Mr. Grundy, and upon the ruins build his own fortune." Bell did not have a competitor this year in the adjoining Nashville district, and his friends were reported to be coming over to the Murfreesboro district "in clouds" to aid Dickinson. Polk and Johnson, on the other hand, were doing all they could to get pro-Grundy candidates elected to the legislature from their districts.[18]

II

Polk was too busy defending himself, however, to do much for his friend Grundy. He had been warned to expect opposition by the pro-Bank agitation in his district during the recharter struggle of 1832. Later that same year, when the legislature was realigning the

[14] Nashville *Republican*, 1 Mar. 1833.

[15] Scott, *White*, 263; Nashville *Republican*, 13, 19 Apr. 1833.

[16] Clement Lyndon Grant, "The Public Career of Cave Johnson," Ph.D. dissertation, Vanderbilt University (1951), 42.

[17] "Letters of James K. Polk to Cave Johnson, 1833-1848," *Tennessee Historical Magazine*, I (Sept. 1915), 213.

[18] J. W. Childress to Polk, 30 Dec. 1832, Polk Papers.

congressional districts, the Erwin party had tried to get Bedford County detached from Maury, so that Theoderick Bradford could run for Congress without encountering the formidable Polk. But the Grundy-White legislators, who were just as anxious to neutralize the Erwinite strength, had succeeded in making a district of Bedford and Maury.

Despite this setback, Bradford continued to act like a candidate and began agitating against the Masonic order as an unscrupulous conspiracy for political power. Though Polk does not seem to have been a Mason, Jackson was, and anti-Masonry had proven to be an effective vehicle for anti-Jacksonism in other parts of the country. But Polk refused to be concerned about this "mere gull to deceive the people and get votes," and thought he would have "but little difficulty in exposing the motives of those who attempt it." He was ready to meet Bradford "*at any point*," he told his supporters, and actually believed he could outpoll him in both counties.[19]

Nevertheless Polk was taking no chances. Through the winter of 1832-1833 he kept the mails from Washington loaded with congressional documents addressed to the innumerable local post offices in his district. His most effective stroke was to persuade the Post Office Department to make the main mail route through Bedford a triweekly service carried in four-horse stages. "Your mail rout . . . has been a quietus upon Theo," wrote one of his supporters. "It has done you more service than all your big speeches in Congress."[20]

All through the winter Bradford kept denying that he was a candidate. Meanwhile he had induced Polk's popular fellow townsman Thomas J. Porter to announce, hoping that after the Maury vote was divided, he could enter the race and win with a big majority in Bedford. When Polk reached home in the spring, he had to go to the Western District on business, and during his absence the Nashville attack on his Bank report and Bradford's candidacy were launched almost simultaneously. Hurrying back to Columbia, Polk counterattacked in a speech on the opening day of the Maury circuit court. Denying that he had undermined western credit, he reiterated his charges against the Bank with such force that Bradford quickly

---

[19] J. K. Polk to L. J. Polk, 19 Oct. 1832, G. W. Polk Papers (SHC); A. C. Hays to Polk, 17 Apr. 1832, Polk Papers; M. W. Campbell to Polk, 29 Nov. 1832, *ibid.*; Jonathan Webster to Polk, 6 Dec. 1832, *ibid.*; Nashville *Republican*, 3, 8, 13, 21 Oct. 1832; Shelbyville *Western Freeman*, 27 Nov., 4 Dec. 1832.

[20] Archibald Yell to Polk, 16 Jan. 1833, Polk Papers; Shelbyville *Western Freeman*, 8 Jan. 1833.

dropped the issue. Henceforth Mr. Biddle's institution was none too popular with the farmers of Polk's district.[21]

Moreover, as Polk predicted, Bradford's heavy anti-Masonic propaganda had fallen flat, and the anti-Polk forces were hard pressed for an issue. When Polk reached Shelbyville for the Bedford county court in May, he found rumors circulating that he had voted against pensions for Revolutionary veterans. At first Polk explained that he had voted against the House pension bill of 1832 because he preferred the Senate's bill, which had later passed the House. But his enemies went outside the district for help and secured from John Bell a statement that Polk had voted for the Senate bill because *"it was the lesser evil* and would take less money out of the Treasury." Polk finally had to publish a detailed account of his record to show that he had opposed pensions only where the recipients were not in need. Thereupon Bradford began denouncing Polk for supporting appropriations for the military academy, for being a Nullifier, and for helping vote a large appropriation for John Randolph's mission to Russia, where the irresponsible diplomat, unnerved by the extreme cold, had remained only ten days.[22]

Thus during the early part of the campaign Polk was kept busy defending himself against the charges of his opponent. But by June he had moved to the offensive. Bradford was particularly vulnerable on the Bank question, having led the pro-Bank forces in the legislature. Polk hunted up his old speeches on the subject and assailed him unmercifully. He also had an ace in the hole, in the form of recommendations sent in for Bradford by a number of notorious anti-Jackson men in 1827, when Bradford was trying to get the Adams administration to appoint him federal marshal. These incriminating documents had been dug out of the State Department files by Polk's friend Andrew Jackson Donelson, and they were devastatingly effective.[23]

By late June Polk felt safe, and the August results were a death knell to the Erwin-Bradford party, even in Bedford. Polk received

[21] James Walker to Polk, 2 Dec. 1832, Polk Papers; W. J. Whitthorne to Polk, 15 Dec. 1832, *ibid.*; Jonathan Webster to Polk, 13 Jan. 1833, *ibid.; Col. Polk's Speech to his Constituents . . . 15 Apr.* [*1833*] . . . , broadside bound in vol. of speeches, *ibid.*; Nashville *Republican*, 6 May 1833.

[22] Shelbyville *Western Freeman*, 4 June 1833; Columbia *Western Mercury*, extra, 17 June 1833; J. K. Polk, *Circular Letter . . . 24 June 1833*, broadside bound in vol. of speeches, Polk Papers; "Polk-Johnson Letters," *loc.cit.*, 211-212.

[23] Polk, *Circular Letter . . . 24 June 1833*; A. J. Donelson to Polk, 30 May 1833, Polk Papers.

over twice as many votes as both his opponents combined. In Maury, Bradford got only seventy-nine votes, while Polk had more than a two-to-one margin over Porter. And in Bedford, Polk's total vote was nearly four times that of each of his opponents. Cave Johnson won almost as decisive a victory, but in the Murfreesboro district Brady lost to Dickinson by fifty-two votes. Polk's victory was almost exclusively personal, for both Maury and Bedford elected the anti-Grundy legislative candidates by narrow margins.[24]

III

The August elections did not end the political excitement, for the legislature still had to choose a senator when it met the next month. Grundy had returned from Washington in March to find the Foster men busily arranging to have their most popular legislative candidates put up in all the counties. Grundy set to work at once to get his friends entered in opposition, at the same time spreading the report that Eaton would not be a candidate. If Eaton should enter the race after the anti-Grundy forces had concentrated behind Foster, Grundy would then profit from dissension among his opponents.

Eaton himself was detained in Washington by his wife's illness, but the *Republican* asserted positively that he would be a candidate. The confusion was increased when Eaton was elected president of the federal board of canal commissioners, and even Grundy seems to have had some genuine doubt as to his intentions. But the August elections gave Grundy's friends such a substantial margin that it was doubtful whether Foster alone could block his reelection. Some of Foster's friends now offered once more to support Eaton if their favorite could not succeed, and when the legislature met, Eaton was present as a candidate. Polk and Johnson were on hand to lobby for Grundy, while Major Lewis had come down from Washington to work for Eaton. Faced with this double opposition, Grundy's friends began organizing public meetings in counties represented by Eaton or Foster supporters to force these legislators to shift to Grundy, who was more popular with the voters. Polk engineered one such meeting in Columbia and succeeded in bringing the Maury delegation over to Grundy's side.[25]

24 Nashville *Republican*, 6 Aug. 1833.

25 *ibid.*, 25 Mar., 22 Apr. 1833; Grundy to [Donelson?], 31 Mar. 1833, Jackson-Donelson Papers, microfilm (JUL); Lewis to Jackson, 26 Apr. 1833, Jackson Papers; Grundy to Jackson, 6 May, 7 Aug. 1833, *ibid.*; Carroll to Jackson, 9 Aug. 1833,

When the balloting opened, Grundy, with 24 votes, was stronger than the year before, while Foster and Eaton trailed with 19 and 17 respectively. Further trials revealed that Foster's friends would again refuse to honor their promise to shift to Eaton, and through forty-one ballots the deadlock held. At this point Eaton withdrew his name, but a few of the former Eaton supporters began to shift toward Grundy rather than Foster, bringing Grundy dangerously close to the 31 votes needed for election. When this became apparent, the anti-Grundy forces played their last card.

It had been recognized in Washington the previous winter that John Bell stood the best chance of uniting the Eaton and Foster followings, and his name was now entered in the senatorial contest. He immediately attracted support from both the Eaton and Foster columns, reaching a total of 23 votes after four ballots. But he could go no higher, and the Eaton and Foster partisans shifted back to their favorites. Finally, on the fifty-fifth ballot, enough of them deserted to Grundy to give him the election. The anti-Grundy forces had failed, but only because they could not yet achieve a firm union. The election demonstrated both the potential strength of this coalition and John Bell's eligibility as its leader.[26]

IV

In the fight for his own reelection to the House and Grundy's reelection to the Senate, Polk was greatly aided by two of his brothers-in-law, James Walker and Adlai O. Harris, partners in one of the leading mercantile firms of Middle Tennessee. Free opportunity to make a dollar counted for more than Jeffersonian dogmas in the political philosophy of these aggressive businessmen. They and others like them furnished substantial support to the Jacksonian war on the national bank, being known in some circles as "Democrats by trade," as distinguished from "Democrats in principle." The animus of these entrepreneurial Democrats against the national bank was closely related to their desire to share in the lucrative profits of the

---

ibid.; Eaton to Jackson, 7 Sept. 1833, *ibid.*, Remnants; Grundy to F. P. Blair and W. T. Barry, 21 June 1833, Blair-Lee Papers; Grundy to Jackson, 6 Aug. 1833, *ibid.*; Cave Johnson to Polk, 25 June 1833, Polk Papers; Grundy to Cave Johnson, 29 Aug. 1833, Personal Papers, Miscellaneous (LC); "Polk-Johnson Letters," *loc.cit.*, 212-213.

26 Washington *United States Telegraph*, 2 Oct. 1833; Nashville *Republican*, 3, 8, 10 Oct. 1833; Carroll to Jackson, 3 Dec. 1833, Jackson Papers.

banking business, both Walker and Harris being greatly interested in a new bank chartered by the Tennessee legislature in 1832.

It was during 1832 that the national bank was making strenuous efforts to reduce its excessive loans in the West, and especially at the Nashville office. The failure of the last two crops had left the planters in debt to the merchants and the merchants to the Bank, and efforts to reduce these loans were producing widespread anxiety, if not distress. " 'Uncle' Saml is taking another turn to the Screw every week or two at Nashville," Adlai Harris complained to Polk. "Mr Biddle writes to the Directors at Nashville that they do not Collect fast enough—to press harder."[27] The Bank Veto intensified these apprehensions. Practically the entire circulating medium of the state, some two million dollars, consisted of national bank notes, but the debts of Tennesseans were estimated at over three million dollars. How were these debts to be paid when the Bank began winding up its business? The inevitable result of these circumstances was a clamor for a state-chartered bank.

During the summer of 1832 businessmen called bank meetings in towns all over the state. In Columbia James Walker organized such a meeting, which in turn called for a state banking convention to meet in Nashville during the legislative session. This statewide assemblage, with Walker presiding, drafted an urgent appeal for the chartering of a state bank. Conceding that an excessive currency "encourages a spirit of speculation," the convention contended on the other hand that too little money was equally harmful. For the hard-money men this body had only contempt. "To suppose for a moment," ran the convention report, "that gold and silver coin would be exclusively relied on as a circulating medium, is to suppose a retrog[r]ade movement in the human intellect and would be a libel on the intelligence of the age." The convention concluded by submitting to the legislature a charter bill providing for a bank half of whose capital would be subscribed in mortgages on real estate.[28]

William Carroll was still governor, however, and hard-money sentiment remained strong. A previous effort to charter a state bank had been frustrated by legislative insistence that the property of all stockholders be liable for any losses, and the legislature now made substantial changes in the convention's bank bill, eliminating the

[27] A. O. Harris to Polk, 11 Dec. 1832, Polk Papers.
[28] Nashville *Republican*, 12 Sept. 1832; *ibid.*, 4, 20, 23, 27, 30 July, 1, 8 Aug., 5, 19 Sept. 1832.

unsound real estate feature entirely. As finally passed the act chartered the Union Bank of Tennessee for thirty years. Its capital was not to exceed three million dollars, of which the state was to subscribe half a million in bonds, and the governor was to appoint five of the directors. The state was to deposit its funds with the bank, receiving interest on them. The bank was also to pay the state a bonus of from five to fifteen thousand dollars a year, and these funds, plus the interest on the state's deposits and the dividends on its stock, were to be devoted to common schools. Directors were to be personally responsible for any losses arising from charter violations, and if their property were insufficient, stockholders were to be liable to the extent of their stock. The bank's issues were not to exceed the stock paid in, and it was forbidden to issue notes for less than five dollars. In addition to the headquarters at Nashville, a branch could be established in each of the three major sections of the state.[29]

Edward B. Littlefield, the leader of the anti-Polk faction in Columbia, made strenuous efforts to become president of the new bank, but James Walker blocked even his appointment as a director of the branch established at Columbia. This branch came under the control of Walker and his friends, and Adlai Harris was made cashier. The Union Bank took over the business of financing the cotton crop as fast as it was relinquished by the national bank and in its first year discounted bills of exchange based on the staple for more than a million dollars. It was probably no accident that the Union Bank became one of the original federal deposit banks in the summer of 1833. There is no direct evidence that Polk facilitated this arrangement, but Grundy interceded with the Treasury several times on behalf of the Tennessee institution.[30]

Shortly afterward the Littlefield group induced the legislature to charter a second bank, the Planter's Bank, under its auspices, and Memphis interests also secured a banking institution for their town. But opposition to the banking principle was still formidable in Tennessee, and Governor Carroll was able to block a strong movement for increasing the state subscription to the new banks.[31]

29 Nashville *Republican*, 13 Oct. 1832; Memphis *Advocate*, 30 Oct. 1832; *Niles' Weekly Register*, XLIII (10 Nov. 1833), 176.

30 J. Knox Walker to Polk, 3 Feb. 1833 (misplaced 1834), Polk Papers; A. O. Harris to Polk, 13 Feb. 1833, *ibid.*; Jackson to Levi Woodbury, 26 July 1834, Levi Woodbury Papers (LC); Woodbury to Grundy, 5 Sept. 1834, copy, *ibid.*, Second Series; Nashville *Republican*, 26, 30 Jan., 5 Apr. 1833; *Executive Documents*: 23rd Cong.: 2nd Sess., No. 27, pp. 48, 62.

31 Thomas Perkins Abernethy, "The Early Development of Commerce and Bank-

Harris was already worth $35,000, but in 1833, perhaps with the aid of his new banking connection, he was able to expand his financial operations by becoming a partner in the important New Orleans mercantile and factorage firm of Caruthers and Harris. The partnership soon engrossed the best business in the Columbia area, and Harris found himself in a position "to make money rapidly, with but little risque."[32]

Walker, too, was arranging "to make money rapidly," presumably with Polk's help. He had entered the stage business, where profits depended on securing government contracts to carry the mail. With the easygoing Major Barry in charge of the Post Office Department, it was not hard to circumvent the requirement for competitive bidding on mail routes, and political influence was the determining factor in awarding the more lucrative contracts. The great prize in the Southwest was the triweekly mail from Nashville to New Orleans, which was carried in four-horse post coaches. Walker was allied with Caruthers and Kinkle, an Alabama stage company backed by Polk's friend Congressman Clement C. Clay, while their chief competitor was a Nashville contractor, John Donly, who had the support of the Eaton-Lewis-Bell combination.

When Donly, aided by Eaton and Lewis, did Walker out of some secondary routes from Nashville to Alabama in 1833, the latter revealed the nature of his Jacksonism. The episode, he complained to Polk, "will teach me the folly of remaining in the ranks of a political party, that totally disregard my feelings and interests." "I was quite inclined to be a Van Buren man," he wrote, still fuming, the next day, "but if his friends treat my interests so lightly, I had better be off. I must be fairly treated, if not served, where I serve hereafter."[33]

Rather than give up, however, Walker contrived a scheme by which Donly might yet be defeated, and he demanded that Polk, Grundy, and Cave Johnson secure the cooperation of the Post Office Department. The necessary cooperation seems to have been forthcoming, since the department divided Donly's original contract in

---

ing in Tennessee," *Mississippi Valley Historical Review*, xiv (Dec. 1927), 321-324; Robert H. White, ed., *Messages of the Governors of Tennessee* (Nashville, 1952-), ii, 440-441; John Sommerville and H. M. Rutledge to Biddle, 10 June 1834, Biddle Papers.

[32] James Walker to Col. William Polk, 22 Aug. 1833, Polk-Yeatman Papers (SHC).
[33] Walker to Polk, 13, 14 Dec. 1833, Polk Papers.

such a way that some of the routes could not be operated at his original low bid for the whole contract. These routes consequently went to Walker and his associates, who had been high bidders. Walker then proposed a corrupt arrangement whereby these routes would be surrendered to a dummy for Donly at the high bid, provided that Donly would pay Walker's associates a bonus of $4,000 a year, or $16,000 for the four-year term of the contract. Donly seems to have rebuffed this proposal, but the upshot of the matter was that the Walker-Caruthers combination finally got the whole contract for the New Orleans mail as far as Natchez, at the handsome compensation of $27,500 a year.[34]

V

The political excitement that preceded the 1833 elections was transmuted promptly into religious excitement, for August was camp meeting time in Maury. The Methodists had erected their brush arbors and prepared for a great festival of the spirit at McPeak's campground near Columbia. Politicians were always alert to large gatherings of the voters, and Polk was on hand to hear a moving sermon by John B. McFerrin, a forceful young preacher who had converted two of the Polk sisters several years before and who later became the bishop of Tennessee Methodism. Polk had always taken religion seriously, and McFerrin's earnest exhortation to embrace the "inheritance incorruptible, and undefiled, and that fadeth not away," which was "reserved in heaven for you," made a deep and lasting impression. To the rigorously predestinarian Presbyterianism of his wife and mother, Polk had never been able to respond, but McFerrin's appeal so affected him that he "went away from the camp-ground a convicted sinner, if not a converted man."

From this time forward Polk was "a Wesleyan in sentiment, and believed in the doctrine and polity of the Methodist Episcopal Church." The conflict of his Methodist leanings with the faith of his wife, plus the scars left by his boyhood encounters with Presbyterianism, prevented him from making an open profession of faith at this time. At the very end of his life, however, he would send for

---

[34] Walker to Polk, 9 Jan. 1834, Polk Papers; Robert Armstrong to A. J. Donelson, 11, 14 Jan. 1834, Andrew Jackson Donelson Papers (LC); *Senate Documents*:21:1, No. 408.

Bishop McFerrin to administer his baptism and receive him into the Methodist church.[35]

Joining the church was a serious matter. Even Sarah, despite her religious upbringing and undoubted piety, could not persuade herself that she was an acceptable Christian according to the rigid Presbyterian standards until a year after James's experience at the campground. When she finally announced her decision to the family, Jane Polk, who had had so little success with her menfolk, took matters into her own hands. The next Sunday at the Presbyterian church in Columbia, Sarah was surprised to hear the minister announce that the church was now ready to receive new members and that she was the only candidate.

While in Washington the Polks usually attended the Presbyterian church, but when Sarah was unable to go, James was often to be found at a Methodist service. Sarah had her own method of discouraging Sunday morning political consultations. She would appear dressed to go out and invite her husband's callers to accompany her to church. After a few experiences of this stratagem, James's impious associates made it a point to stay out of the Polk parlor at church time. Only once did one of these visitors get the best of Sarah. When she announced that she was particularly anxious to go to church because a certain fine preacher was to be in the pulpit, this gentleman responded, "Then I would like to go with you, Madame, for I have played cards all night with him many a time."[36]

VI

During Polk's summer campaign against the Bank in Tennessee, Old Hickory's renewed assault on that "hydra of corruption" had been taking shape at the capital. Polk's minority report had reinforced the warnings of Amos Kendall, Attorney General Taney, and the ubiquitous Reuben Whitney about the danger of leaving the public deposits under Biddle's control. But the only person empowered to remove the federal funds was the secretary of the treasury, and McLane, ambitious for the presidency and unnerved by the House vote upholding the Bank, was reluctant to proceed.

[35] O. P. Fitzgerald, *John B. McFerrin: A Biography* (Nashville, 1893), 219-232; Anson and Fanny Nelson, *Memorials of Sarah Childress Polk: Wife of the Eleventh President of the United States* (New York, 1892), 151.

[36] Nelson, *Sarah Polk*, 43: Milo M. Quaife, ed., *The Diary of James K. Polk during His Presidency, 1845 to 1849* (4 vols., Chicago, 1910), i, 86.

Taney, Kendall, and Whitney soon found a way around the uncooperative secretary. Edward Livingston was persuaded to relinquish the State Department to undertake some delicate diplomatic negotiations in France, and McLane was promoted to the top Cabinet post. Polk was among those considered for the Treasury vacancy, but it finally went to William J. Duane, son of the fiery Pennsylvania Republican of Jefferson's day. Though Duane had been an anti-Bank man, he turned out to be so completely under McLane's influence that the new secretary of state was said to be the head of two departments.

It did not take long for the anti-Bank clique to discover that Duane was no improvement over his predecessor. When Whitney. who had no official position whatever, took it upon himself to tell Duane what was expected of him, Duane complained bitterly to Jackson, arguing that the state banks would not dare defy the still powerful national bank by receiving the deposits. Whereupon Amos Kendall volunteered to sound out the state institutions. After visiting the eastern cities, he assured the president that the state banks would handle the federal funds on satisfactory terms.[37]

The showdown came in September when Jackson informed the Cabinet that the deposits would be transferred to the state banks. The obstinate Duane now refused either to follow the president's directions or to resign. Jackson finally dismissed him peremptorily and appointed Taney in his place. The new secretary issued the necessary instructions: the deposits were not actually withdrawn, but after the first of October all new deposits were to be made in selected state banks, while regular disbursements gradually removed the government funds from the vaults of the national bank.

This action provoked a furious storm of denunciation from opposition politicians and the business community. Rumors of impending removal had given the Bank an excuse to begin reducing its loans in midsummer, and by the time Congress met in December businessmen were under heavy pressure for funds. On the political level, removal caused more defections from Jackson's party than any other measure of his administration. It also enabled the opposition to shift the argument away from recharter and the merits of the Bank, where a majority of the voters had already decided against them, to Jack-

[37] R. M. Whitney to Jackson, 18 Mar., 30 Apr. 1833, Jackson Papers; Amos Kendall to Jackson, 11 Aug. 1833, *ibid.*; Daniel Webster to Biddle, 7 Apr. 1833, Biddle Papers.

son's exercise of an executive leadership far bolder than the country had known before. The cry of "executive usurpation" was raised, and behind this slogan the Calhounites, many of whom opposed the Bank on principle, were able to unite with Webster and Clay against the administration. Soon both Nullifiers and National Republicans were calling themselves "Whigs" in an effort to identify their cause with earlier resisters of tyranny.

In the new Congress the Whig coalition would be in undisputed control of the Senate, and Jackson would have to rely on the House for support. Speaker Stevenson had been slated for appointment as minister to England, but he was called to Washington well in advance of the session and told he would have to remain in the chair until this crisis had passed. The crucial point in the administration defenses was again the Committee of Ways and Means, which would have to be completely reorganized before being ready to bear the brunt of the Whig onslaught. "I feel a deep interest who compose" that committee, wrote Reuben Whitney on the eve of the session. "I have my list made out for that. Polk is my Candidate for Chairman."[38]

The chairman of the Ways and Means Committee was coming to be regarded as the unofficial floor leader for the administration, but Chairman Verplanck had deserted to the Whigs on the Bank question and had been denied reelection by the New York Democrats. It was imperative that the party strategists pick their strongest available man as Verplanck's successor. Polk's yeoman services at the previous session made him the obvious choice. His selection had probably been determined during the summer, since Jackson started supplying him with anti-Bank material in August.

At any rate, when Congress met in December, Polk was taken from the last place on the committee and put at its head. To strengthen the new chairman's hand, five of the ablest Jackson men in the House—Churchill C. Cambreleng of New York City, Isaac McKim of Baltimore, George Loyall of Virginia, Henry Hubbard of New Hampshire, and John McKinley, a personal friend of Polk from Alabama—were assigned to the committee. The Democrats were taking no chances. The Whigs were allotted only three places, but these too were filled by men of great ability: Richard H. Wilde of Georgia, a leader among the Nullifiers; Horace Binney, the bril-

[38] Whitney to William D. Lewis, 24 Nov. 1833, Lewis-Neilson Papers (HSP).

liant Bank counsel from Philadelphia; and Benjamin Gorham of Massachusetts, an intimate of Daniel Webster.[39]

A violent struggle was inevitable. In the heat of his conflict with the president, Nicholas Biddle had lost his head and plunged into a desperate defiance of the government through abuse of the Bank's economic power. Jackson's hostility had made some contraction of the Bank's loans necessary, but Biddle was determined to force such a severe contraction and to create such widespread distress that the government would be forced to restore the deposits and eventually recharter the Bank. "The ties of party allegiance can only be broken by the actual conviction of existing distress in the community," declared Biddle. "Nothing but the evidence of suffering abroad will produce any effect in Congress."[40] Congress was to be deluged, therefore, with a constant stream of distress memorials from businessmen and jeremiads by the Bank's supporters. Removal was to be blamed for all the trouble, and the cry of "executive usurpation" was to ring through the land.

VII

The battle was joined on the third day of the session, when Secretary Taney sent in his report justifying removal. The anti-Bank strategy, as Reuben Whitney described it, was "to imitate Bounaparte" and "attack our enemies before they are prepared for the onset." The secretary's report would be referred promptly "to the Committee of Ways & Means, which will be me, which money cannot corrupt," Whitney continued; inflammatory debate would be suppressed, the Bank's infamy would be exposed through another investigation, and the way would be paved for resolutions approving removal and legislation regulating the state bank deposit system. Thus would the Bank's doom be sealed.[41]

But this strategy backfired badly. The usual procedure was for the House, in committee of the whole, to refer the various parts of the president's annual message, along with the reports from the executive departments, to appropriate committees. Thus when George McDuffie requested that Taney's report be referred also to the committee of the whole, it seemed a reasonable suggestion. Polk took the precaution of asking McDuffie whether his purpose was to

[39] Jackson to Polk, 31 Aug. 1833, Polk Papers; *House Journal*:23:1, p. 28.

[40] Reginald C. McGrane, ed., *The Correspondence of Nicholas Biddle Dealing with National Affairs, 1807-1844* (Boston, 1919), 219.

[41] Whitney to W. D. Lewis, 24 Nov., 4 Dec. 1833, Lewis-Neilson Papers.

have the report referred to a committee along with the section of the president's message dealing with the same subject. McDuffie's reply was indistinct, but both the reporter of debates and John Quincy Adams understood him as replying that this was his intention. Polk therefore agreed to the McDuffie motion.

Apparently Polk suspected nothing until the next day, when in committee of the whole McDuffie moved to exempt from reference those parts of the president's message relating to the Bank. "The motion to refer the clause in the message," asserted the South Carolina Whig, "implies an admission of the authority of the President to remove the deposits, whereas it was well known that he had no such power. . . . The discussion of this topic must now take place."[42]

A motion of reference in the House itself would not have been debatable, but the Whigs had cleverly and rather unscrupulously taken advantage of the fact that debate in committee of the whole was unlimited. The too-trusting Polk had fallen into their trap, and they had succeeded in bringing on the very debate that the Jackson men were determined to avoid at all costs. McDuffie repeated his motion of exemption when Taney's report came up for reference. These maneuvers manifested a high degree of cooperation between the Clay and Calhoun men. The astute Van Buren concluded that McDuffie's adroit strategem had been devised by Clay himself, while McDuffie's chief aide in executing it was Clay's lieutenant, Thomas Chilton of Kentucky.

Polk protested that he had been tricked. It was highly irregular, he complained, to debate reports before a committee had considered them. Chilton replied tartly that he did not propose to see the subject smothered by the Ways and Means Committee. Nor could he "sit by patiently and see the whole weight of this massive Government imposed on the shoulders of his friend from Tennessee."[43]

The only way Polk could now retrieve the situation was by inducing the House to reconsider its reference of Taney's report to the committee of the whole. But this motion was debatable, and debate could be stopped only by passing the previous question, always an unpopular procedure and a dangerous one in view of the uncertain administration majority. Whitney himself admitted that it seemed

---

[42] *Congressional Globe*:21:1, p. 23; *Register of Debates*:23:1, p. 2166; Roger B. Taney to Polk, 3 Dec. 1833, Polk Papers; Charles Francis Adams, ed., *Memoirs of John Quincy Adams, Comprising Portions of His Diary from 1795 to 1848* (12 vols., Philadelphia, 1874-1877), IX, 49.

[43] *Cong. Globe*:23:1, p. 24; Van Buren, *Autobiography*, 717.

"oppugnaceous . . . to gag people," and when Polk tried the previous question, he lost by three votes, even a staunch Democratic member of his committee voting against him. The Bank men had free rein to deliver their inflammatory speeches, and the panic debate quickly began to have effect. The Democrats were obviously unnerved by the growing financial crisis, and the party leaders began to fear for their ostensible majority. When the question of referring a minor Bank matter to the Ways and Means Committee came up, Whitney had to "work all last night and this forenoon with the Wire workers upon this subject" to keep the Democrats in line.[44]

Down at the other end of Pennsylvania Avenue, meanwhile, President Jackson was fuming over the inability of the supposed Democratic majority to control proceedings in the House. He urged Polk to apply the previous question at once, but enough Democrats still could not be brought into line. Polk hoped to shorten the debate by refusing to reply to the Bank men, but their oratorical energies seemed unlimited. Christmas passed as the Whigs continued to regale the House and the country with unnerving accounts of the universal ruin proceeding from the president's rash and autocratic action. And the speeches, combined with Biddle's ever-tightening contraction, were producing results. As banks and commercial houses began to go under, a panic psychology crept over the business community, and wavering Jacksonian congressmen showed signs of surrendering to the enemy. "Unless relief from the present pressure is afforded soon," wrote one of Polk's friends from New York, "the results will be horrible."[45]

Polk finally concluded that the Bank party could go unanswered no longer, and on December 30 he commenced his reply for the administration. This was the most important speech Polk had ever made. Biddle sent urgent instructions for Binney to be ready to answer him "so that he may be demolished outright." Jackson was left alone at the President's House, as everyone went up to the Capitol to hear Polk in the House and Benton's reply to Clay in the Senate. Actually the heated Senate debate drew away most of Polk's

44 Whitney to W. D. Lewis, 13, 18 Dec. 1833, Lewis-Neilson Papers; *Cong. Globe*: 23:1, pp. 23-25, 34-39. McDuffie did finally allow Polk's motion for reconsideration to pass, but he perpetuated the debate by proposing a debatable amendment to Polk's motion referring the report to his committee.

45 John Wurts to Polk, 19 Dec. 1833, Polk Papers; Jackson to Polk, 18 Dec. 1833, *ibid.*

audience, and Watmough reported to his chief that Polk was "puling away to empty benches."[46]

But Polk was little interested in creating a rhetorical effect on his immediate audience. Marshaling exhaustively the whole catalogue of facts damning to the Bank, he relentlessly pursued the conclusion that the Bank's irresponsibility had made removal of the deposits absolutely necessary. Published in pamphlet form, his speech became at once a Bible for Jacksonian editors and politicians. Nor was it wholly lacking in passion. Denouncing the Bank as "a great irresponsible rival power of the Government," Polk concluded that the question was, in fact, "whether we shall have the republic without the bank, or the bank without the republic." If the "power and monopoly" of the Bank were continued for another twenty years, he predicted, it would become

the veriest despot that every ruled over any land—a despotism of money, without responsibility. No man, hereafter, can expect to arrive at the first station in this great republic, without first making terms with the despot. It will control your election of President, of your Senators, and of your Representatives. If such was its power when it stood in the position of an antagonist to the Government, what would it be in the hands of corrupt men, at the head of affairs, whom it would prostitute itself to serve, and whom it could bend to its own purposes?[47]

Despite their professions of contempt, the Bank men were bothered by Polk's address. "The merest milk and water," Biddle called it, but he was compelled to add, "with an infusion of vinegar."[48] A more professional appraisal was that of the former professor of rhetoric at Harvard, John Quincy Adams. "Polk," he recorded in his diary, "is the leader of the Administration in the House, and is just qualified for an eminent County Court lawyer—'par negotiis, neque supra.' He has no wit, no literature, no point of argument, no gracefulness of delivery, no elegance of language, no philosophy, no pathos, no felicitous impromptus; nothing that can constitute an orator, but confidence, fluency, and labor."[49]

The leading Bank organ in New York City described Polk's effort

[46] Watmough to Biddle, 30 Dec. 1833, Biddle Papers; Biddle to Watmough, 28 Dec. 1833, Letter Books, *ibid.*; Jackson to Mrs. Sarah Jackson, 2 Jan. 1834, Jackson Papers.

[47] *Reg. Deb.*:23:1, pp. 2265-2289.

[48] Biddle to Watmough, 6 Jan. 1834, Letter Books, Biddle Papers.

[49] Adams, *Diary*, IX, 64.

as "the most alarming speech that has been made to Congress for some years past." According to this paper's Washington correspondent, Polk was now "the echo of the palace" and "more the organ of the administration than any other individual on the floor of the House of Representatives." This well-informed journalist considered Polk by no means a great man, but warned the Whigs not to underrate his abilities. "Mr. *Polk*," the dispatch concluded, "gives daily evidence of industry and research. And whatever aid he may receive, as it is said he does from others, he possesses the faculty of converting it, advantageously, to his own use."[50]

Jackson men, on the other hand, everywhere hailed Polk as a new Democratic hero. Old Hickory distributed copies of his speech far and wide, and Polk prudently ordered 500 for his constituents. The Tennessee congressman was becoming a national figure. When the Philadelphia Democrats met for their anniversary celebration of Jackson's victory at New Orleans, the first of the volunteer toasts was to "James K. Polk, of Tennessee—an able, honest, and incorruptible champion of the People's rights, in the Congress of the United States."[51]

However gratifying the public reaction, Polk's speech did not accomplish its immediate object. He failed again to pass the previous question, and the Bank forces redoubled their efforts to alarm the country and force recharter. Biddle continued to listen to the advice of men like James Watson Webb, the Bank's chief editorial supporter in New York City. "Nothing will be done to save the Country," this gentleman informed the banker, "unless a general Bankruptcy ensues and the *'experiment'* thus proved to have failed." Such a result would occur in ninety days, he predicted, and then the Bank would be rechartered by a two-thirds vote. Webb's only fear was that Biddle would relax the pressure. If "once having put your hand to the plough," he warned, you

venture to look back, *all is lost*. I do not doubt your determination to persevere, but knowing how strongly you will be urged to relent—what appeals will be made to your best feelings—and what scenes of distress and ruin you will be called upon to witness, I sometimes despair of your withstanding it. But do not forget that the skillful surgeon is frequently compelled to inflict temporary pain to grant permanent relief, & that it is better to loose an unsound limb than that the whole body should become corrupted.[52]

50 New York *Courier and Enquirer,* quoted in Nashville *Banner,* 22 Jan. 1834.
51 Nashville *Banner,* 30 Jan. 1834; James O'Hanlon to Jackson, 24 Apr. 1834, Jackson Papers; receipt, 30 Jan. 1834, Polk Papers.
52 James Watson Webb to Biddle, 26 Feb. 1834, Biddle Papers.

Webb's apprehensions about Biddle were groundless. "My own course is decided," the Bank president remorselessly declared. "All the other Banks and all the merchants may break, but the Bank of the United States shall not break."[53] As the pressure tightened, public clamor mounted, and the Democrats began to despair of forcing the previous question before their ostensible majority melted away. Secretary Taney kept pressing Polk for action, but it was not until February 18 that debate was finally halted by a scant four-vote margin, and the secretary's report went at long last to Polk's committee, more than two months after it was sent to the House.[54]

While Polk was struggling to get his hands on Taney's report, the Ways and Means Committee had been considering another question related to the Bank. In January the secretary of war had ordered Biddle's corporation to give up its long-established business as government agent for paying pensions to Revolutionary veterans. When Biddle refused to turn over the books and funds, pension payments were suspended. The president had referred the controversy to Congress, and the House had passed it on to the Ways and Means Committee. Within a week Polk presented a majority report denouncing Biddle's defiance of the government and blaming the Bank for the suspension of pension payments. Two members of the committee minority, Gorham and Wilde, felt that the Bank was asking for trouble by its conduct, but Biddle demanded vindication. Binney finally whipped the recalcitrants into line, and the minority submitted a report contradicting the majority at every point. The incident, however, did the Bank little good.[55]

Polk meanwhile, anticipating eventual reference of Taney's report to the Ways and Means Committee, had been working on a committee report upholding removal. The flood of petitions on removal had been directed into his hands, and all were grist for his mill. Taney had declined Polk's invitation to draft the committee report himself, but the two men conferred and corresponded on it regularly. Polk was already well along with his task when the Ways and Means Committee finally got the original Taney report on February 18, and two weeks later his own well-documented report of 141 pages (about four fifths of it being supporting evidence) was

---

[53] *Biddle Correspondence*, 221.

[54] *House Journal*:23:1, pp. 344-347; Taney to [Woodbury?], 3 Jan. 1834, Woodbury Papers.

[55] *House Committee Reports*:23:1, No. 263; Adams, *Diary*, IX, 94-95.

ready for the House and the public. Binney, Gorham, and Wilde appended to it a thirty-four-page report for the minority.[56]

The majority report was an elaboration of Polk's speech. The secretary's power over the public funds was argued at length. The reasons Taney had given to justify removal—exclusion of the government directors from the business of the Bank, interference with payment of the public debt, the Bank's demand for damages on a dishonored government draft on France, use of Bank funds to influence public opinion and elections, loans to congressmen, and Biddle's unlimited personal control over Bank resources—were supported by argument and voluminous evidence. The competence of the state banks as government depositories was maintained. One section, defending the secretary's right to make contracts with the deposit banks, was drawn almost verbatim from a letter Taney had written Polk on January 13.

The real dynamite in the report was its brief reference to the current contraction of credit. The Democrats had been pretending up to this point that a panic existed only in the minds and speeches of their opponents, but Polk's report signaled a dramatic tactical shift, suggesting that Biddle had deliberately brought about the pressure in order to force restoration of the deposits and recharter.

While most of the report spoke to the immediate questions at issue, one significant paragraph threw light on the long-range objectives of the Democrats. Jackson and his followers were not trying simply to destroy a hated and overpowerful corporation. With the Bank out of the way, their more fundamental social and economic purposes might be realized. "The main object of legislation," said the committee majority, "should be to enlarge the basis of specie, on which the circulation of the State Banks is to depend for support." By proper execution of the new deposit system, they argued, the currency could be made sounder and "this country rescued permanently from the danger of those sudden expansions and contractions of the paper currency which have been constantly succeeding each other since the Bank of the United States was established, and which have brought such severe and extensive evils upon the country." The reform was to be accomplished by gradually banishing small notes from circulation. This would in turn create a steady

---

[56] Taney to Polk, two letters, n.d. [Dec. 1833; placed at end of 1834], 3 Jan. 1833 [1834], 13 Jan. 1834, Polk Papers. The Polk Papers contain fifty-nine draft pages of the report in Polk's hand (placed at end of 1833).

demand for coin to be used in ordinary transactions and force the banks to keep larger stocks of the precious metals on hand. Here was the first official hint, since Jackson's ambiguous but ominous reference to "a uniform and sound currency" four years before, of the hard-money policy at which the administration was aiming.[57]

Polk's report and the resolutions submitted with it were debated for a month. At first the Whigs were confident that the money pressure was having its desired effect. "We were evidently gaining ground slowly but surely," wrote one pro-Bank congressman, "and we felt great confidence that in the end there would be a majority in the House to disapprove of the act of the Secretary." Biddle's lieutenants pinned their hopes especially on the Pennsylvania delegation, which, though predominantly Democratic, was peculiarly susceptible to Bank influence. At the end of February, however, a Pennsylvania state bond issue went unsubscribed, and the formerly pro-Bank Governor George Wolf publicly excoriated Biddle's corporation for creating the financial stringency.

This was the turning point in the long and bitter struggle. Eleven of the twenty-eight Pennsylvania congressmen held firm against the Bank, and the disintegration of Jackson's majority was halted. After conferring with administration leaders, Polk concluded on April 4 that the time had come to risk a vote on the committee's resolutions. "The pressure of party," a Whig member complained, was "now put down upon the rank and file with more than hydraulic power," and the first resolution, against recharter, carried by the comfortable majority of 134 to 82. Because there were many members against recharter who would not approve removal, the second resolution, against restoring the deposits to the national bank, passed by the narrower margin of 118 to 103. The third, recommending continued deposits in the state banks, was approved by an almost identical vote, while only 32 die-hards opposed the final resolution, calling for an investigation to determine whether the Bank had deliberately provoked the financial panic.[58]

These votes were a death knell to the Bank's hopes for recharter. Biddle had done his utmost, but the very ruthlessness of his tactics brought defeat. By March the Bank's staunchest supporters in the

[57] *House Committee Reports*:23:1, No. 312.

[58] "Selections from the William Greene Papers: II, Letters of Samuel F. Vinton to William Greene, 1833-1861," Historical and Philosophical Society of Ohio, *Quarterly Publication*, XIV (1919), 9-10; Samuel Jaudon to Biddle, 10 Mar. 1834, Biddle Papers; *Reg. Deb.*:23:1, pp. 3474-3477.

business community realized what Biddle was doing, and he was eventually forced to relax his financial pressure to escape public repudiation by the most influential business leaders. Biddle's capitulation, however, served to alienate the men who had been carrying his colors in Congress. "I am as much relieved from duty," wrote the embittered Horace Binney, "as if I were knocked in the head."[59]

The Bank War of 1834 ended on a note of fiasco. The investigating committee authorized by Polk's fourth resolution was armed with wide subpoena powers, including the right to examine all the Bank's books and correspondence, and set off for Philadelphia in high hopes of exposing once and for all the irregularities and corruption with which the corporation was charged. One of the committeemen, John Y. Mason, a Virginia congressman who had been at Chapel Hill in Polk's student days, kept his former schoolmate posted on the committee's progress, or more accurately, lack of progress. The investigators found Biddle still defiant of the government and particularly determined that they should not see any of the correspondence dealing with loans to the Bank's supporters in Congress. The committee was finally denied access to any of the Bank's books, though this was a clear violation of the charter and in contempt of Congress. When the irate investigators returned empty-handed to Washington, they demanded that Biddle and his principal officers be brought to the bar of the House on a citation for contempt. Taney supported this demand, but some of the southern Democrats were unwilling to go so far, and the Bank won a technical victory. Though this episode further damaged the corporation in public esteem, recharter was now so hopeless that it mattered little.[60]

Nicholas Biddle had gambled rashly on his economic power and lost. The country was more convinced than ever that the Bank was a dangerous monopoly. The slim but determined Democratic majority in the House had been driven to an inflexible anti-Bank position. The Bank's warmest supporters were disillusioned, its congressional strategists felt betrayed, and the Whig party was anxious to shed the burden of defending a discredited institution. Except for the formalities of winding up its business, the Second Bank of the United States, as a national institution, was dead.

[59] Charles Chauncey Binney, *The Life of Horace Binney with Selections from His Letters* (Philadelphia, 1903), 118.

[60] John Y. Mason to Polk, 5, 10 May 1834, Polk Papers; [?] to Biddle, 1 June 1834, Biddle Papers.

VIII

The Monster had been slain, but what would take its place? Throughout the long debate the Democrats had been taunted with reminders of previous financial disasters stemming from untrammelled state banking and of previous losses of federal funds deposited in state banks. How could hard-money Democrats, whose professed aim was currency reform, go back to the state bank deposit system? Had not the national bank restrained extravagant inflation by the state banks? With the national bank destroyed, might not the state banks get out of hand before the Democratic reformers could bring them under control?

The difficulties of dealing with the state banks were increased by the fact that the Democrats had been compelled to enlist their political support in the war on the national bank. "The President was not deemed strong enough to encounter all the banks of all the States at once," as Senator Benton explained it. "Temporizing was indispensable."[61] Administration leaders were well aware of the dangers, but they were convinced they had discovered a technique for using the deposit system to secure a general currency reform in the direction of hard money.

Both a rationale and a program for the hard-money men had been developed in a remarkable little book published in 1833 by a Philadelphia editor and economist. William Gouge's *Short History of Paper Money and Banking in the United States*[62] has remained the classic description of the early American banking system. It accomplished the difficult feat of being both economically sound and understandable to the average citizen. On the polemical side Gouge showed workingmen and farmers how they were victimized by the banking system, with its concomitants of periodic depression, unemployment, sagging agricultural markets, and depreciated money. At the same time he bolstered the social argument for hard money with an economic one. Gouge argued convincingly that depressions were attributable mainly to the overextension of credit through bank paper, incidentally misleading the Jacksonians into the assumption that by controlling the issuance of bank paper, they could control the volume of credit. And finally, he gave the hard-money men a concrete program.

Gouge was well aware that a sudden destruction of the existing

---

[61] Thomas Hart Benton, *Thirty Years' View* . . . (2 vols., New York, 1954), I, 158.
[62] Philadelphia, 1833.

system would be disastrous. He was no enemy of legitimate banking, that is, taking money on deposit for interest, loaning at short terms, and dealing in bills of exchange. It was only the current system of inflating the credit structure through overissues of bank notes that he opposed. His proposal for reform was a progressive prohibition of bank notes of higher and higher denominations, until coin replaced small notes in ordinary transactions. Gold and silver were not subject to violent fluctuations, and they did not enrich bankers. Revaluation of gold to bring it back to a parity with silver was a necessary preparatory step. As for governmental fiscal operations, they should be divorced completely from the banking system. The government should deal exclusively in gold and silver coin, keeping its funds in its own independent treasury and subtreasury offices. As a first step, Gouge suggested that Congress require all government dues to be paid in specie. The demand for the precious metals for government payments, coupled with the prohibition of small notes, would bring the entire currency back to a healthy state.

Gouge's ideas had a profound effect on certain Democratic leaders and through them on public opinion. The inchoate antibanking views of men like Jackson, Benton, Kendall, Blair, Taney, and Polk, were strengthened and given focus by an authoritative economic argument and a specific program. Gouge's proposals became, in effect, the long-range fiscal policy of the Jackson party, though it was only gradually unfolded as political and economic circumstances permitted or demanded. The circumstances that evoked and finally frustrated this policy constituted the central theme of Jackson's second term and the administration of Martin Van Buren.

Long before Gouge's book appeared, Jackson had regarded the divorce of government from all banks as an essential element of his hard-money program. The "national bank" he proposed in his first and second annual messages differed little from Gouge's independent treasury, and he had turned to use of the state banks only as a second best solution. Since his own plan had received no support in Congress or from public opinion, he wrote, "I have brought my mind to the belief that the employment of State Banks, if they will enter into reasonable terms is the best if not the only practicable resort." But Jackson was never wholly easy in his mind about the state bank deposit system, and persistently referred to it as his "Experiment," a designation that the Whigs seized on happily.[63]

[63] Jackson to William J. Duane, 17 July 1833, copy, Jackson Papers.

The avidity with which the state banks sought the federal deposits as a basis for vast extensions of their note issues and profits, and their political strength within the Democratic party, were not the only obstacles to rigid controlling legislation. The hard-money Jacksonians were also inhibited by their constitutional scruples. What these men really wanted to do was to regulate the currency, insofar as it consisted of bank paper. But they denied that bank notes were actually currency under the constitutional definition, and hence the federal government had no power over them. They were compelled, therefore, to reach their objectives through indirect and inadequate techniques, supplemented by the naïve hope, expressed in all their pronouncements from Polk's report on, that "the aid and co-operation of the several states may be relied on to banish gradually, the smaller notes, and introduce in their place silver and gold for ordinary domestic purposes."[64]

IX

When Polk's Bank resolutions passed the House, he and the Ways and Means Committee were already at work on a plan to regulate the currency through the deposit system. In a letter to Taney, Polk had voiced the committee's special concern over the impact of the deposit system on the general currency and asked for the secretary's recommendations. Taney's detailed reply constituted the body of a report the committee presented on April 21. Taney proposed that the selection of the favored banks be left to the secretary of the treasury, and also that he be allowed to remove the deposits from any bank, provided he submitted his reasons to Congress. The deposit banks, he recommended, should be required to file monthly statements of their condition, and the government should have the right to inspect their books.

The heart of the report was the section dealing with currency reform. "The dangerous expansion of the paper circulation, compared with its specie basis," the secretary wrote, "shows that there is something essentially vicious in the whole system." The first step in a reform program, destruction of the national bank, was practically accomplished. The second step was revaluation of gold, a measure on which another committee was working. The third step was to be accomplished through the deposit system.

Taney avoided the radical proposal that the government receive

64 *House Committee Reports*:23:1, No. 312, p. 30.

only gold and silver from its debtors. On the other hand he opposed making the notes of deposit banks receivable for all government dues, as the notes of the national bank had been, for this would encourage overissue. What he did recommend was that the deposit banks be required, as a condition of receiving the deposits, to cease issuing themselves, or receiving from other banks, notes under five dollars. Once the economy had adjusted to the demise of the national bank, the prohibition should be extended to notes under ten dollars and eventually to those under twenty dollars. If this were insufficient by itself to reform the currency, he said, "We may safely rely on the co-operation of the several States to impose upon their banks the restrictions necessary to aid in this desirable change in the state of the currency." Specie would then take the place of paper in everyday transactions, and bank credit would be used only for legitimate commercial purposes.

Taney's concluding paragraph echoed the social philosophy of Jackson's Bank Veto. "The laboring classes of the community," wrote the secretary, are paid in small notes, and the most depreciated of these small notes "are too often used in payments to the poorer and more helpless classes of society." If the small notes were banished from circulation, laborers would be paid in gold and silver, "and that portion of society which is most apt to suffer from worthless or depreciated paper, and who are least able to bear the loss, would be guarded from imposition and injustice." In previous provisions for the currency, Taney contended, "we have been providing facilities for those employed in extensive commerce, and have left the mechanic and the laborer to all the hazards of an insecure and unstable circulating medium." "It is time," he thought, "that the just claims of this portion of society should be regarded in our legislation."[65]

Along with this report Polk submitted a bill embodying Taney's recommendations, though there was little hope for passage this late in the session. The Whigs refused to sanction removal even implicitly by supporting such a measure, and when Polk finally got the bill to the floor on June 20, he turned his sarcasm on those who were crying "executive usurpation" while at the same time resisting congressional legislation to regulate the executive's handling of the public funds. He declared emphatically that currency reform was the main object

[65] *House Committee Reports*:23:1, No. 422; [Polk to Taney], 1 Apr. 1834, draft copy, Polk Papers.

of the bill. "The general scope and tenor," he said, "is, to make the public money, wherever deposited, equal to specie," and by eliminating small notes to "gradually introduce in their stead a metallic circulation." Polk was particularly incensed by Whig insinuations that his actions were dictated by servility to Jackson. His course, he insisted, was consistent with "principles and opinions early adopted and steadily maintained from the commencement of my public service."[66] Most of the bill's critics harped on the theme that "Destroying the national bank to expel paper money was like killing the cat to keep the mice away!"[67]

During the debate a Virginia Calhounite, William Fitzhugh Gordon, rose to make a significant and embarrassing proposal. Gordon was one of those old-fashioned state rights doctrinaires who opposed both the national bank and Jackson's removal of the deposits. He denied that Congress had the constitutional power to regulate the currency through either a national bank or state deposit banks, and he now proposed that the government keep its own funds in specie and have nothing whatever to do with any banks. This was essentially the independent treasury plan advanced by Gouge. Gordon seems to have gotten the idea from Condy Raguet, a fellow editor-economist of Gouge in Philadelphia. A free trader and admirer of Calhoun, Raguet had sent an outline of such a system to Senator White several months before. Gordon lived in the same boarding-house with White and had doubtless seen the Raguet proposal. The bill he now presented as a substitute for Polk's deposit bill had been drafted in consultation with Calhoun.

Gordon avowed himself a champion of specie, and "called upon all who were in favor of 'Jackson money' to go with him in support of the old-fashioned constitutional notion of a hard-money Government." The Democrats were not yet prepared to go so far. They were in no mood to accept any proposition emanating from Calhoun, and besides, state bank support was still needed to win elections. Only a handful of members supported Gordon's substitute, and Polk finally succeeded in forcing his own bill through the House, only to see it killed in the Whig Senate. The federal funds remained at the discretionary disposal of the executive, and the Whigs retained an effective campaign issue.[68]

[66] *Reg. Deb.*:23:1, pp. 4602-4622.   [67] *ibid.*, 4749.
[68] *Reg. Deb.*:23:1, pp. 4640-4642; Charles M. Wiltse, *John C. Calhoun* (3 vols., Indianapolis, 1944-1951), II, 229; *House Journal*:23:1, pp. 824-828; *Senate Journal*: 23:1, p. 401.

X

The struggle for a deposit law that would reform the currency was to drag on for two more years. When the second or short session of the twenty-third Congress met in December 1834, the president urgently requested action, and the matter was again referred to the Ways and Means Committee. Within two weeks Polk was ready with a stronger measure than that of the previous session. The prohibition of small notes was to be extended after March 1838 to those under ten dollars, and the deposit banks were required to give collateral security for the government funds and to maintain a specie reserve of one-fourth their note circulation.[69]

Reuben Whitney, now the agent of the deposit banks, was unhappy about these new provisions, particularly the specie reserve requirement, but Polk was under pressures. He doubtless shared the uneasiness of many Jacksonians about any connection with the state banks. The old national bank party was only too eager to tempt the hard-money men with proposals for even harsher restrictions on the deposit banks, while the Calhounites could be counted on to try luring them away entirely from the deposit system with Gordon's independent treasury proposal. "Those of us who have been opposing the B.U.S.," Whitney nervously warned his state bank friends, "have now got to take care that the impetus of opposition to that institution does not extend too far, and injure the state bank interest."[70]

The independent treasury proposal reappeared even before Polk's bill reached the floor, with all the Whigs supporting it in order to embarrass the Democrats. "Sir, it is a remarkable fact," taunted one incorrigible champion of the national bank, "that at a time when the people were taught to believe that they would very soon have in their commerce the exclusive use of the precious metals, that paper money was increasing with unexampled rapidity." Though this gentleman had slight sympathy for hard-money ideas, he professed alarm that the state bank deposit system "will destroy all hope of a hard-money Government, and fasten upon the country a depreciated currency of local value." "Knowing the devotion of the gentleman from Tennessee for eagles and half eagles," the Whig orator hoped he would withdraw further opposition.

[69] *House Journal*:23:2, p. 96; *Reg. Deb.*:23:2, pp. 1266-1277.
[70] Whitney to W. D. Lewis, 6 Nov. 1834, 15 Feb. 1835, Lewis-Neilson Papers.

Polk protested that he was "not an advocate of banks of any kind," but he could not avoid an argument against the independent treasury that would rise to haunt him later. Banks, he maintained, would be "economical, convenient, and useful" fiscal agents. They offered greater security to the government than individual collectors employed by the Treasury Department. Banks could also transfer the public funds from one place to another easily and cheaply. Moreover the state bank deposit system would not affect values and trade adversely by holding large amounts of government specie funds out of circulation. But his primary object was to defend the administration, not the state banks. The provisions in his bill to increase the amount of specie circulation, he said, would give a sounder basis to the paper circulation, "if banks must continue to exist."[71]

The Gordon substitute was made the more embarrassing by daily accumulating evidence of the dangerously inflationary tendency of the state banks. Hard on the heels of the Bank Veto and removal, the states had begun to grant new bank charters by the scores, and the deposit banks themselves, despite the Treasury's restrictions, orders, and entreaties, were using the federal funds for extravagant expansion of their loans and note issues. The country was on the upswing of an inflationary boom that even the national bank could hardly have stemmed, and the Jacksonians were worried. "The present bloat in the paper system cannot continue," thundered "Old Bullion" Benton over in the Senate. "The revulsion will come, as surely as it did in 1819-'20. . . . I did not join in putting down the Bank of the United States, to put up a wilderness of local banks. I did not join in putting down the paper currency of a national bank, to put up a national paper currency of a thousand local banks. I did not strike Caesar to make Anthony master of Rome."[72] But the rise of Anthony was by no means unconnected with Caesar's demise.

The Democrats had had the misfortune to accomplish the first step in their reform program, destruction of the national bank, at the very time when the consequences of this step were most dangerous to their long-range objectives. And now they were virtually bound by political necessity to the state banks. At the moment Polk had no choice but to crack the whip of party discipline, and Gordon's independent treasury proposal was killed, only thirty-three extreme state rights men sticking by it to the end.

71 *Reg. Deb.*:23:2, pp. 897-902, 1266-1280; *Cong. Globe*:23:2, pp. 88-89.
72 Benton, *Thirty Years' View*, I, 703.

Undiscouraged by this failure to lure the Democrats away from the deposit system with the bait of hard money, the Whigs promptly threw their strength behind a long series of amendments offered by Biddle's man Binney. Ostensibly providing further restrictions on the deposit banks and further safeguards for the public funds, these amendments would actually have gone far to destroy the deposit system. Of Binney's more important proposals, one would require the deposit banks to pay interest on federal deposits, which would make it more difficult for the government to control the way the banks used its funds and to secure prompt repayment. Another would require the deposit banks to maintain a specie reserve of one fifth not only of their circulation, but of their public and private deposits as well. This would prevent those banks too remote from the commercial centers for prompt settlements with other banks from accepting large amounts of government deposits in bank notes, and would render the deposit system virtually impossible in the West, where the government was receiving enormous sums from land sales. Still another proposal would require periodic publication of the deposit banks' condition, though this would enable the still potent Bank of the United States to concentrate its resources for the embarrassment or destruction of the weakest members of the deposit system.

Binney's amendments were skillfully designed to appeal to the antibank prejudices of the Jackson men, and Reuben Whitney was soon reporting that "some of our strongest and warmest friends have got the Devil into them." Despite Polk's efforts to show the real effects of the Binney proposals, enough Democrats were seduced to pass them all. "I wish I could be pinned to Polks back as his prompter," Whitney groaned, and he now began beseeching Polk to "*smother*" the whole bill. He finally thought he had committed Polk to an arrangement whereby, "while *seeming* to call up the bill, others shall be permitted to obtain a preference untill the close of the session." But Whitney had mistaken his man, for Polk was still determined to pass the original bill. Days of dogged argument and stringent application of party discipline were necessary, however, before the House was persuaded to reconsider its earlier action and kill the Binney modifications.[73]

Still Whitney and the deposit banks could not rest easy, for Cal-

[73] Whitney to W. D. Lewis, 16, 23 Feb. 1835, Lewis-Neilson Papers; *Reg. Deb.*: 23:2, pp. 1333-1350, 1436-1443.

houn and Webster, prompted by Biddle's cashier, Jaudon, were following Binney's strategy in designing their own deposit bill in the Whig-controlled Senate. The House bill had no chance of passing the Senate, so when the Senate bill came to the House, the Democrats were more tempted than ever to accept additional restrictions on the deposit banks in order to get some kind of deposit law on the books. Even Polk wavered, seeking advice from Levi Woodbury, who had succeeded Taney in the Treasury.

Woodbury was no great friend of the banks, but he was adamant against the Senate bill. It should be entitled, he complained, "a Bill to pave the way to a renewal of the Charter of the United States Bank." Woodbury was positive that few banks would accept deposits on the terms it stipulated, and he urged Polk to provide against this eventuality by inserting a section authorizing the secretary to inaugurate the independent treasury system. Polk was persuaded, and Whitney could finally breathe freely. "Thank god, there are but two days more for mischief to be consummated," he exclaimed. Polk had the Ways and Means Committee draft amendments to bring the Senate bill in line with the House version, but the stalemate between the two houses was so obvious that the subject was not even considered in the rush for adjournment. And so the deposit bill was lost again.[74]

A deposit law was eventually passed by the twenty-fourth Congress in 1836, but it was coupled with the act of that session for distributing the now enormous federal surplus among the states. The deposit provisions of this act followed the original Binney amendments in requiring the banks to pay interest on government funds, and the Treasury was forbidden to deposit with any bank an amount exceeding three-fourths its capital. The result was to alter substantially the deposit system as Taney had designed it. The number of deposit banks increased from the twenty Taney had selected to ninety. No longer a small group of banks, carefully chosen for their soundness and ability to hold the other banks in check, they now recklessly employed the government's money to make speculative profits, and the Treasury lost all control over them.[75]

[74] Woodbury to Polk, 26, 28 Feb. 1835, Polk Papers; Polk to Woodbury, 27 Feb. 1835 [misplaced 1836], *ibid.; id.* to *id.*, 27 Feb. 1834 [1835], Woodbury Papers; Whitney to W. D. Lewis, 1, 4 Mar. 1835, Lewis-Neilson Papers; *Reg. Deb.*:23:2, pp. 619-627; *Senate Journal*:23:2, pp. 196, 199; *House Journal*:23:2, p. 492.

[75] John Spencer Bassett, ed., *Correspondence of Andrew Jackson* (7 vols., Washington, 1926-1935), v, 492.

Jackson was unhappy about both the deposit and distribution features of this measure, but the necessity for some deposit law and the clamor of the states for the federal surplus compelled him to sign it. Instead of checking the dangerous inflationary orgy, this remodeled deposit system stimulated it.

The Jacksonians clearly would have preferred a more far-reaching reform. But they had no control over the states, where banking excesses were rooted, and their attempt to reform the currency through the deposit system was perverted by the votes of the Whigs. Even had there been no partisan opposition, time was running out. The secretary of the treasury had prohibited notes under five dollars on his own responsibility in September 1835, but the boom was rising too fast to be checked by any such limited reform. The inevitable crash was not far away.

XI

These disappointing developments and the ultimate failure of Jackson's "Experiment," however, still lay in the unknown future as the panic session of the twenty-third Congress drew to a close in June 1834. Jubilant over their defeat of Biddle and his bank, the Democrats were little disposed to worry about what lay ahead. Never before had the prospects for the Democracy seemed so bright. And there were few individual Democrats whose prospects seemed brighter than James K. Polk's. The long fight had made him the undisputed administration leader in the House and a hero to Democrats everywhere. Under his guidance the House had stood firm against the worst the cohorts of Biddle, Webster, Calhoun, and Clay could do. The Bank's last hope was dead, and a new, democratic financial policy seemed in the making. All over the country Polk was toasted at Fourth of July celebrations, and Old Hickory himself declared that "Mr. Taney, Benton, and Polk deserve not only golden medals but the gratitude of their country."[76]

The strain and fatigue, however, had taken a physical toll. "The labours you have passed through this session are enough to break down a man of iron," wrote the sympathetic Taney, and Polk had had to spend the last few weeks before adjournment in bed. Sarah did not help matters by exercising her wifely prerogative of poking fun at her husband's views. "Why," she said, "if we must use gold

[76] Jackson to William Findlay, 20 Aug. 1834, copy, Jackson Papers.

and silver all the time, a lady can scarcely carry enough money with her." She was particularly amused at James's insistence on taking along enough coin to meet their expenses while traveling. On one occasion, after turning their trunk upside down to find a bag of specie, she exclaimed, "Don't you see how troublesome it is to carry around gold and silver? This is enough to show you how useful banks are."[77]

[77] Taney to Polk, 24 June 1834, Polk Papers; Nelson, *Sarah Polk*, 38-40.

8

POLK VERSUS BELL

FROM THE STANDPOINT OF POLK'S PERSONAL FORTUNES, the Bank debate was overshadowed by another struggle that occurred during the panic session of 1833-1834. Polk's haste to get to Washington in the late autumn of 1833 had been dictated not only by his new responsibilities as chairman-designate of the Ways and Means Committee, but also by the hope that he might be rewarded with election to the powerful post of speaker of the House.

Rumors that Speaker Andrew Stevenson would be appointed minister to Great Britain had given rise to considerable discussion about his successor the previous spring, and some of the Jackson men had pledged themselves to Polk at that time. Although Stevenson still had not been appointed when Congress adjourned in March 1833, Polk had learned from Major Lewis shortly after reaching home that the appointment was scheduled for early in the coming session. As soon as the elections were over in August, he began lining up his particular friends, while Grundy and Cave Johnson were enlisted to write to their intimates in the House. The initial response to these inquiries was quite favorable, and some members volunteered their support without being approached.

The determining factor would be the wishes of the party leadership, meaning President Jackson, the Kitchen Cabinet, and Martin Van Buren, who controlled the big New York delegation. So anxious was Polk on this point that he adopted the hazardous expedient of appealing to Major Lewis. In the letter setting forth his claims, Polk for the first time explicitly endorsed Van Buren to succeed Jackson.[1] But the wily major was by no means so devoted to the interests of the New Yorker as Polk may have imagined; it would soon be ap-

---

[1] Francis Fry Wayland, *Andrew Stevenson: Democrat and Diplomat, 1785-1857* (Philadelphia, 1949), 100-101; Polk to W. B. Lewis, 13 Aug. 1833, Ford Collection (NYPL); C. C. Clay to Polk, 19 Aug. 1833, James K. Polk Papers (LC; herein cited as Polk Papers, which refers to First Series unless otherwise noted); C. C. Clay to Cave Johnson, 19 Aug. 1833, *ibid.*; W. M. Inge to Polk, 28 Aug. 1833, *ibid.*; Cave Johnson to Polk, 29 Aug. 1833, *ibid.*; Grundy to Polk, 31 Oct. 1833, *ibid.*; "Letters of James K. Polk to Cave Johnson, 1833-1848," *Tennessee Historical Magazine* (Sept. 1915), 212.

parent that Lewis had other loyalties, and Polk's letter served only to expose his plans to a dangerous competitor. For another Tennessean had his eye on the same political plum.

Following a visit to Nashville in October, James Walker warned his brother-in-law that he "saw something which led me to believe there was a perfect understanding between Bell, Eaton, [Robert] Armstrong, Foster, &c. which makes me feel very cautious in saying anything to L[ewis]. upon subjects in which your and Bell's views may clash." This was just after Grundy had defeated Eaton, Foster, and Bell for the Senate, and Walker was convinced that "two parties are organizing in the Jackson ranks, one for Van Buren and the other for Dick Johnson."[2]

A colorful congressman from Kentucky, the red-vested Colonel Richard M. Johnson was a minor national hero by virtue of his reputed slaying of the Indian leader Tecumseh at the Battle of the Thames in the War of 1812. A handsome, jovial, warm-hearted man, Johnson had won the affection of eastern workingmen by his attacks on imprisonment for debt and his opposition to clerical demands that post offices be closed on Sunday. He was now in the field for the Democratic presidential nomination, drawing additional support from westerners, Calhounites, and many nominal Jackson men who were disgruntled by the administration's anti-Bank policy. Devoid of strong convictions on the Bank and most other issues, Johnson was a compromiser by nature, and was now looking for backing where he could find it.

There was little tangible evidence as yet, but the Johnson talk in Tennessee was one more indication that the Eaton-Lewis men, who had contributed so much to Van Buren's triumph over Calhoun, were preparing to abandon him, primarily because of the Bank issue. More immediately Johnson and his friends might help John Bell win the speakership. Bell would be a strong contender if he could get the combined support of the Whigs and these anti-Van Buren Democrats. How clear this whole situation was to Polk and his friends in the fall of 1833 cannot be determined. He could not have understood it when he wrote to Lewis in August, but the cooperation of Eaton, Bell, and Foster in the senatorial election must have opened his eyes. At any rate Polk refused to heed Lewis's suggestion that he forget about running for speaker.

To confuse the situation further, there were other aspirants

2 Walker to Polk, 20 Oct. 1833, Polk Papers.

among those Democrats still faithful to Van Buren. James M.
Wayne of Georgia and Jesse Speight of North Carolina had both
served long and usefully in the House, and either might bring much-
needed southern support to the New Yorker. In a straight popularity contest with these two, Polk could probably get the support of
a majority of the Jackson–Van Buren congressmen, but there was
still another complicating factor, the ambitions of Doctor Joel B.
Sutherland. Sutherland had long been a power in Pennsylvania
politics, where he was allied with the potent Calhoun-Ingham faction. Two years earlier he had thrown a scare into the Van Buren
ranks by almost defeating Stevenson for speaker. Within the last
year he had resigned from Congress to accept a judgeship, then abruptly resigned the judgeship to run again for Congress, being supported by the Van Burenites in his district. Perceptive politicians
at once concluded that Van Buren had offered to make Sutherland
speaker, in return for Pennsylvania support for Van Buren's presidential ambitions. Even Governor Carroll, who still had connections
in his native Pennsylvania, seemed to be in on the intrigue, for he
advised that the speaker should be taken "from some one of the large
States."[3]

From Polk's point of view, there was only one bright spot in the
picture. James Walker had gone on from Nashville to Washington
for negotiations with the Post Office Department about his mail contracts, and he wrote back, just as Polk was leaving for the capital
himself, that the president seemed to be strongly in favor of Polk.
Jackson, indeed had given Van Buren little encouragement in his
flirtation with Sutherland. He was still suspicious, he wrote, of all the
"satelites [*sic*] and tools" of Ingham and Calhoun. "My rule," he
said, "is to repose in all, but place confidence in none, until I find

[3] Carroll to Jackson, 9 Aug. 1833, Andrew Jackson Papers (LC); Duff Green to
Gov. James Hamilton, Jr., 18 July 1831, copy, Duff Green Papers (in possession of
Prof. Fletcher M. Green, Chapel Hill, N.C.); Elisha Whittlesey to John McLean,
3 Mar. 1833, John McLean Papers (LC); Duff Green to McLean, 1 July 1833, *ibid.*;
Van Buren to Jackson, 9 May 1833, Martin Van Buren Papers (LC); Duff Green
to Biddle, 1 Oct. 1833, Nicholas Biddle Papers (LC); Elisha Whittlesey to John
W. Taylor, 10 Oct. 1833, John W. Taylor Papers (NYHS); R. H. Wilde to G. C.
Verplanck, 21 Nov. 1833, Gulian C. Verplanck Papers (NYHS); Charles Francis
Adams, ed., *Memoirs of John Quincy Adams, Comprising Portions of His Diary
from 1795 to 1848* (12 vols., Philadelphia, 1874–1877), VIII, 428-429, 431; John Bassett
Moore, ed., *The Works of James Buchanan: Comprising His Speeches, State Papers,
and Private Correspondence* (12 vols., Philadelphia, 1908-1911), II, 333; Washington
United States Telegraph, 6, 18 Nov. 1833.

they are worthy of it." This rule, he told Van Buren, is "one I would recommend to be adopted by you with our friend Doctor S."[4]

When Polk reached Washington, he found Wayne asserting a special claim to the Jackson party's support. It turned out that Stevenson had told Wayne the preceding spring that he would not be a candidate for reelection to the chair, and, in order to thwart Sutherland, had induced Wayne to announce his candidacy at that time. Neither Wayne nor Bell nor Sutherland nor Polk would retire voluntarily, and both the Cabinet and the Kitchen Cabinet were divided over what should be done. With the crucial panic session about to commence, administration control of the House and its committees was essential, and any division among the Jackson men would be disastrous. Consequently, after frenzied conferences among Polk, Wayne, and the other principals, it was concluded that Stevenson was the only Democrat who could certainly unite the party, his nomination as minister was again postponed, and he was reelected to the chair.[5]

The choice of a new speaker, however, was to be delayed only until the administration forces could come to some agreement, and thus the already turbulent panic session was further agitated by negotiations and intrigues among the various parties and factions over the speakership. The Whigs could not decide whether to run their own candidate or unite on some disaffected Jacksonian. Wayne, Sutherland, and Polk were each rumored to be the regular administration candidate. There were some reports that Polk would be backed by the Nullifiers, but one well-informed Whig doubted "that Mr Calhouns friends have any confidence in or respect for him." "If Mr Polk is other than a subservient tool," declared this member, "he is much changed since last session. He has been in fact the two last sessions, the palace slave, or his part has been much misunderstood."[6]

Actually there was considerable truth in these reports of Cal-

[4] John Spencer Bassett, ed., *Correspondence of Andrew Jackson* (7 vols., Washington, 1926-1935), v, 75; Walker to Polk, 22 Oct., 7 Nov. 1833, Polk Papers.

[5] Jackson to F. P. Blair, 30 Nov. 1833, Jackson Papers; J. M. Wayne to Polk, 1 Dec. 1833, Polk Papers; Murfreesboro *Central Monitor*, extra, 22 Nov. 1834; Elisha Whittlesey to John McLean, 3 Dec. 1833, McLean Papers; Washington *United States Telegraph*, 16 Dec. 1833.

[6] Elisha Whittlesey to John McLean, 30 Nov. 1833, McLean Papers; Washington *United States Telegraph*, 13, 30 Dec. 1833; Nashville *Banner*, 15, 27 Jan., 5 Mar. 1834; Elisha Whittlesey to J. W. Taylor, 2 Jan. 1834, Taylor Papers; David Potts, Jr., to J. W. Taylor, 11 Jan. 1834, *ibid.*

hounite support for Polk. After giving assurances in the proper quarters that he was a Van Buren man, Polk had gone quietly to work to enlist the votes of the Nullifiers. With the aid of Grundy and Cave Johnson he let Calhoun's followers understand that only public opinion in Tennessee had prevented him from taking a firm stand for state rights. After all, Grundy was an old friend of Calhoun, and Johnson had voted against the Force Bill. Though Polk himself had been more discreet, he had opposed the Eaton-Lewis clique's machinations against Calhoun several years earlier, and his strong anti-tariff position was well known. In fact from the very beginning of the contest Polk had been the only prominent Democratic candidate whom Duff Green's *Telegraph* refused to criticize. Grundy went to extreme lengths to strengthen the impression that Polk was sympathetic to the Nullifiers. How far Polk himself went is impossible to determine, but one of Biddle's correspondents passed on a rumor that Polk had denounced Van Buren as having "too much political obliquity for the party to support him, that his unpopularity will break them down." This informant was positive "that Polk has said Van Buren cannot be run for the President."[7]

John Bell's campaign was conducted very quietly at first. Early in the session it was noised about that "Bell is to be the Admin[istration] candidate, though others in the mean time are fed with hope." It is not difficult to see the hand of Major Lewis behind this report, and events steadily discredited it. Though in previous sessions Bell had been a vocal and effective supporter of the administration, he hardly opened his mouth during the protracted struggle over removal and there was even talk that he was preparing to introduce a bill for a new national bank.[8] Succeeding events demonstrated the extent to which the Bank issue was influencing the speakership election and foreshadowed future developments in Tennessee.

Both Bell's candidacy for speaker and Richard M. Johnson's candidacy for president seem to have been sponsored by some thirty Democratic congressmen who were gravely disturbed over Jackson's anti-Bank policy. When it appeared that the House would sustain removal of the deposits, these men set on foot a project to create a

---

[7] [R. L. Colt to Biddle], 17 Apr. 1834, Biddle Papers; Duff Green to Bell, 25 Mar. 1835, copy, Green Papers; "Correspondence of John Bell and Willie Mangum, 1835," *Tennessee Historical Magazine*, III (Sept. 1917), 196-200; Nashville *Banner*, 10 Feb. 1836.

[8] R. H. Wilde to G. C. Verplanck, 24 Dec. 1833, Verplanck Papers; Polk to Cave Johnson, 28 Mar. 1835, draft copy, Polk Papers.

new national bank that might avoid some of the objectionable features of the old one. Thus they hoped to "divert our friends from
wild & impracticable schemes, keep them from deserting us on the
main question, and at last *lock up* in *safe hands,* the power to create
a *new Bank.*"[9] When Colonel Johnson broached this plan for "*a*
Bank" rather than "*the* Bank" to Jackson, "the General opened
his battery in fine style upon the gallant Colonel," and the project
had to be abandoned for the moment. Johnson and his group, however, took their revenge by supporting Bell for speaker.[10]

Bell himself kept well in the background of the movement for "*a*
Bank," since he was counting on substantial support from "*the*
Bank." Biddle's handyman Watmough was hard at work lining up
votes for Bell, and shortly after Polk's resolution for another investigation of the Bank passed the House in April, Watmough wrote
to his chief about a "singular conference" he had just had with his
candidate for speaker. Greatly excited, Bell had taken Watmough
into one of the committee rooms, locked the door, and informed him
that the Ways and Means Committee had found out about some letters he had written to Biddle and intended to expose them through
the impending investigation. Bell was heavily indebted to the Bank,
and in seeking extension of his loans he had assured Biddle that he
favored the Bank and had spoken disparagingly of the Jackson
party, from which, Watmough commented, "he has not courage to
dis-enthrall himself." Bell now told Biddle's representative that "he
looks forward to the time when he will be of use, when Public Sentiment will sustain him &c &c &c & all that sort of thing." Watmough
himself thought that "the time will come when he will be of use."
"If you can," he urged Biddle, "spare him."[11]

The investigating committee did make a particular effort to secure Bell's letters, but Biddle reassured the worried congressman
that, of course, "I would never permit the execution of such an order." It is quite possible that the committee wished to use the letters
to force Bell out of the speakership race, and it is even clearer that
the Bell case was at the bottom of Biddle's risky defiance of the con-

[9] Robert T. Lytle to William Conclin, 5 Mar. 1834, Blair-Lee Papers (PU); R. M.
Johnson to F. P. Blair, 6 June [1835], *ibid.*; T. J. Lacey to Jackson, 4 June 1834,
Jackson Papers; R. M. Whitney to W. D. Lewis, 6 Nov. 1834, Lewis-Neilson Papers
(HSP).

[10] Newark *Daily Advertiser,* 10 June 1834.

[11] Watmough to Biddle, 19 Apr. 1834, Biddle Papers; Bell to Biddle, 5 July 1834,
Etting Papers (HSP).

gressional investigators. The whole episode indicated the importance that Biddle attached to the speakership election.[12]

On May 19, 1834, President Jackson called Polk and the other contenders to the White House for a "confidential communication." This was undoubtedly, at long last, the news that Stevenson would receive his appointment, for the omniscient newspaper correspondents reported the same day that he would resign the chair immediately. But again there was a delay of two weeks while the Democratic leaders made desperate last minute efforts to unite the party on a single candidate. Jackson stuck resolutely by Polk, Van Buren insisted on honoring his commitment to Sutherland, at least on the early ballots, and Bell refused to withdraw. It was pretty clearly understood by now, however, that there was no serious intention of actually electing Sutherland, and Polk was regarded as the administration candidate. Stung by the Bank investigation episode, Bell rejected Polk's proposal for submitting all the aspirants' claims to a Democratic caucus, and made an open bid for Whig support by refusing to endorse Van Buren. He knew he could secure twenty to thirty votes from his and Richard M. Johnson's pro-Bank Democratic supporters, and he was now frankly counting on Whig votes to put him over. It was generally known, on the other hand, that Polk was expecting substantial backing from the Nullifiers.[13]

With the session running out, Stevenson's nomination could be delayed no longer. He resigned the chair on June 2, and the speakership election followed immediately. The first ballot revealed a master stroke on the part of the opposition. Instead of nominating some northern Whig, such as Edward Everett, they had concentrated their entire strength on a Nullifier, Richard H. Wilde of Georgia, and Polk was thus deprived of votes that might have given him a commanding lead at the start. Wilde was ahead with 64 of the 112 votes needed to elect, and Polk was second with 42. Sutherland had 34 votes, mostly from New York and Pennsylvania; Bell had 30, including a few Whigs; and Speight and Wayne brought up the rear with 18 and 15 respectively.

12 Biddle to Bell, 2 May 1834, Letter Books, Biddle Papers.
13 Jackson to Polk, 18 May 1834, Polk Papers; John McKinley to Polk, 13 Aug. 1834, *ibid.*; Cave Johnson to Polk, 12 Sept. 1834, *ibid.*; C. C. Clay to Polk, 13 Sept. 1834, extract, *ibid.*; Watmough to Biddle [May 1834; placed at end of 1834], Biddle Papers; Anonymous to Biddle, 1 June 1834, *ibid.*; James Love to [J. J. Crittenden], 27 May 1834, John J. Crittenden Papers (LC); John L. Blair to John McLean, 31 May 1834, McLean Papers; Boston *Statesman*, 24 May 1834; Washington *United States Telegraph*, 5 June 1834.

On succeeding ballots Sutherland's votes shifted steadily to Polk, while the Speight and Wayne support rapidly evaporated. Wilde's total never increased after the first ballot, and from the second ballot on, with the Whigs shifting to Bell and the Jackson men to Polk, it was clear that Polk and Bell were the real contenders. By the seventh ballot Polk had climbed to 83, but Bell was close behind with 76. This was the critical moment. If Bell could continue to climb, he would attract not only the rest of the Whigs, but some additional Democratic votes as well. But Polk could still succeed also. The Nullifiers intended to shift to Polk as soon as Wilde's chances seemed hopeless, and their aid at this point would probably give him sufficient impetus to achieve a majority in another ballot or two. About this time, however, Bell's friends began to whisper that Kendall, Blair, and Lewis of the Kitchen Cabinet were in the lobby electioneering for Polk, and this caused the Nullifiers to hesitate. Grundy found Duff Green and rushed him into the House to save the situation. To Green, Polk vehemently denied that he was the Kitchen Cabinet's favorite, declaring heatedly that he would "make them smell Hell" for their actions. But the damage had been done. On the eighth ballot Polk slipped to 78, and Bell surged ahead to 97.

In desperation Polk appealed to Senator Willie P. Mangum, a Calhounite from North Carolina, who had just come into the House chamber. If the State Rights men meant to help him, he implored, now was the time. But Mangum was on a different mission. The tension of the tight contest had spread across the rotunda to the Senate chamber, and when word of Bell's big gain on the eighth ballot reached the Senate, the sharp-eyed Mangum had noted consternation in the face of Vice President Van Buren. Concluding instantly that Polk was the Van Buren candidate, Mangum resolved that the Nullifiers should by no means aid him. Polk had accosted the senator just as he was rushing onto the House floor to warn his colleagues to withhold their support.

By now Bell was so confident of success that he was going over the speech he intended to make when elected. So well did the Whig leaders control the situation that they were able to promise Bell a majority in two more ballots. On the ninth ballot his total increased to 104, and Polk made a final appeal to the Nullifiers to save him. But they were now going for Bell, and on the tenth and final vote, when

Bell achieved a majority, only one Nullifier voted for Polk, and he on the ground that he could not stomach Bell's pro-Bank views.[14]

The Whigs' strategy had succeeded brilliantly. Concentration of their entire strength on Wilde at the beginning had withheld the Nullifier votes from Polk long enough for Bell to begin moving ahead with the support of disgruntled Sutherland men and the gradually shifting Whigs. And finally, through carefully planted suspicions, the Nullifiers themselves had been won for Bell. The Whig press was jubilant at this victory over the administration, accurately ascribing Bell's election to his anti-Van Burenism. The Bank men had obviously contributed greatly to the result, and no one was more pleased than Nicholas Biddle. "I am delighted at our friend Bell's success," he told Watmough, "and now that the Committee of Investigation have gone, I wish you would tell him so." The Bank president, whom the investigating committee was just now seeking to bring before the House on a charge of contempt, saw an ironic humor in the situation. "I have amused myself," he wrote, "with the pleasant prospect of standing at the Bar—and receiving a reprimand from Bell for my contumacy in not giving up his letters."[15]

At the White House gloom prevailed. His heart set on Polk's election, Jackson had prepared refreshments for a celebration the moment the election was over. The four-horse official carriage had been held in readiness, and as soon as the end of the election was signaled from the Capitol, it set off at a gallop down Pennsylvania Avenue to carry the new speaker and his friends to the president. When the coachman returned with news of the result, Jackson was bitterly disappointed. There was no festivity at the White House that evening, and a couple who called the next day were told by Patrick, the president's doorkeeper, that "he would as soon conduct them into the President's room as ate a meal of victuals, but if they would take his advice, they would as soon put their fingers into a candle, as to go there, for he was in a miserable bad humor."[16]

14 Duff Green to Bell, 25 Mar. 1835, copy, Green Papers; *Cong. Globe*:23:1, pp. 4371-4373; Washington *United States Telegraph*, 2, 6 June 1834; Baltimore *Patriot*, 3 June 1834; Washington *Globe,* 7 June 1834; Nashville *Banner*, 19 June 1834; Washington *Sun*, 13 Jan. 1836; "Polk-Johnson Letters," *loc.cit.*, 223; "Bell-Mangum Correspondence," *loc.cit.*, 198-200; Ben Hardin to Cave Johnson, 22 Sept. [1834; placed 1836], Polk Papers.

15 Biddle to Watmough, 5 June 1834, Letter Books, Biddle Papers; Newark *Daily Advertiser*, 4, 5 June 1834.

16 Washington *United States Telegraph*, 11 June 1834.

II

Bell was hardly seated in the speaker's chair when the newspapers began to predict that "an attempt will be made to rout him at home." Jackson himself, report had it, was going to Tennessee during the summer "to fight Bell upon his own ground."[17] Bell's position was truly uncomfortable. Having courted Whig votes and defeated the president's candidate for speaker, his only road forward was one that led farther from Jackson. Polk and his friends, on the other hand, now had a splendid opportunity to secure Jackson's support in their designs against the whole Bell-Eaton-Lewis-Foster connection, and this opportunity they resolved to make the most of.

The speakership election was no sooner over than Polk instructed James Walker to circulate accounts of Bell's apostasy as widely as possible in Tennessee. In this effort, and indeed in the whole of the coming contest for political control of the state, the press would be of primary importance. At Columbia the *Western Mercury*, which had generally supported Polk, had gone out of existence in the spring, but it was soon replaced by the *Observer*, and this paper became Polk's most reliable advocate. In addition Polk's friends controlled several small-town weeklies, but their circulation was so limited that they were of little value. Much would depend on the attitude of the powerful and widely read Nashville papers. The *Republican* was hopelessly committed to Bell, but the *Banner* had been more friendly to the Grundy-Polk faction until the Bank question began to make it, too, unreliable.

Though the *Banner* was edited by a faithful Polk–Grundy–Van Buren man, Samuel H. Laughlin, its publisher, W. Hasell Hunt, was a well-to-do businessman and a champion of the Bank. Hurrying to Nashville as soon as he received Polk's instructions, James Walker found Hunt unwilling to cooperate in a campaign against Bell. Bell was a universal favorite with the Nashville business community, Walker discovered, and the Bank interests were strongly for him. In fact, wrote Walker, "this Nashville is a most wretchedly Bank ridden population." Walker had to rely, therefore, on the Columbia *Observer* and various village papers to carry the reports that Bell had been elected by Whig votes. The *Republican*'s defense of the new speaker, of course, got far wider circulation than the original charges.[18]

17 *ibid.*, 10 June 1834.

18 Walker to Polk, 24 June 1834, Polk Papers; Nashville *Republican*, 5 July 1834, 19 May 1835.

Congress did not adjourn until June 30, 1834, and by the time the members began reaching Tennessee late in July, newspapers and public meetings were alive with the controversy. Cave Johnson reported that the old Bank, tariff, and internal improvement party was not very strong in his district, "but when added to the Foster party are pretty formidable." Congressman Balie Peyton was justifying his vote for Bell on the ground that Polk had thrown himself into the arms of the Nullifiers, while Polk's friends were denouncing Bell's silence during the panic debate and circulating charges that he favored "*a* Bank," if not "*the* Bank."[19] The dispute got into Fourth of July celebrations all over the state, and at one such affair the toast was offered: "The Hon. John Bell, a sentinel from Tennessee.—Why silent in the hour of danger?"[20]

The friends of both principals to the quarrel had arranged public dinners to enable their respective favorites to state their positions. These dinners, or barbecues, were always carried off with elaborate preparations and publicity, and the Polk affair at Columbia was no exception. A procession headed by Revolutionary veterans and the guests of honor formed on the public square at one o'clock, and from there escorted Polk to a grove near town for a "splendid dinner." The main business of the day began with a series of toasts prepared by the arrangements committee, and one of these flung down the gauntlet for the coming political war. "The Hon. James K. Polk," proclaimed the toastmaster, "Our *esteemed* fellow citizen, and *faithful representative* in Congress—though not *Speaker of the House*, we hail him the able *Speaker for the people*." Polk responded with a speech "in his usual style of impassioned eloquence," and after some fifty additional toasts the meeting broke up, of course, in the greatest good humor.[21]

At Nashville, meanwhile, Bell had decided against accepting his invitation to a dinner, but he used his letter of declination to notice publicly the "misrepresentations" being circulated about the speakership election. These "sheer inventions of embittered personal or political hostility" he denounced as "the natural and but too common resort of unsuccessful opposition." Denying that he had deserted the administration, he declared that he did not want to become engaged in a general controversy unless it were necessary. "It cannot be expected that I will continue to act on the defensive," the

19 Cave Johnson to Polk, 18 July 1834, Polk Papers.
20 Nashville *Banner,* 16 July 1834.   21 Columbia *Observer,* 8 Aug. 1834.

speaker concluded ominously, "and a contest may be provoked, which may turn out alike unprofitably and disagreeably to all concerned." Thus warned, Polk began to prepare himself for the threatened counterattack by securing statements about the speakership election from various friendly members of the House.[22]

Hard on the heels of the congressmen, Andrew Jackson reached Tennessee for a visit. He was barely settled at the Hermitage before he wrote to Van Buren that Bell had been much injured by his silence on the Bank. "He must come out boldly against a Bank as well as the Bank," said Jackson, "or he is politically gone." Eaton had arrived in Nashville about the same time, and he and Bell, together with Congressmen Peyton, Dickinson, and Forester, immediately went out to the Hermitage to try to mollify the old general. But Jackson was not satisfied with Bell's general protestations of loyalty. Convinced that all of Bell's Nashville friends, with Foster at their head, were for a national bank and against Van Buren, the president doubted whether Bell could break loose from the "Bank junto."[23]

The convention that had finally been called to revise the state constitution was then in session at Nashville, and on August 13 a mammoth celebration and dinner were held in Jackson's honor. Polk, Cave Johnson, Grundy, and their leading allies were all in town for consultation on this festive occasion. After a parade, to the accompaniment of firing guns, ringing bells, and a band, nearly 2,000 Tennesseans sat down to dinner with their distinguished guest. Because of the tense political atmosphere, the arrangements committee had omitted the usual toasts, but they could not avoid toasting Jackson, and he replied with an arresting sentiment:

The true Constitutional currency, gold and silver coin.—It can cover and protect the labor of our country without the aid of a National Bank, an institution which can never be otherwise than hostile to the liberties of the people, because its tendency is to associate wealth with an undue power over the public interests.[24]

The Bell and Bank men were stunned. The toast, said Jackson, "came upon the ears of the Bank aristocracy with as much surprise as the toast I gave at the Jefferson dinner."[25] Bell cursed audibly,

---

[22] Nashville *Banner*, 31 July 1834; letters to Polk from Cave Johnson, C. C. Clay, W. C. Dunlap, James Standifer, and S. W. Mardis, Sept.-Oct. 1834, Polk Papers.
[23] *Jackson Correspondence*, v, 281-282; *ibid.*, 282-283; W. G. Childress to Polk, 9 Aug. 1834, Polk Papers.
[24] Nashville *Banner*, 14 Aug. 1834.
[25] *Jackson Correspondence*, v, 282.

and Foster burst out, "We are broke down. Grundy & Polk are to rule this State, the Bank will have to go down."[26] Polk, one observer was moved to remark, "is the strongest man in the State."[27]

While they were together in Nashville, the Polk-Grundy men laid plans for following up their advantage. First they made preparations to defeat Bell's reelection to Congress the following summer by persuading Governor Carroll to run against him. Polk had aided Carroll when he was in Washington the previous winter seeking his long-deferred appointment as minister to Mexico, and when Bell declared against Van Buren, Carroll had broken with his former lieutenant and was now thoroughly in sympathy with the Polk-Grundy group.[28]

Polk and his friends next turned to the problem of securing a Nashville newspaper organ. Through a combination of pressure on Hunt and agreement with Laughlin, they finally assured themselves, as they thought, of the *Banner*'s support. Laughlin apparently promised to take a strong anti-Bank, anti-Bell, pro-Van Buren course. But Hunt consented to the arrangement with extreme reluctance and seems, indeed, to have been unaware of the full nature of the agreement.[29]

With these arrangements completed, and with the dread cholera appearing in Maury, Polk retired to a nearby watering place for a much-needed rest. From this point he continued to feed Jackson's suspicions of a plot to charter "*a* Bank." He called the president's attention to the fact that Laughlin of the *Banner* had come out against this dangerous alternative to "*the* Bank," but reminded him that Allen A. Hall of the *Republican*, "so far as I have observed has been silent." When Jackson sent Polk a copy of an anti-Bank speech by Henry D. Gilpin, he promptly had it republished in the Columbia paper, and then lost no time in pointing out that "It has not yet, I believe been republished in either of the Nashville papers."[30] Jackson immediately took the speech to Hall and compelled him to print it. These activities further endeared Polk to Old Hickory, and the

26 R. M. Burton to Polk, 27 Aug. 1834, Polk Papers.

27 R. M. Burton to R. L. Caruthers, 17 Aug. 1834, Robert L. Caruthers Papers (SHC).

28 *ibid.*; Daniel Graham to Polk, 2 Jan. 1835, Polk Papers; Carroll to Polk, 19 Dec. 1834, *ibid.*

29 R. M. Burton to Polk, 27 Aug. 1834, Polk Papers; Cave Johnson to Polk, 1 Sept. 1834 [misplaced 1835], *ibid.*; Samuel H. Laughlin to Polk, 4 Sept., 20 Oct. 1834, *ibid.*

30 Polk to Jackson, 23 Aug. 1834, Jackson Papers.

president began telling his callers that "Polk for the hard service done in the cause deserves a Medal from the American people."[31]

Grundy, meanwhile, had been given the assignment of spreading the doctrines of the president's Nashville toast throughout the state. In a speech at Murfreesboro he rang all the changes on "*the* Bank" and "*a* Bank," and even managed to come out for Jackson's hard-money doctrine. The Bell partisans were outraged, and Congressman David Dickinson attempted a reply. Evidently he was not very persuasive, for Polk and White were the only members of Congress singled out for praise in the toasts that followed, and Polk's name was applauded more loudly than anyone else's.[32]

Bell's long-threatened counterattack was finally launched through the editorial columns of the *Republican* on September 4, just before Jackson returned to Washington. Polk and the Columbia *Observer* were charged with a vicious and unwarranted assault on Bell, motivated by personal ambition. The *Observer* replied promptly, trying to shift the argument to Bell's record in Congress. For the next few months the Tennessee press was filled with violent accusations, denials, and counteraccusations.[33]

At this crucial moment Polk and his friends were let down by their Nashville editor. Laughlin was an experienced lawyer, an able polemicist, and an avid political manipulator, but he also proved to be lazy, bibulous, and timid where Hunt was concerned. At any rate he was prevailed upon to reprint the initial *Republican* attack. "I must consult Hunt's interest," he explained weakly to Polk, "with the mercantiles of this blessed town, among whom Bell has his partisans." Besides, he added, this would give him a good excuse to republish the *Observer*'s replies. But almost in the same breath he urged Polk not to press the controversy.[34]

The *Observer*'s replies never appeared in the *Banner*, for Laughlin chose this moment to go on a prolonged drinking bout. His contract as editor expired just at this time, and Hunt dismissed him, borrowing $3,000 from Bell to pay Laughlin's back salary and purchase his share in the paper. According to Laughlin, he and Hunt disagreed on every political question, Hunt being pro-Bank,

[31] R. M. Burton to Polk, 27 Aug. 1834, Polk Papers.

[32] Murfreesboro *Central Monitor*, 6 Sept., 11 Oct. 1834; J. W. Childress to Polk, 19 Aug. [1834; misplaced 1836], Polk Papers.

[33] Nashville *Republican*, 4, 18, 20 Sept., 2 Oct. 1834; Columbia *Observer*, 19, 25 Sept., 2, 15 Oct. 1834.

[34] Laughlin to Polk, 6 Sept. 1834, Polk Papers.

anti-Van Buren, and pro-Bell. "The Banner," complained the dismissed editor, "is now a prostitute open to the embraces of all politicians of all parties, but is the peculiar mistress of the Bank and Bank men."[35] So Bell came to control both the papers of wide circulation in Tennessee, and the Polk-Grundy men were left without any effective means of getting their side of the controversy before the public.

It was not long before the lack of a Nashville organ was bitterly felt. John Bell was temperamentally ill suited to the give and take of political warfare, one of his friends describing him as "a sensitive man & constitutionally jealous hearted."[36] The constant barrage of criticism by the village papers supporting Polk made his position in a party with which he did not sincerely sympathize intolerable. Unable to stand the strain any longer, he unburdened himself in an impassioned tirade at Murfreesboro in October. Not only did he give free rein to his hatred for Polk, but he even allowed himself to speak too freely of Jackson and his policies. Complaining bitterly of the persecution to which he had been subjected, Bell asserted that a national bank was constitutional and went on to denounce the idea of a gold and silver currency as a humbug, though he said he was willing to give Jackson's experiment a fair trial. He also boasted that he had had enough influence to defeat the administration on the deposit question if he had wished to do so.[37]

Both sides realized at once that the speech had been a capital blunder. The little Murfreesboro newspaper, which was just expiring, printed only a fragmentary account, and Polk wrote urging that the speech be published in full. Sarah's brother John Childress and her brother-in-law Doctor William Rucker, who served as Polk's political agents in Rutherford County, had already set about getting a more complete report. They advised Polk to come to Murfreesboro for Sarah, who was visiting there, and to make a speech himself, but he vetoed this proposal. After more than a month of effort, Polk's Murfreesboro friends persuaded the publisher of the defunct paper to get out one last issue containing a fuller account of what Bell had said.

[35] Laughlin to Polk, 20 Oct. 1834, Polk Papers; J. W. Childress to Polk, 19 Sept. 1834, *ibid.*; S. G. Smith to Polk, 20 Sept. 1834, *ibid.*

[36] Balch to Jackson, 30 Oct. 1834, Jackson Papers.

[37] William Brady to Jackson, 7 Oct. 1834, Jackson Papers; J. W. Childress to Polk, 7 Oct. 1834, Polk Papers; Murfreesboro *Central Monitor*, 11, 18 Oct., 22 Nov., extra, 1834.

Bell's Nashville editors could do no better than deny the accuracy of the Murfreesboro reports, but without a newspaper of general circulation, Polk and his friends were helpless to capitalize on the situation. They were particularly incensed because the *Globe* refused to publish anything critical of Bell, though its columns were open to articles in his favor. This was not the first time Polk had had cause to be dissatisfied with Frank Blair. Major Lewis had long ago prejudiced Blair against his own enemies in Tennessee, and the *Globe* had consistently slighted Polk's speeches and services in the House.[38]

Polk was now more determined than ever to have a newspaper at Nashville. Laughlin had sobered up in the meantime and discovered that the *Republican* was so deep in debt that Hall would have to dispose of it. He proposed that the friends of Polk and Grundy assist himself and M. A. Long, an experienced Nashville printer, in purchasing it. But Bell's supporters came to Hall's aid before a bargain could be struck, and Hall eventually refused an offer of $1,000 more than he had originally asked. Polk, Grundy, and their Nashville associates, with no better prospect in sight, then agreed to raise enough money to enable Laughlin and Long to launch a new paper.[39]

Polk was in no position to make heavy expenditures for political purposes. His plantation in the Western District had not been so profitable as he had anticipated, and he was determined to "make more money or loose [*sic*] more." In the fall of 1834 he sold it for $6,000 and entered into partnership with his brother-in-law Doctor Caldwell to buy a new one in the recently opened and booming Chickasaw country of North Central Mississippi. They finally paid ten dollars an acre for an 880-acre tract in Yalibusha County, and in January 1835 Caldwell marched south with about eighteen of each man's slaves to put up cabins and clear lands for the first year's crop. Caldwell soon became discouraged, however, and Polk eventually purchased his share.[40]

---

[38] W. R. Rucker to Polk, 12 Oct. 1834, Polk Papers; Polk to Rucker, 16 Oct. 1834, *ibid.*; William Brady to Polk, 29 Nov. 1834 [misplaced 1833], *ibid.*; J. W. Childress to Polk, 20 Dec. 1834, *ibid.*; Daniel Graham to Polk, 2 Jan. 1835, *ibid.*; Nashville *Banner*, 1 Dec. 1834.

[39] J. W. Childress to Polk, 19 Sept. 1834, Polk Papers; Cave Johnson to Polk, 2 Oct. [1834; misplaced 1837], *ibid.*; Laughlin to Polk, 20 Oct. 1834, *ibid.*; S. G. Smith to Polk, 20 Nov. 1834, *ibid.*

[40] Polk to Mrs. Polk, 26 Sept. 1834, Polk Papers; John Spencer Bassett, ed., *The Southern Plantation Overseer As Revealed in His Letters* (Northampton, Mass., 1929), 39-51, 74-87.

The arrangements for the new plantation and the new newspaper were barely under way before it was time to return to Washington. James's youngest brother, Sam, and the two Walker boys, Knox and Joseph, were entering Yale College this year, and the Polks agreed to escort them and another Columbia youngster to New Haven. The trip was something of an adventure for the gay family party, featuring their first exciting ride on the new railroad from Frederick, Maryland, to Baltimore, shopping and sightseeing in Philadelphia and New York, and a steamboat ride up Long Island Sound to New Haven.[41]

All too soon, James and Sarah were back in Washington, putting up at Clements' boardinghouse. Sarah, to judge from her purchases this winter, was becoming quite a reader of fashionable books,[42] while James had more than enough to keep his mind occupied during the early weeks of the session. Through the haze of the Polk-Bell feud, a second portentous development in Tennessee politics was looming. The two had progressed side by side for a time, but now they showed signs of a coalescence that could be disastrous to Polk and his friends, and even to Jacksonian Democracy.

III

Several months before Polk left for Washington, one of his supporters in Bedford, Archibald Yell, became so enraged by the Nashville *Republican*'s anti-Polk editorials that he wrote to Allen A. Hall canceling his subscription. Hall's reply was both puzzling and ominous. Polk was making a serious mistake by joining Grundy and Carroll in their attacks on Bell, Hall warned, for in six months there would inevitably be a split between Polk and Carroll. "Nay, there will be a split between Polk and the *President*!!" the wily editor added. "Col. Polk by no earthly possibility can continue to maintain his present position in the event of certain future contingencies which are *obliged* to take place." Yell was completely mystified by these enigmatic remarks, but events soon proved that Hall knew whereof he spoke.[43]

Better versed than Yell in the intricacies of Tennessee politics,

---

[41] Receipts, 13, 19, 22, 25 Nov. 1834, Polk Papers; memorandum, 25 Nov. 1834, *ibid.*
[42] C. C. Clay to Mrs. Clay, 15, 26 Dec. 1834, Clement C. Clay Papers (DU); receipt, 31 Jan. 1835, Polk Papers. Sarah's book purchases included Irving's *Sketch Book, Don Quixote,* several of Sterne's works, and the inevitable religious tracts.
[43] Yell to Polk, 25 Sept. 1834, Polk Papers.

Polk could not have mistaken the drift of Hall's remarks. As far back as 1830 one of Polk's correspondents had detected a "powerful but silent effort making for the political power of the state" by men out of sympathy with Jackson's purposes. Rather than foolishly opposing Jackson himself, the dissidents hoped "to bring out a Successor and to give tone to public sentiment in his favour."[44] About the same time Jackson began to make it clear that any such conservative "Successor" would have to beat Martin Van Buren.

Van Buren was obviously unpopular with Tennesseans generally. Besides being a New Yorker, he had too much the reputation of an unscrupulous manipulator and effeminate dandy to appeal to a western agricultural population. But it was business-minded conservatives, alarmed by the administration's anti-Bank policies, who had the strongest reason to distrust Jackson's designated heir. Overton and Eaton's desertion of Van Buren in 1832 and the Overton faction's steady coalescence with the Nashville business community had begun to indicate by 1833 that an anti-Van Buren movement might ultimately succeed in Tennessee, despite all Jackson could do. Bell and Foster had emerged as the darlings of the conservative business interests, and most of the Overton men were working closely with them. Bell's flirtation with Richard M. Johnson was only one sign that these men were seeking an alternative candidate for president.

But who would this new candidate be? Calhoun, Webster, and Clay were all hopelessly discredited in Tennessee; indeed, the impressive victories of Jackson tickets in various elections around the country in 1833 and early 1834 would make their prospects hopeless everywhere. Jackson's second term had hardly begun before most segments of the opposition abandoned hope of electing an outright Whig and began casting about for some conservative candidate who was not conspicuously anti-Jackson and who might defeat Van Buren by leading a substantial secession from the Democratic party. Among those discussed were Richard M. Johnson, former Secretary of the Treasury Louis McLane, Senator Littleton W. Tazewell of Virginia, and Supreme Court Justice John McLean. Duff Green, with his passion for political management, was particularly busy in these maneuvers. For a time he encouraged Judge McLean, who had been on good terms with Green's hero, Calhoun, but he finally decided that a southern candidate could best unite the various constituent

44 S. G. Smith to Polk, 10 Nov. 1830, Polk Papers.

elements of anti-Van Burenism, and during 1833 Green was pushing Richard M. Johnson.[45]

Potentially the strongest of all these candidates in Tennessee was Judge John McLean. A conspicuous Methodist, he had the core of a political organization in his enthusiastic coreligionists. Supreme Court justices still rode circuit in the 1830's, and McLean's regular visits to Nashville to hold court gave him an excellent opportunity to strengthen his forces. His Ohio residence and his bluff, friendly manners made him appealing to westerners, while his opinions were sufficiently flexible, ambiguous, or unknown to enable him to be all things to all men.

McLean's principal promoter in Tennessee, H. R. W. Hill, a Methodist and one of Nashville's wealthiest merchants, was able to build up a surprising amount of underground support for his favorite. Early in 1833 Grundy seemed to be deeply involved in the McLean movement and had Laughlin publishing pro-McLean articles in the *Banner*. Even Governor Carroll, his hopes for the Mexican appointment waning at the moment, seemed friendly, an opening the McLean men promptly exploited by offering to support him for vice president. During the summer the judge was endorsed by meetings in various parts of the state, and by fall several of the smaller newspapers had come out for him. Polk's friend Archibald Yell was responsible for some of this activity, and in September McLean had a conversation with Polk himself at Nashville. According to the judge, Polk declared that "he was not disposed to work into the hands of the Albany Regency." About the same time Grundy assured McLean that Polk was opposed to Van Buren, and the judge was convinced that Senator White felt the same way.[46]

These Tennessee politicians were far from ingenuous. Under strong pressure from Jackson to back Van Buren, they were painfully aware of Van Buren's unpopularity with their constituents. Their enemies, moreover—the men who had just tried to knock Polk

[45] Charles H. Ambler, *Thomas Ritchie: A Study in Virginia Politics* (Richmond, 1913), 156; Duff Green to John McLean, 1 July 1833, McLean Papers; Green to [Calhoun], 22 Sept. 1833, copy, Green Papers; Nashville *Republican*, 14 Sept. 1833.

[46] John McLean to Elisha Whittlesey, 27 Sept. 1833, Elisha Whittlesey Papers (Western Reserve Historical Society, Cleveland); *id.* to *id.*, 6 Sept. 1833, *ibid.*; H. R. W. Hill to McLean, 4 Dec. 1831, 4 Jan., 11 Dec. 1833, 20 May, 1 June 1834, McLean Papers; Archibald Yell to McLean, 22 Sept., 20 Nov. 1833, *ibid.*; W. Hasell Hunt to McLean, 16 May 1834, *ibid.*; John McLean to J. W. Taylor, 7 Sept. 1833, Taylor Papers; Carroll to Van Buren, 11 Nov. 1833, Van Buren Papers; Yell to Polk, 1 Dec. 1833, Polk Papers.

out of the House, who were now opposing Grundy's reelection to the Senate, and who were already laying plans to rob Polk of the speakership—still seemed to be the official representatives of Van Burenism in Tennessee. Nevertheless, after Polk's reelection to Congress in August 1833 and Grundy's victory over Bell, Eaton, and Foster in October, they apparently decided that ultimately they would stick with Jackson and Van Buren, though they certainly tried to mislead McLean in September and Duff Green and the Nullifiers during the speakership contest.

August 13, 1833, was the date of Polk's letter to Major Lewis endorsing Van Buren, and in October, hard on the heels of the senatorial election, Grundy told Governor Carroll that "his feelings were very kind" toward Van Buren. Carroll at once wrote to the vice president impressing on him the importance of conferring with Grundy, and these consultations were evidently fruitful, for Polk came to be the administration favorite for speaker. Meanwhile Grundy sent Laughlin instructions not to endorse McLean or anyone else in the columns of the *Banner*, and Laughlin's pro-McLean employer was soon referring to his editor as "a Van Buren partisan." Unfortunately Archibald Yell was not informed of this shift in direction and continued to promote the McLean boom with enthusiasm until the spring of 1834, when McLean's chances in Tennessee began to wane.[47] But as the McLean boom faded it was replaced by another movement even more portentous for Polk and his friends. It was this movement that was to produce the "future contingencies" of which Allen Hall so mysteriously warned Yell in the fall of 1834.

IV

Ephraim Foster had encouraged Judge McLean for a time, but when the legislature met in the fall of 1833, one of Foster's supporters had come up with the ingenious suggestion that Senator White be nominated for president. Besides being enormously popular with both voters and politicians in Tennessee, White was so closely associated with the Grundy-Polk men that they could hardly oppose the movement. This plan was squelched for the moment by the strenuous efforts of Governor Carroll, Alfred Balch, and White

---

[47] Carroll to Van Buren, 11 Nov. 1833, Van Buren Papers; Polk to Lewis, 13 Aug. 1833, Ford Collection; H. R. W. Hill to McLean, 3 Feb., 12 June 1834, McLean Papers; W. H. Hunt to McLean, 16 May 1834, *ibid.*

himself, but the idea had been planted and was shortly endorsed by several of the smaller newspapers in Tennessee and Alabama.[48]

"Judge" White, as Tennesseans always called him, was a small, emaciated-looking man, but his narrow, high-browed face with its stern, pale features and cold, blue eyes denoted a stubborn puritanic spirit. In a moment of unusual candor White had admitted to his friend Overton that "I am stubborn and unyielding in disposition."[49] Time and again he had adamantly refused to lend himself to the political machinations of the Jackson managers, and as president pro tempore of the Senate during the nullification crisis of 1832-1833 he had demonstrated his independence by appointing a committee that favored Clay's tariff bill over the administration's, an action that Jackson resented as "an insult to me."[50] About this time Alfred Balch, Tennessee's most acute political observer, became suspicious that White wanted the vice presidential nomination in 1836 as a steppingstone to the White House. "The old fellow believes that no man knows that he cherishes this hope as a mother does her darling," wrote Balch. "But, I saw him last fall & conversed with him for 20 minutes. I went away satisfied. Mark it! his object is to succeed Van Buren. The ambition of those men who, like Judge White are ever protesting that they want nothing and are seeking nothing, is hotter than a volcano."[51]

When White's name was first proposed in the fall of 1833, John Bell and his friends were encouraging Richard M. Johnson's pretensions, but they seem to have been sympathetic to the White movement as an alternative possibility. Bell's defiance of the Democratic leaders in the speakership contest of 1833-1834 left him in an awkward position, where he could not remain indefinitely. Either he must creep meekly back into the Van Buren ranks, or he must attach himself to some movement that had a prospect of defeating Van Buren. Feeling his way with extreme caution, he encouraged the White and Johnson partisans alternately. Rumors of White's candidacy circulated in Congress at the height of the speakership con-

48 H. R. W. Hill to McLean, 4 Dec. 1831, McLean Papers; Carroll to Jackson, 3 Dec. 1833, Jackson Papers; Balch to Jackson, 29 Nov. 1833, *ibid.*; A. O. P. Nicholson to Polk, 5 Dec. [1833], Polk Papers; Nashville *Republican*, 17 Dec. 1833; Nashville *Banner*, 31 Jan. 1834, 29 Mar. 1837; Nashville *Union*, 31 Dec. 1835.

49 White to Overton, 22 Feb. 1827, John Overton Papers, Claybrooke Collection (THS); Nashville *Banner*, 21 Nov. 1834.

50 Jackson to Grundy, 13 Feb. 1833, in *American Historical Magazine* (Nashville), v (Apr. 1900), 137.

51 Balch to McLean, 20 Jan. 1833, McLean Papers.

troversy, but as late as the fall of 1834 Bell was still urging Johnson to run, even if he had to defy the Democratic national convention and oppose Van Buren. These exhortations were coupled with intimations that "*the* Bank" or "*a* Bank" must be sustained.[52]

Indications of Van Buren's unpopularity and of widespread support for Judge White continued to multiply in Tennessee during the first half of 1834. White was toasted at the Columbia dinner honoring Polk on his return from Congress in August by two ambitious young politicians, Felix K. Zollicoffer, editor of the Columbia *Observer*, and Alfred O. P. Nicholson. Three weeks later Nicholson sent the *Observer* a long article setting forth White's claims, and from then on the *Observer* was the most zealous White newspaper in the state. Simultaneously the *Observer* was leading Polk's assault on Bell, and Bell complained that Polk's friends were trying to capitalize on White's popularity to his injury. Actually Polk had little control over Zollicoffer with regard to the presidential question.[53]

The White movement came to a head when the state constitutional convention met at Nashville in August 1834. Bell and Foster now definitely took the lead in an attempt to get the convention to nominate White unconditionally, that is, without submitting his claims to the Democratic national convention, which was to meet at Baltimore in May 1835. But the effort to nominate failed again, largely because of Old Hickory's emphatic declaration that Judge White would be ruined if he permitted himself to be run by a splinter of the party. Some of the judge's friends talked with the president, as he traveled through East Tennessee on his trip back to Washington, and came away with the impression that if White would give up his presidential ambitions, the party might support him for vice president, with the prospect of succeeding Van Buren after eight years. Jackson denied ever making such an offer, but he probably had some such arrangement in mind.[54]

52 Duff Green to [Calhoun], 22 Sept. 1833, copy, Green Papers; James Walker to Polk, 20 Oct. 1833, Polk Papers; Dudley Selden to G. C. Verplanck, 15 Feb. 1834, Verplanck Papers; Mr. Ficklen to W. T. Barry, 8 Sept. 1834, extract [placed 3 Oct. 1834], Jackson Papers; R. M. Johnson to F. P. Blair, 14 June 1835, Blair-Lee Papers; T. J. Pew to [F. P. Blair?], 16 July 1835 [placed with the preceding], *ibid.*; Norman L. Parks, "The Career of John Bell of Tennessee in the United States House of Representatives," Ph.D. dissertation, Vanderbilt University (1942), 226-227.

53 S. G. Smith to Polk, 18 Feb. 1834, Polk Papers; Laughlin to Polk, 6 Sept. 1834, *ibid.*; Nashville *Republican*, 19 May 1835; Columbia *Observer*, 8 Aug. 1834; Columbia *Tennessee Democrat*, 12 Nov. 1835.

54 R. M. Burton to Polk, 27 Aug. 1834, Polk Papers; Laughlin to Polk, 9 Sept.

White's friends also reported that the president had threatened to denounce him if he became a candidate, and Polk was painfully embarrassed when the judge complained to him about the president's language. Though Polk was one of White's closest political friends, neither he nor Grundy nor Cave Johnson had any enthusiasm for the White presidential boom. The only reply Polk could manage was a weak "There must be some mistake about it."[55] Jackson's threats and promises backfired so far as their effect on White was concerned. The proud old East Tennessean spurned the vice presidential offer, or any other arrangement "which would operate as a *lure* to induce any person to vote for myself or any other person [i.e. Van Buren] contrary to his judgment."[56]

Jackson's pressure was more effective with the nervous John Bell. Alfred Balch had been sent to warn him of the consequences of further opposition to the administration, while other emissaries had threatened that Carroll would oppose him in the next congressional election unless he mended his ways. In response Bell had led the president to believe that he would support the administration loyally as speaker, and likewise that he would uphold the national convention and Van Buren's nomination. Though he later denied making any specific commitment, he unquestionably wrote to one of Van Buren's New York aides that "the sagacious politicians amongst us are going for Van Buren."[57]

Bell was not yet ready, in fact, to stake his political future on so risky a venture as a White nomination without a last attempt at an understanding with Van Buren. What he wanted from the New Yorker was a promise of support against the Grundy-Polk faction in Tennessee. As soon as he reached Washington for the meeting of Congress in December 1834, he tried to draw Van Buren out on this subject, but the vice president was well aware of Bell's object and parried his several attempts to broach the matter. Finally one of Bell's close friends arranged a dinner at which the speaker and the vice president were the only guests. When Bell again brought up the

---

1834, *ibid.*; William Brady to Polk, 26 Dec. 1834, *ibid.*; Jackson to Balch, 5 Nov. 1835, copy, Jackson Papers; Balch to Jackson, 4 Apr. 1835, *ibid.*; "For the Union and to the Public," undated MS [placed June 1837], *ibid.*; Donelson to Blair, 14 Sept. 1834, Blair-Lee Papers; Nashville *Banner*, 11 May 1835, 12 Sept. 1836, 29 Mar. 1837.

[55] Nancy N. Scott, *A Memoir of Hugh Lawson White* . . . (Philadelphia, 1856), 254.

[56] Nashville *Banner*, 13 Sept. 1836.

[57] Balch to Jackson, 30 Oct. 1834, Jackson Papers; Jackson to Balch, 5 Nov. 1834, copy, *ibid.*; S. G. Smith to Polk, 20 Sept. 1834, Polk Papers; Nashville *Banner*, 11 May 1835.

presidential question, Van Buren suddenly developed a severe tooth-ache and was "compelled to decline the conversation and to retire almost immediately." Bell made a final attempt when the two men found themselves side by side, presiding over a joint session of the House and Senate. The occasion was hardly appropriate, but the speaker was growing desperate. After expressing regret that the party was to be divided by the prospective nomination of White, he whispered that he hoped the matter could be adjusted amicably, but that a point had come when whatever was done must be done immediately. The imperturbable Van Buren, however, turned the conversation into other channels.[58] The only alternatives remaining to the unhappy speaker were abject surrender or open revolt. And there was no more time for temporizing.

V

The fall elections of 1834 had gone so decisively against the Whigs in New York, New Jersey, and Pennsylvania that all factions of the party lost hope of electing their favorite candidates. The New York election meant, observed John Tyler in Virginia, that "*no Bank man* can be elected." To Tyler the prospect was "absolutely one of gloom, unless a Southern man can be found who will unite the whole South, and thereby ensure to himself the support of all the anti-Van Buren States."[59]

It soon appeared that Judge White filled these specifications better than anyone else available, and almost overnight he became a major contender. The Tennessee press was for him vociferously, and papers in Alabama, Mississippi, North Carolina, and Virginia began to advance his claims. From Georgia, Congressman Richard Wilde announced that the Whigs would "endeavor to make a diversion in favour of Hugh L. White, the only man who has the least chance ultimately of taking away the electoral Vote of the State from Mr Van Buren."[60] Even Judge McLean's supporters now conceded that "the only way V.B. can be defeated, is by running Judge White."[61]

---

[58] John C. Fitzpatrick, ed., *The Autobiography of Martin Van Buren*, American Historical Association, *Annual Report*, 1918, ii (Washington, 1920), 225n.-226n.

[59] Armistead C. Gordon, *William Fitzhugh Gordon, A Virginian of the Old School: His Life, Times and Contemporaries (1787-1858)* (New York, 1909), 294.

[60] R. H. Wilde to G. C. Verplanck, 15 Nov. 1834, Verplanck Papers; Pulaski *Tennessee Beacon*, 26 Sept., 17 Oct. 1834; Washington *United States Telegraph*, 8 Nov. 1834.

[61] James Taylor to McLean, 6 Dec. 1834, McLean Papers.

The situation was well summarized by North Carolina's Whig senator, Willie P. Mangum:

> Mark it—*No opposition man can be elected President.* They may mar, but they can't make. . . . Clay is off—Calhoun is off—& Webster, tho anxious for a nomination, must soon find that overwhelming defeat is inevitable.
>
> All that is left to us, is a choice of evils—& that choice will most probably be restricted to Judge McLean, Judge White & Van Buren—of these I most decidedly prefer White.[62]

The strategy of backing White appealed also to demoralized northern Whigs. The influential New York *Evening Star* endorsed the idea, and some officials of the United States Bank were impressed by its possibilities. One of Biddle's most trusted advisers informed him that White was understood to be "sound on the subject of the Judiciary, & currency, & *will not put his veto* on any Bill, unless it is a manifest violation of the Constitution." Admitting that White would not recommend a Bank, this official was convinced that he would sign a recharter bill if Congress passed one. Might it not be well, he asked Biddle, "for our party to carry him into the Presidents Chair, if it is conceded, we cannot carry our own man?" Clay was said to be ready to support White; the only obstacle was Webster. "Mr Webster can make the Judge President," Biddle's correspondent concluded, "& I am almost inclined to say the Judge is the only man who can brake the Kitchen Van Buren course, & that Mr Webster ought to give in."[63]

The most active promoter of the White boom nationally was Duff Green. During the summer of 1834 he had been insisting that the Nullifiers could not support any man who did not agree with their principles, but by October he was cautiously announcing that he favored White over Van Buren, and within a few weeks the *Telegraph* was campaigning wholeheartedly for an endorsement of White by all elements of the opposition. Some ascribed Green's position to a desire to retain his lucrative contract for printing Senate documents. In the previous Congress the Whigs had given the House printing to Gales and Seaton of the *National Intelligencer*, the spokesmen for the National Republican wing of the opposition, while the Senate printing had gone to Green as the Nullifiers' share of the spoils. Since the new Democratic House was sure to transfer its

---

62 W. P. Mangum to W. A. Graham, 17 Dec. 1834, William A. Graham Papers (SHC).

63 R. L. Colt to Biddle, 7 Dec. [1834], Biddle Papers.

printing from Gales and Seaton to Frank Blair, it was expected that the National Republican Whigs would want to give Gales and Seaton the Senate printing. Green's support of White might well secure him enough votes from White's Democratic friends to save his Senate contracts.[64]

Whatever his real motives, Green called on Grundy and Polk as soon as they reached Washington in December 1834 and urged them to have White formally brought into the race by action of the Tennessee congressional delegation. When they refused to commit themselves, the project was pushed in other quarters.[65]

Democratic leaders were perfectly willing to have White submit his claims to the party's national convention, where he would inevitably be overwhelmed by the Van Buren forces, but the big question was whether White would allow his backers to run him in defiance of the convention nomination. The rumors around Washington were that White was ripe for rebellion. "I am assured Judge White *will* stick," reported Richard H. Wilde, "& the Tennesseans are *keen* for him." These impressions were strengthened when White defied the president by opposing a treaty the administration had recently negotiated for removing the Cherokee Indians to the West.[66]

Meanwhile Green's efforts with the Tennesseans were bearing fruit. The members from East Tennessee were sincerely in favor of White out of personal friendship and respect, and Congressman James Standifer finally agreed to take the lead in calling a meeting of the delegation to consider nominating him. On the morning of December 22, Standifer approached Polk in the Ways and Means Committee room and asked him to attend. Standifer had stood solidly with Polk in the Polk-Bell controversy of the previous summer and was clearly acting without reference to the political situation in Tennessee, but his invitation put Polk in an uncomfortable position. He told Standifer that his personal relations with Bell, Peyton, and Dickinson would make it impossible for him to collaborate with them in anything. Unquestionably he also expressed his high regard for Judge White, but just what he said about White's candidacy later became a matter of great dispute. That night Polk canvassed the situation with Grundy, who had likewise declined Standifer's invi-

64 Henry Clay to W. P. Mangum, 26 Aug. 1834, Willie P. Mangum Papers (DU); Washington *United States Telegraph*, 21, 27 Oct., 8, 14 Nov., 4, 20, 22, 23 Dec. 1834.
65 Polk to Cave Johnson, draft copy [placed 20 Jan. 1835], Polk Papers.
66 R. H. Wilde to G. C. Verplanck, 12 Dec. 1834, Verplanck Papers; White to Jackson, 15 Dec. 1834, Jackson Papers.

tation, and both agreed that it was best to stay away. When another East Tennessean, Luke Lea, renewed the invitation the next day as he and Polk walked home from the meeting of the House, Polk stuck to his refusal.[67]

One of the principal reasons why the idea of backing White appealed to Duff Green and other Whig leaders was the success of their similar strategy in the speakership election of the previous spring. Despite his overtures to Van Buren, John Bell, the hero of the earlier maneuver, had returned to Washington ready to commit himself to the White movement. "There is a *bitter controversy* now going on in Tennessee between the friends of Speaker Bell and Polk," reported one extraordinarily well-informed observer shortly after the session commenced. "The friends of the former are about to fix on Judge White for the Presidency and the latter are supposed to be with Mr. Van Buren."[68] Bell and his allies Peyton and Dickinson stayed carefully in the background of the White movement, however, leaving the initiative to Green and the East Tennesseans. Bell even feigned reluctance before accepting Standifer's invitation to attend the delegation meeting, but as soon as the meeting opened, he took command of the proceedings. The whole sequence of events, in fact, suggests prior planning between Bell and Green, though the East Tennesseans had no suspicion that Bell was involved.

Both Polk and Grundy had tried to arouse Standifer's suspicions by telling him about Bell's continuing flirtation with Van Buren, but Standifer concluded that Bell might not be the only Tennessee politician playing a double game. He resolved to get all members of the delegation clearly on record with regard to White's candidacy, and the first order of business at the delegation meeting was to determine the sentiments of the absent members. Lea and Standifer reported that both Polk and Grundy had promised to support the judge in any way he would permit himself to be run, and Cave Johnson remarked, as the close associate of the two absentees, that they had

[67] The account of the meeting of the Tennessee delegation has been pieced together from the following: Polk to James Walker, 24, 25 Dec. 1834, Polk Papers; Polk to John Blair, 19 Jan. 1835, copy, *ibid.*; Polk to J[ohn]. B[ell]. & Co., 20 Jan. 1835, draft copy, *ibid.*; Polk to Grundy, 28 Jan. 1835, copy, *ibid.*; Polk to W. C. Dunlap, 19 Oct. 1838, copy, *ibid.*; Polk to Cave Johnson, n.d., draft copy [placed 20 Jan. 1835], 28, 30 Mar., draft copies, 26 Mar. 1835, *ibid.*; Johnson to Polk [10 Mar. 1835; misplaced 10 Feb. 1838], 3 Apr. 1835. *ibid.*; "Polk-Johnson Letters," *loc.cit.*, 216-226; Nashville *Banner*, 23 Feb., 11 May 1835; Nashville *Union*, 29 June 1835; Scott, *White*, 259-260.

[68] James Graham to W. A. Graham, 8 Dec. 1834, Graham Papers.

earlier expressed themselves in favor of White. When Bell inquired whether they had insisted that White must be nominated by the Democratic national convention, Johnson could recall no mention of a convention in the conversations. Polk and Grundy later asserted repeatedly that they had always made their support of White conditional on his being the choice of a majority of the party, and several of their colleagues corroborated this claim. No doubt they had counted on White's refusing to be a pawn for the Whigs, and in any case, whatever they said was unquestionably as ambiguous as they could make it.

Toward the end of the meeting Bell argued strongly that the delegation should take the lead in sponsoring White's candidacy by establishing a newspaper at Washington to advocate his claims. Subsequent events were to demonstrate that the newspaper project had originated in consultation with Duff Green. Bell opposed a formal nomination by the delegation, because it would look too much like a caucus movement, and also because a movement to have the Alabama legislature nominate White had already been launched by an Alabama politician who was a close friend of Bell and a college classmate of Dickinson.

Worried by the drift of the discussion and Bell's prominent role in it, Cave Johnson asked whether such a movement might not play into the hands of the Whigs and have the ultimate effect of reviving the American System. Bell rejoined that the Whigs would probably not even enter a candidate, and if they did, then would be time enough to consider withdrawing White. Though other remarks indicated a determination to run White in defiance of the national convention, Johnson chose not to argue the point. The meeting closed when Bell persuaded Luke Lea to take charge of the movement.

The next morning Johnson realized that he had blundered in not making his position clear, and he immediately sent Standifer a note saying that he would not support White if he were to be run by only a small fraction of the Jackson men combined with the united opposition. He showed this letter to Polk, and Polk and Grundy saw to it that Jackson got wind of what the delegation was up to. The president "highly approved" the actions of Polk, Grundy, and Johnson, and his outspoken denunciation of the project cooled the enthusiasm of two other congressmen, John Blair from East Tennessee and William C. Dunlap of the Bolivar district.

Within a few days after the meeting, a letter asking White's consent to the use of his name as a candidate for president was handed around the Tennessee delegation for signature. Polk, Johnson, and Grundy reiterated their refusal to have anything to do with the movement, but Dunlap and Blair finally joined the other Tennesseans in signing. White responded promptly on December 30, saying that the people had a right to choose whom they pleased and that no one had a right to refuse the office if he were their choice. According to the judge's subsequent account, he finally consented because of Jackson's threats to "make him odious to society" if he allowed himself to be run. This correspondence was kept secret for almost two months, until after White had been nominated by the Alabama legislature.

On the first day of 1835 the delegation majority met again to sign a reply to Cave Johnson's letter. This document, apparently drafted by John Bell, was designed to indict Johnson, Grundy, and Polk for guile and hypocrisy with regard to White's candidacy. It charged that Polk and Grundy had declared themselves for White without any qualification, and that Johnson had given the impression that he approved of all that was done at the original meeting. William M. Inge appended a note saying that he was somewhat uncertain about the terms in which Grundy and Polk had stated their position, and Standifer added another postscript to the effect that Blair had objected to a formal nomination by the delegation. Standifer wanted to put in still another clarifying note indicating that Grundy and Polk had attached conditions to their endorsement of White, but Bell objected to any more additions, and Standifer did not insist. Blair and Dunlap refused to sign this attack on their colleagues, and Standifer also had misgivings about it, for four days later he told Polk and Grundy what had transpired. The letter was not delivered to Johnson for two weeks, in the meantime being shown to various members of Congress for the purpose of injuring the three Tennesseans it attacked. Realizing that the controversy would ultimately be decided at the Tennessee ballot box, both sides began to prepare for the coming struggle by placing their own versions of the episode on record with a view to future publication.[69]

[69] See Note 67 above.

VI

Duff Green was jubilant over the success of his scheme thus far. White's friends, he exulted, will probably "urge his pretensions in despite of the Baltimore Convention." About this time Polk's friend Henry Hubbard of New Hampshire accidentally saw a letter from Green to Luke Lea urging that the White paper at Washington be established immediately, and on February 7 the first number of the *Appeal* appeared. Backed by Bell and Dixon H. Lewis, the corpulent Calhounite congressman from Alabama, the new paper was edited by a young printer from Duff Green's establishment. The first issue, appealing to the Whigs to unite on White, was circulated surreptitiously, so as not to offend potential White supporters among the Jackson men.[70]

But Duff Green was in for a rude shock. John Bell had never had any use for Green's nullifying principles, he had not forgiven Green for supporting Polk in the speakership election, and he was little disposed to play second fiddle to anyone in the political revolution he was trying to effect. Two weeks after the *Appeal* came out, a second White paper, the *Sun*, was established at the capital. Green was thunderstruck when he learned that Bell was backing the new paper, that Bell considered Green his personal and political enemy, and that the Tennesseans had promised the White party's patronage to the *Sun*, rather than to the *Appeal*. A loan from the national bank had enabled Bell to get this second paper under way, and its opposition to nullification was made crystal clear in its first issue. "We are, therefore, for the Union as it is, 'one and indivisible,' " announced the editors, "and are opposed to any change that is predicated upon speculative theories, and to be tested by doubtful experiments." Soon the *Sun* was engaged in a violent attack on Green for his antilabor policies as publisher of the *Telegraph*.[71]

Green was understandably furious, especially since he learned these things just as he was starting out on a trip through the South to line up Nullifier support for White. "I can no longer permit Mr Bell to play between the curt[a]in," he exploded in a letter to Dixon Lewis. The same day he wrote to White and Bell, making it clear

70 Green to Condy Raguet, 8 Jan. 1835, copy, Green Papers; Green to White, 11 Apr. 1835, copy, *ibid.*; [Polk to Cave Johnson, placed 20 Jan. 1820], draft copy, Polk Papers; *Jackson Correspondence*, v, 327-329; agreement, 11 Feb. 1835, in Hugh Lawson White folder, Personal Papers, Miscellaneous (LC).

71 Washington *Sun*, 21 Feb. 1835; *ibid.*, 1 Apr. 1835; S. F. Bradford to Biddle, 10 Feb. 1835, Biddle Papers.

that they had jeopardized the support of the Nullifiers. Either they must "let the Sun take its course and go down," or the Calhoun men would "denounce White and the whole concern." Bell stuck to his guns, however, and the *Appeal* was forced to sell out to its rival. To Green the episode indicated "a settled purpose of bringing up a party around Mr Bell for his own personal ends," and from this time forward enthusiasm for White ebbed rapidly among the Nullifiers.[72]

Though Green's estimate of Bell's motives undoubtedly contained much truth, the speaker may have been sincerely convinced that the Calhounites would do White's cause more harm than good. In any case he did not want to see the new White party dominated by the Nullifiers. His actions indicated that he was relying for success mainly on disaffected Democrats and the Clay-Webster Whigs. During the early months of 1835 there were signs that this daring strategy might succeed. "This *White* affair is much more serious than I had imagined," reported John Sergeant to Biddle,[73] while another of Biddle's correspondents ventured the opinion that "there is no chance for a Natl. Rep[ublican], & that our best throw is to support White." This writer again passed on the report that "in case of the election of Judge White, there will be still some hope for the Bank— at least so far that he will not veto any act in its favor that a majority of both Houses may please to pass."[74] A Whig congressman from Vermont was surprised to discover that many of his friends favored White; a White paper was established in Boston; there was a strong White movement in Illinois; a portion of the Whig party in New Hampshire came out for White; and Judge McLean's supporters in Ohio began shifting to the Tennessee senator. Bell was so anxious about the backing of the northern Whigs that he tried to persuade White to promise Daniel Webster the chief justiceship of the Supreme Court.[75]

Right up to the adjournment of Congress in March 1835, White's managers continued to receive encouragement from all elements of

[72] Green to D. H. Lewis, 11 Apr. 1835, copy, Green Papers; Green to White, 11 Apr. 1835, copy, *ibid.*; Green to Bell, 11 Apr. 1835, copy, *ibid.*; Washington *Sun*, 18 Apr. 1835; Nashville *Union*, 18 May 1835.

[73] John Sergeant to Biddle, 23 Jan. 1835, Biddle Papers.

[74] Samuel Bradford to Biddle, [2?] Jan. 1835, Biddle Papers.

[75] B. Swift to J. W. Taylor, 13 Feb. 1835, Taylor Papers; Duff Green to W. P. Mangum, 14 Apr. 1835, Mangum Papers (LC); S. S. Southworth to Mangum, 4 May 1835, *ibid.*; Bell to White, 20 May 1835, John Overton Papers, microfilm (JUL).

the Whig party in all sections of the country. But Bell had hardly got back to Tennessee before he began to suspect that he had been monstrously duped, that what the Democrats were saying was true, that the Whigs had encouraged the White movement merely to take southern votes away from Van Buren, so that the election could be decided in the House of Representatives, where one of the Whigs' real leaders could be the final choice. Misled by the success of his strategy in the speakership contest, Bell had not realized that a presidential election was a very different affair. He had failed to get a personal commitment from either Clay or Webster, and even Calhoun had refrained from endorsing Duff Green's enthusiastic efforts on behalf of Judge White. It was soon all too apparent that Calhoun was decidedly cool to the White movement, that Webster's friends had only been strengthened in their determination to push their favorite by the prospect of division among the southern and south-western Jacksonians, and that Clay was using his influence to discourage the White movement.

By June, Bell was writing to northern Whig leaders in despair and indignation. "What do Webster and his friends mean?" he demanded of Gulian Verplanck. "Can any of them—can he be in the interest of Van Buren?" Whatever the intention, he continued, Webster's insistence on running was destroying the White movement and insuring a Van Buren victory. Thousands of voters were being weaned away from White by the Democratic argument that White was being used to prevent a Van Buren majority and throw the election into the House of Representatives, where the Bank "will buy up enough States to elect Webster." "Alabama and Mississippi are half gone already from Judge White," Bell asserted, and even Tennessee was in danger. "It is idle to argue that the politicians in this State cannot desert White," he went on, for "the people *may* & will leave the politicians." The truth of the situation, he implored, must "be beat into the heads of Websters friends," for if things went on as they were, Webster "cannot get into the House even, & he prostrates absolutely every leading man of Judge White's party."[76]

Webster refused, of course, to postpone his ambitions, and worse was yet to come. By fall Clay was backing William Henry Harrison as a competitor with White for anti-Van Buren votes in the North-

[76] Bell to G. C. Verplanck, 22 June 1835, Verplanck Papers. See also Bell to Samuel McKean, 22 Apr. 1835, Simon Gratz Autograph Collection (HSP).

west, and the embittered Duff Green was trying to swing the Virginia Nullifiers from White to Harrison.[77]

The Whig strategy was now clear. As early as June 1835 one of the leading Whig newspapers in New York had announced publicly that "Our strength is in multiplying our presidential candidates, so as to ensure an election by Congress. . . . We have with this view encouraged the nomination of Mr. Webster in the north, Judge White in the south, Mr. Clay or Gen. Harrison in the west."[78] White was not to be considered seriously for the presidency, but the Whig managers tried to avoid making this too obvious to White's supporters. "Harrison's friends dread nothing more than that White should be scared off the field, or his friends discouraged from giving him a zealous support, and perhaps relapsing into Van Burenism," warned Clay's chief of staff, John J. Crittenden. "To avoid this is a point of obvious policy, and I think it is neither right nor politic to exaggerate Harrison's prospects at the expense of White's."[79]

But however considerately they were treated by their fellow Whigs, White's friends could hardly convince themselves any longer that he had much chance to be elected. Indeed, even their chances of serving the over-all Whig strategy by carrying the South for White had been jeopardized by Bell's rebuff to the Calhounites. In Tennessee itself the White cause might go down to defeat, carrying with it all its leaders. Into the struggle for White's own state, therefore, Bell and his associates now poured all their energies and resources. They were fighting for their political lives.

[77] *The Writings and Speeches of Daniel Webster*, National Edition (18 vols., Boston, 1903), XVI, 251; Henry Clay to [?], 14 July 1835, Thomas J. Clay Papers (LC); Duff Green to R. K. Cralle, 5 Oct. 1835, bound vol., Duff Green Papers (LC).

[78] New York *Evening Star*, 9 June 1835.

[79] Mrs. Chapman Coleman, *The Life of John J. Crittenden, with Selections from His Correspondence and Speeches* (2 vols. in 1, Philadelphia, 1873), I, 86.

TENNESSEE DESERTS JACKSON

THE BATTLE FOR TENNESSEE opened even before the congressmen left Washington in the spring of 1835. Late in February there was an acrimonious controversy between Polk and Cave Johnson on one side and Judge White on the other, when the president appointed a man recommended by Polk and Johnson as federal attorney for West Tennessee. White complained that the Nashville bar had not been given a chance to make recommendations, but what really disturbed him was the revelation that the Polk-Grundy group would henceforth control the federal patronage in Tennessee.[1]

The two groups clashed again when the White forces revived the old Jacksonian proposal for a constitutional amendment to prevent presidential elections from being decided by the House of Representatives in case no candidate had a majority in the electoral college. Hoping to attract many nominal Democrats to their favorite, White's managers were greatly disturbed by the Democratic argument that his candidacy would split the party and throw the election into the House, where the people's will might be flouted as in 1824. It was to neutralize this argument that Speaker Bell appointed George Gilmer, a White backer from Georgia, as chairman of a committee to consider a constitutional amendment. When the Van Burenites on the committee raised so many objections to the details of various proposals as to render a report impossible, Gilmer finally presented an amending resolution on his own responsibility.

The Democrats could hardly oppose the measure on its merits, least of all Polk, who had made his first speech in Congress in support of a similar proposition. But party interests now dictated its defeat, and Polk was the administration leader in the House. Consequently he, too, discovered insuperable objections in minor details and suggested that time was too short at this session to give the question the attention it deserved. When Balie Peyton put his finger

---

[1] White to Polk and Johnson, 24, 26 Feb. 1835, James K. Polk Papers (LC; herein cited as Polk Papers, which refers to First Series unless otherwise noted); Polk and Johnson to White, 25 Feb. 1835, draft, 25 Feb. [1835; misplaced 1836], draft, 26 Feb. 1835, two drafts, *ibid.*

on the political motives behind these delaying tactics, Polk replied that he still favored the reform and would vote for the Gilmer resolution. This he did, but enough Democrats voted the other way to defeat it.[2] The frustrated White men taunted Polk with reminders that "A half hour speech from him would have passed it, as the rank and file of the party would then have seen that permission was given them by their leaders to vote for the measure."[3]

The bitterness between the two groups of Tennesseans continued to mount through the closing weeks of the session, reaching a peak in the late hours of March 3, the day on which Congress was compelled to adjourn. The country had been excited during the preceding weeks by the refusal of the French government to carry out its agreement to make certain indemnity payments for depredations on American commerce during the Napoleonic Wars, and Jackson had brought the affair to the saber-rattling stage. Late in the evening, with the regular appropriation bill for fortifications still to be passed before the House could adjourn, administration leaders suddenly offered an amendment appropriating three million dollars to be expended at the president's discretion for military purposes, should any exigency requiring it arise during the recess of Congress. The House approved this bellicose gesture, but the Senate refused to accept it, and near midnight a conference committee under the chairmanship of C. C. Cambreleng was appointed to meet a similar Senate committee to adjust the disagreement.

The conference committee was not ready to report until two in the morning, and at this point Polk objected that the House had no power to transact business after midnight. His apparent object was to defeat the entire fortification bill and throw on the Senate, where Clay, Webster, and Calhoun held sway, the odium for leaving the country defenseless. At any rate Cambreleng refused to make his report; many Democrats refused to answer the roll call; and the session broke up in confusion and rancor. This reckless partisan maneuver may have been aimed particularly at Judge White, who had sided with the Whigs against the three-million-dollar House amendment, and Polk must bear a large share of the responsibility for its execution.[4]

[2] *Register of Debates*: 23rd Cong.: 2nd Sess., 1501-1504; *House Journal*:23:2, p. 377; Nashville *Republican Banner*, 3 Oct. 1838.

[3] Nashville *Republican Banner*, 15 Oct. 1838.

[4] *House Journal*:23:2, pp. 509-532; *Reg. Deb.*:23:2, pp. 1659-1663; *Congressional Globe*:24:1, p. 131; Polk to Laughlin, 30 Jan. 1836, Polk Papers.

II

More concerned about developments in Tennessee than with events in Washington, Polk was anxious to get home. As soon as Congress adjourned he and Sarah joined Grundy and C. C. Clay to charter a private stagecoach to Wheeling, where they boarded a steamboat for the trip down the Ohio and up the Cumberland. Tarrying only a day in Nashville to consult with Laughlin, Balch, and the other leading Van Burenites, he hastened on to Columbia to plunge into the fight to save Tennessee for the national Democratic ticket.[5]

Before leaving Tennessee the previous fall, the Bell men had prepared the ground in Tennessee for White's nomination; and the delegation meeting had no sooner occurred than the politicians back home started falling in line. The old anti-Jackson men and the Eaton-Lewis-Foster-Bell connection had come out en masse for White, creating the impression, in the absence of any open dissent, that the White movement would sweep all before it. All the state offices under the new constitution were to be filled at the August elections, or by the legislature to be chosen at that time, and the lesser politicians flocked to the White standard to stake their claims for a share of the spoils. The village weeklies were almost unanimously for White; the Nashville *Banner* had come out for the judge as soon as Laughlin was fired; and Allen Hall now took the *Republican* into the White camp. "We are *all, all* for White here," Bell announced jubilantly on reaching Tennessee. "There is not more than one Van man for ten White men in the whole State." And one of Polk's friends, after traveling across the state, had to admit that he had never seen "such unanimity of sentiment as prevails for Judge White."[6]

Since January, Bell and his cohorts had kept the Tennessee newspapers filled with denunciations of the approaching Democratic national convention as a rigged caucus of corrupt officeholders, handpicked to nominate Van Buren and representing no one but themselves. Davy Crockett, for example, had lampooned the Democratic arguments by publishing a burlesque letter declining a proposal that he run for president. To his boosters, "Nicholas Banks, Andrew

---

[5] C. C. Clay to Mrs. Clay, 3 Mar. 1835, Clement C. Clay Papers (DU); Catron to Jackson, 21 Mar. 1835, Andrew Jackson Papers (LC).

[6] Bell to Samuel McKean, 22 Apr. 1835, Simon Gratz Autograph Collection (HSP); S. G. Smith to Polk, 13 Feb. 1835, Polk Papers; Daniel Graham to Polk, 2, 29 Jan. 1835, *ibid.*; Pulaski *Tennessee Beacon*, 17 Oct. 1834.

J. Bullion, Thomas B. Goldwire and Martin V. Trashmony," Crockett replied that the Democracy "must hang together like a pitch plaster to a bald pate. No flying off—no thinking for ourselves. One man must think for all. . . . I'll be a 'voter,' . . . and carry any candidate the caucus at Baltimore may set up against the people." Refusing to divide the party by running himself, Crockett suggested that Martin Van Buren was "the most fitting man next to General Jackson, for the President, of any man that now hurrahs for hard money and the people. The way he is a Democrat, is a caution all over. He is dyed in the wool, through and through, and comes as near to the red breeches of Mr. Jefferson as a new patch upon an old garment can be made."[7]

This anticonvention propaganda went virtually unanswered, because the Van Buren men lacked any means of getting their views before the public. The project for a Grundy-Polk newspaper at Nashville had been beset by difficulties and delays. Sam Laughlin had got sober enough to go to Washington to complete the arrangements in December, but much time was consumed raising money for printing equipment, and then it could not be shipped from Cincinnati until the ice broke in the Ohio River. So the first number of the Nashville *Union* appeared only at the end of March, and the congressmen returned home to find that "everything like convention has been rendered odious."[8]

Jackson was so alarmed that he adopted the doubtful expedient of throwing his personal influence into the scales. The *Republican* had published a cleverly worded editorial denying that Jackson opposed White but intimating that any attempt at "dictation" by the president would backfire. Jackson replied publicly, excoriating attempts to divide the party and calling on his fellow Tennesseans to send delegates to the national convention. But his letter had little effect beyond forcing the White press to come out more openly against the president himself.[9]

Polk found his district virtually inundated by the White enthusiasm. The Columbia *Observer* had "hoisted the White flag and nailed it to the mast," and all that numerous class of local politicians who

[7] Randolph *Recorder*, 17 Feb. 1835, quoted in Charles E. Pool, "The Rise of the Whig Party in West Tennessee, 1834-1843," M.A. thesis, University of Mississippi (1950), 9.

[8] "Letters of James K. Polk to Cave Johnson, 1833-1848," *Tennessee Historical Magazine*, I (Sept. 1915), 219; Laughlin to Donelson, 1 Mar. 1835, Andrew Jackson Donelson Papers (LC).

[9] Nashville *Banner*, 20 Mar. 1835.

"watch the popular breeze" had joined Polk's enemies in a public meeting endorsing White. The meeting had shouted James Walker down when he proposed substitute resolutions endorsing White but declaring that the Democrats should unite on the candidate preferred by a majority of the party. The general sentiment seemed to be for White "against the field."[10] A loyal Polk man saw in the whole affair a plot "to get White and the people upon one side & Van Buren & my friend Col. Polk on the other," a suspicion that was confirmed when attacks on Walker's substitute resolutions began appearing in the *Observer*.[11]

Walker had been for Van Buren from the first, and he worked harder in this campaign than he ever had before. His zeal may be understood partly in the light of his mail contracts and partly in the light of the Union Bank's desire to preserve the state bank deposit system. But even the fervent Walker was intimidated by the White juggernaut. He had carefully avoided any direct mention of Van Buren or the national convention in his substitute resolutions, and he met Polk on his return from Congress with the advice, "Non interference may be your true position."[12]

Faced with this situation and threatened with opposition at the August election, Polk had little choice but to follow Walker's counsel. "Be careful," he cautioned his newly launched Nashville editor, Laughlin, "to say nothing of the *Convention* (for that is an abstract question, the discussion of which now can be of no practical use), and say nothing of any potential candidate for the Presidency."[13]

The convention question was indeed abstract, since Tennessee was the only state besides Calhoun's South Carolina that did not send delegates. The only Tennessee politicians who made a serious effort to have the state represented at Baltimore were Van Buren's old champion, Alfred Balch, and Judge John Catron, who was hoping for a seat on the federal Supreme Court. They were especially anxious to prevent Richard M. Johnson's expected nomination for vice president, fearing that his unorthodox domestic relations and mulatto daughters would make him a dead weight to the ticket in the slaveholding states. Balch wanted a Virginian to get the second

---

[10] Walker to Polk, 12, 28 Feb. 1835, Polk Papers; Columbia *Observer*, quoted in Washington *Sun*, 21 Feb. 1835; Nashville *Banner*, 18 Feb. 1835.

[11] J. K. Thomas to Polk, 12 Feb. 1835, Polk Papers.

[12] Walker to Polk, 28 Feb. 1835, Polk Papers.

[13] Polk to Laughlin, 28 Apr. 1835, Polk-Laughlin Letters, special section of Polk Papers.

position, but Catron tried to stir up sentiment for Governor Carroll, whose nomination would make it easier to defeat White in Tennessee. Catron enlisted Polk to write to Jackson on Carroll's behalf, but the project came to nothing, and soon even Balch was informing the president that "The distance is so great to Baltimore and the business of men so pressing that they cannot go however anxious they may be."[14]

Old Hickory was dumbfounded. "What," he exploded in a letter to Polk, "Tennessee, the once Democratic Tennessee apostate from the republican fold . . . and seperated [*sic*] from all her republican brethren! How strange! How humiliating to every real friend to the democracy of our beloved country."[15] The president had little sympathy with the cautious course of his Tennessee lieutenants. "The politicians are mistaken," he asserted. "If there was one bold eficient [*sic*] man, to come out freely and efficiently before the people, . . . *the recoil would be overwhelming.*"[16] Polk was subjected to a barrage of appeals for courageous action. "You and Grundy . . . are looked to," said Jackson, "to take a firm and open stand in favour of the republican principles, *a national convention by the people.*"[17] But Grundy cautioned Polk to "say nothing,"[18] and soon Old Hickory was writing again: "How is it that there is no man in the Republican ranks to take the Stump, and revive Tennessee from her degraded attitude of abandoning principle to sustain men who have apostatised from the republican fold for sake of office?" If he were a mere private citizen, Jackson continued, he could show the voters the fallacies of the White movement, and within a week Tennessee would be "erect upon her republican legs again." These sentiments, he added, were *"for every body."*[19]

When the convention met, Van Buren was duly nominated, but the vice presidential choice turned on the fact that Tennessee was represented after all. An obscure Tennessean, Edmund Rucker, happened to be in Baltimore at the time and was put under heavy pressure by the Kentucky delegation to cast Tennessee's fifteen conven-

[14] Balch to Jackson, n.d. (postmarked 4 Apr.) 1835, Jackson Papers; *id.* to *id.*, 3 Feb., 4 Apr. 1835, *ibid.*; Catron to Jackson, 21 Mar. 1835, *ibid.*; J. K. P[olk]. to [Jackson], 29 Apr. 1835, *ibid.*, Second Series; Balch to Polk, 3 Apr. 1835, Polk Papers.

[15] Jackson to Polk, 12 May 1835, Polk Papers.

[16] Jackson to A. J. Donelson, 12 May 1835, Donelson Papers.

[17] Jackson to Polk, 3 May 1835, Polk Papers.

[18] Grundy to Polk, 11 May 1835, Polk Papers.

[19] Jackson to Polk, 12 May 1835, Polk Papers.

tion votes for Colonel Johnson. The party managers foolishly allowed this to happen, and Rucker's Tennessee votes provided the margin by which Johnson defeated Virginia's candidate. This, of course, furnished the opposition with ready-made gibes at the "Ruckerized" Baltimore "caucus." "Edmund Rucker," ran a toast at the Fourth of July celebration in Columbia, "the political father of Col. Tecumseh Johnson—united with such a matron as the Baltimore Convention, who ever expected their issue to be *White?*"[20]

<h2 style="text-align:center">III</h2>

In the summer of 1835 the long process of realignment among Tennessee's political forces had at last reached its culmination, and two potent aggregations confronted each other for a showdown at the state elections in August. The Bell-Foster group seemed to possess most of the advantages: Judge White's enormous popularity, the prestige and financial backing of the business community, a near monopoly of the press, and the support of scores of lesser politicians scrambling for places on the White band wagon. The Polk-Grundy men could throw into the scales little more than President Jackson's hold on the loyalty of thousands of obscure Tennesseans, but this, they hoped, might be enough to avert catastrophe in August and even, perhaps, to save Tennessee for Van Buren the following year.

John Bell's defeat was the dearest wish of Polk and his friends. The previous summer Governor Carroll had promised to run against the speaker, but as the time for campaigning drew near he hesitated. Carroll was considerably bothered by his rheumatism, and he well realized that he would have an uphill fight in the Nashville district, the stronghold of the conservative business community. Ratification of the new state constitution offered a way out. The governor decided that he was no longer bound by the three-term limitation of the old constitution and that he could easily be reelected to the office he had already won six times. By March he was determined to announce once more for governor.[21]

This was only slightly less alarming to the White party than his running against Bell would have been, for Carroll had come out more forthrightly for Van Buren than any other prominent politician in the state, and his reelection could be interpreted to mean

---

[20] Nashville *Banner*, 15 July 1835.
[21] Daniel Graham to Polk, 2 Jan. 1835, Polk Papers; Carroll to Jackson, 12 Mar. 1835, Jackson Papers, Fragments.

that even Tennessee was against White. Accordingly the White men put up White's fellow townsman Richard G. Dunlap to oppose Carroll, hoping that the White question would defeat the popular governor. But it was quickly apparent that the White question was doing Carroll no harm, and the White newspapers were soon denying that the gubernatorial result would be any test of White's strength. Heavier artillery was brought to bear on Carroll in June, when Newton Cannon, the veteran anti-Jackson leader and Bank champion, announced for the governorship. Dunlap eventually gave up the race, and though another minor candidate was entered, the real fight was between Cannon and Carroll.[22]

The presidential question also dominated the contests for the legislature. Whichever party controlled this body would be able to fill the state offices under the new constitution and lay strong foundations for future political power. Moreover the new legislature would elect a senator, as White's term was expiring, and the White party also counted on it to give the judge a formal presidential nomination. Candidates who were personally for Van Buren found the White fever running so high that they were forced to promise their support to the judge.[23]

The presidential controversy figured less prominently in the congressional races, for the Van Buren men were able to mount candidates in only four of the thirteen districts. William Brady ran against two pro-White candidates for the retiring David Dickinson's seat in the Murfreesboro district, while A. A. Kincannon bore the Polk-Grundy colors in another three-cornered race in lower Middle Tennessee. The greatest disappointment was in John Bell's district. When Governor Carroll refused to offer against the speaker, the Van Buren men turned to Robert M. Burton, a popular lawyer who was related to President Jackson. But Burton was worried about a serious illness in his family, and for two months he resisted the entreaties of Democratic leaders from Jackson down. Finally, at the end of June, he disgraced himself in a brawl, and the idea of running him had to be abandoned. It was too late to enter another can-

22 James Campbell to David Campbell, 5 Apr. 1835, David Campbell Papers (DU); Carroll to Jackson, 3 May 1835, typed copy, Jackson Papers, Second Series; Nashville *Banner*, 27 May, 4 June, 20 July 1835.

23 A. B. Currey to R. L. Caruthers, 1 Aug. 1835, Robert L. Caruthers Papers (SHC); S. J. Garrison to R. L. Caruthers, 29 Aug. 1835, *ibid.*; W. G. Childress to Polk, 10 Jan. 1837, Polk Papers; Nashville *Union*, 16 Aug. 1836.

didate, even if one could have been found, and Bell made the race without opposition.[24]

The White men were thus left free to concentrate their strength against the two Van Burenite incumbents. Their candidate against Cave Johnson, however, was soon forced to withdraw by Johnson's overwhelming strength in the poor and rabidly pro-Jackson Tennessee River counties. But this was a minor disappointment to Bell and his friends. James K. Polk was their real bête noire, and before leaving Washington they had promised Biddle's agent Samuel Jaudon that Polk would be defeated. Immediately on reaching Tennessee they sent Allen Hall to canvass the situation with the anti-Polk politicians in Bedford, and a week later Polk's old foe Theoderick Bradford went up to Nashville for a conference. Polk was certain that Bradford would be his competitor, but that gentleman was still smarting from his defeat at the previous election, and the White managers finally had to look elsewhere for a candidate. Through May and June, Polk kept hearing reports of their negotiations with various politicians in his district. They overlooked few possibilities, even enlisting a Whig senator from Alabama to bring pressure on one of his relatives in the district.[25]

Threatened with opposition at any moment, Polk prudently campaigned through Maury and Bedford almost as zealously as if an opponent were already in the field, inspiring one of his enemies to toast him at a Bedford County White rally as "The political Somnambulist, who walks in his sleep over his district, making speeches on national politics without any opposition."[26] It was well that he did, for more was involved in this election than his personal feud with Bell or even his personal political survival. Though the White movement seemed to be fading as a major factor in national presidential politics, it was unquestionably bringing Jacksonian Democracy to a Thermopylae in the president's own state, and Polk was the only possible Democratic Leonidas in sight.

By a decade of dogged application and painful trial and error, Polk had mastered the techniques of parliamentary maneuver and

[24] Jackson to Donelson, 12 May 1835, Donelson Papers; Grundy to Polk, 5, 7, 9, 28 June 1835, Polk Papers; Grundy to Jackson, 6, 17 June 1835, Jackson Papers.

[25] Cave Johnson to Polk, 1 May [1835; misplaced 1838], 22 May 1835, 15 June [1835; misplaced 1836], Polk Papers; Jaudon to Biddle, 25 Feb. 1835, Nicholas Biddle Papers (LC); "Polk-Johnson Letters," *loc.cit.*, 219-223; John Spencer Bassett, ed., *Correspondence of Andrew Jackson* (7 vols., Washington, 1926-1935), v, 346.

[26] Nashville *Banner*, 20 July 1835.

legislative leadership, and his party had finally and somewhat grudgingly begun to utilize his abilities. In the House of Representatives, however, Polk was still only a tactical leader, wincing under Whig gibes that he was slavishly executing policies formulated by others, and even here the coveted speakership had eluded his grasp. The political crisis at home in the summer of 1835 gave him his first opportunity for party leadership in his own right. If he could rally Jackson's dispirited supporters and stem the White tide in Tennessee, he could dominate the Tennessee Democracy and assert strong claims on his party nationally. But the talents Polk had been developing in Congress would help him little in this situation. The task of reversing a strong tide of public sentiment and building a party press and organization from the ground required those qualities of personal magnetism that excite the popular imagination and inspire confidence and loyalty in other politicians.

Such qualities did not come naturally to Polk. He had none of the urbanity, wit, fire, and capacity for comradery that made Henry Clay, for example, the idol of so many voters and politicians. Cave Johnson seems to have been the only man with whom he ever approached any kind of relaxed intimacy. Even in this relationship, to judge from the two men's correspondence, all the jocularity and personal references proceeded from Johnson, who appeared to sense a warmth in Polk that was never expressed openly.

Yet at thirty-nine this introverted, unrelaxed man presented an impressive front to the world. A trifle under middle height and solidly built, Polk carried himself energetically and with military erectness. His face, with its mop of unruly black hair brushed back from a broad forehead, its long, prominent nose, and its darkish skin stretched tightly over the high cheekbones and pulled down tautly around the strong, narrow chin, suggested the only partly refined ruggedness of the West.

In two of his facial features Polk was revealed to an unusual degree. His eyes, large, steel-gray, and moving restlessly in their deep sockets, afforded the only unobstructed view of the fires that burned within him; while his thin, compressed lips and the rigid set of his mouth expressed the determination and rigorous self-discipline that enabled him, except in these two betraying features, to present himself not as he was but as he wished to be. It was his air of restrained power and passion, suggested by this conjunction of eyes and mouth, that made Polk so impressive to those around him.

Polk's personal and public relations required, in fact, an exertion of will so nearly continuous that it became second nature. His personality seemed unbelievably methodical and calculated, but he worked so hard at making it believable that people were half convinced. With all his outgoing impulses and aspirations turned inward and focused on the satisfactions of politics, he had set himself as a young man to cultivating the qualities requisite for political success. Schooling himself to a rather ceremonial affability, he collected acquaintanceships avidly and cultivated them assiduously.

One of Polk's acquaintances recalled an incident that illustrates this aspect of his personality. Polk was pacing up and down a tavern porch one afternoon when a stranger rode up and hitched his horse. Polk walked up as the man climbed the steps, "offered him his hand and with a smile looked him in the face with an expression of uncertainty and inquiry which seemed to ask the question, 'Am I mistaken?'" When the traveler replied that he was mistaken, that they were unacquainted, Polk rejoined, "I was in doubt, Sir, until you spoke; but now I am sure I know you—this is Colonel Holman, of Lincoln County." "You must have a most remarkable memory," Holman gasped, for the only time they had met was at a Fourth of July barbecue ten years before. "Colonel Holman," said Polk, "I don't think I was ever introduced to a man and talked with him ten minutes, that I ever afterwards forgot him." Such energetic application to the business of personal relations compensated in large measure for his inability to achieve real spontaneity.[27]

By training and practice Polk likewise overcame his lack of the natural gift of eloquence. At Chapel Hill he had preferred logical appeals to reason, but when these proved ineffective with Tennessee audiences, he developed a new style that, despite its incongruity with his personality, eventually made him one of the most celebrated stump speakers in the history of the state. He was still sufficiently dignified to satisfy educated townspeople, and his speches were still full of information and logical argument. But he had learned to spice this fare with sallies of wit and sarcasm that evoked shouts and huzzas from the "wool hat b'hoys." Polk was no windmill orator. He did not need to wave his arms, for he had made his face such an expressive instrument that the sly glances and the grimaces by which

[27] Nathaniel Baxter, "Reminiscences," *American Historical Magazine* (Nashville), VIII (July 1903), 263-264.

he drove home his innuendos were enough to send the crowds into roars of delight.

Polk lacked the imagination for the flowery flights and sonorous periods that made Grundy, for example, so impressive to Tennesseans. Wisely recognizing this limitation on what he could make himself do, he almost never attempted bombast, except in his inevitable apostrophe to Jackson, "that brave old Hero and Patriot, who stood like a wall of fire when England hurled her avalanche of brutal myrmidons upon the ramparts of New Orleans, yelling like demons, their beastly watchword—'Beauty and Booty,' and when the lives and honors of our fair women had no shelter from the storm but his gallant heart, his wise head, his strong arm and indomitable courage." But however much Polk's audiences were informed by his reasoning, entertained by his anecdotes and raillery, or impressed by his occasional rhetorical extravagances, it was something else that convinced them, "something in his manner and delivery that suggested the idea of labor, effort, power," something "deliberate yet vehement," the sense he somehow conveyed of the strength and passion that were pent up and channeled by his disciplined will.[28]

None of these things came easily to Polk. Like all his abilities they were acquired only by dint of unremitting effort over a considerable period of time. But this made them no less effective. Before another decade passed Polk would vanquish the most gifted politician of his generation, Henry Clay, for the highest office in the land. Though circumstances as well as personal qualities would contribute to Polk's ultimate triumph, it nevertheless stands almost unparalleled in the annals of American politics as an achievement of modest endowments, coupled with extraordinary determination and self-discipline.

Polk's development was continuous throughout his career, rarely progressing ahead of the challenges that presented themselves, forcing him to the limit of his abilities in every new situation, but somehow enabling him to meet the demands of each successive episode. By 1835 he was just prepared to move toward statewide political leadership.

IV

Constantly threatened with opposition at the August election, Polk was caught between two fires. To defy his constituents' obvious enthusiasm for White was to court defeat and political oblivion,

[28] *ibid.*, 265-267.

while to acquiesce in the White movement, even by silence, was to forfeit his claims on the Democratic party for the speakership, at the same time delivering Tennessee over to Bell and Foster without a contest. At first, therefore, he was compelled to navigate a hazardous course between Scylla and Charybdis.

Speaking at the courthouse in Columbia on the first day of the April court, Polk carefully avoided any mention of Van Buren or the Baltimore convention, but explained that he had not joined the rest of the Tennessee delegation in sponsoring the White movement because he did not think his constituents had sent him to Washington to engage in president making. It was not his duty to take a position, he said, unless the election finally went to the House of Representatives for decision, and in that event he promised to vote as his district had voted. More important, he believed that the Republicans, if they were to "preserve and perpetuate the great principles they profess," must "unite if possible their whole strength upon some one man of the party, and run but one candidate."

Polk even declared that he personally preferred White, for "all know the intimate personal and political relations, which have for many years existed between us"; and he promised to support the judge, "if at any time hereafter the public sentiment in the Democratic Republican States, in whatever fair mode ascertained or expressed shall indicate him as the choice of the body, or of a majority of the Republican supporters of the present administration." But until this was clearly the case, said Polk, "I will wait and see upon whom the great body of our friends of the same political faith in other states do concentrate; and upon him, whomsoever he may be, in my opinion, all should unite."[29]

These brief remarks about the presidency were set in a context that expressed eloquently Polk's deep commitment to the Old Republican America and the party that championed its principles. Though he never had great enthusiasm for Van Buren, political expediency alone does not account for his loyalty to his party's prospective candidate. Any other course would have violated his ideological bent, for he saw the political struggles of his own day as merely a continuation of the classic conflict between Thomas Jefferson and Alexander Hamilton, between Old Mecklenburg and

[29] *Mr. Polk's Speech . . . on Monday, the 26th of April,* broadside bound in vol. of speeches, Polk Papers.

Philadelphia, between simple morality and a conspiracy of wealth and power.

The White movement, in Polk's eyes, was a genuinely shocking attempt to transfer Tennessee to the enemy's side in this fundamental struggle. Since he would never admit that most Tennesseans did not share his Old Republican convictions, he could only believe that they were being deceived and poisoned by false leaders, and he sprang to the stump to supply the antidote. From this time forward for many years to come he would hammer away at a single theme, the identity of the "new light Whig party" with the "Old Blue Light Federal party." Elaborating this argument in every corner of Maury and Bedford during the summer of 1835, he never after let his constituents forget it.

Polk's standard speech always went back to the royalist and centralist Hamilton. Then passing over George Washington in silence, he would pay his respects to John Adams and the Alien and Sedition Acts. After describing the Federalist Hartford Convention in all its treasonable horror and contrasting it with the patriotism of Republican Tennessee and Jackson's glorious victories, he would come at last to Henry Clay, the younger Adams, and the "bargain, intrigue, and corruption" by which "General Jackson had been cheated out of the Presidency and the people out of their votes" in the election of 1824. The noble line of the Democratic party from Jefferson to Jackson would then be contrasted with the sorry record of the conspiratorial Federalist-Whig alignment. This offering was always interspersed with discussions of the Bank, the tariff, or some other current issue, and through the whole would run a constant stream of anecdotes, mockery, and sarcasm.[30]

But speeches were not enough, for Polk desperately needed an effective organ to put his side of the controversy before the voters. The most fortunate development came in April, when Jackson finally got Frank Blair out from under Major Lewis's influence and the *Globe* began a series of characteristically slashing attacks on Bell and the White movement. Polk was grateful for this help, but he could not forget his bitterness at Blair. "I see the Globe thunders now," he wrote. "If it had done so in time, we would have been saved our present troubles."[31] Bell promptly answered the *Globe*'s charges with a long letter in the *Republican*, and Jackson, as soon as he got

---

[30] Baxter, "Reminiscences," *loc.cit.*, 267-269.
[31] Polk to Donelson, 29 Apr. 1835, Donelson Papers.

hold of a copy, sent it to Blair with peremptory orders to "settle all matters and prostrate him."[32]

Polk still needed a newspaper in his own district, since the Shelbyville paper was for White and the *Observer* had gone over so completely to his enemies that he was no longer on speaking terms with the editor. Late in June the first number of the Columbia *Tennessee Democrat* appeared, bearing the significant motto, "Measures—not men." Once Polk's reelection was certain, it began to speak out boldly for Van Buren. The paper was published by a young printer from Nashville but backed, of course, by Polk and Walker. In fact most of the editorials were written by Walker and Andrew Hays, a longtime Polk supporter who had been rewarded with the town postmastership. Polk was also trying to get control of the Shelbyville paper.[33]

Meanwhile Bell, in a speech before the Nashville elite at the fashionable Vauxhall Gardens, had expressed eloquently the aversion of a conservative, strong-willed individual for political parties. Freed at last from the party discipline under which he had chafed in the Jackson ranks, the independent-minded speaker lashed out at the whole party system, as a grave threat to free institutions. Parties, he argued, were controlled by unscrupulous men who cared more for power and office than for principle, and who would never rest "while there is a shred of constitutional restriction remaining upon the absolute impulsive will of an excited and agitated people." The Jackson party—enforcing its edicts through patronage, conventions, and the president's fearful popularity with this "excited and agitated people"—was to Bell only the most demonic product of the system.[34]

These opinions demonstrated how far out of sympathy Bell was with the powerful democratic currents running through the America of his day. Only a man of Bell's type would have had the courage—or political foolhardiness—to lead the initial breakaway from Jackson in Tennessee, but his temperamental aloofness from the mainstream of his generation's political life was to deprive him of the political advancement that his ambitious nature craved.

Only a few days after the Vauxhall Garden speech, Polk's friends got wind of another example of Bell's ineptitude. In the congres-

32 *Jackson Correspondence*, v, 349; Nashville *Republican*, 9 May 1835, extra.

33 Nashville *Banner*, 1 June 1835; Nashville *Union*, 10 July 1835; A. C. Hays to Polk, 21 Nov. 1835, Polk Papers.

34 Nashville *Republican*, 15 June 1835.

sional district to the south of Maury, which had formerly been part of Polk's district and where he still had many friends, the Polk-Grundy candidate for Congress, A. A. Kincannon, had been capitalizing on Polk's popularity by making an issue of the coming speakership election. Early in May a White supporter, Charles Cassedy, had written to tell Bell about this strategy and also to request a denial of Kincannon's charges that Bell and White were Bank men. Bell replied that it would be a mistake for White to declare that he would veto any Bank bill Congress might pass. As for the speakership, he suggested that even Polk might be put under promise to vote for Bell against any candidate except himself. "My course in appointing him Chairman of the Committee of Ways and Means," he added, "could be used to show that I have not been influenced by personal considerations against him, when the country is concerned."[35]

Unfortunately, Bell's correspondent was greatly addicted to the bottle, and the contents of the speaker's communication soon became generally known. Kincannon heard about it and informed Polk, who immediately appreciated its importance as a revelation of "the machinations of the little *junta* of self-constituted, would-be-great men at Nashville who wish to control the State, and to prostrate all whom they may suppose, stand in the way of their own advancement." After three weeks of strenuous efforts, Polk's friends were able by some means to get a copy of Bell's letter, and it was published in the *Union*.[36]

The Polk-Van Buren men succeeded in creating a great stir over the Cassedy letter, charging that Bell was interfering in elections outside his district, that he was trying to force Polk to support him for speaker by subtle threats to deprive him of his committee chairmanship, and, most damning of all, that White would not veto a bill to recharter the national bank. The only defense that the embarrassed Bell-White press could manage was an attack on Polk's friends for violating private correspondence. The Cassedy letter did Bell serious damage, not only in Tennessee, but also in the subsequent speakership election. Its most immediate effect was to nip in

35 Nashville *Union*, 26 June 1835.
36 Polk to [Kincannon], 1 June 1835, Washburn Papers (MHS), Vol. IX, No. 55; Kincannon to Polk, 1 June 1835, Polk Papers; Grundy to Polk, 7, 18, 21, 25, 26 June 1835, *ibid.*; Laughlin to Polk, 17 June 1835, *ibid.*; Alfred Flournoy to Polk, 21 June 1835, *ibid.*; James Osburn to Laughlin, 22 June 1835, copy, *ibid.*; James Osburn to Polk, 26 June 1835, *ibid.*; Nashville *Banner*, 31 July 1835.

the bud a campaign to compel congressional candidates in the other districts to pledge themselves to support Bell for speaker.[37]

The episode probably also helped convince the Bell-White managers at Nashville that Polk was too strong to be beaten, but not until two weeks before the election did they abandon their efforts to bring out a candidate against him. By that time, the summer's strenuous campaigning, added to the strain of the preceding congressional session, had broken down Polk's chronically precarious health. He stayed at home until the balloting was over and then withdrew to Beaver Dam Springs, a remote watering place, for complete rest and solitude. Seriously ill for a time, he was not able to leave the Springs until the end of August, and even then his strength returned only slowly.[38]

The election results did not aid Polk's recovery. The Polk-Grundy men were stunned, and even the White party was surprised, by Cannon's smashing victory over Carroll for governor, by a majority of 41,852 to 33,030, with the third candidate getting 8,202 votes. Cannon had struck a popular chord in East Tennessee by coming out strongly for a state program of internal improvements, and he carried all but two counties in that area. He also had a small majority in the Western District, which was becoming increasingly anti-Jackson with the spread of large-scale cotton plantations, while Carroll had a small majority in the middle section of the state. Carroll had won Maury by only 52 votes out of more than 3,000 cast, while he lost Bedford, despite Polk's help, by 300 votes. The White men admitted that the presidential question had not been the main factor in Carroll's defeat. What apparently bothered the voters most was the dubious legality of a fourth consecutive term, an issue on which his opponents played strongly in the closing weeks of the campaign.

The congressional results were equally discouraging. Bell and most of his allies had either run unopposed or defeated their competitors, while John Blair and Kincannon had both lost to White supporters. There was some consolation in the reelection of Dunlap, a reluctant White man and friend of Polk, in the Bolivar district, and in Adam Huntsman's victory over Crockett, though Polk could

37 Nashville *Union*, 12, 26 June, 10 July, 3 Aug. 1835; Nashville *Banner*, 12, 26 June, 3, 31 July 1835; Laughlin to Polk, 5 July 1835, Polk Papers; Polk to Laughlin, 7 July 1835, *ibid.*

38 Polk to Jackson, 14 Aug. 1835, Jackson Papers; Polk to Laughlin, 6 Sept. 1835, Polk-Laughlin Letters.

only hope that the eccentric Huntsman "may go right." The biggest disappointment was the Murfreesboro district, where the Polk-Grundy stalwart, William Brady, who was regarded as a sure winner, had died on the eve of the election, leaving the seat to be filled by Abram Maury, a White man who it was hoped would not be under Bell's control. As for the legislature, the White men won big majorities in both houses, and the Tennessee Democracy was left disorganized and dispirited, with little hope of saving the state for Old Hickory's favorite.[39]

V

The August elections produced only the briefest calm in the political storm. The most crucial session of the legislature in years would convene the first week of October; the speakership contest would be renewed when Congress reassembled two months later; and beyond that lay the presidential election. Safely past the danger of personal defeat by the White enthusiasm, the Van Buren men began to come out more boldly on the presidential question, and President Jackson kept the mails filled with urgent summonses to renew the battle. The White forces likewise returned eagerly to the fray, anxious to press their hard-won advantage. The leaders on both sides were now motivated by personal hatreds that began to overshadow their original political differences. Alfred Balch's declaration of "war to the knife & the knife to the hilt," in breaking off his formerly warm friendship with John Bell, was typical of the feeling in both camps.[40]

Polk was the principal target of Bell's friends, who were resolved to discredit him at all costs. Their immediate strategy was to prevent his election as speaker by creating the impression that he was weak in his own state, and to this purpose they bent all their energies. Judge White made a point of going to Columbia early in September, and shortly afterward Bell spent a whole week there, ostensibly visiting relatives. Over a hundred of Polk's local enemies signed an invitation to Bell for a public dinner, but as Polk had predicted, it turned out to be "*a paper* dinner & not an *eating* dinner." The object was to demonstrate Bell's popularity with Polk's fellow towns-

---

[39] "Votes in the Governor's Election in Tennessee in 1835 and 1837," MS placed 31 July 1837, Polk Papers; Polk to Jackson, 14 Aug. 1835, Jackson Papers; Nashville *Banner*, 9 Sept. 1835.

[40] Balch to Jackson, 3 Feb. 1835, Jackson Papers.

men and to give him an opportunity to attack the Tennessee Van Burenites once again in his reply declining the invitation. Bell saw to it that this correspondence was widely publicized in Whig newspapers throughout the country.[41]

One incident during his visit, however, was most embarrassing to the speaker. At a private dinner for Bell, his cousin Judge William E. Kennedy offered a most indiscreet toast: "Tennessee—When a Caesar shall appear in our country to usurp our liberties, Tennessee will furnish a Brutus to redress her wrongs." The town was already, according to Polk, "highly excited,"[42] and the Bell-White men were enraged when the Democrats got hold of Judge Kennedy's toast and published it in the *Tennessee Democrat*. Accompanied by some of his friends, Kennedy promptly invaded the newspaper premises to thrash the editor, but, as Polk reported with relish, he "met with a suitable reception and was unceremoniously thrust from the office, without effecting his object."[43] Though Kennedy lamely denied that he had intended any allusion to Jackson, the Van Buren press was able to make great capital out of the affair.

A month later Polk's enemies staged an elaborate White celebration at Columbia. There were military companies, bands, dignitaries on white horses, and saluting cannon, while the wives and daughters of the anti-Van Buren families waved white handkerchiefs from their windows as the parade went by. The day was climaxed by a dinner for Judge White, attended by over 600 people. Again the White press gave the event wide publicity.[44]

Polk was unable to counter these activities at first, for his physical recovery was so slow and so impeded by relapses that he could not even travel up to Nashville for a conference with Grundy and Johnson until the end of September. His spirits had revived more quickly. While Bell was in Columbia, Polk claimed to be as "calm as a summer's evening." "My reliance is not upon the village politicians," he told his friends, "but upon the *real people*, who have never failed to sustain me, and I have no reason to fear that they will do so, so long as I do my duty."[45]

41 Polk to Laughlin, 17 Sept. 1835 (HEH); Polk to Alfred Flournoy, 14 Sept. 1835, typed copy, Polk-Flournoy Letters, special section of Polk Papers; *Niles' Weekly Register*, XLIX (17 Oct. 1835), 117-118.

42 Nashville *Banner*, 14 Oct. 1835; Polk to Donelson (postmarked 23 Sept. [1835]), Jackson Papers.

43 Polk to F. P. Blair, 3 Oct. 1835, Blair-Lee Papers (PU).

44 Nashville *Banner*, 28 Oct. 1835.

45 Polk to Alfred Flournoy, 14 Sept. 1835, typed copy, Polk-Flournoy Letters.

Before long "the *real people*" justified this confidence. Two days after the White dinner at Columbia, an enormous crowd of rural voters from the southeastern part of Maury County turned out for a dinner to honor Polk at the hamlet of Mooresville. Polk had prepared his speech carefully with an eye to the forthcoming speakership election and took care to distribute copies among his Democratic congressional colleagues. Whereas he had merely declared against dividing the party in his speech at Columbia back in April, he now came out aggressively in defense of the national convention, Jackson, and Van Buren. "I resolved, from the beginning, not to separate myself from the body of [the Republican] party; but to act with them in supporting the candidate of the republican party, and often so declared in my late canvass," he said. "If, in doing this, I may have sacrificed former personal attachments for men, it is a sacrifice for principle, and on which I am ready to stand. I have changed no political opinion or principle I ever entertained; and if I shall sink, politically, I go down like an honest man, and without a regret, standing by my old principles and associations, and having changed neither." Polk went on to complain that his enemies, "some of whom are nullifiers, and others Bank men," had made Columbia "the theatre of greater political excitement and more proscriptive violence than any other spot in the whole state." "It is not so much Judge White's advancement, as my prostration—which they desire," he charged. "What care they for Judge White, further than their own views are advanced?"[46]

The experience at Mooresville was repeated the next week at Mount Pleasant and Williamsport in the western end of the county, and Polk had to decline still other invitations. He was delighted with the reaction to his speeches. "We have had two glorious days at Mt. Pleasant & Williamsport, and you will be surprised when I tell you that the people almost without a division are openly with us on the Presidential question," he assured a friend. "The leading men are talking aloud for Van-Buren. Such a simultaneous moving of the people, such excitement & such a revolution in opinion I have never witnessed. They are become if possible, more unanimous than the Mooresville country."[47]

[46] Nashville *Union*, 19 Nov. 1835.
[47] Polk to A. O. P. Nicholson, 28 Oct. 1835, Alfred O. P. Nicholson Papers (NYHS).

VI

Polk could not, however, concern himself merely with his own district. Much of the responsibility for the Van Buren cause throughout the state was being thrust upon his shoulders, and on his performance depended the party's support in the speakership election. The immediate problem was the legislature, where the pro-White majority hoped to nominate White for president, elect one of their own men to the Senate, and fill all the state offices with White supporters. The Tennessee Van Burenites were at first inclined to a conciliatory strategy, hoping to save some of the state offices for Van Buren men. They also hoped that the legislators might be induced, while nominating White, to refrain from attacking Van Buren and to declare their willingness to support either man rather than see the presidential election thrown into the House of Representatives. Grundy, who could be forced to resign from the Senate by legislative instructions to vote against his principles on some measure, was especially cautious, and could not "be gotten to open his mouth except in a corner."[48]

Such temporizing was not for Andrew Jackson. His former pleas having fallen on deaf ears, he now issued explicit orders. The August elections were barely over when Polk received detailed campaign plans from the White House. Old Hickory demanded that his lieutenants take the offensive by calling on the legislature to instruct Tennessee's senators to support the current test of Democratic loyalty, Thomas Hart Benton's expunging resolutions.

During the panic session of 1833-1834 Henry Clay had pushed through the Senate a resolution declaring that Jackson had violated both the law and the Constitution in removing the deposits. Benton had promptly introduced a set of resolutions to expunge this censure of the president from the Senate journal, and they had become the focal issue in the Democratic campaign to regain control of the Senate, with loyal Democratic legislatures instructing their senators to support the Benton expunging resolutions and replacing those who refused to obey. The expunging question might be especially effective in Tennessee, since Judge White had voted against Benton's resolutions at the previous session of Congress, arguing that they violated the constitutional requirement that the Senate keep a journal of its proceedings. Jackson's strategy was not merely a bid

[48] Balch to Jackson, 26 Aug. 1835, Jackson Papers.

for personal vindication, but an attempt to turn the question in Tennessee from one between White and Van Buren to one between Jackson and Clay.

The president urged Polk, therefore, to see that the necessary instructing resolutions were prepared and that local meetings were organized to instruct the legislators to support them. Prompt action was necessary, he pointed out, to get the instructing resolutions under way before the White men announced their candidate for the Senate, so as to avoid the charge that they were designed for the persecution of any particular senator. Through August and September the president continued to bombard his Tennessee supporters with directions and exhortations. He sent Governor Carroll a draft of the kind of resolutions he thought were appropriate, arranged to have copies of the *Globe* containing Benton's speeches on expunging sent to all members of the legislature, and pleaded with Polk to be at Nashville before the legislature began, to see that the resolutions were introduced at the earliest possible moment.[49]

Polk's illness prevented him from getting to Nashville for the initial meeting at which the Van Buren men made arrangements to carry out Jackson's plans, but he kept busy at home lining up the support of favorably disposed legislators by mail. His most valuable conquest was the able and extremely ambitious young Columbia lawyer A. O. P. Nicholson, who had been one of the early leaders of the White movement in Maury County and who had just been elected to the legislature as a White man. Nicholson's change of heart seems to have been connected with suggestions that Polk would not run for Congress again in 1837 and that Nicholson could be his successor; if this eventuality did not materialize, Nicholson soon indicated, the federal district attorneyship would be almost as acceptable.[50]

Polk finally got to Nashville just before the legislature met. The resolutions of instruction were introduced on the second day of the session, and the Van Buren men threw themselves into a last ditch effort to rally public opinion behind them. As local meetings and petitions instructing the legislators multiplied, the Whigs grew

[49] Jackson to Polk, 3 Aug., 15 Sept. 1835, Polk Papers; *Jackson Correspondence*, v, 367, 371.

[50] Polk to Jackson, 22 Sept. 1835, Jackson Papers, Second Series; A. O. P. Nicholson to Jackson, 26 Jan. 1836, Jackson Papers.

worried. A White paper in the Western District described the methods used in circulating the Democratic petitions as follows:

"Mr. ——" says the solicitor for signers, "you are a friend to General Jackson, a'nt you?" "Certainly" replies the honest farmer, who will not and perhaps cannot read the long string of stuff that fills the paper presented to him. "Well here," continues the Solicitor, "the dam things are abusing General Jackson's character, and we must redeem it," and the man signs the paper of instructions and Van Burenism. Many an unsuspecting friend of Judge White has thus been duped.[51]

The Van Buren men climaxed their campaign on a Saturday late in October with a tremendous dinner in honor of Grundy, Carroll, Polk, and Johnson at Nashville. Jackson ordered his adopted son at the Hermitage to go and take all his neighbors; and nearly 2,000 loyal Democrats, many from distant counties, flocked into the city for the event. Following the customary cannon salutes and parade, the dinner got under way shortly after noon, but the sun had long gone down before the last of the orators had had his say.

Polk's address was by and large a repetition of what he had said at the Maury dinners, but like all the speakers on this occasion he gave special attention to the expunging resolutions. Preceding Polk, Grundy had grandiloquently proclaimed that "the cry of *expunge* would not only be reverberated from the most distant recesses of the mountains, and the hills re-echo the same overwhelming sound, but that the mothers of the land would teach the infant on their knee to lisp the word *expunge*." It was Polk's earthier call to do battle for Old Hickory, however, that brought the partisan crowd to its feet cheering. "Suppose, my fellow countrymen," he asked, "suppose that the old hero should now rush in among you, with a *bloody nose*, crying out '*these rascals, Clay, Calhoun, and Poindexter, are attempting to murder me*,' is there one here who would not rush to his rescue?"[52]

Despite all these efforts, Jackson's plans were upset. Probably through Major Lewis, who had become little better than a spy in the President's household,[53] the Bell forces got advance notice of the Democratic strategy and moved to counter it by pushing White's

[51] Randolph *Recorder*, 18 Dec. 1835, quoted in Powell Moore, "The Establishment of the Whig Party in Tennessee," Ph.D. dissertation, Indiana University (1932), 202; Polk to Jackson, 10 Oct. 1835, Jackson Papers.

[52] Nashville *Commercial Transcript*, quoted in Washington *Sun*, 25 Nov. 1835; *Jackson Correspondence*, v, 373; Nashville *Union*, 7 Nov. 1835.

[53] Donelson to Polk, 24 Sept. 1835, Polk Papers.

reelection to the Senate as soon as the session began and before any instructions could be passed. Firmly in control of both houses, they were able to reelect him even before the governor's message was read. This made the Democratic instructing resolutions seem an instrument for driving White from the Senate, and the White men had no trouble getting them laid on the table. With these victories under their belts, the White forces proceeded to replace most of the Van Buren men in state offices, Judge Catron of the supreme court being the most important victim. The next item on the majority agenda was a formal nomination of White for the presidency, and this they accomplished with relative ease on October 16 and 17.

Yet by the time Polk passed through Nashville again on his way to Washington at the end of October, the White juggernaut had lost its momentum. The filling of the state offices eliminated one of the White managers' most potent means of control over the lesser politicians, and the disappointed aspirants were disgruntled. Moreover some members of the legislature were beginning to feel the pressure of instructions on the expunging resolutions from the voters back home, and Jackson himself was deluging the lawmakers with personal appeals. When the expunging question showed signs of producing some alteration in statewide opinion on the presidency, it began to appear that a good many legislators had little genuine enthusiasm for the White movement.[54]

At any rate, as the session dragged on through November and December into January, the Van Buren men became convinced that they could eventually round up enough votes to take the expunging resolutions off the table and pass them. Soon they had a shaky control of the senate; the rest of the struggle centered in the house. Now the White men began to receive appeals for action from Washington. The White forces must take the instructing resolutions off the table and kill them, wrote Balie Peyton, before the Democrats were strong enough to pass them. "You are giving your opponents the advantage of you," he warned, "every day that they are delayed."[55]

By this time, however, the legislature was so evenly divided that the White leaders were afraid to risk a vote. The emboldened Van Burenites, on the contrary, tried to take the resolutions off the

[54] Polk to Jackson, 10 Oct. 1835, Jackson Papers; Nicholson to Jackson, 26 Jan. 1836, *ibid.*; *Jackson Correspondence*, v, 375.
[55] Balie Peyton to R. L. Caruthers, 1 Feb. 1836, Caruthers Papers.

table themselves, their first attempt failing by a single vote. A final effort was made on February 12, as the session was drawing to a close. Failing again by a narrow margin, the Van Buren forces altered their tactics and called up a resolution endorsing a long series of Democratic measures. The balance of power in the evenly divided legislature was now held by a handful of Nullifiers, who had previously refused to commit themselves to either side. At this point their leader, Major Andrew L. Martin of Madison County in the Western District, gave notice that they would support the White men. Announcing his determination to "try the stomachs of some of his over-righteous whole-hog Jackson friends," he offered an amendment adding the president's starkly nationalistic Nullification Proclamation to the list of measures approved. This amendment was acutely embarrassing to many Democrats of a state rights persuasion, but when it passed nevertheless, Martin followed it with another to the effect "that the President's course in attempting by his influence to secure the election of a successor of his own choice, by his franks and letters, so far as any member had knowledge of such letters and franks, met with the hearty approbation of the General Assembly."

The Van Buren leaders had had enough of this game, so they offered as a substitute for the resolutions of endorsement a proposition instructing Tennessee's senators to support a revised version of the expunging resolution. This provided that instead of blotting out or erasing the Clay resolution of censure, heavy black lines were to be drawn around it and a note saying that it was expunged by vote of the Senate was to be written across its face. This would get around the constitutional objection to defacing the journal that White and others had raised. On this proposition the legislature got into an exciting debate that lasted from Friday morning until Saturday at midnight, when the house adjourned. But after the weekend recess the revised resolution could not be got back to the floor, and there the matter rested.[56]

Though they had failed to pass the expunging resolution, the Van Buren men had conducted themselves with extraordinary ability and success. Starting the session in a tiny minority, they had ended it on nearly even terms with their opponents, and this

[56] Nancy N. Scott, *A Memoir of Hugh Lawson White* . . . (Philadelphia, 1856), 337-339.

revived their hopes of carrying Tennessee after all, in the coming presidential election.

VII

Meanwhile a contest of equal importance for its bearing on the state's future political alignment was taking place at Washington. The circumstances of the previous speakership contest should have made Polk the logical Democratic candidate against Bell at the opening of the twenty-fourth Congress in December 1835, but presidential politics entered into the question to such an extent that this was by no means a foregone conclusion. If Tennessee were clearly lost to the Democrats, Van Buren might want to use the speakership to strengthen his prospects in some other state. Even in Tennessee past factional differences made some of the original Van Buren men lukewarm toward Polk. The previous spring Alfred Balch had suggested that John Y. Mason of Virginia might be the best Democratic candidate for speaker. Virginia was still disgruntled at the way her candidate had been deprived of the vice presidential nomination at Baltimore by Rucker's Tennessee votes, and Balch was anxious that this important but doubtful state be mollified.[57]

Polk's determination to be the instrument by which the Democratic majority in the House punished Bell was increased by the unsolicited endorsements he began receiving from other members, mostly in the Northwest and Southwest. One Illinois congressman supported Polk because he wanted "a 'full hog' Van Buren Speaker." As soon as the August elections were over, Polk had sent James Walker to Nashville to set Grundy, Laughlin, Carroll, Catron, and Johnson to work writing on his behalf to prominent Democrats all over the country. His friends advocated his election chiefly on the ground that, by exposing Bell and the White movement as opposed to Jackson, it would enable Van Buren to carry Tennessee. They also pointed to Polk's faithful service in the House, the sacrifices he had made to uphold the president and vice president in Tennessee, and his intimacy with Jackson.[58]

Paradoxically, the greatest threat to Polk's being the Democratic candidate arose from the machinations of Bell and his friends. Bell knew that if the Jackson men united on Polk he would have no

[57] Balch to Jackson, 4 Apr. 1835, Jackson Papers.
[58] John Reynolds to F. P. Blair and J. C. Rives, 3 Sept. 1835, Blair-Lee Papers; Walker to Polk, 14 Aug. 1835, Polk Papers; Laughlin to Polk, 30 Aug. 1835, *ibid.*

chance, while a defeat by some other Democrat would not be nearly so damaging to his political standing in Tennessee. So he shrewdly tried either to encourage other Democrats to enter the race, so as to divide the majority's vote, or to get the Democrats to unite on some-one other than Polk. Through the White press he sought to create the impression that Polk had been reelected to Congress as a quasi-White man and that Van Buren had no chance whatever to carry the state. At the same time he was artfully stirring discontent in the two most disaffected Democratic states, Pennsylvania and Virginia, by reminding them of the claims of their sons Joel B. Sutherland and John Y. Mason on the speaker's chair.

Bell could rely on Major Lewis to further these schemes at Washington, especially with Frank Blair, who might be induced either to support Mason or to remain neutral. Blair was already in an ambiguous position. As the architect of Colonel Johnson's victory over the Virginia aspirant for the vice presidential nomination at the Baltimore convention in May, he had sought to mollify the Old Dominion by suggesting that Mason might be the party's choice for speaker in December. Giving wide circulation to this story, the White press now kept asserting positively that Mason had already been picked as the Democratic candidate. Bell seems also to have established communication with the friends of Mason and Sutherland, for from these quarters Blair received a thinly veiled threat that the Democratic dissidents might block his reelection as House printer if he did not conduct himself properly with reference to the speakership.[59]

Perfectly aware of what his enemies were about, Polk did everything he could to counter their activities. As proof that he was uncontaminated with Whiteism, he had already had copies of his April speech against dividing the party sent to all Democratic congressmen, and he now printed and distributed 1,500 copies of his pro-Van Buren speech at Mooresville.[60] Andrew Jackson Donelson was working to neutralize Major Lewis's intrigues in Washington, but Polk's greatest asset was the unwavering support of General Jack-

[59] Blair to [H. Haines], 24 Aug. 1835, copy, Blair-Lee Papers; H. Haines to Blair, 27 Aug., 16, 25 Nov. 1835, *ibid.*; Polk to Laughlin, 6 Sept. 1835, Polk-Laughlin Letters; Laughlin to Donelson, 21 Oct. 1835, Jackson-Donelson Papers, microfilm (JUL); Washington *Sun*, 10 Oct., 21, 25 Nov., 2, 5 Dec. 1835.

[60] Polk to Laughlin, 28 Apr. 1835, Polk-Laughlin Letters; Laughlin to Polk, 18 Nov., 1 Dec. 1835, Polk Papers.

son, who seems to have put heavy pressure on Blair to keep the *Globe* in line.

At any rate Blair indignantly spurned the suggestions of the Mason-Sutherland men and warned them of dire consequences to any fomenters of divisive movements. Actually Mason and his friends were too faithful Democrats to follow Bell's example of the previous year. They had to admit that Polk was "honest, loyal and useful," though they hoped that the party would "keep him at the head of an important Committee—send him to Russia or by and by, to France," rather than elect him speaker. Mason and Virginia deserved the speakership, they felt, but if a majority of the party decided for Polk, they would yield rather than aid the enemy. As for Sutherland, these high-minded Virginians could only point aghast to "his own favorite maxim 'that a politician should be a man of principle in proportion to his interest.'" "Give him the *cut direct* at once—send him to Spain—to Jericho—or if possible to the Devil," wrote Mason's leading supporter, "for there he will be in congenial company."[61]

By November, therefore, Polk was quite optimistic about his prospects. Jackson sent word that New England would be for him, probably through the president's influence on such key figures as Levi Woodbury of New Hampshire. Polk's friend Clement C. Clay had been elected governor of Alabama and was busy lining up four of that state's five congressmen for him. Word came that Illinois and Indiana would be solidly for him, and Colonel Johnson was holding Kentucky in line, to atone for his earlier flirtation with Bell.[62]

But all this would go for naught if Van Buren's big New York delegation decided that more electoral votes were to be garnered by supporting Sutherland or Mason. Polk was convinced that Bell would never have won the previous election if New York had not made a diversion in favor of Sutherland. The Albany *Argus*, editorial spokesman for the New York Democracy, had recently paid Polk a glowing tribute for his leadership at the previous session, but he was still anxious about the attitude of the Empire State. Back in August he had written to C. P. White, a prominent Van Burenite congressman from New York City,[63] but when the Polk carriage

---

61 H. Haines to Blair, 25 Nov. 1835, Blair-Lee Papers.

62 Polk to Donelson, 22 Sept. 1835, Jackson Papers, Second Series; Jackson to Andrew Jackson, Jr., 1 Oct. 1835, Jackson Papers.

63 Albany *Argus*, quoted in Nashville *Union*, 19 Oct. 1835; Polk to Laughlin, 10

started up the long road to Washington early in November, no word from New York had yet come. After a journey of three weeks they reached the capital to find C. P. White's long-awaited reply.

White's letter was everything Polk could have hoped for. "All our friends here," wrote Van Buren's spokesman, were greatly impressed by "the moral courage you have displayed in Tennessee." "I am greatly mistaken if your noble and independent course in your own state," he continued, "has not made a deeper impression upon the party, than even the consummate ability which you exhibited in the House of Representatives in the eventful crisis through which we have passed in the defence of the administration as the leader of the Democracy of the country in the last Congress." Racing impatiently through these wordy but gratifying encomiums, Polk came at last to the crucial passage. "All concur with me," announced White, "that it is due to you and to the state of Tenn. that you should be made Speaker." "I feel confident," the New Yorker concluded prophetically, "our country has in store for you her highest honors."[64]

In the negotiations that preceded the opening of Congress, therefore, Mason was forced to withdraw, and Polk was selected as the party candidate. Realizing at last that he had no chance, Bell made a final desperate effort to get Sutherland into the race, but the Pennsylvanians, too, refused to rebel against the party decision. The election came on December 7, with Polk winning on the first ballot by the decisive margin of 132 votes to 84 for Bell and 6 scattered among several others. Polk's victory was far more sweeping than Bell had thought possible. The new speaker was immediately escorted to the chair by Richard M. Johnson and the veteran Maine Jacksonian Leonard Jarvis, and the oath of office was administered by Lewis Williams of North Carolina, the oldest member of the House. Polk then made a little speech of thanks, asking the indulgence of the members and promising to be an impartial presiding officer.[65]

The Whig press tried to salvage something from the result by circulating stories that Mason had been inveigled out of the race by

Aug. 1835 (in possession of Miss Mary A. Benjamin, 18 E. 77th St., New York City); *id.* to *id.*, 6 Sept. 1835, Polk-Laughlin Letters.

[64] C. P. White to Polk, 30 Nov. 1835, Polk Papers.

[65] Washington *Sun*, 2, 5 Dec. 1835; Boston *Age*, 17 Aug. 1836; *Cong. Globe*:24:1, pp. 2-3; Arthur G. Staples, ed., *The Letters of John Fairfield* (Lewiston, Me., 1922), 23; Henry Clay to Mrs. Clay, 9 Dec. 1835, Thomas J. Clay Papers (LC).

a promise that Polk would shortly be appointed secretary of war, whereupon Mason would be made speaker. There was some plausibility to this report, since even Polk's friends seemed to believe for a time that he was in line for some higher position. When these rumors of a promotion to the Cabinet died away, the Whig press explained that the project had been abandoned because of the ambitions of other Democrats for the Cabinet position and because Sutherland threatened to run against Mason for speaker if the chair again became vacant.[66]

Coming in the middle of the legislature's long stalemate over expunging, Polk's triumph did much to rejuvenate the dispirited Tennessee Democracy. When the speakership results became known in Nashville on the evening of December 19, the Van Buren men poured out into the streets for an impromptu parade, to the accompaniment of drum and fife, firing muskets, and the ringing of all the bells in town. The news was not the only stimulant that circulated through the crowd, and one man swaggered about exclaiming, "I am now just fifty three years of age, weigh just one hundred and sixty three pounds, and can whip any man opposed to James K. Polk." The party leaders capped the evening with a celebration at the Vauxhall, where they "screwed the necks off a few dozen of champagne, under the war of 48 rounds of cannon."[67]

The results reached Maury the next day. Columbia, where the White men were in a majority, wore a mournful air. But out in the country there was a different story. Polk's friends in the little village of Mooresville celebrated boisterously. Houses were illuminated by candles in all the windows, and the Democrats paraded up and down the only street firing guns and shouting "Polk and Van Buren forever!" Marsh's store served in lieu of a Vauxhall for the Mooresville celebrants, but their jollification was quite as enthusiastic as the one at Nashville. "Great were the hilarity and rejoicing on the occasion," reported one of the participants. "It was a perfect Van-Buren Democratic Jubilee on rather a small scale. The company dispersed at a proper hour, no lives lost, and only a few wounded (not mortally) by the kicking of their pistols." The next morning

[66] Nashville *Banner*, 30 Dec. 1835, 23, 30 Mar. 1836; Nicholson to Jackson, 26 Jan. 1836, Jackson Papers.

[67] H. M. Watterson to Polk, 21 Dec. 1835, Polk Papers; Nicholson to Polk, 20 Dec. 1835, *ibid.*

it was observed that, "You can tell a White Whig any where in Maury *by the unusual longitudinal attenuation of his phiz.*"[68]

This Democratic rejoicing was not confined to the districts of the two rivals. One of Polk's supporters in Pulaski claimed that he had been "at the point of death with my friends around my bed" when the news came to revive him. At Blountsville in East Tennessee, the Democrats were somewhat hampered by the lack of a cannon to fire, but they felt more than compensated when a Democratic wife opportunely gave birth to a fine son and named him James K. Polk in defiance of her Whig husband. "So much," commented Polk's informant, "for female republicanism."[69]

VIII

For the next seven months Polk was to be preoccupied with the duties and difficulties of his new position, but he was not allowed to forget the political war in Tennessee. Though most of the state enjoyed a degree of calm while the principal partisan gladiators were absent in Washington for the session of Congress, the excitement only increased in Polk's district. Bell, Balie Peyton, and their hot-blooded Virginia ally Congressman Henry A. Wise were using the House floor as a forum for scathing attacks on Polk and sending quantities of their printed speeches into his district under congressional frank.

The Columbia *Democrat* came spiritedly to Polk's defense, at the same time attacking Terry H. Cahal, the state senator from Maury and Bell's principal lieutenant in the county. Cahal, the *Democrat* charged, had always opposed Jackson and in the last election "had swapped off the country for the town." Cahal promptly threatened to cowhide the editor on sight, and feeling soon reached such a height that Van Buren and White men stopped speaking to each other.[70] Even the ladies got involved. One of Sarah's Columbia neighbors was indignant that the local military company of White supporters had held ceremonies honoring two babies who had been named for White. "I intend to name sister's [baby] Martin Van Buren," Sarah's friend announced hotly, "let it be what it may."[71]

[68] H. B. Kelsey to Polk, 24 Dec. 1835, Polk Papers; Bill Polk to J. K. Polk, 21 Dec. 1835, *ibid.*

[69] J. H. Rivers to Polk, 19 Jan. 1836, Polk Papers; George Gammon to Polk, 28 Jan. 1836, *ibid.*

[70] Nashville *Republican*, 9 Feb. 1836; Walker to Polk, 20 May 1836, Polk Papers.

[71] R. L. Houston to Mrs. J. K. Polk, 24 Apr. 1836, Polk Papers.

When A. O. P. Nicholson defended Polk against Bell's charges and attacked White in a two-hour speech to the crowd assembled for the April court, the "town boys" hissed him, and the Democrats in from the country started a near riot. Even the elections for county officials and militia officers were made to turn on the presidential question. The Van Buren men were jubilant when they carried the county offices and elected their candidate for brigadier general over his pro-White opponent. They lost the major-generalship, however, by dividing their strength between two Van Buren candidates.[72]

Before the legislature adjourned in February 1836, the Democratic members had issued an address to the public and made plans for nominating their strongest men as presidential electors. They knew, though, that they were going to have great difficulty in getting their side of the question before the voters. Polk, Grundy, and Johnson helped as much as they could by franking speeches and documents all over the state and soliciting subscriptions to a special campaign edition of the *Globe*. But these measures were no substitute for a strong press. "It is impossible for any party to fight with any reasonable hope of victory," complained Polk to Frank Blair, "when all the forts, and arms and ammunition are in the hands of the enemy."[73]

The triweekly *Union* was still only a weak competitor to the two White dailies at Nashville, the *Banner* and the *Republican*. Laughlin continued to get drunk, his business partner, M. A. Long, was wasting away with tuberculosis, and constant demands were made on Polk and his friends for money. At the crucial moment of the legislature's convening the previous fall, Laughlin had gone off to earn a few hundred dollars from some legal clients, and in January, when the expunging resolutions were about to come up, he left Nicholson and others to edit the paper as best they could while he absented himself in New Orleans for several months. And he would not surrender the paper.

By summer the *Union* had gone from bad to worse. Long had given up and sold his share to Laughlin. The editor was again incapacitated by a long drinking bout, and the whole editorial responsibility was thrown on Judge Catron, who had been trying

72 Nicholson to Polk, 22 Apr. [1836; misplaced 1838], Polk Papers; Walker to Polk, 26 Apr. 1836, *ibid*.; Greenville Cook to Polk, 17 Jan. 1836, *ibid*.

73 Polk to Blair, 3 Oct. 1835, Blair-Lee Papers; bill placed 21 June 1837, Polk Papers; Nicholson to Polk, 7 Feb. 1836, *ibid*.; George Gammon to Polk, 25 May 1836, *ibid*.; Carroll to Van Buren, 27 Feb. 1836, Martin Van Buren Papers (LC).

to reestablish a legal practice since being thrown off the bench. The Columbia *Democrat*, with James Walker doing most of the writing, was the strongest of the Van Buren papers, but the merchants gave it little job work, and subsidies were necessary to keep it in operation. At the end of 1835, there was only one other Democratic paper in the entire state, and the party leaders knew they had no chance unless they could strengthen their press support.[74]

Polk himself guaranteed the necessary financial backing to a young printer who bought out the White paper at Shelbyville and converted it into a Van Buren organ. He tried to do the same thing with another White paper at Pulaski, but here he was outbid by the White men. Through the spring and summer the Van Burenites made strenuous efforts, and by election time they had control of ten small weeklies. The White men, on the other hand, could claim the support of sixteen weeklies, and their papers were generally stronger. The Van Buren press was especially impotent in East Tennessee, where its two little journals weighed insignificantly against the influential Knoxville *Register*; and in the Western District, where the aggressively edited Jackson *Truth Teller* was a source of great strength to the White cause.[75]

The campaigning did not really become intense in the state at large until the members of Congress returned home at the end of July. From that time until the November election the leaders on both sides—White, Bell, Foster, and Peyton for the White party, and Carroll, Grundy, Polk, and Johnson for the Democrats—were continually in motion from political dinner to political dinner. Jackson, too, arrived in Tennessee along with the congressmen, being hailed by large and enthusiastic crowds along his route through the eastern part of the state to the Hermitage. It was a hard trip for him, but the resolute old man was determined to let nothing remain undone that might aid in the redemption of Tennessee.

Polk reached home to find an invitation to a dinner in his honor at Lockridge's campground on Carter's Creek, where he had played as a boy. Nearly 2,000 people turned out to cheer his argument that

---

[74] Johnson to Polk, 11 Sept. 1835, Polk Papers; Laughlin to Polk, 3 Aug. 1836, *ibid.;* Catron to Polk, 6 Sept. 1836, *ibid.;* Walker to Polk, 20 May 1836, *ibid.;* Nicholson to Jackson, 20 Dec. 1835, Jackson Papers.

[75] Greenville Cook to Polk, 16 Oct. [1835; misplaced 1834], Polk Papers; Nicholson to Polk, 7 Feb. 1836, *ibid.;* Polk to Alfred Flournoy, 14 Sept. 1835, typed copy, Polk-Flournoy Letters; Nashville *Banner*, 29 Aug. 1836.

even if White carried all the states where he had electoral tickets, he would still be far short of a majority. The people, exulted the *Union*, "love the old tyrant Jackson, and the young tyrant Speaker Polk, in spite of every thing Ex-Speaker Bell, with the whole Whig press at his command, can do to prevent it."[76]

Only a week after the "young tyrant" was honored, the Democrats held a dinner for the "old tyrant" at Nashville. Jackson's toast on this occasion left the public in no doubt about his attitude. "RE-PUBLICAN TENNESSEE," rasped the president, "Her motto, *'principles not men'*—She will never abandon her good old Jeffersonian Democratic Republican principles which she has so long maintained and practiced, to throw herself (on any occasion) into the embraces of the Federalists, the Nullifiers, or the new born Whigs." From Nashville Jackson started for Alabama to visit the family of his old comrade John Coffee, and Polk persuaded him to stop at Columbia for a Democratic celebration. Over 4,000 people— the largest crowd ever assembled in that part of the state—gathered from all the surrounding country, and the president was nearly worn out from shaking hands. Sarah was equally exhausted, for Jackson and his party spent the night with the Polks before resuming their journey the next day.[77]

Old Hickory's campaigning had an adverse effect on some independent-minded Tennesseans, and when White struck back at this presidential "dictation," Polk admitted in a letter to Senator Silas Wright of New York that he was worried about Van Buren's prospects in Tennessee. To his friends at home, though, he radiated confidence. "The ball is now in motion," he said, "and all that is now necessary, is a vigorous & bold effort on our part." Polk's own efforts could not have been more vigorous. On September 1 he spoke at a dinner in Johnson's district; several days later he was in Bedford County; and from there he campaigned through Giles and Lincoln. All the while he was busy distributing Democratic speeches and pamphlets.[78]

Bell and Peyton invaded Polk's district in the middle of September

[76] Nashville *Union*, 18 Aug. 1836.

[77] *ibid.*, 23 Aug. 1836; Jackson to Andrew Jackson, Jr., 26 Aug. 1836, Jackson Papers.

[78] Polk to Donelson, 3 Sept. 1836, Donelson Papers; Nashville *Banner*, 12 Sept. 1836; Wright to Polk, 3 Oct. 1836, Polk Papers; Polk to J. L. Jones and others, 9 Oct. 1836, copy, *ibid.*; Polk to Laughlin, 28 Sept. 1836, *ibid.*; Nashville *Union*, 27 Sept., 1 Oct. 1836.

for a White dinner a few miles south of Columbia. Polk had been warned that Peyton intended to draw him into a duel by calculated insults, but though many harsh things were said by both the barnstorming congressmen, nothing untoward occurred. The next day Bell's entourage moved over to Shelbyville, where the White men had attracted an audience of some 2,000 people by firing cannon and ringing bells throughout the preceding night. In a bitter tirade Bell charged Polk with being a nullifier at heart and with selling himself for office. When Polk's friends arranged a dinner three days later to permit him to reply, the Bell-White men, according to the Columbia *Democrat*, pulled down all the handbills advertising the meeting. In October Polk followed White and Grundy into the Western District, where the Democrats knew they were running behind. Soon White was admitting that "Polk, Grundy and Johnson are doing me some harm," but he thought they were injuring themselves more.[79]

Polk was determined above all else to carry his district for Van Buren, and he hurried back for a final dinner at Shelbyville on the Saturday preceding the election. Knowing that the Bell men were just as anxious to carry the district, he took elaborate precautions against last minute tricks. Planning himself to stay in Shelbyville through Monday, the day before the election, he ordered Nicholson, who was campaigning in the southern counties, to return to Columbia "immediately" and remain there "until the fight is over." Polk was especially fearful that his enemies would import illegal voters from adjoining counties, but he was hardly prepared for the stratagem they did adopt to produce a last minute reaction in his district.[80]

The Polk dinner at Shelbyville attracted the largest crowd ever assembled in Bedford. The parade was just forming on the packed courthouse square when suddenly—Judge White rode into town. Forewarned, the local White men raised a shout and started a rush toward the judge's cavalcade, followed by many of the curious. The Polk parade was completely disorganized, and for the rest of the afternoon Shelbyville presented the spectacle of a milling mass of humanity that engulfed both Polk and White headquarters in such confusion and contention that neither side was able to get off any

[79] White to T. A. R. Nelson, 24 Oct. 1836, Thomas A. R. Nelson Papers (LM); W. G. Childress to Polk, 15 Sept. 1836, Polk Papers; E. J. Frierson to Polk, 23 Sept. 1836, *ibid.*; Nashville *Union*, 20, 27 Sept. 1836.
[80] Polk to Nicholson, 3 Nov. 1836, Nicholson Papers.

oratory. The quick-witted Polk men won a moral victory, however, by outdistancing White's supporters in the race for the town's only cannon, which they kept thundering away until after sundown.[81]

Polk spent the night before the election riding back to Columbia, arriving in time to see the polls opened and to follow the Nashville *Banner*'s election eve advice: "Van Buren men, get shaved *early* tomorrow! The next day your faces will be so long that the barbers will charge you double price!"[82]

This prediction was all too accurate. White carried the state by the decisive majority of 35,968 to 26,120, winning forty-six of the sixty-five counties. Van Buren took only three counties in East Tennessee and three in the Western District, one of the latter being Hardeman, where Polk's kinfolk were numerous and influential. Van Buren strength was impressive only in the poor farming counties of the Cumberland plateau and in the hilly country along the western section of the Tennessee River. In the wealthier areas of Middle Tennessee, two of the four Van Buren counties were Bedford and Maury, in Polk's district, while a third was Lincoln, which he had once represented and where he was still popular.

Though it was a stunning defeat for the Tennessee Democracy as a whole, the election was something of a personal triumph for Polk. Maury and Bedford had both gone for Van Buren by substantial margins. The two towns, Columbia and Shelbyville, had voted heavily for White, but "the real people" had saved the day, the Democrats carrying nineteen of Maury's twenty-four rural precincts.[83]

In the state at large the Democrats were injured by a stay-at-home vote that was loyal to Jackson but reluctant to vote against a popular native son. Only 62,088 votes were cast at this election, as compared with the 108,680 Tennesseans who would go to the polls four years hence. There were also many Democrats at heart, especially East Tennesseans like the Greenville tailor Andrew Johnson, who could not bring themselves to deny their votes to White.

But this was far from the whole story. White's triumph was more than a personal victory, and the Whig party that grew out of it was more than a White party. For years to come, the political map of Tennessee would show little change from the election of 1836.

[81] Washington *Sun*, 5 Nov. 1836.   [82] Nashville *Banner*, 7 Nov. 1836.
[83] Nashville *Republican Banner*, 2 Sept. 1837; Columbia *Democrat*, 16 Nov. 1836, extra.

Of the sixty-five counties voting in 1836, fifty-three would continue to vote in the elections of 1840, 1844, 1848, and 1852 for the same party they supported in 1836. Six of the remaining twelve were White counties in 1836, but were to be consistently Democratic thereafter. Thus only six of the counties voting in the election of 1836 were destined to shift in subsequent elections from one party to the other.[84] Old Republican, Jacksonian Tennessee was a two-party state, and would long retain the political pattern imposed by the violent political struggles of the mid-thirties.

This political pattern may be explained partly by personal influence, especially in the cases of Polk in Middle Tennessee and White in East Tennessee, but this factor merely modified more fundamental geographic, economic, and social bases of cleavage. Enthusiasm for internal improvements made for Whiggery in the extreme eastern and western sections of the state, while Whig conservatism appealed to Western District planters and the well-to-do farmers of Middle Tennessee. Probably most important of all was the probusiness bias of the Whig party, which won it the unquestioning loyalty of the closely knit business community in Nashville and the smaller towns and brought to it financial resources, newspaper support, and the leadership of men like John Bell and Ephraim H. Foster. The small farmers, on the other hand, dominant in the Cumberland mountain region and the Tennessee River counties and numerous everywhere, constituted the backbone of the Democracy.

The shrewder of the Democratic leaders, sensing some of these implications in the election returns, could see many hard battles ahead. For the moment they could only take comfort from their party's sweeping triumph in the nation at large. Van Buren won a convincing majority over his three competitors combined, while Georgia was the only other state that voted for White. Though White would hold on to his Senate seat until 1840, he would never again be an important political factor.

[84] Ernest Walter Hooper, "The Presidential Election of 1836 in Tennessee," M.A. thesis, University of North Carolina (1949), 147.

10

MR. SPEAKER POLK

FOR ALL ITS VIOLENCE, the Tennessee presidential campaign of 1836 was no more tempestuous than the scenes through which Polk had passed the previous winter in Washington. Never had a speaker been called to the chair under more trying circumstances than was Polk in December 1835. The unprecedented partisan, sectional, and personal animosities displayed in this and the succeeding four sessions demanded tact, coolness, firmness, and even physical bravery on the part of the presiding officer.

These years witnessed the culmination of the trend toward a rigid partisan organization of American politics and a strict enforcement of party discipline. Polk was the first speaker to be regarded frankly as a party leader, responsible for pushing a party program through the House. Moreover, with the Jacksonian political revolution well along into its second phase, the two parties represented more and more a clear-cut division of American politics along economic, class, and sectional lines. The intense partisan conflict that would have arisen in any case from this sharp polarity was further embittered by the schisms, the excommunications, the apostasies, the dissolution of old coalitions, and the formation of new ones, which inevitably accompanied the regrouping of political forces.

It was under these inauspicious conditions that the slavery question made its debut as a major national issue. Slavery, to be sure, had previously entered into debates on many subjects; and at least once, in the Missouri statehood dispute fifteen years before, all the deep-seated emotions surrounding it had come boiling up to demonstrate its ominous potentialities as a political question. But only now did the North begin to elect congressmen filled with a righteous, uncompromising zeal for destruction of the hated slave system. Only now did southern men begin to defend their "peculiar institution" with an intransigence born of insecurity and misgivings, as the most beneficent of all social arrangements. And only now did doctrinaires on both sides begin to question the honor, patriotism, and morality of their opponents.

Bitterness was compounded when events in the Southwest invited an expansive nation to embrace the "manifest destiny" to which it was just awaking. For this new question was wedded to the slavery issue. The tragic consequences of this marriage still lay years ahead, but they were foreshadowed from the first by the shrill indignation of old John Quincy Adams, pale and trembling with fury on the floor of the House, or by the slashing attacks of Henry A. Wise on his colleagues, or by the spectacle of fellow members shooting each other down in cold blood on the field of "honor."

Polk was well equipped for keeping these combustible elements under control. His years of experience in the House had given him an intimate understanding of that body's rules and procedures, while his long and turbulent political career had taught him to avoid trouble whenever possible, and when it could not be avoided, to restrain his temper, think clearly, and act promptly and decisively. The speaker's great powers, moreover, gave him a large degree of control over the House. Appointing all the committees, he had considerable influence on the course of business. Deciding who should have the floor, ruling speakers out of order, and making parliamentary decisions, he dominated the flow of debate. Polk himself greatly augmented the speaker's existing authority through his leadership of the Democratic majority. The House did most of its actual debating in committee of the whole, where the speaker did not have to preside, and this enabled Polk to spend much of his time planning and executing his party's legislative strategy.

The House was still the informal, unpretentious body it had been when Polk first came to Washington. Debate was limited only by the previous question, members wore their hats on the floor, and, according to a freshman representative from New England, they "buzz and talk while the business is going on so that much of the time it sounds like a town meeting, the Speaker only appearing to attend to the business of the House." This Yankee congressman was especially struck by the pronunciation of Speaker Polk and other members from the West and South. Polk, he observed, "says cheer for chair and Clark for Clerk," and others "chew words, and when d u come together as in duty, durance, etc., they pronounce them juty, jurance, etc." Their rhetorical style seemed like "sheer affectation" to the sober-sided New Englander. "The speakers all have abundance of action, of not the most graceful, many of them appearing as if cutting wood," he commented. "Their style of speaking is declamatory, such as you would expect to see in times of great excitement, but unsuited to the sober business of legislation."[1]

The congressmen's day was a busy one. Early in the morning, fortified by a breakfast of beefsteak, mutton, sausage, hominy, flapjacks, biscuits, and tea or coffee, they made their way to the Capitol for committee meetings. The House usually convened at noon, and after a session lasting until three or sometimes four o'clock, there was a general exodus to the boardinghouses along Pennsylvania Avenue for dinner. The landladies spread their tables with an array of roast beef, boiled turkey with oyster sauce, boiled ham, roast duck, puddings, tarts, and apples, a fare that one member had the ill grace to criticize for regarding "fashion and gentility at the expense of real wholesome substance." A light tea early in the evening concluded the day's gastronomic activities, and unless there was a night session, as was usually the case in the last weeks before adjournment, the members had the rest of the evening free for visits, parties, the theater, or letter writing.[2]

Polk's new position carried with it a private office, tucked into a corner off the House chamber, and a personal porter to regulate the constant stream of visitors. Here he consulted committee chairmen and party leaders, interviewed job seekers, and shook hands with curious citizens visiting the Capitol. In addition to his other duties the speaker was responsible for the work of the clerk and doorkeeper and their staffs and for all kinds of petty administrative details, which ranged from enforcing the ban on sale of hard liquor in the basement refreshment stands, through overseeing the remodeling of the House chamber, to coping with Mrs. Anne Royall, the contumacious publisher of *Paul Pry*, who delighted in bullying congressmen with threats to expose their peccadillos in her scandalmongering books and newspaper.

The attempt to improve the acoustics by moving the speaker's desk to the eastern side of the chamber and turning the chairs around to face it had proven a failure, and during Polk's speakership the old arrangement with the speaker's chair facing the main entrance was resumed, and the chamber was refurbished in the process. The handsome new speaker's desk was elevated high above the floor and flanked with a pair of ornate brass lamps, though fastidious observers soon began criticizing the tasseled, crimson

---

[1] Arthur G. Staples, ed., *The Letters of John Fairfield* (Lewiston, Me., 1922), 33.
[2] *ibid.*, 31-32.

canopy whose voluminous folds descended upon it from the ceiling.[3]

II

As a freshman congressman Polk had complained when a pro-administration speaker gave President Adams' supporters "studied majorities" on the House committees, "regardless, it would seem in some instances, of qualifications, talents or experience."[4] Now his own committee appointments showed how much water had flowed over the dam since that time. Cambreleng was placed at the head of Ways and Means; Polk's rivals for the speakership, Mason and Sutherland, were made chairmen of the Foreign Affairs and Commerce committees; all the important committees were given heavy Democratic majorities; and the Whigs were disposed of by being crowded on to those committees whose duties were routine and tedious.

In some cases Speaker Polk recognized the special interests or qualifications of certain Whig leaders. John Quincy Adams was made chairman of the Committee of Manufactures; Charles Fenton Mercer, the grand old man of the internal improvements movement, was left at the head of the Committee on Roads and Canals; and, at the request of that arch-Whig, Edward Everett, Polk designated Caleb Cushing as a member of the Committee of Foreign Affairs. Most remarkable of all, John Bell was restored to his old position as chairman of the important Committee on Indian Affairs. Some Democrats complained of these concessions, but by and large the committees were arranged with a single eye to expediting Democratic policies.[5]

The committee appointments were no sooner announced than Polk's enemies resolved to test his nerve by subjecting him to such an ordeal of harassment as no other speaker had ever suffered. Bell, Peyton, and Wise all lived together in a mess with Judge White, and they now undertook a deliberate campaign against the speaker, compounded of points of order, appeals from his decisions, defiance of the parliamentary rules, and personal insult. Even if they failed

[3] "Glances at Congress," *United States Magazine and Democratic Review*, v (Mar. 1839), 261-263.

[4] J. K. Polk to Col. William Polk, 14 Dec. 1826, Polk Family of North Carolina Papers (LC).

[5] *Congressional Globe*: 24th Cong.: 1st Sess., 21-22; Everett to Polk, 3 Dec. 1835, James K. Polk Papers (LC; herein cited as Polk Papers, which refers to First Series unless otherwise noted); J. K. Paulding to [?], 8 June 1838, Joel R. Poinsett Papers (HSP).

to drive him from the chair, they hoped to create enough turmoil to convince the country that he was incompetent to maintain order in the House. Henry A. Wise, who took a singular delight in being as violent and vituperative as possible, led the attack, with the full support of Balie Peyton. Bell generally refrained from precipitating these incidents himself, but he was always ready to argue at length against the speaker on disputed points. Before long the vendetta against Polk turned into a public spectacle. Projected attacks were announced beforehand at Gadsby's Hotel and other public places, and crowds packed the galleries to see the fireworks.[6]

No question was too petty to be a vehicle for veiled insults to the speaker. Early in the session Wise jumped into a discussion over distribution of House documents to deliver a blast against presidential influence over members of Congress, going on to illustrate his point by the "intriguing and subserviency" through which the speaker had won his election. "There sat the Speaker," he declared, "like a cancer on the body politic."[7]

The Virginia hotspur got another chance to attack Polk when John Quincy Adams offered a resolution blaming the Senate for loss of the fortifications bill in the closing hours of the preceding session. The diplomatic crisis with France had not eased, and the patriotic ex-president was ignoring partisanship and aggressively supporting Jackson's nationalistic diplomacy. With a presidential campaign in full swing, the Whigs were thoroughly exasperated, and Wise tore into Polk for the part he had played in defeating the bill. The whole maneuver, he charged, had been executed by Polk to discredit Judge White. In fact, said Wise, Polk had told one of White's friends in the House that the president favored the three-million-dollar appropriation but asked him to say nothing about the fact. Wise interpreted this to mean that Polk had plotted with Jackson to keep White from learning that the special appropriation was an administration measure and thus to trap him into voting against it. This Wise dared the speaker to deny.

Until now Polk had stood up well against his assailants, hewing to the rules of the House, refusing to let himself be bullied in his decisions, and ignoring their insults, all without losing his temper or judgment. If anything, he had leaned over backward to be fair to Wise and his henchmen, especially in his refusal to stop their

6 Boston *Age*, 17 Aug. 1836; *Congressional Directory*:24:1 (Blair and Rives), 39.
7 Nashville *Banner*, 1, 8 Jan. 1836.

carefully camouflaged personal references. But this debate had aroused great excitement, and Polk had already had to quell one unprecedented outburst of cheering by the Democrats. Wise's challenge could hardly be evaded, and accordingly Polk took the floor for one of the few times during his speakership and dispassionately exposed the absurdities in Wise's interpretation of the episode.[8]

Following this passage at arms, Wise, Peyton, and company redoubled their efforts to provoke the speaker into a false move. Fearing that they would drag him into a duel, James Walker worriedly reminded his brother-in-law that "moral courage is the highest virtue," though he had to admit that a man could not avoid fighting if attacked directly.[9] Events proved Walker's fears well founded, even before his letter reached Washington. One day in March, Polk had to call Wise to order a number of times for inflammatory remarks in a speech on the abolition question. When the House adjourned, Wise met the speaker at the door of the chamber, pointed a finger in his eye, and said, "Sir, you talked in a d- - - -d arbitrary manner to me to-day." Before Polk could reply, the Virginian exploded a volley of deliberate insults. Polk was "a *petty tyrant*," he raged, adding, to remove all doubt about his purpose, "I mean it personal & pocket dam you, pocket it."[10]

Polk ignored this challenge, and the Bell-White newspapers, with the Washington *Sun* leading the pack, promptly branded him a coward. The speaker "wants weight of character to ward off the attacks which his situation provokes," said one editor, "and his talents are not sufficient to give him that authority which can alone render his post pleasant and dignified."[11] Another paper reported that Polk had denied hearing Wise's parting words, with their explicit challenge. "Mr. Wise is known to be a dead shot," this writer continued, "and it is said that the members are not anxious to come in a collision with him."[12]

The most scurrilous accounts of the affair were circulated by Balie Peyton, who wrote to Tennessee that "Wise scared Polk nearly to death." Peyton's report to the Nashville *Banner* asserted that Jackson had denounced Polk for not fighting on the spot. According to

8 *Cong. Globe*:24:1, pp. 131-132.

9 Walker to Polk, 14 Mar. 1836, Polk Papers.

10 Peyton to W. B. Campbell, 9 Mar. 1836, David Campbell Papers (DU); Nashville *Banner*, 26 Mar. 1836.

11 Philadelphia *United States Gazette*, quoted in Nashville *Banner*, 19 Mar. 1836.

12 Boston *Sentinel*, quoted in Nashville *Banner*, 25 Mar. 1836.

Peyton, Jackson had said: "Why did he not knock him down? If he means to submit to such indignities he had better resign and go home! What, let that little splinter of a Virginian denounce him to his face, and pocket the insult?" Old Hickory was furious when he saw Peyton's fabrication, and the *Globe* promptly announced that the president "highly approved" Polk's conduct.[13] "In treating such blackguardism with contempt," Jackson declared later, Polk had "pursued the course which was most consistent with the dignity of the house, and a just self respect."[14]

Before the session was over, Wise and his friends exhausted the patience of the House, a number of the Whigs joined the Democrats in voting them down on every occasion, and they lost the power to be more than a nuisance. "We have struck when & where we could," complained Peyton, "but have been trammeled, & bound by the damnable shackles of 'the party.' "[15] They were especially infuriated because Bell, whom they were holding in reserve for set speeches to supplement the harassing operations of Wise and Peyton, had been unable to get the floor. The Democrats had kept off the floor any resolution that Bell could use as the occasion for a political speech. He finally found an opening when the naval appropriations bill was under discussion, and he delivered himself again during a debate on the harbor appropriations bill. Both of these speeches were arraignments of "party" and "executive patronage," as the instruments by which the administration was controlling the country's politics and erecting a virtual dictatorship. Denying that he had ever called the president a tyrant, Bell did assert that "he may be the master of *slaves* and *menials*." Among those most prominent in these categories, he suggested, were Polk and Grundy, who "are at this moment in the enjoyment of the rewards of their hypocrisy and their treachery to their colleagues."[16]

III

By far the greatest amount of time was consumed at this session by debates over slavery and abolition. The abolitionists were still

[13] Peyton to W. B. Campbell, 9 Mar. 1836, Campbell Papers; Nashville *Banner*, 16 Mar. 1836; Washington *Globe*, 30 Mar. 1836; Jackson to Andrew Jackson, Jr., 29 Mar. 1836, Andrew Jackson Papers (LC).

[14] Nashville *Union*, 3 Nov. 1840.

[15] Peyton to W. B. Campbell, 9 Mar. 1836, Campbell Papers.

[16] *Cong. Globe*:24:1, Appendix, 745; Peyton to R. L. Caruthers, 1 Feb. 1836, Robert L. Caruthers Papers (SHC).

an unpopular minority, even in the North, but this was a reforming age, and their numbers and influence were growing. Though committed to the ultimate extinction of human bondage everywhere, they recognized that the national government had no authority over slavery in the states where it already existed. Consequently their immediate objective was to end the slave trade and slavery itself in the District of Columbia, over which Congress had direct control. These were objectives with which many northern men and women of good will sympathized, and as the thirties wore on a perfect avalanche of petitions for action in the District began to descend on Congress.

Southern concern over slavery and intransigence in its defense mounted alongside the abolition crusade. What stung the southerners most deeply was the flood of antislavery propaganda that began pouring into the South. This material, much of it aimed at the slave himself and picturing the planters as cruel, greedy, immoral monsters, stirred up the most intense anxiety in a section still jittery over the bloody slave revolt led by Nat Turner in Virginia only a few years before.

By 1835 a small group of southerners, most notably John C. Calhoun, had come to regard the defense of slavery as the primary task of southern political leadership. The South Carolina senator recognized that the campaign against slavery arose from deep moral conviction and could not be countered by ordinary political methods. The Constitution, as interpreted by the state rights men, was the only possible bulwark in sight, and Calhoun devoted the rest of his life to persuading the South that defense of the Constitution and slavery was a task so important that it overrode all other political issues. His passionate desire for national leadership frustrated, Calhoun was influenced in adopting this strategy by the hope of placing himself at the head of a united South.

The Calhounites were convinced that the abolition movement had to be stopped at the threshold, if it were to be stopped at all. Interference with slavery in the District of Columbia, they felt, was merely the opening wedge for more sweeping attacks on the southern social system, and they argued that even this was unconstitutional. The Democrats, as a national party seeking a formula satisfactory to a majority in both sections, were feeling their way toward the position that abolition in the states was unconstitutional and that abolition in the District was constitutional but inexpedient. Democratic politicians were well aware that more could not be conceded to the South without destroying the Democracy as a national party. The southern intransigents became equally convinced that any compromise with or toleration of abolition sentiment would mean the ultimate destruction of slavery.

So it was that Calhoun decided to provoke a decisive struggle over the question when the twenty-fourth Congress assembled in December 1835. The fight began in the House with the presentation of the first abolition petition on December 16. Promptly Calhoun's messmate James H. Hammond of South Carolina moved that the petition be not received. Hammond admitted that the House had previously received such petitions before laying them on the table or rejecting them. But, he said, he could not "sit there and see the rights of the southern people assaulted day after day, by the ignorant fanatics from whom these memorials proceed." The flood of petitions must be stopped; more stringent methods must be adopted.[17]

This deliberately aggressive maneuver at once made Polk, who had barely got accustomed to the speaker's chair, the focal point of one of the bitterest controversies in the history of Congress. The question was a procedural one, and the outcome would depend in great degree on the speaker's rulings. Polk decided that Hammond's motion not to receive was unprecedented and out of order. Hammond then moved that the petition be rejected, another member moved that it be laid on the table, and the House got into a long, angry debate, which finally ended in a vote to send the petition to the table.[18]

Other petitions soon appeared, and each was the occasion for rancorous speeches by extremists on both sides. Northern members held forth on the evils of slavery, while the southern hotspurs contended that interference with slavery in the District was unconstitutional and that there was no right to petition for an unconstitutional object. So vital was the issue and so passionately in earnest were the contending parties that the speeches of one side served only to inflame the other with new paroxysms of fury. Political motives, too, were involved. The extremists on both sides were anti-Jackson men, and this violent agitation of the slavery question was calculated to injure Van Buren in the impending presidential election. For six weeks all other business was put aside

[17] *Register of Debates*:24:1, p. 1967.
[18] *House Journal*:24:1, pp. 74, 79.

while the slavery debate raged on, raising tempers to the point where members came to the House armed with knives.

The moderates, including the bulk of the Democrats, were determined to put an end to these dangerously inflammatory discussions, but an acceptable procedure was hard to find. The parliamentary questions were so novel and involved that Polk himself was at first confused in his decisions. After a careful study of the rules he concluded that the House did have a right to refuse to receive a petition. Since the question of whether to receive was debatable, it was almost impossible to prevent an angry debate upon the presentation of each new petition. Any effort to change the rules would have to avoid impairing the constitutional right of citizens to petition for a redress of grievances.[19]

Not until February 8 were the Democrats able to work their way out of the parliamentary tangle. On that day Henry L. Pinckney of South Carolina, who had previously been classed with the southern intransigents, offered a resolution declaring: (1) that Congress could not constitutionally interfere with slavery in the states; (2) that all petitions and papers relating to the slavery controversy should be referred to a special committee; and (3) that the committee be instructed to report that Congress "ought not" to interfere with slavery in the District of Columbia. The Nullifiers were furious at Pinckney's treachery, which, they perceived immediately, would enable Congress to escape making an explicit declaration on the constitutionality of interference with slavery in the District. The extreme antislavery men were equally outraged by this plan to stifle their petitions. But the majority passed Pinckney's resolution with a sigh of relief, and he was made chairman of the committee to receive the petitions and present a report.[20]

A blunder by Polk a week later threatened to reopen the whole question. Another petition was presented, and Wise asked the speaker whether the Pinckney resolution covered it. Though the resolution had apparently been intended to apply to future petitions as well as those already received, Polk replied that it did not, and even entertained Wise's subsequent motion that the petition not be received. This, of course, revived the debate, and Wise, as one disgusted northern Democrat complained, "got on his tall horse & rode off, splashing the mud all over the House." Polk finally had to

[19] *Reg. Deb.*:24:1, pp. 2128-2129; *House Journal*:24:1, p. 128.
[20] *Reg. Deb.*:24:1, pp. 2482-2483, 2495-2502.

call Wise to order for insulting Pinckney personally as a traitor to the South for the sake of party, but the angry discussion raged on through that day and the better part of the next before the Van Buren men were able to stop it by reversing the speaker's ruling and sending the petition to Pinckney's committee.[21]

Throughout the long wrangle Polk's position was one of scrupulous fairness. Without precedents to guide him, he adopted a strict constructionist interpretation of the disputed House rules. The sudden introduction of so many new questions so soon after he became speaker caught him off balance for a moment, but once he had a chance to study the problem, his decisions were consistent and, given his strict constructionist approach, justifiable. Though on several moot points his rulings seemed to favor the southern extremists, there can be no doubt of his personal desire to "stop the mouths of these Southern fanatics, upon the petitions of the Northern fanatics." To his brother-in-law he wrote:

The political agitators of the opposition, in the North and in the South will be unable to get up an excitement on the Slave question, which they can turn to political account. The unanimous vote of the friends of Mr. Van Buren (with less than half a dozen exceptions) on Pinckney's resolutions, must satisfy the country that they are sound upon that subject. Still a few reckless men in the South, will doubtless endeavour still to fan the flame, with a view to produce sectional divisions by which they hope to profit. The old Federalists in the North who are in opposition, are willing to see the discussion go on. It is amusing to witness the operation, and see how they play into each other's hands. An opposition man from the North presents a petition, whereupon a nullifier or Whitite from the South, springs upon it, and makes an inflammatory speech, into which he incorporates the most inflammatory portions of the abolition publications of Tappan, Garrison and Company these he distributes under his frank, and yet cries out lustily against the dissemination of incendiary publications.[22]

Pinckney presented the report of his committee in May, accompanied by three resolutions. The first two asserted that interference with slavery in the states was unconstitutional and in the District inexpedient. The third resolution was the famous gag rule:

Resolved, That all petitions, memorials, resolutions, propositions, or papers, relating in any way, or to any extent whatever, to the subject of slavery, or the abolition of slavery, shall, without either being printed or

[21] *Fairfield Letters,* 105-106.
[22] Polk to W. R. Rucker, 22 Feb. 1836, Polk Papers, Second Series.

referred, be laid upon the table, and that no further action whatever shall be had thereon.[23]

This was clearly as far as any national party could go in meeting southern demands, but the fire eaters denounced the report, if anything, more vehemently than the antislavery men. Tempers got completely out of hand, and Polk had great difficulty maintaining even a semblance of order. When the resolutions finally reached a vote, after days of argument, extremists on both sides defied the rules and refused to answer the roll call. John Quincy Adams replied to his name by shouting out that the gag rule was an unconstitutional violation of the rights of his constituents, but his voice was drowned out by cries of "Order!" The Van Buren ranks held firm, and all three resolutions passed by substantial majorities. The slavery agitation was quelled temporarily, but in the long run the gag rule merely added fuel to the flames. By shifting their propaganda to a defense of the sacred right of petition, the antislavery men won the support of thousands who would not have responded to arguments for abolition itself.[24]

IV

The second session of the twenty-fourth Congress, which convened in December 1836, showed very little in the way of positive accomplishment. The Democrats had at last obtained a majority in the Senate, and Benton had the satisfaction of seeing black lines drawn around Clay's offensive resolution censuring President Jackson. In the House the abolition question again caused some excitement when Polk ruled that the Pinckney resolutions of the previous session were no longer in force. There was heated debate before a new gag rule was adopted, and even after that the speaker clashed with Adams over whether the new rule covered petitions presented before its adoption. The chair's decision against him left the ex-president almost speechless with rage, while Polk "shook with wrath" and "looked savage" when Adams appealed his ruling to the House. But Adams' pertinacity had worn out the patience of almost everyone, and the speaker was sustained by a large majority.[25]

The time of the House at this short session was almost completely consumed by the aggressive minority's savage attacks on the Jackson

---

[23] *Reg. Deb.*:24:1, pp. 2756-2757.   [24] *ibid.*, 4050-4055.
[25] Baltimore *Chronicle*, quoted in Nashville *Banner*, 2 Feb. 1837.

administration. The pacific Cambreleng was ill equipped to cope with this situation, and the president complained that there was "no leader in the House of Representatives and the minority do with the majority as they did last year in the Senate."[26] Under the circumstances, much of the responsibility for administration strategy fell on Polk's shoulders. He had again been warned that Peyton and Wise were planning to draw him into a duel,[27] and these two lost no time in demonstrating their determination to cause trouble.

On Wise's motion a special committee was set up under his chairmanship to investigate the administration's abuse of the patronage. A similar committee, under James Garland, a White partisan from Virginia, undertook an investigation of Reuben M. Whitney's mysterious relationship with the Treasury Department and the deposit banks. Wise called such witnesses as Judge White and John Bell in an effort to demonstrate that Jackson had used federal appointments to control elections, while Peyton, as a member of the Garland committee, tried to implicate Whitney and the administration in all kinds of sinister doings. But Speaker Polk had thoughtfully furnished both investigating committees with Democratic majorities, and their reports generally discounted the opposition charges. This provoked Peyton into a scurrilous philippic accusing the Speaker of buying power by "the *sale* and *prostration* of *every principle of honor, patriotism, independence.*" The speakership had been degraded, he said. "Any man who *crawls* up to that point in *these days,* will never hazard the *consequences* of a *patriotic,* a *generous,* or a *noble* action; it would be fatal to him." Polk ignored these insults, as he had the earlier ones.[28]

The proceedings took on a comic opera touch when Whitney refused to answer a summons from the Wise committee. He was then cited for contempt and hauled up to the bar of the House, where he told how Wise and Peyton had drawn pistols and threatened his life at one of the hearings. He would have returned to complete his testimony, he said, if he had been assured that Wise would not bring a pistol or dirk to the committee meeting. Wise realized too late that the Democratic majority had consented to the contempt proceedings only to make him ludicrous, and despite his furious complaints, Whitney was discharged without punishment. This episode,

26 Jackson to Donelson, 11 Jan. 1837, Emily Tennessee Donelson Papers (LC).
27 Johnson to Polk, 4 Nov. [1836], Polk Papers.
28 *Cong. Globe*:24:2, Appendix, 349-359.

like almost every other in the bitterly divided body, gave rise to sharp controversies over procedure and posed knotty problems for the speaker.[29]

Bell, too, contributed to the general assault with a bill "to ensure the freedom of elections." This measure would have barred federal officeholders from participating in partisan politics. It had no chance of passage, but it gave Bell a chance for another of his characteristic arraignments of "party" and "dictation."[30] Distracted and disorganized by all these partisan forays, the twenty-fourth Congress came to an inconclusive, inglorious end at midnight on March 3, 1837.

Andrew Jackson, whose momentous presidency closed simultaneously with the twenty-fourth Congress, could review his record with far greater satisfaction. The internal improvement craze had been checked, the tariff controversy had been adjusted, the national bank had been destroyed, the federal debt had been paid, the Senate had expunged its mortifying resolution of censure, Roger B. Taney had replaced John Marshall at the head of the Supreme Court, and Jackson's faithful lieutenant had been chosen to succeed him. Old Hickory left the White House at the height of his popularity. Van Buren's inauguration took place on the day after Congress adjourned, but the new president was almost overlooked by the crowds in their anxiety to do honor to his retiring predecessor.

Donelson had to hurry back to Tennessee because one of his children was ill, and he asked Polk to accompany Jackson on his homeward journey and do what he could to shield him from the crowds. This was no light task, for never before had there been such an outpouring of people along the route of a touring American statesman. The Polks themselves narrowly escaped injury when one of the cars on the Baltimore-Frederick railroad became uncoupled, and the aging president showed signs of wilting under the continuous excitement and jostling. He was able to get a little rest when the party boarded a steamboat at Wheeling, but the journey down the Ohio was interrupted by tumultuous celebrations at Cincinnati and other river towns. Jackson caught a cold while on the river, and there was a delay at the mouth of the Cumberland before a boat came along bound for Nashville, but Polk was able to turn his distinguished charge over to Donelson in reasonably good health.[31]

[29] *House Journal*:24:2, pp. 380-446. [30] *Cong. Globe*:24:2, Appendix, 291 ff.
[31] Donelson to Polk, 14 [Mar. 1837; misplaced 1833], n.d. [Mar. 1837; misplaced

Polk himself was considerably worn down by more than three years of hard political warfare without the slightest respite except during his illness in 1835. He had earned a rest, and fortunately, for the first time since 1831, he was not threatened with opposition at the August election. John Catron, who had tarried in Washington to make sure of his own appointment to the Supreme Court, wrote reassuringly of Polk's prospects under the Van Buren administration. "If you can recruit your health and spirits," ran Catron's letter, "you'll live in comfort, unless your conscience should sink under causing some deaths by envy."[32] Both "health and spirits" were badly in need of recruitment, and James and Sarah quickly got away to Murfreesboro for a quiet visit with Sarah's relatives in that sleepy country town.

V

Polk was to have only the briefest vacation from politics. While still on the Ohio River with Jackson, he had begun to hear reports of an unusual financial stringency and rumors of failing banks and business houses at Natchez and New Orleans. Even more disturbing stories followed him to Murfreesboro, and by May the truth was all too clear—the vast structure of speculative credit built up since 1834 had at last come crashing down, and the country was in the middle of the most serious panic in its history. It was 1819 again, and worse. Bank notes were depreciating, debts could not be paid, cotton could not be moved, laborers were thrown out of work, and a pall of fear and want descended over every section of the country.

The Democrats were in for trouble, since it was absurdly easy for the Whigs to pin all the blame on Democratic financial policies. The voters, moreover, were so disgusted with the depreciating state bank notes and so clamorous for a stable circulating medium that almost overnight a new national bank became a distinct possibility. Recognizing the peril at once, Polk hastened back to Columbia, without even stopping for a promised visit at the Hermitage, "to take a tour through my District, in order to preserve a sound state of public opinion."[33]

---

31 Dec. 1838], Polk Papers; Catron to Polk, 13 Mar. [1837], *ibid.*; Jackson to Van Buren, 22 Mar. 1837, Martin Van Buren Papers (LC); Nashville *Union*, 25 Mar. 1837.

32 Catron to Polk, 13 Mar. [1837], Polk Papers.

33 Polk to Jackson, 29 May 1837, Jackson Papers.

For two strenuous months he was constantly making speeches and writing letters on a single theme: "The present pressure could not have been caused by the acts of the government." Over and over that summer Polk pointed out that the panic was worldwide, trouble actually having appeared first in England. The real cause, he argued, was to be found in "that mania of speculation in lands, stocks, merchandise, negroes and every description of property; in that wild and extravagant overtrading which had prevailed during the last two years."[34] All this overtrading, he told his constituents, grew out of the use of "rag money" and the "irredeemable paper" of the banks in place of specie, the only constitutional currency. Citing statistics to show that the country had more than eighty million dollars in specie, an ample amount to furnish a circulating medium, Polk usually wound up his appeals with a eulogy on the "Old Roman" for his efforts "to restore the constitutional currency of Gold and Silver" and usher in a "Golden Age."

Polk's indictment of "overtrading" was sound up to a point, but as one of his Whig auditors noted, "No Inquiry was made in regard to what had produced 'overtrading,' though every moment I expected to hear the question '*popped*,' and if it had, I fear the 'cat would have been let out of the wallet.' " But Polk did not rely merely on reasoning. He was a master at translating abstract arguments into the terms of his audience's experience. In one of his speeches at Shelbyville he illustrated the unsoundness of a paper currency by telling a story about a little boy who had bought a horse.

When he went home his father asked him how he got the horse? "I bought him," said the boy. "You bought him?" rejoined the father. "Yes, I bought him and paid for him too." "How did you do it?" "Why," exclaimed the boy, with great emphasis, "I gave my note for him."

Told in Polk's inimitable style, this not only produced a roar of laughter, but also carried conviction to his listeners.[35]

Along with other Democrats, Polk soon learned that it was impossible to argue with a depression. The only thing that could save the Democracy was affirmative action to alleviate distress or prevent its recurrence. One thing was certain: the deposit system would have to be changed. The law permitted deposits only in specie-paying banks, of which there were none left. Furthermore the federal funds

34 Polk to W. M. Warner, 19 June 1837, copy, Polk Papers.
35 Nashville *Republican Banner*, 8 July 1839.

already in the deposit banks could now be withdrawn only at the depreciated rate. It was to resolve the government's desperate financial crisis and to present the Democratic plan for reform that Van Buren promptly called Congress to meet in special session on the first Monday of September.

But what reform should be adopted? Many Democrats immediately thought of Jackson's old scheme for a "Treasury Bank" and Gouge's similar independent treasury plan, by which the government would divorce itself altogether from banks and deal only in the precious metals. Such a thoroughgoing hard-money policy, however, would encounter strong opposition from the state bank and business-minded element in the Democratic party. There had been signs of rebellion the previous summer, when Jackson tried to check the inflationary boom with his Specie Circular, forbidding the reception of anything but gold and silver in payment for public lands.

A group of "Conservative" Democrats, led by Senators Nathaniel P. Tallmadge of New York and William C. Rives of Virginia, had joined the Whigs in opposition to the Specie Circular. This Whig-Conservative coalition had passed Rives' bill repealing the Circular and requiring the government to accept bank notes, and Jackson's pocket veto of this measure had been one of his last acts as president. Thus the Democratic leaders were already on notice that a respectable portion of the party was unwilling to abandon the state banks.

The panic served to crystallize this incipient division within the party. To men of Jackson's way of thinking, the state banks had now demonstrated their unreliability. The only remaining alternative to a new national bank was a complete divorce of government from banking. Van Buren had no sooner issued his call for a special session than Frank Blair's *Globe* began to argue against "placing the public finances under the control of any grasping corporation," while down in Tennessee Cave Johnson began stumping his district in favor of the Treasury Bank plan.[36]

Other Tennessee Democrats, however, did not see how the business community could get along without a uniform paper currency underwritten by the government. All through the summer James Walker expostulated with Polk against the hard-money philosophy. "I do not believe that the notion of collecting and paying out the public revenue in coin will do," he said, "nor do I see any necessity for dispensing with the convenience of Bank transmissions of the

---

[36] Nashville *Banner*, 12 June 1837.

public money from one section of the country to another." Walker argued further that to resist the demand for a national paper currency would inevitably lead to Whig victories and a national bank on the old plan. This was certainly the Whig objective. At this very time Balie Peyton was writing to William B. Campbell, who was to succeed him in Congress, that "you must have such arrangements made as will *enable* you to vote for the *right* sort of a *Bank*."[37]

Walker advocated a national bank wholly owned by the states, which would be susceptible to local inflationary pressures. Though Polk urged him to wait and see what Van Buren would propose, he insisted on airing his plan through the Columbia *Democrat*. "A National Bank owned by stockholders irresponsible to the people, disposed to rule them with an iron hand, is out of the question," declared the *Democrat*. "If a National Bank was indispensable, *it should be a National Bank in fact; belonging to the American People*, AND UNDER THE CONTROL OF MEN DIRECTLY RESPONSIBLE TO THE PEOPLE, and having the strongest inducements to promote the happiness and welfare of every section of the union."[38]

Also skeptical of the independent treasury was Judge Catron, who came to Columbia to discuss the problem with Polk and Walker. Instead of Walker's bank plan, Catron proposed that a uniform paper currency be furnished by issuing Treasury notes redeemable in specie. The question was settled for Polk when he stopped at the Hermitage on his way to Washington in August and learned from Jackson that Van Buren would advocate the independent treasury plan.[39]

VI

One of the more immediate effects of the panic was to weaken Democratic hopes of winning the Tennessee elections in August 1837. Polk and his friends had entered the campaign moderately optimistic that many of White's supporters would return to their former Democratic allegiance. During the preceding winter Polk had carried on an extensive correspondence with various local politicians in an effort to secure the ablest possible candidates for gov-

[37] Walker to Polk, 19 Aug. 1837, Polk Papers; Peyton to W. B. Campbell, 5 Aug. 1837, Campbell Papers.

[38] Columbia *Democrat*, quoted in Nashville *Banner*, 12 June 1837.

[39] Polk to J. F. H. Claiborne, 26 June 1837, Polk Papers; Jackson to Polk, 6 Aug. 1837, *ibid.*; Catron to Polk, 10 Sept. 1837, *ibid.*

ernor, Congress, and the legislature, and by spring it began to appear that the Democrats would have a strong ticket. The legislature was particularly important. Grundy's senatorial term would expire in March 1839, some months before the 1839 legislature met, and if the Whigs controlled the 1837 session, they would probably seize on this excuse to choose his successor two years ahead of time. A Whig legislature could also instruct Grundy to oppose the independent treasury.

The governorship was the greatest problem. Carroll had originally agreed to be a candidate, but when Van Buren appointed another man to the long-promised post of minister to Mexico, the embittered Carroll published a curt statement refusing "all participation in the approaching election, as a candidate for any office."[40] The Whigs, on the other hand, were determined to wage a strong campaign based on federal issues, in order, as Balie Peyton admitted, "to arouse the state in opposition to Van Buren . . . so as to secure Grundy's defeat." Bell had his eye on Grundy's Senate seat, and the flamboyant Peyton was slated to run for governor in place of the incumbent Newton Cannon, who not only was a colorless campaigner, but also had made himself unpopular in East Tennessee by his lack of enthusiasm for that section's internal improvement projects.[41]

Polk feared that some of the conservative Nashville Democrats would push General Robert Armstrong for governor, so as soon as Carroll declined, he began moving heaven and earth to find an alternative candidate. Though a nominal Democrat, General Armstrong was closely associated with Nashville's commercial and banking interests and was on intimate terms with the Bell-Foster group. Moreover, as Judge Catron pointed out, he "cannot speak, and is radically defective in intelligence."[42] But he had served heroically under Jackson in the Creek campaign, and Old Hickory had demonstrated his devotion to Armstrong by bestowing the lucrative Nashville post-

40 Nashville *Banner,* 17 Mar. 1837; Chauncey S. Boucher and Robert P. Brooks, eds., "Correspondence Addressed to John C. Calhoun 1837-1849," American Historical Association, *Annual Report,* 1929 (Washington, 1930), 168-169.

41 Peyton to W. B. Campbell, 30 Dec. 1836, Campbell Papers; Nashville *Union,* 11 July 1837.

42 Catron to Polk, 16 Apr. 1837, Polk Papers; Walker to Polk, 17 Feb. 1837, *ibid.;* Laughlin to Polk, 29 Mar. 1837, *ibid.;* Samuel Powell to Polk, 10 Apr. 1837, *ibid.;* Grundy to Polk, 25 Apr. 1837, *ibid.;* William Trousdale to Polk, 27 Apr. 1837, *ibid.;* J. H. Bills to Polk, 1 May 1837, *ibid.*

mastership on him and by appointing several members of his family to other offices.

Unfortunately all the men Polk approached declined to run for governor, and the Democrats entered May, the fateful month when the banks suspended specie payments, still without a candidate. Jackson was finally induced to endorse his old friend Armstrong, who was announced as the Democratic candidate on May 16. To mollify the more strait-laced Democrats, Armstrong promised to support the Van Buren administration, but six days later, in response to pressure from the Bell-Foster group, he declared that he "would not be a party Governor."[43] Polk bowed gracefully to the inevitable. "I consider it fortunate that he is a candidate," he wrote to Jackson, "and regard his election certain."[44]

The campaign was a curious affair. Bell, Foster, and Allen Hall, who was now editing the *Banner*, supported Armstrong. This had the effect of killing Peyton's candidacy, and since he had already encouraged William B. Campbell to run for his seat in Congress, left him nowhere to go. It also gave Cannon, who had obstinately refused to withdraw in favor of Peyton or anyone else, the chance to run as the regular Whig nominee. Grundy and Armstrong's other managers at Nashville were anxious above all else to carry their legislative ticket in the Nashville district. They insisted on a campaign "of the neutral character, no excitement, or contestation," so as to prevent the former White supporters from rallying along party lines. In other words the Nashville Democrats hoped to succeed by playing down alignments based on parties and going back to the old alignments based on personalities. In line with this strategy, Armstrong made an agreement with Cannon not to campaign actively.[45]

The Democrats were still crippled by the lack of an effective Nashville newspaper. Laughlin had sunk into an almost uninterrupted debauch, and the *Union* frequently failed to appear, but he stubbornly refused to turn it over to anyone else, declaring that he would have

[43] Nashville *Banner*, 21 May 1837; Jackson to F. P. Blair, 11 May 1837, Jackson Papers; Nashville *Union*, 16 May 1837.

[44] Polk to Jackson, 19 May 1837, Jackson Papers.

[45] Catron to Polk, 7 July 1837, Polk Papers; Daniel Graham to Polk, 17 July 1837, *ibid.*; Nashville *Union*, 27 May 1837; J. S. Yerger to W. B. Campbell, 31 May 1837, Campbell Papers; David Campbell to W. B. Campbell, 19 June 1837, *ibid.*; Nashville *Banner*, 14 July 1837.

to be *"starved out."*[46] By the spring of 1837 his debts were so mountainous that this result was nearly accomplished, but it took Polk, Walker, Grundy, and Donelson three months to work out a new arrangement for carrying on the paper. Even this was not satisfactory. The best that could be obtained in the way of a new editor was an Episcopal divinity student, John O. Bradford, who knew little about Tennessee politics and was forced by the Nashville Democrats to adopt a temporizing policy with regard to the gubernatorial election. The *Union* championed Armstrong solely on the basis of his military record and his refusal to "be a political automaton, a mere machine for 'party purposes.' "[47]

A clue to the meaning of this strange campaign may be found in the simultaneous banking crisis. The first Tennessee firm to suspend specie payments was the private banking house of Yeatman, Woods, and Company, and Allen Hall's *Banner* immediately called for a general suspension. The *Union*, at that time still under Laughlin's control, denounced this proposal, and Old Hickory among others began rumbling that the charters of suspending banks should be revoked. When Armstrong entered the gubernatorial race in the middle of May, Nashville's two federal depositories, the Union and Planter's banks, in which Grundy, Carroll, and other Nashville Democrats were interested, were tottering on the brink of suspension. Five days later they stopped paying specie on their notes. Remembering the violent antibank reaction that had followed suspension in 1819, the state banking interests were anxious to have the state government in friendly hands.[48]

In this crisis the state bank Democrats found common ground with John Bell. Bell's marriage to Thomas Yeatman's widow had given him a substantial interest in Yeatman, Woods, and Company, and it was in defense of this firm that the *Banner* had advocated a general suspension. Now Bell joined the Grundy group in backing Armstrong against Cannon. This explains why Polk was rebuffed in all his entreaties with the Nashville group to bring out a strong candidate against Bell for Congress. One man had announced on his own responsibility, but when he withdrew in June, Polk began

---

[46] Laughlin to Polk, 24 May 1837, Polk Papers; Catron to Polk, 6 Sept., 24 Nov. 1836, 13 Mar., 16, 22 Apr. 1837, *ibid.*

[47] Nashville *Union*, 19 July 1837; Laughlin to Polk, 24 May 1837, Polk Papers; Catron to Walker, 30 May, 17 June, 7 July 1837, *ibid.*; J. O. Bradford to Polk, 8, 22 July 1837, *ibid.*

[48] Nashville *Union*, 6, 16, 27 May 1837; Jackson to Blair, 11 May 1837, Jackson Papers.

bombarding Jackson with appeals to find another, even sending Walker to Nashville and the Hermitage to press for prompt action. Donelson was willing to make the race, but much to Jackson's chagrin "our *knowing ones* at Nashville" vetoed the project, fearing that an "excited contest" would keep the White and Bell men from voting for Armstrong and the Democratic legislative ticket. Old Hickory put his finger more precisely on the trouble. "I fear that there are too many of our friend[s] deeply interested in the State Banks," he observed, "who did not want the Banks treachery & swindling of the people to be exposed."[49]

The Grundy strategy backfired badly, for the panic had served to make party considerations paramount to personalities. The people everywhere were clamoring for a reform in the depreciating "shinplaster" currency of the banks, dividing only over whether the Whig national bank was a better solution than the Democratic independent treasury. And for the moment, at any rate, the Whig solution seemed surprisingly popular. "We shall not stickle about a National Bank, or the Bank of the United States," cried the Memphis *Enquirer*. "We want relief—come whence it may or how it may, so it be really relief—wholesome and permanent." Even one of Polk's staunchest supporters wrote that "if times continue as they are much longer, those who are opposed in principle to the Bank will cease their opposition and let its friends carry it through."[50]

Under these circumstances, many White men swallowed their personal or sectional dislike and voted for Cannon, because he was the candidate identified with regular Whig policies. Conversely, the fact that Bell and Foster were supporting Armstrong made many thoroughgoing Democrats apathetic toward him. Little known in many parts of the state, Armstrong was further injured by his agreement not to campaign. Most important of all, the Whigs succeeded in convincing a majority of the voters that Democratic policies were responsible for the depression. The result was an unexpectedly decisive Whig victory. Cannon defeated Armstrong by a majority of nearly 20,000, as compared with White's majority of less than 10,000 over Van Buren the year before. The Democrats elected only two congressmen besides Polk, the previously unbeatable Cave Johnson be-

[49] Jackson to Blair, 9 July 1837, Jackson Papers; Joseph Howard Parks, *John Bell of Tennessee* (Baton Rouge, 1950), 317-318.

[50] Memphis *Enquirer*, 10 June 1837, quoted in Powell Moore, "The Establishment of the Whig Party in Tennessee," Ph.D. thesis, Indiana University (1932), 285; Alfred Flournoy to Polk, 15 July 1837, Polk Papers.

ing the most prominent victim of the Whig sweep. Polk saved Maury County for Armstrong by a scant 67 votes, while losing Bedford by almost 300.[51]

The results, Jackson observed, were just "as I expected, from the imbecile councils of the Nashville politicians." The *Union*, he complained, "has been muzzled by some unseen hands."[52] Only Polk "acted well his part whilst our leading politicians here at Nashville lost every thing by supineness and temporizing."[53]

VII

Polk had little time to ponder these disastrous results, for the special session of Congress was to meet on the first Monday in September, and it was imperative that he be in Washington well ahead of that time. The Democrats would again have a majority in the House, but the margin would be so narrow that Polk took great precautions to insure his reelection as speaker. At his suggestion Frank Blair sent out urgent circulars to all the Democratic members, warning that the Whigs would be able to organize the House unless all the Democrats were in Washington for the first day of the session.[54] But Polk seems to have been unaware of the threat to his reelection by a defection of the Conservative Democrats.

Up in New York, Senator Tallmadge was making strenuous efforts to persuade Democratic congressmen not to vote for Polk, unless he promised to place the Ways and Means Committee in the hands of the friends of the "credit system." More particularly the Conservatives were prepared to insist on the elimination from the committee of C. C. Cambreleng, whose inflexible hard-money views were well known. When Polk reached Washington a week early, some hectic negotiations awaited him, but in the end the speakership election transpired without any sign of Conservative defection. The united Democracy gave Polk a 116-to-103 victory over John Bell, and he promptly appointed Cambreleng to his old post at the head of Ways and Means.[55]

[51] Nashville *Republican Banner*, 2 Sept. 1837.

[52] Jackson to Polk, 6 Aug. 1837, Polk Papers.

[53] Jackson to Blair, 16 Aug. 1837, Jackson Papers.

[54] Polk to Blair, n.d. (postmarked 30 June [1837]), 16 Aug. 1837, Blair-Lee Papers (PU); Blair to Jackson, 10 Aug. 1837, Jackson Papers.

[55] J[esse] H[oyt] to Van Buren, 30 Aug. 1837, Van Buren Papers; John Arthur Garraty, *Silas Wright* (New York, 1949), 152-153; Nashville *Union*, 7 Oct. 1837; *Cong. Globe*:25:1, p. 3.

The narrowness of his escape was demonstrated, however, when the election of House printer took place the next day. Gales and Seaton of the *National Intelligencer* were nominated by the Whigs, and Blair and his partner Rives of the *Globe* by the Democrats, but there was also a third candidate. Shortly before the new Congress assembled the Conservatives had established a Washington newspaper, the *Madisonian*, and now its publisher, Thomas Allen, was put in nomination for printer. Allen's twenty-two votes on the first ballot prevented a majority for anyone, and after five ballots Blair and Rives were still eleven votes short of a majority. For three days the tug of war continued, until finally all but nine of the Whigs shifted to Allen, and he was elected. This news infuriated Old Hickory. The Conservatives, he wrote to Blair, have "plaid the Bell game on you." The wonder was that they had not also "Bellized Col. Polk."[56]

Van Buren's message came out forthrightly for hard money and a divorce of the government from the banks. But carrying its recommendations into effect would be enormously difficult in a House that could be controlled by a union of the Whigs and Conservatives. Polk had to choose his committees with great care. "The Speaker appears to have had some difficulty in getting clear of all the Whigs," one newspaper correspondent noted; "they are becoming almost too many for him." The minor committees were crowded with Whigs and Conservatives, one of them having not a single Van Buren member, so that loyal Van Burenites could retain safe control of the more important ones. As punishment for their desertion of Blair, the Conservatives were treated as harshly as the outright Whigs. The most crucial spot, Cambreleng's Ways and Means Committee, was given a healthy six-to-three Van Buren majority, and included not a single Conservative.[57]

Most of the important measures originated this session in the Senate, where the administration had a clear majority, thanks to Calhoun's momentous decision to support the independent treasury. The Carolinian was coming to the conclusion that the Democracy, despite its equalitarian tendencies, was a safer defender of slavery than the nationalistic Whig party. Besides Calhoun would have a better chance for national leadership in the Democratic ranks. Van

[56] John Spencer Bassett, ed., *Correspondence of Andrew Jackson* (7 vols., Washington, 1926-1935), v, 511-512; *Cong. Globe*:25:1, pp. 11-16.
[57] Nashville *Republican Banner*, 25 Sept. 1837.

Buren now realized that he must rely on strong southern support to carry his program, and this southward shift of the party's center of gravity was to have far-reaching consequences for both the Democracy and the speaker of the House.

The new political alignment was fundamentally congenial to Polk's state rights predilections. He lost no time in having the Nashville *Union* welcome Calhoun back into the Democratic fold. Meanwhile he cooperated heartily with Francis W. Pickens of South Carolina, the House leader of the Calhounites, in pushing the independent treasury bill.[58]

Calhoun was ready to go further than many Democrats in the direction of hard money, and it was on his demand that the "specie amendment" was inserted in the bill while it was still in the Senate. Some Democratic senators were willing to mollify the Conservatives by making the notes of specie-paying banks receivable for government dues, but Calhoun refused to support the independent treasury unless specie only was recognized, and the bill finally passed the Senate in the form he demanded. When the measure came to the House, the combination of Whigs and Conservatives was too strong to be overcome in the limited time available during the special session. The administration leaders finally consented to tabling the bill, so that it could be taken up at the regular session. Congress did, however, authorize the issuance of ten million dollars in Treasury notes and pass other emergency measures to extricate the government from bankruptcy.

VIII

Polk's position as speaker imposed heavy social responsibilities on him and Sarah. The speaker ranked with the leaders of Washington society—the president, Cabinet officers, foreign ministers, and other dignitaries—who sponsored the more formal social occasions and whose hospitalities ordinary congressmen were not expected to return. Upon his election to the speakership, therefore, Polk followed the precedent of previous speakers by renting a separate suite of rooms, though he and Sarah continued for a time to take their meals with a regular congressional mess next door.

When this arrangement proved unsatisfactory, the Polks moved to Jonathan Elliott's fashionable Pennsylvania Avenue establish-

[58] Nashville *Union*, 16, 23 Nov. 1837; Pickens to Polk, n.d. [Oct. 1837], Polk Papers, LXXXII, No. 8841.

ment, where they had their own parlor and dining room for meals and entertaining. At the same time, when they wanted it, they could have the company of Elliott's other tenants, including Senator Silas Wright of New York; Judge Catron; Polk's old friend Archibald Yell, now a congressman from Arkansas; and, during the Polks' last winter in Washington, most of the Supreme Court justices. The wives of all these gentlemen became famous friends, though Sarah's special confidante was Mrs. Catron, whom she had known since girl-hood.[59]

Sarah thoroughly enjoyed her social role, despite the minor re-straints that her Presbyterian conscience imposed. She absolutely refused to attend the horse races, which were in great vogue among the fashionable, while the local Presbyterian minister's denunciation of theaters as "the devil's protracted meetings" prevented Sarah and James from seeing, for example, the celebrated actor Edwin For-rest.[60]

In spite of, or perhaps because of, these idiosyncrasies, Sarah was extremely popular, and her drawing room was always crowded. The wine bill of $138 that she ran up during a single session was an in-dication of both the moderation of her scruples and the extent of her entertaining. One New England congressman paid Sarah the high compliment of observing that while she was "not by any means handsome," she was "more like our northern women than any that I have met with here." This same member commented that she dressed "with much simplicity" and was "easy & familiar though not in-elegant in her manners."[61]

To maintain his new dignity, Polk ordered a luxurious coach, which he insisted must be "a handsome & fashionable article built after the latest style." It was to have glass windows with venetian blinds, curtains of claret-colored silk, a lining of the same color, and mountings and lanterns of brass. At the same time, it had to be light enough so that he and Sarah could use it on their trips to and from Tennessee. Two years later he acquired still another equipage,

[59] *Congressional Directory*:24:1, p. 38; *ibid.*:24:2, p. 37; *ibid.*:25:1, p. 35; *ibid.*:25:2, p. 35; *ibid.*:25:3, p. 36; Joseph Hall to G. P. Osgood, 25 Dec. 1835, George Bancroft Papers (MHS); Catron to Polk, 8 Dec. [1838], Polk Papers; Carroll to Catron, 9 Nov. 1838, *ibid.*

[60] Anson and Fanny Nelson, *Memorials of Sarah Childress Polk: Wife of the Eleventh President of the United States* (New York, 1892), 48; J. W. Clay to C. C. Clay, Jr., 12 Mar. 1838, Clement C. Clay Papers (DU).

[61] *Fairfield Letters*, 149; receipt, 18 June 1838, Polk Papers.

which the country's leading coachmaker called "the most splendid and best finished ever turned out by me."[62]

These fine vehicles were frequently drawn up before the White House and the homes of the leaders of official society, for the speaker belonged to the select circle that attended the most exclusive affairs. When, for example, King Louis Philippe's son, the Prince de Joinville, visited Washington, the French minister's dinner party for him included only Polk, the vice president, two Cabinet members, a senator, and two members of the House. The biggest party given by the Polks themselves took place in March 1838. Several hundred invitations were sent out, and even the acidulous Anne Royall conceded it to be "the genteelest party that has been given this winter by far."[63]

In addition to this inescapable official social life, the Polks found time to spend with such friends as the Catrons and visiting members of the Polk connection. James's brother and nephews were frequently in Washington on their way to and from Yale College, where they claimed to stand forth "as the fearless champions of equal rights and anti monopolies, 'Loco foco' to the core!"[64] In the winter of 1838 James Walker sent his daughter Jane to the capital for a stay with her aunt and uncle. She arrived to find that her cousin Sam, suspended from Yale for participating in a riot, had come to Washington to continue his studies under the eye of his brother James.

The family soon had more to worry about than Sam's academic difficulties, for in June he began to manifest symptoms of tuberculosis. As soon as Congress adjourned, James took the family to New York to have his brother examined by the best physicians. Here Knox Walker joined them from New Haven, and they all returned to Philadelphia for further medical consultations. The doctors held out little hope for Sam, and James could only do his best to make his brother comfortable on the melancholy journey by Pennsylvania's new railroad and canal boat system to Pittsburgh, then by steamboat to Maysville, Kentucky, and finally by chartered stage to Co-

62 S. Knowles to Polk, 30 Nov. 1838, Polk Papers; Polk to L. Knowles and Co., 5 July 1836, copy, *ibid.*

63 Mrs. Anne Royall to Polk, 19 Mar. 1838, Polk Papers; series of notes acknowledging invitations, 7-12 Mar. 1838, *ibid.*; Charles Francis Adams, ed., *Memoirs of John Quincy Adams, Comprising Portions of His Diary from 1795 to 1848* (12 vols., Philadelphia, 1874-1877), IX, 542-543.

64 J. Knox Walker to Polk, 12 Dec. 1837, Polk Papers.

lumbia. James himself was "much fatigued and broken down" by the long trip, but he had done all he could for his youngest brother.[65]

Sam was still lingering on when James and Sarah left again for the capital in the fall, but they had no sooner reached Washington than they received alarming news about Bill, the next youngest brother. Bill had horsewhipped a young Columbia attorney for calling him a "drunken fellow," and his victim had threatened to kill him. When the two met on Columbia's main street to shoot it out, Bill had escaped unscathed, but the other man was fatally wounded.

The family, and especially Bill's recent bride, Belinda, were distraught. He sold his farm and moved back to his mother's house, while the brothers-in-law tried to prevent an indictment for murder. The grand jury finally decided by a split vote that Bill had acted in self-defense, but he was tried for assault and sentenced to six weeks' imprisonment and a $750 fine. However the Columbia jail was not too uncomfortable; the loyal Belinda was allowed to move in with her young husband; and the family got what consolation it could from the fact that the couple "have as good rooms and accommodations as at home."[66]

Troubles were coming thick and fast for old Mrs. Polk. "My afflictions are light," Belinda told Sarah, "in comparison to Mother's." Jane Polk had now buried three of her six sons, and she knew that Sam, the youngest and her favorite, could not live much longer. Her burden was lightened only by the belief that Sam was "prepared to go." The boy sent word to Sarah that he could never forget her kindness, which had been "more the kindness of a Mother than a Sister." A few days later he died in his mother's arms.[67]

IX

When Congress reassembled for its regular session in December 1837, after a short two-month vacation, the independent treasury bill was the principal item on its agenda. Again the initiative was

[65] Polk to Jackson, 7 Aug. 1838, Jackson Papers; Jeremiah Day to Polk, 5 Jan. 1838, Polk Papers; W. H. Polk to J. K. Polk, 17 June 1838, *ibid.*; entries 12 Feb.–12 July 1838, Sam Polk Account Book, *ibid.*; a small memorandum book in *ibid.* lists other expenses for Polk's young relatives on the journey.

[66] Walker to Polk, 25 May 1839, Polk Papers; Dr. J. B. Hays to Polk, 4 Dec. 1838, 11 Jan. [1839], 13 Jan. [1839; misplaced 1838], *ibid.*; Walker to Polk, 10 Dec. 1838, *ibid.*; W. H. Polk to J. K. Polk, 2 Jan. [misplaced 21 Jan.] 1839, *ibid.*; Brownsville *District Herald*, 11 Dec. 1838; Nashville *Republican Banner*, 18, 22 Jan. 1839.

[67] Mrs. W. H. Polk to Mrs. J. K. Polk, 17 Feb. 1839, Polk Papers; W. H. Polk to J. K. Polk, 24 Feb. 1839, *ibid.*

left to the Senate, but this time a number of Democratic senators voted with the Whigs against Calhoun's specie provision, in a bid for Conservative support. Reasoning that half a loaf was better than none at all, they argued that once the independent treasury was established, it could be perfected by subsequent legislation. They paid a heavy price, however, for Calhoun voted against the bill on its final narrow passage through the Senate, and the defection of even a few of his followers would spell defeat in the more precariously balanced House.

The Democratic House leadership was thus placed in a cruel dilemma. Retention of the specie clause would forfeit Conservative support, while its elimination would cost the votes of the Calhounites; and the loss of either group would bring almost certain defeat. Polk took the correct hard-money position, tempered by realism. "We much prefer the Bill with the specie provision retained," he wrote, but he conceded that it was "better to take it without it than to pass no bill." Still he was convinced that the Conservatives would continue to oppose the independent treasury, specie or no specie, so the House leaders decided to take up the House bill, as reported by Cambreleng's committee with the specie clause, rather than the emasculated Senate version. If they failed to pass the one, then the other could be tried.[68]

But even Providence seemed to intervene against the independent treasury, when the uncertain administration majority was rendered even more precarious by the death of three Democratic members. In addition, two other supporters were lost as the result of a disputed election in Mississippi. Since Mississippi did not elect her congressmen until November, the governor had had to call a special election in July to provide the state with representation at the special session, and two Van Buren men, John F. H. Claiborne and Samuel J. Gholson, had been successful. After some debate the House had declared the two Democrats elected for the entire Congress, but Mississippi had proceeded with its regular November congressional election anyhow. The Democrats refusing to participate in this second election, the Whig candidates, Sergeant S. Prentiss and Thomas J. Word, had won easily, and all four men presented themselves when the regular session convened.

Wise and Bell immediately leapt to the defense of the Whig claim-

[68] Polk to Donelson, 26 Mar. 1838, Andrew Jackson Donelson Papers (LC; herein cited as Donelson Papers).

ants, and the ferocity of the ensuing debate almost brought about a duel between Wise and Gholson. Polk declared that he had "never witnessed more feeling or greater exertions on any other question before Congress."[69] This debate gave the twenty-nine-year-old Prentiss his first national audience for a lavish display of the flamboyant oratory that was to make him one of the most celebrated speakers of his day. His memorable three-day plea swept enough members away from their party moorings to secure a majority for Bell's resolution rescinding the previous decision seating Claiborne and Gholson for the entire Congress.

The Democrats then proposed a compromise denying the seats to Prentiss and Word as well and sending the whole question back to the Mississippi voters for yet a third election. On this proposition feeling again ran high, and the vote stood 117 to 117, leaving the decision to Speaker Polk. When Polk voted against the Whig claimants, all the wrath of the opposition was poured on his head. Polk's vote was "the effect of the most miserable, abject *dependence*," raged the Nashville *Republican*. "*He dared not do otherwise*. He lives and moves, and has his political being in the sunshine of power. He does not look to his own resources and energy of character for promotion, but expects to find his reward in a servile devotion to the higher powers."[70]

The third Mississippi election went against the Democrats, and soon Prentiss was back in the House constantly harassing the speaker and having to be called to order for injecting personalities into debate. One account of his swearing-in that went the rounds of the Whig press was adapted from Davy Crockett's famous coon-hunting story, with Prentiss taking the part of Crockett and Polk playing the coon:

Mr. Prentiss, with a firm step and unquailing eye, advanced to the Speaker's chair to present his credentials. The Speaker looked at him, as if he would say, "is that you, Capt. Prentiss?" Prentiss looked as much as to say "it is." "Then, don't shoot" looked the Speaker, "I'll come down."[71]

Most Democrats had given up all hope for the independent treasury bill by this time, but Polk had been working hard to convert doubtful opposition members to the measure, telling his colleagues that a Democratic victory in Mississippi might provide the margin

69 Polk to Donelson, 4 Feb. 1838, Jackson Papers.
70 Nashville *Republican Banner*, 22 Feb. 1838.
71 Columbia *Observer*, 19 July 1838.

to pass it. The Mississippi defeat, of course, settled any doubt that may have existed about its fate. When the bill reached the floor, the anti-specie men were able to eliminate the specie clause, whereupon it was deserted by the Calhounites and rejected, 111 to 125.[72]

It was now apparent that the opposition controlled the House, while the Democrats held sway in the Senate. Consequently the final session of the twenty-fifth Congress convened the following December to do little constructive business. But with a new Congress about to be elected and with a presidential campaign in the offing, the politician-congressmen were neither idle nor silent. The close division of parties, as a matter of fact, caused this Congress to outdo even the twenty-fourth in partisan wrangling.

One fruit of this political ill feeling was a barbarous duel fought in February 1838 between a Maine Democrat, Jonathan Cilley, and a Kentucky Whig, William Graves. The affair grew out of a trivial controversy, and a challenge was deliberately provoked with the connivance of Wise, who was Graves' second, and Henry Clay. The sanguinary conflict was conducted with rifles fired at eighty yards, but four fires were necessary before Cilley fell dying to the ground. The House was momentarily sobered, but even this bloody event did not moderate the debates for long.[73]

Nowhere was the prevailing partisan bitterness more intense than between the warring Tennessee factions. Three months after the Graves-Cilley duel, Hopkins L. Turney, a new Democratic congressman from the Cumberland mountain district, launched into a searing attack on Bell for deserting his former principles and party. When Turney insinuated that Bell had been influenced by bank loans and ambition for personal advancement, the former speaker, who was sitting just behind him, lost his temper and replied in the most cutting language. This attack, Bell shouted, had been instigated by Polk, who was afraid to meet him directly, either in or out of the House. The speaker, he continued, "was as destitute of private honor as he was of public virtue." As for Turney, Bell concluded, he was merely "a fit and voluntary *conduit* of the malice of others, . . . the dirty scavenger of others—*a tool of tools*."[74] Turney leaped

72 Polk to Jackson, 7 Mar. 1838, n.d. [Apr. 1838], Jackson Papers; Blair to Jackson, 28 May 1838, *ibid.*; Polk to Donelson, 29 May 1838, Donelson Papers; Polk to Jackson, 11 June 1838, *ibid.*; *Cong. Globe*:25:2, p. 478.

73 Charles M. Wiltse, *John C. Calhoun* (3 vols., Indianapolis, 1944-1951), ii, 379.

74 Nashville *Republican Banner*, 9, 11 June 1838; *Fairfield Letters*, 233; W. B. Campbell to David Campbell, 1 June 1838, Campbell Papers.

to his feet exclaiming that Bell was lying, Bell struck him, and within an instant the two men were lashing at each other, while the House was thrown into pandemonium. Polk had not been presiding at the time, but he rushed to the chair and by strenuous efforts was able to restore order. The combatants were compelled to apologize to the House, and Bell was permitted to continue his speech, but he now took care to keep within the rules, and peppery old John Quincy Adams complained that "his discourse was stale and flat, like a pot of small beer after a bumper of pure whiskey."[75]

This affair might easily have had more serious consequences, especially if the fiery Balie Peyton had been on the ground. In political retirement at New Orleans, Peyton could not believe that Turney would refuse to challenge Bell for his insults, and he tried to egg on Bell and Wise by correspondence. Fearful that Bell was "rather too slow" for a formal duel, but convinced that he "would be Hell in a street fight," Peyton implored Wise to have Bell goad Turney into a common brawl. Let Bell "load up those rifle barrell Pistols of his which will kill a Buffaloe [at] 50 yds.," he advised, "& meet him, shooting the 1st at the distance of at least 30 yds. holding it like a rifle in both hands, & aiming low, with a heavy charge."

An even better strategy, Peyton thought, would be "for Bell to pull *Polks* nose on some pretext & get into a fight with him. Let him meet P. & say (taking him by the nose) this is for setting on me that infamous scoundrel Hop. Turney, who no gentleman can notice. I am accountable to *you*—I never will notice *him*." Thus the fighting would be with Polk, and any subsequent challenge from Turney could be ignored on the ground that it was sent only because Bell had declared he would not recognize it. Fortunately Bell did not have a chance to adopt either strategy, since Turney, probably on Polk's advice, never sent a challenge.[76]

It was not until the last session of this Congress that Polk's enemies were able to land a really telling blow on him. An enormous defalcation by Samuel Swartwout, collector of the port of New York, had been exposed, and a congressional investigation was inevitable. Wise seized this opportunity to insist that the investigating committee be chosen by ballot, rather than appointed by the speaker. In a vituperative speech he accused Polk of being a spineless administra-

---

[75] Adams, *Diary*, x, 45.
[76] Peyton to Wise, 17 June 1838, Miscellaneous Collection (HSP).

tion tool and of packing the earlier Wise investigating committee to prevent a real investigation. "Now, sir," he said, addressing himself to Polk on the subject of the earlier investigation,

I propose to show that *your* committee obeyed the will of their master. Yes, as you had done, by *packing* and stocking the committee. It was *your* committee—peculiarly and emphatically *yours*—its *appointment*, its *conduct*, its honor or *infamy*, will forever attach itself, sir, to *your name*. . . . *You*, the Speaker, the President of the United States, the heads of Executive Departments, *your* committee, and your whole party, combined and conspired to stifle investigation.

Wise had the votes to carry his point, and an opposition majority was elected to the investigating group. But nothing startling was discovered, though lengthy majority and minority reports were filed for use as ammunition in the coming campaign.[77]

X

Back of the congressional ill temper of these years burned the imperfectly repressed fires of slavery controversy, fresh fuel for which was accumulating on the plains of the Southwest. Ever since the Missouri Compromise had established the principle of balancing new states, one slave for one free, some southerners had been looking to Texas as their only hope for new territory to balance the vast free expanse of the Northwest. Acquisition of this tremendous Mexican province had been a pet hobby with Jackson, and Sam Houston had gone there in 1833 with the object of eventually annexing it to the United States. The winning of Texas independence and the broaching of the annexation question had come just at the time when Congress was embroiled with the petition controversy.

The Texas question was more than academic for Polk, since members of his family had been deeply involved in the Texas war for independence. He had been speaker only a few months when he received a letter from his great-uncle, Thomas J. Hardeman, giving a firsthand account of Santa Anna's massacre of the Texan defenders of the Alamo. Two of Polk's cousins had been cut off from the Texan forces and had nearly starved before getting back safely. But the old pioneer's letter was more than a family epistle. "We are looking to the United States to acknowledge our Indepindance [*sic*] and give us all the assistance they can," he wrote. The letter

77 *Cong. Globe*:25:3, Appendix, 386-387; Nashville *Republican Banner*, 28 Jan. 1839.

ended with a blunt question: "James, you have an active tongue. Why not use it for Texas, as all true Americans should do under existing circumstances?"[78]

At that time, in early 1836, Polk had a compelling reason for not complying with his uncle's request. Van Buren's election was not yet secure, and suspicious northerners like John Quincy Adams were beginning to see in the whole Texas movement a conspiracy to extend the slave area of the union. The true policy of the Democrats, Van Buren argued, and even Jackson had to agree, was to avoid any question that threatened the unity of northern and southern Democrats. But the Texas question, like every other phase of the slavery problem, was difficult if not impossible to suppress.

Adams himself was determined to agitate the matter, and at the special session of 1837 he demanded that the House call on the president for all his correspondence with the Mexican and Texan authorities. Adams' assertion that a majority of Americans preferred dissolution of the Union to the admission of Texas threw the House into a heated wrangle, and Polk was barely able to restore order. Adams' agitation was not stopped until the House passed a rule confining debate at the special session to subjects mentioned in the president's message. Even then the ex-president continued to make a nuisance of himself by demanding divisions on questions where there was a clear majority, refusing to vote, and similar tactics.[79]

At the opening of the regular session of 1837-1838, William Slade, a Vermont abolitionist, stirred up the stormiest slavery debate Congress had yet experienced. Slade started the fireworks by presenting several abolition petitions, and since the gag rule had not yet been reenacted, he could not be prevented from launching into a thoroughgoing attack on human servitude. Wise, Robert Barnwell Rhett, and other southern hotspurs, almost distracted with rage, kept interrupting, but as long as Slade stayed within the rules, Polk upheld his right to the floor. Finally the southerners began to call out for the southern delegations to withdraw, and an adjournment was carried just as there began to be a general movement from the House.

At a meeting of irate southern members the same evening, some openly advocated secession, while Calhoun pleaded for a convention

[78] T. J. Hardeman to Polk, 31 Mar. 1836, Polk Papers.
[79] *Cong. Globe*:25:1, pp. 21, 24-26; Nashville *Republican Banner*, 26 Oct. 1837.

of the southern states. But more moderate, and from the Democratic point of view more politic, counsels prevailed. It was decided to reenact the gag rule, and this was promptly done, to the accompaniment of Adams' usual objections.[80]

Determined to prevent a recurrence of the Slade speech at the final session of the twenty-fifth Congress, the Democratic leaders laid their plans carefully at a presession caucus in Speaker Polk's apartment. An improved set of gag resolutions was drafted carefully so as to deny to Congress the right to interfere with slavery anywhere, while avoiding the delicate constitutional question as to the District of Columbia. By relentless application of the previous question, the resolutions were pressed to a vote and passed without debate. Adams, for a change, let them go through without protest, though Wise fumed and sputtered that they surrendered principles vital to the South.[81]

Adams' unwonted silence was no sign of acquiescence. At the very moment, he was observing the contempt with which the southerners treated northern men who gave in to their demands. He concluded, in fact, that there was such a difference in manners between the North and the South "that their members could never be very intimate personally together." If southern congressmen had been able to read the ex-president's diary entry on the night after the gag resolutions passed, there would not have been even civility. "The conflict between the principle of liberty and the fact of slavery is coming gradually to an issue," he wrote. "Slavery has now the power, and falls into convulsions at the approach of freedom. That the fall of slavery is predetermined in the counsels of Omnipotence I cannot doubt; it is a part of the great moral improvement in the condition of man, attested by all the records of history. But the conflict will be terrible, and the progress of improvement perhaps retrograde before its final progress to consummation."[82]

Thus fortified with draughts from his liberal Unitarian faith and from the Puritan predestinarianism of his forefathers, John Quincy Adams went up to the Capitol the next morning with a renewed determination to do battle in the cause of righteousness. When the clerk reached his name on the roll call for petitions, Adams com-

[80] *Cong. Globe*:25:2, pp. 41, 451 ff.; Wiltse, *Calhoun*, II, 367-373.
[81] *Cong. Globe*:25:3, pp. 23-28; Adams, *Diary*, x, 60, 62; Nashville *Republican Banner*, 24 Dec. 1838.
[82] Adams, *Diary*, x, 41, 63.

menced a declaration that he considered the gag rule unconstitutional and would refuse to answer. The first words were hardly out of his mouth before the speaker called him to order, insisting that he answer aye or no. When Adams persisted in his statement, the House began to resound with furious shouts of "Order!", the old man from Quincy shrieking above the rest. Polk was shouting at the top of his voice for the House to help him restore order, when Adams suddenly sat down, and the tumult abruptly subsided. One of the Whigs then raised a laugh by asking what aid Polk desired of the House, only to be called out of order by the nettled speaker.[83]

Such were the trials of the presiding officer. It should be said to Polk's credit that he continued to treat Adams with consideration. When that irascible gentleman proposed a bill to punish dueling in the District of Columbia, the speaker promised to appoint a committee favorable to the measure and consulted Adams on its membership.[84]

XI

The twenty-fifth Congress came to a close with a vindictive attack on Speaker Polk, who was ending his fourteen-year career in the House to seek further political honors in a different arena. He had passed through severer trials than any previous speaker and had emerged unscathed from all the traps and frontal assaults of his enemies. They now resolved, mainly for the purpose of discrediting him in his new undertaking, to deny him the customary vote of thanks for the "able, impartial, and dignified manner" in which he had presided over the House.

The assault was led by the vengeful Sergeant S. Prentiss, who had been barred from his seat for a time by Polk's vote and who later complained that Polk subjected him to a "reversed telescope" whenever he tried to get the floor.[85] Prentiss moved to strike the word "impartial" from the resolution. "A more perfectly party speaker," he said, "one who would be more disposed to bend the rules of the House to meet the purposes of his own side in politics, never pressed the soft and ample cushions of that gorgeous chair." But despite the support of Wise, Bell, and other vindictives, the Prentiss motion failed, and the resolution of thanks passed by an ample majority. Polk dispelled the effect of this attack by the good

83 *ibid.*, x, 65. 84 *ibid.*, x, 58.
85 Nashville *Republican Banner*, 4 Jan. 1839.

temper of his remarks of thanks. He valued the resolution the more, he said, because under the circumstances it was not just a meaningless formality.[86]

It was hard for the Polks to say goodbye to Washington and particularly hard for Sarah to give up the capital's active social life. Whig and Democratic ladies alike called to pay their parting respects, for the harsh controversies on Capitol Hill had not yet disrupted the drawing rooms. Sarah would miss most, however, the great men of the country, with their stimulating conversation and flattering compliments. The most precious memento of her leave-taking was the verse composed for the occasion by her fellow boarder at Elliott's, the scholarly Justice Joseph Story of the Supreme Court:

TO MRS. POLK ON HER LEAVING WASHINGTON

> Lady, I heard with saddened heart
>   The melancholy strain:
> So soon from these fair scenes to part
>   Ne'er to return again.
>
> How swift have flown the busy hours,
>   Since we as strangers met;
> And some so bright, so strewed with flowers,
>   Are fresh in memory yet.
>
> For I have listened to thy voice,
>   And watched thy playful mind,
> Truth in its noblest sense thy choice,
>   Yet gentle, graceful, kind.
>
> O, may thy future days be blest
>   With all our hearts approve;
> The sunshine of a spotless breast,
>   The joy of natural love.
>
> Farewell! And when thy distant home,
>   Cheered by thy smile shall be,
> And o'er the past thick fancies come,
>   I ask one thought of me.[87]

"Ne'er to return again"? How James and Sarah must have pondered this question as they boarded "the cars" for Baltimore and home.

[86] *Cong. Globe*:25:3, pp. 251-253; Nashville *Union*, 22 Mar. 1839.
[87] Nelson, *Sarah Polk*, 52-55.

11

TENNESSEE REDEEMED

POLK WAS GOING HOME TO ROUSE TENNESSEE. Consistently and almost unanimously Republican for the first four decades of its history, the state had now lain four years under the spell of White Whiggery. The defeats of 1835 and 1836 had utterly demoralized the Democracy, and the spirit of resistance had been kept alive mainly by the enthusiasm and energy of a single man, the harassed and heavily burdened speaker of the House. Somehow, in spite of the anxieties and responsibilities that pressed upon him during the hectic sessions of Congress in these years, Polk had found time to send a steady stream of speeches, newspapers, pamphlets, and letters of advice and exhortation over the mountains to Tennessee, while the summers saw him riding up and down the state, making speeches and prodding dispirited Democrats into action.

The disastrous defeat of 1837 had discredited the party leadership of Grundy and the Nashville Democrats, and caused Polk to emerge as the generally acknowledged chieftain of the Tennessee Democracy. The special session of 1837 took him out of the state immediately after the August election, but during the short congressional recess in October he rushed back—leaving Sarah to overtake him and making the trip in ten days—to set the Democratic house in order. His ascendancy in the party and its prospective revitalization were both indicated by the dinner given in his honor at Nashville, where prominent Democrats from all parts of the state had assembled for the meeting of the legislature.

Polk's hurried journey had not left him time to prepare a speech, but the infectious optimism of his extemporaneous talk banished the gloom and indifference that pervaded the party's ranks. At the same time he plotted the strategy the Democrats would follow in their march back to power. Polk took as his text a passage from Governor Cannon's recent message to the legislature. Having been reelected by a depression-generated reaction against the party in control at Washington, the governor had sought to solidify the existing party division by excoriating the "blighting effects" of the

Jacksonian monetary policies, "measures more pernicious and unholy than were ever known to be inflicted upon the people of a free and enlightened country." Even while the people were being made "to taste the bitter fruits of an experiment upon the currency," Cannon went on, "we are still threatened with another Experiment, in continuation of the same blind and infatuated policy."

Polk now demanded to know just what pernicious measures the governor meant, recalling that until 1835 all Tennessee politicians, including those now opposed to the Van Buren administration, had professed to favor Jackson's policies. In opposing policies they formerly professed to support, Polk argued, the "new born Whigs" of Tennessee were joining forces with those aristocrats, archconsolidationists, and Bank hirelings, Clay and Webster. This led him into his favorite topic, the descent of "modern Whiggery" from Federalism.

Polk reached the heart of his argument with the assertion that "our people are sternly Democratic and it is only necessary that they shall distinctly see the false position into which certain leading men in the State, who once professed the Democratic faith, but who have now deserted and are found in the Federal ranks, seek to place them, to induce them to act out their principles, and by an immense majority to adhere to their ancient and cherished political faith." This result, he assured his audience, was almost at hand. Since the August election, he pointed out, the White politicians had stopped claiming to be better Jackson men than the Van Burenites and "now for the first time fight under the Whig flag openly." Still more encouraging, the Tennessee Whigs were preparing to support Henry Clay, who was almost certain to be their candidate for president. "In such an issue," said Polk, "before a Democratic Republican people, such as the people of Tennessee are, there cannot be a doubt of the result."[1]

II

The immediate reason for Polk's haste to get back to Tennessee in the autumn of 1837 was his anxiety to save Grundy's Senate seat from the Whig legislature. John Bell and Ephraim Foster were both anxious to succeed Grundy, but the Democrats had raised a furor against electing a senator two years in advance of the vacancy

[1] Nashville *Union*, 14 Nov. 1837.

and were hoping to embarrass their opponents and perhaps stave off the election by supporting Major Andrew L. Martin, the State Rights Whig from the Western District. Polk had anxiously advised the Democratic legislators on strategy by mail, and he brought with him from Washington authority to withdraw Grundy's name or use it in any way that seemed desirable.

Prompt action enabled the Whigs to circumvent all Democratic strategems, and the election was over before Polk reached Nashville. Bell's friends made a strenuous effort, but the Foster men stood fast, and the Whigs finally united on the latter and elected him. The plan of luring Western District Whig votes away from Bell or Foster to Major Martin failed when Martin followed Calhoun into support of the independent treasury, and the Democrats gave their ineffectual votes to former Governor Carroll. But the Democrats were greatly encouraged by the divisions among their opponents and hoped to make political capital out of the legislature's precipitancy in bringing on the election.[2]

The Whigs were not yet through with Grundy. Resolutions were introduced instructing him to vote against the independent treasury, in the expectation that this would force him to resign. Polk had to hurry back to Washington before these resolutions were acted on, but he sent instructions to Maury's representative, A. O. P. Nicholson, to fight them off if possible. "If you find our opponents resolved to instruct on the Sub Treasury," Polk added, "goad them to an expression of opinion upon the Bank question, for that is what they mean." The disciplined Whig majority was not to be denied, however, and the resolutions passed without much trouble. Fortunately Grundy's vote was not needed on the independent treasury bill in the Senate, and he disappointed the Whigs by obeying the legislature's instructions, instead of resigning.[3]

Before leaving Tennessee, Polk had made another effort to rejuvenate the *Union* by employing a highly recommended Democratic editor from Louisville, Kentucky, Joshua Cunningham, to replace the ineffectual Bradford. Bradford retired willingly when Polk promised to secure him a chaplaincy in the navy, but the poor fellow

[2] Nashville *Republican Banner*, 13 Sept. 1837; J. O. Bradford to Polk, 2 Sept. [1837], James K. Polk Papers (LC; herein cited as Polk Papers, which refers to First Series unless otherwise noted); Polk to Nicholson, 9 Oct. 1837, *ibid.*; Grundy to Polk, 17 Oct. 1837, *ibid.*

[3] Polk to Nicholson, 13 Jan. 1838, copy, Polk Papers; Walker to Polk, 25 Jan. 1838, *ibid.*

was unable to regain the requisite ecclesiastical status in the Episcopal church, its governing committee being "all good and true Whigs . . . from whose tender mercies much cannot be expected for a Van Buren editor." Eventually a suitable federal job was found for him.[4]

Polk had also blueprinted a statewide organization for his party and persuaded the Democratic leaders to arrange a series of public meetings to drive home the points elaborated in his Nashville speech. During the winter he kept the mails full of express letters to Jackson, Donelson, Nicholson, and Walker, insisting that these plans be followed up. At the same time he was collecting lists of influential Democrats in all parts of the state and bombarding them with printed speeches and documents. To reinforce the faltering *Union*, he persuaded Frank Blair to issue a special weekly campaign edition of the *Globe* and set his friends at home to circulating it.

Donelson gave especially faithful support to Polk's plans, organizing the first of the public meetings at Nashville on the last day of 1837. A central committee was created, and the work of organizing county committees and county meetings was delegated to the Democratic members of the legislature. Polk's favorite theme, the identity of the "modern Whigs" with the old Federalists, was expounded by the Nashville meeting and echoed by subsequent county meetings in Cave Johnson's district and at Columbia and Shelbyville.[5]

Polk followed all these activities with the greatest solicitude from Washington. When the Whigs tried to break up the Columbia meeting, and Nicholson challenged Terry Cahal to a later debate on the independent treasury, Polk hurried off to Nicholson a detailed outline of the arguments he could use most effectively. The Shelbyville meeting was even more tumultuous than the one at Columbia. Designed to publicize the conversion to Van Burenism of two prominent Whigs, Doctor Joseph Kincaid, a veteran politician who was tired of fighting Polk, and Harvey M. Watterson, an extremely voluble and ambitious younger man, the affair was advertised as a meeting of those who had supported White because they agreed

[4] Bradford to Polk, 18 Dec. 1837, Polk Papers; S. Penn, Jr., to Donelson, 4 Nov. 1837, *ibid.*; Polk to Donelson, 10 Nov. 1837, *ibid.*; Walker to Polk, 7 Dec. 1837, *ibid.*; Van Buren to Jackson, 15 Apr. 1838, Martin Van Buren Papers (LC).

[5] Donelson to Polk, 28 Dec. 1837, 4, 24 Jan. 1838, Polk Papers; Carroll to Polk, 17 Feb. 1838, *ibid.*; Polk to Donelson, 3 Jan. 1838, Andrew Jackson Donelson Papers (LC; herein cited as Donelson Papers); *id.* to *id.*, 4 Feb. 1838, Andrew Jackson Papers (LC); Polk to Jackson, 7 Jan. 1838, typed copy, *ibid.*, Second Series.

with his Republican principles and who now wanted to compare the merits of Clay and Van Buren. After Watterson and Kincaid had lauded Van Buren for several hours, the Whigs began to clamor for a speech by one of their own leaders, and a riot ensued. Watterson and his followers adjourned to the street, where the day's events terminated in a scuffle between Watterson and one of the Whigs. Both sides, of course, claimed the victory.[6]

These signs of Democratic aggressiveness reflected not only Polk's prodding, but also a mounting optimism stemming partly from the passage of an ambitious banking, internal improvement, and education act by the legislature of 1837-1838. Introduced by Major Martin, this measure had been pushed through mainly by the efforts of Nicholson, Democratic leader in the house, and Josephus C. Guild, Democratic leader in the senate. Four million dollars in state bonds were to be issued, with which the state was to subscribe for half the stock of various railroad, turnpike, and river improvement companies. The interest on these bonds was to be paid by the earnings of a new state-owned and state-operated bank, whose five-million-dollar capital was to be furnished partly by the sale of additional state bonds. Besides carrying the internal improvement debt, the new bank was also to pay $100,000 a year for common schools and $18,000 for academies.

Though the division on this omnibus measure was more along sectional than party lines, the Democrats undoubtedly expected it to redound to their political benefit by easing the money shortage. When Polk expressed alarm at this extravagant new venture in paper money banking, James Walker assured him that it "is to have a fine effect for us," while Donelson urged him not to "be uneasy at what the Legislature will do on the subject of a new Bank." The Whigs saw at once what the Democrats were up to. "The object is to give the people money a plenty to stop their mouths on the subject of a National Bank," explained one of Congressman William B. Campbell's correspondents. "Two & a half millions are to be brought into the State for the Bank Capital & four million for Internal Improvements, by the Sale of State bonds. It is calculated that the influx of such a vast amount & its circulation among the people will so swell the tide of their prosperity that they

---

[6] Polk to Nicholson, 20 May 1838, Alfred O. P. Nicholson Papers (NYHS); S. P. Walker to Polk, 8 May 1838, Polk Papers; Nashville *Union*, 25 July, 1 Aug. 1838; Nashville *Republican Banner*, 22 Aug. 1838.

will forget the ills which the Van-tampering of the last four years has brought upon the country."[7]

In the meantime Polk had uncovered some striking corroboration for his charge that the White leaders were attempting to align Tennessee with the "Federal" Whigs of the North. While he was making his flying trip to Tennessee in October, John Bell had been touring the northern states. When Polk got back to Washington, he fortuitously fell in with Charles G. Green, editor of the Democratic Boston *Post*, who told him that Bell had been royally entertained and welcomed as a comrade in arms by the most dyed-in-the-wool Whigs in New York, Boston, Salem, Worcester, and Hartford.[8]

Feverishly collecting accounts of Bell's visits to these places, Polk kept the Tennessee Democratic press filled for weeks with Bell's doings and sayings among the "violent and malignant federalists" of the North. Polk's editors took care to point out that many of Bell's hosts had been associated with the disunionist Hartford Convention during the War of 1812, while "Tennessee furnished a General and her proportion of soldiers, who at New Orleans acquired deathless renown, by beating off an invading foe, and achieving for their country a victory unsurpassed in the annals of history." Bell had been welcomed at Salem, Tennessee readers were told, by "the most devoted disciples of the HARTFORD CONVENTION school." Presented in Boston's Faneuil Hall by none other than Daniel Webster, he had told a cheering crowd of "Hartford Convention federalists" that "Tennessee is in principle with Massachusetts." At Worcester "a Hartford Convention federalist of the first water" had introduced him. And in Hartford itself, where his audience included the secretary of the Hartford Convention, Bell was reported as declaring that he and they were "united in the same great cause." Though Tennessee and Connecticut were separated by a great distance, he had continued, "we tender to you the hand of friendship and alliance, and receive you as members of the great political family."[9]

As the final link in the chain of evidence for "stripping Mr. Bell

---

[7] Walker to Polk, 31 Dec. 1837, Polk Papers; Donelson to Polk, 4 Jan. 1838, *ibid.*; Abraham Caruthers to W. B. Campbell, 28 Jan. 1838, David Campbell Papers (DU); James Campbell to David Campbell, 8 Jan. 1838, *ibid.*; Nashville *Union*, 23 Dec. 1837.

[8] Polk to Donelson, 13, 18 Dec. 1837, Donelson Papers; C. G. Greene to Polk, 26 Dec. 1837, 10, 18, 23, 23 Jan. 1838, Polk Papers.

[9] Nashville *Union*, 28 Dec. 1837, 15, 22 Feb. 1838.

of his mask," Polk dug up a speech by a prominent Pennsylvania Federalist-turned-Whig, who boasted that the "Federalists were again coming into power." Not content with circulating these materials through the newspapers, Polk had his friends at Nashville print them in pamphlet form for distribution in all the counties.[10]

This Democratic propaganda was well timed, for it coincided with indications that the Tennessee Whigs were, as charged, about to support Henry Clay for president in 1840. During the winter Bell began privately preparing his Tennessee associates for this move, only to be embarrassed by the precipitancy of some of his allies. When the Bell interests consolidated their two Nashville newspapers into the *Republican Banner* under Allen Hall's editorship, the more militantly probusiness group that supported Ephraim Foster had established a new Nashville paper, the *Whig*. In Memphis, which was becoming a major cotton-shipping center, similar interests launched the *Enquirer*. Shortly after the election of 1837 these two papers had come out openly for the Kentucky statesman, which forced the hand of the more politically sensitive Bell wing of the party. When the Nashville *Whig* brashly ran up the Clay flag, Bell's more cautious *Banner* was forced to admit that in a contest between Van Buren and Clay, Clay would clearly be preferable. By the summer of 1838 most of the Whig leaders and newspapers were backing Clay unequivocally, and in August Bell persuaded Judge White to withdraw his own pretensions and endorse the Kentuckian publicly.[11]

These developments produced a decided reaction. Several Whig newspapers, mostly in the cotton-planting Western District, declared against Clay. Major Martin's State Rights faction began to lose its enthusiasm for Whiggery, and its newspaper organ, the Jackson *District Telegraph*, denounced the Clay movement. "The truth is Van is gaining in the District rapidly and daily," wrote one former White supporter. "Since Calhoun pulled off his hat and bid good bye to the Northern Whigs, all the Nullifiers who were the bitterest enemies of the administration has changed their abuse and villification into total silence in relation to Van but acknowledge quite frankly they cannot go for Clay or Webster. . . . There never

10 Polk to Jackson, 7 Jan. 1838, typed copy, Jackson Papers, Second Series; Donelson to Polk, 24 Jan. 1838, Polk Papers.

11 F. S. Latham to Clay, 4 Dec. 1837, Henry Clay Papers (LC; herein cited as Clay Papers); Bell to R. L. Caruthers, 17 Mar. 1838, Robert L. Caruthers Papers (SHC); Nashville *Union*, 18 July, 27 Aug., 5 Sept. 1838.

was such a time since Judge White has been defeated for Van's friends to organize a powerful and energetic party and such as would beat Clay and Webster easily."[12]

III

Tennessee's congressmen reached home in the first week of August 1838, and Polk, though "much fatigued and broken down" by his journey, immediately threw all his energies behind the promising political reaction. Three days after his arrival he made a "*war* speech against all Banks" at Lewisburg. Many former White supporters in that area were already "open and loud in opposition to Clay," while others were still on the fence, and Polk's main object was "to cause the latter to alight on the right side." Accordingly he bore down on the theme that "Clay was as certainly the Whig candidate, as though the proposed Convention of '39 had met and had already nominated him."[13]

Regarding Polk as their most dangerous foe, the Whigs tried to pooh-pooh the Lewisburg meeting as "rather a cold-water business." Indeed, long before he resumed the stump in Tennessee, they had recognized Polk as a major source of the renewed Democratic vitality, and for months the Whig press had been concentrating on him a constant stream of partisan vilification.[14] This fear of Polk also explains the scurrilous speech that brought on Bell's collision with Hopkins L. Turney in the House.

A week after the Lewisburg meeting Polk vindicated himself in a speech to an immense crowd at Shelbyville. The only reason for the attacks on him, he said, was that "I have had the temerity stubbornly to refuse to betray the old-fashioned Republican constituents whom I represent, and basely to attempt with covert, selfish and concealed designs, to transfer them, with their principles, to the embraces of their Federal opponents." He then turned to answer Bell's charge that he was "alike destitute of private honor and public principle." "Public principle!" snorted Polk. "A man who has notoriously abandoned and deserted every 'public principle' and

12 Adam Huntsman to Polk, 1 Jan. 1838, Polk Papers; Charles E. Pool, "The Rise of the Whig Party in West Tennessee, 1834-1843," M.A. thesis, University of Mississippi (1950), 65-67.

13 Nashville *Union*, 23 Sept. 1838; Nashville *Republican Banner*, 11 Aug. 1838; Polk to Jackson, 7 Aug. 1838, Jackson Papers; H. B. Kelsey to Polk, 24 July 1838, Polk Papers.

14 Nashville *Republican Banner*, 16 Mar., 26 Apr., 11 Aug. 1838.

political association of his former life, and is now found acting with his former political opponents; and not only opposing, but denouncing the men and measures he but the other day professed zealously to support, has the unblushing effrontery to become a public lecturer on 'public principle.' A man whose double dealing in politics had become notorious, talks of 'public principle.' " Going remorselessly through Bell's entire political career, Polk showed that up to 1835 he had without exception supported all the Democratic measures he now denounced.

And what are Bell's present "public principles"? Polk asked. Does he still oppose federal internal improvements? Would he still vote against a national bank? What are his present "public principles" on Clay's American System? Finally—and here Polk furnished a new weapon to the Democratic arsenal—"What are his opinions on the course of Mr. Adams, Mr. Slade, Mr. Clay himself, and a large portion of the party he has recently joined, upon the subject of Abolition? Does he think Mr. Grundy and myself, and our political friends North and South, with whom we act, destitute of 'public principle,' because we oppose the fanatical, wicked and dangerous agitation of this delicate question, in the public discussions in Congress? Does he not know that the Abolitionists constitute a branch of the Federal or modern Whig party to which he has recently joined himself, and with whom he now acts in general opposition to the Administration of Mr. Van Buren? Does Mr. Bell condemn the course of these fanatical and wicked agitators?" If so, asked Polk triumphantly, why had he failed to vote for the gag rule? Obviously, he insinuated, for fear that "he might offend a large number of the new political friends at the North whom he had recently joined."

In conclusion Polk rang all the changes on Bell's fraternization with the Whigs of New England, insisting that his assurances to them left no doubt of his present "public principles."

Here is "public principle," declared to the Hartford Convention Federalists. They are told that there is "a cordial sympathy of mind, of understanding and of *feeling*" between *us* (the people of Tennessee,) and *them*; that *we* are "identified in the same cause" with *them*; that *"we have been united for years;"* that "we are *battling side by side with them;"* the *"hand of friendship and alliance"* is tendered to them as *"members of the same great political family;"* and they are told that the *"only practical reform"* is to turn out the present Republican incumbent of the Presidential chair, and elect some other "upon whom we may mutually agree;" that is to say, a Federalist, one whose "public principles" would accord with those of himself and his audience. What say the people of Tennessee to this open pledge and transfer of their "public principles" and suffrages, made by Mr. Bell to the Federalists of Hartford.[15]

Between speeches Polk was carrying on some important negotiations to strengthen the party. Before leaving Washington he had commissioned his kinsman John H. Bills of Bolivar to go to Jackson, in the Western District, and sound out the leaders of the State Rights faction on a fusion with the Democracy. Bills' report was waiting when Polk reached home. "I find them & the press at that place decidedly and openly with us, opposed to Mr. Clay heart and soul," wrote Polk's emissary. "Martin & all his party are uproarious against Mr. Clay & now for Van Buren." These new allies, continued Bills, insisted only that a vigorous campaign be waged, with the strongest possible candidates brought out for governor, for Congress, and for the legislature.[16]

Though the August 1839 election was still a year away, there had already been much discussion of which Democrat should run for what office, and some prompt decisions would be necessary to insure united action. Grundy's appointment as Van Buren's attorney general had just been announced, and he was about to leave for Washington. In the middle of August, a few days before his departure, Polk rode up to Nashville for an important consultation with the state's Democratic leaders.

IV

Ever since his reelection the previous August, Polk had been perplexed about his political future. He had now gone as far as he could go in the House, and the slightest Whig gain in the next congressional election would subject him to a galling defeat for the speakership at the hands of John Bell. During the winter it had been rumored around Columbia that Polk would not run again for Congress. He may have expected a Cabinet appointment, but he was definitely beginning to be tantalized by the possibility of securing the Democratic vice presidential nomination in 1840. The latter prospect had been planted in the mind of Polk's Nashville editor, Bradford, by December 1837, and it was hardly without Polk's knowledge that his intimate friend and messmate Judge Catron

---

[15] Nashville *Union*, 7 Sept. 1838.
[16] J. H. Bills to Polk, 1, 25 Aug. 1838, Polk Papers.

wrote to Jackson on the subject from Washington the following month.

It was Catron who had unsuccessfully warned against making Colonel Richard M. Johnson, he of the red vest and mulatto daughters, Van Buren's running mate in 1836. With the Democrats becoming more dependent on southern support, and with the South becoming more sensitive on the slavery question, Catron now argued, it would be unthinkable to nominate Colonel Johnson again. The candidate must come from a slaveholding state, and since Van Buren was a New Yorker, second place on the ticket should go to a man from the West. Among southwestern Democrats, Catron maintained, Polk was the obvious choice. "Never have we had such a speaker to the crowd; nor have we a man of so much energy, or character; nor from Ky. South is there so aceptable [*sic*] a man individually to the Democratic party," declared the judge. "He is good for six states—nay sir for South Carolina, I think also, strange as it may seem. His Station as Speaker has quieted asperity—has drawn to him a weight far above any other man." Catron clinched his argument by appealing to Old Hickory's passionate desire to see Tennessee back in the Democratic fold. "Our state follows men," he shrewdly pointed out, "is clanish [*sic*], has no very strongly fixed creeds, and to a certainty can only be carried by the means of a local candidate." Jackson apparently gave the project his blessing, though he declined for the time being Catron's plea that he urge it on Van Buren.[17]

Polk had already been forced to reveal his hopes to one of his lieutenants. The reports that Polk would not run again for Congress had excited the always lively ambition of A. O. P. Nicholson, and early in January 1838 Nicholson had sent Polk an urgent letter saying that his private affairs made it virtually necessary for him to retire from politics. But, he continued, if Polk were to be the vice presidential candidate, he would feel duty-bound to aid the party by running to succeed Polk in Congress. "Will you be the candidate of our party for Vice President?" he asked point-blank. And, "If not will you again run for Congress?"[18]

Polk's reply from Washington was carefully phrased. As to the vice presidency, he declared that Colonel Johnson would have to be

17 Catron to Jackson, 4 Jan. 1838, Jackson Papers; J. O. Bradford to Polk, 18 Dec. [1837], Polk Papers.
18 Nicholson to Polk, 7 Jan. 1838, Polk Papers.

replaced, and that his replacement would have to come from a south-western state. But, said Polk, it would be imprudent "*at this time*, to agitate the question *here*." He was not ready to commit himself definitely about his future course. There had been some talk of his running for governor in 1839, but Carroll seemed interested in running also, and the matter was not yet settled. For the moment he wanted to be considered a candidate for reelection to Congress. He promised, however, that if he did run, it would be the last time, and urged Nicholson not to think of leaving politics. "I know of no man of your age," he said, "who has so fair or so bright prospects before him, *if you remain where you are*."

At the same time, Polk intimated adroitly that, though it would be unwise to press the vice presidential question in Washington, much would depend on expressions of opinion in the Southwest. The first suggestion should not come from Tennessee, but from Missis-sippi or Alabama. "You can think on this," Polk concluded sig-nificantly, "and act upon your better judgement [*sic*] in this respect."[19]

Walker, too, was set to stirring up Polk sentiment in the other southwestern states, and these efforts had begun to bear fruit in February, when the Florence, Alabama, *Gazette* proposed Polk as the Democratic vice presidential nominee. Soon a Democratic news-paper at Harrisburg, Pennsylvania, endorsed Polk, while additional support came from papers in New England, Ohio, Michigan, and South Carolina. Polk and the Tennesseans, however, carefully main-tained a noncommittal pose. "Mr. Polk is undoubtedly well qualified for the office," said the *Union* in reprinting the Florence editorial, "but we consider any movement in relation to the subject premature at present." And in Washington Polk guarded his intentions so suc-cessfully that one of his closest congressional friends suspected that he was pushing Grundy for second place on the 1840 ticket.[20]

Polk's real dilemma during the winter of 1837-1838 was whether to retain his secure congressional seat or to run for governor in furtherance of his vice presidential ambitions. At first he inclined to the safer plan of remaining in Congress, for late in January Walker was urging Carroll to offer for governor, and it was Polk's Shelbyville newspaper that in March first proposed Carroll publicly.

19 Polk to Nicholson, 13 Jan. 1838, copy, Polk Papers.
20 Nashville *Union*, 22 Feb. 1838; Walker to Polk, 7 Feb. 1838, Polk Papers; R. H. Gillet to Polk, 1 July 1838, *ibid*.

When the *Union*, under the influence of Donelson, who had lost all patience with Carroll, threw cold water on the Carroll movement, it was Polk's Columbia *Democrat* that came to his defense. Carroll was formally nominated by a Democratic meeting in Cave Johnson's district, and the nomination was promptly seconded by a meeting of the Maury Democrats. It is not difficult to see Polk's hand in these developments.[21]

By June, however, heavy pressure was being put on Polk to run himself, and he was beginning to find the idea attractive. Alfred Balch reported that Carroll "has lost his voice and cannot stump it," while other friends pointed out that the redemption of Tennessee would give Polk great claims on the party nationally. But getting Carroll out of the race was a delicate operation. The matter dragged on through the summer, and it was the principal item on the agenda when the state's Democratic leaders met in August, just before Grundy's departure to take up his new Cabinet duties.[22]

The leaders' decision did not become public for nearly two weeks. Meanwhile John H. Bills sounded out the Western District Nullifiers on Polk's candidacy for governor and received a favorable response. Then Polk began preparing a speech and making other important arrangements for a public dinner to which he had been invited at Murfreesboro on Tuesday, August 30.[23]

The widely advertised Murfreesboro dinner attracted some 2,000 people to a pleasant grove just outside the town. Polk climbed on to the speaker's stand promptly at noon, and spoke for two hours. There were few new themes he could introduce, but new emphases were creeping into his treatment of the old ones. The "federal" project of "building up a splendid and extravagant government," which Polk had been denouncing for years on other grounds, now began to take on a sectional character. Such a government, Polk argued, "threw the burden of raising the supplies on the south, and aggrandized the north by lavish expenditures for a system of internal improvements, extravagant appropriations for the construction of artificial harbors, and an immense system of fortifications."

21 Walker to Polk, 25 Jan. 1838, Polk Papers; Nashville *Republican Banner*, 29 Mar. 1838; Nashville *Union*, 31 Mar., 7 Apr., 14 May 1838.

22 Balch to Polk, 15 June 1838, Polk Papers; Johnson to Polk, 1 June 1838, *ibid.*; W. S. Haynes to Polk, 24 July 1838, *ibid.*; H. S. Turney to Polk, 30 July 1838, *ibid.*; Nashville *Republican Banner*, 18 Aug. 1838.

23 J. H. Bills to Polk, 25 Aug. 1838, Polk Papers; Nashville *Republican Banner*, 1 Sept. 1838.

The White movement and the emergence of a Tennessee Whig party he cleverly interpreted as a plot to deceive the people into supporting this odious scheme. The plot was bound to fail, said Polk, because "the farmers and mechanics had no other object in view than the good of the country, and all they required to put them right was a clearer comprehension of the present attitude of parties." This "clearer comprehension" Polk was resolved to give them.

The body of his speech was an argumentative defense of Van Buren and the independent treasury. On the subject of banks and their paper money "trash," Polk hardly sounded like the same man who had defended the deposit system so vigorously in 1834-1835. "What claims have the stockholders of the banks to the use of the public money gratis?" he asked. "The merchants own the principal portion of the bank stock of the country, and are the principal borrowers from the banks—they borrow the public money from the deposite banks in which they are stockholders, and receive in dividends on their stock what they pay in interest on their loans, while the poor tax payer not only reaps no benefit from the operation, but may be doubly taxed, to supply the deficiency created by the refusal of the banks to refund the revenue deposited with them." In closing he could not resist another cut at Bell's fellowship with the "old blue lights" of New England. "Though others had deserted their principles and abandoned their party," Polk declared, "he would fall, if fall he must, with his flag flying and his face to the foe."

Their comprehensions clarified, the hungry voters now descended on the tables nearby to dispatch "forty fat sheep, forty fine shoats, six beeves, three hundred pounds of fine ham, and bread and vegetables without limit." Having washed down this solid fare with "the generous juice of the grape, whisky, and old cogniac [*sic*]," the crowd returned to the speaker's stand. The toasts were the only remaining item on the program, but the day's biggest sensation was still to come.

Governor Carroll had arrived unexpectedly while Polk was speaking, and when the arrangements committee presented a toast endorsing him for governor, he was called on for a speech. After thanking the sons of Rutherford County for their unwavering support, both in war and in the more recent political strife, Carroll made a stunning announcement. He was in poor health "arising from exposure in the late war," he said, and for this reason "and various others" he could not be a candidate.

How unexpected was Carroll's announcement? Apparently the Democratic leaders had agreed at Nashville two weeks before that he should be eliminated from the race, and perhaps they had only now persuaded him to withdraw and hurried him off to Murfreesboro for that purpose. At any rate, a few minutes after Carroll's declaration, the arrangements committee was ready with a toast calling on Polk to be a candidate for governor. Polk promptly rose, professing surprise and dismay at having the question so unexpectedly presented. He expressed regret at the decision of "that 'war-worn veteran' whose feeble frame and declining health gave evidence that he was now suffering the effects of his early toils and privations in his country's service." But, Polk continued, it had been feared for some time that Carroll could not run, and many friends had urged him to be ready to step into the breach. He had reflected on his duty, and his mind was made up. Cheers broke out as he announced that he was a candidate for governor of Tennessee.[24]

V

The enthusiastic reaction to Polk's announcement spread rapidly through the ranks of the Tennessee Democracy. No other man had a chance to reverse the heavy Whig majorities of the past four years, and if Polk could not, the Democrats might well resign themselves to a permanent minority status in Old Hickory's own state. Polk's personal fortunes were also hanging on the outcome. He had exchanged the security of a safe seat in Congress for the hazards of a statewide election, but he was risking his political life for higher stakes than the governorship.

Ever since Doctor McDowell's operation had worked its miraculous transformation, Polk had driven himself to overcome his boyhood sense of inadequacy. Politics was the field in which he had sought self-satisfaction, and politics had become his whole life, aside from which he had no aspirations, intellectual interests, recreations, or even friendships. His wife and family constituted the only break in this almost total commitment of his personality. Behind his matter-of-fact exterior Polk harbored an insatiable appetite for the political success without which his life would lose its meaning.

Other politicians have been inordinately ambitious, but Polk was ambitious with a difference. Lacking intellectual brilliance and great

24 Nashville *Union*, 3 Sept. 1838.

personal magnetism, he drove himself ruthlessly, exploiting the abilities and energies he did possess to an extent that few men ever equal. His good judgment and self-control, moreover, kept his ambition from getting out of hand and damaging his career. In political combat he remained cool and calculating, unruffled by the taunts of his enemies and ever ready to take advantage of mistakes they made in the heat of conflict. At the same time he prided himself on his consistency, eschewing opportunism on grounds of both conviction and long-range expediency. He could wait and work patiently for his opportunities, but when they came, he pursued them with a furious energy that often brought success where other, and perhaps abler, men would have failed.

When Polk resolved to run for governor, therefore, he laid out for himself a campaign the like of which Tennessee had never seen. During September he planned to cover Middle Tennessee, starting with a dinner at Fayetteville only a week after the Murfreesboro announcement. Fayetteville's biggest crowd since a visit by Jackson thirteen years before turned out to greet Polk, but he was already pressing against the limits of his endurance and was so weak that much of the audience was unable to hear him. He was forced to spend the rest of the month, except for an appearance at Franklin, recruiting his strength for an invasion of the crucial Western District during October.[25]

Polk was particularly concerned about the Western District, for here the Whig defections were most numerous, and here the Democrats hoped to make their biggest gains. He had to make his annual visit to the new Mississippi plantation before returning to Washington, and he planned it to coincide with his political tour. Leaving home on September 24 in the middle of a burning drought, he made speeches at Pulaski, Jackson, Brownsville, Covington, and Raleigh on the way to Mississippi; disposed of his plantation business in a flying ten-day trip; and spoke on his return journey at Somerville, Bolivar, Huntington, Paris, and Dresden. Nearly 4,000 people attended the meeting at Jackson, the largest town in the section and the center of the State Rights shift to the Democratic ranks. The Nullifier leader, Major Andrew L. Martin, whose senatorial aspirations Polk seems to have encouraged, formally announced his support for Polk and Van Buren, while Polk followed up this advantage in

25 *ibid.*, 23 Sept., 3 Oct. 1838.

all his speeches by stressing that Clay would be the Whigs' next presidential candidate. There was a little excitement at Huntington, where Polk crossed the trail of John Bell, who was also making speeches through the Western District. Bell's friends boasted that he would drive Polk from the platform, but he stayed in his tavern until Polk had left town.[26]

The Democrats were jubilant over the enthusiasm aroused by Polk's tour. From Amos Kendall, who was visiting at the Hermitage, President Van Buren learned that the state was "in the midst of revolution." "Mr. Polk is rousing up the people," said Kendall, "and pouring floods of light among them in relation to men and things." The Whigs, on the other hand, were dismayed by this persuasive candidate who was so tirelessly riding over the state trying "*to polk* Van Burenism down the throats of our citizens." "The democracy in this State is dying a violent death and Mr. Polk is dispatched as a Democratic physician extraordinary with violent palliatives and a new batch of nostrums from the loco foco laboratory at Washington," declared the Memphis *Enquirer*. "But our people will not swallow them. They have been physicked and operated on by the quacks of the Jackson System until they can hardly stand nor can they be persuaded by Mr. Polk that the hair of the dog is good for the bite."[27]

Try as they might to reassure themselves, however, the Whig editors were worried by "the rattling harangues of the defunct speaker," with his "considerable fund of electioneering tact and trickery."[28] One panicky Whig paper was driven to warning its readers, just before Polk visited the area, not to be seduced:

Do not be led captive by the wiles of the enemy. Jas. K. Polk is an artful, cunning, intriguing man. He will talk *soft* words to you; he has a smooth tongue; but, mind, he is a snake in the grass; he will steal around you and win you away ere you are apprised of it. . . . He will shake hands with you, he will talk friendly and polite to you, get you to say you will vote for him, then persuade you to electioneer for him, and is your best friend and the cleverest fellow on earth; but all this he does while he cares nothing for you; he only wants your votes and your influence. He will go

[26] Polk to Jackson, 23 Sept. 1838, Jackson Papers; Polk to Armstrong, 29 Oct. 1838, *ibid.*; Nashville *Union*, 8, 10 Oct. 1838; Pool, "Whig Party in W. Tenn.," 68-70.

[27] Kendall to Van Buren, 20 Oct. 1838, Van Buren Papers; Paris *West Tennessean*, 19 Oct. 1838; Memphis *Enquirer*, 29 Sept. 1838, quoted in Robert H. White, ed., *Messages of the Governors of Tennessee* (Nashville, 1952-), III, 271.

[28] Memphis *Enquirer*, 20 Oct. 1838, quoted in *ibid.*, III, 272.

home, get among his congressmen of his party, and laugh about it, he will tell how he duped you, that he made you believe he was a good sociable fellow, a patriot, and all this thing.[29]

Polk had hardly a week to rest from his long, hot journey over the dusty roads of West Tennessee and Mississippi. It was time to return to Washington for his last session in the House, and he had planned his route so that he could make speeches through Middle and East Tennessee. The drought broke about the time he left home, and constant rain and cold made the trip thoroughly unpleasant.

Elaborate preparations, including a band and free barbecue, had been made for Polk's appearance at Island Springs outside Nashville, but he had no sooner started speaking than it began to rain. A recess was declared for a soggy dinner, and some of the crowd melted away. To add insult to injury the speaker's stand collapsed when Polk climbed back up, at the insistence of a band of loyal Democrats, to resume his speech; but undismayed by the circumstances, he talked for an hour and a half under a steady downpour. For the next three weeks he spoke at least every other day while making his way slowly over the Cumberland plateau and through East Tennessee.[30]

After all this Polk's duties as speaker might have seemed almost restful had he not been compelled to devote much of his energy to preparing for the coming summer's campaign. If he expected to be elected, he would have to oversee personally every phase of the Democratic campaign, and many matters had to be attended to at once.

One of the biggest problems was securing strong congressional candidates. Polk had got some of the districts in good shape before leaving home. Sarah's cousin William G. Childress had consented to run to succeed Abram Maury in the Franklin-Murfreesboro district, and Nicholson had announced as the candidate for Polk's seat. The Fayetteville-Pulaski district, south of Maury, caused him more trouble. Colonel A. A. Kincannon had announced as a Democratic candidate, but he had been beaten badly by Shields, the Whig incumbent, two years before, and Polk was anxious to have his old friend Aaron Brown in the field. He had finally got Kincannon to withdraw by persuading Brown to resign his job as federal Indian agent and arranging to have Kincannon appointed in his place.

[29] Paris *West Tennessean*, 19 Oct. 1838.
[30] Nashville *Union*, 5, 12 Nov. 1838; Nashville *Republican Banner*, 30 Oct. 1838.

During the winter the Democrats were alarmed by a report that Kincannon's job was about to be abolished, which would bring him back into the race. "If Kincannon's office is to be made void," wrote one man frantically to Polk, "for gods sake have him provided for so as to keep him out of the way." Whether by Polk's intervention or otherwise, Kincannon was kept "out of the way," leaving the field to Brown.[31]

Many other districts were still up in the air, and Polk had to undertake the necessary arrangements by correspondence from Washington. Discouraged by his defeat two years before, the formidable Cave Johnson was reluctant to make another fight. He had just married his childhood sweetheart, recently widowed after many years of marriage to another man, and he feared that spending the winters in Washington would bring back his old rheumatic affliction. In the end, however, the loyal Johnson was induced to take the stump. About the same time, Polk's kinsmen in the Bolivar district got another old friend, William C. Dunlap, into the race.[32]

In January trouble erupted in the quarter where it was least expected, Polk's own district. Abruptly and without consulting the Democrats, Nicholson declared that he was quitting politics to enter a law partnership with Terry Cahal, the most dangerous Whig in Maury. Apparently with the connivance of Nicholson and by a combination of misunderstanding and design, Harvey M. Watterson, the recent convert from Whiggery, was promptly announced as the new Democratic candidate. Watterson was unpopular with many Democrats; there were other men more deserving of promotion; and his precipitate announcement caused one disgruntled Bedford Democrat to announce also and begin appealing for Whig votes. Polk urged his friends to get Watterson to withdraw in favor of some stronger Democrat; but these efforts failed, and the party was forced to take him as its candidate.[33]

The district Polk was most concerned about was John Bell's. Next to his own success, his most cherished wish was the downfall of his hated enemy. Moreover, if Bell were unopposed for reelection, he would be free to harry Polk all over the state in the gubernatorial

[31] J. B. Clements to Polk, 11 Feb. 1839, Polk Papers; Nashville *Republican Banner*, 27 Feb., 31 July 1839.

[32] Johnson to Polk, 28 Nov. [1837], 28 Aug. 1838, Polk Papers; James Ross, *Life and Times of Elder Reuben Ross* (Philadelphia, n.d.), 266.

[33] Dr. J. B. Hays to Polk, 11 Jan. [1839; misplaced 1835], 7 Feb. 1839, Polk Papers; E. J. Frierson to Polk, 1 Feb. 1839, *ibid.*

canvass. As early as September, Polk had spurred Jackson and General Armstrong to get Jackson's kinsman Robert M. Burton into the race against Bell, but Burton had been reluctant to give up his lucrative law practice. The Democrats then shifted their entreaties to General Carroll. He seemed willing to run, but complained about his rheumatism and for months refused to commit himself. By the end of January they had given up the Carroll project in disgust and at Polk's instance were applying heavier pressure on Burton. Finally, after Jackson enlisted Mrs. Burton's aid and virtually commanded him to enter the race, the reluctant Burton consented to be a candidate. But by this time it was April, and the long delay made the uphill battle against the entrenched Bell all the more difficult.[34]

Just as important as getting strong candidates was the old but still-unsolved problem of the Nashville *Union*. Unfortunately Cunningham had been no improvement over Bradford. He was, according to Amos Kendall, "a perfect marplot, having no common sense and being a rowdy to boot." Polk had renewed his search for an able, fearless editor the previous spring, enlisting the aid of sundry prominent Democrats. But all the men Polk approached ended by declining to move to Nashville, and he had gone home in the summer of 1838 still without an editor.[35]

The problem of the *Union* was uppermost in his mind, therefore, when he returned to Washington in December 1838, to be met by word of still another prospect, a Jeremiah George Harris, who had edited a Democratic weekly in New Bedford, Massachusetts, and George Bancroft's *Bay State Democrat* in Boston. In response to Polk's urgent summons, Harris reached Washington on Christmas Day and made an extremely favorable impression on the speaker. Polk, Grundy, and Catron put such pressure on him—even enlisting the president to reinforce their entreaties—that he accepted, and they immediately hurried him off to Nashville, where he took charge of the *Union* on February 1. Harris quickly fulfilled all Polk's ex-

[34] Armstrong to Polk, 22 Sept. 1838, 6 Feb. [1839], Polk Papers; Polk to Jackson, 2 Sept. 1838, typed copy, Jackson Papers, Second Series; Carroll to Jackson, 14 Dec. 1838, Blair-Lee Papers (PU); Jackson to Van Buren, 2 May 1839, Van Buren Papers.

[35] Kendall to Blair, 7 Nov. 1838, Blair-Lee Papers; Polk to Donelson, 26 Mar., 8, 18, 29 May 1838, Donelson Papers; Van Buren to Jackson, 29 Apr. 1838, Van Buren Papers; letters to Polk from Philo White, Dr. J. L. Martin, Edwin Croswell, Isaac Hill, Henry Hubbard, J. J. Gilchrist, Edmund Burke, James Page, S. S. Southworth, dated June-Sept. 1838, Polk Papers.

pectations. The Whigs were soon in dread of his slashing pen, and under his editorship the *Union* became a powerful asset to the Democrats in the campaign of 1839.[36]

Polk also arranged for the financing of a new Democratic paper, the *Argus*, at Knoxville, and secured another young New England Democratic journalist, E. G. Eastman, to edit it. The return of the State Rights faction to the Democracy in the Western District had brought Polk an effective editorial champion in the Jackson *District Telegraph*, and this support was reinforced when another group of State Rights Democrats launched the Memphis *Western World* in January 1839. Thus for the first time the Democrats had an effective statewide organ and strong regional papers in the eastern and western sections, while the number of local Democratic weeklies was also growing.

VI

The most important part of Polk's preparation for the coming campaign was devising a platform for the rejuvenated Democracy. All winter long he worked on a closely printed, twenty-eight-page address to the voters outlining the issues he wanted to emphasize. Distributed by the thousands in the spring, Polk's pamphlet indicated that he would wage the campaign mainly on national issues. Most of it was given over to familiar themes—the genealogy of Federal-Whiggery, the great reforms of the Jackson administration and Polk's consistent support of these reforms, the apostasy of Bell and company, the current Whig plot to deliver Tennessee to Henry Clay, the iniquities of national and state banks, the merits of the independent treasury, and the sterling republicanism of Martin Van Buren. Less than three of the twenty-eight pages concerned state issues, for there were few questions of state policy on which either of the parties had clear-cut positions.

Governor Newton Cannon had assumed all along that he would carry the Whig colors against Polk, despite his unpopularity with some segments of the Whig party. During the winter there were reports of efforts to make him give way to Judge White or John Bell, Bell confiding to Henry Clay that "Our Gov. Cannon is too sluggish

36 C. G. Greene to J. C. Rives, 3 Dec. 1838, Polk Papers; J. G. Harris to George Bancroft, 26 Dec. 1838, George Bancroft Papers (MHS); Polk to Donelson, 3 Jan. 1839, Donelson Papers.

and self sufficient, or we might do better." But Cannon refused to be forced out, and the Whigs had to make the best of him.[37]

Cannon's strict construction of the sweeping internal improvement law of 1838 had gained him many enemies. The governor had insisted that the private stockholders in improvement companies should actually subscribe their entire half of the capital before he would issue bonds for the state's half. Many railroad and turnpike speculators were thus frustrated in their hopes of building their projects mainly on state capital and were correspondingly alienated from Cannon.

Some ingenious speculators, however, still saw a way to capitalize on the state's funds. James Walker was the moving spirit in one such enterprise, the Central Turnpike Company, which was chartered to build a toll road from Columbia to the Tennessee River. He and his associates promptly borrowed $150,000 to subscribe their half of the capital and called on the governor for the state's half. As Walker explained the scheme to Polk, "We calculate that by purchasing the negroes ourselves, we can build the road with the State Stock, have the negroes left and a town on the Tennessee river which will be second to Nashville in the State, and clear our own stock." When Cannon refused to issue the state bonds on this basis, Walker and other promoters pinned their hopes on electing a more cooperative governor.[38]

Cannon's half-hearted support of the ambitious project for a railroad from the Ohio River to Charleston by way of East Tennessee had also alienated this enterprise's strong following in the Knoxville area, including many of Judge White's influential friends. Some of these men, most notably Doctor J. G. M. Ramsey, now became open supporters of Polk.

In capitalizing on this anti-Cannon sentiment, however, Polk had to be extremely cautious. He was no more willing than Cannon to plunge the state into extravagant or unsound projects, or to lend its credit to speculators. Moreover public opinion was beginning to turn against the improvement program, especially in Middle Ten-

---

[37] Bell to Clay, 20 May 1839, Clay Papers; Catron to Polk, 27 Oct. [1838; misplaced 1835], Polk Papers; Armstrong to Polk, 8 Nov. [1838; misplaced 1839], *ibid.*; J. C. Guild to Polk, 24 Jan. 1839, *ibid.*

[38] Walker to Polk, 2 May 1838, Polk Papers; J. G. M. Ramsey to Polk, 5 Jan. 1839, *ibid.*; J. H. Dew to R. L. Caruthers, 23 Apr. 1838, Robert L. Caruthers Papers (SHC).

nessee, which by now had built up a good network of turnpikes and was disinclined to support projects for the other sections.

Polk's address, therefore, was rather equivocal on the subject. He expatiated at length on the benefits the state would derive from improved transportation, but the "liberal system" which he endorsed was "such a system which at the same time it is liberal, shall not be visionary, extravagant or wasteful; such a system as would not burthen the people with onerous taxation, or incur an unreasonable public responsibility in its accomplishment." The public interest, moreover, must be guarded against "abuses." On the whole Cannon was justified in his claim that Polk actually agreed with him. Ramsey, Walker, and other improvement men, however, were confident that Polk would be more friendly than the incumbent, and Walker's Columbia *Democrat* embarrassed Polk by denouncing Cannon's refusal to issue state bonds to speculative enterprises.[39]

The bank question was still more confused. The new Bank of Tennessee had been greatly criticized, but even the Democrats were divided over what was wrong with it. On one point all Democrats agreed: Cannon and the Whig legislature had made it a partisan institution. The central directorate had twice as many Whigs as Democrats, while the Whigs outnumbered the Democrats on the branch boards by nine to three or ten to two. The location of the branches had also caused great dissatisfaction. Of the three branches in Middle Tennessee, two had been situated in Polk's district, at Columbia and Shelbyville, and placed in the hands of his bitterest enemies, while the third was at Clarksville in Cave Johnson's district. The Democrats complained that this was done for political effect, while many towns all over the state, particularly Knoxville and Sparta, were disappointed at not securing banking facilities.

The real issue, however, was what policy the new bank should follow. Should it bend all its resources toward forcing an early resumption of specie payments, or should it expand its issues to make money and credit more abundant, which would inevitably postpone resumption and further depreciate the currency? Unfortunately the bank's ability to do either was limited by the difficulty of selling the state bonds that furnished its capital. This difficulty the Whigs blamed on the Democratic national depression, while the Democrats

[39] *James K. Polk to the People of Tennessee, April 3, 1839* (Columbia, 1839), pamphlet, Polk Papers, p. 25; Nashville *Republican Banner*, 20 May 1839.

naturally traced it to the incompetence of the bank's Whig officers.[40]

In his speeches during the summer and fall of 1838 Polk had lived up to his hard-money professions by calling for resumption, which would necessitate a contraction of loans. Again, however, he was embarrassed by James Walker's Columbia *Democrat*, which lined up with Bell's Nashville *Republican Banner* to argue that "immediate resumption would ruin the country" and denied that Polk favored such a drastic policy. "The existing evil is not a depreciated currency," said the *Democrat*, "but that we scarcely have any currency at all."[41]

To balance this voice of the entrepreneurial Democracy, the *Union* championed the hard-money, Loco-foco Democratic idea of immediate resumption and elimination of bank notes under twenty dollars. "We believe that the *working man's money* should be GOLD AND SILVER," declared the *Union*.

The greater portion of the evils of a depreciated currency fall upon the classes who reap no benefits from banks. The day laborer, the journeyman mechanic, the great majority of our agriculturalists, derive no advantages from banks, either in the shape of discounts, the purchase of bills, or the sale of exchanges. Why, then, should they be taxed from two to twenty-five per cent. upon their hard earnings, to uphold bankrupt banks or grasping shavers. Common sense rejects the idea with abhorrence. Yet such is now the fact. If a merchant, or a man in business of a mercantile character, gets a note receivable in banks, he lays it by to pay his debt in bank; the uncurrent notes are almost invariably paid to their mechanics and laborers. Nor are they alone in this matter; the practice is nearly universal with employers.

This is a crying abuse and cries loudly for a sufficient remedy.[42]

By the time Polk came to compose his address, the banks had resumed. Though the resumption was to prove temporary, it lasted through the August election, aiding the Democrats and making it easier for Polk to stick to the hard-money line. The state should "exercise a constant and strict supervisory inspection and control," he said in his address, to keep the banks "from running into those excesses which are incident to the paper money system in every country in which it exists."

Banks are monopolistic, possessing exclusive privileges not granted to the

[40] Nashville *Union*, 6, 27 July, 8 Aug., 14 Nov. 1838; Memphis *Western World*, 8 Jan. 1839; Polk to Jackson, 11 June 1838, Donelson Papers.

[41] Columbia *Democrat*, quoted in Nashville *Republican Banner*, 21 Sept. 1838.

[42] Nashville *Union*, 14 Nov. 1838.

balance of the community, and should be content with reasonable and moderate profits.—It but too often happens, however, that having once secured their monopoly they look exclusively to an enlargement of their profits, and in seeking after such, unduly expand their business, which is soon followed by a necessity for a sudden contraction, and often a suspension of payment, which brings upon the community loss, suffering and distress. In these seasons of revulsion, the people and not the Banks suffer. Indeed it often happens that during a suspension of specie payments, the banks are doing their most profitable business; but they do it at the expense of the suffering and loss to the community which they have created. It should be the care of the public authorities, as far as practicable, to restrain and keep them within proper bounds.

Such talk boded no good for bankers. In regard to the state bank, Polk intimated doubts about the wisdom of its creation in the first place. As it stood, he criticized its political direction and the unfair distribution of its branches and resources, leaving the implication that under his administration "its benefits should be as generally diffused as possible among all the people of the State."[43]

The only other phase of state policy that Polk discussed in his address had not yet become an important issue, but it had been close to his heart ever since his days in the legislature, and he now pronounced it a subject "of thrilling interest to every patriotic man." This was the extension of popular education to "the great mass of the community." "No people who are not enlightened," he declared, "can long remain free." The Columbia *Democrat* had recently called attention to the achievements of the common school system in Michigan, and Polk bemoaned the fact that Tennessee had fallen behind many states in this important work. Tennessee now had the resources, he concluded, and it was time to devise a workable system for extending schools to every part of the state.[44]

There was one additional issue that Polk was prepared to use. During his last months in Washington he was busy collecting evidence of abolitionist sentiment among northern Whigs, as contrasted with the antiabolitionism of northern Democrats. Nothing was said about this for the moment, but by the time he departed for Tennessee in March, he had accumulated an impressive arsenal of materials on the subject to be used at the proper time.[45]

One of the last things Polk did before leaving the capital was to

43 *Polk to the People*, 26.
44 *ibid.*, 25; Nashville *Union*, 27 July 1838.
45 Henry Hubbard to Polk, 28 Jan. 1839, Polk Papers; J. M. Burt to Polk, 7 Feb. 1839, *ibid.*

settle his account with Blair and Rives for the great quantity of Democratic propaganda with which he had been flooding Tennessee for the past year and a half. The bill came to $251, and covered 8,400 copies of twenty-one different speeches, pamphlets, and documents, all of which he had addressed individually.[46] He had prepared his ground as well as it could possibly be done. Now he had only to fight the hardest political battle the state of Tennessee had yet seen.

VII

Reaching Columbia late in March 1839, Polk spent a week at home seeing his address through the press, making last minute arrangements for Democratic candidates for lesser offices, preparing his coming campaign speeches, and mapping out the most intensive electioneering tour ever undertaken by a Tennessee politician. Having visited the Western District the previous autumn, he now concentrated on exploiting the opportunity for Democratic gains in East Tennessee. The schedule he announced for this part of the state would keep him on the road for two months and cover every county and important town on and beyond the Cumberland plateau. After trying out his basic speech on his faithful constituents at Shelbyville, he proceeded to Nashville for final conferences with Donelson, his new editor Harris, and General Armstrong, who was to serve as general manager for the statewide campaign.[47] Actual hostilities opened in the courthouse at Murfreesboro on Tuesday, April 11.

Governor Cannon appeared for this meeting, and Polk invited him to speak first, but Cannon insisted that he had come mainly to listen, though he might want to reply when Polk was through. Polk's speech covered substantially the same ground as his published address, though enlivened with the anecdotes and mimicry that delighted his Tennessee audiences. Allen Hall was on hand to report the affair for the Nashville *Banner*, and he tried to counter Polk's "mimicking and grimacing propensities" by ridicule. Polk "made an attempt to imitate HENRY CLAY—and such an attempt!" ran the *Banner's* account. "James K. Polk, the narrow minded, superficial, little, grimacing politician attempting to expand his outward man, gesture and voice into something his hearers might

46 Receipt, 6 Mar. 1839, Polk Papers.

47 Nashville *Republican Banner*, 6 Apr. 1839; schedule of appointments, Polk Papers, LXXXI, No. 8618.

take for HENRY CLAY! He also attempted to represent the portly front, the dark, penetrating, majestic look of DANIEL WEB- STER! Drawing himself up to fully five feet seven, and blowing out his cheeks as far as possible (as if he really felt that he then measured, breadth and length with Daniel himself!) he pronounced those celebrated words of Webster, to wit: 'I BREATHE FREER AND DEEPER!' Bless us, how the little man swelled!"[48]

As in his published address, Polk touched briefly on the defects of the state's banking, education, and internal improvement poli- cies, and then, according to the *Banner's* report, "unbuttoned his vest and threw it open, most likely to 'breathe FREER AND DEEPER,' and branched off upon his old hobby—National Poli- tics." Polk was already nettled by a barrage of Whig criticism for his emphasis on national questions in earlier speeches. "They say you must reject Polk because he supports Van Buren!" he com- plained. "But if Polk undertakes to defend himself and say why he supports Van Buren, they then cry out, Oh, Polk is not the man to be elected Governor of Tennessee! he never alludes to the affairs of the State, but is always talking about National Politics!" Polk argued that Tennessee had a great stake in national affairs, and that her governors and legislatures had always discussed them. At any rate, the apostasy of the Whig leaders from the Jackson party was too telling a point to abandon, and the Whig complaints were eloquent testimony to its effectiveness.

So this speech, which was essentially the one he gave everywhere during the campaign, hammered away at all Polk's familiar themes —the virtues of the Old Hero, the iniquities of Henry Clay and John Quincy Adams, the genealogy of "modern Whiggery," the White Whigs' desertion of their principles, and the Whig plot to line up Tennessee for Henry Clay. But the Whig attacks on the in- dependent treasury plan, the expenditures of the Van Buren ad- ministration, and Swartwout's defalcation also forced Polk to spend much of his time on the defensive. He complained frequently of "the slanderous, libelling newspapers," which had "attacked and mis- represented me, my motives, my conduct, and my speeches." But "if they intended to hunt him down in this contest," he declared, "he would pitch his tents in their midst and fight out the war to the last."[49]

[48] Nashville *Republican Banner*, 13 Apr. 1839.
[49] *ibid.*, 15 Apr. 1839.

After Polk had spoken for two and a half hours, Cannon demanded a right to reply and consumed an additional ninety minutes. The audience was rewarded for its patience. More blunt than judicious, Cannon lashed into Jackson's tinkering with the currency and boldly declared himself for a national bank. Jackson was "a tyrant by nature and education," said the governor, and it was impossible to follow him without being "his tool and his slave." During the Creek war, he charged bitterly, Jackson had sent Cannon's regiment to almost certain disaster, while he remained behind in safety. With obvious reference to Polk, the governor boasted that he had never been a favorite with Jackson. "His popularity never bore me along to smiles and fortune. I never clung to the skirts of his coat, or, when danger approached, jumped into his pocket." In applying this point, he recalled a conversation with an old lady who had just read Amos Kendall's public letter eulogizing Polk as an unwavering supporter of Jackson. "Well, Governor," she had said to Cannon, "I suppose Mr. Polk, according to this, was out in the Indian Campaign with you, following the General?" Assured that he was not, she rejoined, "What, not there! Oh, I have it, you couldn't see him Governor; he was in the General's pocket."

The crowd was delighted by these vigorous thrusts, but Cannon had gone too far. In rebuttal, Polk seized on the governor's slap at Jackson, and never again during the campaign did he let the voters forget it. Far superior to Cannon in this kind of rough and tumble, Polk soon had the crowd cheering. Judge White and the whole population of Tennessee, he pointed out, would have to be classified as Jackson's "tools and slaves" under Cannon's interpretation of their support for his administration. The old lady story, too, reinforced Polk's complaints of relentless vilification. Cannon tried to reply briefly to a few of Polk's last points, but he finally had to conclude that his competitor was like "the Irishman's flea—put your finger on him, and he is not there!" He "would be sure to be there," Polk called out, and the first encounter was over.[50]

The next day the two candidates traveled to a nearby militia muster and then on to Lebanon in John Bell's district for another joint debate on Saturday. Word that Bell would be present to meet Polk for the first time on the stump attracted such a large throng that the meeting had to be moved out of doors. The Murfreesboro debate was substantially repeated, with Polk beginning at noon and

[50] *ibid.*, 16 Apr. 1839.

Cannon following him after he had spoken nearly four hours. When Cannon sat down at five-thirty, John Bell mounted the stand "in a rage of passion," demanding to be heard. This was another occasion when Bell lost his temper and discretion. Until it was quite dark, he poured out his hatred for Polk. Before the meeting took a recess for dinner, Polk was able to get in a short reply to Bell, "hurling in his teeth the assault he had made." Again Polk's cool-headedness enabled him to catch an opponent off balance, and his advantage over Bell was so obvious that even in this Whig stronghold he was cheered long and loudly. During dinner Bell's friends calmed him down, and when he resumed his speech in the courthouse that night, he avoided personal references. This did not prevent him from subjecting the Van Buren administration to the kind of remorseless dissection at which he was so skillful, and poor Burton, Bell's Democratic competitor for Congress, did not get a chance to speak until after eleven. Polk was jubilant over the outcome. "The day was clearly ours & our opponents know it," he wrote to Sarah. "Bell did more for us than I and all our friends could have done."[51]

As if to corroborate Polk's contention, Governor Cannon suddenly thought of important state business and returned to Nashville, leaving Polk to traverse the state unopposed, except by such local candidates as might wish to take him on. Two days later he participated in another rhetorical marathon at Carthage with the Whig congressman, William B. Campbell. Again Polk made a long speech, and again the replies and rejoinders were ended only by gathering darkness. Again the meeting was resumed after dinner. Campbell claimed that the crowd was on his side, but he admitted privately that the Democrats were making such gains that he feared for his reelection.[52]

From Carthage, Polk began his ascent into the Cumberland mountain country. In this sparsely populated but strongly Democratic area there were fewer Whigs to oppose him, but the hard, daily horseback rides from town to town were longer, and the crowds were smaller. The enthusiasm of these mountain farmers, however, more than compensated for their lack of numbers. Polk had planned to make an address every other day, but he found himself compelled to speak wherever he stopped. Throngs of voters even met him on

[51] Polk to Mrs. Polk, 14 Apr. 1839, Polk Papers; Nashville *Republican Banner*, 16 Apr. 1839.
[52] W. B. Campbell to David Campbell, 28 Apr. 1839, Campbell Papers.

the road, and on such occasions he would dismount, tie his horse, and talk to them. Editor Harris reported to George Bancroft that Polk was "the happiest *mixer* with the sovereigns (as we say here) that I ever saw." Cannon overtook him while on the plateau, but he stayed only two days before returning again to Nashville.[53]

Traversing the Cumberland country from northwest to southeast, Polk entered East Tennessee at its southern end. He spent a week in the Cherokee section, then moved slowly up through Knoxville and on into the far northeastern corner of the state. After a month away from home his letters to Sarah began confessing that he was "greatly fatigued." His exhausted horse had to be left behind, and he began to wish that he had brought the sulky, instead of traveling by horseback. Nevertheless he instructed Sarah to tell his friends that he would "be able to go through the campaign," and that he was in "high spirits" at his prospects. Indeed he was certain that he would get a majority in East Tennessee, which Armstrong had lost by more than 4,000 votes two years before.[54]

On his return journey Polk crisscrossed the northern section of the Cumberland plateau, speaking in all the counties he had missed on his way out. By the second week of June he was back in Middle Tennessee, devoting two days to Williamson County, and on the seventeenth he wound up his long tour with a speech at Columbia. In a little over two months he had ridden more than 1,300 miles, through thirty-seven of the state's sixty-six counties, making forty-three scheduled and numerous impromptu addresses.

The Democrats were elated and the Whigs correspondingly despondent over the public reaction. Because of Cannon's "self-confidence & consequent unpardonable inactivity," Senator Foster admitted, some of the Whigs were "actually beginning to be tormented with fears." Another Whig confessed that he would not be surprised at a Democratic victory. "Polk has ten times the activity of Cannon," he complained, "& is traversing the state like an emissary, making speeches."[55]

To some Whigs, however, Cannon's ineffectiveness did not seem so great a handicap as Henry Clay's unpopularity in Tennessee. Actually only a handful of Whig leaders realized how deeply Clay's

[53] Harris to Bancroft, 4 May 1839, Bancroft Papers; Polk to Mrs. Polk, 20 Apr. 1839, Polk Papers.

[54] Polk to Mrs. Polk, 2, 8, 12, 22 May, 2 June 1839, Polk Papers.

[55] Foster to [W. B. Campbell], 12 June 1839, Campbell Papers; James Campbell to David Campbell, 16 June 1839, *ibid.*

presidential aspirations were involved in Tennessee's gubernatorial campaign. Bell was resolved to tie the Tennessee party to Clay's fortunes and was basing the Whig strategy on suggestions received from him. "The real question now before the people of this state is will they take Henry Clay to rule over them," Bell told the Kentuckian in May, "and as the vote shall be in August next, so shall it be in 1840. What we have now in hand is to convince the people that you are the greatest man in America, and worthy of all trust."[56]

With both parties expecting this election to determine the ultimate political character of Tennessee, the excitement rapidly mounted to the height of 1835. The early stages of the campaign were punctuated by bloody street fights between Whigs and Democrats in several towns, and the candidates themselves prepared for physical violence. Burton armed himself with pistols for his stump encounters with Bell; the Democrats drove an East Tennessee Whig congressman into paroxysms of fury with "the terrible reports they have on him about the wh – – es at Washington, & particularly respecting, a woman who followed him on, even to his own town!";[57] and on one occasion William B. Campbell and his Democratic challenger "spoke a while, & then fought awhile—no injury done on either side."[58]

The most widely publicized personal controversy was between J. George Harris and the two Whig editors at Nashville. It had not taken the Whigs long to realize that they had a dangerous antagonist in the editorial chair of the *Union*. Unable to counter Harris's barbed paragraphs on the issues, they had shifted to personal attacks. Harris had replied in kind, and fist fights had nearly resulted on several occasions. But the Whig editors held a trump card, which after a month of careful buildup, they played on June 10 by reprinting an old Harris editorial from the New Bedford *Gazette*, urging free Negroes to vote for a Democratic congressional candidate. "We are opposed to slavery in all its shapes," Harris was quoted as saying. This bombshell stunned the Democrats momentarily, but to Polk's credit, he stood behind his editor. Harris never demonstrated his superb controversial talents so well as in the bar-

[56] Bell to Clay, 21 May 1839, Clay Papers.

[57] J. L. Williams to W. B. Campbell, 30 June 1839, Campbell Papers; Joseph Howard Parks, *John Bell of Tennessee* (Baton Rouge, 1950), 160; Nashville *Republican Banner*, 5 Apr. 1839; M. R. Rucker to Mrs. Polk, 13 May 1839, Polk Papers; J. W. Childress to Mrs. Polk, 27 May 1839, *ibid.*

[58] James Campbell to David Campbell, 16 June 1839, Campbell Papers.

rage of countercharges, qualified denials, and general obfuscation that brought him out of this ticklish spot with little damage to himself, the *Union*, or the Democratic party.[59]

Polk tarried at home only a day on his return from East Tennessee before setting out to keep another killing schedule of appointments in the lower counties of Middle Tennessee and those parts of the Western District he had missed the previous autumn. At Purdy on June 23, Cannon again tried matching his "blunt, plain, straightforward" talk against his opponent's aggressive rhetoric, but the results were disheartening, and thereafter the governor stayed out of Polk's way. Sarah, who had been kept busy at home mailing out Democratic literature, arranging Polk's schedule, and handling his correspondence, was alarmed at the demands her husband was making on his none too robust constitution. He wrote her affectionate letters whenever he could and demanded frequent word from her, but she still could not rest easy during his prolonged absences. "I am anxious to hear from you," she wrote while he was in the Western District, "not political prospects only, but your *health*."[60]

Two weeks before the election, the Whig editors discovered Polk's votes in the 1823 legislature against further relief to squatters in the district south of the French Broad River. About the same time, Bell and Foster frightened Cannon into setting off for a tour of East Tennessee. East Tennessee had to be saved, and Polk promptly canceled his other appointments to ride in pursuit of the governor, overtaking him at Rogersville on July 29, three days before the election.[61]

Escorted by a band of hurrahing Democrats, Polk entered Rogersville just as the Whigs, headed by Cannon and Judge White, were parading to their dinner. They could hardly refuse to let Polk speak, and he and Cannon addressed the crowd of nearly 2,000 for an hour and a half each. But Polk then demanded the right to reply to any hostile toasts before he would participate in the dinner. When the Whigs refused to give such an assurance, the uproarious crowd of Democrats marched off, shouting "gag-law, dictation," and Polk

59 Nashville *Republican Banner*, 10 June 1839; Harris to Bancroft, 4 May 1839, Bancroft Papers.

60 Mrs. Polk to Polk, 25 June 1839, Polk Papers; Pool, "Whig Party in W. Tenn.," 74-76.

61 Nashville *Republican Banner*, 18, 21, 22 July 1839.

had a barrel of whisky rolled out into the street and broken open for his followers. For last minute effect the Democrats promptly circulated thousands of handbills describing how the Whigs had mistreated Polk.[62] On this fitting note the tumultuous campaign ended, and Polk barely got back to Columbia before the returns started coming in.

VIII

The results were so close that the outcome was in doubt for more than a week. Not until August 9 were the Democrats confident enough of victory to launch their jubilant celebrations. Polk's bare majority of 2,462 votes was a tremendous achievement. While the Whig total was less than 1,500 below Cannon's total of two years before, Polk's vigorous campaign had so inspired his party and aroused the voters that the Democratic vote increased more than 20,000. Moreover the Democrats won both branches of the legislature—the senate by fourteen to eleven, and the house by forty-two to thirty-three—and doubled their congressional representation from three to six of the state's thirteen seats. The two incumbent Democratic congressmen, Hopkins Turney and Abraham McClellan, were reelected easily; Watterson took over Polk's seat without any trouble; Julius Blackwell won a formerly Whig seat in lower East Tennessee; Aaron Brown captured his lower Middle Tennessee district; and Cave Johnson rewon his old seat in upper Middle Tennessee and the Tennessee River counties. The unsuccessful Democratic candidates ran well in the two Western District races, and though both Bell and Campbell outpolled their Democratic rivals, Bell assured Campbell that "You have had a dreadful campaign & so have I." In fact, Bell was so disheartened over the general results that he mourned, "I am *done done* as a public man, unless we can have some better understanding with each other, & all will agree to give the *working men* more assistance that we have heretofore done."[63]

The Whigs conceded privately that Henry Clay had been a heavy load for them to carry, but their strenuous public denials of this were ample testimony to the zeal with which John Bell was promoting the Kentuckian's cause. Clay himself admitted that Polk's victory was "a most disastrous event, which, I fear, is likely to exercise

---

62 *ibid.*, 17 Aug. 1839.

63 Bell to W. B. Campbell, 10 Aug. 1839, Campbell Papers; *Messages of the Governors of Tenn.*, III, 274.

great, if not fatal, influence far beyond the limits of Tennessee."[64] Already hard pressed by William Henry Harrison and General Winfield Scott for the Whig presidential nomination, Clay well realized that his part in the Tennessee defeat could kill his chances with the Whig convention.

To avert this calamity Allen Hall argued vehemently in Bell's Nashville *Banner* that the trouble arose only because "the numerous and envenomed attacks on Mr. Clay's public character and conduct were left wholly unanswered by the Whig candidates." In Bell's district and the few other places where Clay was openly defended, he insisted, the Whigs had been successful. If, in the face of this "culpable supineness and inactivity of the Whigs," the state had been lost by only a few thousand votes, surely the Whigs would reverse the result when Clay's merits were compared with Van Buren's in the presidential election. Hall reiterated these reassuring conclusions in a private letter to Clay, adding that he was the only Whig candidate who could defeat Van Buren in Tennessee.[65]

Universally the Whigs blamed the result on Polk's unprecedented exertions. Analysis of the campaign and the returns bears out this evaluation. It was Polk who inspired his fellow Democrats, who mapped out the strategy, and who supplied the arguments used on all levels. The Democrats won by wooing away a number of former White supporters with Polk's arguments and by getting to the polls for the first time many citizens of a Democratic persuasion who had not previously been in the habit of voting. Aside from a few areas like Polk's congressional district, where personal influence was important, Democratic strength was concentrated in the less prosperous sections: lower East Tennessee, the Cumberland plateau, the northwestern corner of the state, and the Tennessee River counties. The Whigs, on the other hand, ran strongest in the wealthier counties and in the areas tributary to Knoxville, Nashville, Jackson, and Memphis. To the question, "Where have these new recruits under the banner of locofocoism come from?" the Whig Memphis *Enquirer* replied: "They are the men from the deep gorges of the hills and mountains, and by the side of the creeks, in the far-off corners of the counties—who take no newspapers and come not into the towns.

---

[64] Clay to Thomas Washington, 12 Oct. 1839, Henry Clay Papers (THS; herein cited as Tenn. Clay Papers); S. M. Blythe to W. B. Campbell, 8 Aug. 1839, Campbell Papers; David Campbell to [W. B. Campbell], 15 Aug. 1839, *ibid.*

[65] Nashville *Republican Banner*, 12, 31 Aug. 1839; Hall to Clay, 23 Sept. 1839, Clay Papers.

These are the men—honest but uninformed on the political affairs of the country, and easily led astray by the artful demagogues—who have swelled the loco vote."[66]

Throughout the country jubilant Democrats took Polk's triumph as a portent of Democratic victory in the coming presidential election. Warm congratulations poured in from Cabinet members and Democratic congressmen, while the vacationing Frank Blair reported that "The Tennessee Election burst like a boom among the Whigs" at the White Sulphur Springs of Virginia. Many of the leading Whigs had gathered at the Springs to meet Clay on his return from a visit to New York, and they had struck Blair as "the most Swaggering gasconading knot of politicians that ever enjoyed triumph in anticipation." But once the news came, the Whigs kept to their rooms and soon departed.[67]

Naturally it was among the Democrats of Tennessee that joy reigned most unrestrained. In Nashville the celebrants mounted a stalk of polk bush, a local weed, on a cannon, which they pulled through town, firing one round for every county in the state. A victory dinner of 700 Democrats in Murfreesboro was addressed by the Hero of San Jacinto, Sam Houston, then on a visit to his native state. In the Western District there was a royal melee at Dover, when the Whigs tried to chop down a polk stalk planted as a victory symbol by the Polk men. In East Tennessee the Jonesboro Democrats celebrated with a band, a parade, and an illumination of the town. At Bolivar an anxious crowd of Democrats assembled on the thirteenth to meet the Nashville stage with news of the last East Tennessee returns. Pandemonium broke out when the coach came into sight with a little Democrat sitting on top wildly waving a polk stalk. Pistols were fired in exultation, and one bold Whig who demurred at the proceedings "would have got a Polk stalk across his Countinence" if he had not "backed water."[68]

Polk waited until all the returns were known, and then he and Sarah joined Jackson, Grundy, Harris, and the other leading Demo-

66 Memphis *Enquirer*, 23 Aug. 1839, quoted in Powell Moore, "The Establishment of the Whig Party in Tennessee," Ph.D. dissertation, Indiana University (1932), 329.

67 Blair to Jackson, 20 Aug. 1839, copy, Transcripts of Jackson-Blair Correspondence, Gist Blair Papers (LC); letters to Polk from J. H. Prentiss, John Cramer, J. H. Bronson, Franklin Pierce, Moses Dawson, Thomas Maxwell, Isaac Fletcher, Levi Woodbury, Aug.-Oct. 1839, Polk Papers.

68 Letters to Polk from R. D. Casey, L. P. Cheatham, S. H. Laughlin, W. B. Johnson, J. A. Aiken, 10-22 Aug. 1839, Polk Papers.

crats, for a victory festival at Tyree's Springs, north of Nashville. The gay company assembled on the shady lawn every morning for a moot court, where Judge Grundy imposed fines "for every little trivial offense conceivable, such as failing to bow when passing a lady, or any other slight breach of common courtesy," and the proceeds kept the company supplied with watermelons, canteloupes, peaches, pears, and flowers for the ladies. The strict rule against political discussions should have made this a pleasant respite, but the ever serious governor-elect, with many weighty problems to solve before his inauguration, must have chafed under the restraint.[69]

Victory had raised more difficult problems than had confronted the Democrats in their years of defeat. The little band of Calhounites in the Western District, who despite their small numbers had been and would continue to be essential to Democratic success in the closely divided state, were not going to be easy to manage. While praising Polk and rejoicing in his election, the Jackson *District Telegraph* warned that "we shall not forbear to tell him he has faults as well as other men, and can expect alone to be supported and preferred by freemen, such as Tennesseans, when he shall display those abilities in behalf of that kind of liberty which *they* have secured by a written Consti[tu]tion. . . . Then let Mr. Van Buren and Gov. Polk look to this matter, for just as certain as they do not adhere to the formulary of our faith, they will find the people against them."[70]

Everywhere the Calhoun men were preparing to wrest control of the Democracy from the Van Buren element, and three weeks after the election one of the Tennessee Nullifiers was asking Polk, "Would it not be better to turn some portion of our attention toward South Carolina?" The strategic position Polk would occupy in this coming struggle for power was nowhere more clearly indicated than in the letter he shortly received from the South Carolina fire-eater Robert Barnwell Rhett. "You have probably in your position more power than any man in the South," wrote Rhett, in appealing for decisive Democratic action against the protective tariff. "You are in the South. You know the feelings of the People. You are closely associated with the Administration who are deeply indebted to you."[71]

[69] Anson and Fanny Nelson, *Memorials of Sarah Childress Polk: Wife of the Eleventh President of the United States* (New York, 1892), 60-63.

[70] Jackson *District Telegraph*, 16 Aug. 1839.

[71] D. A. Street to Polk, 20 Aug. 1839, Polk Papers; R. B. Rhett to Polk, 21 Aug. 1839, *ibid.*

A more immediate problem, however, was the division of spoils among the hungry Democrats of Tennessee. Polk would have to "employ some tact and skill," warned the astute Alfred Balch, lest the party "suffer any heart burnings to distract its harmony, in consequence of the disposition of the public offices." But, as Balch reassured President Van Buren, "Polk's temper is amicable and he will exercise a kind influence over the hot ambition of aspirants in our ranks."[72] No one realized better than Polk himself that on his handling of these delicate matters depended not only the future of his party in Tennessee, but also his personal prospects for high national honors.

[72] Balch to Van Buren, 20 Aug. 1839, Van Buren Papers.

12

THE GOVERNORSHIP—AND HIGHER STAKES

NASHVILLE WOKE EARLY ON MONDAY, OCTOBER 14, 1839. By mid-morning its streets were thronged with crowds of men and women drawn from every level of Tennessee life. Weather-beaten circuit riders, in town for the Methodist convention, collided with rustic "messengers" sent by remote Baptist congregations to that denomination's annual association meeting. Both groups of religionists displayed a fascinated aversion for the genteel horse fanciers and rakish gamblers attracted by Nashville's celebrated fall races. Adding variety and bombast to the scene were the members of the legislature, which had been in session for a week. By Whig report, "half the democrats in the State are in attendance for some office,"[1] and this morning they were even more in evidence than usual. This was the Democratic day of jubilee, for after four lean years a Democratic governor was being inaugurated.

Promptly at eleven o'clock the two houses of the legislature assembled in their meeting rooms at the county courthouse and moved off in procession toward the Presbyterian Church, which was already packed for the inaugural ceremonies. The Methodists and Baptists were both present in a body, and a place of honor had been reserved for Tennessee's hero, the aging but indomitable ex-president Jackson, who was making it obvious to all within range that he was *"mighty happy"* about the day's events. After a prayer by the local Baptist minister and a brief, dignified valedictory by the retiring Governor Cannon, the audience leaned forward to see how the new chief executive would acquit himself.[2]

Convention required the incoming governor to state his political principles, and Polk complied with an uncompromising exposition of orthodox Jeffersonian doctrines on federal-state relations. The federal government, he said, might exercise only those powers expressly delegated to it by the Constitution or "necessary and proper" to

[1] W. B. Campbell to David Campbell, 10 Oct. 1839, David Campbell Papers (DU).
[2] Nashville *Republican Banner*, 15 Oct. 1839; Jackson to Van Buren, 18 Oct. 1839, Martin Van Buren Papers (LC).

carry into effect some delegated power. And "necessary and proper," he added, did not mean "convenient" or "expedient." Nor could the federal government "promote the general welfare," except through expressly delegated powers.

However hackneyed or antique these arguments were beginning already to sound, Polk had never been more in earnest. With an idyllic vision of Old Mecklenburg in his mind's eye, he conceived the task of statesmanship to be a restoration of the purity and simplicity of the Old America by removing the unconstitutional excrescences that had accumulated over the years. These excrescences he identified by name: the national bank, the protective tariff, the distribution of federal surpluses among the states, and federal internal improvements.

Though Polk was undoubtedly expressing long-held convictions, his emphasis was at least partly prompted by the rising threat of abolition. Only under a strict construction of the Constitution, he argued, would the Union be safe from the "unholy agitation" of the slavery question. He admitted that a small part of this agitation sprang from the "mistaken philanthropy" of "a few misguided persons," but politician that he was, charged abolitionism mainly to his political foes. Many of the leading abolitionists, Polk declared, were active partisans, "fully identified with and constituting no inconsiderable part of, one of the political parties of the country." Under such circumstances all friends of the Union should rejoice that they had a president pledged to uphold the sacred constitutional compromises on this delicate subject.

Polk's stress on strict construction at this particular time was hardly unrelated also to his need for support from the Calhounites. In fact Polk went a long way toward Calhoun's position on doubtful constitutional powers. "In all such cases," he said, "it is both safest and wisest to appeal to the people, the only true source of power, in the constitutional forms, by an amendment of the fundamental law, to remove such doubt." Yet there was an obvious difference in temper between this statement and the doctrine of the South Carolina theorist. Where Calhoun emphasized the sovereignty of the states, Polk maintained as his fundamental principle that "the ultimate and supreme authority rests in the People." This devotion to political democracy led him to acclaim the beneficial operation of Tennessee's new constitution, under which the people elected nearly all their officials directly, confining even judges to a limited term of years.

Leaving a detailed exposition of his views on state policy for a later message to the legislature, Polk contented himself with promising strict economy, avowing his devotion to state internal improvements and education, and warning that he would seek restrictions on the "curse" of "excessive banking." He concluded his address by invoking "the aid and guidance of the Supreme Ruler of the Universe," after which a local judge administered the oath of office, and the Methodist bishop closed the ceremony with prayer.[3]

Governor Polk threw himself into his new duties with characteristic diligence. The state having no executive mansion, he and Sarah rented a spacious brick house, with kitchen, stables, and a pleasant garden in the rear, on one of Nashville's better streets. Though Sarah tried to draw her husband into the city's active social life, he more often than not begged out of invitations on the plea that he "could not lose half a day just to go and dine." However he encouraged Sarah to attend these social affairs without him, and she soon formed many warm friendships among the Whig families who dominated Nashville society.[4]

Except when Jackson visited Nashville or relatives and friends came up from Murfreesboro or Columbia, the Polks did little entertaining. This was partly because of James's absorption in his duties, and perhaps even more because of the serious financial straits in which he found himself. His congressional salary had never been sufficient for his expenses, he was still in debt for his plantation, and the depression had cut down his plantation income and made it difficult to realize anything on his land holdings. At the same time, he had been pouring his private funds into the effort to reclaim Tennessee for the Democrats. Large expenditures for subsidizing newspapers (especially the *Union*), circulating pamphlets, and personal traveling expenses, had plunged him a good many thousand dollars into debt. The meager governor's salary of $2,000 did not even pay his living expenses, and he had been forced to borrow over $6,000 from the Union Bank on endorsements by James Walker, several thousand more from his old friend Archibald Yell, in Ar-

[3] Nashville *Republican Banner*, 18 Oct. 1839.

[4] Anson and Fanny Nelson, *Memorials of Sarah Childress Polk: Wife of the Eleventh President of the United States* (New York, 1892), 63-64; Catron to Polk, 1 Sept. 1839, James K. Polk Papers (LC; herein cited as Polk Papers, which refers to First Series unless otherwise noted).

kansas, and a small sum from Judge Catron. But this still was not enough, and he made desperate efforts to sell some of his lands and slaves. The only thing that saved him was the plantation, which finally became profitable enough to cover his expenses and to retire enough of his heavy debt each year to satisfy his creditors.[5]

The governor's office itself was little more than a distinguished clerkship. The state government was still a simple affair carried on by the governor and a handful of other officials—the secretary of state, the comptroller, the attorney general, and the superintendent of the common school fund—without secretarial assistance. What state enterprises existed ran along in well-worn grooves, leaving little scope for executive discretion. Polk nevertheless found his endless stream of official correspondence a time-consuming drudgery. There were pardons to be considered, commissions for state officers to be signed, and fugitives from justice to be rendered to or obtained from other states. The greatest amount of work grew out of the internal improvement act of 1838, which required the governor to issue bonds to improvement companies whenever they complied with the complicated provisions of the law.

In all this business Polk's attitude was one of extreme caution to make sure the law was being complied with. He was, if anything, more punctilious than Cannon in his relations with James Walker's Columbia Central Turnpike Company, causing Walker to write peevishly that he was "discouraged and disgusted with political matters." "I have sustained my principles and opinions honestly and fully, at the expense of much time and money," complained the governor's avaricious brother-in-law. "It seems that whenever I have any interest within the power of the general or state government, the very fact of my being interested blights and destroys, plain and fair justice."[6]

The governor of Tennessee traditionally exercised little control over state policy except, as in the case of Carroll, when he had personal influence with individual legislators. Polk was the first governor to function as a party leader in the policy sphere, and it was as political leader that he expended most of his energies. Here

[5] Archibald Yell to Polk, 15 Sept. 1839, Polk Papers; Walker to Polk, 30 Dec. 1839, *ibid.*; J. M. Bass to Polk, 2 Sept. 1840, *ibid.*; E. P. McNeal to Polk, 2 Dec. 1840, *ibid.*; W. H. Polk to J. K. Polk, 4 Dec. 1840, *ibid.*; canceled note, Polk to Catron, 23 Aug. 1839 [placed 1 Aug. 1839], *ibid.*

[6] Walker to Polk, 23 Mar. 1840, Polk Papers; Letter Book of Governor James K. Polk (Tennessee Archives, Nashville), passim.

his task was twofold: first, to maintain Democratic harmony in the face of rival ambitions to fill the offices now at the party's disposal; and second, to guide the Democratic legislative majority in dealing with the ticklish banking and internal improvement questions. In a political sense the first of these tasks was probably the more important and the more difficult, but even the Whigs admitted that Polk, who "now acts as Autocrat of the party in this State," was "worth all in management," and "with his tact may reconcile."[7] If he failed, it would not be for lack of trying.

II

Competition between various Democrats over the legislative speakerships and various state offices was the most immediate danger, and it was imperative that Polk provide leadership in securing some agreement in the party before the legislature met. During the latter part of August he visited Nashville and the Hermitage to consult other prominent Democrats, and it was decided to urge the Democratic legislators to reach Nashville four or five days before the session, in order to settle these matters in advance. Polk was reluctant to attend this caucus himself, lest the Whigs charge that he was dictating all the arrangements, but he finally agreed to go up for the weekend. The caucus was completely successful, and when the legislature met, the Democrats elected their candidates to all the lesser offices without difficulty.[8]

The most troublesome problem was the senatorships. Of the two Whig incumbents, Ephraim Foster had publicly promised to resign if the voters returned a Democratic legislature, while Judge White would probably resign rather than obey legislative instructions to vote for the independent treasury. The Foster seat, which would have to be filled from Middle Tennessee, would undoubtedly be the first vacated, and within ten days after the August election Polk began taking steps to prevent the inevitable "collision between numerous aspirants." He acted none too soon, for Burton, Nicholson, Trousdale, and others had already begun to advance their

---

[7] W. B. Campbell to David Campbell, 10 Oct. 1839, Campbell Papers.

[8] Laughlin to Polk, 20 Aug. 1839, 30 Sept. [1839; misplaced 1830], Polk Papers; R. B. Reynolds to Armstrong, 2 Sept. 1839, *ibid.*; J. P. Hardwicke to Polk, 18 Sept. 1839, *ibid.*; Armstrong to Polk, 27 Sept. [1839], 29 Sept. [1839; misplaced 1840], Polk Papers; Polk to Laughlin and Armstrong, 1 Oct. 1839, *ibid.*; B. Martin and Laughlin to Polk, 2 Oct. 1839, *ibid.*; Tennessee *House Journal*, 1839, pp. 4-5, 25, 46-47.

claims, and even the faithful Cave Johnson was nursing senatorial ambitions.

Though most of the hopefuls professed a willingness to step aside in favor of whoever had the widest Democratic support, the Whigs were playing on the always susceptible ambitions of A. O. P. Nicholson, who might defeat any such arrangement by running against the party's choice with solid Whig support. Fearing this result from the first, Polk had taken the position that Attorney General Grundy was the only man whose claims to the seat were so nearly indisputable as to unite the entire party behind him. But Grundy was reluctant to leave the Cabinet, and President Van Buren did not want to have to replace him on the eve of a presidential nominating convention.[9]

Grundy suggested that the Democrats extricate themselves from their dilemma by using a stratagem the Whigs had employed two years before. Judge White's term would expire in March 1841, while the next legislature would not meet until October of that year, thus leaving Tennessee unrepresented in the event of a special session of Congress during the summer. This was the excuse the Whigs had used to elect Grundy's successor two years before his term expired, and Grundy now proposed that the same thing be done with White's seat. Grundy could be elected to succeed White, with his term starting in March 1841, and thus could finish out his Cabinet appointment. Meanwhile East Tennessee, where there were no such bitter rivalries for the Senate as in Middle Tennessee, could furnish a replacement for Foster. This ingenious scheme Polk rejected. The Whigs' premature election of Foster had been much resented, and he did not want to repeat their mistake.[10]

Anyhow Foster refused to resign before the legislature instructed him to vote for the independent treasury, so Polk devoted his attention to pushing the instructing resolutions. By the first week in November they had passed the state senate, and the approval of the lower house was imminent. At this point Polk decided that Grundy would have to accept. The attorney general, he argued in a letter to Van Buren, "is the only man in the State, upon whom the Demo-

9 Polk to Jackson, 12 Aug. 1839, Andrew Jackson Papers (LC); Nashville *Republican Banner*, 11 July 1839; Dr. J. S. Young to Polk, 21, 25 Aug. 1839, Polk Papers; Armstrong to Polk, 4 Sept. 1839, *ibid.*; Johnson to Polk, 8 Jan. [1840; misplaced 1839], *ibid.*; Milo M. Quaife, ed., *The Diary of James K. Polk during His Presidency, 1845 to 1849* . . . (4 vols., Chicago, 1910), I, 319-320.
10 Grundy to Polk, 17 Oct. 1839, Polk Papers.

cratic members of our Legislature can be united." If Grundy would not accept, Nicholson's machinations would put the party "in imminent danger of being disorganized if not for a time dissolved." Such a plea could not be resisted by loyal party men like Grundy and Van Buren. Within a week the instructions passed, Foster resigned, and Grundy was restored to the Senate as his successor.[11]

Now the Democrats were free to concentrate on Judge White. Here there was no problem of clashing ambitions, for Polk had already picked White's successor. His choice was General Alexander Anderson, a Knoxville lawyer and businessman of some ability, who had formerly been a Whig but who had contributed to the Democratic gains in East Tennessee the previous summer. As a recent convert who still had Whig family connections, and as a promoter of the Hiwassee Railroad, which was competing with Doctor Ramsey's Cincinnati and Charleston Railroad for state aid, Anderson was unpopular with many East Tennessee Democrats. Judge Samuel Powell, a venerable, old-fashioned Republican, who according to Judge Catron was "just of the grade to suit that people— with substance & homely plainness," would have been the most popular selection. The apparent reason for Polk's insistence on Anderson was Anderson's eagerness to serve the governor's vice presidential ambitions.

At any rate Polk had persuaded Powell not to oppose Anderson even before the legislature met, and the only remaining problem was to force White's resignation. When passage of the instructions failed to secure this result, Polk wrote to Senator Benton urging that the independent treasury bill be brought to a vote early in the session, so that White would have to show his hand. Early in January the bill was called up, White resigned his seat, and the legislature obediently designated Anderson to fill the unexpired portion of the term. Anderson implored the governor to have the legislature elect for the term beginning in 1841 also, but Polk was adamant against following the Whig precedent.[12]

As it turned out, the aged White's expulsion from the Senate hurt the Democrats. White was "a patriot and statesman of more than Roman virtue," complained the Whig press from as far off

[11] Polk to Van Buren, 11 Nov. 1839, Van Buren Papers; Nashville *Republican Banner*, 20 Nov. 1839.

[12] Catron to Polk, 3 Jan. 1840, Polk Papers; Anderson to Polk, 22 Aug., 3, 10, 13, 16 Nov., 4 Dec. 1839, *ibid.*; John Blair to Polk, 7 Nov. 1839, *ibid.*; R. B. Reynolds to Polk, 27 Nov. 1839, *ibid.*; T. H. Benton to Polk, 5 Dec. 1839, *ibid.*

as Georgia, "but it was left for the resistless Goths, who follow the beck and nod of such poor cowardly creatures as JAMES K. POLK, to perpetrate this outrage." Returning to Tennessee ill and embittered, White spent his time, according to Grundy, sitting "all day long in the chimney corner, spitting tobacco juice by the gallon, cursing everything and everybody, except his Creator,—but *thinking* devilish hard of Him!" In three months he was dead.[13]

III

As a matter of fact the senatorial problem was more easily solved than the banking problem. The resumption of specie payments in January 1839 had aided the Democrats in their successful campaign, and they now had a chance to frame reform legislation that would prevent another suspension and strengthen the currency by an infusion of gold and silver coin into circulation. But Polk was no sooner in office than fate turned against him. His message was just about ready for the legislature when, three days after the inauguration, Nashville learned that the eastern banks had again suspended specie payments. The next morning, October 18, the Planters and Union banks followed suit, and the president of the state-owned Bank of Tennessee pointedly informed the legislature that his institution was under heavy pressure. Thus the Democrats were suddenly presented with a challenge to their avowed hard-money principles.

Henderson Yoakum, the Democratic senator from Rutherford County, introduced a resolution directing the state bank to "continue to pay its debts as public faith and common honesty require," but other Democrats were not so ready to stand by their principles. Fighting for time, Sam Laughlin, who had conquered his intemperance sufficiently to win election to the senate from a Cumberland mountain district, argued that the legislature should first find out whether the state bank was able to continue paying specie. He succeeded in overriding Yoakum's demand for immediate action, and the senate called on the bank president for the desired information. President William Nichol replied the next morning, October 19, that his institution could continue, but that it would have to "cease all discounts and accommodations, and call in on its discounted

---

[13] Savannah *Daily Republican*, 27 Jan. 1840; John C. Fitzpatrick, ed., *The Autobiography of Martin Van Buren*, American Historical Association, *Annual Report*, 1918, II (Washington, 1920), 226n.

paper." In other words, continuance of specie payment would mean a severe contraction of credit and heavy pressure on debtors. The bank was obviously leaving the whole question to the Democratic legislative majority, which would have to bear the blame for the consequences if it refused to sanction suspension.[14]

Meanwhile the news had reached Columbia, and James Walker, alarmed lest the Democrats stand by their principles and ruin the party, scribbled off a lengthy plea to Polk. The state bank could hold out against all the other banks, he reminded the governor, only by "the most grinding collections," which would "produce a state of ruin and distress among the people unparalleled in the history of the country." The bank's Whig directors, said Walker, would be glad to make the Democrats responsible for these conditions. Walker was not at all averse to suspension, since it would enable the banks to expand their loans and circulation. "If the currency is of inferior value," he said, "we shall at least have something that will pay debts, and produce exchanges of property." The great difficulty, as Walker saw it, was that the country "had scarcely any currency good or bad," so that "Any change must be some relief." He entreated Polk to keep the legislature from taking any action whatever. The bank would have to suspend, and the directors would be responsible.[15]

A substantial number of Democratic legislators agreed with this point of view, and a resolution calling for suspension by all the banks was offered by Andrew Johnson, the ambitious young tailor from East Tennessee. Though Johnson's proposal was ignored, Yoakum's resolution was buried in committee, and the state bank promptly suspended by action of its directors.[16]

Among the Democrats who opposed suspension was Governor Polk. The banking crisis forced him to revise his legislative message at the last minute, but when it came, it was in the spirit of Andrew Jackson. There is "no sufficient ground for the suspension of payments by our banks so long as they have an ability to pay," said the governor. "Like individual debtors, they should meet their liabilities honestly and promptly as long as they are able to pay." It cost the banks nothing to suspend, he pointed out. "The labor of the

[14] Nashville *Republican Banner*, 19 Oct. 1839; Tenn. *Senate Journal*, 1839, pp. 49, 51.

[15] Walker to Polk, 20 Oct. 1839, Polk Papers.

[16] Tenn. *House Journal*, 1839, p. 49.

country bears the loss, whilst the banks during a period of suspension are often doing their most profitable business."

Banks, Polk conceded, had become so "interwoven and intimately connected with all our extensive commercial operations," that "their employment to a reasonable extent, in conducting our trade," had become "conducive to our prosperity." But he argued for legal regulations to exclude all banks not founded on "a solid and substantial specie basis." "Beyond this, Banks and Banking facilities are an evil," Polk declared. "An excess of paper circulation gives a fictitious value to property, paralyzes the industry of the country, produces extravagant habits of living, and excites a thirst for wild and adventurous speculation. An excess of Bank circulation must necessarily be followed by a contraction, which will operate severely upon the debtor classes, and especially upon such as have become so during such excess or abundance of paper money." In fact, the governor continued, it was just such a "wild, extravagant and disastrous speculation" that had brought the current depression on the country. These troubles could not be blamed on the government, for "No government can, without the exercise of despotic powers, control or restrain the individual enterprize of its citizens. In a government like ours the attempt to exercise such a power would be wholly incompatible with individual freedom."

"The only substantial and permanent relief is to be found in habits of economy and industry, and in the productive labour of our people," Polk maintained, in tones reminiscent of William Carroll's pronouncement on the depression of sixteen years earlier. "By the observance of these, another crop, would more than liquidate our Eastern debt. We must bring our expenses within our income. Our merchants and traders must cease to indulge in hazardous and wild speculations which they are unable to meet."

There was one thing government could do, and do at once. It could regulate banking to prevent the currency inflation that bred this dangerous inflationary spirit. The legislature had a clear legal right to control the state bank, and Polk declared that "an early resumption is in my judgment demanded by the interests of the State." As for the stock banks, Polk had argued while a freshman legislator that the state had a right to revise their charters, only to have his arguments refuted by the superior knowledge and skill of Grundy. Now he suggested that the same end could be accomplished by coercing the banks into agreeing to charter revisions.

Suspension was clearly a charter violation, and Polk thought the threat of revocation on this ground could be used as a club to force reform on the banks. First, they should be required to resume specie payment in short order. Second, they should be forbidden to declare any dividends until six months after resumption. Third, the existing prohibition of notes under five dollars should be extended to include notes under ten, and eventually twenty, dollars. And finally, the banks should be compelled to accept "such additional restrictions as the public safety may require and as experience may have shown to be necessary and proper."

With regard to the future operation of the banking system, Polk was adamantly opposed to the perennial appeals for an increase in banks and banking capital. He admitted that the distribution of the state bank's branches had left some sections with legitimate complaints and recommended that such areas (the Cumberland plateau was the section most obviously slighted) be given a branch, but the total capital of the bank should not be increased in the process. At the same time, however, he wanted the state bank to be as strong as possible. It had been hampered so far by its inability to sell more than one million of the two and a half million dollars in state bonds authorized for its capital. Polk suggested that these bonds be made saleable by being converted into sterling bonds, that is, bonds payable in sterling funds at London.[17]

Polk's position was statesmanlike and, in the circumstances, courageous. Though the cure he proposed was a painful one, he knew that no other kind would work, and he was willing to risk the political consequences. But would the Democratic legislators follow his bold leadership? The governor's message had no sooner been read than Yoakum introduced a resolution embodying Polk's proposal that the stock banks be forced to resume immediately and refrain from declaring dividends for six months, on pain of losing their charters. But for two months no action was taken in this direction. Another resolution calling for immediate resumption by the state bank got prompter consideration, though it was killed after a week of debate by a vote of nine to fourteen. Seven of the fourteen Democrats voted for this proposition, six opposed it, and one did not vote.[18]

17 Nashville *Republican Banner*, 24 Oct. 1839.
18 Tenn. *Senate Journal*, 1839, pp. 53-55, 71, 73, 83-85; Nashville *Republican Banner*, 23, 24, 30 Oct. 1839.

The six Democrats voting against resumption included a hard core of four or five Democratic senators who were to oppose effective bank regulation for the rest of the session. Among them were the senators from Bedford and Maury, and they were joined on this occasion by Sam Laughlin. Laughlin, who was closer to Polk than any other member of the senate, was to shift back and forth in subsequent votes on the banking question, guided apparently by no fixed convictions on banking policy except as the legislature's action might affect the political fortunes of the Democratic party. The Democrats "never *really* intended to direct the Bank forthwith to resume, nor in our opinion, wished it to do so," charged the Nashville *Banner.* "If Gov. Polk had been *sincere* in his regrets at the suspension by the Bank, he had only to give the cue to his partisans in the Legislature, and the edict for resumption would immediately have gone forth," the editor continued. "But neither the Governor nor his partisans dared assume the responsibility of such a step, although it would have been in strict accordance with the received and acknowledged doctrines of the party. They therefore, only sought to make a *show* of their desire for immediate specie payments by the Bank of Tennessee, for the sake of political effect."[19]

Despite its grain of truth, this indictment misrepresented the situation as far as Polk was concerned. The real difficulty was in controlling the handful of Democrats who opposed drastic action. Polk's desire to have a united party behind him in his bid for the vice presidential nomination may have made him unduly cautious about forcing the recalcitrants into line, but there can be no doubt of his personal desires. Repeated attempts at bank reform throughout the session revealed a steady pressure that could have come only from the governor's office, while Sam Laughlin's increasingly aggressive attitude was a reliable clue to the governor's position.

The next move came a week later in the house when Thomas Barry, the Democratic chairman of the committee on banks, introduced a bill for forced resumption and for the future regulation of all the banks by a board of bank commissioners. Barry announced that he was "radically opposed to all stock banks and all state banks." He was for "good old Jefferson's doctrines." He was for "going back to the currency contemplated by the wise men who framed the constitution." He was for "the much abused *Tom Benton currency.*"

[19] Nashville *Republican Banner,* 30 Oct. 1839.

The debate dragged on until the middle of December, with opponents contending that the bill would violate the banks' vested charter rights and saddle the state with great expense.[20]

The *Union*, speaking for Polk, finally vented its exasperation at the lawmakers' vacillation. "If in their opinion it be inexpedient to act on the subject at all, let them so decide," declared the Democratic organ. "But if they are for taking up and reforming the whole banking system—if they think the country as a patient can at this time well sustain the pain that it must necessarily undergo in effecting the *cure*—if they are desirous of recovering legislative control over the Banks of the State which by their charters claim a term of independence—if they would in future prevent the suspension of specie payments with impunity on the part of the Banks—we are of opinion that no plan can be more acceptable to the people, than that suggested by Mr. Barry." When the showdown came, seven Democratic representatives joined twenty-nine Whigs to postpone Barry's bill indefinitely by a scant majority of four, only one Whig voting with the thirty-one Democrats against postponement.[21]

Despite the defeat of the bank commissioner bill, the house Democrats were better bank reformers than their senate colleagues, and Barry was more successful with a resolution calling for immediate resumption by all the banks. It passed the house in four days. When the senate buried it in committee, the house passed another resumption resolution, which the Democrats supported thirty-three to eight. In the senate, however, five probank Democrats again joined the Whigs to postpone the resolution indefinitely.[22]

A new resumption resolution was promptly started on its way through the senate, the debate indicating that Governor Polk was trying to find a compromise. Laughlin declared immediate resumption to be a "humbug," only to be told by another Democratic senator that these were not the principles upon which he, Laughlin, had been elected, and that he seemed to be "in the habit of speaking one way and voting another on the Bank question."[23] Here Richard Warner, the probank Democratic senator from Bedford, offered an amendment providing for resumption by June 1, instead of immediately, a proposition that Laughlin supported strongly. By now,

---

[20] *ibid.*, 23 Dec. 1839; Tenn. *House Journal*, 1839, p. 118.

[21] Nashville *Union*, 20 Dec. 1839; Nashville *Republican Banner*, 23 Dec. 1839.

[22] Tenn. *House Journal*, 1839, pp. 138, 338; Tenn. *Senate Journal*, 1839, pp. 109, 124, 302-304; Nashville *Republican Banner*, 14, 17, 18, 19 Dec. 1839.

[23] Nashville *Republican Banner*, 31 Dec. 1839.

however, feeling between the two Democratic factions was so high that the antibank Democrats would not accept the resolution unless resumption were to be immediate, while Laughlin, Warner, and a few others were willing to vote for resumption only with the June 1 proviso. Enough Whigs, of course, sided with one group or the other to defeat either resumption proposition. At one point the resolution for immediate resumption passed, only to be reconsidered. Warner's June 1 amendment was reinserted, and with this change the resolution failed by a tie vote of ten to ten. Even Governor Polk's influence had not been enough to reconcile the warring Democrats.[24]

The Democratic leadership was now desperate for some action, and Laughlin immediately offered a measure to accomplish the purposes of the Barry bank commissioner bill without risking the innovation of commissioners. Laughlin's bill provided that the banks must resume by a certain date and accept four amendments to their charters: first, that they should issue no notes under ten dollars; second, that their charters should be subject to future amendment or repeal by a two-thirds vote of the legislature; third, that they should not pay dividends during suspension or for four months afterward; and fourth, that they should not issue in notes more than twice the amount of specie in their vaults.[25]

This was obviously the Democrats' last chance for thoroughgoing bank reform. A future date for resumption was specified to win over those who had supported the Warner compromise earlier, and heavy pressure was applied to bring the simon pures into line. But some Democrats still held out against resumption. "It is not coin that the people want and must have," insisted James Walker from Columbia, "it is something that will pay debts and relieve the pressure." The Whigs were "goading on our party to harsh measures towards the Banks," he warned, and constantly taunting the Democrats with the cry, "*you are the hard money party*—carry out your doctrines." Actually, said Walker, the Democrats were the "*sound currency party*," and to Walker "sound currency" meant at the moment the depreciated notes of suspended banks. If resumption were forced, he predicted, "the country must be ruined—and I think Democratic ascendancy destroyed." And with a shrewd allusion to Polk's stand for principle, he added, "What do men care for country—when the

---

[24] Tenn. *Senate Journal*, 1839, pp. 319, 326; Nashville *Republican Banner*, 24, 31 Dec. 1839, 1 Jan. 1840.
[25] Nashville *Republican Banner*, 24 Dec. 1839.

country ruins them?" The Democrats must not fall into the Whig trap. "Why break things to pieces, to satisfy the malevolence of the Whig party?"[26]

Such arguments persuaded two of the Democratic senators to hold out against all the pressures brought on them, and in the end their votes gave the Whigs just enough strength to defeat the Laughlin bill. The final tally, on January 21, was twelve to twelve, all the Whigs being in opposition, allied with the two Democratic antiresumptionists.[27]

The session was drawing to a close, and Laughlin tried to salvage something by introducing still another resumption resolution. This time it was forced through the senate, but overnight several Democrats were weaned away. The next day the resolution was reconsidered and defeated, four Democrats joining the Whig opposition, and one of them denouncing the antibank ranting of his colleagues with the statement, "God forbid, *he* should ever sacrifice the interests of his country on the altar of party." This, another Democratic senator retorted tartly, was "as good a *Whig* speech as he had ever heard!" The Democrats, crowed the Whig press, "dared not, as a party, carry out the principles, or rather *professions*, with which they humbugged their dear constituents."[28] So, after several months of feverish maneuvering and furious debate, the crucial banking question came to issue in no action whatever.

The legislature did act on several subsidiary banking matters. The clamor of various areas, especially Knoxville, the strongly Democratic Cumberland plateau, and Memphis, for additional banking capital gave rise to a number of proposals. Reluctant to add to the state bank's seven branches and without hope of satisfying all the discontented sections, the Democrats finally proposed to reduce the number of branches to two, located at Jackson and Knoxville. But enough Democrats came to the defense of the existing branches to defeat this scheme, and the matter was settled by establishing one additional branch at Sparta on the Cumberland plateau. In taking this action the legislature followed Polk's recommendation that the bank's total capital should not be increased, and the new branch's capital was furnished by reducing the capital of the other offices.[29]

26 Walker to Polk, 30 Dec. 1839, Polk Papers.
27 Tenn. *Senate Journal*, 1839, pp. 329, 358, 440, 448.
28 Nashville *Republican Banner*, 27 Jan. 1840.
29 *ibid.*, 16, 17 Jan. 1840; Tenn. *Session Laws*, 1839, chap. 69.

However the legislature ignored Polk's request for strengthening the state bank by converting its million and a half dollars of unsold state securities into sterling bonds. In a mood for drastic retrenchment and exasperated by the inconclusive struggle over resumption, the lawmakers took the opposite tack, ordering the unsold bonds called in and canceled, thus destroying any prospect of a stronger state bank. Though various efforts to extend the restriction on small notes failed to pass, the Democratic majority did beat back numerous Whig attempts to repeal the existing prohibition of notes under five dollars.[30]

Despite the frustrating results of this long struggle over banking, the outcome was probably as advantageous politically as any the Democrats could have devised. Governor Polk and a large majority of the Democratic legislators had registered their strong desire to curb irresponsible banking, but they were saved from the unfavorable reaction their reform measures would have produced if they had been able to enact them. At the same time they could argue that reform legislation had failed through no fault of the bulk of the party.

Another important political aspect of the banking situation was that the Democrats now gained control of the state bank and its branches. In appointing the new board of directors Polk followed Governor Cannon's precedent by naming eight members of his party and four of the opposition. The character of Polk's appointees—who included such universally respected Democrats as Governor Carroll, Judge George W. Campbell, and Dr. Felix Robertson—gave promise that the bank would be administered conservatively and without partisan bias. The new board promptly lived up to these expectations by retaining the incumbent officers of the institution, though they were all Whigs, and though the president, William Nichol, was Ephraim Foster's brother-in-law.

A similar spirit governed the appointment of directors for the eight branches. The central board tried to give the Democrats a majority on each branch board, but at the same time they so readily recognized the greater interest and skill in banking matters of businessmen, most of whom were Whigs, that many of the branches quickly came under Whig control. Within a few years five of the eight branches had Whig presidents and five had Whig cashiers.[31]

[30] Tenn. *Session Laws*, 1839, chap. 75; Tenn. *Senate Journal*, 1839, p. 120; Tenn. *House Journal*, 1839, pp. 217-222, 487; Nashville *Republican Banner*, 20 Dec. 1839.
[31] Nashville *Union*, 22 June 1840; Nashville *Republican Banner*, 27 Jan. 1840.

Polk was particularly anxious about the branch at Columbia, where he had good reason to fear James Walker's inflationary propensities, as well as the political effect of having his brother-in-law prominent in the branch's management. Unable to deny Walker's claim to a seat on the branch board, the governor implored him not to accept the presidency. But the prize was too tempting to a man of Walker's disposition, and he allowed his fellow directors to put him at the head of the branch, despite Polk's pleas. Though he vowed "fairness and impartiality and fidelity to the intent of the state," this promise was negated by the jubilant statement that followed it. At last, Walker rejoiced, "whatever relief the Bank can be fairly and safely made to afford to a suffering community," not forgetting the suffering James Walker, "may be afforded."[32]

IV

Hardly less important than the banking question was that of internal improvements. This legislature showed a radically different temper from the Whig-controlled body that had enacted the grandiose improvement program two years before. The Democrats were by nature more retrenchment-minded than the Whigs, but other factors also contributed to a decided reaction against state aid to transportation companies. Middle Tennessee, having fewer transportation problems than the other sections, and having secured the state aid it desired for its turnpikes, was now almost solidly against the improvement policy. Besides, the continuing depression had made it difficult to raise the private stock subscriptions and to sell the state bonds, and this had cooled enthusiasm for improvements in all sections.

Nevertheless the many companies already chartered were anxious for further state aid and were able to bring strong political pressure on the governor and legislature. The backers of the chief West Tennessee project, the LaGrange and Memphis Railroad, were demanding an increased state subscription and a grant of banking privileges in furtherance of their ambitious undertaking. They hoped to join their road along the southern border of Tennessee with various lines in northern Mississippi and Alabama, and eventually to connect at the present site of Chattanooga with the Georgia railroad system leading to the Atlantic coast.

---

[32] Walker to Polk, 20 June, 23 July 1840, Polk Papers.

The East Tennessee allotment of $1,600,000 in state bonds had been divided among three projects, and the supporters of all three were demanding further aid. Upper East Tennessee wanted river improvements and complained because the $300,000 in 5 per cent state bonds granted for this purpose could not be sold. The major portion of East Tennessee's allotment had been divided between two railway projects. The Knoxville area and the upper counties were committed to the Cincinnati and Charleston railroad scheme and wanted to use their share of the state subscription to build the Tennessee portion of a four-state system connecting the Ohio River with the South Carolina coast by a route crossing the mountains through the Cumberland Gap, past Knoxville, and along the French Broad River. The southern counties of East Tennessee argued, however, that their Hiwassee Railroad project, running from Knoxville to a junction with the Georgia railroad system near Chattanooga, was a much more practical way to reach the Atlantic coast. Neither of these roads had been able to raise enough of its private stock subscriptions to receive more than a small part of the state subscription, and even then, they complained, the bonds had to be sold at far below par, when they could be sold at all.[33]

When the legislature met, both the East Tennessee railroads were in dire straits. The Cincinnati and Charleston company had been granted the special privilege of using its funds as capital for a bank until they were needed for construction in Tennessee. Under the conservative direction of Polk's friend Doctor J. G. M. Ramsey of Knoxville, the Southwestern Railroad Bank was the only one in the state still paying specie. But the difficulty of raising capital was making it doubtful whether the railroad would ever be pushed through the mountains as far as Tennessee, and even the visionary Ramsey lost hope when the project's able and determined champion in South Carolina, Robert Y. Hayne, died. If the railroad were abandoned, its banking privileges would have to be surrendered along with the rest of its charter.[34]

The Hiwassee Railroad had made more progress at construction, but it had now exhausted all its funds and could raise no more from the private subscribers. The construction contractor, who was a

[33] For a full discussion of the Tennessee internal improvement program, see Stanley J. Folmsbee, *Sectionalism and Internal Improvements in Tennessee 1796-1845* (Knoxville, 1939).

[34] J. G. M. Ramsey to Polk, 26 Sept., 1 Nov. 1839, Polk Papers.

heavy subscriber and a Democrat, had persuaded the farmers along the route to work without pay for two more months, but, he informed Governor Polk, "If something is not done when that time expires the death warrant of our improvement is signed."[35] Polk's choice for the Senate, Alexander Anderson, wrote that the Whigs were redoubling their efforts for victory in 1840, and outlined a grandiose scheme whereby the state would make up the deficiencies in the private subscriptions to the Hiwassee road, grant it banking privileges, transfer it from Whig to Democratic control, and, in effect, convert it to Democratic political purposes in East Tennessee. The Democrats had been "made to feel the magnitude of the Rail Road (Hiwassee) power here," he said, and "they want reform, & this must be done from the President throughout! ! ! and Democrats in their place!" "Surely—surely," Anderson pleaded, "our friends will not leave us as naked as women in this last fight."[36]

Polk proved to be considerably more favorable to "a judicious system of Improvements" than his followers in the legislature. No subject was more important to the state, he declared in his message, and no other policy "can so much tend to develope [*sic*] our resources, and add to our wealth and prosperity." He stressed the clearing of navigable streams, especially in isolated East Tennessee; east-west projects to bind the three major sections more closely together; and north-south projects to connect with similar undertakings in other states. Some of these projects, said the governor, were already under construction, the state had encouraged them to proceed, and, "In their continued progress of construction they will probably require further public patronage."

Beyond these general remarks, his most specific proposal was that the state's improvement bonds be given "a character which will insure a ready sale in the market at their par value." This was only equitable, he argued. The legislature of 1837-1838 had clearly intended that the state subscribe an equal share with the stockholders, and it was unjust for the state to make its subscription in bonds that must be sold at a depreciated rate. The logical inference was that the bonds should be converted into sterling bonds and their interest increased from 5 to 6 per cent, as he had recommended in the case of the bank bonds. Moreover, Polk suggested, these bonds

---

[35] Kennedy Lonergan to Polk, 11 Dec. 1839, Polk Papers; E. G. Eastman to Polk, 26 Oct. 1839, *ibid.*

[36] Anderson to Polk, 3 Nov., 4 Dec. 1839, Polk Papers.

should all be marketed by the state bank, instead of being issued to the improvement companies to be "hawked about the streets of our principal commercial cities and sold in the market at ruinous sacrifices." Tennessee had a smaller debt in proportion to its population and resources than any other state, the governor maintained, and if his proposals were adopted, he had no doubt the bonds could be sold at par.

At the same time, however, Governor Polk insisted on more care to avoid wasting the state's money. Too many charters had already been granted to "local and unimportant works," which would return little profit and burden the state with a heavy debt. These charters should be repealed, and in the future the legislature should be careful to charter only such undertakings as would earn enough profit to retire the bonds. If this were done, the governor was convinced that the present state subscription of one half the capital was "not in my judgment too large and should be continued."

To carry out this policy Polk advocated the creation of a board of public works, consisting of two or more competent engineers. They would not only report on the cost, feasibility, and profitability of proposed projects, but also supervise minutely the construction of projects that were approved. The board would have to be paid adequately, he admitted, "but in the end their employment would be real economy."[37]

The legislature promptly proceeded to flout the governor's recommendations. From the first week of the session the clerks were flooded with bills to repeal all laws subscribing state bonds to internal improvement companies. Some of Polk's friends struggled manfully to salvage as much of the internal improvement system as possible, but the public reaction against it was too strong to be resisted by the politically sensitive local politicians who composed the legislature. Reluctant to sponsor a repeal bill themselves, the Democrats finally lined up behind a Whig anti-improvement measure and put it over by thumping majorities in both houses. In addition to ending new bond issues, this act authorized existing companies to surrender their charters or reduce their capital, and directed the attorney general to proceed against any companies guilty of fraud, misrepresentation, or misuse of the state funds. The state was still bound, of course, by its commitments to companies that had begun

[37] Nashville *Republican Banner*, 24 Oct. 1839.

their projects, but they were hedged about with additional regulations. Before further bonds could be issued to any company, the governor had to appoint three commissioners to ascertain whether previous funds had been expended in a bona fide manner, and whether individual stockholders had actually paid an amount equal to the requested state subscription.[38]

The economy-minded lawmakers, moreover, were so bemused by the prospective collapse of such enterprises as the Cincinnati and Charleston Railroad, and the consequent cancellation of the large state subscriptions already authorized, that they uniformly rejected all proposals to carry out Polk's recommendation for making the remaining bonds payable in sterling. Whig members actually furnished more support for these sterling bond propositions than Democrats, but this did not prevent the Whig press from raising a hue and cry against Polk for scheming to create "a *foreign* debt, and that debt to *England*!"[39]

Thus died the grandiose improvement program of 1838. Its greatest accomplishment was the construction of over 400 miles of macadamized turnpikes, mostly in Middle Tennessee, though the managers of these enterprises had usually let construction contracts to themselves at such high prices that the income never sufficed to pay the interest on the state bonds. The Cincinnati and Charleston charter was eventually surrendered, and great sectional bitterness was created when the state subscription was canceled, instead of being transferred to other East Tennessee undertakings. The Hiwassee and the LaGrange and Memphis railroads languished for more than a decade before being reorganized and completed in the 1850's. These results indicated that the legislature may have been wiser than the governor, for no matter what restrictions were placed on the improvement companies, the state would probably have continued to bear most of the expense for constructing poorly planned and badly managed enterprises.[40]

While it was not engaged on these major questions of banking and internal improvement, the legislature busied itself mainly with routine or local matters. In accord with the governor's recommenda-

---

[38] Tenn. *House Journal*, 1839, pp. 77, 86, 94, 101, 111, 352, 395, 396, 468, 476, 497, 539; Tenn. *Senate Journal*, 1839, pp. 35, 152, 154, 356, 359-360, 374-376; Nashville *Union*, 5 Feb. 1840.

[39] Nashville *Republican Banner*, 3 Jan. 1840; Folmsbee, *Internal Improvements*, 202-205.

[40] Folmsbee, *Internal Improvements*, 216-267.

tions, the administration of the common school system was tightened, and arrangements were made for opening and operating the lunatic asylum that had just been completed at Nashville. There was a bitter and in the end abortive fight to move the state capital to Murfreesboro, and two new counties were created. Blandly disregarding their cavalier treatment of the governor's proposals, the legislators named the first of these in honor of Polk, while the other was named for President Van Buren.[41]

Polk's inability to get what he wanted from the legislature should not obscure the fact that he was the first governor of Tennessee to function as legislative leader of his party. There were many reasons for his lack of success. The Democrats had only a narrow majority, and legislative independence was a habit of long standing in the state. It was customary for governors to make recommendations without much hope of seeing them enacted, and to Polk's Democratic followers the idea of party responsibility and party discipline was somewhat novel. On the banking issue, moreover, Polk ran into a hard core of determined opposition within his own party, while in the field of internal improvements he was trying to hold back one of those currents of public feeling that no politician can successfully defy.

It is probably also true that Polk still had much to learn about the techniques of executive leadership, but he had a capacity for learning from failure. As a young congressman he had rebounded from his defeat on the Tennessee land bill to become one of the ablest parliamentary strategists in the House of Representatives; and not many more years were to pass before he would be recognized as a master of executive influence over Congress. Still one other factor remains to be noted. At this moment Polk needed a united and harmonious party behind him more than he needed an impressive array of legislative accomplishments. His failure to bring heavier pressure on recalcitrant Democratic legislators was doubtless related to his ambitious nature, which could not rest content with the governorship of Tennessee.

V

References to Polk's vice presidential aspirations had all but disappeared from the state's Democratic newspapers during the

[41] Tenn. *Session Laws*, 1839, chaps. 10, 54; Polk to J. W. Childress, 24 Feb. 1840, Polk Papers.

gubernatorial campaign, for the Whigs had been predicting that he wanted the governorship only as a steppingstone to the high federal office. Despite this public silence, Polk and his friends were not inactive. J. G. Harris had hardly settled into the *Union*'s editorial chair before Polk had him writing to his former patron, George Bancroft, leader of the Massachusetts Democracy, and these efforts bore fruit in prompt endorsements of Polk by several New England newspapers. Meanwhile, in Washington and on his judicial travels through the West, Judge Catron continued to argue the merits of his fellow Tennessean and to bombard Jackson with appeals to take a hand in the vice presidential situation.[42]

The spring and summer of 1839 had witnessed a growing conviction throughout the Democratic party that Colonel Richard M. Johnson's renomination for vice president would be unwise, and that his place on the ticket should be filled by a southerner or southwesterner. Thomas Ritchie's powerful Richmond *Enquirer* bluntly suggested that Johnson step aside, while Amos Kendall was so disturbed by a reliable informant's account of "Old Tecumseh's" domestic habits that he sent it on to Van Buren, so the president could "see the depth of degradation to which the man has sunk whose name is associated with yours in the government."[43]

Kendall's friend had visited Colonel Johnson's tavern at Great Crossings, Kentucky, and reported that:

The old gentleman seems to enjoy the business of *Tavern Keeping* as well as any host I ever stopped with, and is as bustling a *landlord* as the most fastidious traveller could wish. The example of Cincinnatus laying down his public honors and returning to his plough should no longer be quoted as worthy of imitation, when the Vice President of these United States, with all his civic and military honors clustering around his time-honored brow, is, or seems to be so happy in the inglorious pursuit of tavern-keeping— even giving his personal superintendence to the chicken and egg purchasing and watermellon [*sic*] selling department.

Such undignified behavior was bad enough, but what really affronted Kendall's Yankee morality was the additional report that Colonel

[42] Harris to Polk, 30 Apr. [1839; misplaced 1843], Polk Papers; *Plymouth Rock and County Advertiser*, 9 May 1839, quoted in Arthur M. Schlesinger, Jr., *The Age of Jackson* (Boston, 1946), 441n.; E. D. Beach to Bancroft, 23 July 1839, George Bancroft Papers (MHS); Catron to Donelson, 4 Jan. 1839, Andrew Jackson Donelson Papers (LC; herein cited as Donelson Papers).

[43] Kendall to Van Buren, 22 Aug. 1839, Van Buren Papers; James Buchanan to J. R. Clay, 18 Apr. 1839, Duer Collection (HSP); Leland Winfield Meyer, *The Life and Times of Colonel Richard M. Johnson of Kentucky* (New York, 1932), 433-434.

Johnson "devotes most too much of his time to a young Delilah of about the complexion of Shakespears [*sic*] swarthy Othello." This young lady was "said to be his third *wife*; his second, which he sold for her infidelity, having been the sister of the present *lady*," continued Kendall's informant. "She is some eighteen or nineteen years of age and quite handsome—plays on the piano, calls him my *dear Colonel* and is called *my dear* in return, and is said to be very *loving* and devoted."[44]

As stories like this continued to circulate, many of the national party leaders, probably including President Van Buren, lost their enthusiasm for Johnson. With the party increasingly dependent on southern support, the colonel would clearly be a heavy burden on the Van Buren ticket. Moreover Johnson was not a particularly reliable Democrat. He had won the nomination in 1836 mainly by making a nuisance of himself, and his views in favor of a national bank and federal internal improvements were well known.

But it would not be easy to get rid of the troublesome colonel. The Democrats could not very well criticize their own vice president openly, and since he had run with Van Buren four years before, it would seem unfair to drop him now for no announced reason. Besides, Johnson had some real support. His homespun qualities and the legend that he had slain Tecumseh made him a popular figure throughout the Northwest, while his famous argument for separation of church and state had endeared him to the eastern workingmen, whose support might be decisive in the pivotal and doubtful state of New York.

But the greatest obstacle to eliminating Johnson was the multiplicity of candidates springing forward to claim his place. Thomas Ritchie's Virginia Democracy proposed former Speaker Andrew Stevenson; Alabama nominated Senator William R. King; Georgia presented the claims of Secretary of State John Forsyth; there was some sentiment for the secretary of war, Joel R. Poinsett of South Carolina; and finally, Polk's distinguished congressional services and the quiet but persistent activity of the Tennesseans had brought his name into discussion. It was impossible for the party leaders to throw their support to any one of these candidates without antagonizing all the others on the eve of a national election.[45]

44 Anonymous to Kendall, 12 Aug. 1839, Van Buren Papers.
45 Buchanan to Mrs. F. P. Blair, 15 May 1839, Blair-Lee Papers (PU); Nashville *Republican Banner*, 26, 27 July 1839.

Polk's unexpected redemption of Tennessee—"one of the most astonishing political revolutions which the ballot box ever witnessed," a Michigan newspaper called it—sent a thrill through the national Democracy and made him front runner in the vice presidential sweepstakes. Polk's victory, said the Michigan editor, "was not brought about by the ordinary means of accomplishing a political triumph—it was the achievement of a political campaign the best planned, and the most valiantly fought that ever distinguished a popular election"; and he expressed the reaction of countless loyal Democrats when he called on the party to draft Polk as Van Buren's running mate.[46]

Not until after the August election did Polk's campaign for the nomination come out in the open. The returns were barely in when Democratic newspapers all over Tennessee began running up the Van Buren and Polk flag, while public meetings in county after county called on the legislature to place him in nomination. This apparently spontaneous activity was, of course, carefully planned, though Polk kept in the background and left the work to a handful of confidants. Chief among them were Doctor John S. Young, who was shortly to be elected secretary of state by the legislature; Alexander Anderson, likewise soon to be rewarded; Sam Laughlin; and Doctor Ramsey.[47]

Polk, however, was not completely inactive. His visit to northern Alabama just before the inauguration was hardly unrelated to his vice presidential ambitions, while his inaugural address, with its state rights flavor, was designed to appeal to both old-fashioned Republicans and Calhounites, and was distributed to leading Democrats of this stripe all over the South. "Father" Ritchie of the *Enquirer*, the official guardian of the Jeffersonian tradition, read it with "the strongest approbation," pronouncing it "the best synopsis of the Democratic State Rights Creed, we have seen for some time past," and recommending it to his readers as "a text for these times."[48]

Meanwhile the Columbia *Democrat* launched a vicious attack

[46] *Michigan Free Press*, quoted in Dresden *Tennessee Democrat*, 25 Sept. 1839.

[47] Ramsey to Polk, 20 Aug., 26 Sept. 1839, Polk Papers; Laughlin to Polk, 20 Aug., 6 Sept. 1839, *ibid.*; Anderson to Polk, 22 Aug. 1839, *ibid.*; Young to Polk, 21 Aug., 1 Sept. 1839, *ibid.*; Anderson to Young, 16, 30 Sept. 1839, *ibid.*; Nashville *Union*, 9 Oct. 1839.

[48] Richmond *Enquirer*, quoted in Nashville *Union*, 13 Nov. 1839; Polk to Jackson, 31 Aug. 1839, Jackson Papers.

against "Old Dick" Johnson on the score of his alleged abolitionism, quoting an abolition journal's account of his recent visit to New York. During his stay in the city, Johnson "took much pains to express to some of the gentlemen of color, his deep interest in the question of their rights and prospects, as all he should leave behind him at death (his two daughters) were identified in destiny with them," ran this account. "He also declared that each of his own slaves held a deed of emancipation, and would never serve any but himself. He introduced his colored visitors to many of the public characters that called at his lodgings, and expressed many sentiments highly honorable to his heart."[49]

Polk had been governor only two days when Laughlin confronted the legislature with resolutions proposing him as Van Buren's running mate, and despite Whig obstructionism, less than a week was required to push them through both houses.[50] Polk's campaign now shifted from Tennessee to Washington, where the decisive negotiations would be conducted during the winter. Here Polk was relying on his friends in the Tennessee congressional delegation, especially Hopkins Turney, Aaron Brown, the faithful Cave Johnson, and Senators Grundy and Anderson. Their first task was to persuade the party to hold a national convention for the purpose of replacing Johnson on the ticket. Jackson was enlisted to advocate this plan in letters to Frank Blair, Van Buren, and others, while Polk himself addressed the president, emphasizing the narrow margin by which the Democrats had carried Tennessee and implying that an appealing ticket would be needed to keep the state Democratic in 1840.

When Polk's lieutenants reached Washington early in December, they found themselves in the midst of such a violent struggle over organization of the House that the vice presidential question was nearly forgotten. Neither the Whigs nor the Democrats had a clear majority, and for two weeks the leaderless body wrangled over which of two rival delegations from New Jersey should be seated. When the House was finally able to proceed to the speakership election, conflict broke out again, this time within the Democratic ranks. The trouble arose from the rival ambitions of Benton and Calhoun to succeed Van Buren four years hence, and from the growing sectional divisions that underlay this rivalry.

The Democratic caucus finally settled on George W. Jones, a

[49] Columbia *Democrat*, quoted in Nashville *Republican Banner*, 11 Sept. 1839.
[50] Nashville *Republican Banner*, 22 Oct. 1839; Tenn. *House Journal*, 1839, p. 73.

Virginian of the Benton wing, for speaker, but when five South Carolinians bolted and prevented his election, the party shifted its support to the Alabama Calhounite Dixon H. Lewis. Eleven Democrats refused to support Lewis, however, and in the end the Whigs and Calhounites united to elect Robert M. T. Hunter, a Virginia Whig who was at the same time a devoted disciple of Calhoun. Among the eleven Democrats who refused to support Lewis were three of the six Tennesseans, Cave Johnson, Hopkins Turney, and Julius Blackwell. The "little knot of nullifyers" were trying to coerce the whole party, Johnson charged hotly in a letter to Polk. "I would have lost my right arm before I would have yielded to such conduct. . . . I expect they intended to rule us when they joined us, and if we are to submit to such dictation from such a squad our friends must get a different sort of man from me."[51]

Johnson feared that his conduct would injure Polk's prospects, for the vice presidential question was also deeply involved in the struggle over the presidential succession in 1844. The powerful Pennsylvania Democrat James Buchanan, who was hoping to squeeze between Calhoun and Benton into first place on the 1844 ticket, already saw in Polk a possible rival and moved to counter this threat by booming his close personal friend Senator King of Alabama for the 1840 vice presidential nomination. The Van Burenites, in turn, sought to clip Buchanan's wings by organizing a movement to throw Pennsylvania to Secretary Forsyth for vice president. It was even rumored that Van Buren was trying to place Forsyth ahead of Benton for the presidential succession in 1844, and for a time this induced Benton's supporters to rally around Polk. But the Forsyth movement failed to take hold, and the Benton men eventually came to share Buchanan's fears that Polk might develop into a presidential rival by 1844.[52]

These apprehensive aspirants were not the only ones who perceived that Polk was possible presidential timber. "Your pretensions are put on stilts after this success for Gov.," wrote Judge Catron from Washington, "so as to induce the belief, that you are to be worth more than any man in the west." Even before the Tennessee

---

51 Johnson to Polk, 16 Dec. [1839], Polk Papers.

52 Johnson to Polk, 10 Nov. [1839], 4 Dec. [1839], Polk Papers; Catron to Polk, 3 Jan. 1840, *ibid.*; J. M. Niles to Bancroft, 25 Nov. 1839, Bancroft Papers; Buchanan to Mrs. F. P. Blair, 15 May 1839, Blair-Lee Papers; W. B. Lewis to Buchanan, 1 June 1839, James Buchanan Papers (HSP); King to Buchanan, 20 June 1839, *ibid.*; S. Pleasanton to Buchanan, 24 June 1839, *ibid.*

election, a Massachusetts newspaper had observed that "Mr. Polk is yet a young man—but a little more than forty, we believe—and will by and by be President of these United States." Shortly after his victory, a leading Democrat reported that "there are a very considerable portion of our *common people that are looking forward to seeing James K. Polk as the successor of Mr Van Buren*";[53] and one of these common people himself informed the newly elected governor that "The plan that I had laid off was for you to be our Governor six years and then Senator Six and at the end of Benton's eight years make you President."[54]

Similar plans were in the minds of several experienced politicians. Both Joshua Martin, a former congressional colleague, soon to be governor of Alabama, and Polk's old friend Archibald Yell, just now making a successful race for governor of Arkansas, warned him against endangering his ultimate chances for the presidency by running prematurely for vice president and antagonizing the other hopefuls; while a Mississippi and an Arkansas congressman expressed similar views to Cave Johnson. At the same time Johnson had to caution a North Carolina congressman against venting too openly his enthusiasm for Polk as a presidential candidate in 1844.[55]

Yell advised Polk to run for reelection as governor, so as to consolidate the Democratic position in Tennessee. Then, he assured his friend, he would have no difficulty obtaining either a Cabinet seat or the vice presidency in 1844. "Recollect you are only about 40 years of age, too young for the Presidency," he admonished, "at 53 will be young enough and younger than any former President." That Polk himself was harboring some such thoughts might be taken for granted, even if Yell had not confidently employed the phrase, "your *ultimate wishes*," in speaking of the presidency. But Polk would not accept his friends' counsel of patience and discretion. Rather, he sought to allay the suspicions of other politicians by an unequivocal declaration that, if nominated for vice president, he would not be a candidate in 1844 for either the first or second office.[56]

53 Catron to Polk, 3 Jan. 1840, Polk Papers; *Plymouth Rock and County Advertiser*, 9 May 1839, quoted in Schlesinger, *Age of Jackson*, 441n.; W. H. Humphreys to Polk, 25 Sept. [1839; misplaced 1838], Polk Papers.

54 Amos Kirkpatrick to Polk, 17 Oct. 1839, Polk Papers.

55 J. L. Martin to Polk, 2, 20 Nov. 1839, Polk Papers; Johnson to Polk, 12 Dec. [1839; misplaced 1842], 8 Jan. [1840; misplaced 1839], *ibid.*

56 Yell to Polk, 12 Dec. 1839, Polk Papers; Ramsey to Polk, 26 Sept. 1839, *ibid.*; Johnson to Polk, 4 Dec. [1839], *ibid.*

VI

The early reports from Polk's friends at Washington were optimistic. Cave Johnson had been assuring the Benton men that Polk would probably support the Missourian in 1844, and Benton, without committing himself, sought to leave the impression that he favored Polk. Calhoun was openly on Polk's side, partly because he regarded him as the strongest southern candidate against Johnson, partly because of Polk's inaugural address, and partly because of some missionary work Doctor Ramsey had done in South Carolina while attending a directors' meeting of the Cincinnati and Charleston Railroad. Even Frank Blair tried to impress the Tennesseans with his friendliness to Polk's aspirations.[57]

The most encouraging development was the agreement that a national convention should be held. The New Yorkers and some other prominent Democrats were cool to this proposal, since Van Buren's renomination was a foregone conclusion and his New York delegation would run the risk of alienating some of the vice presidential hopefuls in a convention. Senator Silas Wright, Van Buren's principal strategist, preferred to let each aspirant run in his own section, leaving the final choice to the Senate, if no one got a majority in the electoral college. But Polk was confident that the mere calling of a convention would be sufficiently indicative of dissatisfaction with "Uncle Dick" to make him step aside. The Tennessee papers and Polk's letters to Washington harped continually on this theme, and here he had the support of King and Forsyth. It was arranged for the New Hampshire Democrats to lead the way, and following their call for a convention to meet at Baltimore in May, state after state endorsed the idea. Meanwhile Polk had been receiving assurances that he was second choice in King's Alabama and Forsyth's Georgia and first choice in the other southern states; J. George Harris's appeals to George Bancroft seemed to be bringing New England into the Polk camp; and there were even newspaper endorsements of Polk here and there through the northwestern states.[58]

But shortly after the first of the year, the tide began to turn.

[57] Ramsey to Polk, 18 Dec. 1839, Polk Papers; Nashville *Republican Banner*, 26 Dec. 1839; Johnson to Polk, 10 Nov. [1839], 8 Jan. [1840; misplaced 1839], Polk Papers; A. V. Brown to Polk, 4 Feb. 1840, *ibid.*

[58] Johnson to Polk, 12 Dec. [1839; misplaced 1842], 1 Jan. 1840, Polk Papers; Nashville *Union*, 25 Nov., 9 Dec. 1839, 24, 31 Jan. 1840.

When the Whig national convention at Harrisburg in December unexpectedly dropped Clay and nominated General William Henry Harrison, "Uncle Dick" Johnson's stock had begun rising rapidly. The Whigs had finally learned the lesson of the Jacksonian democratic revolution. In this campaign they would appeal to the common man with a homespun westerner, whose chief claim to fame was his victory at Tippecanoe over the forces of the same Tecumseh whom Johnson had reputedly slain later at the Thames. Now it was more important than ever, Johnson's friends argued cogently, that he should remain on the Van Buren ticket.

How great a blow this development was to Polk's chances became apparent when the Ohio Democratic convention endorsed Johnson, despite the previous commitment of many of the state's top party leaders to Polk. In North Carolina the situation was reversed; wide popular support for Polk was thwarted when the state leaders prevented any endorsement whatever.[59] Meanwhile Silas Wright had brought the Tennessee congressmen around to his point of view, by promising them that if no nomination were made, New York would support Polk in the electoral college, where his election would be assured. Early in February all but one member of the delegation addressed to Polk a joint appeal to abandon his insistence on a nomination by the national convention. "If the Convention could be dissolved harmoniously, without making nominations at all," wrote his friends in Congress, "it would accord better with our views than any other course." Calhoun, too, sent word by Aaron Brown that he favored no nomination.[60]

These suggestions Polk stubbornly rejected. The memories of 1835-1836, when he had denounced Judge White for running as a sectional candidate, were too fresh to allow him to consider for a moment being only one of several candidates. "I have acted a passive part," he wrote somewhat disingenuously to a Calhounite who had urged the no-nomination strategy. "I resolved that if I should be selected as the candidate of the party, with whom I agree in political sentiment, I should not feel at liberty to decline the nomination, but on the contrary regard it, as a high distinction. This is the only position which I could consent to occupy." Polk regarded the scheme

[59] Nashville *Republican Banner*, 6, 13 Feb. 1840; T. L. Hamer to T. P. Moore, 23 Jan. 1840, Polk Papers; Harris to Bancroft, 19 Feb. 1840, Bancroft Papers.

[60] Grundy, McClellan, Watterson, Turney, Johnson, and Brown to Polk, 3 Feb. 1840, Polk Papers; Brown to Polk, 4 Feb. 1840, *ibid*.

to strengthen the ticket by running sectional vice presidential candidates as a departure from principle. His back up, he expressed with unusual clarity the inflexible though narrow adherence to principle that characterized his whole career. "As regards the political principles which I entertain," he wrote,

they are not as of yesterday. They were formed upon mature consideration, and have been long acted on. They were boldly and fearlessly avowed every where, in my canvass last Summer, both orally and in writing. And after the election was over they were deliberately re-iterated and placed in a durable form in my Inaugural Address and Message to the Legislature. They are unchanged, and I am quite sure I shall live and die with them, and this too even though they should prostrate or annihilate me, as a public man. I have during my whole course been opposed to a tariff of protection, Internal Improvements by Federal Authority, a Bank of the U. States, and shall be equally so, to large standing armies of any kind whether of militia or regulars.[61]

So Polk renewed his demands that his friends press for his nomination at Baltimore and left early in March for his annual visit to the Mississippi plantation, where for a month he was out of touch with Washington. Meanwhile Harris was urging Bancroft to bring out the Massachusetts Democracy officially for Polk, and Jackson was writing peremptory letters in a similar vein to Blair, Catron, and Van Buren.[62]

Polk's managers at Washington, however, remained cool to this strategy. Cave Johnson wrote the governor a long letter carefully explaining once more that the Northwest was sure to go for "Old Dick" in the convention and most of the South for Polk, leaving the decision to the northeastern Democrats. Though they preferred Polk personally, Johnson continued, they would make their decision on the basis of expediency, that is, whether to risk the Northwest by nominating Polk or the South by nominating Johnson. The Northwest was more doubtful territory for the Democrats, and Cave Johnson was sure that "in despite of all that can be said or done by your friends the Convention will give it to RMJ."[63]

Grundy was less patient. He was "mortified" by the implication in recent letters from Tennessee that "we who are here, are not

61 Polk to David Hubbard, 7 Feb. 1840, copy, Polk Papers.
62 Johnson to Polk, 27 Feb. [1840; misplaced 1841], Polk Papers; Harris to Bancroft, 19 Feb. 1840, Bancroft Papers; Jackson to Blair, 15 Feb. 1840, Jackson Papers; Jackson to Van Buren, 17 Feb. 1840, Van Buren Papers.
63 Johnson to Polk, 27 Feb. [1840; misplaced 1841], Polk Papers.

acting as zealously as we should." "I will not do a foolish thing knowingly," he wrote with some warmth.[64] Even Donelson, who had gone to Washington to stiffen the backs of Polk's friends, was converted to the Wright-Grundy no-nomination strategy. All these men, though, on the basis of Wright's assurances, were confident that Polk would be the ultimate choice, if the convention did not make a nomination.

By the time Polk got back to Nashville and read these and similar letters, events had strengthened Grundy's arguments. The Virginia Democratic convention had endorsed Polk but refused to send delegates to the national convention, while South Carolina, another Polk state, would likewise be unrepresented. Besides, King's chances had become so slim that he was no longer a serious contender, and he and Buchanan were shifting over to Johnson, who would not be in Buchanan's way in 1844, carrying the big Pennsylvania delegation with them.[65]

Even now Polk did not abandon hope. The time had come for plainer talk. Knowing that the party needed him on its ticket in the South, he began to intimate that he would not run without a convention nomination. New York and New England could still save the party, he threatened subtly, by taking a stand in the convention. Jackson again appealed to Van Buren. "Could a man of high honorable feelings & character continue a candidate," Old Hickory asked indignantly, if he were merely being used along with others to strengthen the ticket; "for one, I am sure, Col Polk would not."[66] Harris was simultaneously making a last effort with Bancroft. "We prize Polk too highly to enter him on a *scrub-race*," the Nashville editor wrote. "He is too good a man—and unless we are *cornered* he shall not run such a tilt, if it can be prevented." These tactics produced some results. Bancroft was finally persuaded, and the Democratic members of the Massachusetts legislature duly endorsed the Tennessean. About the same time, Polk's hopes were further encouraged by a letter from Thomas Hamer, an influential Ohio Democrat, who promised to carry his state's Baltimore delegation for Polk, despite the state convention's endorsement of Johnson.[67]

---

[64] Grundy to Polk, 2 Mar. 1840, Polk Papers.

[65] Donelson to Polk, 4 Mar. 1840, Polk Papers.

[66] Jackson to Van Buren, 3 Apr. 1840, Van Buren Papers; Polk to Johnson, 30 Mar. 1840, copy, Polk Papers.

[67] Harris to Bancroft, 27 Mar. 1840, Bancroft Papers; Nashville *Union*, 6 Apr. 1840; T. L. Hamer to T. P. Moore, 23 Jan. 1840, Polk Papers.

Polk was playing a dangerous game. Despite all he could do, there was a good chance that the convention would not nominate; and unless he wanted to alienate the party leaders irrevocably, he could no longer delay a careful statement of what his ultimate course would be. If the convention did not nominate, he announced finally, he would wait to see whether he was taken up by a majority of the Democratic states, and if this occurred, he would not withdraw his name. But under no circumstances would he "consent to be run by a *minority*, against the *majority*, of my own party, . . . *merely* for the purpose of strengthening the ticket in a few States, in the Presidential election. To be *used* in a few States, merely for that purpose, would be a sacrifice of myself and of all my future prospects, to which I ought not voluntarily to agree, and which the party ought not to require of me."[68] Polk went on to point out that

That was the unenviable position occupied by Judge White in the Presidential election of 1836, when he was used only in a few States merely to answer a purpose, and with the certainty that he could not be elected, even though he received all the votes, in all the States where he was run. His fate is now a matter of history. By permitting himself to be so used he was destroyed. I was among those who objected to his position at that time, and made it a chief ground of attack, that he was used by a minority, to answer a purpose merely, and without hope or prospect of his own election.

Under these circumstances, Polk thought he should not be "required to act a part which would sacrifice the little public character which I have been labouring so many years to make for myself."[69]

The position that Polk outlined here still did not represent so great a concession to the Wright-Grundy strategy as may appear at first glance. The New Yorkers were obviously so fearful of having Johnson on the ticket in the South that they were willing to promise Polk success in the electoral college, in order to keep him in the running without a convention nomination. Thus New York could avoid antagonizing the other aspirants until after the election. Polk's position amounted, in effect, to a threat. If he were not endorsed following the convention by a clear majority of the party, including New York, then he would withdraw and endanger Van Buren's success in the South. This is what he meant by his constantly

68 Polk to Johnson, 30 Mar. 1840, copy, Polk Papers.
69 Polk to David Hubbard, 8 Apr. 1840, photostat, George Washington Campbell Papers (LC), Box III. The phrasing of this letter is almost identical to that of the letter to Johnson above. Presumably Polk was writing similar letters to other Democratic politicians about this time.

reiterated suggestion that New York "must *finally* take her position, and would give no more offense now, than she would at a later period, when it may be out of her power to avert the danger which threatens the party." "If New York makes a misstep," as he stated it more baldly in another letter, "she may put to hazard the main election, whereas by a prudent but decided course taken *now*, she may put our success beyond all doubt."[70] In other words, if the New Yorkers wanted to keep him in the running, the best way to do it was by forcing his nomination at Baltimore.

But such final, halfhearted efforts as Polk's friends at Washington made to win over the Empire State failed. Senator Anderson, who was so sensitive to Polk's wishes that he had refused to join the rest of the Tennessee delegation in recommending the no-nomination strategy, reported that the attempt had been made, "in all the modes in which it could be done," but that "New York will not consent to be constrained." Even Anderson was now forced to admit that a nomination was virtually out of the question. Van Buren had already replied to Jackson's letters with expressions of "a great deal of uneasiness" over the vice presidential question. "The exertions made by Govr Polk in the great struggle in Tennessee," the president wrote, "added to his previous strong claims upon the confidence & affection of the Democracy of the nation, are so highly appreciated, that I for a season supposed that he would in the sequel be most likely to carry the question in the convention." However, he continued tactfully, it would be impossible for him to intervene, and both Johnson's availability as Harrison's equal in military fame, and a widespread disinclination to cut the popular colonel off the ticket had made Polk's nomination unlikely.[71]

Polk's pertinacity had placed Grundy in an embarrassing position with his New York friends, and he was thoroughly exasperated. "You know," he reminded the governor,

my Judgment has uniformly been against a nomination at Baltimore and if the Ten. delegation had not been urged from home to act against their own convictions, the Convention would not have met, or no nomination of Vice-president would have been made—and you would have been Vicepresident, beyond all doubt. It is true, we have not acted against our Judgment— but we have not felt authorised to act agreeably to it—with that energy

70 Polk to Laughlin, 1, 2 Apr. 1840, Polk-Laughlin Letters, special section of Polk Papers.
71 Anderson to Polk, 14 Apr. 1840, Polk Papers; Van Buren to Jackson, 7 Apr. 1840, Jackson Papers, Second Series.

with which we might have acted—as it was expedient that every letter, newspaper paragraph &c from Ten. indicated a different course from the one, we deemed Judicious. Should there be no nomination at Baltimore, you will probably be elected. But the prospect is not as good as it would have been if the proper steps had been taken—but which seemed to be interdicted by our Constituents. I have at no time in my life, seen my way so clear, as I have on this whole matter, and I have never been so thwarted & vexed by opinions of a contrary character from those who have not the means of Judging correctly.

"To all I have heard upon the subject," Grundy concluded devastatingly, "I have one answer to make—you cannot be nominated by that convention—that I suppose is sufficient."[72]

At the very moment Grundy was thus venting his exasperation in Washington, Polk was conferring in Nashville with Sam Laughlin, whom he had pressed into service to go to Baltimore and make one last effort for Polk's nomination. Polk had induced General Jackson to come in from the Hermitage for a visit, and as soon as Laughlin reached town, the governor had taken him and several other convention delegates to his house for tea with Old Hickory. Jackson assured the delegates that he was "very deeply impressed with the importance of the nomination of President and Vice President," particularly Polk's nomination for the second place. The next morning, just before their departure for Washington and Baltimore, the delegates again met with Polk and "heard his views at large, and his determination." Polk stressed the fact that his friends at Washington had not known of the Massachusetts endorsement when they advocated the no-nomination strategy, and he carefully instructed Laughlin and the others to impress the party leaders with his determination not to run, unless he were supported by a majority of the party.[73]

Reaching Washington ten days later, Laughlin found Polk's friends so fearful of Johnson's nomination that the only hope for Polk seemed to lie in preventing any nomination whatever. "All were now agreed that Gov. Polk could not be nominated," Laughlin noted in his diary, "that Johnson could not without New York, and that [the] best way, if possible, was to make no nomination."[74] But it appeared that even this might be difficult to accomplish. The

[72] Grundy to Polk, 15 Apr. 1840, Polk Papers.
[73] "Diaries of S. H. Laughlin, of Tennessee, 1840, 1843," *Tennessee Historical Magazine*, II (Mar. 1916), 45-47.
[74] *ibid.*, 52.

Buchanan-King men were urging the Johnson and Polk backers to unite on King as a compromise candidate, and this failing, were ready to insist on Johnson's nomination. The Kentuckian's grass roots popularity in New York City threatened to drag even the Empire State into the Johnson movement. Grundy, working closely with Wright, was moving heaven and earth to commit the New Yorkers and Benton's northwestern supporters solidly to the no-nomination strategy. Massachusetts had decided that the best way to aid Polk and prevent a nomination was by sending no delegates to Baltimore, but at the last minute the Johnson movement became so ominous that one of the Massachusetts congressmen hastened home to round up a delegation to vote against a nomination. When the Tennesseans held their final caucus in Washington on Saturday night, May 2, they decided, as a last resort, to refuse to attend the convention, if it looked as though a nomination would be made in spite of all their efforts.[75]

Everything hinged on whether the New York delegation could be held to the no-nomination strategy. Grundy took the six a.m. train to Baltimore on Sunday for a meeting with the New Yorkers' floor leader, General John A. Dix. Grundy "did wonders," Aaron Brown reported admiringly, but he required the aid of "every thing every man from Tennessee could do." Not only was New York firmly committed to the no-nomination strategy, but the important Ohio delegation was also brought into line.[76]

When the convention was finally called to order on Tuesday, May 5, the problem was referred to a committee on nominations, headed by Polk's old friend Senator Clement C. Clay of Alabama, and including a representative from every delegation. The committee unanimously endorsed Van Buren for president, and after heated debate Clay was able to carry a preamble and resolution recommending no nomination for vice president. The vote in committee, based on the electoral vote of each state represented, was 99 for nominating and 132 against.[77]

Johnson's friends now recognized the impossibility of obtaining the two-thirds majority that the Democrats had begun to require for nomination. But they heatedly demanded that the convention

---

75 Laughlin to Polk, 29 Apr. [misplaced 29 Aug.], 29 Apr., 2, 3 May 1840, Polk Papers.
76 Brown to Polk, 8 May 1840, Polk Papers; Laughlin to Polk, 6 May 1840, *ibid.*
77 Laughlin to Polk, 6 May 1840, Polk Papers.

at least ballot, confident that the results would show Johnson so far ahead that he would become the choice of the whole party in the fall election. Grundy finally silenced their clamor with a sally of wit. The party had "a commander-in-chief, and a brave one, too," he pointed out, adding that "if we could get the head along, the tail would not be far behind." In the general laughter that greeted this pleasantry, the committee's resolution passed unanimously, even the Johnson men remaining silent to create an appearance of harmony.[78]

Polk's friends regarded the outcome as a distinct victory. Grundy, according to the other Tennesseans, had "surpassed himself," and though he was "so nearly broke down" that he could not write to Polk immediately, he sent word through Aaron Brown to "keep your flag flying—& all will be well yet."[79]

VII

The decisions of the Baltimore convention were reported in the Nashville newspapers on May 18 and immediately placed Polk in an embarrassing position. Grundy's plan was to discourage any further talk of the vice presidency during the campaign, leaving New York and other uncommitted states free to vote for Polk in the electoral college. But the reaction of the Whig press indicated that this would not be easy. Polk's situation was made even more uncomfortable by the manner in which the vexed John Forsyth resigned his vice presidential aspirations. As soon as the convention failed to nominate, Forsyth had issued a statement declaring that "no friend of the Administration can hope for an election by the people," and that the successful candidate must be elected by the Senate and consequently would hold his place "against the decision of a majority of his fellow-citizens." Under these circumstances, said the secretary of state, he did not want his name "mixed up in the contest" any longer. Forsyth's statement was gleefully seized upon by the Nashville *Banner*. "We shall see whether his Excellency, Gov. Polk, is willing to seek office on terms which the high-spirited Georgian has so contemptuously spurned," Allen Hall taunted. "Our opinion is, that he will resort to any means and accept the office on any terms."[80]

[78] *Niles' National Register*, LVIII (9 May 1840), 151.
[79] Turney to Polk, 8 May 1840, Polk Papers; Brown to Polk, 8 May 1840, *ibid.*
[80] Nashville *Republican Banner*, 18 May 1840.

The same day, however, the *Union* indicated that Polk had no such intention. The Democrats in the other states, demanded Harris, should promptly declare their preference. Here again was a veiled threat to New York that Polk would withdraw unless explicit support were forthcoming. Jackson was characteristically blunt in letters to Van Buren and Blair. Though Tennessee and probably other states would be lost without Polk on the ticket, he warned, "the declared principles of Govr. Polk will cause him, in due time, to withdraw from the canvass, unless from the demonstrations of the states a sufficient number come out in his favour that if they adhere to him will elect him." These facts, Jackson told the president, should be made known to the New York leaders, for if a New York convention endorsed Polk, the whole South and West would fall into line, and the election would be safe.[81]

But the trend to Johnson, reinforced by politicians averse to building up potential rivals for 1844, was so strong that the New Yorkers could hardly reverse it, even if they wanted to. The Maryland Democrats had endorsed Johnson before the national convention adjourned, and Vermont, Pennsylvania, and New Jersey followed suit in rapid order. Whig editors in Tennessee featured these and other evidences of Johnson's strength prominently.[82] This deriding of Polk's pretensions reached a climax on May 28, when the Whig press republished a New York Democratic editorial approving the action of the Baltimore convention, on the ground that "by inciting our friends to active exertions in behalf of their favorite candidates," it would "call out greater strength for our candidate for the Presidency." Allen Hall fairly pounced on this admission of the Democratic strategy. "If Gov. Polk is willing to disgrace his station by playing the part of 'cats-paw' for Mr. Van Buren—a part which Mr. *Forsyth* contemptuously scorned—the people of Tennessee have quite too much self-respect to countenance the degradation," the *Banner* proclaimed. "We predict that Gov. Polk will be compelled by the indignant voice of his fellow citizens to abandon the humiliating position he now occupies in relation to the Vice Presidency."[83]

Polk had already decided that his position was intolerable, and

[81] Jackson to Van Buren, 21 May 1840, Van Buren Papers; Nashville *Union*, 18 May 1840.

[82] *Niles' National Register*, LVIII (30 May 1840), 147, 194, 199; Nashville *Republican Banner*, 19, 20, 22, 26 May 1840.

[83] Nashville *Republican Banner*, 28 May 1840.

he had spent the previous day drafting an important letter to Grundy for publication in the *Globe*. Ever since he was "unexpectedly placed in nomination by a portion of my Republican Fellow-citizens," he wrote, he had resolved to be governed by the wishes of a majority of the party, and "in no possible contingency to yield *my own consent*, to the use of my name as a candidate by a *minority* of my own political friends." He thought it essential that Democratic sentiment should be sufficiently concentrated to ensure an election by the people, rather than the Senate. "I trust," he continued, "I may be permitted to express my sincere desire—*should the further use of my name in connection with the Vice Presidency, be found to interpose the slightest obstacle to the entire and cordial union of the Democratic party, that it may be promptly withdrawn by my friends from before the public*." "If in my public career, I have heretofore evinced any becoming ardour and zeal, in the maintenance of our principles," the governor concluded, "that ardour is unabated. that zeal is undiminished, and though my position may be that of an individual citizen in the ranks of my party, I shall be found faithfully acting with my political friends and upon all suitable and proper occasions, resolutely exercising my rights as a free man, in maintaining the Republican principles of our fathers—and carrying them successfully through the 'ordeal of the popular suffrage.' "[84]

Polk's letter appeared in the *Globe* on June 6 and was interpreted everywhere as a withdrawal. Though Van Buren must have shared Grundy's irritation at Polk's persistent efforts to force New York to declare itself, and though Polk's withdrawal was a blow to Democratic chances in the South, the sagacious president made the best of this latest development. "Gov Polks letter has called forth expressions of the warmest admiration from the Democratic Press & raised him still higher in the estimation of the Democracy," he wrote blandly to Jackson. "Do me the favor to remember me most kindly to him & his good lady when you see them."[85]

Polk's letter was highly embarrassing in Tennessee, where the Democratic press had been denouncing Johnson as an impossible candidate and claiming that Polk was by far the strongest contender. The *Union* at first insisted that Polk had not withdrawn and kept his name beside Van Buren's on its masthead, but this left too much room for Whig gibes at "the contemptible *juggle* which Gov. Polk

[84] Polk to Grundy, 27 May 1840, copy, Polk Papers.
[85] Van Buren to Jackson, 17 June 1840, Van Buren Papers.

and his organ are attempting to carry on in relation to the Vice Presidency." "Pull down the flag, Sir Union," taunted the *Banner*. "You can't come it!" Not until July 13 did the Polk banner finally disappear from the *Union*'s columns.[86]

Why did Polk insist so stubbornly on a convention nomination or an endorsement by New York, flouting the advice of his most loyal friends and risking the hostility of the most powerful men in the party? Whether Grundy's strategy would actually have made Polk the Democratic choice in the electoral college is impossible to say, though it can be said that Silas Wright was a man whose word could be relied on, and that the experienced Grundy was not likely to be fooled in a situation like this. The facts suggest, however, that Polk was a far shrewder and more ambitious politician than either his friends or enemies suspected.

One of Polk's archfoes, Allen A. Hall, may have come closest to the truth. The *Banner*'s perceptive editor was greatly puzzled, not only by the governor's tactics, but also by the strong backing he received from the Massachusetts Democrats. Ruminating on all the circumstances in his editorial column, Hall ventured a canny guess. "Their support of him," he wrote,

is probably founded on their abundant faith in Gen. Jackson's power and influence, which they no doubt deem sufficient to make Gov. P. President after Mr. Van Buren. In that event, they would count upon receiving a very valuable *quid pro quo*—very *substantial rewards* for their early support of his Excellency. They would look upon him in some sort as *their* President. By what train of reasoning, or through what sources of information they have arrived at the conclusion, that Gen. Jackson's influence will be exerted in behalf of Gov. Polk, is also a matter of conjecture with us. . . . These Yankees are shrewd hands at guessing, but how far Gov. Polk's Boston *clique* may be right in their expectations of seeing him appointed by Gen. Jackson to succeed Mr. Van Buren, remains to be hereafter developed.

On the basis of these conjectures, the *Banner* concluded that Polk's position was that of a "minority candidate who desires to run, not with any expectation of being elected, but as a *training for another race hereafter*, should Gen. Jackson live. To have the vote of the *South* and *South West* concentrated upon him now, for Vice President, as the representative of *southern principles*, would, he no doubt imagines, be the means of keeping him before the public, and giving him a *pretty start* hereafter."[87]

[86] Nashville *Republican Banner*, 26 June 1840.
[87] *ibid.*, 20 June 1840.

In a party that was on the brink of a deep split between its northern and southern wings, Polk was almost the only prominent Democratic politician who could bid strongly for the support of both the Calhoun and the Van Buren-Benton factions. His behavior throughout the vice presidential maneuvering indicated that he wanted the nomination only with the open support of both Calhoun and Van Buren and that he would have it on no other terms. In fact, Polk's actions suggested that he recognized the signs of Democratic defeat in 1840, and that he wanted the vice presidential nomination less than he wanted these endorsements, which would put him in a strong position for 1844. Why else was he willing to pledge that, if elected, he would seek no national nomination in 1844? Polk must have regarded a Whig victory as inevitable, for he was too young and too ambitious to think of ending his career with the vice presidency.

Following its shrewd conjectures about Polk's motives, the *Banner* had a final bit of prophecy about his future as a politician:

His party will be overthrown, "horse, foot and dragoons," and he along with it of course. But in any event, the *leaders* at *Washington* have done as much for him as they intend to do. They think, no doubt, that when they made him *Speaker*, they paid him amply for all he had ever done, or could ever after do. Having received his reward in *advance*, he need expect nothing more in any contingency.

"HENCEFORTH," Hall concluded, "HIS CAREER WILL BE DOWNWARDS."[88] But was Hall's prophecy as sound as his analysis? For a time it seemed to be.

88 *ibid.*

13

FRUSTRATION

Polk's failure to secure the vice presidential nomination was hardly a fatal blow to his political prospects. At forty-four he was younger than any other Democrat of equal prominence, and given his superb strategic position in relation to the party's factions, he could afford to wait for the highest political honors. But he could not afford to be quiescent. His hopes and even his political survival depended on maintaining both his own political standing and the Democratic hegemony in Tennessee for the next four years, an undertaking that would require all his energies and a good bit of luck besides.

Accordingly Polk's withdrawal as a candidate made it no less important to hold Tennessee for the Democratic ticket in the presidential election. Early in the winter of 1839-1840 this task had not seemed too difficult. Though the Whig leadership presented a solid front in favor of Clay's nomination as the Whig candidate, a widespread sentiment for General Winfield Scott among local Whig politicians betrayed grave misgivings about Clay's popularity in Tennessee.[1] When the national convention at Harrisburg unexpectedly bestowed the nomination on William Henry Harrison, the unpretending clerk of an Ohio court, who years before had commanded western troops in some Indian campaigns, the news fell "heavily & cold" upon Tennessee Whigs of all persuasions. "If Gen. Harrison be the nominee," the editor of the Memphis *Enquirer* had declared on the eve of the convention, "we shall almost despair"; and the *Enquirer* greeted the first reports from Harrisburg with threats that the southern Whigs would support a candidate of their own. In Nashville, where the legislature was in session, Ephraim Foster moaned that the nomination "struck many of us dumb," adding that he, for one, was "sunk down to the very earth by the blow."[2]

---

[1] W. B. Campbell to David Campbell, 4, 6, 9 Dec. 1839, David Campbell Papers (DU).

[2] Memphis *Enquirer*, 29 Nov., 13 Dec. 1839, quoted in Charles E. Pool, "The Rise of the Whig Party in West Tennessee, 1834-1843," M.A. thesis, University of Mississippi (1950), 92-94; E. H. Foster to [W. B. Campbell], 16 Jan. 1840, Campbell Papers.

But while the Democrats were looking forward to an easy conquest, the Whigs swallowed their disappointment and pulled themselves together for a prodigious effort. In this campaign, leadership of the Tennessee Whigs passed from John Bell to Ephraim Foster. Though Bell's aptitude for intrigue and his boldness, born of personal bitterness and desperation, had been indispensable to the initial success of the revolt against Jackson in Tennessee, the aloof, temperamental former speaker was poorly suited to inspire and harmonize a going party. While Bell was still sulking over the Harrisburg nomination, the more adaptable Foster was impressing the Whig forces with the importance of victory in the presidential election and whipping them into line behind the national nominee and the national strategy.

After a decade of defeats by the self-styled champions of the people, the national Whig leaders had now decided to "out loco foco Van"[3] by themselves appealing boisterously to the common man. This strategy Foster vigorously applied in Tennessee. Throughout the winter the Whigs were busy organizing campaign committees down to the neighborhood level, and by February they had their electoral ticket in the field. Before the Democrats realized the campaign was under way, colorful Whig festivals, featuring bands, parades, log cabins, hard cider, and coons, were attracting enormous crowds in every section. Foster was ranging the whole state as a Whig electoral candidate, and despite his elegant Nashville manners, he was proving most adept at the common touch dictated by the new Whig strategy. "Brother Epm. tells a story about a *Bull calf*," reported an alarmed Democrat, "and . . . it is *funny*."[4]

By the time the Democrats woke up to the fact that they had "a mighty struggle" on their hands, they were already at a decided disadvantage. Polk's personal stake in the campaign made him acutely sensitive to the Whig revival, and since the first of the year he had been hard at work arousing the Democrats. He succeeded in assembling a Democratic state convention at Nashville on February 11, to select candidates for electors and delegates to the Baltimore convention. This gathering also appointed a state central committee and urged that every county set up its own campaign committee and that every Democrat aid in circulating party newspapers and

---

[3] Arthur Campbell to [David Campbell], 7 Jan. 1840, Campbell Papers.

[4] Robert H. White, ed., *Messages of the Governors of Tennessee* (Nashville, 1952-), III, 416.

pamphlets. Soon after, J. George Harris began issuing a special weekly campaign paper, the *Advance Guard of Democracy*. But these arrangements were no match for the Whig enthusiasm, and the Democrats were completely baffled by the new Whig tactics. "The Vans here are certainly lowspirited," exulted Foster. "They dont understand the 'racket' . . . now so constantly sounding into their air."[5]

Polk did everything he could to dispel this Democratic discouragement. He sent the party's ablest speaker, A. O. P. Nicholson, who was trying to reinstate himself in the governor's good graces, off to East Tennessee to help Andrew Johnson answer Foster, and the ailing Carroll was dispatched to various critical points in Middle Tennessee. Polk himself visited the Western District to get the Democratic orators there into action. But the party still lagged, and worried Democrats began demanding that Polk take the stump. When, however, he made several speeches attacking Harrison as a Federalist and, for good measure, an abolitionist, the Whig press castigated him for neglecting his executive duties.[6]

Itching to plunge into the struggle and determined to find some way around this criticism, Polk accepted an invitation to a Democratic rally at Knoxville, and there, on July 4, announced that he was a candidate for reelection as governor in 1841. For three weeks he traversed lower East Tennessee and the Cumberland plateau on behalf of Van Buren, while the Whig press denounced the "traveling executive," and the grand jury of Sevier County brought in a presentment complaining that he was a common nuisance. While Polk was speaking in Monroe County, several hundred Whigs rode up on horseback, carrying dead polk stalks, a canoe (a reminder of Tippecanoe), and various other Harrison emblems and flags. "$2,000 *a year salary as Governor, not as Elector*," proclaimed the biggest banner. "THE PEOPLE WILL ELECT THEIR OWN PRESIDENT."[7]

[5] Foster to W. B. Campbell, 12 Apr. 1840, Campbell Papers; Carroll to Van Buren, 23 Jan. 1840, Martin Van Buren Papers (LC); Nashville *Union*, 21 Feb. 1840.

[6] J. W. Goode to W. B. Campbell, 13 May 1840, Campbell Papers; Nicholson to Polk, 9 Feb. [1840; misplaced 1838], James K. Polk Papers (LC; herein cited as Polk Papers, which refers to First Series unless otherwise noted); Polk to Dr. W. R. Rucker, 4 Apr. 1840, *ibid.*; Polk to Nicholson, 28 May 1840, Alfred O. P. Nicholson Papers (NYHS); *Messages of the Governors of Tenn.*, III, 416-417.

[7] Nashville *Republican Banner*, 22 July 1840; Nashville *Union*, 13, 20 July 1840; James Phelan, *History of Tennessee; the Making of a State* (Boston, 1889), 387.

Such demonstrations did not prevent Polk from venting his spleen at "the log cabin, hard cider, and raccoon humbuggery" by which the Whigs were trying to deceive the people. These "clap-traps" were "an insult to their understanding," he declared, and he was sure that "the people were too intelligent to be gulled by such trickery and flummery, and could not be induced by it to vote for Gen. Harrison, the federal Whig candidate for the presidency." Polk argued that the Whigs kept Harrison from saying anything, so as to conceal their lack of principles and policies. This point he demonstrated dramatically by holding up seven different campaign biographies of "old Tippecanoe," which he said were "designed to suit the politics of different sections in the Union. One for the abolitionists, one for those opposed to abolition, one for the United States Bank folks, one for those opposed to a Bank, &c. &c." The Whig orators generally kept out of Polk's way, preferring showmanship to serious discussion, but at the last meeting of his tour the governor was challenged by James C. Jones, a freshman legislator who was winning a wide reputation by his ability to amuse the common man.[8]

After spending a few days in Nashville to catch up with his executive business, Polk was off for a tour of the Western District, where the Democrats hoped to make great gains by emphasizing the abolitionists' connection with Harrison and the northern Whigs. Polk was back in this part of the state late in August; he spent most of September, except for a week of sickness, campaigning in Middle Tennessee; and in October he was again in the Western District, accompanying General Jackson, whom the desperate Democrats were bringing actively into the campaign.

By the time Polk reached the Western District, his collection of Harrison biographies had increased to fourteen, and he had a powerful new weapon. A Whig congressman from New York had sent him under official frank the published proceedings of an abolitionist convention in London, and Polk seized on this opportunity to write a blistering reply, which the Democrats circulated far and wide. "Are you so deliberately reckless of consequences," the governor demanded,

as to be willing to lend the aid of your official privilege to countenance and abet foreigners in proceedings calculated if not designed to excite sectional

8 Nashville *Union*, 20 July 1840; Nashville *Republican Banner*, 3 Aug. 1840.

jealousies and heart burnings to divide the States by geographical lines to array one section against another and that too at the imminent perral [*sic*] of producing domestic insurrections and a servile war? Have you yet to be informed that slavery existed in the Colonies long before Independence was achieved? Have you yet to learn that at the adoption of the Constitution the adjustment of the slave question provided one of the chief difficulties in the formation of the Union which had to be encountered and that it was ultimately settled upon principles of mutual concession & compromise? Would you disturb the fundamental compact upon which the Union of the States rests? But I will not argue the question, it is not one which is debatable.

"The only further notice which I shall take of this infamous proceedings of foreigners with whom you stand associated," Polk's reply had concluded, "will be to expose them to the indignant reprobation of the people of Tennessee."[9] This he lost no time in doing. Speaking at Jackson in the heart of the Tennessee plantation country, Polk excoriated "the incendiary and intermeddling ethers of the Abolition Convention lately held in London," though he could not quote from the proceedings, since they were "too dangerous to be made known to the numerous slaves within hearing."[10]

By August the governor's efforts had roused the Democrats to a vigor almost rivaling that of the Whigs. The Democratic candidates for elector were out every day in their respective districts, aided by the Democratic congressmen home from Washington, while Polk, Grundy, and Nicholson roamed over the entire state making speeches. Tennessee, in fact, was alive with stump orators. "There never has been anything to compare with it, in the world before, of the kind," observed one man. "The very children are as deeply imbued with the party *Spirit* as the grown people." Violence was predicted, and in numerous cases the prediction was fulfilled. Levin Coe, a Democrat in the Western District, shot a Whig politician after several heated encounters on the stump, and J. George Harris was involved in a less dangerous fight with a Nashville Whig.[11]

Harris's trenchant pen kept him continually in hot water, for the Whigs winced under his editorial blows and were doing everything they could to destroy him. The stories about his former sympathies

[9] Polk to S. M. Gates, 2 Oct. 1840, copy, Letter Book of Governor James K. Polk (State Archives, Nashville); Nashville *Union*, 3 Sept. 1840.

[10] Nashville *Union*, 15 Oct. 1840.

[11] James Campbell to [a sister], 9 Sept. 1840, Campbell Papers; Polk to Laughlin, 9, 15 Aug. 1840, Polk-Laughlin Letters, special section of Polk Papers; Polk to Laughlin, 2 Oct. 1840, Polk Papers; Coe to Polk, 4 Aug. 1840, *ibid.*

for abolition were refurbished and given a prominent place in the Whig press. Harris was "a stranger in this community—with no character whatever, other than a very infamous one—wholly irresponsible," sneered the *Banner*, "—a man [who] for eighteen months past has poured down upon the most upright and distinguished of your fellow-citizens, an uninterrupted stream of calumny and detraction that is without parallel in the history of the partisan press of this country."[12] A Western District paper that had felt Harris's lash was even more vituperative. "That ugly, blear-eyed, monkey faced, '*free nigger*' editor of the Nashville Union—J. GEO. HARRIS—than whom there is not a more contemptible being roaming the face of the earth," raged the editor, "has opened the flood-gates of his abuse upon us in his filthy sheet of the 19th inst."[13]

The most vicious newspaper in this era of vicious political journalism, however, was "Parson" William G. Brownlow's *Whig* in East Tennessee. Brownlow's principal contribution to the campaign was to give currency to rumors that Polk's grandfather, old Ezekiel, had been a Tory during the Revolution. But it was the Parson's style, rather than his content, that gave him his dubious distinction. His pungent epithets had led to an unsuccessful assassination attempt at Elizabethtown in March, and when he moved his paper to Jonesboro in May, he promptly got into a brawl with the Democratic editor, coming off with a bullet in his thigh.[14]

All the fighting, speaking, and writing of the Democrats, however, could not match the log cabins, coons, parades, costumes, and mammoth festivals of their rivals. The Whigs attracted thousands of voters from North Carolina, Virginia, Tennessee, and Kentucky to a tremendous political camp meeting at Cumberland Gap in September and to another one in the same area the following month. Lesser festivals were held in most of the principal towns, but all of them were overshadowed by the great Southwestern Whig Convention at Nashville in August. Its sponsors claimed an attendance of 30,000, which would make it the largest political meeting ever held in Tennessee up to that time. Henry Clay and John J. Crittenden of Kentucky were the principal orators, assisted by a score of local Whig champions. The day after Clay arrived, a Sunday, Polk com-

---

[12] Nashville *Republican Banner*, 10 Sept. 1840; *ibid.*, 8 Sept. 1840.
[13] Brownsville *District Herald*, 31 Oct. 1840.
[14] E. Merton Coulter, *William G. Brownlow: Fighting Parson of the Southern Highlands* (Chapel Hill, 1937), 36-39.

plained of the cannon fire, drum beating, and marching through the streets, but he professed to be "heartily rejoiced that he has come," for "It can not fail to revive old recollections."[15]

The most fastidious of the Whig leaders joined gladly in the fanfaronade. When a Whig delegation from Indiana visited Nashville to present their Tennessee brethren with an Indian canoe, a caged coon, and similar Harrison emblems, John Bell and the other leading Whigs personally built a log cabin on the main street to house these relics. Quoting the refrain of a popular Negro song in celebration of this event, the *Banner* caught the mood of the whole campaign:

> Possum up a gum-tree
> Cooney in the hollow.

The *Union* promptly picked the ditty up and threw it back in this form:

> Whiggies to the rescue,
> Cooney in a cage,
> Go it with a rush, boys,
> Go it with a rage.
>
> Mum is the word, boys,
> Brag is the game;
> Cooney is the emblem
> Of Old Tip's fame.
>
> Go it, then, for cooney,
> Cooney in a cage;
> Go it with a rush, boys,
> Go it with a rage.

That the Whigs seized upon Harris's burlesque and made it one of their most popular campaign songs spoke volumes about the nature of this contest.[16] The Whigs used their "Old Tip" jingles on every possible occasion and saw to it that a supply of Harrison song books was always available. Thomas D. Arnold broke up one of Grundy's meetings in East Tennessee by distributing song books to a crowd outside. When Grundy gave up trying to compete with the "unearthly noise" and left in his carriage, Arnold shouted, "Get out

[15] Polk to Anderson, 16 Aug. 1840, copy, Polk Papers; Thomas B. Alexander, "The Presidential Campaign of 1840 in Tennessee," *Tennessee Historical Quarterly*, I (Mar. 1942), 21-43.

[16] Phelan, *History of Tenn.*, 385-386.

of the way, get out of the way there, you common people, or those lordly aristocrats will drive right over you!"[17]

Harris fought back by composing a number of catchy songs for the Democrats. The *Union* carried, for example, a musical tribute to Ephraim Foster, said to have been written by "the youngest member of the Slick family":

> I 'spose you think as how, Efe,
>   That cause we live up there
> In them 'are hills and cedars, Efe,
>   You'll lead us any where.
>
> I tell you what it is, Efe,
>   We know a thing or two
> We really think we know, Efe,
>   Almost as much as you.
>
> We like your anecdotes, Efe,
>   We like to hear you laugh,
> We like the puppy story, Efe,
>   And that about the calf.
>
> You talk so plaguey honest, Efe,
>   And so so plaguey winning,
> We feel right sorry for you, Efe,
>   And yet can't keep from grinning.[18]

Try as they might, though, the Democrats could not bring themselves to adopt the Whig tactics or to believe that the voters would be fooled by them. At one meeting where Polk spoke, a Democratic reporter rejoiced to see "the lugubrious and elongated faces of the Whigs as the 'up-the-branch-boys,' as they call the Democrats, marched in by battalions, like the Northern hordes upon the effeminate and luxurious Romans in their decline from virtue and greatness, and to hear them ask and echo, both in sorrow and anger, 'where can the people come from!' " "The ruffle shirt, silk stockings, city Whig gentry," concluded this writer, "cannot make us backwoods folks believe that we ought to be coon-catchers for them and Gen. Harrison." But this was whistling in the dark, as the election returns demonstrated. Tennessee gave Harrison 60,000 votes to 48,000 for Van Buren.[19]

---

[17] Oliver P. Temple, *Notable Men of Tennessee from 1833 to 1875: Their Times and Their Contemporaries* (New York, 1912), 60.

[18] Quoted in Alexander, "Campaign of 1840," *loc.cit.,* 42.

[19] Nashville *Union,* 3 Sept. 1840; Nashville *Republican Banner,* 2 Dec. 1840.

II

The crushing defeat of 1840 might well have demoralized the Tennessee Democrats for years to come. Not only did it virtually extinguish the hopes aroused by Polk's victory in 1839, but more seriously, it shook the very foundation of the Democratic ethos: faith in the people's ability to judge the issues and support the party that stood for sound principles. "The fact is," ran a characteristic postelection lament, "the people like coonery and foolery better than good argument."[20]

But one Democrat refused to be discouraged, and once again the fate of the Tennessee Democracy came to depend on his determination and energy. Not only was Polk's personal future at stake in the survival of a vigorous party, but his faith in the people, on which all his other convictions rested, was virtually unshakable. While the last disheartening results were still coming in, he was at his desk feverishly writing scores of letters to Democratic leaders all over the state, to counteract the demoralizing effects of defeat. "We are *beaten*," he had to admit, but only "*beaten* by the superior organization and industry of our opponents." The whole trouble had been the Democrats' early overconfidence, which had enabled the Whigs to begin campaigning three months before them, "and thus to give an impulse to public sentiment which it was difficult to resist." The state was still Democratic, Polk insisted, and "with proper *organization* and *energy* on our part she will recover herself at the next Election." "We must take up courage," he exhorted the faithful, " 'lick the flint and try it again.' " Polk closed his letters by urging the leaders to come to Nashville for a meeting to get a Democratic revival under way in time for the next summer's gubernatorial campaign.[21]

As usual, Polk had set himself an uphill task. Most of the dispirited politicians professed to share his optimism, but they found various excuses for not being at the Nashville meeting. Undiscouraged, or at least betraying no signs of discouragement, Polk undertook the party's reorganization singlehanded. A circular outlining his plans was issued through the Nashville Democrats in December. There was to be a five-man campaign committee in each county, and these groups were to appoint three-man committees in each

[20] Isaac Goladay to Polk, 9 Nov. 1840, Polk Papers.
[21] Polk to Nicholson, 7 Nov. 1840, Nicholson Papers.

civil district. The district committees were to distribute Democratic literature, convert doubtful voters, and make sure that each Democratic voter got to the polls on election day. Maury County went to work early in 1841 to effect its organization and provide a model for other counties, while Polk pleaded with individual leaders to get the system instituted wherever possible. All of this required infinite time and an incredible amount of labor, but by February and March results were beginning to show.[22]

The Whigs needed only to retain the similar network of committees they had already established, and by early spring Tennessee was more thoroughly organized politically than ever before in its history. Each civil district, as one politician later remembered the Whig system, "was placed under a kind of political martial law. Those voters who were unalterably attached to the Democratic or the Whig parties were polled. Those who were doubtful were turned over to some Whig friend or neighbor to be persuaded, wheedled, and argued into voting the Whig ticket. All who were halt, maim, or blind were each assigned to some individual whose duty it was to procure a vehicle and bring them to the polls."[23]

Simultaneously Polk was writing scores of letters designed to bring out the strongest Democrats as candidates for Congress and the legislature. Though Cave Johnson, Hopkins Turney, and Aaron Brown were anxious to retire from Congress, Polk eventually prevailed on them all to run one more time. Again there was trouble in Maury. Congressman Watterson was still so unpopular with many Democrats that a split seemed unavoidable. Polk and James Walker finally persuaded all the aspirants to submit their claims to a district Democratic convention, but this solution was threatened when Polk's brother, Bill, who wanted to run for the legislature, began making speeches against a convention. Walker probably put his finger on the trouble when he intimated that Polk was not as prudent as usual in dealing with his brother. "You *command him too much*," Walker wrote, "& have too little patience with him." In the end Bill was mollified by the Democratic legislative nomination, and the district convention united the party once more behind Watterson.[24]

[22] Letters to Polk from E. A. Keeble, H. L. Turney, H. M. Watterson, Bolling Gordon, A. O. P. Nicholson, W. H. Polk, S. C. Pavatt, W. B. Harris, R. M. Woods, 9 Nov. 1840–6 Jan. 1841, Polk Papers.

[23] Phelan, *History of Tenn.*, 393.

[24] James Walker to Polk, 18 Mar. 1841, Polk Papers; S. P. Walker to Polk, 6 Nov. 1840, *ibid.*; Nicholson to Polk, 13 Jan., 12 Feb. 1841, *ibid.*; James Walker to Polk, 24 Feb., 10 Mar. 1841, *ibid.*

One phase of the campaign Polk did not have to worry about. He could count on the *Union* for the ferocious editorial warfare needed to arouse the Democratic voters. Harris's kind of journalism required a rough and ready temperament that did not appeal to refined sensibilities; Sarah, for one, never warmed to "Mr. Jerry George," as she deprecatingly called him. Indeed Harris had as much need of physical bravery as of editorial skill. The Nashville Whigs had been demeaning him personally for months, and early in January two of Foster's sons shot him down in the barroom of the Nashville Inn. He was dangerously wounded in the arm and chest but returned to his editorial chair after a five-week convalescence and was soon slashing away again with unabated vigor. The Foster boys were brought to trial and acquitted; meanwhile one of them had involved his father in a bloody altercation with another leading Democrat.[25]

At the same time the Whigs were running into difficulties created by their own successes. Though nearly all the leaders were determined to jettison Cannon as their gubernatorial candidate, it was not so easy to agree on a replacement. Bell and Foster were the obvious choices, but neither was willing to run. Foster hoped to be returned to the Senate by a Whig legislature; Bell was moving heaven and earth to get into Harrison's Cabinet. There was little love lost between these two, and each sought to get the other out of his way by pressing him on the party as a gubernatorial candidate. "Would you take me from my present position, where I may either be Speaker, or perhaps a member of the Cabinet if I wish the place," Bell complained to one friend, "& reduce me to the subordinate situation of Governor, an office which would leave me without any hope of preferment or further usefulness in all probability?" Meanwhile Bell was becoming unpopular with many Tennessee Whigs. He was the most influential Tennessean in the national councils of the party, and some Tennessee aspirants for national office began to complain of his selfishness and indifference to his friends.[26]

The rivalry between Bell and Foster complicated the competition

[25] Nashville *Republican Banner*, 15, 21 Jan., 26 Feb. 1841; Nashville *Union*, 14 Jan., 25 Feb. 1841; John Campbell to David Campbell, 17 Apr., 4 June 1841, Campbell Papers.

[26] Bell to T. A. R. Nelson, 21 Dec. 1840, Thomas A. R. Nelson Papers (LM); W. B. Campbell to David Campbell, 20 Jan., 24 Mar. 1841, Campbell Papers; David Campbell to W. B. Campbell, 8 Feb. 1841, *ibid.*; Arthur Campbell to David Campbell, 22 Mar. 1841, *ibid.*; M. P. Gentry to W. B. Campbell, 4 Apr. 1841, *ibid.*; Peyton to W. B. Campbell, 18 Apr. 1841, *ibid.*; Boyd McNairy to R. L. Caruthers, 24 May, 20 June 1841, Robert L. Caruthers Papers (SHC).

among Whig politicians of the second rank for the gubernatorial nomination. Of the dozen or more mentioned, the contest quickly narrowed down to four Middle Tennesseans: Judge Robert L. Caruthers, Congressman Meredith P. Gentry, former Congressman David W. Dickinson, and James C. Jones, whose mastery of the Whigs' newly discovered political techniques convinced his supporters that he would "make a perfect 'Tippecanoe candidate.' "[27]

All the candidates urged their claims vigorously, and to avoid a disastrous intraparty fight, Bell set in motion a plan for a state nominating convention, which met at Murfreesboro the first week in March. Bell was doing all he could to secure the nomination for his brother-in-law, David Dickinson, and this fact eventually caused the other candidates to unite in a stop-Dickinson movement. On the eve of the convention Caruthers withdrew from the race and threw his support to Jones, announcing at the same time for the congressional seat that Bell was abandoning to enter the Cabinet. Gentry also seems to have been a party to this arrangement and was no longer a serious contender. So when the convention met, the contest was between Jones and Dickinson.[28]

The convention sat in the same Presbyterian church where Polk had begun his public career as a member of the legislature. Sarah's Presbyterian mother was so outraged by this desecration that she told the minister "she would never feel at home in her own church again," and for a time she threatened to become a Methodist. By the end of the first day, Dickinson discovered that he could not succeed and withdrew, paving the way for Jones's unanimous nomination the following morning.[29]

Though Jones owed much of his success to John Bell's growing unpopularity with his fellow Whigs in Tennessee, this was by no means the whole story. Many of the Whig leaders had been impressed by his adept use of "coonery and foolery" in the recent presidential campaign, and were now convinced that these were the only techniques that would defeat Polk. "They will attempt to run Jones," one of

27 Columbia *Observer,* quoted in Nashville *Republican Banner,* 12 Dec. 1840; Murfreesboro *Tennessee Telegraph,* 21 Nov. 1840; Memphis *Enquirer,* 4 Dec. 1840; Nashville *Republican Banner,* 12, 14 Dec. 1840, 6 Jan. 1841; William Martin to W. B. Campbell, 12 Dec. 1840, Campbell Papers.

28 Bell to [various Whigs], 8 Nov. 1840, copy, Nelson Papers; Bell to Nelson, 9 Nov. 1840, *ibid.;* Boyd McNairy to R. L. Caruthers, 20 June 1841, Caruthers Papers; Nashville *Republican Banner,* 1 Mar. 1841.

29 Joanna Rucker to Mrs. Polk, 7 Mar. 1841, Polk Papers; Nashville *Republican Banner,* 6, 8 Mar. 1841.

Polk's friends predicted, "as the log cabin boy taken from the plough." Actually, continued this informant, who lived near Jones, "he never ploughed a day in his life—lives in a fine brick house—owns one third of a large rope and hemp factory—a large store in full operation—sold his farm for ten thousand dollars to be paid in State bonds."[30]

Though all this was true enough, the thirty-one-year-old Jones had such an uncommon share of the "common touch" as to make the facts irrelevant. His spindly six-foot frame was topped by a solemn, almost grotesque, face that was enough by itself to bring shouts of merriment from his audiences. But people laughed with James C. Jones, not at him. He had a simple, friendly, unaffected manner that enabled him to circulate through crowds, complimenting farmers' wives and admiring their babies, without the least suggestion of condescension. And in debate he maintained such an air of courtesy and magnanimity that an opponent could not attack the absurdities in his arguments without arousing sympathy for Jones.[31]

III

Polk quickly learned that he had a dangerous antagonist on his hands. Two years before, he had carried the fight to Cannon, but this time Jones was determined to reverse the process. Only ten days after his nomination, the Whig standard bearer was back in Murfreesboro for a speech declaring that he "was going into the contest *to be elected*," and that he was prepared to discuss both national and state issues from one end of Tennessee to the other. The patriotic voters who had given Harrison a 12,000 majority, he predicted, would not rest until they had "rid Tennessee of every vestige of Loco Focoism."

Jones went down the line for the national Whig policies, coming out flatly for a national bank and distribution of land revenues among the states, and against the independent treasury, which, he said, was calculated to "bring our Republican government into an elective Monarchy." The tariff was the only item in the Whigs' federal program that he ignored.

As for state matters, Jones wanted the internal improvement system stopped in its tracks. Admitting that the banking and in-

30 R. M. Burton to Polk, 9 Mar. 1841, Polk Papers.
31 Phelan, *History of Tenn.*, 399-404.

ternal improvement act of 1838 was passed by a Whig legislature, he charged correctly that the *"master spirits"* behind it were such Democrats as Nicholson. Boasting of having introduced a bill to burn those bonds that were still unsold, he derided Governor Polk's recommendation that "these Bonds should take the form of Sterling Bonds, so that they might be sold in London for British Gold, to British Capitalists!"

But more alarming than Jones's forthright policy position was his aggressive manner. Though Polk's anecdotes and raillery had practically driven Cannon from the stump in the previous contest, Jones now announced boldly that "if he can beat me at that game, he shall be welcome to the victory." To demonstrate his own prowess in this field, Jones defined "Modern Democracy" by telling a story about a bright schoolboy who had been asked to describe a bat. "Why, said the hopeful pupil, it has a bald head, india-rubber wings, a shoe string tail, sees best with its eyes shut, and bites like the devil!" This, Jones concluded drolly, was the best description he could find of "Modern Democracy." The audience's delighted reaction was a warning that Polk must look to his laurels.

Jones concluded by announcing that he was going to East Tennessee for a two-month tour "among those free sons of the mountains to set the state on fire." The whole eastern end of the state, he promised, would "blaze into a conflagration." And, he added characteristically, "it was the best part of the world, excepting Middle and West Tennessee."[32]

Breaking all other engagements to accompany Jones, Polk spent his last week in Nashville seeing his forty-page address to the people through the press. This document defended his consistent and unchanging adherence to Old Republican doctrines, and traced the course by which the Tennessee Whigs had moved from their "no-party party" position of 1835, through stages when they called themselves successively "the White-Jackson party," "the White party," and "the White Whig party," until recently, when they had dared to come out openly as a branch of the national Whig party and to endorse its Federalist policies. Again Polk defended the independent treasury and attacked the national bank, but he bore down hardest on Clay's plan for distributing the public land proceeds to the states, which he pictured as a scheme to promote a high tariff and to "as-

[32] Nashville *Republican Banner*, 24 Mar. 1841.

similate ours to the British Constitution and policy, and by latitudi-
nous constructions, make the confederacy rather a *consolidation*, than
a Government regulated by the checks and limitations of a written
Constitution."[33]

These preliminaries out of the way, the two champions measured
each other's mettle on a rainy Saturday, March 27, in the courthouse at Murfreesboro. The Harrison administration, in office only
three weeks, had provided few targets for Democratic criticism beyond the Cabinet appointments, but Polk made the most of these.
Daniel Webster, the new secretary of state, was a shining target,
and Polk had his saddlebags full of documents with which he demonstrated Webster's opposition to the War of 1812. Scarcely less
vulnerable was Francis Granger, Harrison's postmaster general, for
Polk was able to show that Judge White himself had suspected Granger of abolitionism. The other Cabinet members were handled in
similar fashion, with John Bell, who had finally received his appointment as secretary of war, getting, of course, somewhat more
than his due. For the rest, Polk's speech was an exposition of his
consistent loyalty to Republican principles over two decades, contrasted with the changed position now occupied by the Tennessee
Whigs. To his opponent he referred not at all, except once by in-
nuendo. Putting on his spectacles to read from a document, Polk
remarked with what the Whigs always called his "ghastly smile," "*I
was young once!*"

When Jones's turn came, he had some difficulty meeting Polk's
charges and arguments, but he countered Polk's personal allusion by
repeated references to his "*venerable* competitor." This hit he followed up with some embarrassing material bearing on Polk's boast
of consistency over twenty years. First he produced Polk's speech
opposing Gordon's independent treasury proposal in 1835. Then
he pulled out an old circular that showed Polk, as a freshman legislator, arguing that federal improvements were both expedient and
constitutional. As for Polk's twenty-year career, he concluded, the
good old Republican doctrine of rotation in office indicated that it
was time for the governor to retire. "Why, boys, at this rate it will
never be your turn," Jones told his hearers. "You will never get to
be constables even!"[34]

[33] Polk's address was published serially in the Nashville *Union*, 29 Mar., 29 Apr.,
10 May 1841.
[34] Nashville *Republican Banner*, 30 Mar. 1841.

But Jones was not to have the last word. Polk was up for a rejoinder, and for thirty minutes he made the welkin ring with what the Whigs called "his old practice of grinning and telling anecdotes." The governor alleged that "he did not deal in anecdotes to any great extent," but, he promised, "if his friend Jones went into that business he would tell what few ditties he could command, and when he got through he would borrow Jones' *joke book*." His competitor was "a promising young man," said Polk, "but as for his being Governor, that's all a notion." Even the Whig reporter had to admit that Polk's rollicking rebuttal aroused "considerable merriment" and tended to counteract the effect of Jones's arguments.[35]

The joint canvass had no sooner got under way than it was interrupted. Polk had planned to spend Saturday night in Murfreesboro and go on the next day to Lebanon, where he and Jones were to debate again on Monday. But early Saturday evening he learned that President Harrison had issued his long-anticipated proclamation for a special session of Congress to meet on the last day of May. This made it necessary for the governor to call a special election for Tennessee's congressmen, since the incumbents' terms had expired on March 3, and new members would not ordinarily be chosen until the regular election in August. Early Sunday morning, therefore, Polk called on Jones to explain that he would not be able to keep the next few appointments, and then hurried off to Nashville to issue his proclamation for the special election.

IV

Polk had much to think about during his thirty-five mile ride from Murfreesboro, for the special session also raised a serious problem with regard to Tennessee's representation in the Senate, and Polk's decision might have great influence on the approaching election and his whole political future. The problem had first arisen back in December, when the Tennessee Democracy was saddened by the death of Senator Grundy. Polk had had to appoint a successor to sit until the legislature could meet and elect someone for the remaining four years of Grundy's term and in making a choice he had encountered again the disruptive rivalries of the previous autumn.

It was while wrestling with this problem that he had first learned from his faithful friends at Washington, Johnson, Brown, and Tur-

[35] Nashville *Union*, 29 Mar. 1841; Nashville *Republican Banner*, 30 Mar. 1841.

ney, that Harrison would probably call a special session of Congress as soon as he was inaugurated. These friends reminded him that, regardless of whom he appointed, Senator Anderson's term would expire on March 3, 1841, and Tennessee would be left with only one senator at the special session. They urged him, therefore, to be ready to convene a special session of the Democratic legislature to fill both senatorial vacancies, one for four years and the other for six.

This proposal was closely connected with the exalted ambitions that Polk's associates were beginning to cherish for him. The crushing defeat of the previous autumn had convinced the three congressmen that Polk's chances for reelection were exceedingly slim. "If successful you would certainly hold a very conspicuous position *for any thing* your friends might think proper to seek," wrote Aaron Brown. "I repeat it *for any* thing they might desire." But the consequences of failure "might greatly retard if they did not finally defeat purposes in relation to you which I know your friends now contemplate." Under these circumstances, the Tennessee congressmen urged the governor to allow a special session of the legislature to elect him to Grundy's seat in the Senate.[36]

Whether or not he called the legislature, Polk had had to make an interim appointment for the remaining two months of the regular congressional session. After offering the position to several Democratic elder statesmen, he had finally bestowed it on the importunate Nicholson. Nicholson's ardent services in the presidential campaign had atoned somewhat for his past waywardness, and Polk probably hoped that he would now be sufficiently satisfied to be more cooperative. But future trouble was indicated when the new senator complained bitterly about the *Union*'s announcement that the interim appointment "could, in itself, have no direct or indirect influence on the action of the next legislature."[37]

In the early months of 1841, Polk had come under increasing pressure from Washington to convene the legislature, so that Tennessee would have a full senatorial representation at the special session of Congress. The Senate would be so evenly divided that a single Tennessee senator might tip the balance for or against a new national bank, and the Whigs considered the matter so vital that they were threatening to block an election by boycotting any special legislative session. When Frank Blair enlisted Old Hickory to intercede

---

[36] Brown to Polk, 21 Dec. 1840, Polk Papers; Turney to Polk, 21 Dec. 1840, *ibid.*
[37] Nicholson to Polk, 13 Jan. 1841, Polk Papers; Nashville *Union*, 28 Dec. 1840.

with Polk, the governor had ridden out to the Hermitage and impressed Jackson with the possible disadvantages of a special session. Not only would the Whigs be able to charge the Democrats with the $40,000 cost of assembling the lawmakers, Polk argued, but it would look as though the Democrats expected to lose their legislative majority in the August elections and were trying to defy the popular verdict by insuring the two Senate seats to themselves for four and six years to come. Besides, Polk told Jackson, he wanted to use the special session of Congress as an argument against the Whigs in the summer campaign.[38]

The governor had left the Hermitage still without committing himself, but when Harrison's proclamation convening Congress reached him at Murfreesboro, he could delay a decision no longer. Arriving in Nashville late Sunday afternoon, he spent that evening and the next morning outlining his views for publication in the *Union*. It is doubtful whether Polk had ever been seriously tempted by the idea of a special session and his own election to the Senate. One of his most frequent boasts was that he had never received an office except directly from the hands of the people, and Sarah, whose thinking doubtless reflected her husband's, had been cool to the scheme from the beginning.[39]

At any rate Polk's circular denounced Harrison for taxing the people with a $500,000 expense for a special congressional session and refused to follow his example. To allow the present legislature to choose the senators, argued the governor, would be to flout the people's right to make the choice through the new legislature that they would elect in August. "It is better that the State should be for a short time without the services of one of her Senators," he declared, "than that a vital principle, affecting the popular sovereignty should be violated."[40]

V

These matters disposed of, Polk rode all night and all day to overtake Jones some forty miles east of Nashville, missing only two

[38] Blair to Jackson, 28 Dec. 1840, Andrew Jackson Papers (LC); Jackson to Blair, 19 Feb. 1841, *ibid.*; Anderson to Polk, 12 Jan. 1840 [1841], 17 Feb. 1841, Polk Papers; Nicholson to Polk, 2, 12 Feb., 8 Mar. 1841, *ibid.*; Jackson to Polk, 8 Feb. 1841, *ibid.*; Turney to Polk, 19 Feb. 1841, *ibid.*; Adam Huntsman to Polk, 9 Mar. 1841, *ibid.*

[39] Mrs. Polk to Polk, 31 Dec. 1840, Polk Papers.

[40] Nashville *Union*, 1 Apr. 1841.

of their scheduled appointments. He thus started the campaign exhausted and quickly fell prey to a severe cold, which gave the Whigs a chance to boast that Jones had already given the governor the chills.[41] The chills, however, did not prevent Polk from making full use of his allotted time at the daily "speakings," as the two candidates moved off across the Cumberland plateau toward the southeastern corner of the state. After a week in this section, they turned northward up the valley of the Tennessee River and reached Knoxville on April 22.

The time of their arrival at each town was announced weeks ahead, and on the appointed day the roads were choked with crowds of people coming in from the surrounding countryside. "Speakings" had long since become major social and recreational events in Tennessee, but the throngs attracted by the candidates in 1841—ranging from three or four hundred in sparsely populated areas to two or three thousand in the more important towns—were regarded by the politicians as enormous. Polk had won great renown as a stump speaker two years before, and the voters were anxious to see how the youthful Whig challenger would stand up against him. The campaigns of 1839 and 1840, moreover, had accentuated the entertainment value of politics and aroused the interest of previously indifferent segments of the population.

Beginning about noon, the speaking was usually held in the courthouse, or a church, or a nearby grove traditionally used for such purposes. Sometimes a barbecue would be served. Polk and Jones alternately spoke first, each for two hours and a half, unless they had arrived so late from the previous speaking as to make a shorter time necessary. Each man then had thirty minutes for a rebuttal. After this strenuous afternoon and an evening of conferring with local politicians and writing letters, the candidates were more than ready for bed—occasionally the same bed—since morning would bring another hard ride to the next speaking point.

Polk had been unable to shake off his cold under this grueling schedule, but he had the consolation that Jones "is much more fatigued than I am." Back home in Nashville, Sarah worried continually about her husband's health and longed for the end of the campaign. "When I think of the labour and fatigue you have to undergo," she wrote, "I feel *sad* and mela[n]choly, and conclude

41 *ibid.*, 13 May 1841.

that *success* is not worth the labour." She professed not to believe the Whig claims that Jones had her husband on the run, but added, "If *Jones* does frighten you home by the 15th you may tell him your wife will be glad to see you." James, for his part, wrote affectionately whenever he could find time, reassuring Sarah about his health and political prospects and demanding frequent letters in return.[42]

As a matter of fact the redoubtable "Lean Jimmy" was proving quite troublesome. Knowing Jones to be a prosperous farmer and merchant and irritated by his constant talk of "the log cabin, the plough handles and all that," Polk originally argued that he had as good a claim to simple rural origins as his competitor. In his first speech after the joint debates were resumed, Polk boasted that "he was here cutting the cane a third of a century ago," and that he had "drove the team afield and followed the plough over the soil of Tennessee many a day." Indeed he threatened to turn the canvass into a plowing contest. "*Bring on your team fellow-citizens*," he challenged, "*and I will stake my prospects of election against those of my competitor that I will turn a furrow through yonder field straighter and fairer and quicker than my opponent can.*"[43]

The futility of such appeals was soon apparent. The contrast between Polk's dignity and Jones's homely simplicity was too great. Jones had only to amble to the stand stroking a coon skin and remarking in his comical manner, "Did you ever see such fine fur?" to send the crowd into gales of laughter and settle conclusively the disputed question of rural pedigree. After a few experiences of this kind, Polk tried ridiculing his exasperating rival. Throughout the campaign he continued to call Jones his "young friend," while Jones regularly referred to Polk as his "venerable competitor." The governor complained that though he tried to discuss serious matters of state in a serious way, his opponent "wisely made a jest of things which indeed were beyond his comprehension." But whether Polk used humor, serious appeal, or ridicule, Jones was too often able to best him with wit.

The governor finally decided that the best he could do was to make his customary argumentative speeches, hoping that the voters would resent Jones's levity and superficiality. This strategy was

---

[42] Mrs. Polk to Polk, 8 Apr. 1841, Polk Papers; Polk to Mrs. Polk, 11, 16 Apr. 1841, *ibid.*; "Letters of James K. Polk to Cave Johnson, 1833-1848," *Tennessee Historical Magazine*, I (Sept. 1915), 228.
[43] Nashville *Union*, 8 Apr. 1841.

not wholly successful before an electorate still tipsy from the heady drafts of political foolery administered to them in the presidential campaign. "Mr. Polk made an ass of himself, talking sense to a lot of d- - - -d fools," a loyal Democrat complained furiously after one speaking. When asked what Jones had said, he replied that neither he nor anyone else knew. But, he said, "I know this much. If I were Mr. Polk I wouldn't allow any one to make a laughing-stock of me. He ought to get a stick and crack Jones's skull, and end this tom-foolery."[44]

Polk gave the same basic speech everywhere, though it was varied by local allusions, and some new issues were introduced in the later stages of the campaign. He always began by defending his record as governor, especially his efforts to get the banks to resume specie payments and his course on the internal improvements question. On the latter point, he tended to stress his friendship for improvements in those areas where the program was still popular and his insistence on retrenchment and inspection in other sections. His opponent's unremitting attacks on his sterling bond proposal forced Polk to devote special attention to this question, arguing that sterling bonds would give the state bank enough capital to afford relief to debtors while at the same time resuming specie payments.

But the main body of his speeches focused, as always, on national politics and particularly on the "federalism" of Webster and the other members of Harrison's Cabinet. He inevitably defended the independent treasury and conjured up all the old fears connected with a national bank, but his emphasis shifted more and more to attacks on Clay's distribution proposal, which many Tennessee Whigs opposed, as a device to raise the tariff and consolidate all power in the federal government. Polk invariably wound up with an appeal to nostalgia. Reminding his hearers of Tennessee's long devotion to old-fashioned Republican doctrines, he boasted of his consistent support for these doctrines, as contrasted with his opponents' desertion to "federal whiggery."

Jones, by contrast, was rambling and extemporaneous. He resolutely upheld the national bank and the distribution policy, and though his reasoning was superficial, it was no less effective. When Polk tried to expose his fallacies, the detailed arguments required were hard to follow; and Jones went on repeating the same hollow

[44] Phelan, *History of Tenn.*, 400-403.

but momentarily plausible statements.[45] For example, Polk frequently pressed Jones to say what kind of national bank would be constitutional and beneficial. All Jones would say was that the Supreme Court had three times decided that a national bank was constitutional and that, besides, if Tennessee did not like the particular bank chartered, she could keep it from operating within her borders. Polk immediately pounced on this contention, demonstrating that the very decisions upholding the Bank's constitutionality had been directed against states trying to keep it out. But the audience grew restive under the long constitutional exposition necessary to show Jones's error, and "Lean Jimmy" continued to make the same assertions.[46]

Polk would have made little show against this astute politician had he not been Jones's match in storytelling and humorous illustration. Here the honors were about evenly divided, with sometimes one and sometimes the other emerging triumphant. One of Polk's best weapons was his "sucking colt story," in which "the neighing, whinnying and whickering of a regiment of colts, starving for want of the teat, was compared to the crying and screaming which is daily heard from Mr. Jones and his party in their greedy scramble for office under the new federal administration."[47] Polk told this story repeatedly with great effect until Jones finally devised a suitable rejoinder. He admitted that the Whigs were young colts, but said that "the governor himself was an old sucker who had been at it for fifteen years." The farmers in his section, Jones continued, "generally let a live, healthy colt be weaned by his dam, but that in the case of a scrubby, unpromising fellow, they generally weaned him about the first Thursday in August," which was, of course, the day of the election.[48]

At the end of April, just as the candidates were approaching the Democratic strongholds in the northeastern corner of the state, Polk was again called back to Nashville by his executive duties. The special congressional election took place on May 6, and the governor had to be at the seat of government to issue commissions to the

[45] For descriptions of the two candidates' speeches at various points, see Nashville *Union*, 8, 22 Apr., 3, 21 May, 10, 17, 21 June, 5, 8, 15 July, 2 Aug. 1841; Nashville *Republican Banner*, 5, 21 May, 18 June, 2, 12, 24 July, 2 Aug. 1841; Columbia *Observer*, 8 July 1841.

[46] Nashville *Union*, 10, 17 June 1841.

[47] *ibid.*, 17 June 1841.

[48] Phelan, *History of Tenn.*, 401.

successful candidates. Accordingly he informed Jones that the joint appointments would have to be interrupted and planned a separate schedule of daily speeches along the route to Middle Tennessee. Jones finally decided to accompany the governor on the two-week trip to Nashville.

With most political interest centered on the gubernatorial race and with only a month for congressional campaigning, the congressional election attracted little attention, and its results were inconclusive. McClellan, Turney, Johnson, Watterson, and Brown were all returned, but the Democrats lost one marginal district in East Tennessee, and Robert J. Caruthers swamped a weak Democratic candidate for Bell's seat. On the whole, the Democratic showing was not bad in the light of the previous year's Whig landslide.[49]

The congressional commissions signed, Polk and Jones retraced their steps to the Cumberland plateau to keep as many of their original appointments as they could. The exhausted campaigners then had a few days at home. Polk got little rest, for he was busy making final arrangements about candidates for the legislature that would soon elect two United States senators. He was both assiduous and skillful at this phase of party leadership, and even those Whigs who were optimistic about the gubernatorial result confessed "some fear of another Democratic legislature." Many Whigs were convinced that Polk, with no hope of reelection, was counting on a Democratic legislature to send him to the Senate, and the Whig press was full of warnings against "the deep laid schemes of the juggling Governor." But "with regard to this matter," as Newton Cannon confessed, "Little Jimmy outmanaged Lean Jimmy [I] fear very much."[50]

While in Middle Tennessee, Polk made a discovery that enabled him to demolish at least one of Jones's hypocritical arguments. All through East Tennessee "Lean Jimmy" had kept up a steady fire on Polk's sterling bond proposal, which he interpreted as a degrading scheme to deliver the state's resources over to "the Lords and Ladies of Europe." When the candidates reached Lebanon in Jones's home county, however, Polk noticed that his opponent omitted his usual reference to this matter. Mentioning it casually to some of the local Democrats after the speaking, Polk was startled to learn that

49 Nashville *Union,* 3, 13, 17 May 1841.
50 Knoxville *Post,* quoted in *Messages of the Governors of Tenn.,* III, 491; Cannon to R. L. Caruthers, 28 May 1841, Caruthers Papers.

Jones himself, as a candidate for the legislature two years before, had advocated making the state bonds payable in sterling. The governor jubilantly instructed his friends to procure signed statements to this effect and forward them to him.[51]

Two weeks later at Lawrenceburg, as the candidates were moving through the south central part of the state toward the Western District, Jones again waxed indignant at Polk's proposal "to sell the faith and credit of this young and chivalrous State to the *Lords* and *Ladies* of foreign potentates." Following in rebuttal, Polk asked Jones point-blank if he had not advocated sterling bonds while a candidate for the legislature. When Jones responded "that he never had," the governor read off the names of six of Jones's neighbors in Wilson County and inquired "whether they were honorable men." Jones had to answer that three or four of them were, whereupon Polk handed him a set of signed statements, requesting that he "be so good as to read them to the people." "I shall do no such thing," the embarrassed Jones retorted hotly, "they may say what they please, they are clever men, but are all Democrats." Polk then proceeded to read the affidavits himself, and Jones could only reply weakly that "these gentlemen were mistaken, though he did while a candidate in 1839, argue *both sides*! of this question in order that the people might instruct him." After this episode, no more was heard from Jones on the subject of sterling bonds.[52]

The canvass had by now become an endurance contest. Jones looked "wearied and worn" and was so hoarse that his supporters wondered how much longer he would be able to continue. Polk, too, was feeling the strain. The weather got sultrier as they entered the unhealthy swamplands bordering the Mississippi River, and he began to worry about his old susceptibility to dysentery. He finally became ill at Dyersburg and was unable to speak or to journey on to Troy for the next appointment. He recovered sufficiently to overtake Jones at Trenton two days later, but the effort prostrated him again. Three days in bed gave him enough strength to travel by easy stages and catch his rival before the important speaking at Jackson. Jones was only slightly better off, but the two men continued to drive themselves for another week on the road back to

[51] Nashville *Union*, 14 Aug. 1843.
[52] *ibid.*, 21 June 1841.

Nashville. Though the formal joint canvass was now completed, there was to be no rest for the weary, for Polk had promised to visit the northeastern counties he had missed in May. He spent only a single day at home before taking the stage for East Tennessee and a final round of speeches, with Jones in hot pursuit.[53]

With the election less than three weeks away, Polk was frankly worried. Old Hickory was decrying the "humiliative" apathy of the Democratic leaders around Nashville, and the governor found his supporters in East Tennessee discouraged. But there was one encouraging development. The policies of the new Whig administration in Washington were finally giving the Democrats something to shoot at. Harrison's death only a month after his inauguration had elevated John Tyler to the presidency, the special session had begun, Henry Clay had unveiled the Whig program, and now for the first time Polk could move to the offensive.[54]

His desperation for issues was indicated by his rash attack on the Whig proposal to pension Harrison's widow. He had a better issue in the national bank bill introduced by the Whig leadership. Here at last was the specific bank proposal he had been pressing Jones for, and he now forced his competitor to endorse it as the best that could be secured. Having put a stop to Jones's demagogic forays on the sterling bond question, Polk found an excuse to indulge in some anti-British ranting of his own, in the current dispute over the murder of an American citizen in connection with the recent rebellion in Canada. Secretary of State Webster's conciliatory handling of the matter he denounced as "truckling to the 'Mistress of the Ocean.' "[55]

Though Polk's presence had roused the Democrats in those parts of East Tennessee he had been able to reach, he still had reason to fear discouragement and apathy in other sections. The recent developments at Washington had produced a reaction wherever he had had a chance to discuss them, but, he had to admit, "the time is so short before the election that it is difficult to say to what extent they may operate." Remaining on the stump in East Tennessee

[53] Polk to Mrs. Polk, 1, 6 July 1841, Polk Papers; Nashville *Republican Banner*, 21 July 1841; Nashville *Union*, 19 July 1841.

[54] Emma Inman Williams, *Historic Madison: The Story of Jackson and Madison County, Tennessee, from the Prehistoric Moundbuilders to 1917* (Jackson, 1946), 416.

[55] Nashville *Republican Banner*, 2 Aug. 1841; Nashville *Union*, 2 Aug. 1841.

right up to election day, he then boarded a stage to race the returns to Nashville.[56]

The results were so close that the outcome was uncertain until the last votes were counted, but in the end Polk's fears were confirmed. Out of a total of over 100,000 votes, Jones had triumphed by a margin of slightly over 3,000. The Democracy had only one consolation. Polk's careful work on the legislative races had given the Democrats a majority of one in the new state senate, though they would be in a minority on the joint ballot by which the two houses customarily elected senators. But the election was not a total defeat for Polk personally. The 12,000-vote Whig majority of the year before had been reduced to 3,000, and this was due almost entirely to Polk's individual efforts. Polk "fought the battle unaided," Jackson informed Frank Blair with considerable accuracy, and was beaten "intirely by the apathy of the Democracy." To Van Buren, he reported in similar strain. "Govr. Polk deserves the thanks of the Democracy of the whole union," declared Old Hickory, "he fought the battle well & fought it alone."[57]

VI

During the closing weeks of his administration, Polk was busy preparing an account of his stewardship, which he sent as his final message to the new legislature on October 7. The most prominent feature of this statesmanlike review of state policy was its masterly analysis of the banking problem. "There is no sound principle of ethics, or of public policy," the retiring governor declared again, "which should exempt Banks from the moral and legal obligation which rests upon individuals to pay their debts." He recommended once more that a fixed day for compulsory resumption be set, that the banks be forbidden to pay further dividends until they resumed, and that in the future suspending banks be liquidated. He further recommended that the Lunatic Hospital be expanded so that it could care for more of these unfortunates, that separate quarters be provided for female convicts at the state penitentiary, and that the governor be authorized to commute death sentences to life imprisonment. This strain of humanitarian concern was also reflected

[56] Polk to Jackson, 2 Aug. 1841, Jackson Papers.
[57] Jackson to Blair, 12 Aug. 1841, Jackson Papers; Jackson to Van Buren, 16 Aug. 1841, Van Buren Papers; Tenn. *Senate Journal*, 1841, pp. 46-47.

in the governor's report that he had pardoned ten convicts and exercised to the limit his legal power to reduce the terms of convicts for good behavior.[58]

Governor Jones was inaugurated a week later, and the following evening the Polks bade an official farewell to their Nashville friends with a splendid party, to which the entire membership of the legislature was invited. The builders were still working on an addition to the house in Columbia, so James and Sarah remained in Nashville for the rest of the month.[59]

In November they set out for Mississippi to make the annual inspection of the plantation. The leisurely journey provided the first real relaxation Polk had known for years. They took their own carriage, with an additional horse behind for riding, which was Polk's only recreation. Solicitous as always for her husband's health, Sarah kept him from sitting up all night with the men who crowded in to talk politics at every stop, though she could not prevent the urgent requests that he speak at several Democratic celebrations that sprung up in their path. But aside from these interruptions, the long days of jogging over the roads of West Tennessee with Sarah beside him, the isolation from the political whirlpool, the relaxation of the cumulative tensions of the past twenty years, the convivial visits with the Polk kin at Bolivar, and the satisfaction of riding over his own land and talking cotton prices and farming methods with his overseer, furnished a long-needed balm to the sore and restless spirit of the ambitious and momentarily thwarted politician.[60]

While at the plantation, the Polks stayed with Isaac H. Dismukes, the overseer. Dismukes was especially glad to see his employer at this time, because he had recently been having a great deal of trouble with that perennial overseer's problem, runaway slaves. Under constant pressure from the owner for increased production, an overseer had to keep the slaves at work. But the slaves could always hope to appeal to the owner against the overseer's cruelty or alleged cruelty, and it was exceedingly difficult for the owner to judge the truth of the matter. Determined not to tolerate cruelty, Polk had had to dismiss two previous overseers because of repeated

58 Nashville *Republican Banner*, 8 Oct. 1841.

59 Polk to Donelson, 12 Oct. 1841, Andrew Jackson Donelson Papers (LC; herein cited as Donelson Papers); Nathan Vaught to Polk, 10 Sept. 1841, Polk Papers.

60 Anson and Fanny Nelson, *Memorials of Sarah Childress Polk: Wife of the Eleventh President of the United States* (New York, 1892), 68; Nashville *Union*, 6 Dec. 1841.

flights of slaves to Doctor Caldwell's plantation or to Columbia with tales of unjustified whippings and assaults. But Dismukes was an efficient manager, who had at last made the plantation profitable, and Polk now decided that the two most recent runaways must be brought back and punished, though he directed that the whipping be done in the presence of a nearby friend, who acted as his business agent in Mississippi.[61]

Polk's presence served to restore Dismukes' control and quiet the slaves, but only because they recognized both their owner's ultimate authority and his sense of justice. Polk's approach to his slaves was by no means essentially humanitarian. He was interested in his plantation primarily as a paying enterprise and unquestionably regarded the slaves as a part of his plantation investment. But at the same time—and this was the anomaly of the slaveholder's position—he could not help regarding them also as human beings and wanting to have them treated fairly and humanely. Polk saw to it that his slaves had adequate food, clothing, and medical care, and that they were not overworked. This was as much good business as kindliness. Though he did not go beyond this point by providing such things as religious instruction, education, and supervision of morals and domestic relations, he did steadfastly refuse to break up slave families or sell his slaves to Negro traders, even when he was hard pressed for money to pay his debts.[62]

With his personal servants and the older slaves who had come down through the family, Polk undoubtedly had kindlier relations. This was best illustrated by a letter he received from Harry, a blacksmith who had belonged to his father and whom he had hired out to work in Carrollton, Mississippi, some forty miles south of the plantation:

Dear Master as a servant I want to subscribe my friendship to you & famly as I am still in Carrollton yet & doing Good Labor for my imploier but tho I am feling [failing] in some stages my Eys site is falling of me I am well Trated by my imployer he feeds well & dont work me Tow Hard. I would wish to be Remembrd to all of my people old mistrs aspsherly Tell the old Lady Harry is hir servent untill deth & would be Gld to see Hir onc more I Expect to come out a cristmust to see you. the Hardness of Times & casness [scarceness] of mony is Her & will Reduce wages.
Dear mastr I have Eleven children. I have been faitheful over the anvill

61 John Spencer Bassett, ed., *The Southern Plantation Overseer As Revealed in His Letters* (Northampton, Mass., 1925), 152-160.
62 *ibid.*, passim.

Block Ever cin 1811 & is still old Harry my childrens names 1 Daniel 2 morcel [Marshall, for Polk's brother?] 3 Ben 4 Elis 5 Carrell 6 Charles 7 Elushey 8 David 9 mooney 10 Carline 11 Ophuley [Ophelia, for Polk's sister?] Some Resquest from you please to send me a letter How all of the people ar doing in your country   Derrect your letter to—

Harry your Servent[63]

It was the middle of December before James and Sarah got back to Columbia, where they were welcomed warmly by their fellow townspeople, and James settled down to the novel life of a politician out of office.

VII

Polk's defeat did not mean even a momentary retirement from politics. On the contrary, as before it was Polk who rallied the vanquished Democracy to rise and fight again. Six weeks after the election he announced defiantly to a Democratic gathering that though he "might be cast down, he was not destroyed." Though he was now only "an humble soldier" in the Democratic ranks, he "kept his armor on, and would still be found battling for the rights of the people." He carried with him into retirement, said Polk, "the same devotion to Equal Rights—the same opposition to a moneyed aristocracy, and the same determination to persevere in the maintenance of Republican principles that had marked his course hitherto." As in previous years, he was also ready with plausible explanations for Democratic defeat and abundant reasons for renewed Democratic hopes.[64]

Polk had an opportunity to elaborate on these reasons at a dinner given in his honor by the Democratic members of the legislature in October, and his published speech became a political manual for Democratic politicians all over the state. The Whigs had won power, he charged, by the "ridiculous, unmeaning and disgusting pageants" of 1840. Knowing that they could accomplish their evil purposes only while the excitement lasted, they had called a special session of Congress, promising the people relief, retrenchment, and reform. But instead of relief, retrenchment, and reform, the special session had produced such conclusive evidence of the Whigs' devotion to the old "federal" program of consolidation and extravagance that Tennessee's eyes had been opened. "Such a scene

63 Harry to Polk, 10 May 1842, Polk Papers.
64 Nashville *Union*, 16 Sept. 1841.

as that enacted before her people in 1840," Polk predicted, "can never again occur until the old men shall have passed off the stage of action and a new generation shall have taken their places."

Lest any miss the import of the reprehensible "federal" measures of the special session, Polk dissected them one by one. Instead of achieving retrenchment, the special session itself had cost $376,477 and had increased appropriations by over five million dollars. One of the very first actions of the Whig Congress had been to repeal the gag rule, "that salutary rule of proceeding which shut out from the Hall of Representatives the agitation of the abolitionists," so that the first month of the session was almost completely taken up with "agitating and alarming scenes." Polk reiterated what was to remain his fixed opinion, "that modern abolitionism with rare and few exceptions, had become a purely political question." He was equally sure that the bulk of the abolitionists were Whigs, while "the great body of the Democracy of the North" were "the natural and faithful allies of the South and of Southern interests."

Called ostensibly to fill a fictitious shortage of public funds, the special session had passed Clay's distribution bill, which was "a tariff measure in disguise" and unconstitutional besides. The people had been told, Polk continued, that the money taken from the Treasury by distribution would be made up by tariffs on luxuries, which would not affect the poor. "And what now do we see?" The new tax bill levied a tariff of 20 per cent on salt, "that article of indispensable necessity to man and beast." "Every farmer's cow that is well fed," Polk underscored the point, "consumes more of it in a year than the richest money-broker in *Wall Street*." In addition, to pay for distribution and the increased appropriations, "a funded national debt" of twelve million dollars had been "fastened on the country in a period of peace" by this *"relief Congress."*

Polk reserved his choicest invective for Clay's Bankrupt Law, which, he predicted, would not only "operate in favor of bankrupt merchants and traders alone, and to the prejudice of all honest and solvent merchants, and to the balance of the community," but would also increase the number of "reckless gamblers in trade." All that was missing to complete this system of speculation and favoritism was a national bank, from which the bankrupt might borrow money to set up in business again. And the only thing that had prevented the chartering of a new national bank had been Harrison's death and the repeated vetoes of his successor, John Tyler. President Tyler was entitled to "the lasting gratitude of his country," said Polk, for "arresting the dominant majority in Congress in their mad career, and saving his country from the dominion and political incubus of the money-power in the form of a National Bank." By his defiance of Clay, Tyler had brought on the resignation of most of his Cabinet and had been read out of his party by the Whig congressional caucus.

And what had been the political consequences of all this? In state after state that had voted for Harrison, the fall elections were going Democratic by heavy majorities. "The whole country is roused to a sense of the dangerous tendency of these consolidating measures. The 'sober second thought of the people' is every where producing its effect." Tennessee Democrats could only regret bitterly that the revelations had not come quite in time to affect the August elections. But "Tennessee only waits another opportunity to come to the ballot-box," Polk declared confidently, "to demonstrate to her Republican sister States, that she is now where she was in the political struggle of 1800, where she was when war was on our borders, and where she was in 1825 and 1828."

In these cheering circumstances, Polk concluded to thunderous applause, "we must keep on the armor of our political warfare and continue to do battle in the cause of sound principles." As for himself,

I retire to private life. I go to my home, the home of my early youth. I cheerfully and without complaint yield to the will of the people, as expressed in the last election. Though expressed by a diminished popular vote, and without the lights which have since broke in upon the public mind from Washington, it should be regarded as their will until they shall again speak in the constitutional forms. In that contest I fought the battle of principle, and honestly kept my political faith. If I fell in the conflict, I fell with my principles, and I am proud to know that more than fifty thousand freemen, who are still unterrified and undismayed, stood by me.[65]

Polk's optimism was no mere whistling in the dark. The Democrats had solid grounds for hope. The Whigs were split among themselves as no party had ever been before. The special session had raised issues on which they were vulnerable, and Democratic victories in all parts of the country were unmistakable evidence of the fact. Enthusiasm actually seemed to be replacing the apathy and discourage-

[65] *Speech of Governor James K. Polk, . . . October 23, 1841*, pamphlet in Polk Papers.

ment that had pervaded the Democratic ranks before their August defeat. In fact it was this spreading mood of optimism that led the Democrats unwittingly into a predicament more uncomfortable than those that politicians are usually required to endure.

VIII

The close division in the new legislature, with the Democrats having a narrow margin of thirteen to twelve in the upper house and the Whigs a majority of three in the lower house, had set the politicians to speculating about the coming senatorial elections almost before the August returns were counted. The Whigs were committed to electing Foster and Spencer Jarnagin, an East Tennessean who had done yeoman service as a Whig candidate for presidential elector in 1840, but the composition of the legislature raised some doubts about whether they could succeed. The immemorial practice had been to elect senators in a joint convention of the two houses, where the Whigs would have a majority of two. The increasingly bumptious Democrats, however, could use their control of the upper house to prevent a joint convention except on their own terms, and they were soon busily hatching schemes that might give them one or both of the senators.

The Whig hopes for defeating these Democratic machinations rested on Sam Turney, brother of Congressman Hopkins Turney and state senator from a Cumberland plateau district. Though a Democrat, Turney had been elected with bipartisan support, and the Whigs claimed that he had pledged himself to vote for Whig senators. Hopkins Turney assured Polk, however, that his brother would be faithful to the party. To make certain, the Democrats elected him speaker of the upper house.

With Turney under control, the Democrats were confident that they had the game in their own hands and set about making the most of their advantage. Polk himself must bear much of the responsibility for this rash partisan attempt to flout the electoral decision. It was Polk who began sending his subordinates in various parts of the state urgent instructions to contest elections that had gone against them by small majorities in normally Democratic counties and to put heavy pressure on wavering Whigs. This risky departure from his usually cautious course and from his frequently expressed devotion to majority rule can be explained partly by the intensity of his conviction that recent events had really changed the complexion of political opinion in Tennessee. Probably more important was his dismay at the fading of his prospects for high national office, in the wake of the successive defeats suffered by the Tennessee Democracy. To avoid complete eclipse, he seems to have been toying with the idea of going to the Senate himself.[66]

At first the Democrats had hoped only to thwart Foster and disorganize the Whigs by supporting their discarded ex-governor, Newton Cannon, for one of the Senate seats. Then, under the impetus of Polk's driving will and signs of increasing Democratic strength, they began to talk of forcing the Whigs to compromise on one senator from each party. But by the time the legislature met in October, it appeared that two or three Whigs might be weaned away from their party in the lower house, and the Democrats were soon scheming for both Senate seats.

Nicholson and Anderson argued that as the retiring incumbents they had first claim on the party's support, but a strong sentiment rapidly developed to elect Polk. It began with Polk's friends in Congress. Immediately after the August election Hopkins Turney had written from the capital that Polk's defeat for governor might turn out to be fortunate, for, he said, if Polk could come to the Senate, "I believe your chance for a nomination for the Pres. would be better than any other mans."[67] During the campaign Polk had denied vehemently the Whig charges that he had no hope of being elected governor and that he was merely trying to carry a Democratic legislature so he could go to the Senate. He "wanted nothing that the people of Tennessee cannot bestow," he had said in one of his last campaign speeches; he "had never asked or accepted and never would accept office from any other power." Nevertheless, the "Polk for Senator" cry was soon taken up by Harris's *Union* and Sam Laughlin's McMinnville *Gazette*, both the editors being among Polk's closest associates. Polk was the man whom the doubtful Whigs were being asked to vote for, and it was reported that he and no other

[66] Nashville *Whig*, quoted in *Messages of the Governors of Tenn.*, III, 595-596; Nashville *Republican Banner*, 10 Aug. 1841; Nashville *Union*, 30 Aug. 1841; J. J. Hinton to R. L. Caruthers, 15 Aug. 1841, Caruthers Papers; Anderson to Polk, 20 Aug. 1841, Polk Papers; H. L. Turney to Polk, 24 Aug. 1841, *ibid.*; J. W. Blackwell to Polk, 1 Sept. 1841, *ibid.*; W. H. Polk to J. K. Polk, 7 Sept. 1841, *ibid.*; G. W. L. Marr to Polk, 7 Sept. 1841, *ibid.*; "Polk-Johnson Letters," *loc.cit.*, 228-229.

[67] H. L. Turney to Polk, 12 Aug. 1841, Polk Papers; Anderson to Polk, 27, 28 Sept. 1841, *ibid.*

Democrat could get their support. That Polk himself was behind this policy was indicated when he informed Cave Johnson that the Democrats had already made enough converts to create a tie on joint ballot "so far at least as one of the Senators is concerned." He wanted Johnson's aid in securing a doubtful Whig from his district to tip the balance. Even the Whigs conceded at the beginning of the session that Polk would probably get one of the seats.[68]

For some reason this plan did not work out. Perhaps Polk had a "sober second thought" himself. Certainly the Whig press was doing everything it could to show the retiring governor the folly of his apparent intention. "Before the reverberation of the thunder-tones of the people's condemnation of his claims to their confidence and support, has died away among the mountains," trumpeted the *Banner*, "we find him obtruding his repudiated pretensions before their representatives and setting up his claim to even a higher station than that which, but yesterday, they so signally declared he was unfit to occupy." On the other hand, the Democrats may simply have failed to corral enough Whig votes to elect him. A letter Andrew Johnson wrote on October 24 gives support to either conjecture. "We have been defeated in every move as yet," he said, but he also reported that "Polk is not and will not be a candidate for Senator." This determination Polk had announced the previous evening at the Nashville Democratic dinner. "If I shall ever again rise," he declared as though he had never considered accepting office at the hands of the legislature, "I expect to *rise from the people*."[69]

There still remains one other possible explanation for Polk's equivocal behavior. It may be that he never had any intention of letting himself be elected, and was merely using himself as a stalking horse. Not only would his name woo more Whigs away from their party allegiance than any other, but it would also unite the contentious Democrats for a real fight over the senatorships, before they were split by the rivalries of various aspirants. If this was Polk's strategy, it succeeded in one important respect. By the time he announced his determination not to be a senator and departed

---

[68] Nashville *Republican Banner*, 2 Aug. 1841; "Polk-Johnson Letters," *loc.cit.*, 228; Laughlin to Polk, 1, 12 Sept. 1841, Polk Papers; J. F. Gillespy to Polk, 21 Sept. 1841, *ibid.*; C. W. Nelson to [T. A. R. Nelson], 6 Oct. 1841, Nelson Papers; Nashville *Union*, 16, 30 Sept. 1841; Knoxville *Post*, 29 Sept. 1841, quoted in *Messages of the Governors of Tenn.*, III, 429.

[69] Nashville *Republican Banner*, 4 Oct. 1841; Andrew Johnson to William Lowery, 24 Oct. 1841, Andrew Johnson Papers (LC); *Speech of Governor James K. Polk, . . . October 23, 1841*, p. 10.

for Mississippi, the Democrats were so committed to holding out for at least one of the seats that they were resolved to stand their ground, even if Polk would not be their candidate.

Before Polk departed, the thirteen Democrats in the upper house —soon to be known as the "Immortal Thirteen"—caucused and agreed to make their stand on the contention that the long-practiced method of electing senators by joint convention was unconstitutional. They gave the Whigs to understand that an election could be secured only by conceding the Democrats one of the seats, while to strengthen their position they addressed a circular to all the senatorial aspirants asking their views on the principal measures of the special session and inquiring specifically, "Do you admit the right of the General Assembly, as a constituent body, to instruct Senators in Congress, and their duty, when instructed, to obey or resign?" When Foster and Jarnagin contemptuously refused to answer these questions, the Democrats charged them with disrespect for the legislature and defiance of the cardinal democratic doctrine of instruction. They also charged that during the campaign, when it was expected that the Whigs would control the upper house and the Democrats would have a majority on joint ballot, Governor Jones had proposed that the Whigs refuse to go into convention to elect senators.[70]

Favorable replies to the Democratic "interrogatories" were received, however, from Hopkins Turney and Thomas Brown, the latter a doubtful Whig from East Tennessee whom the Democrats had encouraged to enter the race. Turney was no doubt brought into the running both because of his faithful service to the party, and also to keep his brother Sam in line. The "Thirteen" now attempted to elect Hopkins Turney and Brown by joint resolution of the two houses, counting on a few wavering Whigs to provide the margin of victory for this hybrid slate in the lower house. But one of the "Thirteen" refused to support this coupling of a Whig with a Democrat, and the resolution had to be divided and was thus doomed to defeat in the lower house.[71]

At this point Sam Turney gave in to the heavy Whig pressure from his district and announced that he would vote with the Whigs for a joint convention. The crucial factors in Turney's reversal seem

[70] Nashville *Republican Banner*, 22 Oct. 1841; Nashville *Union*, 3, 24 Dec. 1841.
[71] Nashville *Republican Banner*, 19, 26, 30 Nov. 1841; Nashville *Union*, 1 Dec. 1841; J. P. Hardwicke to Polk, 12 Nov. 1841, Polk Papers; Laughlin to Polk, 13 Nov. 1841, *ibid.*; W. H. Polk to J. K. Polk, 6 Jan. 1842, *ibid.*

to have been a conviction that his brother could not be elected, his brother's departure to Washington for the regular session of Congress, and the arguments of Judge Catron, who was then in Nashville. Catron was one of the few Democrats who perceived the dangers in the course of the "Thirteen," and he had warned Jackson that the attempt to force the election of Democratic senators "is running into extremes, & is ultra."[72] Catron feared that this might became the main issue in the next campaign and thus sacrifice all the advantages the Democrats now had on national issues. These views the judge expressed to Sam Turney, who was obviously impressed.

Having failed, then, to elect Brown and Hopkins Turney, and with Sam Turney, "shivering in the wind," the Democrats would have been wise to give up the struggle. But when Sam Turney's shift enabled the joint convention to meet, the other twelve Democratic senators refused to attend, sending word that they were in their chamber ready for "constitutional business," and the convention had to adjourn for lack of a quorum. By dint of threats and expostulation, Turney was finally brought back into line, and the "Thirteen" were again "safe against the world."[73]

A contest of such bitterness could hardly occur among Tennessee politicians without physical violence. Fisticuffs broke out during a heated debate in the lower house, and though the two combatants were quickly separated, tempers continued to boil. On the way out of the hall at the end of the day, they began to curse one another again, each drew and fired two pistols in rapid succession, and each was in the act of firing another when the bystanders intervened to prevent further bloodshed. One of the lawmakers had been shot through the hand. The *Union*'s comment indicated how close Tennessee still stood to the frontier: "It is acknowledged by all that both gentlemen behaved very gallantly on the occasion."[74]

By the time Polk returned from Mississippi, even the "Immortal Thirteen" realized that they were in a dangerous position and were imploring him to come up from Columbia and extricate them. The senatorial question might now have been comprised but for internal difficulties in both parties. Foster would probably have joined Sam Turney in a move to get himself and Sam's brother elected to the

[72] Catron to Jackson, n.d., Jackson Papers, cxviii, No. 62.
[73] Nashville *Republican Banner*, 23, 30 Nov. 1841; W. H. Polk to J. K. Polk, 22 Nov. 1841 [misplaced 1840], Polk Papers; Laughlin to Polk, 24 Nov. 1841, *ibid.*
[74] Nashville *Union*, 1 Dec. 1841; Nashville *Republican Banner*, 30 Nov. 1841.

Senate, except that a few of Jarnagin's Whig friends "would not let the machine move without he was in it." The situation was further complicated when Bell, having just sacrificed his Cabinet post to party loyalty, came home hoping to be rewarded with a seat in the Senate. At the same time Nicholson was making almost as much trouble for the Democrats by turning his friends against Hopkins Turney, so as to pave the way for a compromise on himself and either Foster or Bell.[75]

With the session drawing to a close, the Democrats were becoming panicky at the prospect of being blamed for a failure to elect senators. From Washington, Judge Catron wrote that it was "nonsense" to argue that an election by joint ballot was unconstitutional and urged "an election at any hazzard," even if it meant taking Foster and Thomas Brown.[76] With these sentiments Polk agreed, but it was almost impossible to find a way for the "Thirteen" to recede gracefully from the position they had so militantly assumed.

The crisis came in the middle of January, when Bell's friends proposed a compromise on himself and Hopkins Turney, which prompted the Foster men to suggest a similar proposition involving their favorite. But the Nicholson-Turney feud was causing such trouble that it was now hard to bring the Democrats together on either of these propositions. Nettled already by Nicholson's unreliability, Polk was infuriated at this latest manifestation of his unscrupulous ambition. He could no longer avoid taking a personal hand in the situation. To his more reliable friends in the legislature he wrote of Nicholson:

Every day convinces me more and more, that he (N) is now travelling in the broad road that John Bell travelled for several years before his apostacy, whilst he was making loud professions of his adhesion to our principles. We all know where John Bell now is. *And mark what I now say to you,* that five years, perhaps not one will pass, before he is found where Bell now is, unless it shall be his personal interest shall make him seem to be otherwise. I am not mistaken. I speak from no personal or malignant feeling. I would prefer to day, an open opponent, to a hypocritical friend in disguise.[77]

[75] J. P. Hardwicke to Polk, 15 Dec. 1841, Polk Papers; Harris to Polk, 13 Dec. 1841, *ibid.*; J. P. Hardwicke to Polk, 13, 31 Dec. 1841, *ibid.*; W. H. Polk to J. K. Polk, 15 Dec. 1841, *ibid.*; H. L. Turney to Polk, 26 Dec. 1841 [misplaced 1839], 2 Jan. 1842, *ibid.*

[76] Catron to Polk, 2 Jan. 1842, Polk Papers.

[77] Polk to Lackfield Maclin, 17 Jan. 1842, Johnson Papers; J. P. Hardwicke to Polk, 9, 16 Jan. 1842, Polk Papers; Laughlin to Polk, 10 Jan. 1842, *ibid.*; H. L. Turney to Polk, 16 Jan. 1842, *ibid.*; Armstrong to Polk, 22 Jan. 1842, *ibid.*; Lackfield Maclin to Polk, 26 Jan. 1842, *ibid.*

At the same time Polk sent James Walker to Nashville with authority to use his own name for one of the Senate seats, if this were the only way to get a compromise without splitting the Democrats. Polk was unwilling to see Bell elevated by Democratic votes, however, and was equally adamant against any compromise including Nicholson. In short, Walker was to persuade the Democratic leaders to compromise on Foster and Polk, though he had to do so without letting it appear that the initiative came from Columbia.[78]

Polk's position left the game in Foster's hands, and he played his cards adroitly. Foster appreciated the partisan advantage the Whigs would derive from a failure to elect senators, and he had permitted his friends to talk of compromise only for the purpose of luring the Democrats away from the propositions being made by Bell's friends. Once he perceived that the Democrats were resolved not to take Bell, he discouraged any further talk of a compromise involving himself. Thus the session neared its end, with the unhappy Democrats attempting one desperate scheme for compromise after another. They all failed, and when the legislature adjourned, the Whigs had a ready-made issue with which to counter their disadvantages on national questions. The "Thirteen" had compounded their difficulties by refusing to sanction Governor Jones's nominations for directors of the state bank, thus leaving the Democratic directors appointed by Polk in office.[79]

Foster had good reason to be jubilant. "Most of the 'immortal thirteen' for weeks before the adjournment, were in unspeakable travail," he gloated to a friend. "They saw the error of their way, & would have been glad to retrace their steps, but that a retrograde march would have damned them with double infamy. Leper as they made me out, I could have gone to the Senate with their hearty prayers & good wishes, if I would have condescended to relieve their embarrassments, by taking with me . . . 'a little bit of a democrat,' & I could myself have chosen the 'little creature.' "[80]

But the end was not yet. A special session of the legislature would have to be convened in the autumn of 1842 to lay off new congressional districts, and the leaders of the "Thirteen," fully realizing

[78] Walker to Polk, 13, 16 Jan. 1842, Polk Papers; Polk to Walker, 17 Jan. 1842 [misplaced 1841], *ibid.*; W. H. Polk to J. K. Polk, 17 Jan. 1842, *ibid.*

[79] J. P. Hardwicke to Polk, 26 Jan. 1842, Polk Papers; Laughlin to Polk, 29 Jan. 1842, *ibid.*; Armstrong to Polk, n.d. (postmarked 29 Jan. [1842]), *ibid.*; James Campbell to David Campbell, 10 Feb. 1842, Campbell Papers; Nashville *Republican Banner*, 7, 25 Feb., 11 May 1842.

[80] Foster to R. L. Caruthers, 13 Feb. 1842, Caruthers Papers.

their peril, issued an address at the end of the regular session proposing "to return the power to elect Senators pure and undefiled to the hands of the people." The Whigs shrewdly construed this as a proposition for a resignation of all members of the upper house, where they were in a minority, and an election of new state senators to settle the question at the special session. In this form they accepted the proposal, but at Polk's prompting the Democrats insisted that the whole legislature must resign. By frantic efforts during the summer of 1842, they succeeded in having ready the resignations from all the Democratic members.[81]

This put the Whigs at a real disadvantage. The new editor of the *Banner*, Felix K. Zollicoffer, privately confessed his fear that not all the Whigs would resign, which would "give our opponents such an advantage in the next regular contest as to lose us all our vantage ground on their factious course in the Senate." And even if a general resignation took place, Zollicoffer added, the Whigs were so "entombed in apathy" that they would be defeated. Moreover the Bell-Foster rivalry prevented the Whig leadership from coming to any agreement about what should be done, and in the end the Whigs merely let the matter drop. Thus the Democrats succeeded in partially neutralizing the senatorial question as a political issue. When the special session of 1842 met, efforts at compromise were again unsuccessful, though the deadlock might have been broken had the Democrats been willing to accept Bell. At this session the "Thirteen" also blocked an effort by Governor Jones to investigate the affairs of the state bank.[82]

Which party had profited most from the outcome of the long controversy would not be known until August 1843. Meanwhile it was apparent to all that the struggle had further embittered the political life of the strife-torn state. "The contest that is to come off in Tennessee in 1843," wrote Governor Jones to a friend, "is to be fierce and fearfull and who will conquer or be vanquished in the struggle time must determine." The governor, for one, felt that he had "received in the last three years campaign scars enough to entitle me to an honorable discharge."[83]

81 Nashville *Republican Banner*, 30 May, 13 July, 17 Aug. 1842; Polk to Laughlin, 1 June 1842, Polk-Laughlin Letters; Anderson to Polk, n.d. [July 1842; misplaced at end of 1840], 24 July 1842, Polk Papers.
82 F. K. Zollicoffer to R. L. Caruthers, 19 July 1842, Caruthers Papers; Armstrong to Polk, 22 July 1842, Polk Papers; Harris to Polk, 11 Dec. 1842, *ibid.*; W. H. Polk to J. K. Polk, 14 Feb. 1843, *ibid.*; Nashville *Republican Banner*, 10 Oct., 18 Nov. 1842.
83 Jones to R. L. Caruthers, 4 Feb. 1842, Caruthers Papers.

14

FINIS?

WHILE GOVERNOR JONES WAS DREADING THE COMING BATTLE and longing for the freedom and repose of private life, his restless foe, James K. Polk, was trying to make the best of that situation. Even the Whigs had to confess that Polk's "course at home is most unexceptionable." The personal bitterness that had estranged him from many of his neighbors through years of political warfare began to wear off and even to be replaced by cordiality. "He is a plain, dignified gentleman," one of the leading Columbia Whigs conceded grudgingly, "polite to every body, but cringing to none."[1]

Polk entered dutifully into the routine of domestic and social activities expected of a gentleman of some leisure. There was much visiting and dining with the various branches of the Polk clan in and around Columbia, and he and Sarah often made the trip to Murfreesboro, sometimes for the wedding of a niece, but often enough without any particular occasion. There were the regular spring and fall journeys to the Mississippi plantation, with Sarah usually insisting on going along. There was also time now to attend to the long-neglected estates of his father and deceased brothers. This meant riding horseback through the Western District to supervise the sale and renting of lands, most of which were still unsold because of the depression.[2]

Without the stimulation of immediate involvement in the political whirlpool, James as well as Sarah began to feel ever more poignantly their failure to have children. They had tried to keep some of their many nieces and nephews around them in Washington and Nashville, but this was no real substitute for children of their own. James had always felt a particular responsibility for the small boy and

[1] Edmund Dillahunty to R. L. Caruthers, 5-6 May 1842, Robert L. Caruthers Papers (SHC).

[2] Anson and Fanny Nelson, *Memorials of Sarah Childress Polk: Wife of the Eleventh President of the United States* (New York, 1892), 67-68; receipt (placed 6 Mar. 1842), James K. Polk Papers (LC; herein cited as Polk Papers, which refers to First Series unless otherwise noted); Polk to Laughlin, 1 June 1842, *ibid*.

girl, Marshall and Eunice, left by his brother Marshall, though their legal guardian was now the North Carolina physician whom Marshall's widow had married. James's inquiries to Doctor Tate about the children became more and more frequent, and he insisted on sending some of his own funds to insure a good education for Eunice, who was now of school age. He had almost persuaded the Tates to send both children to Columbia for schooling when Eunice died tragically, and it took another year to persuade Mrs. Tate to give up Marshall. By then it was late in the fall of 1843, and the boy's delicate health made it necessary to postpone the trip until spring, when Polk was at last able to welcome the lad to whom he would henceforth be a father.[3]

Polk's personal finances also required attention. The long years of trying to make his landed property and plantation profitable under depression conditions, while living on modest government salaries and spending heavily for political purposes, had kept him deep in debt. Besides loans from John Catron and other individuals, he owed nearly $6,000 to various banks, over half of this amount to the state bank, whose directors he had appointed. Though his plantation was beginning to pay, he was constantly having to anticipate his crop proceeds to meet pressure from the banks for at least a partial retirement of his notes, and little was left for living expenses. It was this pressing necessity that forced him to form a law partnership with his brother Bill and another Columbia attorney and to ride the circuit once more, defending murderers and serving litigants for healthy fees.[4]

But Polk's heart was not really in any of these things, for his political ambition would not let him rest. He equally begrudged the time he gave to the law, business affairs, or the social activities Sarah arranged. Night and day, whenever he could escape from other duties, he was in his study, reading newspapers and correspondence and busily writing to political friends. Even Sarah, whose word ordinarily carried much weight in family matters, could make

[3] Polk to Dr. W. C. Tate, 1 Nov. 1841, copy, 18 Nov. 1843 [misplaced 1842], copy, Polk Papers; Tate to Polk, 13 Oct. 1842, 14 Oct. 1843, *ibid.*; Polk to Mrs. Polk, 26 Oct. 1843, *ibid.*

[4] Armstrong to Polk, 14, 15 Apr., 30 Aug. [on reverse side of Polk to Dr. William McNeill, 2 Aug.] 1842, Polk Papers; articles of agreement, 5 Sept. 1842, 17 Aug. 1843, *ibid.*; Abbott Lawrence to Polk, 21 Sept. 1842, *ibid.*; Catron to Polk, 25 Dec. 1842, *ibid.*; W. S. Pickett to Polk, 6 Nov. 1843, *ibid.*; notices of notes due at several banks, 20 Feb. 1842, 7 May, 1, 4 July, 3 Sept., 1 Oct., 1, 11 Nov. 1843, *ibid.*

little headway against this constant toil. "You work too much," she would remonstrate on going into the study. But her husband, hardly pausing to glance up, would hand her a newspaper, saying, "Sarah, here is something I wish you to read," and she, too, would be put to work.[5]

As well as she had learned to manage her husband in other respects, Sarah knew better than to oppose this absorbing political passion. Instead she wisely tried to share his political interests, seeking only to guard his health against the constant danger of overexertion and to provide him with occasional diversions. Indeed Sarah herself was not immune to the allurements of political life.

James, for his part, fully recognized his dependence on his wife for both emotional stability and political counsel. Her judgment was usually sound, and he frequently sought and accepted it. Alfred Balch probably had Sarah also in mind when he commented acidly of her friend Mrs. Catron, "These women you know who do not breed must always be busy either in making matches or making and unmaking Statesmen or such things provided they have enough money to buy fine clothes and ride in their own carriages." At any rate, whenever one of those frequent summonses to a political consultation at Nashville arrived, James would urge Sarah to go along. "Why should you stay at home?" he would ask, brushing aside her feeble protests. "To take care of the house? Why if the house burns down, we can live without it."[6]

These trips came more and more frequently. The Tennessee Democracy was looking to Polk as the David who would slay the Whig Goliath in August 1843. Beyond that epic battle might lie the vice presidency or, in the minds of Polk's enthusiastic friends, an even higher post. With many a calculating glance at the increasingly chaotic condition of the Democratic party, they were beginning to tell Polk that his success in bringing Tennessee back to its Democratic faith would "lead on certainly to your election to the Presidency."[7] Such suggestions accounted for the feverish energy with which the defeated governor labored in his quiet study at Columbia to launch his battered bark once more on the turbulent sea of national politics.

[5] Nelson, *Sarah Polk*, 67-68.

[6] Balch to [Van Buren], 22 Nov. 1842, Martin Van Buren Papers (LC); Nelson, *Sarah Polk*, 68.

[7] Nicholson to Polk, 13 Jan. 1841, Polk Papers.

II

Both great national parties entered the 1840's, the decade so crucial to the fate of the American Union, more deeply split than ever before and incapable of mastering or moderating the powerful disruptive currents that were running uncontrolled through the country. The internecine battles for the 1844 presidential nominations, in fact, encouraged reckless exploitation of dangerously divisive sectional and economic differences. With agriculture and commerce still languishing under depressed conditions, the old economic issues were charged with additional bitterness as ambitious politicians made them weapons in the struggle for power. Simultaneously both northern abolitionism and southern apprehensions over slavery were growing apace. Northern constituencies were sending a growing number of out and out antislavery men to Congress, the petition battles were becoming more furious, and the passionate deliverances of the Henry Wises on one side and the John Quincy Adamses on the other were forcing the slavery controversy toward a showdown on the Texas question.

Old Hickory's forceful leadership and Van Buren's courage and shrewdness in the crisis of 1837 had made the Democracy a truly national party, with great power to subordinate, or at least harmonize, the sectional and parochial loyalties of its adherents. But the disaster of 1840 virtually destroyed the authority of the party's high command. The federal patronage, which had served Van Buren so well in weathering the Panic of 1837 and realigning the party behind his radical economic policy, was gone, while the Jacksonian idealism and enthusiasm that had previously bound the party together had withered seriously under the blight of defeat.

Murmurings against Van Buren spread rapidly as "Democrats by trade," who had never favored the hard-money ideas of the Jackson–Van Buren group, began to argue that new leaders and new policies were needed to restore Democratic ascendancy in 1844. These sentiments were eagerly embraced by other politicians, who, regardless of opinions on economic issues, were reluctant to postpone their own ambitions so that Van Buren could have another chance at the White House. At the same time the increasing concentration of Democratic strength in the southern states was enhancing the party stature of John C. Calhoun, and he was more obsessed with presidential ambitions than ever. Though Calhoun was determined to bend the Democracy to his extreme free trade, state rights, proslavery position, his obvious ability and conciliatory behavior were making him the real leader of the Democratic minority in Congress.

These elements of Democratic discord were all too apparent by the time the special session of Congress adjourned in September 1841. The Whigs were no better off, and their repudiation of President Tyler intensified the struggle among the Democrats by increasing Democratic hopes for victory in 1844. For the next two and a half years the Democracy would be torn with strife, as Calhoun and other dissidents sought to build up organizations that could control the national convention, while Van Buren tried desperately to maintain his grip on the party machinery. The vice presidential aspirants were mere pawns in this constantly shifting contest among the principals.

Nevertheless it was necessary for the lesser contenders to stake their claims early, and Polk was already campaigning indirectly when he visited his Mississippi plantation in the autumn of 1841. Mississippi's support was essential to his claim to be regarded as the candidate of the Southwest, and his friends in Yalabusha County, where his plantation was located, had arranged a dinner in his honor. "The agriculturists and working men of the country to the distance of more than forty miles, and from all the adjacent counties," said the *Union*'s account, "come [*sic*] in crowds on horseback and on foot, in waggons and two on a horse, to see, hear, and talk to the great Tennessee orator, statesman, and patriot." After describing Polk's characteristic denunciation of the Whigs, the *Union*'s correspondent concluded significantly, "Gov. Polk is more endeared to the democracy of north Mississippi than any man in the Union, and his name is intimately associated with the next Vice Presidency of the United States."[8]

Meanwhile the Calhounites had begun to cultivate Polk. Through Doctor Ramsey, Calhoun's managers at Charleston proposed that Polk run for vice president on the Calhoun ticket and tried to induce the Tennessee Democrats to stir up sentiment for such a combination. Inexperienced at political intrigue but delighted to have a hand in it, Ramsey thought this a capital suggestion, though he did have the good sense to insist that the first move come from Calhoun's friends in some other state, preferably North Carolina. The good doctor learned eventually that the Calhoun men would initiate

8 Nashville *Union*, 6 Dec. 1841.

no such movement, since Calhoun's running mate must obviously come from the North. In fact the South Carolinians were dangling the same proposition under Silas Wright's nose, while expecting ultimately to fall back on Levi Woodbury of New Hampshire.[9]

The more astute Calhoun leaders hardly expected Polk to swallow this kind of bait, but they had other lures ready. Calhoun himself took pains to forward copies of his Senate speeches to Polk and showered attentions on a puzzled J. George Harris, when the editor visited Washington. At the same time Polk's friends were being told that Calhoun wanted to adopt the "one term system," by which he would serve four years in the White House with Wright as vice president, Wright would then serve four years with Polk as vice president, and then Polk would be in line for the succession. Similar intimations were repeated in many forms. One politician told Polk that Calhoun's friends "look upon you as their next leader in the South," while a principal Calhoun strategist, Franklin H. Elmore, held out the more concrete prospect of a Cabinet post.[10]

All this put Polk in a delicate position, as it was intended to do. From the very first he had been determined to support Van Buren and to claim second place on his ticket. But even if Van Buren defeated Calhoun for the presidential nomination, Polk would probably still need the convention votes of the Calhounites to insure his own nomination for vice president. So he was careful to maintain a cordial attitude toward the South Carolina leader. To Elmore he replied that he considered both Van Buren and Calhoun well qualified for the presidency, and denied that he had committed himself to Van Buren. Beyond this he would only say, "Whoever may be thus fairly selected in a general convention, in which the body of the people shall be truly represented I will cheerfully support." Elmore complained that this was "perfectly non committal," and the Calhoun men became suspicious "that Tennessee is for Van B. & that the fact is suppressed from policy." They demanded to know how Tennessee would vote in the convention, but Polk could not afford to say more.[11]

[9] Ramsey to Polk, 9 Nov. 1841, 2, 26 Feb., 18 Apr., 10 May 1842, Polk Papers.

[10] W. M. Gwin to Polk, 5 Nov. 1842, Polk Papers; Harris to Polk, 13 Dec. 1841, *ibid.*; Brown to Polk, 9 Apr. 1842, *ibid.*; Johnson to Polk, 20 July 1842, *ibid.*; F. H. Elmore to Polk, n.d. [postmarked 12 May] 1842, *ibid.*; J. Franklin Jameson, ed., *Correspondence of John C. Calhoun*, American Historical Association, *Annual Report*, 1899, II (Washington, 1900), 844–845.

[11] Polk to F. H. Elmore, 13 June 1842, copy, Polk Papers; Brown to Polk, 27 Dec. 1842, *ibid.*

While this byplay with the Calhounites was going on in the early months of 1842, Polk had his friends hard at work trying to stir up public sentiment for the Van Buren and Polk ticket in Mississippi and Alabama. Here he ran into trouble, because Calhoun was also trying to get endorsements in these states. Developments were especially disappointing in Mississippi, where Senator Robert J. Walker had countered the Calhoun activity by organizing a Democratic meeting to endorse Van Buren. Walker was just emerging as Polk's rival for preeminence among southwestern Democrats, and he adroitly sought to discourage Polk's pretensions by having the Van Buren meeting endorse Richard M. Johnson for vice president. Polk's supporters, most of them from northern Mississippi, had tried to defeat this action by arguing that any vice presidential nomination was premature, but they had been outvoted by the well-organized Walker forces. Having taken a position against a premature nomination, it was then hard for them to get up their own meetings to endorse Van Buren and Polk. Even when they did so, they were dismayed to find their actions apparently deprecated by Polk's Nashville *Union,* for the *Union* was following the national Van Buren strategy and vigorously discouraging any agitation of the presidential question at this time.[12]

The most important maneuvering was simultaneously going on among the congressmen in Washington, where it appeared that Van Buren and Calhoun were by no means the only contenders for first place on the ticket. The cautious James Buchanan was pressing his claims, arguing that Pennsylvania had served proudly for years as "the keystone of the Democratic arch" without adequate reward. Buchanan was appealing mainly to the conservative wing of the party, and again, as in the previous campaign, William R. King of Alabama was seeking the vice presidential nomination as his running mate.

But Buchanan had enemies within the Pennsylvania Democracy, and these men constituted a considerable portion of the heterogeneous following that was gathering around the candidacy of Richard M. Johnson. "Old Dick" had persuaded himself that he was the choice of the masses for the first office itself, and he was touring the North

---

12 J. M. Howry to Polk, 15 Feb., 9 Sept. 1842, Polk Papers; L. H. Coe to Polk, 30 Apr., 30 May, 2 June, 30 July 1842, *ibid.*; Lackfield Maclin to Polk, 4 May 1842, *ibid.*; James E. Saunders to L. H. Coe, 11 May 1842 [placed with Coe to Polk, 30 May 1842], 22 July 1842 [placed with Coe to Polk, 30 July 1842], *ibid.*; J. M. Howry to Coe, 10 May 1842, *ibid.*

and West in search of encouragement. Many suspected, however, that the red-vested colonel would be willing to settle for second place on the Van Buren ticket. When it appeared that Johnson's martial renown no longer elicited much response, most of the conservative support attracted by his flexible views on banking and other questions began shifting to the phlegmatic Lewis Cass of Michigan, a former member of Jackson's Cabinet who had just resigned as minister to France.[13]

Thus there were many groups besides the Calhounites who were ready to aid in Van Buren's downfall, and Polk, with his long record of support for the Jackson–Van Buren policies, could expect little at the hands of these generally conservative Democrats. In addition, those Democrats with national aspirations, whether opponents of Van Buren or not, would hardly help put Polk in a position that strengthened his ultimate claims on the White House. Even if Van Buren were nominated, all these elements could be expected to prefer a running mate like Johnson or King, who would not be in their way in the future. It was for this reason that maintaining good relations with the Calhounites was so important for Polk. If their chief failed to get the presidential nomination, they might be willing to help Polk get second place on the ticket.

Amid the ceaseless maneuvering for advantage among all these groups, Polk's hopes alternately rose and fell. For a time his friends suspected that Benton was promoting Colonel Johnson for vice president. Actually the Missouri senator was so irritated by Johnson's presumptuous competition with Van Buren for the first place that he eventually denounced him openly. At the same time, however, Benton refused to endorse Polk, while secretly trying to start a boom for Joel R. Poinsett, an anti-Calhoun Democrat from South Carolina. Another danger arose when Thomas Ritchie, boss of the Virginia Democracy, demanded that Van Buren reward Virginia's long fealty by securing the vice presidential nomination for former Speaker Andrew Stevenson.[14]

13 W. B. Lewis to Jackson, 20 Dec. 1841 (HEH); Catron to Polk, 7 Jan. [1842; misplaced 1840], Polk Papers; Johnson to Polk, 20 Mar. 1842, *ibid.*; W. M. Gwin to Jackson, 16 Feb., 14 Mar. 1842, Andrew Jackson Papers (LC); John Law to Van Buren, 13 July 1842, Van Buren Papers; Nashville *Republican Banner*, 4 May, 22 Aug. 1842.

14 Johnson to Polk, 20 Mar. 1842, 29 Jan. 1843, Polk Papers; Turney to Polk, 4, 31 Jan. 1843, *ibid.*; John Letcher to [T. H. Benton], 15 Dec. 1842, Van Buren Papers; A. P. Stinson to Levi Woodbury, 30 Sept. 1843, Levi Woodbury Correspondence, Gist Blair Papers (LC); Grace E. Heilman and Bernard S. Levin, eds., *Calendar of*

Every letter from Washington made it clearer that Polk's fate depended on Van Buren's attitude, and he soon had a golden opportunity to sound out the ex-president. In April 1842 Van Buren reached Tennessee in the course of a long, leisurely, "non-political" tour of the South and West, in company with his former secretary of the navy, James K. Paulding. Polk had enlisted the cooperation of Jackson and Donelson, and when the distinguished visitors' steamboat reached Nashville on Monday, April 25, he hastened up from Columbia and the next day accompanied them to the Hermitage, where they remained all day Wednesday. A great Democratic celebration had been arranged for Thursday in Nashville, and the party returning from the Hermitage was greeted with the firing of cannon, the ringing of bells, military companies, and a parade through the city, after which Van Buren was introduced to the Democrats who had come in from all parts of the state to meet him. When the ex-president returned to the Hermitage that evening, Polk was forced to depart for home without having been able to engage Van Buren in conversation on the all-important subject.[15]

However Polk had persuaded Van Buren to visit Columbia the following week. Though General Armstrong and Donelson made further efforts to broach the matter of the vice presidency in the intervening period, all they could extract from their evasive guest were effusive expressions of "kind feelings &c &c." But Armstrong assured Polk that "The old Genl. will tell him before leaving the Hermitage to have a conversation with you."[16]

Van Buren reached Columbia late in the afternoon of Saturday, May 7, and was saluted with a demonstration only slightly less elaborate than Nashville's. After shaking hands with the crowd at the tavern, he inspected Columbia's vaunted Female Institute, where the jaundiced Whigs were waiting to compare his etiquette with that of the punctilious rector, having laid many wagers "as to who will out bow." Van Buren then retired to the Polks' house, where there was a large party in the evening. The ex-president remained with the Polks all day Sunday, but when he left for Nashville Monday morning, Polk still had not been able to draw

---

Joel R. Poinsett Papers in the Henry D. Gilpin Collection (Philadelphia, 1941), 173-174.

[15] Nashville *Union*, 28 Apr. 1842; Nashville *Republican Banner*, 29 Apr., 4 May 1842.

[16] Armstrong to Polk, 4 May 1842, Polk Papers.

him into "the conversation," and was as much in the dark as before.[17]

Van Buren's visit was of considerable value to the Democratic cause in Tennessee. Many discovered that the Van Buren they had disliked was the supercilious, effeminate dandy of Whig propaganda, not the courteous, unpretentious man they saw before them. The Whigs tried to counteract this reaction by making an issue of his "shabby genteel" dress. "He had on his old clothes," they said, and "had left his new suit at home thinking his old hat & striped pantaloons would do for the West."[18] Polk, however, probably derived more personal harm than good from the visit. "The bargain is struck, *we think*," trumpeted the Whig press as the ex-president left Columbia,[19] while Calhoun's friends were now convinced that "Van has effected his purpose with Polk." Polk could only try to erase this impression by sending Calhoun assurances that "there is no understanding" between him and Van Buren.[20]

Several months passed, and Polk's anxiety to see how his cause was faring in Washington, coupled with his urgent need for a substantial loan, caused him to make a trip to the North. Sarah was extremely reluctant to let him go, since he had just been ill again, but he made good steamboat connections on the Ohio, and by the end of June was in Washington, "figuring about on some party expedient," as his suspicious enemies reported. Actually there was little he could do, so he moved on to Philadelphia and New York, to seek out funds and renew his acquaintance with prominent Democrats who might be helpful in his vice presidential quest. The northern capitalists, he found, had no funds to risk, at least not on southwestern real estate; and though he was hospitably received by C. P. White and other leading Van Burenites, he was no more successful in extracting assurances from them than he had been with their chieftain.[21]

Admonished by the noncommittal attitude of the New Yorkers,

[17] Edmund Dillahunty to R. L. Caruthers, 5 May 1842, Caruthers Papers; Nashville *Republican Banner*, 13 May 1842; Johnson to Polk, 20 May 1842, Polk Papers.

[18] G. A. Henry to R. L. Caruthers, 31 May 1842, Caruthers Papers.

[19] Nashville *Republican Banner*, 13 May 1842.

[20] Eugene Irving McCormac, *James K. Polk: A Political Biography* (Berkeley, 1922), 203n.; Charles H. Ambler, ed., *Correspondence of Robert M. T. Hunter, 1826-1876*, American Historical Association, *Annual Report*, 1916, II (Washington, 1918), 49.

[21] W. B. Campbell to David Campbell, 30 June 1842, David Campbell Papers (DU); Mrs. Polk to Polk, 19, 24 June, 1 July 1842, Polk Papers; Henry Horn to Polk, 6 July 1842, *ibid.*; C. P. White to Polk, 9 July 1842, *ibid.*; Nashville *Republican Banner*, 20 July 1842.

Polk returned home resolved to demonstrate more unmistakably his loyalty to Van Buren, even at the risk of offending Calhoun. By the autumn of 1842 several Democratic papers in Alabama had run up the Van Buren and Polk flag, and though one of them took an embarrassingly severe cut at Calhoun, Polk had Harris endorse their sentiments cautiously in the *Union*. In Mississippi, too, Polk's friends were beginning to act more boldly, despite their fear of antagonizing Calhoun's supporters.[22]

Polk's most decisive move, however, was made through the Democratic legislators at the special session of 1842. The Calhoun partisans, beset by the difficulties of perfecting their national organization, had begun to agitate for postponing the Democratic convention to the latest date possible, probably May 1844; while it was to Van Buren's interest to have the convention meet early, since a majority of the existing state organizations were in the hands of his friends. Polk's real allegiance was demonstrated clearly, therefore, when the Democratic members of the Tennessee legislature resolved that the national convention should be held in November 1843. This action was duly noted by the New Yorkers, and though they eventually decided to concede the later convention date in the interest of harmony, the Van Buren men began to adopt a warmer tone toward Polk's aspirations. It was at this juncture that Benton declared against Colonel Johnson, and by the spring of 1843 it was generally conceded in congressional circles that Polk would be the logical choice to complete the Van Buren ticket.[23]

But Polk's shift in strategy raised new problems, for the more openly he pressed for Van Buren, the more opposition to the New Yorker developed in the ranks of the Tennessee Democracy. South Carolina's earlier flirtation with the Polk men had won Doctor Ramsey and most of the other East Tennessee party leaders over to Calhoun, and Silas Wright's vote for the Whig tariff of 1842 had turned such Tennesseans as Aaron Brown in the same direction.

[22] L. H. Coe to Polk, 30 July 1842, Polk Papers; J. E. Saunders to L. H. Coe, 22 July 1842 [placed with the above], *ibid.*; Harris to Polk, 24 Aug. 1842, *ibid.*; J. M. Howry to Polk, 9 Sept. 1842, *ibid.*; W. M. Gwin to Polk, 5 Nov. 1842, *ibid.*; Williamson Smith to Polk, 8 Dec. 1842, *ibid.*; Nashville *Republican Banner*, 10 Aug. 1842; Chauncey S. Boucher and Robert P. Brooks, eds., "Correspondence Addressed to John C. Calhoun 1837-1849," American Historical Association, *Annual Report*, 1929 (Washington, 1930), 179-180.

[23] Nashville *Union*, 13 Jan. 1843; Albany *Argus*, quoted in *ibid.*, 20 June 1843; Turney to Polk, 31 Jan. 1843, Polk Papers; L. D. Ewing to Polk, 4 Feb. 1843, *ibid.*; Johnson to Polk, 28 Feb. 1843, *ibid.*

Even Judge Catron, who had never liked the radical Democratic policies with which Van Buren was identified, tried for a time to win Polk over to Buchanan. The Democratic legislative caucuses at Nashville revealed a widespread feeling that Van Buren's unpopularity had been a major factor in the party's recent lack of success. "I assure you Sir," reported one of Polk's most trustworthy lieutenants from Nashville, "there is a plain disinclination on the part of our friends to take up Van Buren." Many of the lesser politicians, he continued, seemed to be turning to Cass as the most available candidate.[24]

This was not all Polk had to worry about. He realized full well that Van Buren's backing was conditional on Tennessee's return to the Democratic column in August 1843. More than the vice presidency might be at stake in the coming state election. Almost a quarter century of hard political struggle had at last brought Polk to the point where he dared to think of the highest office in the land. As he plunged into the most strenuous battle of his career, he was urged on by the laconic observations of the canny Armstrong. "If you succeed as you must and we carry the State," ran the general's hasty scrawl, "we must then look to the Convention for Electing . . . a Candidate for President & Vice President . . . Their [*sic*] may be a clash between the friends of Van Buren & Calhoun that cannot be settled[.] Then your prospects as a compr[om]ise is best. The friends of V. B. & C. are Democrats, and could with great propriety agree upon you."[25] But the Tennessee battle must first be won, or even the lesser prizes would be beyond his grasp.

III

The Tennessee election of 1843 was watched with intense interest by politicians all over the country for an indication of the next year's presidential result. Tennesseans, too, considered it crucial, for the outcome would reveal whether Tennessee had become an irretrievably Whig state, or whether the reaction against the national Whig program had erased the effects of the coonskin campaign of 1840 and made the state debatable ground once more.

There was some uncertainty about when the campaign would

---

[24] J. P. Hardwicke to Polk, 13 Nov. 1842, Polk Papers; Catron to Polk, 7 Jan. [1842; misplaced 1840], *ibid.*; Johnson to Polk, 28 Aug. 1842, *ibid.*; Williamson Smith to Polk, 10 Jan. 1843, *ibid.*; Nashville *Republican Banner*, 17 Mar. 1843.

[25] Armstrong to Polk, 12 June 1843, Polk Papers.

open. When the two parties began to gird themselves for the coming conflict in the summer of 1842, they were still maneuvering for advantage on the question of electing senators. If the Whigs fell in with the Democratic plan for a general resignation of the legislature and a new election before the special session in the fall, the gubernatorial candidates would want to start their canvass along with the legislators. There had never been any doubt that Polk would bear the Democratic standard, and he had scheduled a speech for August 11 at Rogersville in East Tennessee. "Polk will most certainly I think declare himself there a candidate for Governor," Foster predicted, ". . . the war-whoop will sound along the entire line of the enemy & the state will soon be in a bright blaze from one extreme to the other."[26]

The general resignation scheme failed, however, and Polk told his Rogersville audience that he would not reveal his intentions yet. "Perhaps at the putting forth of the buds I may conclude to become a candidate," he said, "at which time you will hear from me again." During the fall and winter Polk continued to speak intermittently in various parts of the state, publishing one of his addresses as an outline of the issues on which he would conduct the campaign. Asked to declare himself at a meeting in January, he alluded to the signs of an early spring and promised to make his position known very soon.[27]

Meanwhile the Democrats were busy perfecting their organization. A Democratic caucus at the special session had issued an address to the voters, and the Maury Democrats again called on the other counties to adopt their system of party committees in every election district. The Democratic press was working up to a fighting pitch, while the Columbia *Democrat* was already so vituperative that the Nashville *Banner* denounced its editor as "the brainless poltroon who blackguards us so incessantly," and the Whig editor in Columbia felt called upon to give him a thrashing.[28]

The problem of candidates for Congress and the legislature fell, as usual, on Polk's shoulders. Tennessee had lost two of its thirteen congressional seats by reapportionment, and in the process of re-

26 Foster to Caruthers, 22 June 1842, Caruthers Papers.

27 Nashville *Republican Banner*, 19 Aug. 1842; *ibid.*, 26 Aug., 5 Dec. 1842; Nashville *Union*, 7 Feb., 13 Mar. 1843.

28 Nashville *Republican Banner*, 23 May 1842; Laughlin to Polk, 11 Oct. 1842, Polk Papers; Polk to Laughlin, 6 Jan. 1843, Polk-Laughlin Letters, special section of *ibid.*

districting the state, the Democratic legislators had managed to arrange five districts that were Democratic on the basis of their vote in 1840, as well as two others that the Democrats would have a good chance of carrying.[29]

Cave Johnson and Aaron Brown were both reluctant to run again in enlarged and more precarious districts, but letters from Jackson and other forms of pressure from Polk finally induced them to make one more race. As a member of the legislative redistricting committee, Andrew Johnson had carved out a Democratic district for himself in the northeastern part of the state, and here he was opposed by a nominal Democrat whom the Whigs were supporting. Harvey Watterson and Hopkins Turney were thrown into the same district by the new arrangement, but President Tyler, who was now wooing Democrats with the federal patronage, helped Polk get rid of the unreliable Watterson by giving him a minor diplomatic appointment. Watterson was no sooner disposed of, however, than two other Democratic candidates announced. Polk could induce neither of them to give way, and Turney loyally retired, leaving the two Democrats in the field with no Whig opposition.[30]

The most painful situation arose in the solidly Democratic district on the Cumberland plateau, where Sam Laughlin had long wanted to run for Congress. Here the Whigs had encouraged another Democrat, Alvan Cullom, to enter the race. This intraparty contest, like the one in the Watterson-Turney district, was a real threat to Democratic harmony and success. In both cases the Whigs deliberately refrained from entering their own candidates, expecting to trade their support to one of the Democratic congressional candidates, in return for Democratic votes for the Whig legislative and gubernatorial candidates. Polk repeatedly implored Laughlin and Cullom to submit their claims to a Democratic district convention, but Cullom steadfastly refused, and the faithful Laughlin eventually withdrew to insure the success of the state ticket.[31]

The Whigs, meanwhile, were having troubles of their own. The

[29] Balch to [Van Buren], 22 Nov. 1842, Van Buren Papers.

[30] Brown to Polk, 4 Feb. 1843, Polk Papers; H. L. Turney to Polk, 1 Apr. 1843, *ibid.*; Johnson to Jackson, 18 Feb. 1843, Jackson Papers; Nashville *Republican Banner*, 6 Feb. 1843; Oliver P. Temple, *Notable Men of Tennessee from 1833 to 1875: Their Times and Their Contemporaries* (New York, 1912), 62, 216-217.

[31] Polk to R. L. Caruthers, 6 June 1842, Caruthers Papers; Polk to Laughlin, 6, 27 Jan., 20 Mar. 1843, Polk-Laughlin Letters; Laughlin to Polk, 27 Mar. 1843, Polk Papers; Polk to Alvin Cullom, 20 Mar. 1843, *ibid.*, in special bundle labeled "Polk to Others."

Bell-Foster feud was the major disturbing factor, though some of the leaders also doubted Jones's ability to stem the Democratic upsurge in another campaign. "If Jones is his competitor," one Whig predicted, "Polk will beat at the lowest estimate 15,000 votes." Some suggested that Foster run for governor, leaving Bell to go to the Senate and putting Foster in line for a subsequent Cabinet appointment, but Foster was unwilling to gratify his rival in this way. The Whigs were generally discouraged and apathetic, and one of their expiring newspapers blamed its demise on "the coldness and luke-warmness which has palsied the energies of the political party with which we are associated."[32]

That the Whigs were able to overcome this despondency was owing almost entirely to the insight, energy, and ambition of Ephraim H. Foster. It was Foster who convinced his party that Tennessee was truly a Whig state, and it was Foster who, like Polk in the Democratic party, aroused local leaders, got counties and districts organized, kept newspapers financed and staffed, and arranged slates. Foster's greatest achievement was to persuade the Whigs to take their stand boldly for Henry Clay and all his measures. By the summer of 1842, the Whig newspapers began running up the "Clay for President" flag, and Clay "Coonventions," as the Democrats called them, were being held all over the state, reaching a climax in the mammoth celebration of Clay's visit to Memphis in February 1843. Whether this policy was shrewd or foolhardy, only August and the election could tell.[33]

The most important convert to Foster's strategy and its ablest practitioner was Governor James C. Jones. Foster aside, no one else was conceded a chance to defend the new-model Whiggery against the redoubtable Polk. Despite a genuine reluctance to run, Jones was loyal to his party and to Foster's leadership, and early in February he was announced as the Whig standard bearer. This was the "putting forth of the buds" that Polk had been waiting for. Promptly declaring his own candidacy, he gave notice that he would open the campaign with an address at Jackson on April 3.

[32] Edmund Dillahunty to R. L. Caruthers, 5 May 1842, Caruthers Papers; Athens *Watchman*, 9 July 1842; Daniel Graham to Polk, 11 Aug. 1842, Polk Papers; Foster to W. B. Campbell, 20 June 1843, Campbell Papers.
[33] Foster to W. B. Campbell, 1 Jan. 1843, Campbell Papers; Foster to Harry Brown, 12 Feb. 1843, copy, Caruthers Papers; Foster to R. L. Caruthers, 22 May 1843, *ibid.*; Charles E. Pool, "The Rise of the Whig Party in West Tennessee, 1834-1843," M.A. thesis, University of Mississippi (1950), 138-139.

A week later Jones promised to be at Jackson with Polk and scheduled six appointments on the way to Jackson, the first one at Springfield, north of Nashville, on March 24. Polk responded by publishing a list of seventy-five additional appointments throughout the state, extending to election day. And so the ground was laid for one of the most thorough statewide campaigns ever attempted in the history of American politics.[34]

Polk was well aware of what this meant for the candidates who had to go through it. "The labour of canvassing a State like this, of more than six hundred miles in extent, and reaching from the mountains of Virginia & Carolina to the Swamps of the Mississippi, and of visiting and addressing the people in more than eighty Counties," he wrote to Van Buren, "is greater than can be estimated by any one who has not performed it. It requires four months of unceasing riding and speaking."[35] Polk had first traversed the entire state in 1839, and the campaign of 1841 had set the pattern of the joint canvass, but never had the state seen anything like this. The route laid out zigzagged back and forth across Tennessee for some 2,300 miles, and this to be covered on horseback in four months, with five or six hours of speaking almost every day.

Though Jones was dismayed by the prospect of such "an active and unprecedented canvass before the people on the *stump*," he resolved "to go with his competitor wherever he may go, and to be with him wherever he may be."[36] The only comfort to be derived from the forbidding schedule was that Polk, profiting from his previous experience, had planned the appointments so that the candidates would be out of the hot, unhealthy Western District by the middle of May and would spend most of June and July in the cooler regions of East Tennessee.

No one felt the hardships of campaigning more than Polk's wife. "I must confess that I feel sad & melancholy at the prospect before me, or I should say before you," she wrote to her husband shortly after he left home. "The fatigue, exposure and absence for four months cannot present to me a bright prospect. I have not the assurance that the body and constitution can keep up under such labours as you have to go through, and it is only the *hope* that you

34 Nashville *Union*, 10 Feb., 31 Mar. 1843; Nashville *Republican Banner*, 17 Feb. 1843.

35 Polk to Van Buren, 8 Dec. 1842, Van Buren Papers.

36 Nashville *Republican Banner*, 17 Feb., 12 July 1843.

can live through it, that gives me a prospect of enjoyment. Let me beg and pray that you will take care of yourself, and do not become to[o] much excited."[37] Sarah's despondency continued to depress Polk throughout the campaign. Even the five days he spent at home while on his way from the Western District to East Tennessee did not cheer her. "I was pleased to find that you had time to play the *beaux* in receiving flowers from young ladies," she wrote after he had set out again, "for I am sure that you did not *act* the *beaux* towards your wife when at home." Despite her jealousy of her husband's absorption in politics, Sarah loyally contributed her bit toward his success by helping to mediate a nasty intraparty feud that had arisen among the Maury Democrats.[38]

IV

Hoping to revive the color and pageantry of 1840, the Whigs had arranged parades, flags, and fiddlers to enliven the first encounter between the two candidates at Springfield. These demonstrations Polk promptly resented. This election "was to be decided by an appeal to reason and not by flags and fiddling," he declared, adding that "the people had been flagged and fiddled to their heart's content in 1840." When the Whigs kept up their displays at subsequent meetings, Polk warned that they were making a mistake by trying to inoculate the people with the "flag disorder," for though the country had been infected with this disease in 1840, "it was like the small pox, nobody ever took it but once."[39]

The Whig editors taunted "his ex-excellency" with having "a holy horror of any thing which reminds him of 1840,"[40] but Polk was not far wrong. For all the Whig efforts, this was the quietest campaign in years. The constant political excitement had become intolerable, and even the Whigs had to admit on the eve of the election that "The people seem weary of politics, and talk but little about candidates or the Government affairs."[41] However the Whigs kept right on trying to stir up excitement. Thousands of dollars were raised for Whig betting pools, and on election day itself seventy-odd young Nashville Whigs, who were voting for the first

[37] Mrs. Polk to Polk, 29 Mar. 1843, Polk Papers.
[38] Mrs. Polk to Polk, 3 May, 17 Apr. 1843, Polk Papers.
[39] Nashville *Union*, 25 Apr., 16 June 1843.
[40] Nashville *Republican Banner*, 14 July 1843.
[41] W. B. Campbell to David Campbell, 29 July 1843, Campbell Papers.

time, marched to the polls in a body wearing badges inscribed, "First Fire of the Young Whigs of 1843."[42]

Polk was not so fortunate in his attempts to parry Jones's low comedy platform techniques. No feature of this campaign testified more eloquently to Polk's unshakable faith in the good sense of the electorate than his dogged determination to pitch his speeches on the level of the real issues. Having tried matching wits with Jones two years before without winning the confidence of a majority, he entered this canvass resolved to stick steadfastly to argumentative appeals. This resolution he adhered to with few exceptions, and the voters saw a new Polk, all serious demonstration, with little of the raillery and wit that had delighted them in previous contests. Only occasionally was he so irritated by the governor's endless repetition of fallacious arguments that "he threw off his coat and fought with him to his heart's content."

"No man relished a good joke better than he did," Polk would declare at such times, "but when it came to telling over Eph Foster's old, stale, wornout stories, he could *not* laugh." Then, throwing caution to the winds and reveling in the style of campaigning he had first introduced to Tennessee politics, he would let go "a perfect volley of humorous anecdotes and hard hits" that soon had his audience convulsed.[43] But the next morning he would return to his original resolution of seriousness, and weeks would pass before he was again tempted from it. The Whigs found this new Polk hard to account for. "What is most strange of all," wrote a puzzled Whig reporter after one speaking, "he actually grew *facetious* towards the close of his speech and did *try to get up a laugh.* You may rely upon it he is getting *funny* again, but still he would not tell an anecdote, not him. We can't tell why it was, but suppose that he just puts that *pretty* smile on his face to win the influence of the *ladies.*"[44]

Jones began the campaign with a slashing attack on the "Immortal Thirteen." He particularly criticized them for blocking an investigation of the state bank and refusing to confirm his nominees for bank directors. He hinted darkly of "astounding developments," and charged that half the directors "deserved to be hung."[45] In fact, he shouted, turning to Polk, the institution "is still under the

[42] Nashville *Republican Banner*, 4 Aug. 1843; C. C. Norvell to R. L. Caruthers, 26 July 1843, Caruthers Papers.

[43] Nashville *Union*, 28 Apr. 1843; *ibid.*, 31 Mar., 1 Apr. 1843.

[44] Nashville *Republican Banner*, 31 July 1843.

[45] Clarksville *Jeffersonian*, 15 Apr. 1843.

administration of my *illustrious predecessor.*" This made the conduct
of the "Thirteen" most suspicious, and "for an anti-Bank, DEMO-
CRATIC, BANK-HATING Senate, they held on *to the Bank* with
most astonishing tenacity." Jones challenged Polk to defend or
denounce the policy of the "Thirteen" on this point, as well as their
position on electing senators.[46]

Polk refused to become involved in a discussion of the state bank
until some specific charges were made, and Jones, unable to find
evidence of any mismanagement, eventually dropped the issue. A
subsequent Whig investigation showed that Polk's directors had
administered the institution with spectacular honesty and impartiality. The senatorial question was more embarrassing. Polk recognized that the course of the "Thirteen" had not been popular, but
he could not afford to repudiate the Democratic legislators. He
declined to intervene, therefore, in what he called a dispute between
the governor and the state senate, adding only that Jones had urged
the Whigs to follow the same strategy at a time when he thought
the Democrats would have a majority on joint ballot, and quoting
a letter from a respected Knoxville Democrat, Arthur Crozier, to
prove it. Jones never denied this allegation, but seized on the fact
that several of the Democratic witnesses to his statement were free
Negroes, and tried to escape by asserting that the charge was made
by *"three free negroes, and one Arthur Crozier, a little democrat
about four feet four, in East Tennessee."* When the candidates
reached East Tennessee, Polk forced the governor to admit that
Crozier was "a man of truth and veracity," but he was never able
to get him either to stop denouncing the "Thirteen" or to admit that
he had proposed the same strategy to the Whigs.[47]

On a second group of issues, Jones followed Foster's strategy by
taking a bold and unequivocal stand for the national Whig position
and defending it resourcefully against Polk's counterattacks. In his
very first speech he pointed proudly to a Whig flag emblazoned
"CLAY AND A U.S. BANK," and declared, "THERE IS MY
BANNER—AND UNDER THAT FLAG I WILL EITHER
CONQUER OR DIE! ! !" The governor made it plain that there
would be no more apologizing for Henry Clay in Tennessee. "I am
for CLAY first, CLAY last, and CLAY *all the time*," he announced

[46] Nashville *Republican Banner*, 29 Mar. 1843.

[47] Nashville *Union*, 2 May 1843; *ibid.*, 3 Mar., 11 Apr., 23 June 1843; Robert H.
White, ed., *Messages of the Governors of Tennessee* (Nashville, 1952-   ), III, 680.

defiantly.[48] Polk did his best to revive the "bargain, intrigue, and corruption" charges of 1825, leaning heavily on the denunciations of Clay by Bell and the Tennessee legislature at that time. Clay almost challenged Polk to a public debate on the subject, but wisely changed his mind, since a debate would have served to recall an eighteen-year-old issue that had largely lost its force. Jones merely asserted that these "exploded charges" had since been abandoned by many of their original sponsors, and went calmly on eulogizing "Harry of the West" as the greatest statesman of the age.[49]

Jones's equally open advocacy of a national bank indicated a marked change in the attitude of Tennesseans toward this once reviled institution. Jones made no bones about being for a national bank, arguing that it was the only agency that could bring relief from the long depression. He insisted that the Supreme Court and many of the founding fathers had upheld the Bank's constitutionality, reminded the voters of past losses from depreciating state bank notes, and asked anyone who had ever lost money by depreciation of a national bank note to speak up.

The governor was particularly effective in taunting the Democrats with inconsistency on the bank question. Some Democrats, he said, were for hard money, some were for a mixed currency of metals and paper, and some had realized the necessity of a national bank. He challenged Polk to "say what kind of currency *he* was for? if for a mixed currency, how he wished it mixed?" "Are you, Col., for a metallic currency?" he continued. "If so, say it; and you'll never know what hurt you, for," and here Jones turned to the audience, "Boys there's not enough of *that* to buy your marriage licenses." Between hard money and a national bank, the only alternative was a state bank currency, and Jones assured the voters that while the Democrats considered the national bank a *"monster,"* he would "prefer even a *large monster* to *a thousand little monsters,* stuck all around and sucking out his life blood." "I am for a United States Bank," Jones regularly concluded the bank section of his speeches, "between this and a hard money currency—*choose ye.*"[50]

Old Hickory had recently dashed off a public letter reasserting his fealty to the simon pure hard-money gospel, but Polk, his ears

[48] Nashville *Republican Banner*, 29 Mar. 1843.
[49] Clay to Polk, 20 May 1843, Henry Clay Papers (LC); Nashville *Republican Banner*, 31 May, 3 July 1843.
[50] Nashville *Republican Banner*, 29 Mar. 1843.

filled with the clamor for money, any kind of money, was in no position for such heroism. He merely reminded his hearers of the despotic and dangerous tendencies of Biddle's Bank and maintained that Clay's plan for a bank was "in substance, the old bank charter —the government put in partnership with money dealers who had the control of the public money for purposes of speculation—that it was made the public treasury, and not under the control of officers, elected by and responsible to the people, and in a time of emergency, such as war—it might in truth get under the control of the enemies of our country, and the very monies collected of the people, be withheld from us in time of utmost need."[51] Polk denied that a national bank could possibly afford any immediate relief, if for no other reason because President Tyler was sure to veto any bank bill passed. Moreover, he pointed out, the federal government had no power to abolish the state banks; the remedy was to make them live up to their obligations. As for monsters, big or little, "it was preposterous to set one *large* Bank to watch a set of little ones, the consequence would be to make a larger one to watch it in a short time if little ones could not get along without a monster."[52]

These arguments unfortunately, like the old charges against Clay, seemed timeworn and lacked their former impact. Some of Polk's supporters devised an effective reply, however, to Jones's claim that no one had ever lost money by national bank notes. At Shelbyville the Democrats secured an old, worthless ten-dollar note of Biddle's now bankrupt institution and put it up for auction. Finally the Whig sheriff offered five dollars for it, and it was knocked down "for fifty cents in the dollar in the Strong hold of Whiggery." When the Whigs tried to counter this demonstration by organizing their own auction and bidding in the same bill for ten dollars, the Democrats scoured the country for more bills of this type, and the Whigs had to admit that they had had enough.[53]

Still another category of issues found Polk on the offensive, carrying the war to his tantalizing antagonist over those parts of the Whig record that were least popular in Tennessee—the tariff, federal expenditures, and the Bankrupt Law that Clay had pushed through the special session of 1841. But it was on precisely such questions that Jones was most irritating, for by imposture and

---

[51] Nashville *Union*, 31 Mar. 1843.
[52] *ibid.*, 16 May 1843; *ibid.*, 2 May 1843.
[53] Robert Matthews to Armstrong, 10 June 1843, Polk Papers.

burlesque he succeeded in enveloping them in such a cloud of confusion that he escaped virtually unscathed, if not actually the victor.

The Whigs were most vulnerable on the Bankrupt Law, and Polk had given notice in speeches the previous autumn that they could expect a raking fire at this point. "The temptation has been held out to *reckless traders, gambling speculators* and to the *unscrupulous of every class*," he had trumpeted, "to convert their property into money, conceal it beyond the power of discovery or detection, and be released forever from all legal liability or compulsion to pay their honest debts. Should they afterwards draw out their concealed treasure or by other means become possessed of wealth and live in affluence and ease they could not be made to pay. Their creditors, whose property they had bought, whose money they had borrowed or who were their securities or endorsers and had been ruined and with their families had been reduced to penury and want by them had no remedy against them."[54]

The alarmed Whigs soon discovered that Polk's arguments were making the law "odious all over Tennessee." A hundred Whig votes had been lost in a single county, the editor of the *Banner* reported, and this was "not the only such tale that might be told of other counties."[55] The entreaties of the Tennessee Whigs probably contributed to the haste with which the Whig Congress repealed the law just before the gubernatorial canvass commenced.

Polk naturally refused to surrender a good issue merely because the law had been repealed. He gave the Whigs credit for redeeming one of "their numerous and magnificent promises," the promise to provide a sound currency that would pay debts everywhere, for their Bankrupt Law was "current every where in the payment of debts, and magically available in the release of obligations," and "the bankrupt's certificate was the currency made for that purpose."[56] Jones was too astute to defend the unpopular law. "Admitting it all to be wrong," he said, this was still no reason for a Whig to turn to "the foul ranks of Modern Democracy."[57]

As the campaign progressed, Jones developed a more effective method of dealing with this troublesome question. Polk's arguments, he maintained, were like sticking a spear into a dead Indian. The law

[54] Nashville *Union*, 17 Mar. 1843.
[55] F. K. Zollicoffer to R. L. Caruthers, 9 Jan. 1843, Caruthers Papers.
[56] Nashville *Union*, 31 Mar., 9 June 1843.
[57] Nashville *Republican Banner*, 29 Mar. 1843.

had been repealed and repealed by the Whigs. Polk was like a farmer whose premises were invaded by a bear. Retreating to the loft of his cabin and leaving his wife to deal with the intruder, he cried out, "Lay on Nancy!" "lay on Nancy." Only after Nancy had slain the bear did her husband descend from the loft, exclaiming, "What soldiers *we* are!"[58]

After listening to this story for several weeks, Polk lost his patience. "Sir," he finally shouted, "I wish to discuss these questions gravely, and not resort to things so undignified as 'lay on Nancy' 'lay on Nancy!' and here, according to a Whig reporter, he roared out, "lay on Nancy!" some eight or ten times, to the accompaniment of "his most horrible ugly *grinning*." "Sirs," Polk continued, as soon as the laughter and applause subsided, "if the citizen of some other State had stopped here to hear the candidates for Governor of Tennessee make speeches, and had slipped up about the time Gov. Jones was exclaiming 'lay on Nancy,' he would have said that it was not a candidate for Governor. That man ought to be painted and put on a straight jacket and turned loose in the ring of a circus."

This sally brought gales of merriment, but as usual Jones had a rejoinder. "Gentlemen," said the governor, with a gesture toward his spindly legs, "I am willing to be painted, put on the straight jacket, and enter the ring of the circus as the clown"; but, he went on, "suppose some stranger had come up about the time my competitor was making such horrible faces, and bawling out, 'lay on Nancy,' what would they have said of my competitor?" Why, the governor concluded, they would have said that Polk was even better fitted for the little grinning monkey in a red jacket, "*the little fellow on the bob-tailed pony*." This was regarded as a capital hit, and for the rest of the campaign the Whigs taunted Polk as "the little fellow on the pony."[59]

Another question on which Polk failed to gain the advantage he expected was the tariff. His tariff debate with the Whigs had actually begun with his October 1841 speech in Nashville, when he attacked the Whig special session of Congress for laying duties on tea, coffee, and other previously duty-free items. Milton Brown, a Whig congressman from the Western District, promptly charged on the floor of the House that in 1832 Polk himself had joined the

[58] Nashville *Union*, 9 June 1843.
[59] Nashville *Republican Banner*, 10 July 1843; James Phelan, *History of Tennessee: The Making of a State* (Boston, 1889), 402.

Ways and Means Committee in sponsoring a bill to lay duties on tea and coffee. Replying to Brown in various speeches during the fall of 1842, Polk had maintained that the 1832 bill actually reduced the duties below the level of the Tariff of Abominations, and had threatened to meet Brown face to face "at Philippi" to set this "little matter" straight.[60]

Too impatient to wait for "Philippi," Brown had published a blistering rejoinder in the newspapers. "Philippi," he revealed, alluded to an incident in the life of Brutus, when an apparition appeared in his tent at midnight. "Who art thou?" Brutus had inquired. "Thy evil genius," the phantom replied, *"we will meet again at Philippi."* But Brown's research had revealed that this apparition was raised against Brutus by Antony, who, like Polk, "relied on his popular eloquence, his appeals to popular prejudices, his stratagems and his artifices to mislead the popular mind and give success to his vaulting ambitions." "Brutus was threatened by the phantom raised by Antony," continued Brown, "and I am threatened with the ghostly grin and contortion of face with which Gov. Polk is wont to fight when the weapons of truth and argument fail him." Nevertheless, he was well armed with facts, the Whig congressman concluded boldly, so "Let the conflict come!"[61]

Meanwhile the Whig Congress had passed a clearly protective tariff, raising the general level of duties substantially above the 20 per cent prescribed by the sacred Compromise of 1833. Thus, when the campaign opened in March, there was considerable public interest in the tariff question and eager anticipation of the promised meeting between Polk and Brown "at Philippi." Jones, of course, picked up Brown's charges with alacrity, and in his first speech warned Polk that "I'll make you sick of Tea and Coffee before I am done with you." When Polk replied that he had *"another to meet at Philippi,"* Jones retorted, "I now notify you that I shall give you more than you desire on that subject, *before* you get to Philippi."[62]

"Lean Jimmy" was armed with some ingenious arguments of his own on the tariff question. The most novel was his proposition that a high tariff made the price of protected goods lower, and this doctrine he defended in speech after speech, despite Polk's demonstrations of its patent absurdity. More effective was his unscrupulous indictment of Polk's tariff record. Holding a House journal in his

60 Nashville *Republican Banner,* 5 Dec. 1842; *ibid.,* 2 Sept. 1842.
61 *ibid.,* 20 Jan. 1843.   62 *ibid.,* 29 Mar. 1843.

hand, he would leaf through page after page of roll calls on various items in the Tariff of 1832, asking in each case, "who do you think voted for it?" and then, pointing to Polk, would answer his own question, "As Nathan said unto David, 'thou art the man.' " Polk explained repeatedly that the Tariff of 1832 actually reduced the high duties that had prevailed before, but Jones continued to pretend that Polk had helped impose all these duties for the first time. And the dramatic repetition of his indictment, "thou art the man," undoubtedly convinced many voters that "Lean Jimmy's" charges were true.[63]

Under this daily bombardment Polk could only console himself with the fact that the candidates were approaching Milton Brown's congressional district. But when Brown appeared for the meeting at Trenton on Saturday, April 1, Jones refused to let him speak. Polk promptly declared that "the Spectre should meet Brutus (alias Brown) at the appointed time at Philippi, notwithstanding the generous interference of Gov. Jones," and he spent all day Sunday preparing a special effort for Monday's speaking at Jackson, where an enormous crowd was gathering from all over the Western District. Here Polk's three-and-a-half-hour excoriation of the protective system and Brown's tariff record produced the desired result, Governor Jones announcing that Brown would debate the question with Polk the following day. Philippi had come at last.[64]

The Whigs actually had a much sounder case against Polk than Jones's specious arguments indicated. Brown had discovered that tea and coffee were temporarily duty-free at the time Polk had voted to tax them. However he was honest enough to admit that the antitariff men had generally favored revenue duties on tea and coffee to avoid protective duties on manufactured items, and that the 1832 bill had merely restored revenue duties that the protectionists had managed to eliminate only the year before. Brown's real complaint was not against Polk's votes for tea and coffee duties, but against his unfair criticism of the Whigs for adopting similar revenue duties at the special session of 1841. Though Brown had given this information to Governor Jones, "Lean Jimmy" stuck to his demagogic technique of making Polk out to be a protectionist.

Brown, on the other hand, while he had better arguments than Jones, lacked the debating ability to make them stand against the

---

63 Nashville *Union*, 16 May 1843; *ibid.*, 1 Apr., 2, 5 May 1843.
64 Nashville *Union*, 7 Apr. 1843; *ibid.*, 11 Apr., 5, 19 May 1843.

experienced Polk, and "at Philippi" he was completely routed. "I suppose it will not be immodest for me to say to my wife that my speech was perhaps the happiest effort of my life," Polk wrote jubilantly to Sarah. "I drove him to the wall upon the facts and the argument, and as in his speech he had made a great effort to turn the occasion into a frolic, I concluded to close my speech by fighting the old boy with fire, and accordingly turned the laugh upon him & almost laughed him out of the Court House. Without going into further details the result is, that my victory is the most triumphant I have ever achieved." Polk exaggerated very little. His speech made a tremendous impression throughout the Western District, and no more was heard from Brown.[65] Unfortunately this did not prevent the imperturbable Jones from repeating his "thou art the man" performance over the rest of the state.

The candidates spent the better part of a week at Jackson, and during this time the Whig strategists supplied Jones with ammunition for repelling Polk's attacks on the extravagance of the Whig regime in Washington. When the canvass was resumed, this question replaced the tariff as the leading issue. Polk had been contrasting the Whigs' promises to reduce expenditures with their performance. The expenditures had been increased rather than decreased, he maintained, and the federal debt of seven millions left by Van Buren had grown to twenty-seven millions. To frugal Tennessee farmers this was a serious matter.

In rebutting Polk's charges Jones garbled and juggled the complicated federal balance sheets so as to create a wholly misleading impression of Democratic profligacy and Whig thrift. When Polk tried to correct these misinterpretations, he found himself enmeshed in such involved explanation that Jones was able to escape unscathed in the maze of figures. After a week of this Polk concluded that the only way to catch his wily antagonist was by making him put an argument on paper. Accordingly, while they were debating at Carrollsville, he suggested that the two candidates publish within a month's time their arguments on public expenditures, and to this proposition Jones had to agree.[66]

This was the beginning of a paper war that ran parallel to the stump war for the rest of the campaign. Jones decided that he also

65 Polk to Mrs. Polk, 4 Apr. 1843, Polk Papers; Nashville *Union*, 11 Apr. 1843; Nashville *Republican Banner*, 17 May 1843.
66 Nashville *Union*, 21, 25 Apr. 1843.

wanted to smoke Polk out on some points, and since they were now approaching Memphis, he arranged to have a group of Memphis Whigs submit a series of seven questions to the candidates, requesting publication of the answers. Polk promptly got a group of Memphis Democrats to submit a list of interrogatories on eleven other points where he wanted to press Jones to an explicit stand. Jones answered both of the Memphis interrogations briefly and promptly, but not until the candidates reached home in the middle of May for a scheduled week of rest did Polk find time for the more elaborate replies he proposed to make. Neither man got much rest, since they were both busy preparing the statements they had agreed on at Carrollsville. All these documents, answers to them, and answers to the answers flowed in a steady stream from Tennessee's political presses right up to election day.

Through the Memphis interrogatories, Jones forced Polk to approve publicly the actions of the "Thirteen" in the senatorial election. Polk also had to declare that he favored a mixed currency of specie and paper, though he insisted that suspending banks should be liquidated and that in future charters the stockholders should be made liable for the banks' obligations.[67]

Polk, on the other hand, compelled Jones to come out explicitly for Clay's bank bill and the Whig tariff of 1842. Jones did say that the tariff rates should be lowered if they produced more revenue than the government needed, but his position was weakened when he was forced to reavow his support of distribution. Here he could only revive his old argument, repeatedly refuted by Polk, that the loss of revenue would be made up by higher duties on "foreign luxuries, silks, wines, &c. &c.," tea and coffee presumably being included among the unenumerated et ceteras.

The most important admission the Democrats managed to extract from the governor was that "The Legislature has the right to prescribe the mode by which Senators shall be elected," though he added that he favored election by convention of the two houses, as the long-established precedent in Tennessee. Jones was also induced to say that he opposed the Democratic compromise proposition to elect one senator from each party, while Polk was able to answer this question with a plausible argument for the equity of such a compromise in the evenly divided legislature.[68]

[67] *ibid.*, 2 June 1843.
[68] Memphis *American Eagle*, 2 May 1843.

The statements about federal expenditures agreed upon at Carrollsville followed close after the replies to the Memphis interrogatories. Polk buttressed his case with page upon page citing chapter and verse from the official Treasury documents, but Jones was able to carry off in print the same kind of plausible obscurantism that he managed on the stump. "If he had sought to involve the subject in still more confusion, than he had done in his speeches," complained the irritated Polk, "he could not have done it more successfully than he has in his attempts to make it clear." But at least, Polk consoled himself, "The people can now have the benefit of my competitor's 'facts and figures.' "[69]

Having at last got Jones committed on paper, Polk lost no time when the canvass resumed in probing the chinks in his statistical armor. The governor was now forced to admit the essential point, that federal expenditures had been lower in 1840, Van Buren's last year, than in either 1841 or 1842. Meanwhile Polk was spending his evenings feverishly composing an exposé of Jones's errors on expenditures, and he had it ready for publication in less than a week. In like manner Polk now compelled Jones to say in debate that he opposed repealing the Tariff of 1842, "*until it was tried*," and he published a second installment of his reply to Jones, dealing with this subject, four days after the first one came out.[70]

Jones was ready to let the tariff matter drop, but he continued to argue the expenditures question. When Polk's vigorous attack reduced his argument to the contention that the register of the Treasury, on whose official reports Polk was relying, was a "rank democrat," the governor published a reply to Polk's replies. He twitted Polk with having turned to the press after failing on the stump, and he promised his rival that "when you have tested this new mode of conducting this canvass, you are at perfect liberty to choose any other mode that your fancy may suggest, and *I am your man.*" Polk doubtless wished there was still some other mode, for Jones's latest publication merely reiterated his most blatant deception: distorting the comparative expenditures of the two administrations by adding to get Van Buren's total both the amount he expended and the amount he borrowed to help pay for these expendi-

[69] *Gov. Polk's Reply to Gov. Jones*, pamphlet in Polk Papers, p. 1; Nashville *Republican Banner*, 22 May 1843; *Address of James K. Polk to the People of Tennessee*, pamphlet dated 17 May 1843, Polk Papers.
[70] *Gov. Polk's Reply to Gov. Jones*, 2-3.

tures.[71] Thus, as with the tariff and the bankrupt law, the resourceful "Lean Jimmy" succeeded in blunting one of his opponent's dangerous weapons.

As the candidates moved into East Tennessee for the final stage of the campaign, Jones went on the offensive with several new arguments. In all his later speeches he endorsed Henry Clay for president and John Sergeant for vice president and then demanded that Polk reveal his preferences. Polk usually replied that he would support the candidates nominated by the Democratic convention, and countered by demanding that Jones name his choices for senator. "Sir," Jones would rejoin, "I dare you to name your men, if you do I will hammer them until you won't know them."[72] Failing to elicit a satisfactory response, Jones would wax indignant. In 1840 the Democrats had "called the lamented Harrison in derision, General Mum," he complained. This same party had abused Foster and Jarnagin for refusing to answer the interrogatories of the "Thirteen." "And now," he would shout, "when I call upon my competitor to tell the people who is his favorite for the presidency, he is *Mum*! ! Yes, as *dumb* as a *sun fish*."[73]

Even this was not so trying as Jones's reintroduction of the sterling bond question in the last week of the campaign, too late for Democratic refutations to overtake his assertions. True, Polk had been arguing that if Clay's bank bill passed, "we would have witnessed the humiliating spectacle of beholding the government of the United States, hawking her bonds through the streets of London and Paris, and bowing at the feet of the aristocrats of the crowned heads of Europe to get money to bank upon."[74] He was understandably nettled when Jones grew tired of this argument and threatened to read Polk's proposal to make the state bonds payable in sterling, so they could be sold abroad. Polk thought he had spiked this gun in the last campaign, but fortunately he had brought along the affidavits indicating that Jones had once advocated the same policy.

Jones now had the effrontery to do what he had not dared to do two years before, assert flatly that these allegations were false. Polk broke in here to ask if Jones was questioning the truth of the wit-

71 Nashville *Republican Banner*, 12 July 1843; Nashville *Union*, 13 June 1843.

72 Nashville *Republican Banner*, 10 July 1843; *ibid.*, 3 July 1843; Nashville *Union*, 30 June 1843.

73 Nashville *Republican Banner*, 31 July 1843.

74 *ibid.*, 10 July 1843.

nesses' statements. *"I do,"* shouted Jones, "they are false—utterly untrue." "That sir," responded Polk, "is all I want to hear." The Democrats made haste to publish the affidavits, but Jones went blithely on denying their truth.[75] Meanwhile Jones's friends undertook to discredit one of the witnesses, a Colonel Matlock, by forcing him into a fight, which ended in the death of his assailant and Matlock's flight in fear of his life to Columbia, where he surrendered to the authorities. Thus when the candidates reached Jones's home county just before the election, the way had been prepared for the unscrupulous governor to deny before his lifelong neighbors a charge that had gone two years unanswered. The "Sterling Bond slander" against him had been "fished up," he said, from such "foul receptacles of party filth" as Matlock, who had "fled his county because of the indignation excited by the basest *political villainy.*"[76]

Four more days brought the candidates to the last of the scheduled speakings, at Murfreesboro on Monday of election week. Here Jones announced that he would move on to Columbia for a speech in his opponent's home town on the day before the election, while Polk planned to visit Franklin and then spend election day in Nashville. But at the last minute, fearful of letting the unscrupulous Jones go unanswered, Polk cut short his Franklin speech and hurried home, arriving in time to close the campaign with a reply to "Lean Jimmy" before his fellow townsmen.[77]

In no recent election had both parties been so uncertain about the outcome. Everything hinged on the voters' response to Polk's argumentative appeals on the one hand and Jones's entertaining casuistry on the other. Polk had been optimistic in the early stages of the campaign, and had left the Western District confident of greatly increased strength. This time it was Jones's health that had broken down under the ordeal of campaigning. The governor had had to miss an entire week of meetings in the Western District and continued to be bothered by hoarseness and rheumatism for the rest of the campaign, while Polk had never felt fitter. "East Tennessee only waits your coming to set every thing in motion," General Armstrong had assured Polk as he left home after the brief respite in

[75] Nashville *Union,* 14 July 1843.

[76] Nashville *Republican Banner,* 31 July 1843; Armstrong to Polk, 22 July 1843, Polk Papers.

[77] Nashville *Republican Banner,* 4 Aug. 1843.

May. "You will see as you advance Whiggery flying in every direction."[78]

But Polk had begun to grow discouraged during the last month and to lose his temper, as he watched the voters being taken in by "Lean Jimmy's" humbuggery. The governor's bold and unprincipled handling of the sterling bond question, which might have a decisive eleventh hour effect on the result, was a final dispiriting blow. And while the Democrats were generally more aggressive than they had been in the last campaign, there were disturbing hints that local Democratic politicians were making deals that would sacrifice Polk to buy Whig votes for Democratic legislative and congressional candidates.[79]

Polk was not long in doubt, for the first returns from Middle Tennessee showed "the most unexpected giving-way" in favor of Whiggery. Such banner Democratic counties as Bedford and Giles were lost for the first time, Maury was saved by a mere 400 votes, and there were proportionate losses throughout the middle section of the state. In East Tennessee the Democrats almost held their own, while in the Western District they made substantial gains. These gains were more than counterbalanced, however, by the heavy losses in the middle counties, and Jones won by a slightly larger margin than before, 3,833 votes out of some 110,000.[80] Though both houses of the legislature were lost, the Democrats won six—almost seven—of the eleven congressional races, which doubtless explains in part the gubernatorial result.

Polk's initial reaction was automatic. This "is no time to indulge in a desponding feeling," he wrote bravely to Armstrong. "There must be an immediate and a bold rally of our friends throughout the Union. Let them be urged to keep their armour on, and to fight for principle. For myself so far from surrendering my sword is still unsheathed & I am still ready to do battle for our principles."[81] But the Democracy would not be roused again, and even Polk could not maintain his posture. For nearly a month after the election his usually bulging correspondence file contained not a single letter.

[78] Armstrong to Polk, 22 May [1843; misplaced 22 Mar. 1841], Polk Papers; Polk to Laughlin, 8 May 1843, Polk-Laughlin Letters; James Campbell to David Campbell, 10 May 1843, Campbell Papers.

[79] Nashville *Republican Banner*, 17 July 1843.

[80] Polk to Armstrong, 7 Aug. 1843, Jackson Papers; Tenn. *House Journal*, 1843, p. 92.

[81] Polk to Armstrong, 7 Aug. 1843, Jackson Papers.

V

August 1843 was the darkest hour of Polk's political life. There were none of the plausible explanations he had been able to use in urging his fellow Democrats to "lick the flint and try it again" after previous defeats. Jones had come out squarely for a national bank and Henry Clay and had met the best debater the Democrats had to offer on this and all other questions. No resource of stump or printing press had been spared in presenting both sides to the voters, and they had decided for the Whigs by an increased majority. Polk himself admitted that "the *bank question* was the great cause" of defeat.[82] And all this on the heels of a succession of Democratic victories in every other part of the country. "The election in Tennessee was by far the most important of the year, & its successful issue more than compensates for any partial defeats which we have sustained elsewhere," exclaimed a jubilant Henry Clay, who had awaited the result as almost decisive of his chances for the presidency. ". . . Such an event cannot fail to exert a powerful and salutary influence throughout the whole Union." In short, it was virtually impossible to dispute the *Banner*'s exultant claim that Tennessee was now "A WHIG STATE—A NATIONAL BANK STATE—A TARIFF STATE—A CLAY STATE."[83]

This was shattering to a man of Polk's temper, for not only did it threaten all prospects for future Democratic success in Tennessee, but it also struck at the fervent faith in the people's virtue and wisdom that had animated his whole political career and sustained him in previous defeats. Had the commercial, speculative spirit so undermined the people's Old Republican virtue that the politics of nostalgia could no longer win elections? Had those visions of countless Old Mecklenburgs, of the simple honesty and steady habits of the fathers, to which Polk had always appealed, been inundated by the craze for bank notes, turnpikes, and paper prosperity? Had the towns at last corrupted the sturdy yeomen of the countryside, or enough of them anyhow so that Tennessee might never be pulled "erect on her republican legs," as Old Hickory was wont to phrase it? The explanation that the people had simply been fooled again was even more shattering, for to believe that the voters preferred

---

[82] "Diaries of S. H. Laughlin, of Tennessee, 1840, 1843," *Tennessee Historical Magazine*, II (Mar. 1916), 60.

[83] Clay to W. B. Campbell, 19 Aug. 1843, Campbell Papers; Nashville *Republican Banner*, 11 Aug. 1843.

Whig "coonery" to solid Democratic argument was to believe, in fact, that the people were incapable of self-government.

The blow was only the more cruel because it came at the very moment when Polk's long and faithful championing of the Old Republican faith seemed about to be rewarded with high national honors. A man of less burning ambition would have given up at this point all hope for the vice presidency, to say nothing of any more exalted office. Surveying the results from his placid retreat above the Hudson, a shocked Van Buren read Polk a lecture that was unusually stern for this tactful man. "It is as mortifying, as it is incomprehensible," he wrote, "that Tennessee, which in time past knew not Federalism, should have been proof agst. the feelings & convictions which have within the last two or three years brought all the rest of the old Democratic States into their former, & true positions."[84]

The national leader of the Democracy was blunter, if still obscure, in his comments to his intimate advisers. "The politics of Tenessee [*sic*] have been badly managed on our part," he observed to Frank Blair. "I think I could lay my finger on the causes that have led to the overthrow of our friends, but it is contrary to my habit & feelings to complain of those who design to do well."[85] Seizing upon these hints, other members of the Van Buren circle were quick to promote several of their number to the vacancy in the Democratic line of succession presumably created by the Tennessee defeat, and in the process they had no scruples about supplying the specifications against Polk that their chief had delicately omitted. "The Tennessee Dynasty," wrote one New York politician in proposing Joel R. Poinsett as the new choice for vice president, "were never true to Mr. Van Buren, nor would they be to any man who did not squirt tobacco juice."[86] And a Mississippi newspaper, boosting Senator Robert J. Walker for second place on the ticket, proclaimed that "MR. POLK HAS NOT HIMSELF KEPT UP WITH THE PROGRESS OF THE DEMOCRATIC PARTY, NOR WITH THE SPREAD OF ITS PRINCIPLES." "While the republican party, and the tendencies of the times, are for the return of a hard money currency and the utter prostration of the late corrupt and rotten paper system," this editor went on to explain, "he loiters on

[84] Van Buren to Polk, 27 Dec. 1843, Polk Papers.
[85] Van Buren to Blair, 5 Sept. 1843, Van Buren Letters, Gist Blair Papers.
[86] *Calendar of Poinsett Papers*, 173.

the way and finally becomes the apologist of the State Bank system, and their defender in his own State."[87]

If these reactions were not by themselves a conclusive estoppage to Polk's vice presidential hopes, the interpretations placed on the Tennessee election by Van Buren's rivals for the presidential nomination should have settled the question. The waning hopes of the Calhounites were revived by the argument that Polk's connection with Van Buren had defeated him. "In Tennessee the influence of V.B. Jackson and Polk was perfectly united without any disturbing cause whatever," Calhoun himself observed, "and yet that is the only state, in which the Whigs have gained and the Democrats lost ground."[88] This theme the Calhoun press promptly took up, reminding the country that "Mr. Polk ran as the candidate, 'in expectancy' of the Vice Presidency, with Mr. Van Buren—that he canvassed the whole State with uncompromising zeal and ability, and is defeated." "Will Mr. Van Buren's friends persist in running him a third time," inquired the Calhoun men triumphantly, "and once more throw the Government into the hands of the Whigs?"[89] These arguments produced a measurable reaction against Van Buren on the eve of the national convention, and the New Yorkers could hardly be expected to reward the man they held responsible with a place on the ticket.

Most assuredly not, when Polk's own Tennessee Democrats were blaming their defeat on Van Buren and turning to other aspirants for the presidential nomination. The Calhoun Democrats in East Tennessee now had a perfect excuse to abandon Van Buren; and the Knoxville *Argus* maintained that the Whigs had won by "making Van Burenism (not Democracy) nearly as odious here as black cockade Federalism was in 1800," and by identifying Polk "with the waning fortunes of Mr. Van Buren." Polk, continued the editor, would have won by a majority of ten thousand or more "with another—ANY OTHER—new Democratic candidate for the Presidency." The Tennessee Whig press did all it could to create the impression that this editorial, as well as other signs of disloyalty to Van Buren, stemmed from Polk, while Frank Blair made sure that it came to the attention of Van Buren and the entire Democracy by reprinting it prominently in the *Globe*.[90]

[87] Quoted in Nashville *Republican Banner*, 28 Aug. 1843.
[88] *Correspondence of Calhoun*, 547.
[89] Quoted in Nashville *Republican Banner*, 4 Sept. 1843.
[90] Knoxville *Argus*, quoted in Nashville *Union*, 29 Sept. 1843; Cave Johnson to

As he pondered all these things, Polk may have been reminded of Allen Hall's taunt three years before in the *Banner*. "HENCE-FORTH HIS CAREER WILL BE DOWNWARDS," the veteran Whig editor had written, and everything that had happened since— Polk's failure to win the vice presidential nomination in 1840, the disastrous defeat in the presidential balloting later the same year, Jones's first galling victory, the senatorial fiasco, and now this last and worst defeat—seemed to prove Hall a good prophet. Was this the end? Would Polk, after years of struggle had brought him within striking distance of the greatest prize in political life, now be compelled to follow his hated rival John Bell into a possibly permanent retirement?

Van Buren, 9 Oct. 1843, Van Buren Papers; Nashville *Republican Banner*, 4 Sept. 1843.

SOURCES

THE FOLLOWING PAGES describe briefly the more important sources that contribute directly to Polk's biography down to 1843. Additional sources that were of infrequent use are indicated in the notes.

PHYSICAL REMAINS

The Polks have left only their dead behind in Mecklenburg County, North Carolina. The graveyard where Ezekiel Polk buried his first wife and several of his children has recently been discovered several miles northwest of the town of Pineville, on a heavily wooded slope just east of Sugar Creek. Here are buried also a number of Ezekiel's relatives and neighbors, among them Ezra Alexander. James K. Polk's maternal grandfather, Captain James Knox, is buried in the graveyard of Hopewell Church in the northwestern corner of the county. A marker on Highway 521, a short distance south of Pineville, indicates the site of Sam Polk's cabin.

Ezekiel Polk's tombstone is now in the Polk Graveyard at Bolivar, Tennessee, where many of his descendants lie buried. "Mecklen," the house he was planning at the time of his death, was still standing in a dilapidated condition a short distance west of Bolivar when the author visited it in the spring of 1950.

Sam Polk's house in Columbia has been restored to its ante-bellum condition, and here visitors may inspect a good collection of the Polks' furniture, clothing, portraits, and other articles. Sam Polk and many members of his family are buried in Greenwood Cemetery. The home of James K. Polk has undergone alteration and is now occupied as a private residence.

ARCHIVES

County records are a prime source for the early activities of the Polks in North Carolina and Tennessee. The minutes of the Mecklenburg county court for 1786-1808 are in the North Carolina Department of Archives and History at Raleigh, but all other Mecklenburg records, including the court minutes for 1774-1785, will books, deed books, and the index to deeds, are in the courthouse at Charlotte.

A microfilm of the Tryon county court minute book is in the Department of Archives and History.

In Tennessee, court minutes, will books, and deed indexes for Maury, Robertson, and Hardeman counties are conveniently accessible in the indexed typescripts prepared by the W.P.A. Historical Records Survey and deposited in the State Library at Nashville.

Useful state records in the North Carolina Department of Archives and History are the Governors' Letter Book and Journal of the Council of State, 1795-1855, which contains material on Ezekiel Polk's part in the Zachariah Cox project; and the Revolutionary Account Books and Revolutionary Vouchers, which document the military service of Ezekiel and his brothers. The land records in the office of the secretary of state at Raleigh, including a card index to grants, grant books, and original warrants and surveys filed by counties, are essential for establishing the Polks' land transactions, both in Mecklenburg and the area that is now Tennessee.

Other land records are in the Tennessee Archives at Nashville, especially the Book of Warrants Issued by John Armstrong's Office. Here also are the Tennessee Legislative Papers, comprising committee reports and bills and resolutions, which are important for the periods of Polk's legislative service and governorship; and the record of Polk's official actions while governor, as contained in the Letter Book of Governor James K. Polk.

A few significant items are in the National Archives in Washington. Some information on the families and military services of the early Mecklenburg Polks can be gleaned from the Revolutionary pension papers in the Veterans Administration Section. A number of letters in State Department, Domestic Letters, 1792-1906, and Miscellaneous Letters, 1789-1906, are important for Ezekiel Polk's part in the Zachariah Cox project.

The records of the University of North Carolina are in the North Carolina Collection of the University Library at Chapel Hill. Especially useful are the volumes of Trustee Minutes and Faculty Reports and the volume of miscellaneous letters, 1796-1835. This material is supplemented by the University of North Carolina Papers, in the Southern Historical Collection, University of North Carolina Library.

PRINTED PUBLIC RECORDS

Much information on the Polks and early Mecklenburg is found in William L. Saunders, ed., *The Colonial Records of North Carolina* (10 vols., Raleigh, 1886-1890), and Walter Clark, ed., *The State Records of North Carolina* (vols. xi-xxvi, Winston and Goldsboro, 1895-1905).

For Ezekiel Polk's checkered career in South Carolina, see: [Peter Force, ed.,] *American Archives* . . . (Six Series, Washington, 1837-1853) ; "Journal of the Council of Safety for the Province of South Carolina, 1775," South Carolina Historical Society, *Collections*, ii (Charleston, 1858), 22-74; Alexander S. Salley, Jr., ed., "Historical Notes," *South Carolina Historical and Genealogical Magazine*, v (July 1904), 189-193, and vii (Apr. 1906), 99-113; A. S. Salley, Jr., ed., "Papers of the First Council of Safety of the Revolutionary Party in South Carolina, June-November, 1775," *ibid.*, i (1900), 41-75, 119-135, 183-205, 279-310, ii (1901), 3-26, 97-107, 167-193, 259-267, iii (1902), 3-15, 69-85, 123-138; A. S. Salley, Jr., ed., *Journal of the General Assembly of South Carolina, September 17, 1776–October 20, 1776* (Columbia, 1909).

Of primary importance for James K. Polk's public career in Tennessee, especially in the periods of his legislative service and governorship, are the *House Journals*, *Senate Journals*, and *Session Laws* of that state. Robert H. White's edition of the *Messages of the Governors of Tennessee* (Nashville: Tennessee Historical Commission, 1952-), of which three volumes have now been published, contains a running legislative and political history of the state and a miscellaneous selection of excerpts from contemporary newspapers and correspondence, in addition to the messages.

Of similar importance for Polk's congressional career are the *House Journals*, the Congressional Documents Series, the *Congressional Globe*, the *Register of Debates*, and the *Congressional Directories* for the nineteenth through the twenty-fifth Congress, 1825-1839. The presidential messages are conveniently collected in James D. Richardson, comp., *A Compilation of the Messages and Papers of the Presidents 1789-1902* (10 vols., Washington, 1905).

MANUSCRIPTS

The chief source for Polk's biography is, of course, the magnificent collection of his own papers in the Library of Congress.

Soon after he went to Congress Polk began saving all the letters he received, though he only occasionally retained a copy of an important letter written by himself; consequently the collection consists mainly of letters received. The all too infrequent Polk letters are mostly addressed to his wife or other members of his family, his letters to James Walker being the most valuable. An important group of letters from Polk to Samuel H. Laughlin has recently been acquired and added to the collection, and there is also a handful of letters written to Dr. Alfred Flournoy. Nearly all the documents prior to 1844 are in the First Series of eighty-three bound volumes. In addition to letters the collection includes printed speeches and pamphlets, a number of memorandum books, and the account books for Polk's legal partnerships with Madison L. Caruthers and Aaron V. Brown.

Much information on the various Polks in North Carolina and Tennessee can be gleaned from a number of smaller family collections, consisting largely of the papers of Colonel William Polk of North Carolina and his children, some of whom lived in Maury County. The Polk Family of North Carolina Papers are in the Library of Congress. In the Southern Historical Collection (University of North Carolina Library, Chapel Hill) are the following: Dillon-Polk Papers, Polk-Brown-Ewell Papers, Polk-Yeatman Papers, G. W. Polk Papers, Leonidas Polk Papers, and Lucius J. Polk Papers. The North Carolina Department of Archives and History at Raleigh has a collection of William Polk Papers and another collection listed as Polk Papers, consisting of the papers of James K. Polk's younger brother William H. Polk.

Births, marriages, and deaths in Sam Polk's family are recorded in the Family Bible, on display at the Sam Polk House in Columbia. James K. Polk's certificates of proficiency from his first two teachers and his marriage license are among the Miscellaneous MSS of the Tennessee Historical Society, Nashville.

The best information on Polk's college days comes from the records of the Dialectic Society, including minutes, committee minutes, and treasurers' accounts, in the North Carolina Collection, University of North Carolina Library. The bound vols. of Addresses of the Dialectic Society contain three important James K. Polk MSS. Miscellaneous letters and documents, some bearing on Polk's impeachment proceedings against one of his fellow members, are in the Dialectic Society Papers, Southern Historical Collection.

Next to Polk's own papers, the most valuable source is the voluminous collection of Andrew Jackson Papers in the Library of Congress, containing rich documentation for both Tennessee and national politics, a number of Polk letters, and frequent references to Polk. The Jackson Papers are supplemented by: Letters to William B. Lewis (mainly from Jackson, but including one important Polk letter), Ford Collection, New York Public Library; Andrew Jackson Donelson Papers (the correspondence of Jackson's nephew, including many letters to and from Polk), Library of Congress; Emily Tennessee Donelson Papers, Library of Congress; and Jackson-Donelson Papers, microfilm, Joint University Library, Nashville.

Some extremely significant letters on Tennessee politics in the 1820's and early 1830's are found in the John Overton Papers, Claybrooke Collection, Tennessee Historical Society. A less important collection of Overton's correspondence is on microfilm at the Joint University Library. The sparse Hugh Lawson White Papers, Library of Congress, and Felix Grundy Papers, Southern Historical Collection, contain several significant items. Though full only in the years after 1843, the Alfred O. P. Nicholson Papers, New-York Historical Society, and Andrew Johnson Papers, Library of Congress, include some important letters for the earlier period.

None of the top Whigs in Tennessee have left more than scattered papers, but the Whig side of the story is fairly well documented in the letters of three secondary party leaders. The correspondence of William B. Campbell, Whig congressman from Middle Tennessee, is found in the David Campbell Papers, Duke University Library, while the congressman from an adjoining district has left the Robert L. Caruthers Papers, Southern Historical Collection. The Thomas A. R. Nelson Papers, McClung Collection, Lawson-McGhee Library, Knoxville, are scattered before 1844, but they contain some valuable letters to this East Tennessee Whig from the party leaders in Middle Tennessee.

The Martin Van Buren Papers, Library of Congress, and the Francis P. Blair correspondence in the Blair-Lee Papers, Princeton University Library, are the most important collections for Democratic leaders outside Tennessee. The papers of Clement Claiborne Clay, one of Polk's longtime friends and allies, are in the Duke University Library. The George Bancroft Papers, Massachusetts Historical Society, Boston, throw light on Polk's efforts to win the Democratic vice presidential nomination, as do the James Buchanan

Papers, Historical Society of Pennsylvania, Philadelphia. The Levi Woodbury Papers, Library of Congress, yield information on the Polks' life in Washington and the attempt to pass a bill regulating the state bank deposit system. The many letters from Reuben M. Whitney to William D. Lewis, cashier of the Girard Bank, in the Lewis-Neilson Papers, Historical Society of Pennsylvania, afford valuable insights into the struggle over removal of the deposits and the operation of the state bank deposit system. Relevant letters from Jackson, Blair, Van Buren, and Woodbury are in the Gist Blair Papers, Library of Congress.

On the Whig side, the Nicholas Biddle Papers, Library of Congress, are indispensable for Polk's role in the Bank controversy. The Duff Green Papers (in the possession of Professor Fletcher M. Green, Chapel Hill, N.C.) throw a flood of light on the movement to run Hugh Lawson White for president; a smaller body of Duff Green Papers is in the Library of Congress. The Willie P. Mangum Papers, Library of Congress, include some important letters about Polk's contest with John Bell for the speakership of the House and about the White movement; other Mangum Papers are in the Duke University Library. The John McLean Papers, Library of Congress, are valuable for the preliminaries to the election of 1836 in Tennessee. Comment on the speakership contest, the White movement, and other matters involving Polk may be found in the Gulian C. Verplanck Papers and the John W. Taylor Papers in the New-York Historical Society. The Henry Clay Papers, Library of Congress, though not abundant, contain a number of very important letters on Tennessee politics from the 1820's through the 1840's: a smaller collection of equally valuable Clay Papers is in the Tennessee Historical Society.

PUBLISHED CORRESPONDENCE

R. W. Gibbes, ed., *Documentary History of the American Revolution* . . . (3 vols., Columbia, S.C., and New York, 1853-1857), includes material on Ezekiel Polk's Revolutionary career. Isaac J. Cox has assembled most of the relevant "Documents Relating to Zachariah Cox," in Historical and Philosophical Society of Ohio, *Quarterly Publication*, VIII (Apr.-June, July-Sept. 1913), though Ezekiel Polk's role must be derived from other sources. Much information on Tennessee land speculation in the 1820's and the legislature's handling of the land question is found in William Henry Hoyt, ed., *The Papers of Archibald D. Murphey* (2 vols., Raleigh, 1914); also included is William Polk's autobiographical sketch, the best source for the early North Carolina Polks.

The most important group of James K. Polk letters outside the Polk Papers is "Letters of James K. Polk to Cave Johnson, 1833-1848," *Tennessee Historical Magazine*, I (Sept. 1915), 209-256. John Spencer Bassett has published Polk's correspondence with his plantation overseers and described his plantation experience in *The Southern Plantation Overseer as Revealed in His Letters* (Northampton, Mass., 1925). J. S. Bassett, ed., *Correspondence of Andrew Jackson* (7 vols., Washington, 1926-1935), collects the best Jackson letters from various sources. Amelia W. Williams and Eugene C. Barker, eds., *The Writings of Sam Houston 1813-1863* (8 vols., Austin, Tex., 1938-1943), throws light on Polk's relationships with Houston and Jackson, Tennessee politics, and Houston's trial for contempt of the House of Representatives. Biddle's attitudes in the Bank controversy are sampled in Reginald C. McGrane, ed., *The Correspondence of Nicholas Biddle Dealing with National Affairs, 1807-1844* (Boston, 1919). Arthur G. Staples, ed., *The Letters of John Fairfield* (Lewiston, Me., 1919), pictures in intimate detail the Washington life of a congressman.

Information on the maneuverings for the Democratic presidential and vice presidential nominations in the early 1840's is found in: Charles H. Ambler, ed., *Correspondence of Robert M. T. Hunter*, American Historical Association, *Annual Report*, 1916, II (Washington, 1918); J. Franklin Jameson, ed., *Correspondence of John C. Calhoun, ibid.*, 1899, II (Washington, 1900); Chauncey S. Boucher and Robert P. Brooks, eds., "Correspondence Addressed to John C. Calhoun 1837-1849," *ibid.*, 1929 (Washington, 1930), 125-533, 551-570; Grace E. Heilman and Bernard S. Levin, eds., *Calendar of Joel R. Poinsett Papers in the Henry D. Gilpin Collection* (Philadelphia, 1941).

DIARIES, AUTOBIOGRAPHIES, AND MEMOIRS

Milo Milton Quaife, ed., *The Diary of James K. Polk during His Presidency, 1845 to 1849* (4 vols., Chicago, 1910), contains occasional entries illumining events in Polk's earlier life. William B. Hesseltine, ed., *Dr. J. G. M. Ramsey: Autobiography and Letters*

(Nashville, 1954), affords information on Polk's forebears and reveals the nostalgia for Old Mecklenburg felt by many of her sons and grandsons in Tennessee. James Ross, *Life and Times of Elder Reuben Ross* (Philadelphia, n.d.), includes a vivid narrative of the author's journey with his family from North Carolina to Middle Tennessee at about the same time Sam Polk's family made the trip. Samuel H. Laughlin gives his recollections of James K. Polk as a student at Murfreesboro in John H. DeWitt, ed., "Sketches of Notable Men," *Tennessee Historical Magazine*, IV (Mar. 1918), 73-78. For the college memories of one of Polk's classmates, see *Memoirs of Edward J. Mallett. A Birthday Gift for Each of His Children, May 1st, 1880* (n.p., n.d.). Life in Columbia, Tennessee, in the 1820's is described by Mrs. Alfred O. P. Nicholson in "Reminiscences of an Octogenarian," typescript copy of a series of articles in the Columbia *Maury Democrat*, 1894, in the Southern Historical Collection, University of North Carolina Library. An important description of Polk's personality and style of oratory is Judge Nathaniel Baxter, "Reminiscences," *American Historical Magazine* (Nashville), VIII (July 1903), 262-270.

For recollections of Tennessee politics and politicians in Polk's day, see: Josephus C. Guild, *Old Times in Tennessee, with Historical, Personal, and Political Scraps and Sketches* (Nashville, 1878); Joshua W. Caldwell, *Sketches of the Bench and Bar of Tennessee* (Knoxville, 1898); and Oliver P. Temple (Mary B. Temple, ed.), *Notable Men of Tennessee from 1833 to 1875: Their Times and Their Contemporaries* (New York, 1912). The "Diaries of S. H. Laughlin, of Tennessee, 1840, 1843," *Tennessee Historical Magazine*, II (Mar. 1916), 43-85, are important for two crucial episodes in Polk's quest for the Democratic vice presidential nomination.

The two outstanding personal documents of Jacksonian politics are John C. Fitzpatrick, ed., *The Autobiography of Martin Van Buren*, American Historical Association, *Annual Report*, 1918, II (Washington, 1920); and Charles Francis Adams, ed., *Memoirs of John Quincy Adams, Comprising Portions of His Diary from 1795 to 1848* (12 vols., Philadelphia, 1874-1877). The former throws important light on the Calhoun–Van Buren struggle of Jackson's first administration and reveals John Bell's last minute overtures to Van Buren in 1834, while the latter contains frequent comments on Polk and is especially revealing on the petition fight during Polk's speakership.

NEWSPAPERS

Newspapers are indispensable for Polk's biography. In Tennessee the statewide organs published at Nashville by the different factions and parties are of the first importance. The Nashville *Clarion*, 1806-1822, reported events in Middle Tennessee during Polk's boyhood years and reflected the views of the Erwin faction. Its successor, Patrick H. Darby's Nashville *Constitutional Advocate*, 1822-1824, is a major source for the political struggles over banking and land speculation in these years. Paralleling the *Clarion* and the *Constitutional Advocate* is the Nashville *Whig*, 1812-1826, a spokesman for the Overton faction before 1819 and for the Erwins in its last years. The Nashville *Gazette*, 1819-1827, replaced the *Whig* as the Overton organ and recorded the beginnings of the movement to make Jackson president. The fragmentary accounts carried by these journals provide our only knowledge of legislative debates during the period of Polk's service in the state house of representatives.

In the later 1820's and earlier 1830's the leading Nashville papers were the *Republican*, 1824-1837, which spoke for the Overton-Eaton-Lewis group, and the *National Banner, and Nashville Whig* (commonly called the *Banner*), 1825-1837, which was friendly to Governor Carroll, the Nashville business community, and the Grundy-Polk-White group. By 1833 both of these newspapers were turning against Jackson on the Bank question, and they led the campaign to make White president. In 1837 John Bell united them under the name Nashville *Republican Banner*, 1837-1875, as the unofficial organ of Tennessee Whiggery, but the Foster wing of the party quickly established an influential competitor, the Nashville *Whig*, 1838-1855. Meanwhile Grundy, Polk, and other leaders of what came to be the Democratic party, had founded the Nashville *Union*, 1835-1875, to uphold their point of view.

The scattered surviving copies of various village newspapers are occasionally helpful, and several deserve special mention. Seven different newspapers lived and died at Columbia in this period. Five of them are known by only one or two extant issues. A sixth, Polk's local organ, the Columbia *Democrat*, is represented by a few more copies, all of which are valuable. The fullest file is of the Columbia *Observer*, 1834-1845, which backed Polk against Bell in 1834, simultaneously led the agitation for White for president, and shortly emerged as one of the best-edited Whig newspapers in the state.

The Shelbyville *Western Freeman,* 1831-1835, published at the only other town in Polk's congressional district, throws light on his campaign for reelection in 1833. In the Western District the Jackson *Gazette,* 1824-1830, is an important source for the land question, the emergence of Crockett, and the effort to get the vacant lands relinquished to Tennessee. The Murfreesboro *Central Monitor,* 1833-1834, is indispensable for the Polk-Bell controversy of 1834.

The more important regional papers are available and useful in varying degrees. For the Whigs there are: Parson Brownlow's *Tennessee Whig,* 1839-1883, published successively at Elizabethton, Jonesboro, and Knoxville; the Knoxville *Register,* 1816-1863; the Knoxville *Post,* 1841-1848; the Jackson *Truth Teller,* 1834-?; the Jackson *District Intelligencer,* 1841; the Jackson *West Tennessee Whig,* 1842-1863; and the Memphis *Enquirer,* 1836-1851. On the Democratic side are: the Knoxville *Argus,* 1839-1844; the Jackson *District Telegraph,* 1837-1839, a spokesman for the Nullifier group; the Jackson *Republican,* 1842-1845; the Memphis *Western World,* 1839-1840, another newspaper with Nullifier leanings; and the Memphis *Appeal,* 1840-1894.

The party organs at Washington are indispensable for political developments at the national level. The *National Intelligencer,* 1800-1869, represented the National Republican–Whig point of view. Duff Green's *United States Telegraph,* 1826-1837, was the organ of the Jackson party until Calhoun's break with Jackson, after which it spoke for the Nullifier wing of the Whig party. The *Telegraph* is especially valuable for the Polk-Bell speakership contest and the White movement. Frank Blair's *Globe,* 1831-1845, was established to support Van Buren's interests in the Jackson party and quickly became the party organ. Blair was never overly friendly to Polk. Of special importance for the White movement in 1835-1836 and for the attacks on Polk by the White men are the *Appeal,* published at Georgetown during April 1835, and the *Sun,* 1835-1837, which supplanted it as the organ of the White party.

PAMPHLETS AND BROADSIDES

The most systematic expositions of Polk's views on state and national issues are found in his campaign circulars and biennial circulars to his constituents while a member of Congress, and in his published speeches and other campaign documents for the state campaigns of 1837, 1839, 1841, and 1843. These are cited individually in the notes, and copies are in the Polk Papers.

Much information on the Polk family and on Ezekiel Polk's Revolutionary career is collected in *Vindication of the Revolutionary Character and Services of the Late Col. Ezekiel Polk, of Mecklenburg, N.C.*, published at Nashville by the Democratic State Central Committee during the presidential campaign of 1844. The Library of Congress and the University of North Carolina Library have copies.

The University of North Carolina Library also possesses the following useful pamphlets bearing on Polk's college days: William Hooper, *Fifty Years Since: An Address, Delivered before the Alumni of the University of North-Carolina on the 7th of June, 1859* (Raleigh, 1859); Edward J. Mallett, *Address to the Graduating Class at the University of North Carolina, at Commencement, June 2d, 1881* (Raleigh, 1881); John Y. Mason, *Address before the Alumni Association of the University of North Carolina, Delivered in Gerard Hall, June 2, 1847* (Washington, 1847); *Catalogus Universitatis Carolinae Septentrionalis* (Raleigh, 1817); *Catalogue of the Faculty and Students of the University of North Carolina. September, 1821* (Hillsborough, 1821); *Catalogue of Books Belonging to the Dialectic Society, Chapel-Hill, February, 1821* (Hillsborough, 1821); *The Laws of the University of North-Carolina. As Revised in 1813* (Hillsborough, 1822).

Indispensable to an understanding of the early American banking system and Jacksonian monetary policies is William M. Gouge, *A Short History of Paper Money and Banking in the United States, Including an Account of Provincial and Continental Paper Money. To Which Is Prefixed an Inquiry into the Principles of the System* ... (Philadelphia, 1833).

BIOGRAPHIES

For nearly three quarters of a century after Polk's death, the only full account of him was the eulogistic and unscholarly biography by John S. Jenkins, *The Life of James Knox Polk, Late President of the United States* (Auburn, N.Y., 1850). As a result Polk's reputation remained enveloped in the obloquy engendered by the myth that both the Mexican War and the Civil War were part of a "slave power conspiracy." Not until publication of Eugene

Irving McCormac's thoroughly documented *James K. Polk: A Political Biography* (Berkeley, 1922) did scholars come to recognize that Polk was an outstandingly successful president. Though his impressive work is the necessary starting point for any further investigation of Polk, Professor McCormac did not exhaust the subject. He was not particularly interested in the prepresidential years, where an anti-Jackson bias made it hard for him to treat Polk sympathetically; he explicitly eschewed the task of writing a personal biography, which left Polk, the man, a figure still to be evoked; and he did not have access to many materials that have since become available to add depth to the picture.

For Polk genealogy, see [William Harrison Polk,] *Polk Family and Kinsmen* [Louisville, 1912], which is poorly organized and inaccurate at many points; Mary Winder Garrett, "Pedigree of the Pollock or Polk Family from Fulbert the Saxon (A.D. 1075) to the Present Time," *American Historical Magazine* (Nashville), I (1896), 154-173, 263-270, II (1897), 376-395, III (1898), 32-73, 155-190, 230-240, IV (1899), 46-65, 124-162, which exhibits the genealogical temperament at its worst; and the more reliable findings of Mrs. Frank M. Angelotti, in "The Polks of North Carolina and Tennessee," *New England Historical and Genealogical Register*, LXXVII (1923), 133-145, 213-227, 250-270, LXXVIII (1924), 33-53, 159-177, 318-330. By all odds the fullest and most reliable genealogy is Wilmot Polk Rogers, "Ezekiel Polk and His Descendants" (San Francisco, 1939), typescripts in the Library of Congress and the Tennessee Historical Society, Nashville. For Polk's maternal forebears, see Hattie S. Goodman, *The Knox Family: A Genealogical and Biographical Sketch of the Descendants of John Knox of Rowan County, North Carolina, and Other Knoxes* (Richmond, 1905). William H. Whitsitt, "Annals of a Scotch-Irish Family: The Whitsitts of Nashville, Tenn.," *American Historical Magazine* (Nashville), IX (1904), 58-82, 113-140, 231-251, 352-398, contains some information on the family of Sarah Childress Polk.

James K. Polk's kinsmen General Thomas Polk and Colonel William Polk of North Carolina are described by Albert Ray Newsome and J. G. de R. Hamilton respectively in Allen Johnson and Dumas Malone, eds., *Dictionary of American Biography* (21 vols., New York, 1937), xv, 42-44. Three volumes of medical biography contain information on Polk's boyhood operation for gallstone: Archibald H. Barkley, *Kentucky's Pioneer Lithotomists* (Cincinnati,

1913) ; the sketch of Ephraim McDowell in Samuel D. Gross, ed., *Lives of Eminent American Physicians and Surgeons of the Nineteenth Century* (Philadelphia, 1861), 207-230; and Mary Young Ridenbaugh, *The Biography of Ephraim McDowell, M.D., "The Father of Ovariotomy"* (New York, 1890). O. P. Fitzgerald, *John B. McFerrin: A Biography* (Nashville, 1893), is the principal source for Polk's religious experiences. Much extremely valuable information about Polk's personal life is contained in his wife's reminiscences as recorded by Anson and Fanny Nelson, *Memorials of Sarah Childress Polk: Wife of the Eleventh President of the United States* (New York, 1892).

There are good studies of many prominent Tennessee figures with whom Polk associated. James Parton, *Life of Andrew Jackson* (3 vols., New York, 1861), contains important documentary material. Samuel Gordon Heiskell, *Andrew Jackson and Early Tennessee History* (3 vols., Nashville, 1920-1921), illuminates several phases of Tennessee and national politics. John Spencer Bassett, *Life of Andrew Jackson* (New York, 1928), and Marquis James, *The Life of Andrew Jackson* (2 vols. in 1, Indianapolis, 1938), are excellent scholarly biographies. Joseph Howard Parks has recounted the careers of *Felix Grundy, Champion of Democracy* (University, La., 1940) and *John Bell of Tennessee* (Baton Rouge, 1950) as thoroughly as the surviving manuscript materials permit, while Norman L. Parks treats more intensively "The Career of John Bell of Tennessee in the United States House of Representatives" in his Ph.D. dissertation at Vanderbilt University (1942). The latter is summarized in Norman L. Parks, "The Career of John Bell as Congressman from Tennessee, 1827-1841," *Tennessee Historical Quarterly*, I (Sept. 1942), 229-249. In other Vanderbilt dissertations, Clement Lyndon Grant describes "The Public Career of Cave Johnson" (1951), and Lunia Paul Gresham ably covers "The Public Career of Hugh Lawson White" (1943). Gresham has published excerpts from his dissertation in "Hugh Lawson White as a Tennessee Politician and Banker, 1807-1827," East Tennessee Historical Society, *Publications*, No. 18 (1946), 25-46; "Hugh Lawson White, Frontiersman, Lawyer, and Judge," *ibid.*, No. 19 (1947), 3-24; and "The Public Career of Hugh Lawson White," *Tennessee Historical Quarterly*, III (Dec. 1944), 291-318; while Grant has summarized "The Public Career of Cave Johnson" in *Tennessee Historical Quarterly*, X (Sept. 1951), 195-223. Nancy N. Scott, *A Memoir of Hugh*

Lawson White, Judge of the Supreme Court of Tennessee, Member of the Senate of the United States, Etc., Etc.: with Selections from His Speeches and Correspondence (Philadelphia, 1856), reproduces significant documentary material. Other Tennesseans are well portrayed in E. Merton Coulter, *William G. Brownlow: Fighting Parson of the Southern Highlands* (Chapel Hill, 1937), and Marquis James, *The Raven: A Biography of Sam Houston* (Indianapolis, 1929).

Among biographies of national figures, Charles M. Wiltse, *John C. Calhoun* (3 vols., Indianapolis, 1944-1951), despite an excessive pro-Calhoun bias, stands out as the finest study of national politics in this period. Carl Brent Swisher, *Roger B. Taney* (New York, 1936), contains the most balanced account of the Bank controversy. Other biographies with special relevance for Polk are: Leland Winfield Meyer, *The Life and Times of Colonel Richard M. Johnson of Kentucky* (New York, 1932); Robert W. July, *The Essential New Yorker: Gulian Crommelin Verplanck* (Durham, 1951); John Arthur Garraty, *Silas Wright* (New York, 1949); and Charles Chauncey Binney, *The Life of Horace Binney with Selections from His Letters* (Philadelphia, 1903). [Ansel Wold, comp.,] *Biographical Directory of the American Congress 1774-1927* (Washington, 1928), is often the only source of information about the more obscure members of Congress.

STATE AND LOCAL HISTORIES

For Mecklenburg County, North Carolina, the following are valuable: Daniel A. Tompkins, *History of Mecklenburg County and the City of Charlotte from 1740 to 1903* (2 vols., Charlotte, 1903); John Brevard Alexander, *Biographical Sketches of the Early Settlers of the Hopewell Section* . . . (Charlotte, 1897), and *The History of Mecklenburg County from 1740 to 1900* (Charlotte, 1902); William Henry Foote, *Sketches of North Carolina, Historical and Biographical, Illustrative of the Principles of a Portion of Her Early Settlers* (New York, 1846); Cyrus Lee Hunter, *Sketches of Western North Carolina, Historical and Biographical* . . . (Raleigh, 1877).

Thomas Perkins Abernethy, *From Frontier to Plantation in Tennessee: A Study in Frontier Democracy* (Chapel Hill, 1932), is an admirably perceptive and suggestive interpretation of Tennessee history to the Civil War, marred only by a perverse bias against Andrew Jackson. James Phelan, *History of Tennessee: The Making of a State* (Boston, 1889), is rich with material on Tennessee politics in the Jackson-Polk era.

For Maury County, see: W. S. Fleming, *A Historical Sketch of Maury County, Read at the Centennial Celebration in Columbia, Tennessee, July 4th, 1876* (Columbia, 1876) ; *History of Tennessee: From the Earliest Times to the Present: Together with an Historical and a Biographical Sketch of Maury, Williamson, Rutherford, Wilson, Bedford and Marshall Counties* . . . (Nashville, 1886) ; *Century Review, 1805-1905, Maury County, Tennessee* (Columbia, 1905).

Other local histories relevant to Polk are: Warner Wardell Clifft, "Early History of Hardeman County, Tennessee," M.A. thesis, George Peabody College for Teachers (1930); C. C. Henderson, *The Story of Murfreesboro* (Murfreesboro, 1929) ; Samuel Cole Williams, *Beginnings of West Tennessee: In the Land of the Chickasaws 1541-1841* (Johnson City, Tenn., 1930).

SPECIAL STUDIES

The most thorough study of the North Carolina–Tennessee land question is Albert Lincoln Bramlett, "North Carolina's Western Lands," Ph.D. dissertation, University of North Carolina (1928); while Alice Barnwell Keith, "Three North Carolina Blount Brothers in Business and Politics, 1783-1812," Ph.D. dissertation, University of North Carolina (1940), throws light on the Polks' connection with the Great Speculation. Authoritative accounts of the University of North Carolina in Polk's time may be found in Kemp P. Battle, *History of the University of North Carolina* (2 vols., Raleigh, 1907, 1912) ; and Archibald Henderson, *The Campus of the First State University* (Chapel Hill, 1949).

Arthur M. Schlesinger, Jr., has made a stimulating rediscovery of Jacksonian politics in *The Age of Jackson* (Boston, 1946); though some of his interpretations are subject to revision, his many fresh insights have influenced the present volume. Sister M. Grace Madeleine, *Monetary and Banking Theories of Jacksonian Democracy* (Philadelphia, 1943), brings together much useful material, while Ralph C. H. Catterall, *The Second Bank of the United States* (Chicago, 1903), is authoritative and indispensable.

Useful studies of Tennessee politics are: Stanley J. Folmsbee, *Sectionalism and Internal Improvements in Tennessee 1796-1845* (Knoxville, 1939); Ernest Walter Hooper, "The Presidential Election of 1836 in Tennessee," M.A. thesis, University of North Carolina (1949); Powell Moore, "The Establishment of the Whig Party in Tennessee," Ph.D. dissertation, Indiana University (1932); Charles E. Pool, "The Rise of the Whig Party in West Tennessee, 1834-1843," M.A. thesis, University of Mississippi (1950).

ARTICLES

[J. L. Martin,] "Political Portraits with Pen and Pencil. (No. VI.): James K. Polk," *United States Magazine and Democratic Review*, II (May 1838), 197-208, is the first published biographical sketch of Polk; particularly valuable are the statements about Polk's early life, which are presumably derived from Polk himself. Charles G. Sellers, Jr., "Colonel Ezekiel Polk: Pioneer and Patriarch," *William and Mary Quarterly*, Third Series, x (Jan. 1953), 80-98, treats the career of Polk's grandfather in somewhat greater detail than the present volume. Flournoy Rivers describes "The Beginnings of Maury County" in *American Historical Magazine* (Nashville), III (Apr. 1898), 139-150. Albert V. Goodpasture brings together many facts about "The Boyhood of President Polk" in *Tennessee Historical Magazine*, VII (Apr. 1921), 36-50. For Polk's first school, see Mrs. Mary Wagner Highsaw, "A History of Zion Community in Maury County, 1806-1860," *Tennessee Historical Quarterly*, v (1946), 3-34, 111-140, 222-233.

There are many articles on Tennessee politics in the Jackson period. Thomas Perkins Abernethy, "The Early Development of Commerce and Banking in Tennessee," *Mississippi Valley Historical Review*, XIV (Dec. 1927), 311-325, is the indispensable introduction to this subject. Charles G. Sellers, Jr., "Banking and Politics in Jackson's Tennessee, 1817-1827," *Mississippi Valley Historical Review*, XLI (June 1954), 61-84, documents more fully the interpretation followed in the present volume, while Sellers, "James K. Polk's Political Apprenticeship," East Tennessee Historical Society, *Publications*, No. 25 (1953), 37-53, likewise provides greater detail on Polk's service in the Tennessee legislature. St. George L. Sioussat, "Some Phases of Tennessee Politics in the Jackson Period," *American Historical Review*, XIV (Oct. 1908), 51-69, discusses Crockett's alienation from the Jackson party over the Tennessee land bill and Catron's attack on the national bank.

The fullest account of Tennessee politics during the 1830's and 1840's in print is the series of four excellent articles by Powell Moore: "The Political Background of the Revolt against Jackson in Tennessee," East Tennessee Historical Society, *Publications*, No. 4 (1932), 45-66; "The Revolt against Jackson in Tennessee," *Journal of Southern History*, II (Aug. 1936), 335-359; "James K. Polk and Tennessee Politics, 1839-1841," East Tennessee Historical Society, *Publications*, No. 9 (1937), 31-52; "James K. Polk and the 'Immortal Thirteen,'" *ibid.*, No. 11 (1939), 20-33. Other valuable articles are: Thomas Perkins Abernethy, "The Origin of the Whig Party in Tennessee," *Mississippi Valley Historical Review*, XII (Mar. 1926), 504-522; and Thomas B. Alexander, "The Presidential Campaign of 1840 in Tennessee," *Tennessee Historical Quarterly*, I (Mar. 1942), 21-43. Still other useful articles will be found in the files of the *American Historical Magazine* (Nashville), 1896-1904, *Tennessee Historical Magazine*, 1915-1926, 1930-1937, *Tennessee Historical Quarterly*, 1942- , and East Tennessee Historical Society, *Publications*, 1929- .

INDEX

Note: In the entries for the North Carolina–Tennessee Polks, superior numbers are used to indicate the generation of each individual, as reckoned from William Polk[1] of Pennsylvania.

abolitionism, *see* petition question; slavery question; Texas question
Adams, John, 26, 280
Adams, John Quincy, 108, 132, 157, 161, 165, 215, 217, 280, 305, 307, 308, 335, 349, 367, 461; candidate for president in 1824, 87, 89, 96; nationalistic policies as president, 102-04; leads fight on gag rule, 315, 338-39; agitates Texas question, 337
Advance Guard of Democracy, 421
Albany (N.Y.) *Argus,* 294
Alexander, Ezra: aids Ezekiel Polk in propagating deism, 25, 27
Alexander, Mark, 188, 192
Alexander family, 9, 11, 17, 25
Allen, Thomas, 327
Anderson, Alexander, 396, 402, 403, 411, 435, 451; elected to Senate in 1839, 384
Anderson, William E., 175
anti-Masonry: used against Polk in 1833, 203-04
Armstrong, Gen. Robert, 235, 370, 466, 469, 487, 488; defeated by Cannon for governor in 1837, 322-26; manages Democratic campaign of 1839, 366
Arnold, Thomas D., 182, 197, 425; defeated for Congress in 1827, 136; dispute with Polk, 162

Balch, Alfred, 175, 253, 254, 256, 269, 271, 272, 292, 353, 377, 459; influences Overton men in favor of Van Buren, 137-42
Bancroft, George, 360, 370, 408; supports Polk for Democratic vice presidential nomination in 1840, 400, 406, 409, 417
Bank of Tennessee, 392; chartered in 1838, 345-46; issue in campaign of 1839, 363-64, 365; Democrats fail to prevent suspension or force resumption, 385-92; Polk advocates making bonds payable in sterling, 388, 393; new directors appointed by Polk, 393-94; Democratic senate refuses to confirm Whig directors appointed by Jones, 456; Democratic senate blocks investigation

demanded by Jones, 457; issue in Tenn. campaign of 1843, 475-76; Polk indebted to, 459; administration by Polk's directors, 476. *See also* banks (state); sterling bonds
Bank of the State of Tennessee (Knoxville Bank), 68, 172, 173. *See also* banks (state)
Bank of the United States (Second): and political strategy in the first Jackson administration, 143-44; charter and early history, 168-69, 171; Jackson hostile to, 171-76; Nashville branch blocked in 1817, 172; hostility to, 170-71, 177-78; Nashville branch established, 173; effort to obtain recharter, 178-82; Jackson vetoes recharter bill, 168, 182-83; investigation of 1833, 187-95; bill to sell government stock in, 189-90; postpones liquidation of federal debt, 192-93; overextension at western branches, 193-94; tries to defeat Polk's re-election in 1833, 200-01; forces contraction in Tenn., 207; federal deposits removed from, 211-12; struggle over removal of deposits at Panic Session, 212-22; House resolves against recharter and upholds removal of deposits, 221. *See also* banking and fiscal policies; Biddle, Nicholas
banking and fiscal policies: issue in Tenn. campaign of 1839, 363-65; issue in Tenn. campaign of 1843, 477-78, 484
  elimination of small notes, 364, 393; advocated by Polk's report of 1834, 220-21; proposed by Gouge, 224; state cooperation needed, 225, 232; recommended by Taney as feature of state bank deposit system, 226; inaugurated by Taney in 1835, 232; advocated by Polk in 1839, 388
  hard money, 221, 227, 228, 230, 247, 328, 364, 389; sentiment for in Tenn. election of 1821, 71-72; Bank of the U.S. opposed by advocates of, 169-70, 177, 178; favored by Jackson, 172, 176,